THE CENTURY PSYCHOLOGY SERIES

Richard M. Elliott, *Editor*

READINGS IN THE HISTORY OF PSYCHOLOGY

THE CENTURY PSYCHOLOGY SERIES

EDITED BY
RICHARD M. ELLIOTT, Ph.D., *University of Minnesota*

LEARNING MORE BY EFFECTIVE STUDY, by Charles and Dorothy Bird.

SOCIAL PSYCHOLOGY, by Charles Bird.

HISTORY OF EXPERIMENTAL PSYCHOLOGY, by Edwin G. Boring.

THE PHYSICAL DIMENSIONS OF CONSCIOUSNESS, by Edwin G. Boring.

SENSATION AND PERCEPTION IN THE HISTORY OF EXPERIMENTAL PSYCHOLOGY, by Edwin G. Boring.

BEAUTY AND HUMAN NATURE, by Albert R. Chandler.

GREAT EXPERIMENTS IN PSYCHOLOGY, Rev. Ed., by Henry E. Garrett.

DEVELOPMENTAL PSYCHOLOGY, 2nd Ed., by Florence L. Goodenough.

EXPERIMENTAL CHILD STUDY, by Florence L. Goodenough and John E. Anderson.

PHYSIOLOGICAL PSYCHOLOGY, by S. R. Hathaway.

SEVEN PSYCHOLOGIES, by Edna Heidbreder.

CONDITIONING AND LEARNING, by Ernest R. Hilgard and Donald G. Marquis.

HYPNOSIS AND SUGGESTIBILITY, by Clark L. Hull.

PRINCIPLES OF BEHAVIOR, by Clark L. Hull.

THE WILD BOY OF AVEYRON, by Jean-Marc-Gaspard Itard, translated by George and Muriel Humphrey.

DEVELOPMENT IN ADOLESCENCE, by Harold E. Jones.

THE DEFINITION OF PSYCHOLOGY, by Fred S. Keller.

THE CULTURAL BACKGROUND OF PERSONALITY, by Ralph Linton.

CHILD GUIDANCE PROCEDURES, by Members of the Staff of the Institute for Juvenile Research, Chicago.

PRINCIPLES OF APPLIED PSYCHOLOGY, by A. T. Poffenberger.

THE BEHAVIOR OF ORGANISMS: AN EXPERIMENTAL ANALYSIS, by B. F. Skinner.

THE DYNAMICS OF HUMAN ADJUSTMENT, by Percival M. Symonds.

DIAGNOSING PERSONALITY AND CONDUCT, by Percival M. Symonds.

THE PSYCHOLOGY OF PARENT-CHILD RELATIONSHIPS, by Percival M. Symonds.

HUMAN LEARNING, by Edward L. Thorndike.

INTRODUCTION TO METHODS IN EXPERIMENTAL PSYCHOLOGY, by Miles A. Tinker, 2nd Edition.

THE PSYCHOLOGY OF HUMAN DIFFERENCES, by Leona E. Tyler.

DRIVES TOWARD WAR, by Edward C. Tolman.

THEORIES OF LEARNING, by Ernest R. Hilgard.

Readings in the History of PSYCHOLOGY

COMPILED AND EDITED BY

WAYNE DENNIS

University of Pittsburgh

APPLETON–CENTURY–CROFTS, Inc.

New York

469

MANUFACTURED IN THE UNITED STATES OF AMERICA

PREFACE

THE only set of readings in the history of psychology which has been compiled prior to the present volume is Rand's *The Classical Psychologists,* which was published in 1912. It has long been out of print. Nor would a reprinting of Rand meet contemporary needs. Psychology has changed greatly in the past thirty-six years. Several of the more active "schools" of psychology were barely born, or were unborn, at the time the earlier readings were published. In another respect, also, *The Classical Psychologists* is out-dated. While recent psychological progress has been achieved primarily through investigation and experimentation, Rand's book is devoted chiefly to the philosophical backgrounds of psychology. The readings end approximately where modern psychological research began. The most recent authors cited by Rand are Wundt and James.

In teaching a course in the development of modern psychology, one feels continually that the student needs to read many of the classical contributions in psychology. It is not sufficient for the psychologist-in-training to read about Bell, Weber, Galton, Binet and Watson (to cite some examples), he should read the very words of these authors. His education should not be second-hand. Yet many of the works with which he should make himself familiar are not available in every library. If certain ones are on the shelves of the library, they exist, unfortunately, in single, frequently rare, copies which cannot be exposed year after year to classroom use. The classics in psychology must be reproduced if they are to be studied. The aim of the present compilation is to render many of them, or selections from them, available in one volume.

In selecting the materials to be included, a provisional list of forty-eight titles was first compiled. While this was done without benefit of tabulation, those titles were chosen which very frequently are referred to in current textbooks on the history of psychology or on schools of psychology. This list was then submitted to fourteen psychologists for criticism. Some of these were selected because they were personal friends, whose excessive frankness has been proven over a period of years; others were chosen because they are men of wisdom and responsibility, who, it was felt, could be depended upon to check ill-advised choices and to point out serious omissions. I owe a considerable debt of gratitude to these men, each of whom replied in a most helpful manner. I trust they will be willing to receive my acknowledgment of their assistance anonymously. To cite them as having approved most of my choices might give the appearance of borrowing for my book the very considerable prestige of their names.

Although there was agreement that the original table of contents included valuable material, the criticism frequently was made that serious omissions had occurred. Many specific suggestions were made concerning additional works which should be included. At about the time these comments were received, I also received a note from the publishers expressing their ideas concerning the number of pages which they could accept. I have had to achieve a balance of forces between these two vectors. The final list consists of sixty-one selections. It is regrettable that many important contributions to psychology could not be included.

I wish to make clear that in selecting material for this volume, I have not proposed to measure accurately the relative value of various contributions to psychology. While I believe the selections which comprise this book of readings will be of value to the student and are worthy of reprinting, I have no doubt that many publications just as valuable to the student and just as worthy of reprinting are unavoidably omitted. I see no way to prevent this unfortunate circumstance. Perhaps a later volume may permit a wider inclusion.

A few points concerning the selections: they are arranged chronologically by date of publication; the year of publication follows the title of each selection; the readings are chosen from articles, monographs, and books. With few exceptions, the articles are reprinted in full; the monographs and books are represented by excerpts. Full bibliographic data, together with acknowledgments of permission to reprint, are given with each reading.

In most instances the heading of a selection is the verbatim title of the article, monograph, or book, from which the material was taken. In a few cases, a chapter heading has been used rather than the title of the book from which the reading was taken, because the chapter heading was more descriptive of the contents; for instance, in the case of Helmholtz, "Concerning the Perceptions in General," a chapter title, was used instead of *Physiological Optics*. In some instances, (Newton, Mariotte, and Brown,) a title had to be supplied since none was used by the author.

The authors' footnotes and references, with few exceptions, have been excluded. Practically never are these essential to the sense of the reading; they have been reproduced only in instances in which they are essential.

WAYNE DENNIS

University of Pittsburgh

CONTENTS

Aristotle: 384-322 B.C.

ON MEMORY AND RECOLLECTION *

ca. 330 B.C.

CHAPTER I

WE have, in the next place, to treat of memory and remembering, considering its nature, its cause, and the part of the soul to which this experience, as well as that of recollecting, belongs. For the persons who possess a retentive memory are not identical with those who excel in power of recollection; indeed, as a rule, slow people have a good memory whereas those who are quick-witted and clever are better at recollecting.

We must first form a true conception of the objects of memory, a point on which mistakes are often made. Now to remember the future is not possible, but this is an object of opinion or expectation, like that of divination, in which some believe; nor is there memory of the present, but only sense-perception. For by the latter we know not the future nor the past, but the present only. But memory relates to the past. No one would say that he remembers the present, when it is present, e.g. a given white object at the moment when he sees it; nor would one say that he remembers an object of scientific contemplation at the moment when he is actually contemplating it, and has it full before his mind;—of the former he would say only that he perceives it, of the latter only that he knows it. But when one has scientific knowledge, or perception apart from the actualizations of the faculty concerned, he thus remembers as to the former, that he learned it, or thought it out for himself, as to the latter, that he heard, or saw it, or had some such sensible experience of it. For whenever one exercises the faculty of remembering, he must say within himself: "I formerly heard this" or "I formerly had this thought."

Memory is, therefore, neither perception nor conception, but a state or affection of one of these, conditioned by lapse of time. As already observed, there is no such thing as memory of the present while present, for the present is object only of perception, and the future, of expectation, but the object of memory is the past. All memory, therefore, implies a time elapsed; consequently only those animals which perceive time

* Many of Aristotles's treatises were concerned in part with psychological topics. The treatise presented here, and the one "On Dreams" which follows are perhaps the most distinctly psychological. They are reproduced from *The Works of Aristotle Translated into English*, Vol. 3, by permission of the Oxford University Press.

remember, and the organ whereby they perceive time is also that whereby they remember.

The subject of presentation has already considered in our work *de Anima.* Without a presentation intellectual activity is impossible. For there is in such activity an incidental affection identical with one also incidental in geometrical demonstrations. For in the latter case, though we do not for the purpose of the proof make any use of the fact that the quantity in the triangle is determinate, we nevertheless draw it determinate in quantity. So likewise when one exerts the intellect although the object may not be quantitative, one envisages it as quantitative, though he thinks it in abstraction from quantity; while, on the other hand, if the object of the intellect is essentially of the class of things that are quantitative, but indeterminate, one envisages it as if it had determinate quantity, though subsequently, in thinking it, he abstracts from its determinateness. Why we cannot exercise the intellect on any object absolutely apart from the continuous, or apply it even to non-temporal things unless in connexion with time, is another question. Now, one must cognize magnitude and motion by means of the same faculty by which one cognizes time and the presentation is an affection of the *sensus communis;* whence this follows that the cognition of these qualities is effected by the primary faculty of perception. Accordingly, memory even of intellectual objects involves a presentation: hence we may conclude that it belongs to the faculty of intelligence only incidentally, while directly and essentially it belongs to the primary faculty of sense-perception.

Hence not only human beings and the beings which possess opinion or intelligence, but also certain other animals, possess memory. Whenever one actually remembers having seen or heard, or learned, something, he includes in this act (as to have already observed) the consciousness of 'formerly' and the distinction of 'former' and 'latter' is a distinction in time.

Accordingly, if asked, of which among the parts of the soul memory is a function, we reply: manifestly of that part to which presentation appertains; and all objects capable of being presented are immediately and properly objects of memory, while those which necessarily involve presentation are objects of memory incidentally.

One might ask how it is possible that though the affection alone is present, and the (related) fact absent, the latter—that which is not present—is remembered. This question arises, because it is clear that we must conceive that which is generated through sense-perception in the sentient soul, and in the part of the body which is its seat—viz. that affection the state whereof we call memory—to be some such thing as a picture. The process of movement involved in the act of perception stamps in, as it were, a sort of impression of the percept, just as persons do who make an impression with a seal. This explains why, in those who are strongly moved owing to passion, or time of life, no mnemonic impression is formed; just as no impression would be formed if the movement of the seal were to impinge on running water; while there are others in whom, owing to the receiving surface being frayed, as happens to old walls, or owing to the hardness of the receiving surface, the requisite impression is not implanted at all. Hence both very young and very old persons are defective in memory; they are in a state of flux, the former because of their growth, the latter, owing to their decay. In like manner, also, both those who are too quick and those who are too slow have bad memories. The former are too soft, the latter too hard in the texture of their perceiving organs, so that in the case of the former the presented image though imprinted does not remain in the soul, while on the latter it is not imprinted at all.

But then, if this truly describes what happens in the genesis of memory, when one remembers, is it this impressed affection that he remembers, or is it the objective thing from which this was derived? If the former, it would follow that we remember nothing which is absent; if the latter, how is it possible that, though perceiving directly only the impression, we remember that absent thing which we do not perceive? Granted that there is in us something like an impression or picture, why should the perception of the mere impression be memory of something else, instead of being related to this impression alone? For when one actually remembers, this impression is what he contemplates, and this is what he perceives. How then does he remember what is not present? One might as well suppose it possible also to see or hear that which is not present. In reply, we suggest that this very thing is quite conceivable, nay actually occurs in experience. A picture painted on a panel is at once a picture and a likeness: that is, one may contemplate it either as a picture, or as a likeness. Just in the same way we have to conceive that the mnemonic presentation within us is something which by itself is merely an object of contemplation, while, in relation to something else, it is also a presentation of that other thing. In so far as it is regarded in itself, it is only an object of contemplation, or a presentation; but when considered as relative to something else, e.g. as its likeness it is also a mnemonic token. Hence whenever the residual sensory soul perceives this in so far as it is something absolute, it appears to occur as a mere thought or presentation; but if the soul perceives it as related to something else, then—just as when one contemplates the painting in the picture as being a likeness, and without having at the moment seen the actual Koriskos, contemplates it as a likeness of Koriskos, and in that case the experience involved in this contemplation of it is different from what one has when he contemplates it simply as a painted figure—so in the case of memory we have the analogous difference of the objects in the soul, the one (the unrelated object) presents itself simply as a thought, but the other (the related object) just because, as in the painting, it is a likeness, presents itself as a mnemonic token.

We can now understand why it is that sometimes, when we have such processes, based on some former act of perception, occurring in the soul, we do not know whether this really implies our having had perceptions corresponding to them, and we doubt whether the case is or is not one of memory. But occasionally it happens that while thus doubting we get a sudden idea and recollect that we heard or saw something formerly. This occurrence of the sudden idea happens whenever, from contemplating a mental object as absolute, one changes his point of view, and regards it as relative to something else.

The opposite also occurs, as happened in the cases of Antipheron of Oreus and others suffering from mental derangement; for they were accustomed to speak of their mere phantasms as facts of their past experience, and as if remembering them. This takes place whenever one contemplates what is not a likeness as if it were a likeness.

Mnemonic exercises aim at preserving one's memory of something by repeatedly reminding him of it; which implies nothing else on the learner's part than the frequent contemplation of something (viz. the mnemonic, whatever it may be) as a likeness, and not as out of relation.

As regards the question, therefore, what memory or remembering is, it has now been shown that it is the state of presentation, related as a likeness to that of which it is a presentation; and as to the question of which of the faculties within us memory is a function it has been shown that it is a function of the primary faculty of sense-perception, i.e. of that faculty whereby we perceive time.

CHAPTER II

Next comes the subject of Recollection, in dealing with which we must assume as fundamental the truths elicited above in our introductory discussions. For recollection is not the recovery or acquisition of memory; since at the instant when one at first learns or experiences, he does not thereby recover a memory, inasmuch as none has preceded nor does he acquire one *ab initio*. It is only at the instant when the aforesaid state or affection is implanted in the soul that memory exists, and therefore memory is not itself implanted concurrently with the implantation of the original sensory experience.

Further: at the very individual and concluding instant when first the sensory experience or scientific knowledge has been completely implanted, there is then already established in the person affected the sensory affection or the scientific knowledge if one ought to apply the term scientific knowledge to the (mnemonic) state or affection; and indeed one may well remember, in the incidental sense, some of the things which are properly objects of scientific knowledge, but to remember, strictly and properly, is an activity which will not be immanent until the original experience has undergone lapse of time. For one remembers now what one saw or otherwise experienced formerly; the moment of the original experience and the moment of the memory of it are never identical.

Again it is obviously possible, without any present act of recollection, to remember as a continued consequence of the original perception or other experience; whereas when one recovers some scientific knowledge which he had before, or some perception, or some other experience, the state of which we above declared to be memory, it is then and then only, that this recovery may amount to a recollection of any of the things aforesaid. But though as observed above, remembering does not necessarily imply recollecting, recollecting always implies remembering, and actualized memory follows upon the successful act of recollecting. But secondly, even the assertion that recollection is the reinstatement in consciousness of something which was there before but had disappeared requires qualification. This assertion may be true, but it may also be false; for the same person may twice learn or twice discover the same fact. Accordingly, the act of recollecting ought to be distinguished from these acts; i.e. recollecting must imply in those who recollect the presence of some spring over and above that from which they originally learn.

Acts of recollection, as they occur in experience, are due to the fact that one movement has by nature another that succeeds it in regular order.

If this order be necessary, whenever a subject experiences the former of two movements thus connected, it will experience the latter; if however, the order be not necessary, but customary, only in the majority of cases will the subject experience the latter of the two movements. But it is a fact that there are some movements, by a single experience of which persons take the impress of custom more deeply than they do by experiencing others many times; hence upon seeing things but once we remember them better than others which we may have seen frequently.

Whenever, therefore, we are recollecting, we are experiencing certain of the antecedent movements until finally we experience the one after which customarily comes that which we seek. This explains why we hunt up the series having started in thought either from a present intuition or some other, and from something either similar, or contrary, to what we seek, or else from that which is contiguous with it. Such is the empirical ground of the process of recollection; for the mnemonic movements involved in these starting-points are in some cases identical, in others again, simultaneous with those of the idea we seek, while in others they comprise a portion of them, so that the remnant which one experienced after that portion and which still requires to be excited in memory is comparatively small.

Thus, then, it is that persons seek to recollect and thus too, it is that they recollect even without the effort of seeking to do so, viz. when the movement implied in recollection has supervened in some other which is its condition. For as a rule, it is when antecedent movements of the classes here described have first been excited, that the particular movement implied in recollection follows. We need not examine a series of which the beginning and end lie far apart in order to see how we remember; one in which they lie near one another will serve equally well. For it is clear that the method is in each case the same, that is, one hunts up the objective series, without any previous search or previous recollection. For by the effect of custom the mnemonic movements tend to succeed one another in a certain order. Accordingly therefore, when one wishes to recollect this is what he will do; he will try to obtain a beginning of movement whose sequel shall be the movement which he desires to reawaken. This explains why attempts at recollection succeed soonest and best when they start from a beginning. For, in order of succession, the mnemonic movements are to one another as the objective facts. Accordingly, things arranged in a fixed order, like the successive demonstrations in geometry, are easy to remember, while badly arranged subjects are remembered with difficulty.

Recollecting differs also in this respect from relearning that one who recollects will be able, somehow, to move solely by his own effort to the term next after the starting-point. Whenever one cannot do this of himself, but only by external assistance, he no longer remembers, i.e. he has totally forgotten, and therefore of course cannot recollect. It often happens that, though a person cannot recollect at the moment, yet by seeking he can do so, and discovers what he seeks. This he succeeds in doing by setting up many movements, until finally he excites one of a kind which will have for its sequel the fact he wishes to recollect. For remembering is the existence, potentially, in the mind of a movement capable of stimulating it to the desired movement, and this, as has been said, in such a way that the person should be moved from within himself, i.e. in consequence of movements wholly contained within himself.

But one must get hold of a starting-point. This explains why it is that persons are supposed to recollect sometimes by starting from mnemonic loci. The cause is that they pass swiftly in thought from one point to another, e.g. from milk to white, from white to mist, and thence to moist, from which one remembers Autumn if this be the season he is trying to recollect.

For as regular sequence of events is in accordance with nature, so, too, regular sequence is observed in the actualization of memory, and here frequency tends to produce nature. And since in the realm of nature occurrences take place which are even contrary to nature, or fortuitous, the same happens in the sphere swayed by custom, since in this sphere natural law is not similarly established. Hence it is that the mind receives an impulse to move sometimes in the required direction, and at other times otherwise, particularly when something else somehow deflects the mind from the right direction and attracts it to itself. This last consideration explains too how it happens that, when we want to remember a name, we remember one somewhat like it, indeed, but blunder in reference to pronouncing the one we intended.

Thus, then, recollection takes place.

But the point of capital importance is that for the purpose of recollection one should cognize determinately or indeterminately, the time-relation of that which he wishes to recollect. There is, let it be taken as a fact, something by which one distinguishes a greater and a smaller time; and it is reasonable to think that one does this in a way analogous to that in which one discerns magnitudes. For it is not by the mind's reaching out towards them, as some say a visual ray from the eye does, that one thinks of large things at a distance in space; but one does so by a proportionate mental movement. For there are in the mind the like figures and movements (i.e. like to those of objects and events). Therefore, when one thinks the greater objects, in what will his thinking those differ from his thinking the smaller. In nothing because all the internal though smaller are as it were proportional to the external.

When, therefore, the movement corresponding to the object and that corresponding to its time concur, then one actually remembers. If one supposes without really doing so, he supposes himself to remember. For one may be mistaken, and think that he remembers when he really does not. But it is not possible, conversely, that when one actually remembers he should not suppose himself to remember, but should remember unconsciously. For remembering, as we have conceived it, essentially implies consciousness of itself. If, however, the movement corresponding to the objective fact takes place without that corresponding to the time, or, if the latter takes place without the former, one does not remember.

The movement answering to the time is of two kinds. Sometimes, in remembering a fact one has no determinate time notion of it, no such notion as that, e.g. he did something or other on the day before yesterday, while in other cases he has a determinate notion of the time. Still, even though one does not remember with actual determination of the time, he genuinely remembers, none the less. Persons are wont to say that they remember something but yet do not know when it occurred, as happens whenever they do not know determinately the exact length of time implied in the "when."

It has been already stated that those who have a good memory are not identical with those who are quick at recollecting. But the act of recollecting differs from that of remembering, not only chronologically but also in this, that many also of the other animals as well as man have memory, but of all that we are acquainted with, none, we venture to say, except man, shares in the faculty of recollection. The cause of this is that recollection is, as it were a mode of inference. For he who endeavours to recollect infers that he formerly saw, or heard, or had some such experience, and the process by which he succeeds in recollecting is, as it were, a sort of investigation. But to investigate in this way belongs naturally to those animals alone which are also endowed with the faculty of deliberation; which proves what was said above, for deliberation is a form of inference.

That the affection is corporeal, i.e. that recollection is searching for an "image" in a corporeal substrate, is proved by the fact that in some persons, when, despite the most strenuous application of thought, they have been unable to recollect, it excites a feeling of discomfort which, even though they abandon the effort at recollection, persists in them none the less; and especially in persons of melancholic temperament. For these are most powerfully moved by presentations. The reason why the effort of recollection is not under the control of their will is that, as those who throw a stone cannot stop it at their will when thrown, so he who tries to recollect and "hunts" sets up a process in a material part, in which resides the affection. Those who have moisture around that part which is the centre of sense perception suffer most discomfort of this kind. For when once the moisture has been set in motion it is not easily brought to rest, until the idea which was sought for has again presented itself, and thus the movement has found a straight course. For a similar reason bursts of anger or fits of terror when once they have excited such motions, are not at once allayed even though the angry or terrified persons by efforts of will set up counter motions, but the passions continue to move them on, in the same direction as at first, in opposition to such counter motions. The affection resembles also that in the case of words, tunes, or sayings, whenever one of them has become inveterate on the lips. People give them up and resolve to avoid them; yet again and again they find themselves humming the forbidden air, or using the prohibited word.

Those whose upper parts are abnormally large, as is the case with dwarfs, have abnormally weak memory, as compared with their opposites, because of the great weight which they have resting upon the organ of perception, and because of their mnemonic movements are, from the very first, not able to keep true to a course, but are dispersed, and because, in the effort at recollection, these movements do not easily find a direct onward path. Infants and very old persons have bad memories owing to the amount of movement going on within them; for the latter are in process of rapid decay, the former in process of vigorous growth; and we may add that children, until considerably advanced in years, are dwarf-like in their bodily structure. Such then is our theory as regards memory and remembering, their nature and the particular organ of the soul by which animals remember; also as regards recollection, its formal definition, and the manner and causes of its performance.

Aristotle: 384-322 B.C.

ON DREAMS *

ca. 330 B.C.

CHAPTER I

We must, in the next place, investigate the subject of the dream, and first inquire to which of the faculties of the soul it presents itself, i.e. whether the affection is one which pertains to the faculty of intelligence or that of sense-perception; for these are the only faculties within us by which we acquire knowledge.

If, then, the exercise of the faculty of sight is actual seeing, that of the auditory faculty, hearing, and, in general that of the faculty of sense-perception, perceiving; and if there are some perceptions common to the senses, such as figure, magnitude, motion, etc., while there are others, as colour, sound, taste, peculiar each to its own sense; and further, if all creatures, when the eyes are closed in sleep, are unable to see, and the analogous statement is true of the other senses, so that manifestly we perceive nothing when asleep; we may conclude that it is not by sense-perception we perceive a dream.

But neither is it by opinion that we do so. For in dreams we not only assert, e.g., that some object approaching is a man or a horse but that the object is white or beautiful, points on which opinion without sense-perception asserts nothing either truly or falsely. It is, however, a fact that the soul makes assertions in sleep. We seem to see equally well that the approaching figure is a man, and that it is white. In dreams, too, we think something else, over and above the dream presentation, just as we do in waking moments when we perceive something; for we often also reason about that which we perceive. So, too, in sleep we sometimes have thoughts other than the mere phantasms immediately before our minds. This would be manifest to anyone who should attend and try immediately on arising from sleep to remember his dreaming experiences. There are cases of persons who have seen such dreams, those, for example, who believe themselves to be mentally arranging a given list of subjects according to the mnemonic rule. They frequently find themselves engaged in something else besides the dream, viz. in setting a phantasm which they envisage into its mnemonic position. Hence it is plain

* Reprinted by permission of the Oxford University Press from Vol. 3 of *The Works of Aristotle Translated into English.*

that not every phantasm in sleep is a mere dream-image and that the further thinking which we perform then is due to an exercise of the faculty of opinion.

So much at least is plain on all these points, viz. that the faculty by which, in waking hours, we are subject to illusion when affected by disease, is identical with that which produces illusory effects in sleep. So, even when persons are in excellent health, and know the facts of the case perfectly well, the sun, nevertheless, appears to them to be only a foot wide. Now, whether the presentative faculty of the soul be identical with, or different from, the faculty of sense perception, in either case the illusion does not occur without our actually seeing or otherwise perceiving something. Even to see wrongly or to hear wrongly can happen only to one who sees or hears something real, though not exactly what he supposes. But we have assumed that in sleep one neither sees, nor hears, nor exercises any sense whatever. Perhaps we may regard it as true that the dreamer sees nothing, yet as false that his faculty of sense-perception is unaffected, the fact being that the sense of seeing and the other senses may possibly be then in a certain way affected, while each of these affections, as duly as when he is awake, gives its impulse in a certain manner to his primary faculty of sense, though not in precisely the same manner as when he is awake. Sometimes, too, opinion says to dreamers just as to those who are awake, that the object seen is an illusion; at other times it is inhibited, and becomes a mere follower of the phantasm.

It is plain therefore that this affection, which we name dreaming is no mere exercise of opinion or intelligence, but yet is not an affection of the faculty of perception in the simple sense. If it were the latter it would be possible when asleep to hear and see in the simple sense.

How then, and in what manner, it takes place, is what we have to examine. Let us assume, what is indeed clear enough, that the affection of dreaming pertains to a sense-perception as surely as sleep itself does. For sleep does not pertain to one organ in animals and dreaming to another; both pertain to the same organ.

But since we have in our work on the Soul, treated of presentation, and the faculty of presentation is identical with that of sense-perception, though the essential notion of faculty of presentation is different from that of a faculty of sense-perception; and since presentation is the movement set up by a sensory faculty when actually discharging its function, while a dream appears to be a presentation (for a presentation which occurs in sleep—whether simply or in some particular way—is what we call a dream) it manifestly follows that dreaming is an activity of the faculty of sense perception, but belongs to this faculty qua presentative.

CHAPTER II

We can best obtain a scientific view of the nature of the dream and the manner in which it originates by regarding it in the light of the circumstances attending sleep. The objects of sense-perception corresponding to each sensory organ produce sense-perception in us, and the affection due to their operation is present in the organs of sense not only when the perceptions are actualized, but even when they have departed.

What happens in these cases may be compared with what happens in the case of projectiles moving in space. For in the case of these the movement continues even when that which set up the movement is no longer in contact with the things that are moved. For that which set them in motion moves a certain portion of air, and this, in turn, being moved excites motion in another portion; and so accordingly, it is in this way that the bodies whether in air or in liquids continue moving, until they come to a standstill.

This we must likewise assume to happen in the case of qualitative change; for that part which has been heated by something hot, heats the part next to it, and this propagates the affection continuously onwards until the process has come round to its point of origination. This must also happen in the organ wherein the exercise of sense-perception takes place, since sense-perception as realized in actual perceiving is a mode of qualitative change. This explains why the affection continues in the sensory organs, both in their deeper and in their more superficial parts, not merely while they are actually engaged in perceiving, but even after they have ceased to do so. That they do this, indeed is obvious in cases where we continue for some time engaged in a particular form of perception, for then, when we shift the scene of our perceptive activity, the previous affection remains; for instance we have turned our gaze from sunlight to darkness. For the result of this is that one sees nothing, owing to the motion excited by the light still subsisting in our eyes. Also, when we have looked steadily for a long while at one colour, e.g. at white or green, that to which we next transfer our gaze appears to be of the same color. Again if, after having looked at the sun or some other brilliant object, we close the eyes, then, if we watch carefully, it appears in a right line with the direction of vision, at first in its own colour; then it changes to crimson, next to purple, until it becomes black and disappears. And also when persons turn away from looking at objects in motion, e.g. rivers and especially those which flow very rapidly, they find that the visual stimulations still present themselves, for the things really at rest are then seen moving; persons become very deaf after hearing loud noises and after smelling very strong odours their power of smelling is impaired; and similarly in other cases. These phenomena manifestly take place in the way above described.

In order to answer our original question, let us now, therefore, assume our original proposition, which is clear from what precedes, viz., that even when the external object of perception has departed, the impressions it has made persist, and are themselves objects of perception; and besides that we are easily deceived respecting the operations of sense perception when we are excited by emotions, and different persons according to their different emotions; for example, the coward when excited by fear, the amorous person by amorous desire; so that, with but little resemblance to go upon, the former thinks he sees his foes approaching, the latter that he sees the object of his desire; and the more deeply one is under the influence of the emotion, the less similarity is required to give rise to these illusory impressions. Thus, too, both in fits of anger, and also in all states of appetite, all men become easily deceived, and more so the more their emotions are excited. This is the reason too why persons in the delirium of fever sometimes think they see animals on their chamber walls, an illusion arising from the faint resemblance to animals of the markings thereon when put together in patterns; and this sometimes corresponds with the emotional states of the sufferers, in such a way that, if the latter be not very ill, they know well enough that it is an illusion; but if the illness is more severe they actually move according to the appearances. The cause of these occurrences is that the faculty in virtue of which the controlling sense judges is not identical with that in virtue of which presentations come before the mind. A proof of this is that the sun presents itself as only a foot in diameter, though often something else gainsays the presentation. Again when the fingers are crossed, the one object is felt by the touch as two, but yet we deny that it is two; for sight is more authoritative than touch. Yet, if touch stood alone, we should actually have pronounced the one object to be two. The ground of such false judgments is that any appearances whatever present themselves, not only when its object stimulates a sense, but also when the sense by itself alone is stimulated, provided only it be stimulated in the same manner as it is by the object. For example, to persons sailing past, the land seems to move when it is really the eye that is being moved by something else (the moving ship).

CHAPTER III

From this it is manifest that the stimulatory movements based upon sensory impressions, whether the latter are derived from external objects or from causes within the body, present themselves not only when persons are awake, but also then, when this affection which is called sleep has come upon them, with even greater impressiveness. For by day while the senses and the intellect are working together, they (i.e. such movements) are extruded from consciousness or obscured, just as a smaller is beside a larger fire, or as small beside great pains or pleasures, though, as soon as the latter have ceased, even those which are trifling emerge into notice. But by night (i.e. in sleep) owing to the inaction of the particular senses, and their powerlessness to realize themselves, which arises from the reflux of the hot from the exterior to the interior they are borne in to the headquarters of sense-perception and there display themselves as the disturbance of waking life subsides. We must suppose that, like the little eddies which are being ever formed in rivers, so the sensory movements are each a continuous process, often remaining like what they were when first started but often too broken into other forms by collisions with obstacles. This last mentioned point moreover gives the reason why no dreams occur in sleep immediately after meals, or to sleepers who are extremely young, e.g. to infants. The internal movement in such cases is excessive, owing to the heat generated from the food. Hence, just as in a liquid, if one vehemently disturbs it, sometimes no reflected image appears, while at other times one appears indeed, but utterly distorted, so as to seem quite unlike its original; while, when once the motion has ceased, the reflected images are clear and plain; in the same manner during sleep the phantasms or residuary movements, which are based upon the sensory impressions, become sometimes quite obliterated by the above described motion when too violent; while at other times the sights are indeed seen but confused and weird, and the dreams are unhealthy, like those of persons who are atrabilious or feverish, or intoxicated with wine. For all such affections, being spirituous, cause much commotion and disturbance. In sanguineous animals in proportion as the blood becomes calm as its purer are separated from its less pure elements, the fact that the movement based on impressions derived from each of the organs of sense is preserved in its integrity, renders the dreams healthy, causes a clear image to present itself, and makes the dreamer think, owing to the effects borne in from the organ of sight, that he actually sees, and owing to those which come from the organ of hearing, that he really hears; and so on with those also which proceed from the other sensory organs. For it is owing to the fact that the movement which reaches the primary organ of sense comes from them, that one even when awake believes himself to hear, or see or otherwise perceive; just as it is from a belief that the organ of sight is being stimulated, though in reality not so stimulated, that we sometimes erroneously declare ourselves to see, or that, from the fact that touch announces two movements, we think that the one object is two. For as a rule, the governing sense affirms the report of each particular sense, unless another particular sense, more authoritative, makes a contradictory report. In every case an appearance presents itself, but what appears does not in every case seem real, unless when the deciding faculty is inhibited, or does not move with its proper motion. Moreover, as we said that different men are subject to illusions, each according to the different emotion present in him, so it is that the sleeper, owing to sleep, and to the movements then going on in his sensory organs, as well as to the other facts of the sensory process, is liable to illusion so that the dream presentation, though but little like it, appears as some actual given thing. For when one is asleep in proportion as most of the blood sinks inwards to its fountain (the heart) the internal (sensory) movements, some potential, others actual, accompany it inwards. They are so related that if anything move the blood some one sensory movement will emerge from it, while if this perishes another will take its place; while to one another also they are related in the same way as the artificial frogs in water which severally rise to the surface in the order in which the salt which keeps them down becomes dissolved. The residuary movements are like these: they are within the soul potentially, but actualize themselves only when the impediment to their doing so has been relaxed; and according as they are thus set free, they begin to move in the blood which remains in the sensory organs, and which is now but scanty, while they possess verisimilitude after the manner of cloud-shapes, which in their rapid metamorphoses one compares now to human beings and a moment afterwards to centaurs. Each of them is however, as it has been said, the remnant of a sensory impression taken when sense was actualizing itself; and when this, the true impression, has departed, its remnant is still immanent, and it is correct to say of it, that though not actually Koriskos, it is like Koriskos. For when the person was actually perceiving, his controlling and judging sensory faculty did not call it Koriskos, but, prompted by this impression called the genuine person yonder Koriskos. Accordingly, this sensory impulse, which, when actually perceiving, it so describes, (unless completely inhibited by the blood) it now (in dreams) when quasi-perceiving, receives from the movements persisting in the sense organs, and mistakes it—an impulse that is merely like the true (objective) impression—for the true impression itself, while the effect of sleep is so great that it causes this mistake to pass unnoticed accordingly, just as if a finger be inserted beneath the eyeball without being observed, one object will not only present two visual images, but will create an opinion of its being two objects; while if the finger be observed, the presentation will be the same, but the same opinion will not be formed of it; exactly so it is in states of sleep: if the sleeper perceives that he is asleep and is conscious of the sleeping state during which the perception comes before his mind, it presents itself still, but something within him speaks to this effect: the image of Koriskos presents itself but the real Koriskos is not present; for often, when one is asleep there is something in consciousness which declares that what then presents itself is but a dream. If, however, he is not aware of being asleep, there is nothing which will contradict the testimony of the bare presentation.

That what we here urge is true, i.e. that there are such presentative movements in the sensory organs, any one may convince himself, if he attends to and tries to remember the affections we experience when sinking into slumber or when being awakened. He will sometimes in the moment of awakening, surprise the images which present themselves to him in sleep, and find that they are really but movements lurking in the organs of sense. And indeed some very young persons, if it is dark, though looking with wide open eyes, see multitudes of phantom figures moving before them, so that they often cover up their heads in terror.

From all this, then, the conclusion to be drawn is, that the dream is a sort of presentation, and, more particularly, one which occurs in sleep; since the phantoms just mentioned are not dreams, nor is any other a dream which presents itself when the sense-perceptions are in a state of freedom. Nor is every presentation which occurs in sleep necessarily a dream. For in the first place, some persons when asleep actually, in a certain way, perceive sounds, light, savour, and contact; feebly, however, and, as it were, remotely. For there have been cases in which persons while asleep, but with the eyes partly open, saw faintly in their sleep as they supposed the light of a lamp, and afterwards, on being awakened, straightway recognized it as the actual light of a real lamp; while, in other cases, persons who faintly heard the crowing of cocks or the barking of dogs identified these clearly with the real sounds as soon as they awoke. Some persons, too, return answers to questions put to them in sleep. For it is quite possible that, of waking or sleeping, while the one is present in the ordinary sense, the other also should be present in a certain way. But none of these occurrences should be called a dream. Nor should the true thoughts as distinct from the mere presentations which occur in sleep be called dreams. The dream proper is a presentation based on the movement of sense impressions, when such presentation occurs during sleep, taking sleep in the strict sense of the term.

There are cases of persons who in their whole lives have never had a dream, while others dream when considerably advanced in years, having never dreamed before. The cause of their not having dreams appears somewhat like that which operates in the case of infants, and that which operates immediately after meals. It is intelligible enough that no dream-presentation should occur to persons whose natural constitution is such that in them copious evaporation is borne upwards, which, when borne back downwards, causes a large quantity of motion. But it is not surprising that, as age advances, a dream should at length appear to them. Indeed it is inevitable that, as a change is wrought in them in proportion to age or emotional experience, this reversal from non-dreaming to dreaming should occur also.

Galileo: 1564-1642

MATHEMATICAL DISCOURSES CONCERNING TWO NEW SCIENCES RELATING TO MECHANICS AND LOCAL MOTION *

1638

SALVIATI: Impelled by your queries I may give you some of my ideas concerning certain problems in music, a splendid subject, upon which so many eminent men have written: among these is Aristotle himself who has discussed numerous interesting acoustical questions. Accordingly, if on the basis of some easy and tangible experiments, I shall explain some striking phenomena in the domain of sound, I trust my explanations will meet your approval.

SAGREDO: I shall receive them not only gratefully but eagerly. For, although I take pleasure in every kind of musical instrument and have paid considerable attention to harmony, I have never been able to fully understand why some combinations of tones are more pleasing than others, or why certain combinations not only fail to please but are even highly offensive. Then there is the old problem of two stretched strings in unison; when one of them is sounded, the other begins to vibrate and to emit its note; nor do I understand the different ratios of harmony and some other details.

SALVIATI: Let us see whether we cannot derive from the pendulum a satisfactory solution of all these difficulties. And first, as to the question whether one and the same pendulum really performs its vibrations, large, medium, and small, all in exactly the same time, I shall rely upon what I have already heard from our Academician. He has clearly shown that the time of descent is the same along all chords, whatever the arcs which subtend them, as well along an arc of 180° (i.e., the whole diameter) as along one of 100°, 60°, 10°, 2°, ½°, or 4′. It is understood, of course, that these arcs all terminate at the lowest point of the circle, where it touches the horizontal plane.

* Galileo was the first to relate pitch to frequency of vibration. This discovery was first published in 1638, in dialogue form. The translation, from which quotations are here presented, is by Henry Crew and Alfonso de Salvio, The Macmillan Co., 1914, pp. 95-104. This material is reprinted through the courtesy of Northwestern University.

If now we consider descent along arcs instead of their chords then, provided these do not exceed 90°, experiment shows that they are all traversed in equal times; but these times are greater for the chord than for the arc, an effect which is all the more remarkable because at first glance one would think just the opposite to be true. For since the terminal points of the two motions are the same and since the straight line included between these two points is the shortest distance between them, it would seem reasonable that motion along this line should be executed in the shortest time; but this is not the case, for the shortest time—and therefore the most rapid motion—is that employed along the arc of which that straight line is the chord.

As to the times of vibration of bodies suspended by threads of different lengths, they bear to each other the same proportion as the square roots of the lengths of the thread; or one might say the lengths are to each other as the squares of the times; so that if one wishes to make the vibration-time of one pendulum twice that of another, he must make its suspension four times as long. In like manner, if one pendulum has a suspension nine times as long as another, this second pendulum will execute three vibrations during each one of the first; from which it follows that the lengths of the suspending cords bear to each other the (inverse) ratio of the squares of the number of vibrations performed in the same time.

SAGREDO: Then, if I understand you correctly, I can easily measure the length of a string whose upper end is attached at any height whatever even if this end were invisible and I could see only the lower extremity. For if I attach to the lower end of this string a rather heavy weight and give it a to-and-fro motion, and if I ask a friend to count a number of its vibrations, while I, during the same time-interval, count the number of vibrations of a pendulum which is exactly one cubit in length, then knowing the number of vibrations which each pendulum makes in a given interval of time one can determine the length of the string. Suppose, for example, that my friend counts 20 vibrations of the long cord during the same time in which I count 240 of my strings which is one cubit in length; taking the squares of the two numbers, 20 and 240, namely 400 and 57600, then, I say, the long string contains 57600 units of such length that my pendulum will contain 400 of them; and since the length of my string is one cubit, I shall divide 57600 by 400 and thus obtain 144. Accordingly I shall call the length of the string 144 cubits.

SALVIATI: Nor will you miss it by as much as a hand's breadth, especially if you observe a large number of vibrations.

SAGREDO: You give me frequent occasion to admire the wealth and profusion of nature when, from such common and even trivial phenomena, you derive facts which are not only striking and new but which are often far removed from what we would have imagined. Thousands of times I have observed vibrations especially in churches where lamps, suspended by long cords, had been inadvertently set into motion; but the most which I could infer from these observations was that the view of those who think that such vibrations are maintained by the medium is highly improbable: for, in that case, the air must needs have considerable judgment and little else to do but kill time by pushing to and fro a pendent weight with perfect regularity. But I never dreamed of learning that one and the same body, when suspended from a string a hundred cubits long and pulled aside through an arc of 90° or even 1° or ½°, would employ the same time in passing through the least as through the largest of these arcs; and, indeed, it still strikes me as somewhat unlikely. Now I am waiting to hear how these same simple phenomena can furnish solutions for those acoustical problems—solutions which will be at least partly satisfactory.

Salviati: First of all one must observe that each pendulum has its own time of vibration so definite and determinate that it is not possible to make it move with any other period than that which nature has given it. For let any one take in his hand the cord to which the weight is attached and try, as much as he pleases, to increase or diminish the frequency of its vibrations; it will be time wasted. On the other hand, one can confer motion upon even a heavy pendulum which is at rest by simply blowing against it; by repeating these blasts with a frequency which is the same as that of the pendulum one can impart considerable motion. Suppose that by the first puff we have displaced the pendulum from the vertical by, say, half an inch; then if, after the pendulum has returned and is about to begin the second vibration, we add a second puff, we shall impart additional motion; and so on with other blasts provided they are applied at the right instant, and not when the pendulum is coming toward us since in this case the blast would impede rather than aid the motion. Continuing thus with many impulses we impart to the pendulum such momentum that a greater impulse than that of a single blast will be needed to stop it.

Sagredo: Even as a boy, I observed that one man alone by giving these impulses at the right instant was able to ring a bell so large that when four, or even six, men seized the rope and tried to stop it they were lifted from the ground, all of them together being unable to counterbalance the momentum which a single man, by properly-timed pulls, had given it.

Salviati: Your illustration makes my meaning clear and is quite as well fitted, as what I have just said, to explain the wonderful phenomenon of the strings of the cittern or of the spinet, namely, the fact that a vibrating string will set another string in motion and cause it to sound not only when the latter is in unison but even when it differs from the former by an octave or a fifth. A string which has been struck begins to vibrate and continues the motion as long as one hears the sound; these vibrations cause the immediately surrounding air to vibrate and quiver; then these ripples in the air expand far into space and strike not only all the strings of the same instrument but even those of neighboring instruments. Since that string which is tuned to unison with the one plucked is capable of vibrating with the same frequency, it acquires, at the first impulse, a slight oscillation; after receiving two, three, twenty, or more impulses, delivered at proper intervals, it finally accumulates a vibratory motion equal to that of the plucked string, as is clearly shown by equality of amplitude in their vibrations. This undulation expands through the air and sets into vibration not only strings, but also any other body which happens to have the same period as that of the plucked string. Accordingly if we attach to the side of an instrument small pieces of bristle or other flexible bodies, we shall observe that, when a spinet is sounded, only those pieces respond that have the same period as the string which has been struck; the remaining pieces do not vibrate in response to this string, nor do the former pieces respond to any other tone.

If one bows the base string on a viola rather smartly and brings near it a goblet of fine, thin glass having the same tone as that of the string, this goblet will vibrate and audibly resound. That the undulations of the medium are widely dispersed about the sounding body is evinced by the fact that a glass of water may be made to emit a tone merely by the friction of the finger-tip upon the rim of the glass; for in this water is produced a series of regular waves. The same phenomenon is observed to better advantage by fixing the base of the goblet upon the bottom of a rather large vessel of water filled nearly to the edge of the goblet; for if, as before, we sound the glass by friction of the finger, we shall see ripples spreading with the utmost regularity and with high speed to large distances about the glass. I have often remarked, in a rather large glass nearly full of water, that at first the waves are spaced with great uniformity, and when, as sometimes happens, the tone of the glass jumps an octave higher I have noted that at this moment each of the aforesaid waves divides into two; a phenomenon which shows clearly that the ratio involved in the octave is two.

SAGREDO: More than once have I observed this same thing, much to my delight and also to my profit. For a long time I have been perplexed about these different harmonies since the explanations hitherto given by those learned in music impress me as not sufficiently conclusive. They tell us that the diapason, i.e. the octave, involves the ratio of two, that the diapente which we call the fifth involves a ratio of 3:2, etc.; because if the open string of a monochord be sounded and afterwards a bridge be placed in the middle and the half length be sounded one hears the octave; and if the bridge be placed at 1/3 the length of the string, then on plucking first the open string and afterwards 2/3 of its length the fifth is given; for this reason they say that the octave depends upon the ratio of two to one and the fifth upon the ratio of three to two. This explanation does not impress me as sufficient to establish 2 and 3/2 as the natural ratios of the octave and the fifth; and my reason for thinking so is as follows. There are three different ways in which the tone of a string may be sharpened, namely, by shortening it, by stretching it and by making it thinner. If the tension and size of the string remain constant one obtains the octave by shortening it to one-half, i.e., by sounding first the open string and then one-half of it; but if length and size remain constant and one attempts to produce the octave by stretching he will find that it does not suffice to double the stretching weight; it must be quadrupled; so that, if the fundamental note is produced by a weight of one pound, four will be required to bring out the octave.

And finally if the length and tension remain constant, while one changes the size of the string he will find that in order to produce the octave the size must be reduced to 1/4 that which gave the fundamental. And what I have said concerning the octave, namely, that its ratio as derived from the tension and size of the string is the square of that derived from the length, applies equally well to all other musical intervals. Thus if one wishes to produce a fifth by changing the length he finds that the ratio of the lengths must be sesquilateral, in other words he sounds first the open string, then two-thirds of it; but if he wishes to produce this same result by stretching or thinning the string then it becomes necessary to square the ratio 3/2 that is by taking 9/4; accordingly, if the fundamental requires a weight of 4 pounds, the higher note will be produced not by 6, but by 9 pounds; the same is true in regard to size, the string which gives the fundamental is larger than that which yields the fifth in the ratio of 9 to 4.

In view of these facts, I see no reason why those wise philosophers should adopt 2 rather than 4 as the ratio of the octave, or why in the case of the fifth they should employ the sesquilateral ratio, 3/2, rather than that of 9/4. Since it is impossible to count the vibrations of a sounding string on account of its high frequency, I should still have been in doubt as to whether a string, emitting the upper octave, made twice as many vibrations in the same time as one giving the fundamental, had it not been for the following fact, namely, that at the instant when the tone jumps to the octave, the waves which constantly accompany the vibrating glass divide up into smaller ones which are precisely half as long as the former.

Salviati: This is a beautiful experiment enabling us to distinguish individually the waves which are produced by the vibrations of a sonorous body, which spread through the air, bringing to the tympanum of the ear a stimulus which the mind translates into sound. But since these waves in the water last only so long as the friction of the finger continues and are, even then, not constant but are always forming and disappearing, would it not be a fine thing if one had the ability to produce waves which would persist for a long while, even months and years, so as to easily measure and count them?

SAGREDO: Such an invention would, I assure you, command my admiration.

SALVIATI: The device is one which I hit upon by accident; my part consists merely in the observation of it and in the appreciation of its value as a confirmation of something to which I had given profound consideration; and yet the device is, in itself, rather common. As I was scraping a brass plate with a sharp iron chisel in order to remove some spots from it and was running the chisel rather rapidly over it, I once or twice, during many strokes, heard the plate emit a rather strong and clear whistling sound; on looking at the place more carefully, I noticed a long row of fine streaks parallel and equidistant from one another. Scraping with the chisel over and over again, I noticed that it was only when the plate emitted this hissing noise that any marks were left upon it; when the scraping was not accompanied by this sibilant note there was not the least trace of such marks. Repeating the trick several times and making the stroke, now with greater now with less speed, the whistling followed with a pitch which was correspondingly higher and lower. I noted also that the marks made when the tones were higher were closer together; but when the tones were deeper, they were farther apart. I also observed that when, during a single stroke, the speed increased toward the end the sound became sharper and the streaks grew closer together, but always in such a way as to remain sharply defined and equidistant. Besides whenever the stroke was accompanied by hissing I felt the chisel tremble in my grasp and a sort of shiver run through my hand. In short we see and hear in the case of the chisel precisely that which is seen and heard in the case of a whisper followed by a loud voice; for, when the breath is emitted without the production of a tone, one does not feel either in the throat or mouth any motion to speak of in comparison with that which is felt in the larynx and upper part of the throat when the voice is used, especially when the tones employed are low and strong.

At times I have also observed among the strings of the spinet two which were in unison with two of the tones produced by the aforesaid scraping; and among those which differed most in pitch I found two which were separated by an interval of a perfect fifth. Upon measuring the distance between the markings produced by the two scrapings it was found that the space which contained 45 of one contained 30 of the other, which is precisely the ratio assigned to the fifth.

But now before proceeding any farther I want to call your attention to the fact that, of the three methods for sharpening a tone, the one which you refer to as the fineness of the string should be attributed to its weight. So long as the material of the string is unchanged, the size and weight vary in the same ratio. Thus in the case of gut-strings, we obtain the octave by making one string 4 times as large as the other; so also in the case of brass one wire must have 4 times the size of the other; but if now we wish to obtain the octave of a gut-string, by use of brass wire, we must make it, not four times as large, but four times as heavy as the gut-string: as regards size therefore the metal string is not four times as big but four times as heavy. The wire may therefore be even thinner than the gut notwithstanding the fact that the latter gives the higher note. Hence if two spinets are strung, one with gold wire the other with brass, and if the corresponding strings each have the same length, diameter, and tension it follows that the instrument strung with gold will have a pitch about one-fifth lower than the other because gold has a density almost twice that of brass. And here it is to be noted that it is the weight rather than the size of a moving body which offers resistance to change of motion contrary to what one might at first glance think. For it seems reasonable to believe that a body which is large and light should suffer greater retardation of motion in thrusting aside the medium than would one which is thin and heavy; yet here exactly the opposite is true.

Returning now to the original subject of discussion, I assert that the ratio of a musical interval is not immediately determined either by the length, size, or tension of the strings but rather by the ratio of their frequencies, that is, by the number of pulses of air waves which strike the tympanum of the ear, causing it also to vibrate with the same frequency. This fact established, we may possibly explain why certain pairs of notes, differing in pitch produce a pleasing sensation, other a less pleasant effect, and still others a disagreeable sensation. Such an explanation would be tantamount to an explanation of the more or less perfect consonances and of dissonances. The unpleasant sensation produced by the latter arises, I think, from the discordant vibrations of two different tones which stroke the ear out of time. Especially harsh is the dissonance between notes whose frequencies are incommensurable; such a case occurs when one has two strings in unison and sounds one of them open, together with a part of the other which bears the same ratio to its whole length as the side of a square bears to the diagonal; this yields a dissonance similar to the augmented fourth or diminished fifth.

Agreeable consonances are pairs of tones which strike the ear with a certain regularity; this regularity consists in the fact that the pulses delivered by the two tones, in the same interval of time, shall be commensurable in number, so as not to keep the ear drum in perpetual torment, bending in two different directions in order to yield to the ever-discordant impulses.

The first and most pleasing consonance is, therefore, the octave since, for every pulse given to the tympanum by the lower string, the sharp string delivers two; accordingly at every other vibration of the upper string both pulses are delivered simultaneously so that one-half the entire number of pulses are delivered in unison. But when two strings are in unison their vibrations always coincide and the effect is that of a single string; hence we do not refer to it as consonance. The fifth is also a pleasing interval since for every two vibrations of the lower string the upper one gives three, so that considering the entire number of pulses from the upper string one-third of them will strike in unison, i.e., between each pair of concordant vibrations there intervene two single vibrations; and when the interval is a fourth, three single vibrations intervene. In case the interval is a second where the ratio is 9/8 it is only every ninth vibration of the upper string which reaches the ear simultaneously with one of the lower; all the others are discordant and produce a harsh effect upon the recipient ear which interprets them as dissonances.

René Descartes: 1596-1650

THE PASSIONS OF THE SOUL *

1650

ARTICLE VII

A Brief Explanation of the Parts of the Body and Some of its Functions

In order to render this more intelligible, I shall here explain in a few words the whole method in which the bodily machine is composed. There is no one who does not already know that there are in us a heart, a brain, a stomach, muscles, nerves, arteries, veins, and such things. We also know that the food that we eat descends into the stomach and bowels where its juice, passing into the liver and into all the veins, mingles with, and thereby increases the quantity of the blood which they contain. Those who have acquired even the minimum of medical knowledge further know how the heart is composed, and how all the blood in the veins can easily flow from the vena cava into its right side and from thence pass into the lung by the vessel which we term the arterial vein, and then return from the lung into the left side of the heart, by the vessel called the venous artery, and finally pass from there into the great artery, whose branches spread throughout the body. Likewise all those whom the authority of the ancients has not entirely blinded, and who have chosen to open their eyes for the purpose of investigating the opinion of Harvey regarding the circulation of the blood, do not doubt that all the veins and arteries of the body are like streams by which the blood ceaselessly flows with great swiftness, taking its course from the right cavity of the heart by the arterial vein whose branches are spread over the whole of the lung, and joined to that of the venous artery by which it passes from the lung into the left side of the heart; from these, again, it goes into the great artery whose branches, spread throughout all the rest of the body, are united to the branches of the vein, which branches once more carry the same blood into the right cavity of the heart. Thus these two cavities are like sluices through each of which all the blood passes in the course of each circuit which it makes in the body. We further know

* Descartes presented one of the earliest attempts at a physiological psychology. The present quotations are reprinted by permission of Charles Scribner's Sons from *Descartes Selections,* edited by Ralph M. Eaton, 1927.

that all the movements of the members depend on the muscles, and that these muscles are so mutually related one to another that when the one is contracted it draws toward itself the part of the body to which it is attached, which causes the opposite muscle at the same time to become elongated; then if at another time it happens that this last contracts, it causes the former to become elongated and it draws back to itself the part to which they are attached. We know finally that all these movements of the muscles, as also all the senses, depend on the nerves, which resemble small filaments, or little tubes which all proceed from the brain, and thus contain like it a certain very subtle air or wind which is called the animal spirits.

ARTICLE VIII

What is the Principle of All These Functions?

But it is not usually known in what way these animal spirits and these nerves contribute to the movements and to the senses, nor what is the corporeal principle which causes them to act. That is why, although I have already made some mention of them in my other writings, I shall not here omit to say shortly that so long as we live there is a continual heat in our heart, which is a species of fire which the blood of the veins there maintains, and that this fire is the corporeal principle of all the movements of our members.

ARTICLE X

How the Animal Spirits are Produced in the Brain

But what is here most worthy of remark is that all the most animated and subtle portions of the blood which the heat has rarefied in the heart, enter ceaselessly in large quantities into the cavities of the brain. And the reason which causes them to go there rather than elsewhere, is that all the blood which issues from the heart by the great artery takes its course in a straight line towards that place, and not being able to enter it in its entirety, because there are only very narrow passages there, those of its parts which are the most agitated and the most subtle alone pass through, while the rest spreads abroad in all the other portions of the body. But these very subtle parts of the blood form the animal spirits; and for this end they have no need to experience any other change in the brain, unless it be that they are separated from the other less subtle portions of the blood; for what I here name spirits are nothing but material bodies and their one peculiarity is that they are bodies of extreme minuteness and that they move very quickly like the particles of the flame which issues from a torch. Thus it is that they never remain at rest in any spot, and just as some of them enter into the cavities of the brain, others issue forth by the pores which are in its substance, which pores conduct them into the nerves, and from there into the muscles, by means of which they move the body in all the different ways in which it can be moved.

ARTICLE XI

How the Movements of the Muscles Take Place

For the sole cause of all the movements of the members is that certain muscles contract, and that those opposite to them elongate, as has already been said; and the sole cause of one muscle contracting rather than that set against it, is that there comes from the brain some additional amount of animal spirits, however little it may be, to it rather than to the other. Not that the spirits which proceed immediately from the brain suffice in themselves to move the muscles, but they determine the other spirits which are already in these two muscles, all to issue very quickly from one of them and to pass into the other. By this means that from which they issue becomes longer and more flaccid, and that into which they enter, being rapidly distended by them, contracts, and pulls the member to which it is attached. This is easy to understand provided that we know that there are but very few animal spirits which continually proceed from the brain to each muscle, but that there are always a quantity of others enclosed in the same muscle, which move there very quickly, sometimes by only turning about in the place where they are–that is, when they do not find any passage open from which to issue forth from it–and sometimes by flowing into the opposite muscle; and inasmuch as there are little openings in each of these muscles by which the spirits can flow from one to the other, and which are so arranged that when the spirits that come from the brain to one of them have ever so little more strength than those that proceed to the other, they open all the entrances by which the spirits of the other muscle can pass into this one, and at the same time close all those by which the spirits of this last can pass into the other. By this means all the spirits formerly contained in these two muscles very quickly collect in one of them and then distend and shorten it, while the other becomes elongated and flaccid.

ARTICLE XVI

How All the Members May Be Moved by the Objects of the Senses and by the Animal Spirits Without the Aid of the Soul

We must finally remark that the machine of our body is so formed that all the changes undergone by the movement of the spirits may cause them to open certain pores in the brain more than others, and reciprocally that when some one of the pores is opened more or less than usual (to however small a degree it may be) by the action of the nerves which are employed by the senses, that changes something in the movement of the spirits and causes them to be conducted into the muscles which serve to move the body in the way in which it is usually moved when such an action takes place. In this way all the movements which we make without our will contributing thereto (as frequently happens when we breathe, walk, eat, and in fact perform all those actions which are common to us and to the brutes), only depend on the conformation of our members, and on the course which the spirits, excited by the heat of the heart, follow naturally in the brain, nerves, and muscles, just as the movements of a watch are produced simply by the strength of the springs and the form of the wheels.

ARTICLE XVII

What the Functions of the Soul Are

After having thus considered all the functions which pertain to the body alone, it is easy to recognise that there is nothing in us which we ought to attribute to our soul excepting our thoughts, which are mainly of two sorts, the one being the actions of the soul, and the other its passions. Those which I call its actions are all our desires, because we find by experience that they proceed directly from our soul, and appear to depend on it alone: while, on the other hand, we may usually term one's passions all those kinds of perception or forms of knowledge which are found in us, because it is often not our soul which makes them what they are, and because it always receives them from the things which are represented by them.

ARTICLE XXXI

That There is a Small Gland in the Brain in Which the Soul Exercises Its Functions More Particularly than in the Other Parts

It is likewise necessary to know that although the soul is joined to the whole body, there is yet in that a certain part in which it exercises its functions more particularly than in all the others; and it is usually believed that this part is the brain, or possibly the heart: the brain, because it is with it that the organs of sense are connected, and the heart because it is apparently in it that we experience the passions. But, in examining the matter with care, it seems as though I had clearly ascertained that the part of the body in which the soul exercises its functions immediately is in nowise the heart, nor the whole of the brain, but merely the most inward of all its parts, to wit, a certain very small gland which is situated in the middle of its substance and so suspended above the duct whereby the animal spirits in its anterior cavities have communication with those in the posterior, that the slightest movements which take place in it may alter very greatly the course of these spirits; and reciprocally that the smallest changes which occur in the course of the spirits may do much to change the movements of this gland.

ARTICLE XXXII

How We Know that This Gland is the Main Seat of the Soul

The reason which persuades me that the soul cannot have any other seat in all the body than this gland wherein to exercise its functions immediately, is that I reflect that the other parts of our brain are all of them double, just as we have two eyes, two hands, two ears, and finally all the organs of our outside senses are double; and inasmuch as we have but one solitary and simple thought of one particular thing at one and the same moment, it must necessarily be the case that there must somewhere be a place where the two images which come to us by the two eyes, where the two other impressions which proceed from a single object by means of the double organs of the other senses, can unite before arriving at the soul, in order that they may not represent to it two objects instead of one. And it is easy to apprehend how these images or other impressions might unite in this gland by the intermission of the spirits which fill the cavities of the brain; but there is no other place in the body where they can be thus united unless they are so in this gland.

ARTICLE XXXV

Example of the Mode in Which the Impressions of the Objects Unite in the Gland Which is in the Middle of the Brain

Thus, for example, if we see some animal approach us, the light reflected from its body depicts two images of it, one in each of our eyes, and these two images form two others, by means of the optic nerves, in the interior surface of the brain which faces its cavities; then from there, by means of the animal spirits with which its cavities are filled, these images so radiate towards the little gland which is surrounded by these spirits, that the movement which forms each point of one of the images tends toward the same point of the gland towards which tends the movement which forms the point of the other image, which represents the same part of this animal. By this means the two images which are in the brain form but one upon the gland, which, acting immediately upon the soul, causes it to see the form of this animal.

ARTICLE XXXVI

Example of the Way in which the Passions Are Excited in the Soul

And, besides that, if this figure is very strange and frightful—that is, if it has a close relationship with the things which have been formerly hurtful to the body, that excites the passions of apprehension in the soul and then that of courage, or else that of fear and consternation according to the particular temperament of the body or the strength of the soul, and according as we have to begin with been secured by defence or by flight against the hurtful things to which the present impression is related. For in certain persons that disposes the brain in such a way that the spirits reflected from the image thus formed on the gland, proceed thence to take their places partly in the nerves which serve to turn the back and dispose the legs for flight, and partly in those which so increase or diminish the orifices of the heart, or at least which so agitate the other parts from whence the blood is sent to it, that this blood being there rarefied in a different manner from usual, sends to the brain the spirits which are adapted for the maintenance and strengthening of the passion of fear, i.e., which are adapted to the holding open, or at least reopening, of the pores of the brain which conduct them into the same nerves. For from the fact alone that these spirits enter into these pores, they excite a particular movement in this gland which is instituted by nature in order to cause the soul to be sensible of this passion; and because these pores are principally in relation with the little nerves which serve to contract or enlarge the orifices of the heart, that causes the soul to be sensible of it for the most part as in the heart.

ARTICLE XL

The Principal Effect of the Passions

For it is requisite to notice that the principal effect of all the passions in men is that they incite and dispose their soul to desire those things for which they prepare their body, so that the feeling of fear incites it to desire to fly, that of courage to desire to fight, and so on.

ARTICLE XLII

How We Find in the Memory the Things Which We Desire to Remember

Thus when the soul desires to recollect something, this desire causes the gland, by inclining successively to different sides, to thrust the spirits towards different parts of the brain until they come across that part where the traces left there by the object which we wish to recollect are found; for these traces are none other than the fact that the pores of the brain, by which the spirits have formerly followed their course because of the presence of this object, have by that means acquired a greater facility than the others in being once more opened by the animal spirits which come towards them in the same way. Thus these spirits in coming in contact with these pores, enter into them more easily than into the others, by which means they excite a special movement in the gland which represents the same object to the soul, and causes it to know that it is this which it desired to remember.

ARTICLE XLIII

How the Soul Can Imagine, Be Attentive, and Move the Body

Thus when we desire to imagine something we have never seen, this desire has the power of causing the gland to move in the manner requisite to drive the spirits towards the pores of the brain by the opening of which pores this particular thing may be represented; thus when we wish to apply our attention for some time to the consideration of one particular object, this desire holds the gland for the time being inclined to the same side. Thus, finally, when we desire to walk or to move our body in some special way, this desire causes the gland to thrust the spirits towards the muscles which serve to bring about this result.

Thomas Hobbes: 1588-1679

HUMANE NATURE *

1651

CHAPTER I

Introduction

1. The true and perspecuous explication of the elements of laws natural and politic (which is my present scope) dependeth upon the knowledge of what is human nature, what is body politic, and what it is we call a law; concerning which points, as the writings of men from antiquity downwards have still increased, so also have the doubts and controversies concerning the same: and seeing that true knowledge begetteth not doubt nor controversy, but knowledge, it is manifest from the present controversies, that they, which have heretofore written thereof, have not well understood their own subject.

2. Harm I can do none, though I err no less than they; for I shall leave men but as they are, in doubt and dispute: but, intending not to take any principle upon trust, but only to put men in mind of what they know already, or may know by their own experience, I hope to err the less; and when I do, it must proceed from too hasty concluding, which I will endeavour as much as I can to avoid.

3. On the other side, if reasoning aright win not consent, which may very easily happen, from them that being confident of their own knowledge weight not what is said, the fault is not mine, but theirs; for as it is my part to shew my reasons, so it is theirs to bring attention.

4. Man's nature is the sum of his natural faculties and powers, as the faculties of nutrition, motion, generation, sense, reason, etc. These powers we do unanimously call natural, and are contained in the definition of man, under these words, animal and rational.

5. According to the two principal parts of man, I divide his faculties into two sorts, faculties of the body, and faculties of the mind.

6. Since the minute and distinct anatomy of the powers of the body is nothing necessary to the present purpose, I will only sum them up in these three heads, power nutritive, power motive, and power generative.

* Hobbes was the first of the English empiricists and associationists. His psychological ideas were presented both in *Leviathan* (1650) and in *Humane Nature* (1651). The present selections are from *Hobbes' English Works*, collected and edited by Sir William Molesworth, London, 1839, Vol. 4.

7. Of the powers of the mind there be two sorts, cognitive, imaginative, or conceptive, and motive; and first of cognitive.

For the understanding of what I mean by the power cognitive, we must remember and acknowledge that there be in our minds continually certain images or conceptions of the things without us, inasmuch that if a man could be alive, and all the rest of the world annihilated, he should nevertheless retain the image thereof, and all those things which he had before seen or perceived in it; every one by his own experience knowing, that the absence or destruction of things once imagined doth not cause the absence or destruction of the imagination itself. This imagery and representations of the qualities of the thing without, is that we call our conception, imagination, ideas, notice or knowledge of them; and the faculty or power by which we are capable of such knowledge, is that I here call cognitive power, or conceptive, the power of knowing or conceiving.

CHAPTER II

The Sense and its Main Deception

1. Having declared what I mean by the word conception, and other words equivalent thereunto, I come to the conceptions themselves, to shew their differences, their causes, and the manner of the production, so far as is necessary for this place.

2. Originally all conceptions proceed from the action of the thing itself, whereof it is the conception: now when the action is present, the conception it produceth is also called sense; and the thing by whose action the same is produced, is called the object of the sense.

3. By our several organs we have several conceptions of several qualities in the objects; for by sight we have a conception of image composed of colour and figure, which is all the notice and knowledge the object imparteth to us of its nature by the eye. By hearing we have a conception called sound, which is all the knowledge we have of the quality of the object from the ear. And so the rest of the senses are also conceptions of several qualities, or natures of their objects.

4. Because the image in vision consisting of colour and shape is the knowledge we have of the qualities of the object of that sense; it is no hard matter for a man to fall into this opinion, that the same colour and shape are the very qualities themselves; and for the same cause, that sound and noise are the qualities of the bell, or of the air. And this opinion hath been so long received, that the contrary must needs appear a great paradox; and yet the introduction of species visible and intelligible (which is necessary for the maintenance of that opinion) passing to and fro from

the object, is worse than any paradox, as being a plain impossibility. I shall therefore endeavour to make plain these points:

That the subject wherein colour and image are inherent, is not the object or thing seen.

That there is nothing without us (really) which we call an image or colour.

That the said image or colour is but an apparition unto us of the motion, agitation, or alteration, which the object worketh in the brain, or spirits, or some internal substance of the head.

That as in vision, so also in conceptions that arise from the other senses, the subject of their inherence is not the object, but the sentient.

5. Every man hath so much experience as to have seen the sun and the other visible objects by reflection in the water and glasses; and this alone is sufficient for this conclusion, that colour and image may be there where the thing seen is not. But because it may be said that notwithstanding the image in the water be not in the object, but a thing merely phantastical, yet there may be colour really in the thing itself: I will urge further this experience, that divers times men see directly the same object double, as two candles for one, which may happen from distemper, or otherwise without distemper if a man will, the organs being either in their right temper, or equally distempered; the colours and figures in two such images of the same thing cannot be inherent therein, because the thing seen cannot be in two places.

One of these images therefore is not inherent in the object: but seeing the organs of the sight are then in equal temper or distemper, the one of them is no more inherent than the other; and consequently neither of them both are in the object; which is the first proposition, mentioned in the precedent number.

6. Secondly, that the image of any thing by reflection in a glass or water or the like, is not any thing in or behind the glass, or in or under the water, every man may grant to himself; which is the second proposition.

7. For the third, we are to consider, first that upon every great agitation or concussion of the brain (as it happeneth from a stroke, especially if the stroke be upon the eye) whereby the optic nerve suffereth any great violence, there appeareth before the eye a certain light, which light is nothing without, but an apparition only, all that is real being the concussion or motion of the parts of that nerve; from which experience we may conclude, that apparition of light is really nothing but motion within. If therefore from lucid bodies there can be derived motion, so as to affect the optic nerve in such manner as is proper thereunto, there will follow an image of light somewhere in that line by which the motion was last derived to the eye; that is to say, in the object, if we look directly

on it, and in the glass or water, when we look upon it in the line of reflection, which in effect is the third proposition; namely, that image and colour is but an apparition to us of that motion, agitation, or alteration which the object worketh in the brain or spirits, or some internal substance in the head.

8. But that from all lucid, shining and illuminate bodies there is a motion produced to the eye, and, through the eye, to the optic nerve, and so into the brain, by which that apparition of light or colour is affected, is not hard to prove. And first, it is evident that the fire, the only lucid body here upon earth, worketh by motion equally every way; insomuch as the motion thereof stopped or inclosed, it is presently extinguished, and no more fire. And further, that that motion, whereby the fire worketh, is dilation, and contraction of itself alternately, commonly called scintillation or glowing, is manifest also by experience. From such motion in the fire must needs arise a rejection or casting from itself of that part of the medium which is contiguous to it, whereby that part also rejecteth the next, and so successively one part beateth back another to the very eye; and in the same manner the exterior part of the eye presseth the interior, (the laws of refraction still observed). Now the interior coat of the eye is nothing else but a piece of the optic nerve; and therefore the motion is still continued thereby into the brain, and by resistance or reaction of the brain, is also a rebound into the optic nerve again; which we not conceiving as motion or rebound from within, do think it is without, and call it light; as hath been already shewed by the experience of a stroke. We have no reason to doubt, that the fountain of light, the sun, worketh by any other ways than the fire, at least in this matter. And thus all vision hath its original from such motion as is here described: for where there is no light, there is no sight; and therefore colour also must be the same thing with light, as being the effect of the lucid bodies: their difference being only this, that when the light cometh directly from the fountain to the eye, or indirectly by reflection from clean and polite bodies, and such as have not any particular motion internal to alter it, we call it light; but when it cometh to the eye by reflection from uneven, rough, and coarse bodies, or such as are affected with internal motion of their own that may alter it, then we call it colour; colour and light differing only in this, that the one is pure, and the other perturbed light. By that which hath been said, not only the truth of the third proposition, but also the whole manner of producing light and colour, is apparent.

9. As colour is not inherent in the object, but an effect thereof upon us, caused by such motion in the object, as hath been described: so neither is sound in the thing we hear, but in ourselves. One manifest sign thereof is, that as a man may see, so also he may hear double or treble,

by multiplication of echoes, which echoes are sounds as well as the original; and not being in one and the same place, cannot be inherent in the body that maketh them. Nothing can make any thing which is not in itself: the clapper hath no sound in it, but motion, and maketh motion in the internal parts of the bell; so the bell hath motion, and not sound, that imparteth motion to the air; and the air hath motion, but not sound; the air imparteth motion by the ear and nerve unto the brain; and the brain hath motion but not sound; from the brain, it reboundeth back into the nerves outward, and thence it becometh an apparition without, which we call sound. And to proceed to the rest of the senses, it is apparent enough, that the smell and taste of the same thing, are not the same to every man; and therefore are not in the thing smelt or tasted, but in the men. So likewise the heat we feel from the fire is manifestly in us, and is quite different from the heat which is in the fire: for our heat is pleasure or pain, according as it is great or moderate; but in the coal there is no such thing. By this the fourth and last proposition is proved, viz. that as in vision, so also in conceptions that arise from other senses, the subject of their inherence is not in the object, but in the sentient.

10. And from hence also it followeth, that whatsoever accidents or qualities our senses make us think there be in the world, they be not there, but are seeming and apparitions only: the things that really are in the world without us, are those motions by which these seemings are caused. And this is the great deception of sense, which also is to be by sense corrected: for as sense telleth me, when I see directly, that the colour seemeth to be in the object; so also sense telleth me, when I see by reflection, what colour is not in the object.

CHAPTER III

Imagination and Dreams

1. As standing water put into motion by the stroke of a stone, or blast of wind, doth not presently give over moving as soon as the wind ceaseth, or the stone settleth: so neither doth the effect cease which the object hath wrought upon the brain, so soon as ever by turning aside of the organs the object ceaseth to work; that is to say, though the sense be past, the image or conception remaineth; but more obscure while we are awake, because some object or other continually plieth and soliciteth our eyes, and ears, keeping the mind in a stronger motion, whereby the weaker doth not easily appear. And this obscure conception is that we call phantasy, or imagination: imagination being, to define it, conception remaining, and by little and little decaying from after the act of sense.

2. But when present sense is not, as in sleep, there the images re-

maining after sense, when there be many, as in dreams, are not obscure, but strong and clear, as in sense itself. The reason is, that which obscured and made the conceptions weak, namely sense, and present operation of the object, is removed; for sleep is the privation of the act of sense, (the power remaining) and dreams are the imagination of them that sleep.

3. The causes of dreams, if they be natural, are the actions or violence of the inward parts of a man upon his brain, by which the passages of sense by sleep benumbed, are restored to their motion. The signs by which this appeareth to be so, are the differences of dreams (old men commonly dream oftener, and have their dreams more painful than young) proceeding from the different accidents of man's body, as dreams of lust, as dreams of anger, according as the heart, or other parts within, work more or less upon the brain, by more or less heat; so also the descents of different sorts of phlegm maketh us a dream of different tastes of meats and drinks; and I believe there is a reciprocation of motion from the brain to the vital parts, and back from the vital parts to the brain; whereby not only imagination begetteth motion in those parts; but also motion in those parts begetteth imagination like to that by which it was begotten. If this be true, and that sad imaginations nourish the spleen, then we see also a cause, why a strong spleen reciprocally causeth fearful dreams, and why the effects of lasciviousness may in a dream produce the image of some person that had caused them. Another sign that dreams are caused by the action of the inward parts, is the disorder and casual consequence of one conception or image to another: for when we are waking, the antecedent thought or conception introduceth, and is cause of the consequent, as the water followeth a man's finger upon a dry and level table; but in dreams there is commonly no coherence, and when there is, it is by chance, which must needs proceed from this, that the brain in dreams is not restored to its motion in every part alike; whereby it cometh to pass, that our thoughts appear like the stars between the flying clouds, not in the order which a man would choose to observe them, but as the uncertain flight of broken clouds permits.

4. As when the water, or any liquid thing moved at once by divers movements, receiveth one motion compounded of them all; so also the brain or spirit therein, having been stirred by divers objects, composeth an imagination of divers conceptions that appeared single to the sense. As for example, the sense sheweth at one time the figure of a mountain, and at another time the colour of gold; but the imagination afterwards hath them both at once in a golden mountain. From the same cause it is, there appear unto us castles in the air, chimeras, and other monsters which are not in *rerum natura*, but have been conceived by the sense in pieces at several times. And this composition is that which we commonly call fiction of the mind.

5. There is yet another kind of imagination, which for clearness contendeth with sense, as well as a dream; and that is, when the action of sense hath been long or vehement: and the experience thereof is more frequent in the sense of seeing, than the rest. An example whereof is, the image remaining before the eye after looking upon the sun. Also, those little images that appear before the eyes in the dark (whereof I think every man hath experience, but they most of all, who are timorous or superstitious) are examples of the same. And these, for distinction-sake, may be called phantasms.

6. By the senses, which are numbered according to the organs to be five, we take notice (as hath been said already) of the objects without us; and that notice is our conception thereof: but we take notice also some way or other of our conceptions: for when the conception of the same thing cometh again, we take notice that it is again; that is to say, that we have had the same conception before; which is as much as to imagine a thing past; which is impossible to the sense, which is only of things present. This therefore may be accounted a sixth sense, but internal, (not external, as the rest) and is commonly called remembrance.

7. For the manner by which we take notice of a conception past, we are to remember, that in the definition of imagination, it is said to be a conception by little and little decaying, or growing more obscure. An obscure conception is that which representeth the whole object together, but none of the smaller parts by themselves; and as more or fewer parts be represented, so is the conception or representation said to be more or less clear. Seeing then the conception, which when it was first produced by sense, was clear, and represented the parts of the object distinctly; and when it cometh again is obscure, we find missing somewhat that we expected; by which we judge it past and decayed. For example, a man that is present in a foreign city, seeth not only whole streets, but can also distinguish particular houses, and parts of houses; but departed thence, he cannot distinguish them so particularly in his mind as he did, some house or turning escaping him; yet is this to remember; when afterwards there escape him more particulars, this is also to remember, but not so well. In process of time, the image of the city returneth but as a mass of building only, which is almost to have forgotten it. Seeing then remembrance is more or less, as we find more or less obscurity, may not we well think remembrance to be nothing else but the missing of parts, which every man expecteth should succeeed after they have a conception of the whole? To see at a great distance of place, and to remember at a great distance of time, is to have like conceptions of the thing: for there wanteth distinction of parts in both; the one conception being weak by operation at distance, the other by decay.

8. And from this that hath been said, there followeth, that a man can never know he dreameth; he may dream he doubteth, whether it be a

dream or no: but the clearness of the imagination representeth every thing with as many parts as doth sense itself, and consequently, he can take notice of nothing but as present; whereas to think he dreameth, is to think those his conceptions, that is to say dreams, obscurer than they were in the sense; so that he must think them both as clear, and not as clear as sense; which is impossible.

9. From the same ground it proceedeth, that men wonder not in their dreams at place and persons, as they would do waking: for waking, a man would think it strange to be in a place where he never was before, and remember nothing of how he came there; but in a dream, there cometh little of that kind into consideration. The clearness of conception in a dream, taketh away distrust, unless the strangeness be excessive, as to think himself fallen from on high without hurt, and then most commonly he waketh.

10. Nor is it impossible for a man to be so far deceived, as when his dream is past, to think it real: for if he dream of such things as are ordinarily in his mind, and in such order as he useth to do waking, and withal that he laid him down to sleep in the place where he findeth himself when he awaketh; all which may happen: I know no mark by which he can discern whether it were a dream or not, and therefore do the less wonder to hear a man sometimes to tell his dream for a truth, or to take it for a vision.

CHAPTER IV

Thought

1. The succession of conceptions in the mind, series or consequence of one after another, may be casual and incoherent, as in dreams for the most part; and it may be orderly, as when the former thought introduceth the latter; and this is discourse of the mind. But because the word discourse is commonly taken for the coherence and consequence of words, I will, to avoid equivocation, call it discursion.

2. The cause of the coherence or consequence of one conception to another, is their first coherence or consequence at that time when they are produced by sense: as for example, from St. Andrew the mind runneth to St. Peter, because their names are read together; from St. Peter to a stone, for the same cause; from stone to foundation, because we see them together; and for the same cause, from foundation to church, and from church to people, and from people to tumult: and according to this example, the mind may run almost from anything to anything. But as in the sense the conception of cause and effect may succeed one another; so may they after sense in the imagination: and for the most part they do so; the cause whereof is the appetite of them, who, having a conception of the end, have next unto it a conception of the next means to that end:

as, when a man, from a thought of honour to which he hath an appetite, cometh to the thought of wisdom, which is the next means thereunto; and from thence to the thought of study, which is the next means to wisdom.

3. To omit that kind of discursion by which we proceed from anything to anything, there are of the other kind divers sorts: as first, in the senses there are certain coherences of conceptions, which we may call ranging; examples whereof are; a man casteth his eye upon the ground, to look about for some small thing lost; the hounds casting about at a fault in hunting; and the ranging of spaniels: and herein we take a beginning arbitrary.

4. Another sort of discursion is, when the appetite giveth a man his beginning, as in the example before, where honour to which a man hath appetite, maketh him think upon the next means of attaining it, and that again of the next, etc. And this the Latins call sagacitas, and we may call hunting or tracing, as dogs trace beasts by the smell, and men hunt them by their footsteps; or as men hunt after riches, place, or knowledge.

5. There is yet another kind of discursion beginning with the appetite to recover something lost, proceeding from the present backward, from thought of the place where we miss at, to the thought of the place from whence we came last; and from the thought of that, to the thought of a place before, till we have in our mind some place, wherein we had the thing we miss: and this is called reminiscence.

6. The remembrance of succession of one thing to another, that is, of what was antecedent, and what consequent, and what concomitant, is called an experiment; whether the same be made by us voluntarily, as when a man putteth any thing into the fire, to see what effect the fire will produce upon it: or not made by us, as when we remember a fair morning after a red evening. To have had many experiments, is that we call experience, which is nothing else but remembrance of what antecedents have been followed by what consequents.

7. No man can have in his mind a conception of the future, for the future is not yet: but of our conceptions of the past, we make a future; or rather, call past, future relatively. Thus after a man hath been accustomed to see like antecedents followed by like consequents, whensoever he seeth the like come to pass to any thing he had seen before, he looks there should follow it the same that followed then: as for example, because a man hath often seen offences followed by punishment, when he seeth an offence in present, he thinketh punishment to be consequent thereunto; but consequent unto that which is present, men call future; and thus we make remembrance to be the prevision of things to come, or expectation or presumption of the future.

8. In the same manner, if a man seeth in present that which he hath seen before, he thinks that that which was antecedent to that which he saw

before, is also antecedent to that he presently seeth: as for example, he that hath seen the ashes remain after a fire, and now again seeth ashes, concludeth again there hath been fire: and this is called again conjecture of the past, or presumption of the fact.

9. When a man hath so often observed like antecedents to be followed by like consequents, that whensoever he seeth the antecedent, he looketh again for the consequent; or when he seeth the consequent, maketh account there hath been the like antecedent; then he calleth both the antecedent and the consequent, signs one of another, as clouds are signs of rain to come, and rain of clouds past.

10. This taking of signs by experience, is that wherein men do ordinarily think, the difference stands between man and man in wisdom, by which they commonly understand a man's whole ability or power cognitive; but this is an error: for the signs are but conjectural; and according as they have often or seldom failed, so their assurance is more or less; but never full and evident; for though a man have always seen the day and night to follow one another hitherto; yet can he not thence conclude they shall do so, or that they have done so eternally: experience concludeth nothing universally. If the signs hit twenty times for one missing, a man may lay a wager of twenty to one of the event; but may not conclude it for a truth. But by this it is plain, that they shall conjecture best, that have most experience, because they have most signs to conjecture by: which is the reason old men are more prudent, that is, conjecture better, *cateris paribus*, than young: for, being old, they remember more; and experience is but remembrance. And men of quick imagination, *cateris paribus*, are more prudent than those whose imaginations are slow: for they observe more in less time. Prudence is nothing but conjecture from experience, or taking of signs from experience warily, that is, that the experiments from which he taketh such signs be all remembered; for else the cases are not alike that seem so.

11. As in conjecture concerning things past and future, it is prudence to conclude from experience, what is like to come to pass, or to have passed already; so it is an error to conclude from it, that it is so or so called; that is to say, we cannot from experience conclude, that anything is to be called just or unjust, true or false, or any proposition universal whatsoever, except it be from remembrance of the use of names imposed arbitrarily by men: for example, to have heard a sentence given in the like case, the like sentence a thousand times is not enough to conclude that the sentence is just; though most men have no other means to conclude by: but it is necessary, for the drawing of such conclusion, to trace and find out, by many experiences, what men do mean by calling things just and unjust. Further, there is another caveat to be taken in concluding by experience, from the tenth section of the second chapter; that is, that we conclude such things to be without, that are within us.

Edmé Mariotte: 1620-1684

THE DISCOVERY OF THE BLIND SPOT *

1668

SIR:

This concerns my observation of the lack of vision which occurs when an image of an object falls solely on the optic nerve. I have told you that for a long time I have been curious to know if vision is more or less strong than normal at the point of entrance of the optic nerve. This has caused me to observe a phenomenon to which I had not previously given attention. I hold it certain that vision is caused by the reception of rays which form a picture of objects at the back of the eye, and that this picture is inverted in respect to the objects which are represented. Moreover, I have often observed by dissection of the human eye as well as animal eyes that the optic nerve does not coincide exactly with the center of the back of the eye, that is to say, with the spot on which falls the object at which one looks directly. In man, the origin of the optic nerve is a little higher than the area of distinct vision, and on the side toward the nose. In order to make the rays from an object fall on the optic nerve of my eye, I fastened on a dark background at about the level of my eyes a small disc of white paper to serve as a point of fixation. Then I placed another disc to the right of the first at a distance of about two feet, and a little below the first, in order that its image might fall on the optic nerve of my right eye when I held the left eye closed. I placed myself opposite the fixation point and increased the distance between myself and the fixation point little by little, keeping my right eye on the first disc. When I was at a distance of about nine feet, the second disc, which was nearly four inches in diameter, disappeared from my view. Moreover, I could not attribute this to the oblique position of this object, for I noticed other objects which were even further to the side. Indeed I could have believed that the disc had subtly disappeared if I had not refound it in moving my eye a bit. As soon as I again looked fixedly at the first paper, the one on the right disappeared instantly. I could recover it without moving the eye by making a slight change of position. I then performed the same experiment at other distances,

* From "Nouvelle decouverte touchant la vue, contenue en plusiers lettres écrites par Messrs. Mariotte, Pecquet, et Perrault" in *Oeuvres de Mariotte*, La Haye, Jean Neaulme, 1740. The letter of Mariotte which describes his discovery of the blind spot was written to Pecquet in 1668. It is on pages 496-498 of Mariotte's *Oeuvres* referred to above. The translation is by the present editor.

changing the distance between the papers in proportion. I repeated it with the left eye, holding the right closed, after placing the test paper to the left of my fixation point, so that from its location there was no doubt that its falling upon the optic nerve was the cause of its disappearance.

It is a surprising thing that when in this way one loses sight of a disc of black paper attached to a white background, one does not see any shadow or obscurity where the black paper is located; the background appears white in its entirety.

I communicated this discovery to several of my friends, who found the same thing to be true, but not always at the same distances. I attribute this to the differences in the location of the optic nerve. M. de Billy was one of the first on whom I tried this experiment. You have tried it yourself in the Royal Library, where I demonstrated it to the gentlemen of the assembly, and you remarked that, at the distance employed, some persons lost from view a disc of eight inches, while others did not lose the paper from view unless it was smaller. This can be due only to differences in the size of the optic nerve in different eyes.

The experiment thus confirmed, doubt arises that the seat of vision is in the retina as is commonly believed. I am led to believe that it is in the membrane behind the retina, called the choroid. If vision were located in the retina, it seems that there should be vision wherever the retina is located. Since it covers the origin of the optic nerve as well as the rest of the posterior surface of the eye, there is no reason why there should be an absence of vision at that point. However, if the choroid is the organ of vision, the reason for the insensitivity of the eye at the entrance of the nerve is clear because this membrane does not cover the nerve as it does the remainder of the eye.

You know the other reasons which I have prepared in writing, which I have presented to your assembly, and which you may review, which cause me to conclude more in favor of the choroid than the retina. I shall be pleased to have you write me your frank opinions, as I am not among those who wish to have conjectures taken as proofs. I shall continue to conduct researches on this matter. If I encounter anything worthy of your interest I shall bring it to your attention.

MARIOTTE

Isaac Newton: 1642-1727

A NEW THEORY OF LIGHT AND COLORS *

1672

Sir, To perform my late promise to you, I shall without further ceremony acquaint you, that in the beginning of the Year 1666 (at which time I applyed my self to the grinding of Optick glasses of other figures than Spherical,) I procured me a Triangular glass-prisme, to try therewith the celebrated phenomen of Colours. And in order thereto having darkened my chamber, and made a small hole in my window-shuts, to let in a convenient quantity of the Suns light, I placed my Prisme at his entrance, that it might be thereby refracted to the opposite wall. It was at first a very pleasing divertisement, to view the vivid and intense colours produced thereby; but after a while applying my self to consider them more circumspectly, I became surprised to see them in an oblong form; which, according to the received laws of Refraction, I expected should have been circular.

They were terminated at the sides with streight lines, but at the ends the decay of light was so gradual, that it was difficult to determine justly, what was their figure; yet they seemed semicircular.

Comparing the length of this coloured Spectrum with its breadth, I found it about five times greater; a disproportion so extravagant, that it excited me to a more than ordinary curiosity of examining, from whence it might proceed. I could scarce think that the various Thickness of the glass, or the termination with shadow or darkness, could have any Influence on light to produce such an effect; yet I thought it not amiss, first to examine those circumstances, and so tryed, what would happen by transmitting light through parts of the glass of divers thicknesses, or through holes in the window of divers bignesses, or by setting the Prisme without so, that the light might pass through it, and be refracted before it was terminated by the hole: But I found none of those circumstances material. The fashion of the colours was in all these cases the same.

Then I suspected, whether by any unevenness in the glass, or other contingent irregularity, these colours might be thus dilated. And to try this, I took another Prisme like the former, and so placed it, that the light, passing through them both, might be refracted contrary ways, and so by

* Newton's discovery of the physical basis of color was transmitted to the Royal Society of London and published in the *Philosophical Transactions* of the Royal Society in 1672. It is here reprinted in full.

the latter returned into that course, from which the former had diverted it. For by this means I thought, the regular effects of the first Prisme would be destroyed by the second Prisme, but the irregular ones more augmented, by the multiplicity of refractions. The event was, that the light, which by the first Prisme was diffused into an oblong form, was by the second reduced into an orbicular one with as much regularity, as when it did not at all pass through them. So that, what ever was the cause of that length, 'twas not any contingent irregularity.

I then proceeded to examin more critically, what might be effected by the difference of the incidence of Rays coming from divers parts of the Sun; and to that end, measured the several lines and angles belonging to the Image. Its distance from the hole or Prisme was 22 foot; its utmost length 13¼ inches; its breadth 2⅝; the diameter of the hole ¼ of an inch; the angle, with the Rays, tending towards the middle of the image, made with those lines, in which they would have proceeded without refraction, was 44 deg. 56′. And the vertical Angle of the Prisme, 63 deg. 12′. Also the Refractions on both sides the Prisme, that is, of the Incident, and Emergent Rays, were as near, as I could make them, equal, and consequently about 54 deg. 4′. And the Rays fell perpendicularly upon the wall. Now subducting the diameter of the hole from the length and breadth of the Image, there remains 13 Inches the length, and 2⅜ the breadth, comprehended by those Rays, which passed through the center of the said hole, and consequently the angle of the hole, which that breadth subtended, was about 31′, answerable to the Suns Diameter; but the angle, which its length subtended, was more than five such diameters, namely 2 deg. 49′.

Having made these observations, I first computed from them the refractive power of that glass, and found it measured by the ratio of the sines, 20 to 31. And then, by that ratio, I computed the Refractions of two Rays flowing from opposite parts of the Sun's discus, so as to differ 31′ in their obliquity of Incidence, and found, that the emergent Rays should have comprehended an angle of about 31′, as they did, before they were incident.

But because this computation was founded on the Hypothesis of the proportionality of the sine of Incidence, and Refraction, which though by my own Experience I could not imagine to be so erroneous, as to make that Angle but 31′, which in reality was 2 deg. 49′; yet my curiosity caused me again to take my Prisme. And having placed it at my window, as before, I observed, that by turning it a little about its axis to and fro, so as to vary its obliquity to the light, more then an angle of 4 or 5 degrees, the Colours were not thereby sensibly translated from their place on the wall, and consequently by that variation of Incidence, the quantity of Refraction was not sensibly varied. By this experiment therefore, as well as by the former computation, it was evident, that the difference of the Incidence of Rays, flowing from divers parts of the Sun, could not make them after decussation diverge at a sensibly greater angle, that that at which they before converged; which being, at most, but about 31 or 32 minutes, there still remained some other cause to be found out, from whence it could be 2 degr. 49′.

Then I began to suspect, whether the Rays, after their trajection through the Prisme, did not move in curve lines, and according to their more or less curvity tend to divers parts of the wall. And it increased my suspition, when I remembered that I had often seen a Tennis ball, struck with an oblique Racket, describe such a curve line. For, a circular as well as a progressive motion being communicated to it by that stroak, its parts on that side, where the motions conspire, must press and beat the contiguous Air more violently than on the other, and there excite a reluctancy and reaction of the Air proportionately greater. And for the same reason, if the Rays of light should possibly be globular bodies, and by their oblique passage out of one medium into another acquire a circulating motion, they ought to feel the greater resistance from the ambient Aether, on that side, where the motions conspire, and thence be continually bowed to the other. But notwithstanding this plausible ground of suspition, when I came to examine it, I could observe no such curvity in them. And besides (which was enough for my purpose) I observed, that the difference 'twixt the length of the Image, and diameter of the hole, through which the light was transmitted, was proportionable to their distance.

The gradual removal of these suspitions, at length led me to the Experimentum Crucis, which was this: I took two boards, and placed one of them close behind the Prisme at the window, so that the light might pass through a small hole, made in it for the purpose, and fall on the other board, which I placed at about 12 feet distance, having first made a small hole in it also, for some of that Incident light to pass through. Then I placed another Prisme behind this second board, so that the light, trajected through both the boards, might pass through that also, and be again refracted before it arrived at the wall. This done, I took the first Prisme in my hand, and turned it to and fro slowly about its Axis, so much as to make the several parts of the Image, cast on the second board, successively pass through the hole in it, that I might observe to what places on the Wall the second Prisme would refract them. And I saw by the variation of those places, that the light, tending to that end of the Image, towards which the refraction of the first Prisme was made, did in the second Prisme suffer a Refraction considerably greater then the light tending to the other end. And so the true cause of the length of that Image was detected to be no other, then that Light consists of Rays differently refrangible, which without any respect to a difference in their incidence, were, according to their degrees of refrangibility, transmitted towards divers parts of the wall.

When I understood this, I left off my aforesaid Glass works; for I saw, that the perfection of Telescopes was hitherto limited, not so much for want of glasses truly figured according to the prescriptions of Optick Authors, (which all men have hitherto imagined,) as because that Light itself is a heterogeneous mixture of differently refrangible Rays. So that, were a glass so exactly figured, as to collect any one sort of rays into one point, it could not collect those also into the same point, which having the same incidence upon the same Medium are apt to suffer a different refraction. Nay, I wondered, that feeling the difference of refrangibility was so great, as I found it, Telescopes should arrive to that perfection they are now at. For, measuring the refractions in one of my Prismes, I found, that supposing the common sine of Incidence upon one of its planes was 44 parts, the sine of refraction of the Utmost Rays on the red end of the Colours, made out of the glass into the Air, would be 68 parts: So that the difference is about a 24th or 25th part of the whole refraction. And consequently, the object-glass of any Telescope cannot collect all the rays, which come from one point of an object so as to make them convene at its focus in less room then in a circular space, whose diameter is the 50th part of the Diameter of its Aperature; which is an irregularity, some hundreds of times greater, then a circularly figured Lens, of so small a section as the Object glasses of long Telescopes are, would cause by the unfitness of its figure, were light uniform.

This made me take Reflections into consideration, and finding them regular, so that the Angle of Reflection of all sorts of Rays was equal to their Angle of Incidence; I understood, that by their mediation Optick instruments might be brought to any degree of perfection imaginable, provided a Reflecting substance could be found, which would polish as finely as Glass, and reflect as much light, as glass transmits, and the art of communicating to it a Parabolick figure be also attained. But there seemed very great difficulties, and I have almost thought them insuperable, when I further considered, that every irregularity in a reflecting superficies makes the rays stray 5 or 6 times more out of their due course, than the like irregularities in a refracting one: So that a much greater curiosity would be here requisite, than in figuring glasses for Refraction.

Amidst these thoughts I was forced from Cambridge by the Intervening Plague, and it was more than two years, before I proceeded further. But then having thought on a tender way of polishing, proper for metall, whereby, as I imagined, the figure also would be corrected to the *last*; I began to try, what might be effected in this kind, and by degrees so far perfected an Instrument (in the essential parts of it like that I sent to

London,) by which I could discern Jupiters 4 Concomitants, and shewed then divers times to two others of my acquaintance. I could also discern the Moon-like phase of Venus, but not very distinctly, nor without some niceness in disposing the Instrument.

From that time I was interrupted till this last Autumn, when I made the other. And as that was sensibly better then the first (especially for Day-Objects,) so I doubt not, but they will be still brought to a much greater perfection by their endeavours, who, as you inform me, are taking care about it at London.

I have sometimes thought to make a Microscope, which in like manner would have, instead of an Object-glass, a Reflecting piece of metall. And this I hope they will also take into consideration. For those Instruments seem as capable of improvement as Telescopes, and perhaps more, because but one reflective piece of metall is requisite in them, as you may perceive by the annexed diagram, where AB representeth the object metall, CD the eye glass, F their common Focus, and O the other focus of the metall, in which the object is placed.

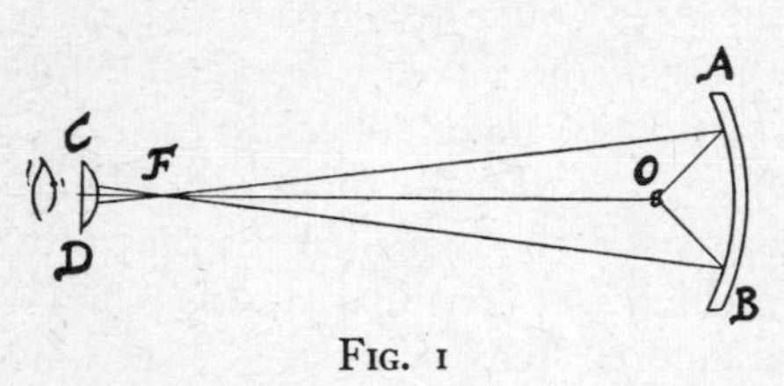

Fig. 1

But to return from this digression, I told you, that Light is not similar, or homogeneal, but consists of difform Rays, some of which are more refrangible than others: So that of those, which are alike incident on the same medium, some shall be more refracted than others, and that not by any virtue of the glass, or other external cause, but from a predisposition, which every particular Ray hath to suffer a particular degree of Refraction.

I shall now proceed to acquaint you with another more notable difformity in its Rays, wherein the Origin of Colours is unfolded: Concerning which I shall lay down the Doctrine first, and then, for its examination, give you an instance or two of the experiments, as a specimen of the rest.

The Doctrine you find comprehended and illustrated in the following propositions:

1. As the Rays of light differ in degrees of Refrangibility, so they also differ in their disposition to exhibit this or that particular colour. Colours are not Qualifications of Light, derived from Refractions, or Reflections of natural bodies (as 'tis generally believed,) but Original and connate properties, which in divers Rays are divers. Some Rays are disposed to exhibit a red colour and no other; some a yellow and no other, some a green and no other, and so of the rest. Nor are there only Rays proper and particular to the more eminent colours, but even to their intermediate gradations.

2. To the same degree of Refrangibility ever belongs the same colour, and to the same colour ever belongs the same degree of Refrangibility. The least Refrangible Rays are all disposed to exhibit a Red colour, and contrarily those Rays, which are disposed to exhibit a Red colour, are all the least refrangible: So the most refrangible Rays are all disposed to exhibit a deep violet colour, and contrarily those which are apt to exhibit such a violet colour, are all the most Refrangible. And so to all the intermediate colours in a continued series belong intermediate degrees of refrangibility, is very precise and strict; the Rays always either exactly agreeing in both, or proportionally disagreeing in both.

3. The species of colour, and degree of Refrangibility proper to any particular sort of Rays, is not mutable by Refraction, nor by Reflection from natural bodies, nor by any other cause, that I could yet observe. When any one sort of Rays hath been well parted from those of other kinds, it hath afterward obstinately retained its colour, notwithstanding my utmost endeavours to change it. I have refracted it with Prismes, and reflected it with Bodies, which in Day-light were of other colours; I have intercepted it with the coloured film of Air interceding two compressed plates of glass; transmitted it through coloured Mediums irradiated with other sorts of Rays, and diversly terminated it; and yet could never produce any new colour out of it. It would by contracting or dilating become more brisk, or faint, and by the loss of many Rays, in some cases very obscure and dark; but I could never see it changed in specie.

4. Yet seeming transmutations of Colours may be made, where there is any mixture of divers sorts of Rays. For in such mixtures, the component colours appear not, but, by their mutual allaying each other, constitute a midling colour. And therefore, if by refraction, or any other of the aforesaid causes, the difform Rays, latent in such a mixture, be separated, there shall emerge colours different from the colour of the composition. Which colours are not New generated, but only made Apparent by being parted; for if they be again intirely mix't and blended together, they will again compose that colour, which they did before separation. And for the same reason, Transmutations made by the convening of divers colours are not real; for when the difform Rays are again severed, they will exhibit the very same colours, which they did before they entered the composition; as you see, Blew and Yellow powders, when finely mixed, appear to the naked eye Green, and yet the Colours of the Component corpuscles are not thereby really transmuted, but only blended. For, when viewed with a good Microscope, they still appear Blew and Yellow interspersedly.

5. There are therefore two sorts of Colours. The one original and simple, the other compounded of these. The Original or primary colours are, Red, Yellow, Green, Blew, and a Violet-purple, together with Orange, Indico, and an indefinite variety of intermediate gradations.

6. The same colours in Specie with these Primary ones may be also produced by composition: For, a mixture of Yellow and Blew makes Green; of Red and Yellow makes Orange; of Orange and Yellowish green makes yellow. And in general, if any two Colours be mixed, which in the series of these, generated by the Prisme, are not too far distant from one another, they by their mutual alloy compound that colour, which in the said series appeareth in the mid-way between them. But those which are situated at too great a distance, do not so. Orange and indico produce not the intermediate Green, nor Scarlet and Green the intermediate yellow.

7. But the most surprising, and wonderful composition was that of Whiteness. There is no one sort of Rays which alone can exhibit this. 'Tis ever compounded, and to its composition are requisite all the aforesaid primary Colours, mixed in a due proportion. I have often with Admiration beheld, that all the Colours of the Prisme being made to converge, and thereby to be again mixed as they were in the light before it was Incident upon the Prisme, reproduced light, intirely and perfectly white, and not at all sensibly differing from a direct Light of the Sun, unless when the glasses I used, were not sufficiently clear; for then they would a little incline it to their colour.

8. Hence therefore it comes to pass, that Whiteness is the usual Colour of Light; for, Light is a confused aggregate of Rays indued with all sorts of Colours, as they are promiscuously darted from the various parts of luminous bodies. And of such a confused aggregate, as I said, it generated Whiteness, if there be a due proportion of the Ingredients; but if any one predominate, the light must incline to that colour; as it happens in the Blew flame of Brimstone; the yellow flame of a Candle; and the various colours of the Fixed stars.

9. These things considered, the manner, how colours are produced by the Prisme, is evident. For, of the Rays, constituting the incident light, since those which differ in Colour proportionally differ in Refrangibility, they by their unequall refractions must be severed and dispersed into an oblong form in an orderly succession from the least refracted Scarlet to the most refracted Violet. And for the same reason it is, that objects, when looked upon through a Prisme, appear coloured. For, the difform Rays, by their unequal Refractions, are made to diverge towards several parts of the Retina, and there express the Images of things coloured, as in the former case they did the Suns Image upon a wall. And by this inequality of refractions they become not only coloured, but also very confused and indistinct.

10. Why the Colours of the Rainbow appear in falling drops of Rain, is also from hence evident. For those drops, which refract the Rays, disposed to appear purple, in greatest quantity to the Spectators eye,

refract the Rays of other sorts so much less, as to make them pass beside it; and such are the drops on the inside of the Primary Bow, and on the outside of the Secondary or exteriour one. So those drops, which refract in greatest plenty the Rays, apt to appear red, toward the Spectators eye, refract those of other sorts so much more, as to make them pass beside it; and such are the drops on the exteriour part of the Primary, and interiour part of the Secondary Bow.

11. The odd Phaenomena of an infusion of Lignum Nephriticum, Leaf gold, Fragments of coloured glass, and some other transparently coloured bodies, appearing in one position of one colour, and of another in another, are on these grounds no longer riddles. For, those are substances apt to reflect one sort of light and transmit another; as may be seen in a dark room, by illuminating them with similar or uncompounded light. For, then they appear of that colour only, with which they are illuminated, but yet in one position more vivid and luminous than in another, accordingly as they are disposed more or less to reflect or transmit the incident colour.

12. From hence also is manifest the reason of an unexpected Experiment, which Mr. Hook somewhere in his Micrography relates to have made with two wedg-like transparent vessels, fill'd the one with a red, the other with a blew liquor: namely, that though they were severally transparent enough, yet both together became opake; For, if one transmitted only red, and the other only blew, no rays could pass through both.

13. I might add more instances of this nature, but I shall conclude with this general one, that the Colours of all natural Bodies have no other origin than this, that they are variously qualified to reflect one sort of light in greater plenty then another. And this I have experimented in a dark Room by illuminating those bodies with uncompounded light of divers colours. For by that means any body may be made to appear of any colour. They have there no appropriate colour, but ever appear of the colour of the light cast upon them, but yet with this difference, that they are most brisk and vivid in the light of their own daylight colour. Minium appeareth there of any colour indifferently, with which 'tis illustrated, but yet most luminous in red, and so Bise appeareth indifferently of any colour with which 'tis illustrated, but yet most luminous in blew. And therefore Minium reflecteth Rays of any colour, but most copiously those indued with red; and consequently when illustrated with day-light, that is, with all sorts of Rays promiscuously blended, those qualified with red shall abound most in the reflected light, and by their prevalence cause it to appear of that colour. And for the same reason Bise, reflecting blew most copiously, shall appear blew by the excess of those Rays in its reflected light; and the like of other bodies. And that this is the intire and adequate cause of their colours, is manifest,

because they have no power to change or alter the colours of any sort of Rays incident apart, but put on all colours indifferently, with which they are inlightned.

These things being so, it can be no longer disputed, whether there be colours in the dark, nor whether they be the qualities of the objects we see, no nor perhaps, whether Light be a Body. For, since Colours are the qualities of Light, having its Rays for their intire and immediate subject, how can we think those Rays qualities also, unless one quality may be the subject of and sustain another; which in effect is to call it substance. We should not know Bodies for substances, were it not for their sensible qualities, and the Principal of those being now found due to something else, we have as good reason to believe that to be a Substance also.

Besides, whoever thought any quality to be a heterogeneous aggregate, such as Light is discovered to be. But, to determine more absolutely what Light is, after what manner refracted, and by what modes or actions it produceth in our minds the Phantasms of Colours, is not so easie. And I shall not mingle conjectures with certainties.

Reviewing what I have written, I see the discourse it self will lead to divers Experiments sufficient for its examination: And therefore I shall not trouble you further, than to describe one of those, which I have already insinuated.

In a darkened Room make a hole in the shut of a window, whose diameter may conveniently be about a third part of an inch, to admit a convenient quantity of the Suns light: And there place a clear and colourless Prisme, to refract the entering light towards the further part of the Room, which as I said, will thereby be diffused into an oblong coloured Image. Then place a Lens of about three foot radius (suppose a broad Object-glass of a three foot Telescope,) at the distance of about four or five foot from thence, through which all those colours may at once be transmitted, and made by its Refraction to convene at a further distance of about ten or twelve feet. If at that distance you intercept this light with a sheet of white paper, you will see the colours converted into whiteness again by being mingled. But it is requisite, that the Prisme and Lens be placed steady, and that the paper, on which the colours are cast, be moved to and fro; for, by such motion you will not only find, at what distance the whiteness is most perfect, but also see, how the colours gradually convene, and vanish into whiteness, and afterwards having crossed one another in that place where they compound Whiteness, are again dissipated, and severed, and in an inverted order retain the same colours, which they had before they entered the composition. You may also, that, if any of the Colours at the Lens be intercepted, the Whiteness will be changed into the other colours. And therefore that the composition of whiteness be perfect, care must be taken, that none of the colours fall besides the Lens. In the annexed design of this Experiment, A B C expresseth the Prism set endwise to sight, close by the hole F of the window E G. Its vertical Angle ACB may conveniently be about 60 degrees: M N designeth the Lens. Its breadth 2½ or 3 inches. S F one of the straight lines, in which difform Rays may be conceived to flow successively from the Sun. FP, and F R two of those Rays unequally refracted, which the Lens makes to converge towards Q, and after decussation to diverge again. And H I the paper, at divers distances, on which the colours are projected: which in Q constitute Whiteness, but are Red and Yellow in R, r, and s, and Blew and Purple in P, p, and n.

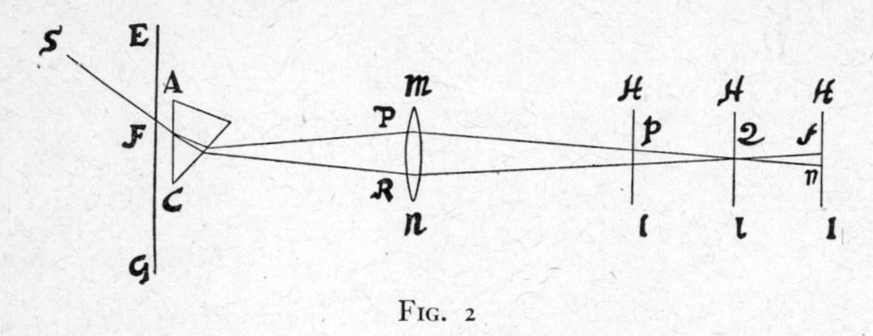

FIG. 2

If you proceed further to try the impossibility of changing any uncompounded colour (which I have asserted in the third and thirteenth propositions,) 'tis requisite that the Room be made very dark, least any scattering light, mixing with the colour, disturb and allay it, and render it compound, contrary to the design of the Experiment. 'Tis also requisite, that there be a perfecter separation of the Colours, than, after the manner above described, can be made by the Refraction of one single Prisme, and how to make such further separations, will scarce be difficult to them, that consider the discovered laws of Refractions. But if tryal shall be made with colours not throughly separated, there must be allowed changes proportionable to the mixture. Thus, if compound Yellow light fall upon Blew Bise, the Bise will not appear perfectly yellow, but rather green, because there are in the yellow mixture many rays indued with green, and Green being less remote from the usual blew colour of Bise than yellow, is the more copiously reflected by it.

In like manner, if any one of the Prismatick colours, suppose Red, be intercepted, on design to try the asserted impossibility of reproducing that Colour out of the others which are pretermitted; 'tis necessary, either that the colours be very well parted before the red be intercepted, or that together with the red the neighbouring colours, into which any red is secretly dispersed, (that is, the yellow, and perhaps green too) be intercepted, or else, that allowance be made for the emerging of so much red out of the yellow green, as may possibly have been diffused, and scatteringly blended in those colours. And if these things be observed, the new Production of Red, or any intercepted colour will be found impossible.

This, I conceive, is enough for an Introduction to Experiments of this kind; which if any of the R. Society shall be so curious as to prosecute, I should be very glad to be informed with what success: That, if any thing seem to be defective, or to thwart this relation, I may have an opportunity of giving further direction about it, or of acknowledging my errors, if I have committed any.

John Locke: 1632-1704

AN ESSAY CONCERNING HUMAN UNDERSTANDING *

1690

NO INNATE PRINCIPLES IN THE MIND

1. *The way shown how we come by any knowledge, sufficient to prove it not innate*—It is an established opinion amongst some men that there are in the understanding certain innate principles; some primary notions or characters, as it were, stamped upon the mind of man, which the soul receives in its very first being, and brings into the world with it. It would be sufficient to convince unprejudiced readers of the falseness of this supposition, if I should only show (as I hope I shall in the following parts of this discourse) how men, barely by the use of their natural faculties, may attain to all the knowledge they have, without the help of any innate impressions, and may arrive at certainty, without any such original notions or principles. For I imagine any one will easily grant that it would be impertinent to suppose the ideas of colours innate in a creature to whom God hath given sight, and a power to receive them by the eyes from external objects: and no less unreasonable would it be to attribute several truths to the impressions of nature and innate characters, when we may observe in ourselves faculties fit to attain as easy and certain knowledge of them, as if they were originally imprinted on the mind.

But because a man is not permitted without censure to follow his own thoughts in the search of truth, when they lead him ever so little out of the common road I shall set down the reasons that made me doubt of the truth of that opinion, as an excuse for my mistake, if I be in one; which I leave to be considered by those who, with me, dispose themselves to embrace truth wherever they find it.

2. *General assent the great argument*—There is nothing more commonly taken for granted than that there are certain principles, both

* Although Hobbes also was an empiricist, Locke is usually considered the founder of empiricism because of the extensive treatment which he gave to it in his "Essay." Only a small fraction of it is reproduced here. The chapter on the association of ideas did not appear until the fourth edition in 1700. The present text is from *The Philosophical Works of John Locke*, edited by J. A. St. John, London, G. Bell and Sons, 1913, I, 134-143, 205-211, 534-541.

speculative and practical, (for they speak of both), universally agreed upon by all mankind, which therefore, they argue, must need be constant impressions, which the souls of men receive in their first beings, and which they bring into the world with them, as necessarily and really as they do any of their inherent faculties.

3. *Universal consent proves nothing innate*—This argument, drawn from universal consent, has this misfortune in it, that if it were true in matter of fact, that there were certain truths wherein all mankind agreed, it would not prove them innate, if there can be any other way shown how men may come to that universal agreement in the things they do consent in, which I presume may be done.

4. *"What is, is" and "it is impossible for the same thing to be and not to be" not universally assented to*—But, which is worse, this argument of universal consent, which is made use of to prove innate principles, seems to me a demonstration that there are none such; because there are none to which all mankind give an universal assent. I shall begin with the speculative, and instance in those magnified principles of demonstration, "whatsoever is, is," and "it is impossible for the same thing to be and not to be"; which, of all others, I think have the most allowed title to innate. These have so settled a reputation of maxims universally received, that it will no doubt be thought strange if anyone should seem to question it. But yet I take liberty to say, that these propositions are so far from having an universal assent, that there are a great part of mankind to whom they are not so much as known.

5. *Not on the mind naturally imprinted, because not known to children, idiots, etc.*—For, first, it is evident that all children and idiots have not the least apprehension or thought of them; and the want of that is enough to destroy that universal assent which must needs be the necessary concomitant of all innate truths; it seeming to me near a contradiction to say that there are truths imprinted on the soul which it perceives or understands not; imprinting, if it signify anything, being nothing else but the making certain truths to be perceived. For to imprint anything on the mind without the mind's perceiving it, seems to me hardly intelligible. If therefore children and idiots have mind, with those impressions upon them, they must unavoidably perceive them, and necessarily know and assent to these truths; which since they do not, it is evident that there are no such impressions. For if they are not notions naturally imprinted, how can they be innate? and if they are notions imprinted, how can they be unknown. To say a notion is imprinted on the mind, and yet at the same time to say that the mind is ignorant of it, and never yet took notice of it, is to make this impression nothing. No proposition can be said to be in the mind which it was never yet conscious of. For if any one may, then, by the same reason, all propositions that are true, and the mind is

capable of ever assenting to, may be said to be in the mind, and to be imprinted; since, if anything can be said to be in the mind, which it never yet knew, it must be only because it is capable of knowing it, and so the mind is of all truths it ever shall know. Nay, thus truths may be imprinted on the mind which it never did nor ever shall know; for a man may live long, and die at last in ignorance of many truths which his mind was capable of knowing, and that was certainty. So that if the capacity of knowing be the natural impression contended for, all the truths a man ever comes to know. will by this account, be every one of them innate; and this great point will amount to no more, but only to a very improper way of speaking; which, whilst it pretends to assert the contrary, says nothing different from those who deny innate principles. For nobody, I think, ever denied that the mind was capable of knowing several truths. The capacity, they say, is innate, the knowledge acquired. But then to what end such contest for certain innate maxims? If truths can be imprinted on the understanding without being perceived I can see no difference there can be between any truths the mind is capable of knowing in respect of their original; they must all be innate or all adventitious; in vain shall a man go about to distinguish them. He therefore that talks of innate notions in the understanding, cannot (if he intend thereby any distinct sort of truths) mean such truths to be in the understanding as it never perceived, and is yet wholly ignorant of. For if these words (to be in the understanding) have any propriety, they signify to be understood; so that to be in the understanding and not to be understood, to be in the mind and never to be perceived, is all one as to say anything is and is not in the mind or understanding. If therefore these two propositions, "Whatsoever is, is," and "it is impossible for the same thing to be and not to be," are by nature imprinted, children cannot be ignorant of them; infants, and all that have souls, must necessarily have them in their understandings, know the truth of them, and assent to it.

6. *That men know them when they come to the use of reason, answered* —To avoid this, it is usually answered, that all men know and assent to them, when they come to the use of reason, and this is enough to prove them innate. I answer:

7. Doubtful expressions, that have scarce any signification, go for clear reasons to those who, being prepossessed, take not the pains to examine even what they themselves say. For, to apply this answer with any tolerable sense to our present purpose, it must signify one of these two things; either that as soon as men come to the use of reason these supposed native inscriptions come to be known and observed by them, or else that the use and exercise of men's reason assists them in the discovery of these principles, and certainly makes them known to them.

8. *If reason discovered them, that would not prove them innate*—If they

mean, that by the use of reason men may discover these principles, and that this is sufficient to prove them innate, their way of arguing will stand thus, viz., that whatever truths reason can certainly discover to us, and make us firmly assent to, those are all naturally imprinted on the mind; since that universal assent, which is made the mark of them, amounts to no more but this, that by the use of reason we are capable to come to a certain knowledge of and assent to them; and, by this means, there will be no difference between the maxims of the mathematicians, and theorems they deduce from them: all must be equally allowed innate, they being all discoveries made by the use of reason, and truths that a rational creature may certainly come to know, if he apply his thoughts rightly that way.

9. *It is false that reason discovers them*—But how can these men think the use of reason necessary to discover principles that are supposed innate, when reason (if we may believe them) is nothing else but the faculty of deducing unknown truths from principles or propositions that are already known? That certainly can never be thought innate which we have need of reason to discover; unless as I have said, we will have all the certain truths that reason ever teaches us, to be innate. We may as well think the use of reason necessary to make our eyes discover visible objects, as that there should be need of reason, or the exercise thereon to make the understanding see what is originally engraven on it, and cannot be in the understanding before it be perceived by it. So that to make reason discover those truths thus imprinted, is to say that the use of reason discovers to a man what he knew before; and if men have those innate impressed truths originally, and before the use of reason, and yet are always ignorant of them till they come to the use of reason, it is in effect to say, that men know and know them not at the same time.

10. It will here perhaps be said that mathematical demonstrations and other truths that are not innate, are not assented to as soon as proposed, wherein they are distinguished from these maxims and other innate truths. I shall have occasion to speak of assent, upon the first proposing, more particularly by and by. I shall here only, and that very readily, allow, that these maxims and mathematical demonstrations are in this different: that the one have need of reason, using of proofs to make them out and to gain our assent; but the other as soon as understood, are, without any the least reasoning, embraced and assented to. But I withal beg leave to observe, that it lays open the weakness of this subterfuge, which requires the use of reason for the discovery of these general truths; since it must be confessed that in their discovery there is no use made of reasoning at all. And I think those who give this answer will not be forward to affirm that the knowledge of this maxim, "that it is impossible for the same thing to be and not to be," is a deduction of our reason. For this

would be to destroy that bounty of nature they seem so fond of, whilst they make the knowledge of those principles to depend on the labour of our thoughts. For all reasoning is search, and casting about, and requires pains and application. And how can it with any tolerable sense be supposed that what was imprinted by nature, as the foundation and guide of our reason, should need the use of reason to discover it?

11. Those who will take the pains to reflect with a little attention on the operations of the understanding, will find that this ready assent of the mind to some truths, depends not either on native inscription, or the use of reason, but on a faculty of the mind quite distinct from both of them, as we shall see hereafter. Reason, therefore, having nothing to do in procuring our assent to these maxims, if by saying that men know and assent to them, when they come to the use of reason, be meant, that the use of reason assists us in the knowledge of these maxims, it is utterly false; and were it true, would prove them not to be innate.

12. *The coming to the use of reason not the time we come to know these maxims*—If by knowing and assenting to them when we come to the use of reason, be meant that this is the time when they come to be taken notice of by the mind; and that as soon as children come to the use of reason, they come also to know and assent to these maxims; this also is false and frivolous. First, it is false, because it is evident these maxims are not in the mind so early as the use of reason; and therefore the coming to the use of reason is falsely assigned as the time of their discovery. How many instances of the use of reason may we observe in children, a long time before they have any knowledge of this maxim, "that it is impossible for the same thing to be and not to be"! And a great part of illiterate people and savages pass many years, even of their rational age, without ever thinking on this and the like general and more abstract reason. Which is so because, till after they come to the use of reason, those general abstract ideas are not framed in the mind, about which those general maxims are, which are mistaken for innate principles, but are indeed discoveries made and verities introduced and brought into the mind by the same way, and discovered by the same steps, as several other propositions, which nobody was ever so extravagant as to suppose innate. This I hope to make plain in the sequel of this discourse. I allow therefore, a necessity that men should come to the use of reason before they get the knowledge of general truths, but deny that men's coming to the use of reason is the time of their discovery.

13. *By this they are not distinguished from other knowable Truths*—In the meantime it is observable, that this saying that men know and assent to these maxims when they come to the use of reason, amounts in reality of fact to no more but this that they are never known nor taken notice of before the use of reason, but may possibly be assented to

some time after, during a man's life; but when is uncertain: and so may all other knowable truths, as well as these, which therefore have no advantage nor distinction from others by this note of being known when we come to the use of reason, nor are thereby proved to be innate but quite the contrary.

14. *If coming to the use of reason were the time of their discovery would not prove them innate*—But, secondly, were it true that the precise time of their being known and assented to were when men come to the use of reason, neither would that prove them innate. This way of arguing is as frivolous as the supposition itself is false. For by what kind of logic will it appear that any notion is originally by nature imprinted in the mind in its first constitution, because it comes first to be observed and assented to when a faculty of the mind, which has quite a distinct province, begins to exert itself? And therefore the coming to the use of speech if it were supposed the time that these maxims are first assented to, (which it may be with as much truth as the time when men come to the use of reason) would be as good a proof that they were innate, as to say they are innate because men assent to them when they come to the use of reason. I agree then with these men of innate principles, that there is no knowledge of these general and self-evident maxims in the mind till it comes to the exercise of reason; but I deny that the coming to the use of reason is the precise time when they are first taken notice of; and if that were the precise time, I deny that it would prove them innate. All that can with any truth be meant by this proposition, is no more but this that the making of general abstract ideas and the understanding of general names being concomitant of the rational faculty, and growing up with it, children commonly get not those general ideas, nor learn the names that stand for them, till, having for a good while exercised their reason about familiar and more particular ideas, they are, by their ordinary discourse and actions with others, acknowledged to be capable of rational conversation. If assenting to these maxims when men come to the use of reason can be true in any other sense, I desire it may be shown; or at least, how in this, or any other sense, it proves them innate.

15. *The steps by which the mind attains several truths*—The senses at first let in particular ideas, and furnish the yet empty cabinet; and the mind by degrees growing familiar with some of them, they are lodged in the memory, names got to them. Afterwards, the mind proceeding further abstracts them, and by degrees learns the use of general names. In this manner the mind comes to be furnished with ideas and language, the materials about which to exercise its discursive faculty; and the use of reason becomes daily more visible, as these materials that give it employment increase. But though the having of general ideas and the use of general words and reason usually grow together, yet I see not how

this any way proves them innate. The knowledge of some truths, I confess, is very early in the mind; but in a way that shows them not to be innate. For if we will observe, we shall find it still to be about ideas not innate but acquired; it being about those first which are imprinted by external things, with which infants have earliest to do, which make the most frequent impressions on their senses. In ideas thus got the mind discovers that some agree and others differ, probably as soon as it has any use of memory, as soon as it is able to retain and perceive distinct ideas. But whether it be then or no, this is certain it does so long before it has the use of words, or comes to that which we commonly call "the use of reason." For a child knows as certainly before it can speak the difference between the ideas of sweet and bitter (i.e., that sweet is not bitter), as it knows afterwards (when it comes to speak) that wormwood and sugarplums are not the same things.

OF IDEAS IN GENERAL, AND THEIR ORIGINAL

1. *Idea is the object of thinking*—Every man being conscious to himself that he thinks, and that which his mind is applied about whilst thinking, being the ideas that are there, it is past doubt that men have in their minds several ideas, such as are those expressed by the words whiteness, hardness, sweetness, thinking, motion, man, elephant, army, drunkenness, and others. It is in the first place then to be inquired how he comes by them. I know it is a received doctrine that men have native ideas and original characters stamped upon their minds in their very first being. This opinion I have at large examined already; and I suppose what I have said in the foregoing book will be much more easily admitted when I have shown whence the understanding may get all the ideas it has, and by what ways and degrees they may come into the mind; for which I shall appeal to everyone's own observation and experience.

2. *All ideas come from sensation or reflection*—Let us then suppose the mind to be, as we say, white paper, void of all characters, without any ideas; how comes it to be furnished? Whence comes it by that vast store which the busy and boundless fancy of man has painted on it with an almost endless variety? Whence has it all the materials of reason and knowledge? To this I answer in one word, from experience; in that all our knowledge is founded, and from that it ultimately derives itself. Our observation employed either about external and sensible objects, or the internal operations of our minds, perceived and reflected on by ourselves, is that which supplies our understanding with all the materials of thinking. These two are the fountains of knowledge from whence all the ideas we have or can naturally have do spring.

3. *The objects of sensation one source of ideas*—First, our senses, con-

versant about particular sensible objects, do convey into the mind several distinct perceptions of things, according to those various ways therein those objects do affect them: and thus we come by those ideas we have, of yellow, white, heat, cold, soft, hard, bitter, sweet, and all those which we call sensible qualities; which when I say the senses convey into the mind, I mean they from external objects convey into the mind what produces there those perceptions. This great source of most of the ideas we have, depending wholly upon our senses, and derived by them to the understanding, I call *Sensation.*

4. *The operations of our minds, the other source of them*—Secondly, the other fountain, from which experience furnisheth the understanding with ideas, is the perception of the operations of our own mind within us, as it is employed about the ideas it has got; which operations, when the soul comes to reflect on and consider, do furnish the understanding with another set of ideas, which could not be had from things without; and such are perception, thinking, doubting, believing, reasoning, knowing, willing, and all the different actings of our own minds; which we being conscious of, and observing in ourselves, do from these receive into our understandings as distinct ideas, as we do from bodies affecting our senses. This source of ideas every man has wholly in himself; and though it be not sense, as having nothing to do with external objects, yet it is very like it, and might properly enough be called internal sense. But as I call the other Sensation, so I call this Reflection, the ideas it affords being such only as the mind gets by reflecting on its own operations within itself. By reflection then, in the following part of this discourse, I would be understood to mean that notice which the mind takes of its own operations, and the manner of them by reason whereof there come to be ideas of these operations in the understanding. These two, I say, viz., external material things, and the objects of reflection; are to me the only originals from whence all our ideas take their beginnings. The term operations here I use in a large sense, as comprehending not barely the actions of the mind about its ideas, but some sort of passions arising sometimes from them, such as is the satisfaction or uneasiness arising from any thought.

5. *All our ideas are of the one or the other of these*—The understanding seems to me not to have the least glimmering of any ideas which it doth not receive from one of these two. External objects furnish the mind with the ideas of sensible qualities, which are all those different perceptions they produce in us; and the mind furnishes the understanding with ideas of its own operations.

These when we have taken a full survey of them, and their several modes, combinations, and relations, we shall find to contain all our whole stock of ideas; and that we have nothing in our minds, which did not come in one of these two ways. Let anyone examine his own thoughts, and thoroughly search into his understanding; and then let him tell me, whether all the original ideas he has there, are any other than of the objects of his reflection; and how great a mass of knowledge soever he imagines to be lodged there, he will, upon taking a strict view, see that he has not any idea in his mind, but what one of these two have imprinted—though, perhaps, with infinite variety compounded and enlarged by the understanding, as we shall see hereafter.

6. *Observable in children*—He that attentively considers the state of a child, at his first coming into the world, will have little reason to think him stored with plenty of ideas, that are to be the matter of his future knowledge: it is by degrees he comes to be furnished with them. And though the ideas of obvious and familiar qualities imprint themselves before the memory begins to keep a register of time or order, yet it is often so late before some unusual qualities come in the way, that there are few men that cannot recollect the beginning of their acquaintance with them; and if it were worth while, no doubt a child might be so ordered as to have but a very few, even of the ordinary ideas till he were grown up to a man. But all that are born into the world being surrounded with bodies that perpetually and diversely affect them, variety of ideas, whether care be taken of it or not, are imprinted on the minds of children. Light and colours are busy at hand everywhere, when the eye is but open; sounds and some tangible qualities fail not to solicit their proper senses, and force an entrance to the mind; but yet, I think, it will be granted easily, that if a child were kept in a place where he never saw any other but black and white till he were a man he would have no more ideas of scarlet or green, than he that from his childhood never tasted an oyster or a pine-apple has of those particular relishes.

7. *Men are differently furnished with these, according to the different objects they converse with*—Men then come to be furnished with fewer or more simple ideas from without, according as the objects they converse with afford greater or less variety; and from the operations of their minds within, according as they more or less reflect on them. For though he that contemplates the operations of his mind, cannot but have plain and clear ideas of them; yet, unless he turns his thoughts that way, and considers them attentively, he will no more have clear and distinct ideas of all the operations of his mind, and all that may be observed therein, than he will have all the particular ideas of any landscape, or of the parts and motions of a clock, who will not turn his eyes to it, and with attention heed all the parts of it. The picture or clock may be so placed, that they may come in his way every day; but yet he will have but a confused idea of all the parts they are made up of, till he applies himself with attention to consider them in particular.

8. *Ideas of reflection later, because they need Attention*—And hence we see the reason why it is pretty late before most children get ideas of the operations of their own minds; and some have not any very clear or perfect ideas of the greatest part of them all their lives; because, though they pass there continually, yet, like floating visions they make not deep impressions enough to leave in their mind clear, distinct, lasting ideas till the understanding turns inward upon itself, reflects on its own operations, and makes them the objects of their own contemplation. Children when they come first into it, are surrounded with a world of new things, which, by a constant solicitation of their senses, draw the mind constantly to them, forward to take notice of new, and apt to be delighted with the variety of changing objects. Thus the first years are usually employed and diverted in looking abroad. Men's business in them is to acquaint themselves with what is to be found without; and so growing up in a constant attention to outward sensations, seldom make any considerable reflection on what passes within them till they come to be riper years, and some scarce ever at all.

OF THE ASSOCIATION OF IDEAS

1. There is scarce any one that does not observe something that seems odd to him, and is in itself really extravagant in the opinions, reasonings, and actions of other men. The least flaw of this kind, if at all different from his own, every one is quick sighted enough to espy in another, and will by the authority of reason forwardly condemn, though he be guilty of much greater unreasonableness in his own tenets and conduct, which he never perceives, and will very hardly, if at all, be convinced of.

2. This proceeds not wholly from self-love, though that has often a great hand in it. Men of fair minds, and not given up to the overweening of self-flattery, are frequently guilty of it; and in many cases one with amazement hears the arguings, and is astonished at the obstinacy of a worthy man, who yields not to the evidence of reason, though laid before him as clear as daylight.

3. This sort of unreasonableness is usually imputed to education and prejudice, and for the most part truly enough, though that reaches not the bottom of the disease, nor shows distinctly enough whence it rises, or wherein it lies. Education is often rightly assigned for the cause, and prejudice is a good general name for the thing itself; but yet, I think, he ought to look a little further, who would trace this sort of madness to the root it springs from, and so explain it, as to show whence this flaw has its original in very sober and rational minds, and wherein its consists.

4. I shall be pardoned for calling it by so harsh a name as madness, when it is considered that opposition to reason deserves that name, and

is really madness; and there is scarce a man so free from it, but that if he should always, on all occasions, argue or do as in some cases he constantly does, would not be thought fitter for Bedlam than civil conversation. I do not here mean when he is under the power of an unruly passion, but in the steady calm course of his life. That which will yet more apologize for this harsh name, and ungrateful imputation on the greatest part of mankind, is, that inquiring a little by the bye into the nature of madness, I found it to spring from the very same root, and to depend on the very same cause we are here speaking of. This consideration of the thing itself, at a time when I thought not the least on the subject which I am now treating of, suggested it to me. And if this be a weakness to which all men are so liable, if this be a taint which so universally infects mankind, the greater care should be taken to lay it open under its due name thereby to excite the greater care in its prevention and cure.

5. Some of our ideas have a natural correspondence and connexion one with another: it is the office and excellency of our reason to trace these, and hold them together in that union and correspondence which is founded in their peculiar beings. Besides this, there is another connexion of ideas wholly owing to chance or custom. Ideas that in themselves are not all of kin, come to be so united in some men's minds, that it is very hard to separate them; they always keep in company, and the one no sooner at any time comes into the understanding, but its associate appears with it; and if they are more than two which are thus united, the whole gang, always inseparable, show themselves together.

6. This strong combination of ideas, not allied by nature, the mind makes in itself either voluntarily or by chance; and hence it comes in different men to be very different, according to their different inclinations, education, interests, &c. Custom settles habits of thinking in the understanding, as well as of determining in the will, and of motions in the body: all which seems to be but trains of motions in the animal spirits, which, once set a going, continue in the same steps they have been used to; which, by often treading, are worn into a smooth path, and the motion in it becomes easy, and as it were natural. As far as we can comprehend thinking, thus ideas seem to be produced in our minds; or, if they are not, this may serve to explain their following one another in an habitual train, when once they are put into their track, as well as it does to explain such motions of the body. A musician used to any tune will find that, let it but once begin in his head, the ideas of the several notes of it will follow one another orderly in his understanding, without any care or attention, as regularly as his fingers move orderly over the key of the organ to play out the tune he has begun, though his unattentive thoughts be elsewhere a wandering. Whether the natural cause of these ideas, as well as of that regular dancing of his fingers be the motion of his animal

spirits, I will not determine, how probable soever, by this instance, it appears to be so: but this may help us a little to conceive of intellectual habits, and of the tying together of ideas.

7. That there are such associations of them made by custom, in the minds of most men, I think nobody will question, who has well considered himself or others; and to this, perhaps, might be justly attributed most of the sympathies and antipathies observable in men, which work as strongly, and produce as regular effects as if they were natural; and are therefore called so, though they at first had no other original but the accidental connexion of two ideas, which either the strength of the first impression, or future indulgence so united, that they always afterwards kept company together in that man's mind, as if they were but one idea. I say most of the antipathies, I do not say all; for some of them are truly natural, depend upon our original constitution, and are born with us; but a great part of those which are counted natural, would have been known to be from unheeded, though perhaps early, impressions, or wanton fancies at first, which would have been acknowledged the original of them, if they had been warily observed. A grown person surfeited with honey no sooner hears the name of it, but his fancy immediately carries sickness and qualms to his stomach, and he cannot bear the very idea of dislike, and sickness, and vomiting, presently accompany it, and he is disturbed; but he knows from whence to date this weakness, and can tell how he got this indisposition. Had this happened to him by an overdose of honey when a child, all the same effects would have followed; but the cause would have been mistaken, and the antipathy counted natural.

8. I mention this, not out of any great necessity there is in this present argument to distinguish nicely between natural and acquired antipathies; but I take notice of it for another purpose, viz. that those who have children, or the charge of their education, would think it worth their while diligently to watch, and carefully to prevent the undue connexion of ideas in the minds of young people. This is the time most susceptible of lasting impressions; and though those relating to the health of the body are by discreet people minded and fenced against, yet I am apt to doubt that those which relate more peculiarly to the mind, and terminate in the understanding or passions, have been much less heeded than the thing deserves: nay, those relating purely to the understanding, have as I suspect, been by most men wholly overlooked.

9. This wrong connexion in our minds of ideas in themselves loose and independent of one another, has such an influence, and is of so great force to set us awry in our actions, as well moral as natural, passions, reasonings, and notions themselves, that perhaps there is not any one thing that deserves more to be looked after.

10. The ideas of goblins and sprites have really no more to do with darkness than light: Yet let but a foolish maid inculcate these often on the mind of a child, and raise them there together, possibly he shall never be able to separate them again so long as he lives, but darkness shall ever afterwards bring with it those frightful ideas, and they shall be so joined, that he can no more bear the one than the other.

11. A man receives a sensible injury from another, thinks on the man and that action over and over, and by ruminating on them strongly, or much, in his mind, so cements those two ideas together, that he makes them almost one; never thinks on the man, but the pain and displeasure he suffered comes into his mind with it, so that he scarce distinguishes them, but has as much an aversion for the one as the other. Thus hatreds are often begotten from slight and innocent occasions, and quarrels propagated and continued in the world.

12. A man has suffered pain or sickness in a place; he saw his friend die in such a room; though these have in nature nothing to do one with another, yet when the idea of the place occurs to his mind, it brings (the impression being once made) that of the pain and displeasure with it: he confounds them in his mind, and can as little bear the one as the other.

13. When this combination is settled, and while it lasts, it is not in the power of reason to help us, and relieve us from the effects of it. Ideas in our minds, when they are there, will operate according to their natures and circumstances. And here we see the cause why time cures certain affections, which reason, though in the right, and allowed to be so, has not power over, nor is able against them to prevail with those who are apt to hearken to it in other cases. The death of a child that was the daily delight of its mother's eyes, and joy of her soul, rends from her heart the whole comfort of her life, and gives her all the torment imaginable: use the consolations of reason in this case, and you were as good preach ease to one on the rack, and hope to allay, by rational discourses, the pain of his joints tearing asunder. Till time has by disuse separated the sense of that enjoyment and its loss, from the idea of the child returning to her memory, all representations, though ever so reasonable, are in vain; and therefore some in whom the union between these ideas is never dissolved, spend their lives in mourning, and carry an incurable sorrow to their graves.

14. A friend of mine knew one perfectly cured of madness by a very harsh and offensive operation. The gentleman who was thus recovered, with great sense of gratitude and acknowledgment owned the cure all his life after, as the greatest obligation he could have received; but, whatever gratitude and reason suggested to him, he could never bear the sight of the operator: that image brought back with it the idea of that agony

which he suffered from his hands, which was too mighty and intolerable for him to endure.

15. Many children, imputing the pain they endured at school to their books they were corrected for, so join those ideas together, that a book becomes their aversion, and they are never reconciled to the study and use of them all their lives after; and thus reading becomes a torment to them, which otherwise possibly they might have made the great pleasure of their lives. There are rooms convenient enough, that some men cannot study in, and fashions of vessels, which, though ever so clean and commodious, they cannot drink out of, and that by reason of some accidental ideas which are annexed to them, and make them offensive; and who is there that hath not observed some man to flag at the appearance, or in the company of some certain person, not otherwise superior to him, but because, having once on some occasion got the ascendant, the idea of authority and distance goes along with that of the person, and he that has been thus subjected, is not able to separate them.

16. Instances of this kind are so plentiful everywhere, that if I add one more, it is only for the pleasant oddness of it. It is of a young gentleman, who, having learnt to dance, and that to great perfection. There happened to stand an old trunk in the room where he learnt. The idea of this remarkable piece of household stuff had so mixed itself with the turns and steps of all his dances, that though in that chamber he could dance excellently well, yet it was only whilst that trunk was there; nor could he perform well in any other place, unless that or some such other trunk had its due position in the room. If this story shall be suspected to be dressed up with some comical circumstances, I answer for myself that I had it some years since from a very sober and worthy man, upon his own knowledge, as I report it; and I dare say there are very few inquisitive persons who read this, who have not met with accounts, if not examples, of this nature, that may parallel, or at least justify this.

17. Intellectual habits and defects this way contracted, are not less frequent and powerful though less observed. Let the ideas of being and matter be strongly joined, either by education or much thought; whilst these are still combined in the mind, what notions, what reasonings, will there be about separate spirits? Let custom from the very childhood have joined figure and shape to the idea of God, and what absurdities will that mind be liable to about the Deity? Let the idea of infallibility be inseparably joined to any person, and these two constantly together possess the mind; and then one body in two places at once, shall unexamined be swallowed for a certain truth, by an implicit faith, whenever that imagined infallible person dictates and demands assent without inquiry.

George Berkeley: 1685-1753

AN ESSAY TOWARD A NEW THEORY OF VISION *

1709

1. My design is to show the manner wherein we perceive by sight, the distance, magnitude, and situation of objects. Also to consider the difference there is betwixt the ideas of sight and touch, and whether there be any idea common to both senses. In treating of all which, it seems to me, the writers of optics have proceeded on wrong principles.

2. It is, I think, agreed by all, that distance of itself, and immediately, cannot be seen. For distance being a line directed end-wise to the eye, it projects only one point in the fund of the eye. Which point remains invariably the same, whether the distance be longer or shorter.

3. I find it also acknowledged, that the estimate we make of the distance of objects considerably remote, is rather an act of judgment grounded on experience than of sense. For example, when I perceive a great number of intermediate objects, such as houses, fields, rivers, and the like, which I have experienced to take up a considerable space; I thence form a judgment or conclusion, that the object I see beyond them is at a great distance. Again, when an object appears faint and small, which, at a near distance, I have experienced to make a vigorous and large appearance; I instantly conclude it to be far off. And this, it is evident, is the result of experience; without which, from the faintness and littleness, I should not have inferred any thing concerning the distance of objects.

4. But when an object is placed at so near a distance, as that the interval between the eyes bears any sensible proportion to it, it is the received opinion that the two optic axes (the fancy that we see only with one eye at once being exploded) concurring at the object, do there make an angle, by means of which, according as it is greater or lesser, the object is perceived to be nearer or further off.

5. Betwixt which, and the foregoing manner of estimating distance, there is this remarkable difference. That whereas there was no apparent, necessary connexion between small distance and a large and strong appearance, or between great distance, and a little and faint appearance, yet

* Empiricism is applied by Berkeley to the perception of distance and magnitude. Space does not permit the reprinting of the entire essay. In the text, the Everyman's Library edition has been followed.

there appears a very necessary connexion between an obtuse angle and near distance, and an acute angle and further distance. It does not in the least depend upon experience, but may be evidently known by any one before he had experienced it, that the nearer the concurrence of the optic axes, the greater the angle, and the remoter their concurrence is, the lesser will be the angle comprehended by them.

6. There is another way, mentioned by the optic writers, whereby they will have us judge of those distances, in respect of which, the breadth of the pupil hath any sensible bigness. And that is the greater or lesser divergency of the rays, which, issuing from the visible point, do fall on the pupil: that point being judged nearest, which is seen by most diverging rays; and that remoter, which is seen by less diverging rays. And so on, the apparent distance still increasing, as the divergency of the rays decreases, till at length it becomes infinite, when the rays that fall on the pupil are to sense parallel. And after this manner it is said we perceive distances when we look only with one eye.

7. In this case also, it is plain we are not beholding to experience: it being a certain, necessary truth, that the nearer the direct rays falling on the eye approach to a parallelism, the further off is the point from whence they flow.

8. I have here set down the common, current accounts that are given of our perceiving near distances by sight, which, though they are unquestionably received for true by mathematicians, and accordingly made use of by them in determining the apparent places of objects, do, nevertheless, seem to me very unsatisfactory: and that for these following reasons:—

9. First, It is evident that when the mind perceives any idea, not immediately and of itself, it must be by the means of some other idea. Thus, for instance, the passions which are in the mind of another, are of themselves to me invisible. I may nevertheless perceive them by sight, though not immediately, yet by means of the colours they produce in the countenance. We do often see shame or fear in the looks of a man, by perceiving the changes of his countenance to red or pale.

10. Moreover it is evident, that no idea which is not itself perceived, can be to me the means of perceiving any other idea. If I do not perceive the redness or paleness of a man's face themselves, it is impossible I should perceive by them the passions which are in his mind.

11. Now from Sect. 2, it is plain that distance is in its own nature imperceivable, and yet it is perceived by sight. It remains, therefore, that it be brought into view by means of some other idea that is itself immediately perceived in the act of vision.

12. But those lines and angles, by means whereof mathematicians pretend to explain the perception of distance, are themselves not at all per-

ceived, nor are they, in truth, ever thought of by those unskilful in optics. I appeal to any one's experience, whether, upon sight of an object, he compute its distance by the bigness of the angle made by the meeting of the two optic axes? Or whether he ever think of the greater or lesser divergency of the rays, which arrive from any point to his pupil? Nay, whether it be not perfectly impossible for him to perceive by sense the various angles wherewith the rays, according to their greater or lesser divergence, do fall on his eye. Every one is himself the best judge of what he perceives, and what not. In vain shall all the mathematicians in the world tell me, that I perceive certain lines and angles which introduce into my mind the various ideas of distance; so long as I myself am conscious of no such thing.

13. Since, therefore, those angles and lines are not themselves perceived by sight, it follows from Sect. 10, that the mind does not by them judge of the distance of objects.

14. Secondly, the truth of this assertion will be yet further evident to any one that considers those lines and angles have no real existence in nature, being only an hypothesis framed by mathematicians, and by them introduced into optics, that they might treat of that science in a geometrical way.

15. The third and last reason I shall give for my rejecting that doctrine is, that though we should grant the real existence of those optic angles, &c., and that it was possible for the mind to perceive them; yet these principles would not be found sufficient to explain the phenomena of distance. As shall be shown hereafter.

16. Now, it being already shown that distance is suggested to the mind by the mediation of some other idea which is itself perceived in the act of seeing, it remains that we inquire what ideas or sensations there be that attend vision, unto which we may suppose the ideas of distance are connected, and by which they are introduced into the mind. And first, it is certain by experience, that when we look at a near object with both eyes, according as it approaches or recedes from us, we alter the disposition of our eyes, by lessening or widening the interval between the pupils. This disposition to turn of the eyes is attended with a sensation, which seems to me, to be that which in this case brings the idea of greater or lesser distance into the mind.

17. Not that there is any natural or necessary connexion between the sensation we perceive by the turn of the eyes, and greater or lesser distance. But because the mind has by constant experience found the different sensations corresponding to the different dispositions of the eyes, to be attended each with a different degree of distance in the object: there has grown an habitual or customary connexion, between those two sorts of ideas. So that the mind no sooner perceives the sensation arising

from the different turn it gives the eyes, in order to bring the pupils nearer or further asunder, but it withal perceives the different idea of distance which was wont to be connected with that sensation. Just as upon hearing a certain sound, the idea is immediately suggested to the understanding, which custom had united with it.

18. Nor do I see, how I can easily be mistaken in this matter. I know evidently that distance is not perceived of itself. That by consequence, it must be perceived by means of some other idea which is immediately perceived, and varies with the different degrees of distance. I know also that the sensation arising from the turn of the eyes is of itself immediately perceived, and various degrees thereof are connected with different distances: which never fail to accompany them into my mind, when I view an object distinctly with both eyes, whose distance is so small, that in respect of it the interval between the eyes has any considerable magnitude.

19. I know it is a received opinion, that by altering the disposition of the eyes, the mind perceives whether the angle of the optic axes is made greater or lesser. And that accordingly by a kind of natural geometry, it judges the point of their intersection to be nearer, or further off. But this is not true, I am convinced by my own experience, since I am not conscious that I make any such use of the perception I have by the turn of my eyes. And for me to make those judgments, and draw those conclusions from it, without knowing that I do so, seems altogether incomprehensible.

20. From all which it plainly follows, that the judgment we make of the distance of an object, viewed with both eyes, is entirely the result of experience. If we had not constantly found certain sensations arising from the various disposition of the eyes, attended with certain degrees of distance, we should never make those sudden judgments from them, concerning the distance of objects; no more than we would pretend to judge of a man's thoughts, by his pronouncing words we had never heard before.

21. Secondly, an object placed at a certain distance from the eye, to which the breadth of the pupil bears a considerable proportion, being made to approach, is seen more confusedly. And the nearer it is brought, the more confused appearance it makes. And this being found constantly to be so, there arises in the mind an habitual connexion between the several degrees of confusion and distance. The greater confusion still implying the lesser distance, and the lesser confusion, the greater distance of the object.

22. This confused appearance of the object, doth therefore seem to me to be the medium, whereby the mind judges of distance in those cases, wherein the most approved writers of optics will have it judge by the different divergency with which the rays flowing from the radiating

point fall on the pupil. No man, I believe, will pretend to see or feel those imaginary angles, that the rays are supposed to form according to their various inclinations on his eye. But he cannot choose seeing whether the object appear more or less confused. It is therefore a manifest consequence from what has been demonstrated, that instead of the greater or less divergency of the rays, the mind makes use of the greater or less confusedness of the appearance, thereby to determine the apparent place of an object.

23. Nor doth it avail to say, there is not any necessary connexion between confused vision, and distance, great or small. For I ask any man, what necessary connexion he sees between the redness of a blush and shame? and yet no sooner shall he behold that colour to arise in the face of another, but it brings into his mind the idea of that passion which has been observed to accompany it.

24. What seems to have misled the writers of optics in this matter is, that they imagine men judge of distance, as they do of a conclusion in mathematics: betwixt which and the premises, it is indeed absolutely requisite there be an apparent, necessary connexion. But it is far otherwise, in the sudden judgments men make of distance. We are not to think that brutes and children, or even grown reasonable men, whenever they perceive an object to approach, or depart from them, do it by virtue of geometry and demonstration.

25. That one idea may suggest another to the mind, it will suffice that they have been observed to go together: without any demonstration of the necessity of their coexistence, or without so much as knowing what it is that makes them so to coexist. Of this there are innumerable instances, of which no one can be ignorant.

26. Thus greater confusion having been constantly attended with nearer distance, no sooner is the former idea perceived, but it suggests the latter to our thoughts. And if it had been the ordinary course of nature, that the further off an object were placed, the more confused it should appear; it is certain, the very same perception that now makes us think an object approaches, would then have made us imagine it went further off. That perception, abstracting from custom and experience, being equally fitted to produce the idea of great distance, or small distance, or no distance at all.

27. Thirdly, an object being placed at the distance above specified, and brought nearer to the eye, we may nevertheless prevent, at least for some time, the appearance's growing more confused, by straining the eye. In which case, that sensation supplies the place of confused vision, in aiding the mind to judge of the distance of the object. It being esteemed so much the nearer, by how much the effort, or straining of the eye in order to distinct vision, is greater.

28. I have here set down those sensations or ideas that seem to me to be the constant and general occasions of introducing into the mind the different ideas of near distance. It is true in most cases, that divers other circumstances contribute to frame our idea of distance, viz., the particular number, size, kind, &c., of the things seen. Concerning which, as well as all other the forementioned occasions which suggest distance, I shall only observe, they have none of them, in their own nature, any relation or connexion with it: nor is it possible they should ever signify the various degrees thereof, otherwise than as by experience they have been found to be connected with them.

52. I have now done with distance, and proceed to show how it is, that we perceive by sight the magnitude of objects. It is the opinion of some that we do it by angles, or by angles in conjection with distance. But neither angles nor distance being perceivable by sight, and the things we see being in truth at no distance from us, it follows, that as we have shown lines and angles not to be the medium the mind makes use of in apprehending the apparent place, so neither are they the medium whereby it apprehends the apparent magnitude of objects.

53. It is well known, that the same extension at a near distance shall subtend a greater angle, and at a further distance a lesser angle. And by this principle, we are told, the mind estimates the magnitude of an object, comparing the angle under which it is seen with its distance, and thence inferring the magnitude thereof. What inclines men to this mistake (beside the humour of making one see by geometry) is, that the same perceptions or ideas which suggest distance, do also suggest magnitude. But if we examine it, we shall find they suggest the latter, as immediately as the former. I say they do not first suggest distance, and then leave it to the judgment to use that as a medium, whereby to collect the magnitude; but they have as close and immediate a connexion with the magnitude as independently of distance, as they do distance independently of magnitude. All which will be evident to whoever considers what hath been already said, and what follows.

54. It hath been shown, there are two sorts of objects apprehended by sight; each whereof hath its distinct magnitude, or extension. The one is properly tangible, i.e. to be perceived and measured by touch, and not immediately falling under the sense of seeing: the other, properly and immediately visible, by mediation of which the former is brought in view. Each of these magnitudes are greater or lesser, according as they contain in them more or fewer points; they being made up of points or minimums. For, whatever, may be said of extension in abstract, it is certain, sensible extension is not infinitely divisible. There is a minimum tangible, and a minimum visible, beyond which sense cannot perceive. This every one's experience will inform him.

55. The magnitude of the object which exists without the mind, and is at a distance, continues always invariably the same: but the visible object still changing as you approach to, or recede from the tangible object, it hath no fixed and determinate greatness. Whenever therefore we speak of the magnitude of any thing, for instance a tree or a house, we must mean the tangible magnitude; otherwise there can be nothing steady and free from ambiguity spoken of it. But though the tangible and visible magnitude in truth belong to two distinct objects, I shall nevertheless (especially since those objects are called by the same name and are observed to coexist) to avoid tediousness and singularity of speech, sometimes speak of them as belonging to one and the same thing.

56. Now in order to discover by what means the magnitude of tangible objects is perceived by sight, I need only reflect on what passes in my own mind, and observe what those things be which introduce the ideas of greater or lesser into my thoughts, when I look on any object. And these I find to be, first, the magnitude or extension of the visible object, which being immediately perceived by sight, is connected with that other which is tangible, and placed at a distance; secondly, the confusion or distinctness: and thirdly, the vigorousness or faintness of the aforesaid visible appearance. *Caeteris paribus*, by how much the greater or lesser the visible object is, by so much the greater or lesser do I conclude the tangible object to be. But be the idea immediately perceived by sight never so large, yet if it be withal confused, I judge the magnitude of the thing to be but small: if it be distinct and clear, I judge it greater: and if it be faint, I apprehend it to be yet greater.

57. Moreover the judgments we make of greatness do, in like manner, as those of distance, depend on the disposition of the eye; also on the figure, number, and situation of objects, and other circumstances that have been observed to attend great or small tangible magnitudes. Thus, for instance, the very small quantity of visible extension, which in the figure of a tower doth suggest the idea of great magnitude, shall in the figure of a man suggest the idea of much smaller magnitude. That this is owing to the experience we have had of the usual bigness of a tower and a man, no one, I suppose, need be told.

58. It is also evident, that confusion or faintness have no more a necessary connexion with little or great magnitude, than they have with little or great distance. As they suggest the latter, so they suggest the former to our mind. And by consequence, if it were not for experience, we should no more judge a faint or confused appearance to be connected with great little magnitude, than we should that it was connected with great or little distance.

59. Nor will it be found, that great or small visible magnitude hath any necessary relation to great or small tangible magnitude; so that the one

may certainly be inferred from the other. But, before we come to the proof of this, it is fit we consider the difference there is betwixt the extension and figure which is the proper object of touch, and that other which is termed visible; and how the former is principally, though not immediately, taken notice of, when we look at any object. This has been before mentioned, but we shall here inquire into the cause thereof. We regard the objects that environ us, in proportion as they are adapted to benefit or injure our own bodies, and thereby produce in our minds the sensations of pleasure or pain. Now bodies operating on our organs by an immediate application, and the hurt or advantage arising therefrom depending altogether on the tangible, and not at all on the visible, qualities of any object; this is a plain reason why those should be regarded by us much more than these: and for this end the visive sense seems to have been bestowed on animals, to wit, that by the perception of visible ideas (which in themselves are not capable of affecting, or any wise altering the frame of their bodies) they may be able to foresee (from the experience they have had, what tangible ideas are connected with such and such visible ideas) the damage or benefit which is like to ensue, upon the application of their own bodies to this or that body which is at a distance: which foresight how necessary it is to the preservation of an animal, every one's experience can inform him. Hence it is, that when we look at an object, the tangible figure and extension thereof are principally attended to; whilst there is small heed taken of the visible figure and magnitude, which, though more immediately perceived, do less concern us, and are not fitted to produce any alteration to our bodies.

60. That the matter of fact is true, will be evident to any one, who considers that a man placed at ten foot distance, is thought as great, as if he were placed at the distance of only five foot; which is true, not with relation to the visible, but tangible greatness of the object. The visible magnitude being far greater at one station than it is at the other.

61. Inches, feet, &c., are settled, stated lengths, whereby we measure objects, and estimate their magnitude. We say, for example, an object appears to be six inches or six foot long. Now, that this cannot be meant of visible inches, &c., is evident, because a visible inch is itself no constant, determinate magnitude, and cannot therefore serve to mark out and determine the magnitude of any other thing. Take an inch marked upon a ruler; view it successively, at the distance of half a foot, a foot, a foot and a half, &c., from the eye: at each of which, and at all the intermediate distances, the inch shall have a different visible extension, i.e. there shall be more or fewer points discerned in it. Now I ask, which of all these various extensions is that stated, determinate one, that is agreed on for a common measure of other magnitudes? No reason can be assigned, why we should pick on one, more than another: and except there be some

invariable, determinate extension fixed on to be marked by the word inch, it is plain, it can be used to little purpose; and to say, a thing contains this or that number of inches, shall imply no more than that it is extended, without bringing any particular idea of that extension into the mind. Further, an inch and a foot, from different distances, shall both exhibit the same visible magnitude, and yet at the same time you shall say, that one seems several times greater than the other. From all which it is manifest, that the judgments we make of the magnitude of objects by sight, are altogether in reference to their tangible extension. Whenever we say an object is great or small, of this or that determinate measure, I say, it must be meant of the tangible, and not the visible extension, which though immediately perceived, is nevertheless little taken notice of.

62. Now, that there is no necessary connexion between these two distinct extensions, is evident from hence; because our eyes might have been framed in such a manner, as to be able to see nothing but what were less than the minimum tangible. In which case, it is not impossible we might have perceived all the immediate objects of sight, the very same that we do now: but unto those visible appearances, there would not be connected those different tangible magnitudes, that are now. Which shows, the judgments we make of the magnitude of things placed at a distance, from the various greatness of the immediate objects of sight, do not arise from any essential or necessary, but only a customary tie, which has been observed between them.

63. Moreover, it is not only certain, that any idea of sight might not have been connected with this or that idea of touch, which we now observe to accompany it; but also, that the greater visible magnitudes might have been connected with, and introduced into our minds lesser tangible magnitudes, and the lesser visible magnitudes greater tangible magnitudes. Nay, that it actually is so, we have daily experience; that object which makes a strong and large appearance, not seeming near so great as another, the visible magnitude thereof is much less, but more faint, and the appearance upper, or which is the same thing painted lower on the retina, which faintness and situation suggest both greater magnitude and greater distance.

64. From which, and from Sect. 57, 58, it is manifest, that as we do not perceive the magnitude of objects immediately by sight, so neither do we perceive them by the mediation of any thing which has a necessary connexion with them. Those ideas that now suggest unto us the various magnitudes of external objects, before we touch them, might possibly have suggested no such thing: or they might have signified them, in a direct contrary manner; so that the very same ideas, on the perception whereof we judge an object to be small, might as well have served to make us conclude it great. Those ideas being in their own nature equally

fitted to bring into our minds the idea of small, or great, or no size at all of outward objects; just as the words of any language are in their own nature indifferent to signify this or that thing, or nothing at all.

65. As we see distance, so we see magnitude. And we see both, in the same way that we see shame or anger in the looks of a man. Those passions are themselves invisible: they are nevertheless let in by the eye along with colours and alterations of countenance, which are the immediate object of vision, and which signify them for no other reason, than barely because they have been observed to accompany them: without which experience, we should no more have taken blushing for a sign of shame, than of gladness.

66. We are nevertheless exceeding prone to imagine those things, which are perceived only by the mediation of others, to be themselves the immediate objects of sight; or, at least, to have in their own nature a fitness to be suggested by them, before ever they had been experienced to coexist with them. From which prejudice every one, perhaps, will not find it easy to emancipate himself, by any but the clearest convictions of reason. And there are some grounds to think, that if there was one only invariable and universal language in the world, and that men were born with the faculty of speaking it, it would be the opinion of many, that the ideas in other men's minds were properly perceived by the ear, or had at least a necessary and inseparable tie with the sounds that were affixed to them. All which seems to arise from a want of due application of our discerning faculty, thereby to discriminate between the ideas that are in our understandings, and consider them apart from each other; which would preserve us from confounding those that are different, and make us see what ideas do, and what do not include or imply this or that other idea.

67. There is a celebrated phenomenon, the solution whereof I shall attempt to give, by the principles that have been laid down, in reference to the manner wherein we apprehend by sight the magnitude of objects. The apparent magnitude of the moon, when placed in the horizon, is much greater than when it is in the meridian; though the angle under which the diameter of the moon is seen, be not observed greater in the former case, than in the latter: and the horizontal moon doth not constantly appear of the same bigness, but at some times seemeth far greater than at others.

68. Now in order to explain the reason of the moon's appearing greater than ordinary in the horizon, it must be observed, that the particles which compose our atmosphere intercept the rays of light proceeding from any object to the eye; and by how much the greater is the portion of atmosphere interjacent between the object and the eye, by so much the more are the rays intercepted; and by consequence, the appearance of the object

rendered more faint, every object appearing more vigorous or more faint, in proportion as it sendeth more or fewer rays into the eye. Now, between the eye and the moon, when situated in the horizon, there lies a far greater quantity of atmosphere, than there does when the moon is in the meridian. Whence it comes to pass, that the appearance of the horizontal moon is fainter, and therefore by Sect. 51 it should be thought bigger in that situation, than in the meridian, or in any other elevation above the horizon.

69. Further, the air being variously impregnated, sometimes more and sometimes less with vapours and exhalations fitted to retund and intercept the rays of light, it follows, that the appearance of the horizontal moon hath not always an equal faintness, and by consequence, that luminary, though in the very same situation, is at one time judged greater than at another.

70. That we have here given the true account of the phenomena of the horizontal moon, will, I suppose, be further evident to any one from the following considerations. First, it is plain, that which in this case suggests the idea of greater magnitude, must be something which is itself perceived; for, that which is unperceived cannot suggest to our perception any other thing. Secondly, it must be something that does not constantly remain the same, but is subject to some change or variation, since the appearance of the horizontal moon varies, being at one time greater than at another. And yet, thirdly, it cannot be the visible figure or magnitude, since that remains the same, or is rather lesser, by how much the moon is nearer to the horizon. It remains therefore, that the true cause is that affection or alteration of the visible appearance, which proceeds from the greater paucity of rays arriving at the eye, and which I term faintness, since this answers all the forementioned conditions, and I am not conscious of any other perception that doth.

71. Add to this, that in misty weather it is a common observation, that the appearance of the horizontal moon is far larger than usual, which greatly conspires with, and strengthens our opinion. Neither would it prove, in the least, irreconcilable with what we have said, if the horizontal moon should chance sometimes to seem enlarged beyond its usual extent, even in more serene weather. For we must not only have regard to the mist which happens to be in the place where we stand; we ought also to take into our thoughts the whole sum of vapours and exhalations, which lie betwixt the eye and the moon: all which co-operating to render the appearance of the moon more faint, and thereby increase its magnitude, it may chance to appear greater than it usually does, even in the horizontal position, at a time when, though there be no extraordinary fog or haziness just in the place where we stand; yet, the air between the eye and the

moon, taken altogether, may be loaded with a greater quantity of interspersed vapours and exhalations, than at other times.

72. It may be objected, that in consequence of our principles, the interposition of a body in some degree opaque, which may intercept a great part of the rays of light, should render the appearance of the moon in the meridian as large, as when it is viewed in the horizon. To which I answer, it is not faintness any how applied, that suggests greater magnitude, there being no necessary, but only an experimental connexion between those two things: it follows, that the faintness, which enlarges the appearance, must be applied in such sort, and with such circumstances, as have been observed to attend the vision of great magnitudes. When from a distance we behold great objects, the particles of the intermediate air and vapours, which are themselves unperceivable, do interrupt the rays of light, and thereby render the appearance less strong and vivid; now, faintness of appearance, caused in this sort, hath been experienced to coexist with great magnitude. But when it is caused by the interposition of an opaque sensible body, this circumstance alters the case, so that a faint appearance this way caused, doth not suggest greater magnitude, because it hath not been experienced to coexist with it.

David Hartley: 1705-1757

OBSERVATIONS ON MAN, HIS FRAME, HIS DUTY AND HIS EXPECTATIONS *

1749

INTRODUCTION

Man Consists of Two Parts, Body and Mind

The first is subjected to our senses and inquiries, in the same manner as the other parts of the external material world.

The last is that substance, agent, principle, etc. to which we refer the sensations, ideas, pleasures, pains, and voluntary motions.

Sensations are those internal feelings of the mind, which arise from the impressions made by external objects upon the several parts of our bodies.

All our other internal feelings may be called ideas. Some of these appear to spring up in the mind of themselves, some are suggested by words, others arise in other ways. Many writers comprehend sensations under ideas; but I every where use these words in the senses here ascribed to them.

The ideas which resemble sensations, are called ideas of sensation: all the rest may therefore be called intellectual ideas.

It will appear in the course of these observations, that the ideas of sensation are the elements of which all the rest are compound. Hence ideas of sensation may be termed simple, intellectual ones complex.

The pleasures and pains are comprehended under the sensations and ideas, as these are explained above. For all our pleasures and pains are internal feelings, and, conversely, all our internal feelings seem to be attended with some degree either of pleasure or pain. However, I shall, for the most part, give the names of pleasure and pain only to such degrees as are considerable; referring all low, evanescent ones to the head of mere sensations and ideas.

* Hartley is noteworthy for having included movements as well as ideas in his formulation of associationism, and for his numerous genetic applications of the doctrine. The present quotations are from an edition, published by J. Johnson, London, 1791, I, 1-12, 103-110.

The pleasures and pains may be ranged under seven general classes, viz.

1. Sensation;
2. Imagination;
3. Ambition;
4. Self-interest;
5. Sympathy;
6. Theopathy; and
7. The moral sense; according as they arise from,
    1. The impressions made on the external senses;
    2. Natural or artificial beauty or deformity;
    3. The opinions of others concerning us;
    4. Our possession or want of the means of happiness, and security from, or subjection to, the hazards of misery;
    5. The pleasures and pains of our fellow-creatures;
    6. The affection excited in us by the contemplation of the Deity; or
    7. Moral beauty and deformity.

The human mind may also be considered as inbued with the faculties of memory, imagination or fancy, understanding, affection, and will.

Memory is that faculty, by which traces of sensations and ideas recur, or are recalled, in the same order and proportion, accurately or nearly, as they were once actually presented.

When ideas, and trains of ideas, occur, or are called up, in a vivid manner, and without regard to the order of former actual impressions and perceptions, this is said to be done by the power of imagination or fancy.

The understanding is that faculty, by which we contemplate mere sensations and ideas, pursue truth, and assent to, or differ from, propositions.

The affections have the pleasures and pains for their objects; as the understanding has the mere sensations and ideas. By the affections we are excited to pursue happiness, and all its means, fly from misery, and all its apparent causes.

The will is that state of mind, which is immediately previous to, and causes, those express acts of memory, fancy, and bodily motion, which are termed voluntary.

The motions of the body are of two kinds, automatic and voluntary. The automatic motions are those which arise from the mechanism of the body in an evident manner. They are called automatic, from their resemblance to the motions of automata, or machines, whose principle of motion is within themselves. Of this kind are the motion of the heart, and peristaltic motion of the bowels. The voluntary motions are those which arise from ideas and affections, and which therefore are referred to the mind; the immediately preceding state of the mind, or of the ideas and affections, being termed will, as noted in the last article. Such are the actions of walking, handling, speaking, &c. when attended to, and performed with an express design.

This may serve as a short account of the chief subjects considered in the first part of these observations. These subjects are so much involved in each other, that it is difficult, or even impossible, to begin any where upon clear ground, or so as to proceed entirely from the Data to the Quasita, from things known to such as are unknown. I will endeavour it as much as I can, and for that purpose shall observe the following order.

First, I shall lay down the general laws, according to which the sensations and motions are performed, and our ideas generated.

Secondly, I shall consider each of the sensations and motions in particular, and inquire how far the phenomena of each illustrate, and are illustrated by, the foregoing general laws.

Thirdly, I shall proceed in like manner to the particular phenomena of ideas, or of understanding, affection, memory, and imagination; applying to them what has been before delivered.

Lastly, I shall endeavour to give a particular history and analysis of the six classes of intellectual pleasures and pains, viz. those of imagination, ambition, self-interest, sympathy, theopathy, and the moral sense.

OF THE GENERAL LAWS ACCORDING TO WHICH THE SENSATIONS AND MOTIONS ARE PERFORMED, AND OUR IDEAS GENERATED

My chief design in the following chapter, is, briefly, to explain, establish, and apply the doctrines of vibrations and association. The first of these doctrines is taken from the hints concerning the performance of sensation and motion, which Sir Isaac Newton has given at the end of his Principia, and in the questions annexed to his Optics; the last, from what Mr. Locke, and other ingenious persons since his time have delivered concerning the influence of association over our opinions and affections, and its use in explaining those things in an accurate and precise way, which are commonly referred to the power of habit and custom, in a general and indeterminate one.

The doctrine of vibrations may appear at first sight to have no connection with that of associations; however, if these doctrines be found in fact to contain the laws of the bodily and mental powers respectively, they must be related to each other, since the body and mind are. One may expect that vibrations should infer association as their effect, and association point to vibrations as its cause. I will endeavour, in the present chapter, to trace out this mutual relation.

The proper method of philosophizing seems to be, to discover and establish the general laws of action from certain select, well-defined, and well-attested phenomena, and then to explain and predict the other phenomena by these laws. This is the method of analysis and synthesis recommended and followed by Sir Isaac Newton.

I shall not be able to execute, with any accuracy, what the reader might expect of this kind, in respect of the doctrines of vibrations and associations, and their general laws, on account of the great intricacy, extensiveness, and novelty of the subject. However, I will attempt a sketch in the best manner I can, for the service of future inquirers.

OF THE DOCTRINE OF VIBRATIONS, AND ITS USE FOR EXPLAINING THE SENATIONS

Proposition I. The White Medullary Substance of the Brain, Spinal Marrow, and Nerves Proceeding from Them, is the Immediate Instrument of Sensation and Motion

Under the word brain, in these observations, I comprehend all that lies within the cavity of the skull, i.e. the cerebrum, or brain properly so called, the cerebellum, and the medulla oblongata.

This proposition seems to be sufficiently proved in the writings of physicians and anatomists; from the structure and functions of the several organs of the human body; from experiments on living animals; from the symptoms of diseases, and from diffections of morbid bodies. Sensibility, and the power of motion, seem to be conveyed to all the parts, in their natural state, from the brain and spinal marrow, along the nerves. These arise from the medullar, not the cortical part, every where, and are themselves of a white medullary substance. When the nerves of any part are cut, tied, or compressed in any considerable degree, the functions of that part are either entirely destroyed, or much impaired. When the spinal marrow is compressed by a dislocation of the vertebrae of the back, all the parts, whose nerves arise below the place of dislocation, become paralytic. When any considerable injury is done to the medullary substance of the brain, sensation, voluntary motion, memory, and intellect, are either entirely lost, or much impaired; and if the injury be very great, this extends immediately to the vital motions also, viz. to those of the heart, and organs of respiration, so as to occasion death. But this does not hold equally in respect of the cortical substance of the brain; perhaps not at all, unless as far as injuries done to it extend themselves to the medullary substance. In dissections after apoplexies, palsies, epilepsies, and other distempers affecting the sensations and motions, it is usual to find some great disorder in the brain, from preternatural tumors, from blood, matter, or serum, lying upon the brain, or in its ventricles, &c. This may suffice as general evidence for the present. The particular reasons of some of these phenomena, with more definite evidences, will offer themselves in the course of these observations.

Proposition II. The White Medullary Substance of the Brain is also the Immediate Instrument by which Ideas Are Presented to the Mind

The evidence for this proposition is also to be taken from the writings of physicians and anatomists; but especially from those parts of these writings, which treat of the faculties of memory, attention, imagination, &c. and of mental disorders. It is sufficiently manifest from hence, that the perfection of our mental faculties depends upon the perfection of this substance; that all injuries done to it, affect the trains of ideas proportionably; and that these cannot be restored to their natural course, till such injuries be repaired. Poisons, spirituous liquors, opiates, fevers, blows upon the head, &c. all plainly affect the mind, by first disordering the medullary substance. And evacuations, rest, medicines, time, &c. as plainly restore the mind to its former state, by reversing the foregoing steps. But there will be more and more definite evidence offered in the course of these observations.

Proposition III. The Sensations Remain in the Mind a Short Time after the Sensible Objects are Removed

This is very evident in the sensations impressed on the eye. Thus, to use Sir Isaac Newton's words:

> If a burning coal be nimbly moved round in a circle, with gyrations continually repeated, the whole circle will appear like fire; the reason of which is, that the sensation of the coal, in the several places of that circle, remains impressed on the sensorium, until the coal return again to the same place. And so in a quick consecution of the colours (viz. red, yellow, green, blue, and purple, mentioned in the experiment, whence this passage is taken) the impression of every colour remains on the sensorium, until a revolution of all the colours be completed, and that first colours return again. The impressions therefore of all the successive colours, are at once in the sensorium—and beget a sensation of white. Opt. B.I. p.2 Experiment 10.

Thus also, when a person has had a candle, a window, or any other lucid and well-defined object before his eyes, for a considerable time, he may perceive a very clear and precise image thereof to be left in the sensorium, fancy, or mind (for these I consider as equivalent expressions in our entrance upon these disquisitions), for some time after he has closed his eyes. At least this will happen frequently to persons, who are attentive to these things, in a gentle way: for as this appearance escapes, the notice of those who are entirely inattentive, so too earnest a desire and attention prevents it, by introducing another state of mind or fancy.

To these may be referred the appearance mentioned by Sir Isaac Newton, Opt. Qu. 16. viz.

> When a man in the dark presses either corner of his eye with his finger, and turns his eye away from his finger, he will see a circle of colours like those in the feather of a peacock's tail. And this appearance continues about a second of time, after the eye and finger have remained quiet.

The sensation continues therefore in the mind about a second of time after its cause ceases to act.

The same continuance of the sensations is also evident in the ear. For the sounds which we hear, are reflected by the neighbouring bodies; and therefore consist of a variety of sounds, succeeding each other at different distances of time, according to the distances of the several reflecting bodies; which yet causes no confusion, or apparent complexity of sound, unless the distance of the reflecting bodies be very considerable, as in spacious buildings. Much less are we able to distinguish the successive pulses of the air, even the gravest sounds.

As to the senses of taste and smell, there seems to be no clear direct evidence for the continuance of their sensation, after the proper objects are removed. But analogy would incline one to believe, that they must resemble the senses of sight and hearing in this particular, though the continuance cannot be perceived distinctly, on account of the shortness of it, or other circumstances. For the sensations must be supported to bear such an analogy to each other, and so to depend in common upon the brain, that all evidences for the continuance of sensations in any one sense, will extend themselves to the rest. Thus all the senses may be considered as so many kinds of feeling; the taste is nearly allied to the feeling, the smell to the taste, and the sight and hearing to each other. All which analogies will offer themselves to view, when we come to examine each of these senses in particular.

In the sense of feeling, the continuance of heat, after the heating body is removed, and that of the smart of a wound, after the instant of infliction, seem to be of the same kind with the appearances taken notice of in the eye and ear.

Proposition IV. External Objects Impressed upon the Senses Occasion Vibrations of the Small, and, as one may say, Infinitesimal, Medullary Particles

These vibrations are motions backwards and forwards of the small particles; of the same kind with the oscillations of pendulums, and the tremblings of the particles of sounding bodies. They must be conceived to be exceedingly short and small, so as not to have the least efficacy to disturb or move the whole bodies of the nerves or brain. For that the nerves themselves should vibrate like musical strings, is highly absurd; nor was it ever asserted by Sir Isaac Newton, or any of those who have embraced his notion of the performance of sensation and motion, by means of vibrations.

In like manner, we are to suppose the particles which vibrate, to be of the inferior orders, and not those biggest particles, on which the operations in chemistry, and the colours of natural bodies, depend, according to the opinion of Sir Isaac Newton. Hence, in the proposition, I term the medullary particles, which vibrate, infinitesimal.

Now that external objects impress vibratory motions upon the medullary substance of the nerves and brain (which is the immediate instrument of sensation, according to the first proposition), appears from the continuance of the sensations mentioned in the third; since no motion, besides a vibratory one, can reside in any part for the least moment of time. External objects, being corporeal, can act upon the nerves and brain, which are also corporeal, by nothing but impressing motion on them. A vibrating motion may continue for a short time in the small medullary particles of the nerves and brain, without disturbing them, and after a short time would cease; and so would correspond to the above-mentioned short continuance of the sensations; and there seems to be no other species of motion that can correspond thereto.

Cor. As this proposition is deduced from the foregoing, so if it could be established upon independent principles (of which I shall treat under the next), the foregoing might be deduced from it. And, on this supposition, there would be an argument for the continuance of the sensations, after the removal of their objects; which would extend to the senses of feeling, taste, and smell, in the same manner as to those of sight and hearing.

Proposition XXI. The Voluntary and Semivoluntary Motions are Deducible from Association

In order to verify this proposition, it is necessary to inquire, what connections each automatic motion has gained by association with other motions, with ideas, or with foreign sensations, according to the third, fourth, and sixth corollaries of the last proposition, so as to depend upon them, i.e. so as to be excited no longer, in the automatic manner described in the nineteenth proposition, but merely by the previous introduction of the associated motion, idea, or sensation. If it follows that idea, or state of mind (i.e. set of compound vibratiuncles), which we term the will, directly, and without our perceiving the intervention of any other idea, or of any sensation or motion, it may be called voluntary, in the highest sense of this word. If the intervention of other ideas, or of sensations and motions (all which we are to suppose to follow the will directly), be necessary, it is imperfectly voluntary; yet still it will be called voluntary, in the language of mankind, if it follow certainly and readily upon the intervention of a single sensation, idea, or motion, excited by the power of the will: but if more than one of these be required, or if the motion do not follow with certainty and facility, it is to be esteemed less and less voluntary, semi-voluntary, or scarce voluntary at all, agreeably to the circumstances. Now, if it be found, upon a careful and impartial inquiry, that the motions which occur every day in common life, and which follow the idea called the will, immediately or mediately, perfectly or imperfectly, do this, in proportion to the number and degree of strength in the associations, this will be sufficient authority for ascribing all which we call voluntary in actions to association, agreeably to the purport of this proposition. And this, I think, may be verified from facts, as far as it is reasonable to expect, in a subject of inquiry so novel and intricate.

In the same manner as any action may be rendered voluntary, the cessation from any, or a forcible restraint upon any, may be also, viz. by proper associations with the feeble vibrations in which inactivity consists, or with the strong action of the antagonist muscles.

After the actions, which are most perfectly voluntary, have been rendered so by one set of associations, they may, by another, be made to depend upon the most diminutive sensations, ideas, and motions, such as the mind scarce regards, or is conscious of; and which therefore it can scarce recollect the moment after the action is over. Hence it follows, that association not only converts automatic actions into voluntary, but voluntary ones into automatic. For these actions, of which the mind is scarce conscious, and which follow mechanically, as it were, some precedent diminutive sensation, idea, or motion, and without any effort of the mind, are rather to be ascribed to the body than the mind, i.e. are to be referred to the head of automatic motions. I shall call them automatic motions of the secondary kind, to distinguish them both from those which are originally automatic, and from the voluntary ones; and shall now give a few instances of this double transmutation of motions, viz. of automatic into voluntary, and of voluntary into automatic.

The fingers of young children bend upon almost every impression which is made upon the palm of the hand, thus performing the action of grasping, in the original automatic manner. After a sufficient repetition of the motory vibrations which concur in this action, their vibratiuncles are generated, and associated strongly with other vibrations or vibratiuncles, the most common of which, I suppose are those excited by the sight of a favourite play thing which the child used to grasp, and hold in his hand. He ought, therefore, according to the doctrine of association, to perform and repeat the action of grasping, upon having such a play thing presented to his sight. But it is a known fact, that children do this. By pursuing the same method of reasoning, we may see how, after a sufficient repetition of the proper associations, the sound of the words grasp, take hold, &c. the sight of the nurse's hand in a state of contraction, the idea of a hand, and particularly of the child's own hand, in that state, and innumerable other associated circumstances i.e. sensations, ideas, and motions, will put the child upon grasping, till, at last, that idea, or state of mind which we may call the will to grasp, is generated, and sufficiently associated with the action to produce it instantaneously. It is therefore perfectly voluntary in this case; and, by the innumerable repetitions, of it in this perfectly voluntary state, it comes, at last, to obtain a sufficient connection with so many diminutive sensations, ideas, and motions, as to follow them in the same manner as originally automatic actions do the corresponding sensations, and consequently to be automatic secondarily. And, in the same manner, may all the actions performed with the hands be explained, all those that are very familiar in life passing from the original automatic state through the same degrees of voluntariness till they become perfectly voluntary, and then repassing through the same degrees in an inverted order, till they become secondarily automatic on many occasions, though still perfectly voluntary on some, viz. whensoever an express act of the will is exerted.

I will, in the next place, give a short account of the manner in which we learn to speak, as it may be deduced from the foregoing proposition. The new-born child is not able to produce a sound at all, unless the muscles of the trunk and larynx be stimulated thereto by the impression of pain on some part of the body. As the child advances in age, the frequent returns of this action facilitate it; so that it recurs from less and less pains, from pleasures, from mere sensations, and lastly, from slight associated circumstances, in the manner already explained. About the same time that this process is thus far advanced, the muscles of speech act occasionally, in various combinations, according to the associations of the motory vibratiuncles with each other. Suppose now the muscles of speech to act in these combinations at the same time that sound is produced from some agreeable impression, a mere sensation, or a slight associated cause, which must be supposed to be often the case, since it is so observable, that young children, when in a state of health and pleasure, exert a variety of actions at the same time. It is evident, that an articulate sound, or one approaching thereto, will sometimes be produced by this conjoint action of the muscles of the trunk, larynx, tongue, and lips; and that both these articulate sounds, and inarticulate ones, will often recur, from the recurrence of the same accidental causes. After they have recurred a sufficient number of times, the impression which these sounds, articulate and inarticulate, make upon the ear, will become an associated circumstance (for the child always hears himself speak, at the same time that he exerts the action) sufficient to produce a repetition of them. And thus it is, that children repeat the same sounds over and over again, for many successions, the impression of the last sound upon the ear exciting a fresh one, and so on, till the organs be tired. It follows therefore, that if any of the attendants make any of the sounds familiar to the child, he will be excited from this impression, considered as an associated circumstance, to return it. But the attendants make articulate sounds chiefly; there will therefore be a considerable balance in favour of such, and that of a growing nature: so that the child's articulate sounds will be more and more frequent every day—his inarticulate ones grow into disuse. Suppose now, that he compounds these simple articulate sounds, making complex ones, which approach to familiar words at some times, at others such as are quite foreign to the words of his native language, and that the first get an ever-growing balance in their favour, from the cause just now taken notice of; also, that they are associated with visible objects, actions, &c. and it will be easily seen, that the young child ought, from the nature of association, to learn to speak much in the same manner as he is found in fact to do. Speech will also become a perfectly voluntary action, i.e. the child will be able to utter any word or sentence proposed to him by others, or by himself from a mere exertion of the will, as much as to grasp: only here the introductory circumstance, viz. the impression of the sound on the ear, the idea of this sound, or the preceding motion in pronouncing the preceding word, is evident; and therefore makes it probable, that the same thing takes place in other cases. In like manner, speech, after it has been voluntary for a due time, will become secondarily automatic, i.e. will follow associated circumstances, without any express exertion of the will.

From the account here given of the actions of handling and speaking, we may understand in what manner the first rudiments are laid of that faculty of imitation, which is so observable in young children. They see the actions of their own hands, and hear themselves pronounce. Hence the impressions made by themselves on their own eyes and ears become associated circumstances, and consequently must, in due-time, excite to the repetition of the actions. Hence like impressions made on their eyes and ears by others will have the same effect; or, in other words, they will learn to imitate the actions which they see, and the sounds which they hear.

In the same manner may be explained the evident powers which the will has over the actions of swallowing, breathing, coughing, and expelling the urine and faeces, as well as the feeble and imperfect ones over sneezing, hiccoughing, and vomiting. As to the motion of the heart, and peristaltic motion of the bowels, since they are constant, they must be equally associated with every thing, i.e. peculiarly so with nothing, a few extraordinary cases excepted. They will therefore continue to move solely in the original automatic manner, during the whole course of our lives. However, association may, perhaps, have some share in keeping these motions, and that of respiration, up for a time, when the usual automatic causes are deficient in any measure; and may thus contribute to their equability and constancy. It seems certain, at least, that where unequable and irregular motions of the heart and bowels are generated, and made to recur for a sufficient number of times, from their peculiar causes, in full quantity, a less degree of the same causes, or even an associated circumstance, will suffice to introduce them afterwards. And the same thing may be observed of hysteric and epileptic fits. These recur from less and less causes perpetually, in the same manner, and for the same reasons, as original automatic motions are converted into voluntary ones.

I will add one instance more of the transition of voluntary actions into automatic ones of the secondary kind, in order to make that process clearer, by having it singly in view. Suppose a person who has a perfectly voluntary command over his fingers, to begin to learn to play upon the harpsicord: the first step is to move his fingers from key to key, with a slow motion, looking at the notes, and exerting an express act of volition in every motion. By degrees the motions cling to one another, and to the impressions of the notes, in the way of association so often mentioned, the acts of volition growing less and less express all the time, till at last they become evanescent and imperceptible. For an expert performer will play from notes, or ideas laid up in the memory, or from the connection of the several complex parts of the decomplex motions, some or all; and, at the same time, carry on a quite different train of thoughts in his mind, or even hold a conversation with another. Whence we may conclude, that the passage from the sensory, ideal, or motory vibrations to the original automatic motions corresponding to them; and consequently, that there is no intervention of the idea, or state of mind, called will. At least, the doctrine of association favours this, and the fact shows, that there is no perceptible intervention, none of which we are conscious.

And thus, from the present proposition, and the nineteenth taken together, we are enabled to account for all the motions of the human body, upon principles which, though they may be fictitious, are, at least, clear and intelligible. The doctrine of vibrations, explains all the original automatic motions, that of association the voluntary and secondarily automatic ones. And, if the doctrine of association be founded in, and deducible from, that of vibrations, in the manner delivered above, then all the sensations, ideas, and motions, of all animals, will be conducted according to the vibrations of the small medullary particles. Let the reader examine this hypothesis by the facts, and judge for himself. There are innumerable things, which, when properly discussed, will be sufficient tests of it. It will be necessary, in examining the motions, carefully to distinguish the automatic state from the voluntary one, and to remember, that the first is not to be found pure, except in the motions of the new-born infant, or such as are excited by some violent irritation or pain.

Friedrich Anton Mesmer: 1734-1815

ANIMAL MAGNETISM *

1779

PROPOSITIONS CONCERNING ANIMAL MAGNETISM

1. A RESPONSIVE influence exists between the heavenly bodies, the earth, and animated bodies.

2. A fluid universally diffused, so continuous as not to admit of a vacuum, incomparably subtle, and naturally susceptible of receiving, propagating, and communicating all motor disturbances, is the means of this influence.

3. This reciprocal action is subject to mechanical laws, with which we are not as yet acquainted.

4. Alternative effects result from this action, which may be considered to be a flux and reflux.

5. This reflux is more or less general, more or less special, more or less compound, according to the nature of the causes which determine it.

6. It is by this action, the most universal which occurs in nature, that the exercise of active relations takes place between the heavenly bodies, the earth, and its constituent parts.

7. The properties of matter and of organic substance depend on this action.

8. The animal body experiences the alternative effects of this agent, and is directly affected by its insinuation into the substance of the nerves.

9. Properties are displayed, analogous to those of the magnet, particularly in the human body, in which diverse and opposite poles are likewise to be distinguished, and these may be communicated, changed, destroyed, and reinforced. Even the phenomenon of declination may be observed.

10. This property of the human body which renders it susceptible of the influence of the heavenly bodies, and of the reciprocal action of those which environ it, manifests its analogy with the magnet, and this has decided me to adopt the term of animal magnetism.

11. The action and virtue of animal magnetism, thus characterized, may

* What are known today as suggestion and hypnotism received much attention in the last quarter of the eighteenth century at the instigation of Mesmer. Mesmer, however, attributed these phenomena to a form of energy which he called animal magnetism. His propositions concerning it are taken from the English translation of Alfred Binet and Charles Fere's *Animal Magnetism,* D. Appleton and Co., New York, 1888, p. 4-8.

be communicated to other animate or inanimate bodies. Both these classes of bodies, however, vary in their susceptibility.

12. This action and virtue may be strengthened and diffused by such bodies.

13. Experiments show that there is a diffusion of matter, subtle enough to penetrate all bodies without any considerable loss of energy.

14. Its action takes place at a remote distance, without the aid of any intermediary substance.

15. It is, like light, increased and reflected by mirrors.

16. It is communicated, propagated, and increased by sound.

17. This magnetic virtue may be accumulated, concentrated, and transported.

18. I have said that animated bodies are not all equally susceptible; in a few instances they have such an opposite property that their presence is enough to destroy all the effects of magnetism upon other bodies.

19. This opposite virtue likewise penetrates all bodies: it also may be communicated, propagated, accumulated, concentrated, and transported, reflected by mirrors, and propagated by sound. This does not merely constitute a negative, but a positive opposite virtue.

20. The magnet, whether natural or artificial, is like other bodies susceptible of animal magnetism, and even of the opposite virtue: in neither case does its action on fire and on the needle suffer any change, and this shows that the principle of animal magnetism essentially differs from that of mineral magnetism.

21. This system sheds new light upon the nature of fire and of light, as well as on the theory of attraction, of flux and reflux, of the magnet and of electricity.

22. It teaches us that the magnet and artificial electricity have, with respect to diseases, properties common to a host of other agents presented to us by nature, and that if the use of these has been attended by some useful results, they are due to animal magnetism.

23. These facts show, in accordance with the practical rules I am about to establish, that this principle will cure nervous diseases directly, and other diseases indirectly.

24. By its aid the physician is enlightened as to the use of medicine, and may render its action more perfect, and he can provoke and direct salutary crises, so as completely to control them.

25. In communicating my method, I shall, by a new theory of matter, demonstrate the universal utility of the principle I seek to establish.

26. Possessed of this knowledge, the physician may judge with certainty of the origin, nature, and progress of diseases, however complicated they may be; he may hinder their development and accomplish their cure without exposing the patient to dangerous and troublesome consequences,

irrespective of age, temperament, and sex. Even women in a state of pregnancy, and during parturition, may reap the same advantage.

27. This doctrine will finally enable the physician to decide upon the health of every individual, and of the presence of the diseases to which he may be exposed. In this way the art of healing may be brought to absolute perfection.

Thomas Young: 1773-1829

OBSERVATIONS ON VISION *

1793

IT is well known that the eye, when not acted upon by any exertion of the mind, conveys a distinct impression of those objects only which are situated at a certain distance from itself; that this distance is different in different persons, and that the eye can, by the volition of the mind, be accommodated to view other objects at a much less distance: but how this accommodation is affected, has long been a matter of dispute, and has not yet been satisfactorily explained. It is equally true, though not commonly observed, that no exertion of the mind can accommodate the eye to view objects at a distance greater than that of indolent vision, as may easily be experienced by any person to whom this distance of indolent vision is less than infinite.

The principal parts of the eye, and of its appertenances, have been described by various authors. Winslow is generally very accurate; but Albinus, in Musschenbroek's *Introductio*, has represented several particulars more correctly. I shall suppose their account complete, except where I mention or delineate the contrary.

The first theory that I find of the accommodation of the eye is Kepler's. He supposes the ciliary processes to contract the diamater of the eye, and lengthen its axis, by a muscular power. But the ciliary processes neither appear to contain any muscular fibres, nor have they any attachment by which they can be capable of performing this action.

Descartes imagined the same contraction and elongation to be effected by a muscularity of the crystalline, of which he supposed the ciliary processes to be the tendons. He did not attempt to demonstrate this muscularity, nor did he enough consider the connection with the ciliary processes. He says, that the lens in the meantime becomes more convex, but attributes very little to this circumstance.

De La Hire maintains that the eye undergoes no change, except the contraction and dilatation of the pupil. He does not attempt to confirm this opinion by mathematical demonstration; he solely rests it on an experiment which has been shewn by Dr. Smith to be fallacious. Haller

* This paper appeared in the *Philosophical Transactions* of the Royal Society of London, 1793, pp. 169-178. It was Young's first paper on visual accommodation; it contains the first correct account of accommodation. He published further evidence for his theory in the *Philosophical Transactions*, 1801, pp. 23-88.

too has adopted this opinion, however inconsistent it seems with the known principles of optics, and with the slightest regard to hourly experience.

Dr. Pemberton supposes the crystalline to contain muscular fibres, by which one of its surfaces is flattened while the other is made more convex. But, besides that he has demonstrated no such fibres, Dr. Jurin has proved that a change like this is inadequate to the effect.

Dr. Porterfield conceives that the ciliary processes draw forward the crystalline, and make the cornea more convex. The ciliary processes are, from their structure, attachment, and direction, utterly incapable of this action; and, by Dr. Jurin's calculations, there is not room for a sufficient motion of this kind, without a very visible increase in the length of the eye's axis: such an increase we cannot observe.

Dr. Jurin's hypothesis is, that the uvea, at its attachment to the cornea, is muscular, and that the contraction of this ring makes the cornea more convex. He says, that the fibres of this muscle may as well escape our observation, as those of the muscle of the interior ring. But if such a muscle existed, it must, to overcome the resistance of the coats, be far stronger than that which is only destined to the uvea itself; and the uvea, at this part, exhibits nothing but radiated fibres, losing themselves, before the circle of adherence to the sclerotica, in a brownish granulated substance, not unlike in appearance to capsular ligament, common to the uvea and ciliary processes, but which may be traced separately from them both. Now at the interior ring of the uvea, the appearance is not absolutely inconsistent with an annular muscle. His theory of accommodation to distant objects is ingenious, but no such accommodation takes place.

Musschenbroek conjectures that the relaxation of his ciliary zone, which appears to be nothing but the capsule of the vitreous humour where it receives the impression of the ciliary processes, permits the coats of the eye to push forwards the crystalline and cornea. Such a voluntary relaxation is wholly without example in the animal economy, and were it to take place, the coats of the eye would not act as he imagines, nor could they so act unobserved. The contraction of the ciliary zone is equally inadequate and unnecessary.

Some have supposed the pressure of the external muscles, especially the two oblique muscles, to elongate the axis of the eye. But their action would not be sufficiently regular, nor sufficiently strong; for a much greater pressure being made on the eye, than they can be supposed capable of effecting, no sensible difference is produced in the distinctness of vision.

Others say that the muscles shorten the axis: these have still less reason on their side.

Those who maintain that the ciliary processes flatten the crystalline, are ignorant of their structure, and of the effect required: these processes are yet more incapable of drawing back the crystalline, and such an action is equally inconsistent with observation.

Probably other suppositions may have been formed, liable to as strong objections as those opinions which I have enumerated.

From these considerations, and from the observation of Dr. Porterfield, that those who have been couched have no longer the power of accommodating the eye to different distances, I had concluded that the rays of light, emitted by objects at a small distance, could only be brought to foci on the retina by a nearer approach of the crystalline to a spherical form; and I could imagine no other power capable of producing this change than a muscularity of a part, or the whole, of its capsule.

But in closely examining, with the naked eye in a strong light, the crystalline from an ox, turned out of its capsule, I discovered a structure which appears to remove all the difficulties with which this branch of optics has long been obscured. On viewing it with a magnifier, this structure became more evident.

The crystalline lens of the ox is an orbicular, convex, transparent body, composed of a considerable number of similar coats, of which the exterior closely adhere to the interior. Each of these coats consists of six muscles, intermixed with a gelatinous substance, and attached to six membranous tendons. Three of the tendons are anterior, three posterior; their length in about two thirds of the semi-diameter of the coat; their arrangement is that of three equal and equidistant rays, meeting in the axis of the crystalline; one of the anterior is directed towards the outer angle of the eye, and one of the posterior towards the inner angle, so that the posterior are placed opposite to the middle of the interstices of the anterior; and planes passing through each of the six, and through the axis, would mark on either surface six regular equidistant rays. The muscular fibres arise from both sides of each tendon; they diverge till they reach the greatest circumference of the coat, and, having passed it, they again converge, till they are attached respectively to the sides of the nearest tendons of the opposite surface. The anterior or posterior portion of the six viewed together, exhibits the appearance of three penniformi-radiated muscles. The anterior tendons of all the coats are situated in the same planes, and the posterior ones in the continuations of these planes beyond the axis. Such an arrangement of fibres can be accounted for on no other supposition than that of muscularity. This mass is inclosed in a strong membranous capsule, to which it is loosely connected by minute vessels and nerves; and the connection is more observable near its greatest circumference. Between the mass and its capsule is found a considerable quantity of an aqueous fluid, the liquid of the crystalline.

I conceive, therefore, that when the will is exerted to view an object at a small distance, the influence of the mind is conveyed through the lenticular ganglion, formed from branches of the third and fifth pairs of nerves, by the filaments perforating the sclerotica, to the orbiculus ciliaris, which may be considered as an annular plexus of nerves and vessels; and thence by the ciliary processes to the muscle of the crystalline, which, by the contraction of its fibres, becomes more convex, and collects the diverging rays to a focus on the retina. The disposition of fibres in each coat is admirably adapted to produce this change; for, since the least surface that can contain a given bulk is that of a sphere, (Simpson's *Fluxions*, p. 486) the contraction of any surface must bring its contents nearer to a spherical form. The liquid of the crystalline seems to serve as a synovia in facilitating the motion, and to admit a sufficient change of the muscular part, with a smaller motion of the capsule.

It remains to be inquired, whether these fibres can produce an alteration in the form of the lens sufficiently great to account for the known effects.

In the ox's eye, the diameter of the crystalline is 700 thousandths of an inch, the axis of its anterior segment 225, of its posterior 350. In the atmosphere it collects parallel rays at the distance of 235 thousandths. From these data we find, by means of Smith's *Optics*, Art. 366, and a quadratic, that its ratio of refraction is as 10000 to 6574. Hauksbee makes it only as 10000 to 6832.7, but we cannot depend on his experiment, since he says that the image of the candle which he viewed was enlarged and distorted; a circumstance that he does not explain, but which was evidently occasioned by the greater density of the central parts. Supposing, with Hauksbee and others, the refraction of the aqueous and vitreous humours equal to that of water, viz. as 10000 to 7465, the ratio of refraction of the crystalline in the eye will be as 10000 to 8806, and it would collect parallel rays at the distance of 1226 thousandths of an inch: but the distance of the retina from the crystalline is 550 thousandths, and that of the anterior surface of the cornea 250; hence (by Smith, Art. p. 367,) the focal distance of the cornea and aqueous humour alone must be 2329. Now, supposing the crystalline to assume a spherical form, its diameter will be 642 thousandths, and its focal distance in the eye 926. Then, disregarding the thickness of the cornea, we find (by Smith, Art. p. 370,) that such an eye will collect those rays on the retina, which diverge from a point at the distance of 12 inches and 8 tenths. This is a greater change than is necessary for an ox's eye, for if it be supposed capable of distinct vision at a distance somewhat less than 12 inches, yet it probably is far short of being able to collect parallel rays. The human crystalline is susceptible of much greater change of form.

The ciliary zone may admit of as much extension as this diminution of the diameter of the crystalline will require; and its elasticity will assist the cellular texture of the vitreous humour, and perhaps the gelatinous part of the crystalline, in restoring the indolent form.

It may be questioned whether the retina takes any part in supplying the lens with nerves; but, from the analogy of the olfactory and auditory nerves, it seems more reasonable to suppose that the optic nerve serves no other purpose than that of conveying sensation to the brain.

Although a strong light and close examination are required, in order to see the fibres of the crystalline in its entire state, yet their direction may be demonstrated, and their attachment shewn, without much difficulty. In a dead eye the tendons are discernible through the capsule, and sometimes the anterior ones even through the cornea and aqueous humour. When the crystalline falls, it very frequently separates as far as the centre into three portions, each having a tendon in its middle. If it be carefully stripped of its capsule, and the smart blast of a fine blow-pipe be applied close to its surface in different parts, it will be found to crack exactly in the direction of the fibres above described, and all these cracks will be stopped as soon as they reach either of the tendons. The application of a little ink to the crystalline is of great use in shewing the course of the fibres.

When first I observed the structure of the crystalline, I was not aware that its muscularity had ever been suspected. We have, however, seen that Descartes supposed it to be of this nature; but he seems to think that the accommodation of the eye to a small distance is principally performed by the elongation of the eye's axis. Indeed as a bell shakes a steeple, so much the coats of the eye be affected by any change in the crystalline; but the effect of this will be very inconsiderabe; yet, as far as it does take place, it will co-operate with the other change.

But the laborious and accurate Leeuwenhoek, by the help of his powerful microscopes, has decribed the course of the fibres of the crystalline, in a variety of animals; and he has even gone so far as to call it a muscle; but no one has pursued the hint, and probably for this reason, that from examining only dried preparations, he has imagined that each coat consists of circumvolutions of a single fibre, and has entirely overlooked the attachment of the fibres to tendons; and if the fibres were continued into each other in the manner that he describes, the strict analogy to muscle would be lost, and their contraction could not have that effect on the figure of the lens, which is produced by help of the tendons. Yet notwithstanding neither he, nor any other physiologist, has attempted to explain the accommodation of the eye to different distances by means of these fibres, still much anatomical merit must be allowed to the faithful description, and elegant delineation, of the crystallines of various animals, which he has given in the *Philosophical Transactions*, XIV, 780, and XXIV, 1723. It appears, from his descriptions and figures, that the crystalline of hogs, dogs, and cats, resembles what I have observed in oxen, sheep, and horses; that in hares and rabbits, the tendons on each side are only two, meeting in a straight line in the axis; and that in whales they are five, radiated in the same manner as where there are three. It is evident that this variety will make no material difference in the action of the muscle. I have not yet had an opportunity of examining the human crystalline, but from its readily dividing into three parts, we may infer that it is similar to that of the ox. The crystalline in fishes being spherical, such a change as I attribute to the lens in quadrupeds cannot take place in that class of animals.

It has been observed that the central part of the crystalline becomes rigid by age, and this is sufficient to account for presbyopia, without any diminution of the humours; although I do not deny the existence of this diminution, as a concomitant circumstance.

John Dalton: 1766-1844

EXTRAORDINARY FACTS RELATING TO THE VISION OF COLOURS: WITH OBSERVATIONS *

1798

It has been observed, that our ideas of colours, sounds, tastes, &c. excited by the same object may be very different in themselves, without our being aware of it; and that we may nevertheless converse intelligibly concerning such objects, as if we were certain the impressions made by them on our minds were exactly similar. All, indeed, that is required for this purpose, is, that the same object should uniformly make the same impression on each mind; and that objects which appear different to one should be equally so to others. It will, however, scarcely be supposed, that any two objects, which are every day before us, should appear hardly distinguishable to one person, and very different to another, without the circumstance immediately suggesting a difference in their faculties of vision; yet such is the fact, not only with regard to myself, but to many others also, as will appear in the following account.

I was always of opinion, though I might not often mention it, that several colours were injudiciously named. The term pink, in reference to the flower of that name, seemed proper enough; but when the term red was substituted for pink, I thought it highly improper; it should have been blue, in my apprehension, as pink and blue appear to me very nearly allied; whilst pink and red have scarcely any relation.

In the course of my application to the sciences, that of optics necessarily claimed attention; and I became pretty well acquainted with the theory of light and colours before I was apprized of any peculiarity in my vision. I had not, however, attended much to the practical discrimination of colours, owing, in some degree, to what I conceived to be a perplexity in their nomenclature. Since the year 1790, the occasional study of botany obliged me to attend more to colours than before. With respect

* From the *Memoirs* of the Literary and Philosophical Society of Manchester, V (1798), 5, 28-45. The article is reprinted in full. As noted by Dalton, a brief note concerning a similar case was published in the *Philosophical Transactions* of the Royal Society of London in 1777. The account presented was second-hand and quite incomplete, so that Dalton's description of his own case is the first adequate description of an instance of color blindness.

to colours that were white, yellow, or green, I readily assented to the appropriate term. Blue, purple, pink, and crimson appeared rather less distinguishable; being, according to my ideas, all referable to blue. I have often seriously asked a person whether a flower was blue or pink, but was generally considered to be in jest. Notwithstanding this, I was never convinced of a peculiarity in my vision, till I accidentally observed the colour of the flower of the *Geranium zonale* by candle-light, in the Autumn of 1792. The flower was pink, but it appeared to me almost an exact sky-blue by day; in candle-light, however it was astonishingly changed, not having then any blue in it, but being what I called red, a colour which forms a striking contrast to blue. Not then doubting but that the change of colour would be equal to all, I requested some of my friends to observe the phaenomenon; when I was surprised to find they all agreed, that the colour was not materially different from what it was by day-light, except my brother who saw it in the same light as myself. This observation clearly proved, that my vision was not like that of other persons;—and, at the same time, that the difference between day-light and candle-light, on some colours, was indefinitely more perceptible to me than to other. It was nearly two years after that time, when I entered upon an investigation of the subject, having procured the assistance of a friend, who, to his acquaintance with the theory of colours, joins a practical knowledge of their names and constitutions. I shall now proceed to state the facts ascertained under the three following heads:

I. An account of my own vision.
II. An account of others whose vision has been found similar to mine.
III. Observations on the probable cause of our anomalous vision.

I. OF MY OWN VISION

It may be proper to observe, that I am short-sighted. Concave glasses of about five inches focus suit me best. I can see distinctly at a proper distance; and am seldom hurt by too much or too little light; nor yet with long application.

My observations began with the solar spectrum, or coloured image of the sun, exhibited in a dark room by means of a glass prism. I found that persons in general distinguish six kinds of colour in the solar image; namely, red, orange, yellow, green, blue, and purple. Newton, indeed, divides the purple into indigo and violet; but the difference between him and others is merely nominal. To me it is quite otherwise:—I see only two or at most three distinctions. These I should call yellow and blue; or yellow, blue, and purple. My yellow comprehends the red, orange, yellow, and green of others; and my blue and purple coincide with theirs. That part of the image which others call red, appears to me little more than a shade, or defect of light; after that the orange, yellow, and green seem one colour, which descends pretty uniformly from an intense to a rare yellow, making what I should call different shades of yellow. The difference between the green part and the blue part is very striking to my eye: they seem to be strongly contrasted. That between the blue and purple is much less so. The purple appears to be blue much darkened and condensed. In viewing the flame of a candle by night through the prism, the appearances are pretty much the same, except that the red extremity of the image appears more vivid than that of the solar image.

I now proceed to state the results of my observations on the colours of bodies in general, whether natural or artificial, both by day-light and candle-light. I mostly used ribbands for the artificial colours.

Red

(By day-light)

Under this head I include crimson, scarlet, red, and pink. All crimsons appear to me to consist chiefly of dark blue; but many of them seem to have a strong tinge of dark brown. I have seen specimens of crimson, claret, and mud, which were very nearly alike. Crimson has a grave appearance, being the reverse of every shewy and splendid colour. Woollen yarn dyed crimson or dark blue is the same to me. Pink seems to be composed of nine parts of light blue, and one of red, or some colour which has no other effect than to make the light blue appear dull and faded a little. Pink and light blue therefore compared together, are to be distinguished no otherwise than as a splendid colour from one that has lost a little of its splendour. Besides the pinks, roses, &c. of the gardens, the following British flora appear to me blue; namely, *Statice Armeria, Trifolium pratense, Lychnis Flos-cuculi, Lynchnis Dioca*, and many of the *Gerania*. The colour of a florid complexion appears to me that of a dull, opake, blackish blue, upon a white ground. A solution of sulphate of iron in the tincture of galls (that is, dilute black ink) upon white paper, gives a colour much resembling that of a florid complexion. It has no resemblance of the colour of blood. Red and scarlet form a genus with me totally different from pink. My idea of red I obtain from vermilion, minium, sealing wax, wafers, a soldier's uniform, &c. These seem to have no blue whatever in them. Scarlet has a more splendid appearance than red. Blood appears to me red; but it differs much from the articles mentioned above. It is much more dull, and to me is not unlike that colour called bottle-green. Stockings spotted with blood or with dirt would scarcely be distinguishable.

Red

(By candle-light)

Red and scarlet appear much more vivid than by day. Crimson loses its blue and becomes yellowish red. Pink is by far the most changed; indeed it forms an excellent contrast to what it is by day. No blue now appears; yellow has taken its place. Pink by candle-light seems to be three parts yellow and one red, or a reddish yellow. The blue, however, is less mixed by day than the yellow by night. Red, and particularly scarlet, is a superb colour by candle-light; but by day some reds are the least shewy imaginable: I should call them dark drabs.

Orange & Yellow

(By day-light and candle-light)

I do not find that I differ materially from other persons in regard to these colours. I have sometimes seen persons hesitate whether a thing was white or yellow by candle-light, when to me there was no doubt at all.

Green

(By day-light)

I take my standard idea from grass. This appears to me very little different from red. The face of a laurel-leaf *(Prunus Lauro-cerasus)* is a good match to a stick of red sealing-wax; and the back of the leaf answers to the lighter red of wafers. Hence it will be immediately concluded, that I see either red or green, or both, different from other people. The fact is, I believe that they both appear different to me from what they do to others. Green and orange have much affinity also. Apple green is the most pleasing kind to me; and any other that has a tinge of yellow appears to advantage. I can distinguish the different vegetable greens one from another as well as most people; and those which are nearly alike or very unlike; to others are so to me. A decoction of bohea tea, a solution of liver of sulphur, ale, &c. &c. which others call brown, appear to me green. Green woollen cloth, such as is used to cover tables, appears to me a dull, dark, brownish red colour. A mixture of two parts mud and one red would come near it. It resembles a red soil just turned up by the plough. When this kind of cloth loses its colour, as other people say, and turns yellow, then it appears to me a pleasant green. Very light green paper, silk, &c. is white to me.

Green

(By candle-light)

I agree with others, that it is difficult to distinguish greens from blues by candle-light; but, with me, the green only are altered and made to approach the blues. It is the real greens only that are altered in my eye; and not such as I confound with them by day-light, as the brown liquids abovementioned, which are not at all tinged with blue by candle-light, but are the same as by day, except that they are paler.

Blue

(By day-light and candle-light)

I apprehend this colour appears very nearly the same to me as to other people, both by day-light and candle-light.

Purple

(By day-light and candle-light)

This seems to me a slight modification of blue. I seldom fail to distinguish purple from blue; but should hardly suspect purple to be a compound of blue and red. The difference between day-light and candle-light is not material.

Miscellaneous Observations

Colours appear to me much the same by moonlight as they do by candle-light.

Colours viewed by lightning appear the same as by day-light; but whether exactly so, I have not ascertained.

Colours seen by electric light appear to me the same as by day-light. That is, pink appears blue, &c.

Colours viewed through a transparent sky-blue liquid, by candle-light, appear to me as well as to others the same as by day-light.

A light drab woollen cloth seems to me to resemble a light green by day. These colours are, however, easily distinguished by candle-light, as the latter becomes tinged with blue, while the former does not. I have frequently seen colours of the drab kind, said to be nearly alike, which appeared to me very different.

My ideas of brown I obtain from a piece of white paper heated almost to ignition. This colour by day-light seems to have a great affinity to green, as may be imagined from what I have said of greens. Browns seem to me very diversified; some I should call red:—dark brown woollen cloth I should call black.

The light of the rising or setting sun has no particular effect; neither has a strong or weak light. Pink appears rather duller, all other circumstances alike, in a cloudy day.

All common combustible substances exhibit colours to me in the same light; namely, tallow, oil, wax, pit-coal.

My vision has always been as it is now.

II. AN ACCOUNT OF OTHERS WHOSE VISION HAS BEEN FOUND SIMILAR TO MINE

It has been already observed that my brother perceived the change in the colour of the geranium such as myself. Since that time having made a great number of observations on colours, by comparing their similarities, &c. by day-light and candle-light, in conjunction with him, I find that we see as nearly alike as any other persons do. He is shorter sighted than myself.

As soon as these facts were ascertained, I conceived the design of laying our case of vision before the public, apprehending it to be a singular one. I remembered, indeed, to have read in the *Philosophical Transactions* for 1777, an account of Mr. Harris of Maryport in Cumberland, who, it was said, "could not distinguish colours;" but his case appeared to be different from ours. Considering, however, that one anomaly in vision may tend to illustrate another, I reperused the account; when it appeared extremely probable that if his vision had been fully investigated, and a relation of it given in the first person, he would have agreed with me. There were four brothers in the same predicament, one of whom is now living. Having an acquaintance in Maryport, I solicited him to propose a few queries to the survivor, which he readily did (in conjunction with another brother, whose vision has nothing peculiar), and from the answers transmitted to me, I could no longer doubt of the similarity of our cases. To render it still more circumstantial, I sent about twenty specimens of different coloured ribbands, with directions to make observations upon them by day-light and candle-light: the result was exactly conformable to my expectation.

It then appeared to me probable, that a considerable number of individuals might be found whose vision differed from that of the generality, but at the same time agreed with my own. Accordingly I have since taken every opportunity to explain the circumstances amongst my acquaintance, and have found several in the same predicament. Only one or two I have heard of who differ from the generality and from us also. It is remarkable that, out of twenty-five pupils I once had, to whom I explained this subject, two were found to agree with me; and, on another similar occasion, one. Like myself, they could see no material difference betwixt pink and light blue by day, but a striking contrast by candle-light. And, on a fuller investigation, I could not perceive they differed from me materially in other colours. They, like all the rest of us, were not aware of their actually seeing colours different from other people; but imagined there was great perplexity in the names ascribed to particular colours. I think I have been informed already of nearly twenty persons whose vision is like mine. The family at Maryport consisted of six sons and one daughter; four of the sons were in the predicament in question. Our family consisted of three sons and one daughter who arrived at maturity; of whom two sons are circumstanced as I have described. The others are mostly individuals in families, some of which are numerous. I do not find that the parents or children in any of the instances have been so, unless in one case. Nor have I been able to discover any physical cause whatever for it. Our vision, except as to colours, is as clear and distinct as that of other persons. Only two or three are short sighted. It is remarkable that I have not heard of one female subject to this peculiarity.

From a great variety of observations made with many of the above-mentioned persons, it does not appear to me that we differ more from one another than persons in general do. We certainly agree in the principal facts which characterize our vision, and which I have attempted to point out below. It is but justice to observe here, that several of the resemblances and comparisons mentioned in the preceding part of this paper were first suggested to me by one or other of the parties, and found to accord with my own ideas.

Characteristics Facts of our Vision

1. In the solar spectrum three colours appear, yellow, blue, and purple. The two former make a contrast; the two latter seem to differ more in degree than in kind.

2. Pink appears, by day-light, to be sky-blue a little faded; by candle-light it assumes an orange or yellowish appearance, which forms a strong contrast to blue.

3. Crimson appears a muddy blue by day; and crimson woollen yarn is much the same as dark blue.

4. Red and scarlet have a more vivid and flaming appearance by candle-light than by day-light.

5. There is not much difference in colour between a stick of red sealing wax and grass, by day.

6. Dark green woollen cloth seems a muddy red, much darker than grass, and of a very different colour.

7. The colour of a florid complexion is dusky blue.

8. Coats, gowns, &c. appear to us frequently to be badly matched with linings, when others say they are not. On the other hand, we should match crimsons with claret or mud; pinks with light blues; browns with reds; and drabs with greens.

9. In all points where we differ from other persons, the difference is much less by candle-light than by day-light.

III. OBSERVATIONS TENDING TO POINT OUT THE CAUSE OF OUR ANOMALOUS VISION

The first time I was enabled to form a plausible idea of the cause of our vision, was after observing that a sky-blue transparent liquid modified the light of a candle so as to make it similar to day-light; and, of course, restored to pink its proper colour by day, namely, light blue. This was an important observation. At the same time that it exhibited the effect of a transparent coloured medium in the modification of colours, it seemed to indicate the analogy of solar light to that resulting from combustion; and that the former is modified by the transparent blue atmosphere, as the latter is by the transparent blue liquid. Now the effect of a transparent coloured medium, as Mr. Delaval has proved, is to transmit more, and consequently imbibe fewer of the rays of its own colour, than of those of other colours. Reflecting upon these facts, I was led to conjecture that one of the humours of my eye must be a transparent, but coloured, medium, so constituted as to absorb red and green rays principally, because I obtain no proper ideas of these in the solar spectrum; and to transmit blue and other colours more perfectly. What seemed to make against this opinion however was, that I thought red bodies, such as vermilion, should appear black to me, which was contrary to fact. How this difficulty was obviated will be understood from what follows.

Newton has sufficiently ascertained, that opake bodies are of a particular colour from their reflecting the rays of light of that colour more copiously than those of the other colours; the unreflected rays being absorbed by the bodies. Adopting this fact, we are insensibly led to conclude, that the more rays of any one colour a body reflects, and the fewer of every other colour, the more perfect will be the colour. This conclusion, however, is certainly erroneous. Splendid coloured bodies reflect light of every colour copiously; but that of their own most so. Accordingly we find, that bodies of all colours, when placed in homogeneal light of any colour, appear of that particular colour. Hence a body that is red may appear of any other colour to an eye that does not transmit red, according as those other colours are more copiously reflected from the body, or transmitted through the humours of the eye.

It appears therefore almost beyond a doubt, that one of the humours of my eye, and of the eyes of my fellows, is a coloured medium, probably some modification of blue. I suppose it must be the vitreous humour; otherwise I apprehend it might be discovered by inspection, which has not been done. It is the province of physiologists to explain in what manner the humours of the eye may be coloured, and to them I shall leave it; and proceed to shew that the hypothesis will explain the facts stated in the conclusion of the second part.

1. This needs no further illustration.

2. Pink is known to be a mixture of red and blue; that is, these two colours are reflected in excess. Our eyes only transmit the blue excess, which causes it to appear blue; a few red rays pervading the eye may serve to give the colour that faded appearance. In candle-light, red and orange, or some other of the higher colours, are known to abound more proportionately than in day-light. The orange light reflected may therefore exceed the blue, and the compound colour consist of red and orange. Now, the red being most copiously reflected, the colour will be recognized by a common eye under this small modification; but the red not appearing to us, we see chiefly the orange excess: it is consequently to us not a modification but a new colour.

3. By a similar method of reasoning, crimson, being compounded of red and dark blue, must assume the appearances I have described.

4. Bodies that are red and scarlet probably reflect orange and yellow in greatest plenty, next after red. The orange and yellow, mixed with a few red rays, will give us our idea of red, which is heightened by candle-light, because the orange is then more abundant.

5. Grass-green is probably compounded of green, yellow, and orange, with more or less blue. Our idea of it will then be obtained principally from the yellow and orange mixed with a few green rays. It appears, therefore, that red and green to us will be nearly alike. I do not, however, understand, why the greens should assume a bluish appearance to us and to every body else, by candle-light, when it should seem that candle-light is deficient in blue.

6. The green rays not being perceived by us, the remaining rays may, for aught that is known, compound a muddy red.

7. The observations upon the phaenomena of pink and crimson, will explain this fact.

8. Suppose a body to reflect red rays as the number 8, orange rays as the number 6, and blue as 5; and another body red 8, orange 6, and blue 6: then it is evident that a common eye, attending principally to the red, would see little differences in those colours; but we, who form our ideas of colours from the orange and blue, should perceive the latter to be bluer than the former.

9. From the whole of this paper it is evident, that our eyes admit blue rays in greater proportion than those of other people; therefore when any kind of light is less abundant in blue, as is the case with candle-light compared to day-light, our eyes serve in some degree to temper that light, so as to reduce it nearly to the common standard. This seems to be

the reason why colours appear to us by candle-light, almost as they do to others by day-light.

I shall conclude this paper by observing, that it appears to me extremely probable, that the sun's light and candle-light, or that which we commonly obtain from combustion, are originally constituted alike; and that the earth's atmosphere is properly a blue fluid, and modified the sun's light so as to occasion the commonly perceived difference.

Thomas Young: 1773-1829

ON THE THEORY OF LIGHT AND COLOURS *

1802

Now, as it is almost impossible to conceive each sensitive point of the retina to contain an infinite number of particles, each capable of vibrating in perfect unison with every possible undulation, it becomes necessary to suppose the number limited, for instance, to the three principal colours, red, yellow, and blue, of which the undulations are related in magnitude nearly as the numbers 8, 7, and 6; and that each of the particles is capable of being put in motion less or more forcibly, by undulations differing less or more from a perfect unison; for instance, the undulations of green light being nearly in the ratio of 6½, will affect equally the particles in unison with yellow and blue, and produce the same effect as a light composed of those two species: and each sensitive filament of the nerve may consist of three portions, one for each principal colour. Allowing this statement, it appears that any attempt to produce a musical effect from colours, must be unsuccessful, or at least that nothing more than a very simple melody could be imitated by them; for the period, which in fact constitutes the harmony of any concord, being a multiple of the periods of the single undulations, would in this case be wholly without the limits of sympathy of the retina, and would lose its effect; in the same manner as the harmony of a third or a fourth is destroyed, by depressing it to the lowest notes of the audible scale.

* This very brief statement is Young's theory of color vision, and his anticipation of the doctrine of the specific energy of nerves. It appeared, as a small part of the article whose title is given above, in the *Philosophical Transactions* of the Royal Society of London, 1802, p. 20.

Charles Bell: 1774-1842

IDEA OF A NEW ANATOMY OF THE BRAIN *

1811

THE want of any consistent history of the brain and nerves, and the dull unmeaning manner which is in use of demonstrating the brain, may authorize any novelty in the manner of treating the subject.

I have found some of my friends so mistaken in their conception of the object of the demonstrations which I have delivered in my lectures, that I wish to vindicate myself at all hazards. They would have it that I am in search of the seat of the soul; but I wish only to investigate the structure of the brain, as we examine the structure of the eye and ear.

It is not more presumptuous to follow the tracts of nervous matter in the brain and to attempt to discover the course of sensation, than it is to trace the rays of light through the humours of the eye, and to say, that the retina is the seat of vision. Why are we to close the investigation with the discovery of the external organ?

It would have been easy to have given this Essay an imposing splendour, by illustrations and engravings of the parts, but I submit it as a sketch to those who are well able to judge of it in this shape.

The prevailing doctrine of the anatomical schools is, that the whole brain is a common sensorium; that the extremities of the nerves arc organized, so that each is fitted to receive a peculiar impression; or that they are distinguished from each other only by delicacy of structure, and by a corresponding delicacy of sensation, that the nerve of the eye, for example, differs from the nerves of touch only in the degree of its sensibility.

It is imagined that impressions, thus differing in kind, are carried along the nerves to the sensorium, and presented to the mind; and that the mind, by the same nerves which receive sensation, sends out the mandate of the will to the moving parts of the body.

It is further imagined, that there is a set of nerves, called vital nerves, which are less strictly connected with the sensorium, or which have upon

* Best known for its distinction between the sensory and motor nerves, Bell's publication is also noteworthy for its statements concerning the specific energy of nerves. It was first published privately in 1811. It was reprinted in the *Journal of Anatomy and Physiology*, III (1869), 153-166. The full text of the reprint is reproduced here.

them knots, cutting off the course of sensation, and thereby excluding the vital motions from the government of the will.

This appears sufficiently simple and consistent, until we begin to examine anatomically the structure of the brain, and the course of the nerves,—then all is confusion; the divisions and subdivisions of the brain, the circuitous course of nerves, their intricate connections, their separation and re-union, are puzzling in the last degree, and are indeed considered as things inscrutable. Thus, it is, that he who knows the parts the best, is most in a maze, and he who knows least of anatomy, sees least inconsistency in the commonly received opinion.

In opposition to these opinions, I have to offer reasons for believing, that the cerebrum and cerebellum are different in function as in form; that the parts of the cerebrum have different functions; and that the nerves which we trace in the body are not single nerves possessing various powers, but bundles of different nerves, whose filaments are united for the convenience of distribution, but which are distinct in office, as they are in origin from the brain:

That the external organs of the senses have the matter of the nerves adapted to receive certain impressions, while the corresponding organs of the brain are put in activity by the external excitement: That the idea or perception is according to the part of the brain to which the nerve is attached, and that each organ has a certain limited number of changes to be wrought upon it by the external impression:

That the nerves of sense, the nerves of motion, and the vital nerves, are distinct through their whole course, though they seem sometimes united in one bundle; and that they depend for their attributes on the organs of the brain to which they are severally attached.

The view which I have to present, will serve to show why there are divisions, and many distinct parts in the brain; why some nerves are simple in their origin and distribution, and others intricate beyond description. It will explain the apparently accidental connection between the twigs of nerves. It will do away with the difficulty of conceiving how sensation and volition should be the operation of the same nerve at the same moment. It will show how a nerve may lose one property, and retain another; and it will give an interest to the labours of the anatomist in tracing the nerves.

When in contemplating the structure of the eye we say, how admirably it is adapted to the laws of light! We use language which implies a partial, and consequently an erroneous view. And the philosopher takes not a more enlarged survey of nature when he declares how curiously the laws of light are adapted to the constitution of the eye.

This creation, of which we are a part, has not been formed in parts.

The organ of vision, and the matter or influence carried to the organ, and the qualities of bodies with which we are acquainted through it, are parts of a system great beyond our imperfect comprehension, formed as it should seem at once in wisdom; not pieced together like the work of human ingenuity.

When this whole was created, (of which the remote planetary system, as well as our bodies, and the objects more familiar to our observation, are but parts), the mind was placed in a body not merely suited to its residence, but in circumstances to be moved by the materials around it; and the capacities of the mind, and the powers of the organs, which are as a medium betwixt the mind and the external world, have an original constitution framed in relation to the qualities of things.

It is admitted that neither bodies nor the images of bodies enter the brain. It is indeed impossible to believe that colour can be conveyed along a nerve; or the vibration in which we suppose sound to consist can be retained in the brain: but we can conceive, and have reason to believe, that an impression is made upon the organs of the outward senses when we see, or hear, or taste.

In this inquiry it is most essential to observe, that while each organ of sense is provided with a capacity of receiving certain changes to be played upon it, as it were, yet each is utterly incapable of receiving the impressions destined for another organ of sensation.

It is also very remarkable that an impression made on two different nerves of sense, though with same instrument, will produce two distinct sensations; and the ideas resulting will only have relation to the organ affected.

As the announcing of these facts forms a natural introduction to the Anatomy of the Brain, which I am about to deliver, I shall state them more fully.

There are four kinds of Papillae on the tongue, but with two of those only we have to do at present. Of these, the Papillae of one kind form the seat of the sense of taste; the other Papillae (more numerous and smaller) resemble the extremities of the nerves in the common skin, and are the organs of touch in the tongue. When I take a sharp steel point and touch one of *these* Papillae, I feel the sharpness. The sense of touch informs me of the shape of the instrument. When I touch a Papilla of taste, I have no sensation similar to the former. I do not know that a point touches the tongue, but I am sensible of a metallic taste, and the sensation passes backward on the tongue.

In the operation of couching the cataract, the pain of piercing the retina with a needle is not so great as that which proceeds from a grain of sand under the eyelid. And although the derangement of the stomach sometimes marks the injury of an organ so delicate, yet the pain is occasioned by piercing the outward coat, not by the affection of the expanded nerve of vision.

If the sensation of light were conveyed to us by the retina, the organ of vision, in consequence of that organ being as much more sensible than the surface of the body as the impression of light is more delicate than that pressure which gives us the sense of touch; what would be the feelings of a man subjected to an operation in which a needle were pushed through the nerve. Life could not bear so great a pain.

This fact is corroborated by experiments made on the eye. When the eyeball is pressed on the side, we perceive various coloured light. Indeed the mere effect of a blow on the head might inform us, that sensation depends on the exercise of the organ affected, not on the impression conveyed to the external organ; for by the vibration caused by the blow, the ears ring, and eye flashes light, while there is neither light nor sound present.

It may be said, that there is here no proof of the sensation being in the brain more than in the external organ of sense. But when the nerve of a stump is touched the pain is as if in the amputated extremity. If it be still said that this is no proper example of a peculiar sense existing without its external organ, I offer the following example: *Qŭando penis glandem exedat ŭlcŭs, ĕt nihil nisi granulatio maneat, ad extremam nervi pudicae partem ubi terminatŭr sensus supersunt, et exquisitissima sensŭs gratificatio.*

If light, pressure, galvanism, or electricity produce vision, we must conclude that the idea in the mind is the result of an action excited in the eye or in the brain, not of anything received, though caused by an impression from without. The operations of the mind are confined not by the limited nature of things created, but by the limited number of our organs of sense. By induction we know that things exist which yet are not brought under the operation of the senses. When we have never known the operation of one of the organs of the five senses, we can never know the ideas pertaining to that sense; and what would be the effect on our minds, even constituted as they now are, with a superadded organ of sense, no man can distinctly imagine.

As we are parts of the creation, so God has bound us to the material world by this law of nature, that it shall require excitement from without, and an operation produced by the action of things external to rouse our faculties: But that once brought into activity, the organs can be put in exercise by the mind, and be made to minister to the memory and imagination, and all the faculties of the soul.

I shall hereafter shew, that the operations of the mind are seated in the great mass of the cerebrum, while the parts of the brain to which the nerves of sense tend, strictly form the seat of the sensation, being the internal organs of sense. These organs are operated upon in two directions. They receive the impression from without, as from the eye and ear: and as their action influences the operations of the brain producing perception, so are they brought into action and suffer changes similar to that which they experience from external pressure by the operation of the will; or, as I am now treating of the subject anatomically, by the operation of the great mass of the brain upon them.

In all regulated actions of the muscles we must acknowledge that they are influenced through the same nerves, by the same operation of the sensorium. Now the operations of the body are as nice and curious, and as perfectly regulated before Reason has sway, as they are at any time after, when the muscular frame might be supposed to be under the guidance of sense and reason. Instinctive motions are the operations of the same organs, the brain and nerves and muscles, which minister to reason and volition in our mature years. When the young of any animal turns to the nipple, directed by the sense of smelling, the same operations are performed, and through the same means, as afterwards when we make an effort to avoid what is noxious, or desire and move towards what is agreeable.

The operations of the brain may be said to be threefold: 1. The frame of the body is endowed with the characters of life, and the vital parts held together as one system through the operation of the brain and nerves; and the secret operations of the vital organs suffer the control of the brain, though we are unconscious of the thousand delicate operations which are every instant going on in the body. 2. In the second place, the instinctive motions which precede the development of the intellectual faculties are performed through the brain and nerves. 3. In the last place, the operation of the senses in rouzing the faculties of the mind, and the exercise of the mind over the moving parts of the body, is through the brain and nerves. The first of these is perfect in nature, and independent of the mind. The second is a prescribed and limited operation of the instrument of thought and agency. The last begins by imperceptible degrees, and has no limit in extent and variety. It is that to which all the rest is subservient, the end being the calling into activity and the sustaining of an intellectual being.

Thus we see that in as far as is necessary to the great system, the operation of the brain, nerves, and muscles are perfect from the beginning; and we are naturally moved to ask, Might not the operations of the mind have been thus perfect and spontaneous from the beginning as well as slowly excited into action by outward impressions? Then man would have been an insulated being, not only cut off from the inanimate world around him, but from his fellows; he would have been an individual, not a part of a whole. That he may have a motive and a spring to action, and suffer pain and pleasure, and become an intelligent being, answerable for his actions,—sensation is made to result from external impression, and reason and passion to come from the experience of good and evil; first as they are in reference to his corporeal frame, and finally as they belong to the intellectual privations and enjoyments.

The brain is a mass of soft matter, in part of a white colour, and generally striated; in part of a grey or cineritous colour having no fibrous appearance. It has grand divisions and subdivisions: and as the forms exist before the solid bone incloses the brain; and as the distinctions of parts are equally observable in animals whose brain is surrounded with fluid, they evidently are not accidental, but are a consequence of internal structure; or in other words they have a correspondence with distinctions in the uses of the parts of the brain.

On examining the grand divisions of the brain we are forced to admit that there are four brains. For the brain is divided longitudinally by a deep fissure; and the line of distinction can even be traced where the sides are united in substance. Whatever we observe on one side has a corresponding part on the other; and an exact resemblance and symmetry is preserved in all the lateral divisions of the brain. And so, if we take the proof of anatomy, we must admit that as the nerves are double, and the organs of sense double, so is the brain double; and every sensation conveyed to the brain is conveyed to the two lateral parts; and the operations performed must be done in both lateral portions at the same moment.

I speak of the lateral divisions of the brain being distinct brains combined in function, in order the more strongly to mark the distinction betwixt the anterior and the posterior grand divisions. Betwixt the lateral parts there is a strict resemblance in form and substance: each principal part is united by transverse tracts of medullary matter; and there is every provision for their acting with perfect sympathy. On the contrary, the cerebrum, the anterior grand division, and the cerebellum the posterior grand division, have slight and indirect connection. In form and division of parts, and arrangement of white and grey matter, there is no resemblance. There is here nothing of that symmetry and correspondence of parts which is so remarkable betwixt the right and left portions.

I have found evidence that the vascular system of the cerebellum may be affected independently of the vessels of the cerebrum. I have seen the whole surface of the cerebellum studded with spots of extravasated blood as small as pin heads, so as to be quite red, while no mark of disease was upon the surface of the cerebrum. The action of vessels it is needless to say is under the influence of the parts to which they go; and in this we have a proof of a distinct state of activity in the cerebrum and cerebellum.

From these facts, were there no others, we are entitled to conclude, that in the operations excited in the brain there cannot be such sympathy or corresponding movement in the cerebrum and cerebellum as there is betwixt the lateral portions of the cerebrum; that the anterior and posterior grand divisions of the brain perform distinct offices.

In examining this subject further, we find, when we compare the relative magnitude of the cerebrum to the other parts of the brain in man and in brutes, that in the latter the cerebrum is much smaller, having nothing of the relative magnitude and importance which in man it bears to the other parts of the nervous system; signifying that the cerebrum is the seat of those qualities of mind which distinguish man. We may observe also that the posterior grand division, or cerebellum remains more permanent in form: while the cerebrum changes in conformity to the organs of sense, or the endowments of the different classes of animals. In the inferior animals, for example, where there are two external organs of the same sense, there is to be found two distinct corresponding portions of cerebrum, while the cerebellum corresponds with the frame of the body.

In thinking of this subject, it is natural to expect that we should be able to put the matter to proof by experiment. But how is this to be accomplished, since any experiment direct upon the brain itself must be difficult, if not impossible?—I took this view of the subject. The medulla spinalis has a central division, and also a distinction into anterior and posterior portions of the brain. Further we can trace down the crura of the cerebellum into the posterior fasciculus. I thought that here I might have an opportunity of touching the cerebellum, as it were, through the posterior portion of the spinal marrow, and the cerebrum by the anterior portion. To this end I made experiments which, though they were not conclusive, encouraged me in the view I had taken.

I found that injury done to the anterior portion of the spinal marrow, convulsed the animal more certainly than injury done to the posterior portion; but I found it difficult to make the experiment without injuring both portions.

Next considering that the spinal nerves have a double root, and being of opinion that the properties of the nerves are derived from their connections with the parts of the brain, I thought that I had an opportunity of putting my opinion to the test of experiment, and of proving at the same time that nerves of different endowments were in the same cord, and held together by the same sheath.

On laying bare the roots of the spinal nerves, I found that I could cut across the posterior fasciculus of nerves, which took its origin from the posterior portion of the spinal marrow without convulsing the muscles of the back; but that on touching the anterior fasciculus with the point of the knife, the muscles of the back were immediately convulsed.

Such were my reasons for concluding that the cerebrum and the cerebellum were parts distinct in function, and that every nerve possessing a double function obtained that by having a double root. I now saw the meaning of the double connection of the nerves with the spinal marrow; and also the cause of that seeming intricacy in the connections of nerves throughout their course, which were not double at their origins.

The spinal nerves being double, and having their roots in the spinal marrow, of which a portion comes from the cerebrum and a portion from the cerebellum, they convey the attributes of both grand divisions of the brain to every part; and therefore the distribution of such nerves is simple, one nerve supplying its destined part. But the nerves which come directly from the brain, come from parts of the brain which vary in operation; and in order to bestow different qualities on the parts to which the nerves are distributed, two or more nerves must be united in their course or at their final destination. Hence it is that the 1st nerve must have branches of the 5th united with it: hence the portio dura of the 7th pervades everywhere the bones of the cranium to unite with the extended branches of the 5th: hence the union of the 3rd and 5th in the orbit: hence the 9th and 5th are both sent to the tongue: hence it is, in short, that no part is sufficiently supplied by one single nerve, unless that nerve be a nerve of the spinal marrow, and have a double root, a connection (however remotely) with both the cerebrum and cerebellum.

Such nerves as are single in their origin from the spinal marrow will be found either to unite in their course with some other nerve, or to be such as are acknowledged to be peculiar in their operation.

The 8th nerve is from the portion of the medulla oblongata[1] which belongs to the cerebellum: the 9th nerve comes from the portion which belongs to the cerebrum. The first is a nerve of the class called vital nerves, controlling secretly the operation of the body; the last is the motor nerve of the tongue, and is an instrument of volition. Now the connections formed by the 8th nerve in its course to the viscera are endless; for everywhere it is accompanied by others, and the 9th passes to the tongue, which is already profusely supplied by the 5th.

Understanding the origin of the nerves in the brain to be the source of their powers, we look upon the connections formed betwixt distant nerves, and upon the combination of nerves in their passage, with some interest; but without this the whole is an unmeaning tissue. Seeing the seeming irregularity in one subject, we say it is accident; but finding that

[1] The medulla oblongata is only the commencement of the spinal marrow.

the connections never vary, we say only that it is strange, until we come to understand the necessity of nerves being combined in order to bestow distinct qualities on the parts to which they are sent.

The cerebellum when compared with the cerebrum is simple in its form. It has no internal tubercles or masses of cineritous matter in it. The medullary matter comes down from the cineritious cortex, and forms the crus; and the crus runs into union with the same process from the cerebrum; and they together form the medulla spinalis, and are continued down into the spinal marrow; and these crura or processes afford double origin to the double nerves of the spine. The nerves proceeding from the Crus Cerebelli go everywhere (in seeming union with those from the Crus Cerebri) they unite the body together, and control the actions of the bodily frame; and especially govern the operation of the viscera necessary to the continuance of life.

In all animals having a nervous system, the cerebellum is apparent, even though there be no cerebrum. The cerebrum is seen in such tribes of animals as have organs of sense, and it is seen to be near the eyes, or principal organ of sense; and sometimes it is quite separate from the cerebellum.

The cerebrum I consider as the grand organ by which the mind is united to the body. Into it all the nerves from the external organs of the senses enter; and from it all the nerves which are agents of the will pass out.

If this be not at once obvious, it proceeds only from the circumstance that the nerves take their origin from the different parts of the brain; and while those nerves are considered as simple cords, this circumstance stands opposed to the conclusion which otherways would be drawn. A nerve having several roots, implies that it propagates its sensation to the brain generally. But when we find that the several roots are distinct in their endowments, and are in respect to office distinct nerves; then the conclusion is unavoidable, that the portions of the brain are distinct organs of different functions.

To arrive at any understanding of the internal parts of the cerebrum, we must keep in view the relation of the nerves, and must class and distinguish the nerves, and follow them into its substance. If all ideas originate in the mind from external impulse, how can we better investigate the structure of the brain than by following the nerves, which are the means of communication betwixt the brain and the outward organs of the senses?

The nerves of sense, the olfactory, the optic, the auditory, and the gustatory nerve, are traced backwards into certain tubercles or convex bodies in the base of the brain. And I may say, that the nerves of sense either form tubercles before entering the brain, or they enter into these convexities in the base of the cerebrum. These convexities are the constituent parts of the cerebrum, and are in all animals necessary parts of the organs of sense: for as certainly as we discover an animal to have an external organ of sense, we find also a medullary tubercle; whilst the superiority of animals in intelligence is shown by the greater magnitude of the hemispheres or upper parts of the cerebrum.

The convex bodies which are seated in the lower part of the cerebrum, and into which the nerves of sense enter, have extensive connection with the hemisphere, again, there pass down, converging to the crura Striae, which is the medullary matter taking upon it the character of a nerve; for from the Crura Cebebri, or its prolongation in the anterior Fasciculi of the spinal marrow, go off the nerves of motion.

But with these nerves of motion which are passing outward there are nerves going inwards; nerves from the surfaces of the body; nerves of touch; and nerves of peculiar sensibility, having their seat in the body or viscera. It is not improbable that the tracts of cineritious matter which we observe in the course of the medullary matter of the brain, are the seat of such peculiar sensibilities; the organs of certain powers which seem resident in the body.

As we proceed further in the investigation of the function of the brain, the discussion becomes more hypothetical. But surely physiologists have been mistaken in supposing it necessary to prove sensibility in those parts of the brain which they are to suppose the seat of the intellectual operations. We are not to expect the same phenomena to result from the cutting or tearing of the brain as from the injury to the nerves. The function of the one is to transmit sensation; the other has a higher operation. The nature of the organs of sense is different; the sensibilities of the parts of the body are very various. If the needle piercing the retina during the operation of couching gives no remarkable pain, except in touching the common coats of the eye, ought we to imagine that the seat of the higher operations of the mind should, when injured, exhibit the same effects with the irritation of a nerve? So far therefore from thinking the parts of the brain which are insensible, to be parts inferior (as every part has its use), I should even from this be led to imagine that they had a higher office. And if there be certain parts of the brain which are insensible, and other parts which being injured shake the animal with convulsions exhibiting phenomena similar to those of a wounded nerve, it seems to follow that the latter parts which are endowed with sensibility like the nerves are similar to them in function and use, while the parts of the brain which possess no such sensibility are different in function and organization from the nerves, and have a distinct and higher operation to perform.

If in examining the apparent structure of the brain, we find a part consisting of white medullary Striae and fasciculated like a nerve, we should conclude that as the use of a nerve is to transmit sensation, not to perform any more peculiar function, such tracts of matter are media of communication, connecting the parts of the brain; rather than the brain itself performing the more peculiar functions. On the other hand, if masses are found in the brain unlike the matter of the nerve, and which yet occupy a place guarded as an organ of importance, we may presume that such parts have a use different from that of merely conveying sensation; we may rather look upon such parts as the seat of higher powers.

Again, if those parts of the brain which are directly connected with the nerves, and which resemble them in structure, give pain when injured, and occasion convulsion to the animal as the nerves do when they are injured; and if on the contrary such parts as are more remote from the nerves, and of a different structure, produce no such effect when injured, we may conclude, that the office of the latter parts is more allied to the intellectual operations, less to mere sensation.

I have found at different times all the internal parts of the brain diseased without loss of sense; but I have never seen disease general on the surface of the hemispheres without derangement or oppression of the mind during the patient's life. In the case of derangement of mind, falling into lethargy and stupidity, I have constantly found the surface of the hemispheres dry and preternaturally firm, the membrane separating from it with unusual facility.

If I be correct in this view of the subject, then the experiments which have been made upon the brain tend to confirm the conclusions which I should be inclined to draw from strict anatomy; viz. that the cineritious and superficial parts of the brain are the seat of the intellectual functions. For it is found that the surface of the brain is totally insensible, but that the deep and medullary part being wounded the animal is convulsed and pained.

At first it is difficult to comprehend, how the part to which every sensation is referred, and by means of which we become acquainted with the various sensations, can itself be insensible; but the consideration of the wide difference of function betwixt a part destined to receive impressions, and a part which is the seat of intellect, reconciles us to the phenomenon. It would be rather strange to find, that there were no distinction exhibited in experiments on parts evidently so different in function as the organs of the senses, the nerves, and the brain. Whether there be a difference in the matter of the nervous system, or a distinction in organization, is of little importance to our enquiries, when it is proved that their essential properties are different, though their union and cooperation be necessary to the completion of their function—the development of the faculties by impulse from external matter.

All ideas originate in the brain: the operation producing them is the remote effect of an agitation or impression on the extremities of the nerves of sense; directly they are consequences of a change or operation in the proper organ of the sense which constitutes a part of the brain and over these organs, once brought into action by external impulse, the mind has influence. It is provided, that the extremities of the nerves of the senses shall be susceptible each of certain qualities in matter; and betwixt the impression of the outward sense, as it may be called, and the exercise of the internal organ, there is established a connection by which the ideas excited have a permanent correspondence with the qualities of bodies which surround us.

From the cineritious matter, which is chiefly external, and forming the surface of the cerebrum; and from the grand center of medullary matter of the cerebrum, what are called the crura descend. These are fasciculated processes of the cerebrum, from which go off the nerves of motion, the nerves governing the muscular frame. Through the nerves of sense, the sensorium receives impressions, but the will is expressed through the medium of the nerves of motion. The secret operations of the bodily frame and the connections which unite the parts of the body into a system, are through the cerebellum and nerves proceeding from it.

Thomas Brown: 1778-1820

THE SECONDARY LAWS OF LEARNING *

1820

AFTER the remarks which I have already frequently made on this subject, I trust it is now unnecessary for me to repeat, that the term *laws*, as employed in the physics, whether of matter or of mind, is not used to denote any thing different from the phenomena themselves,—that, in short, it means nothing more than certain circumstances of general agreement in any number of phenomena. When Mr. Hume reduced to the three orders of resemblance, contiguity, and causation, the relations on which he believed association to depend, he considered himself as stating only facts which were before familiar to every one, and *did* state only facts that were perfectly familiar. In like manner, when I reduce under a few heads those modifying circumstances, which seem to me as *secondary* laws, to guide, in every particular case, the momentary direction of the primary, my object is not to discover facts that are new, or little observed, but to arrange facts that, separately, are well known.

The *first* circumstance which presents itself, as modifying the influence of the primary laws, in inducing one associate conception rather than another, is the length of time during which the original feelings from which they flowed, continued, when they co-existed, or succeeded each other. Every one must be conscious, that innumerable objects pass before him, which are slightly observed at the time, but which form no permanent associations in the mind. The longer we dwell on objects, the more fully do we rely on our future remembrance of them.

In the *second* place, the parts of a train appear to be more closely and firmly associated, as the original feelings have been more lively. We remember brilliant objects, more than those which are faint and obscure. We remember for our whole life-time, the occasions of great joy or sorrow; we forget the occasions of innumerable slight pleasures or pains, which occur to us every hour. That strong feeling of interest and curiosity, which we call attention, not only leads us to dwell longer on the

* In his *Lectures on the Philosophy of the Human Mind*, 1820, Brown stated for the first time principles which have come to be spoken of as laws of learning. According to Brown's terminology, they were laws of suggestion. Suggestion was his term for association. The statements here reproduced are taken from Vol. I, Lecture 37, pp. 371-372 and 375-377, of an 1828 edition published by Hallowell, Boston.

consideration of certain objects, but also gives more vivacity to the objects on which we dwell,—and in both these ways tend, as we have seen, to fix them more strongly in the mind.

In the *third* place, the parts of any train are more readily suggested, in proportion as they have been more *frequently renewed.* It is thus, we remember, after reading them three or four times over, the verses which we could not repeat when we had read them only once.

In the *fourth* place, the feelings are connected more strongly in proportion as they are *more* or *less recent.* Immediately after reading any single line of poetry, we are able to repeat it, though we may have paid no particular attention to it;—in a very few minutes, unless when we have paid particular attention to it, we are no longer able to repeat it accurately—and in a very short time we forget it altogether. There is, indeed, one very striking exception to this law, in the case of old age: for events, which happened in youth, are then remembered, when events of the year preceding are forgotten. Yet, even in the case of extreme age,—when the time is not extended so far back,—the general law still holds; and events, which happened a few hours before, are remembered, when there is total forgetfulness of what happened a few days before.

In the *fifth* place, our successive feelings are associated more closely, as *each has co-existed less with other feelings.* The song, which we have never heard but from one person, can scarcely be heard again by us, without recalling that person to our memory; but there is obviously much less chance of this particular suggestion, if we have heard the same air and words frequently sung by others.

In the *sixth* place, the influence of the primary laws of suggestion is greatly modified by *original constitutional differences*, whether these are to be referred to the mind itself, or to varieties of bodily temperament. Such constitutional differences affect the primary laws in two ways,—first, by augmenting and extending the influence of all of them, as in the varieties of the general power of remembering, so observable in different individuals. Secondly, they modify the influence of the primary laws, by giving greater proportional vigor to one set of tendencies of suggestion than to another.

The primary laws of association, then, it appears, as far as they operate in our intellectual exertions, are greatly modified by original constitutional diversities. They are not less modified by constitutional diversities of another kind. These are the diversities of what is called temper, or disposition. It is thus we speak of one person of a *gloomy*, and another of a *cheerful* disposition; and we avoid the one, and seek the company of the other, as if with perfect confidence, that the trains of thought which rise by spontaneous suggestion to the minds of each will be different, and will be in accordance with that variety of character which we have supposed. To the cheerful, almost every object which they perceive is cheerful as themselves. In the very darkness of the storm, the cloud which hides the sunshine from their eye, does not hide it from their heart: while, to the sullen, no sky is bright, and no scene is fair. There are future fogs, which to their eyes, pollute and darken the purest airs of spring; and spring itself is known to them less as the season which follows and repairs the desolation of winter that is past, than as the season which announces its approaching return.

The next secondary law of suggestion to which I proceed, is one akin to the last which we have considered. The primary laws are modified, not by constitutional and permanent differences only, but by differences which occur in the same individual, according to the varying emotion of the hour. As there are persons, whose general character is gloomy or cheerful, we have, in like manner, our peculiar days or moments in which we pass from one of these characters to the other, and in which our trains of thought are tinctured with the corresponding varieties. A mere change of fortune is often sufficient to alter the whole cast of sentiment. Those who are in possession of public station, and power and affluence, are accustomed to represent affairs in a favorable light: the disappointed competitors for place to represent them in the most gloomy light; and though much of this difference may, unquestionably, be ascribed to wilful mis-statement in both cases, much of it is, as unquestionably, referable to that difference of colouring in which objects appear to the successful and the unsuccessful.

If even a slight momentary feeling of joy or sorrow have the power of modifying our suggestions, in accordance with it, emotions of a stronger and lasting kind must influence the trains of thought still more; —the meditations of every day rendering stronger the habitual connexions of such thoughts as accord with the peculiar frame of mind. It is in this way that every passion, which has one fixed object,—such as love, jealousy, revenge, derives nourishment from itself, suggesting images that give it in return, new force and liveliness. We see, in every thing, what we feel in ourselves; and the thought which external things seem to suggest, are thus, in part at least, suggested by the permanent emotion within.

The temporary diversities of state, that give rise to varieties of suggestion, are not mental only, but corporeal; and this difference of bodily state furnishes another secondary law, in modification of the primary. I need not refer to the extreme cases of intoxication or actual delirium, —the copious flow of follies, which a little wine, or a few grains of opium, may extract from the proudest reasoner. In circumstances less striking, how different are the trains of thought in health and in sickness,—after a temperate meal and after a luxurious excess! It is not to the animal powers only, that the burthen of digestion may become oppressive, but to the intellectual also; and often to the intellectual powers even more than to the animal. In that most delightful of all states, when the bodily frame has recovered from disease, and when in the first walk beneath the open sunshine, amid the blossoms and balmy air of summer, there is a mixture of corporeal and mental enjoyment, in which it is not easy to discriminate what images of pleasure arise from every object, that, in other states of health, might have excited no thought or emotion whatever.

There is yet another principle which modifies the primary laws of suggestion with very powerful influence. This is the principle of habit. I do not speak of its influence in suggesting images which have been already frequently suggested in a certain order,—for it would then be simpler to reduce the habit itself to the mere power of association. I speak of cases, in which the images suggested may have been of recent acquisition, but are suggested more readily in consequence of general tendencies produced by prior habits. When men of different professions observe the same circumstances, listen to the same story, or peruse the same work, their subsequent suggestions are far from being the same; and could the future differences of the associate feelings that are to rise, be foreseen by us at the time, we should probably be able to trace many of them to former professional peculiarities, which are thus always unfortunately apt to be more and more aggravated by the very suggestions to which they have themselves given rise. The most striking example, however, of the power of habit in modifying suggestion, is in the command which it gives to the orator, who has long been practiced in extemporary elocution; a command not of words merely, but of thoughts and judgments, which, at the very moment of their sudden inspiration, appear like the long-weighed calculations of deliberate reflection. The whole divisions of his subject start before him at once; image after image as he proceeds, arises to illustrate it; and proper words in proper places are all the while embodying his sentiments, as if without the slightest effort of his own.

In addition then, to the primary laws of suggestion, which are founded on the mere relations of the objects or feelings to each other, it appears that there is another set of laws, the operation of which is indispensable to account for the variety in the effects of the former. To these I have given the name of secondary laws of suggestion;—and we have seen accordingly that the suggestions are various as the original feelings have been, 1st, of longer or shorter continuance; 2dly, more or less lively; 3dly, more or less frequently present; 4thly, more or less recent; 5thly, more or less pure, if I may so express it, from the mixture of other feelings; 6thly, that they vary according to differences of original constitution; 7thly, according to differences of temporary emotion; 8thly, according to changes produced in the state of the body; and 9thly, according to general tendencies produced by prior habits.

Pierre Flourens: 1794-1867

EXPERIMENTAL RESEARCHES ON THE PROPERTIES AND FUNCTIONS OF THE NERVOUS SYSTEM IN THE VERTEBRATE ANIMAL *

1824

ON THE DETERMINATION OF THE PROPERITIES OF THE VARIOUS PARTS OF THE CEREBRAL MASS

1. I REMOVED both frontal lobes from a small rabbit. The animal lost little blood and was as well after the operation as before. Carefully avoiding injury to the vascular system, I cut through the dura on both sides. I also cut through the arachnoides and removed both. Then I pushed through the cerebral hemisphere along the entire extent without producing anywhere the least effect or the slightest muscular contraction.

2. I also removed by succeeding layers both hemispheres from a pigeon. Throughout the operation the animal remained passive.

3. I pushed a needle through the cerebellum of another pigeon. The animal did not move even when I extirpated the cerebellum by successive layers.

I moved on to the cerebral hemispheres; the animal still remained passive. Then I pushed a needle through the corpora quadrigemina. This resulted in some slight trembling and convulsions. These tremblings and convulsions increased as I went further into the medulla oblongata.

4. Although I repeated this experiment innumerable times, the result always remained the same.

5. The entire cranial portion of a young dog was removed. I pushed a needle through the cerebral lobes, cut them in all directions, and also cut through the cerebellum on that side. The animal seemed neither disturbed nor agitated.

6. I pushed a needle through the corpora quadrigemina of an older dog. This resulted in feeble convulsions. I pushed through the medulla, the convulsions became more violent.

* Flourens introduced extirpation upon experimental animals as a method of studying the function of various parts of the nervous system. The present translation of selections from Flouren's monograph is by Jules Kann of the Department of Psychology of the University of Pittsburgh.

7. Using a rabbit, I first probed the corpus striata and the optic layers from all directions. Next, I completely removed both by successive layers. No agitation accompanied this double test. It had been thought that pressure on the optical layers abolished the contraction of the iris. The same had been thought of the corpus striata. The paralysis takes place in this case only because the optic nerve situated underneath these parts is also affected by the pressure applied.

8. I pushed a needle—in all directions and on all possible points—through the corpus striata and the optic layers of a guinea pig. The iris of its eyes remained undisturbed. I pushed through the corpora quadrigemina and immediately there was a manifest contraction of both irises.

9. I removed both cerebral hemispheres of a pigeon, including the optical layers. The iris retained all of its ability to contract. However, I had only to push through the optic nerves or the corpora quadrigemina to elicit strong and prolonged contractions.

10. This experiment was repeated on several other pigeons. The result was always the same.

11. Consequently the cerebral hemispheres are not responsible for muscular contractions.

EXPERIMENTS ON THE DETERMINATION OF THE ROLE AND FUNCTIONS OF THE CEREBRAL LOBES

1. I removed the right cerebral lobe from a pigon. The animal immediately became blind in the eye opposite to the lobe removed. However, the ability of the iris of that eye to contract persisted nevertheless. I plan to return to that surprising fact at a later time—for the moment though I let it go.

A fairly marked feebleness manifested itself on the entire left side of the pigeon. This feebleness of the side opposite the removed lobe is a very variable phenomenon. This feebleness is pronounced in some animals; in others it is slight; and in still others it is hardly perceivable. In all animals though the strength returns soon to its equilibrium and the disproportion between the two sides soon disappears. As far as the pigeon was concerned, it saw very well through the eyes lateral to the removed lobe; it could hear; stand erect; walk; fly; and appeared generally calm. I wish to remark here that certain animals seem quite anxious after such mutilation. This anxiety does not last long.

2. I removed both cerebral lobes simultaneously from a pigeon. This removal is ordinarily followed by a general profound feebleness because —as will be seen later—there is not a single part of the nervous system which influences the energies of the other parts; rather the degree of this influence varies with each one of the parts. In this pigeon the general

feebleness was not marked; it survived the removal of its lobes for a long time. It stood up erect; flew when thrown into the air; walked when pushed. The iris of its eyes remained mobile in spite of the fact that it could not see. It could not hear, never moved spontancously, acted almost always in the manner of a sleeping animal, and when irritated during this sort of lethargy, the pigeon acted like an animal that is just waking up. In whatever position it was put, it assumed a perfect equilibrium and did not rest until it actually had effected such equilibrium.

I put the pigeon on its back; it got up. I put water in its mouth; it swallowed it. It resisted the efforts I made to open its mouth. It resisted when I bothered it. The pigeon eliminated regularly. The least irritation agitated and disturbed it.

When I let it alone, it remained calm and as if absorbed. In no instance did the pigeon give any signs of volition. In short, picture for yourself an animal condemned to eternal sleep and even deprived of the ability to dream during this sleep, and thus ended, little by little, the pigeon whose cerebral lobes were removed.

3. I removed the right cerebral lobe from a third pigeon. The pigeon immediately lost the sight of the contralateral eye. However, it walked, flew, and moved around just as before. It was only bothered by a little feebleness, which appeared first in the left side and which disappeared soon afterwards. I removed the other lobe. From then on, all spontaneous movements disappeared without returning. Sight was lost in both eyes, although the two irises remained mobile.

The animal was calm as if asleep. It stood up perfectly well; it flew when thrown into the air; and if by force I kept its nostrils closed, it moved—took several steps without any goal or determination and stopped as soon as it was no longer irritated.

When pricked, pinched, or burned, it moved, became agitated, walked, but always in the same place or position. The pigeon no longer knew how to flee. When confronted with an obstacle, it would repeatedly throw itself against it without ever thinking of avoiding this obstacle. It did this in spite of the fact that all pigeons in their natural state, or even blindfolded, are able by some means or other to avoid such an obstacle.

4. Operating on a frog, I began by removing only one of the two cerebral lobes. The frog jumped, walked, and became agitated after the extirpation. It saw very well on the side lateral to the removed lobe. If I placed an obstacle immediately in front of the blind eye, it would at first hit the object when it jumped, but reminded by the shock, it would later remember its position and did not fail to avoid it, even though I had blindfolded its other eye. I removed the second lobe. The frog immediately lost sight and memory. It threw itself twenty times against

the same obstacle, something which no frog does either in the intact state or with one lobe removed nor even if both eyes are extirpated. In addition the frog, which had both cerebral lobes removed, had neither hearing nor sight. Nor did it move unless irritated. However, under the influence of irritation, the frog would jump and flutter about. When put on its back, it regained normal position, balanced itself and again became immobile.

5. I have often repeated these experiments; I publish here only those showing the best results and which, therefore, demonstrate in a better manner the average of all results. It seems demonstrated then by these experiments that the cerebral lobes are neither the origin of muscular reaction nor are they the origin of the control of movements, such as marching, jumping, flying, or just standing, but it also seems demonstrated that they are the exclusive origin of volition and sensation. As far as volition is concerned, it suffices doubtlessly to state that the cerebral lobes once removed there is no vestige left of volition. As far as sensation is concerned, I would like here to return to some preceding statements.

6. If one lobe is removed, the animal loses sight in the contralateral eye. If both lobes are removed, it loses sight in both eyes. The ability of the iris to contract, however, persists in spite of the extirpation. If one irritates the conjunctiva or the optic nerve or the corpora quadrigemina, this contraction becomes convulsive. I feel it proper to show here, in all of its respects, the singular relation between loss of sensation and retention or even exaltation of muscular movements. In short, in this situation, there is convulsion of the iris together with loss of vision. This is true because vision is part neither of the ability of the iris to contract nor is it caused by the irritation of the optic nerve. These contractions and irritations are merely necessary accompanying conditions. Vision is caused by the sensations aroused by these irritations or even better it is the sensation itself.

Or, the origin of these sensations reside in the cerebral lobes but the origin of the contraction of the iris does not reside there. Extirpation of the cerebral lobes may then abolish vision without abolishing either the excitability of the optic nerve nor consequently the ability of the iris to contract.

7. Thus extinction of sensation does not necessarily entail paralysis of movement. One exists without the other. Paralysis of movement comes only from an alteration of the excitable parts of the nervous system. Extinction of sensation comes only from the part of the nervous system which is the origin and receptacle of sensation. It is clear then that these are distinct parts. The effect of their lesions should be distinct also.

8. One lobe removed, the animal retains its memory; both lobes re-

moved it loses it. One lobe removed, it hears; both removed, it does not. The animal has volition when it has one lobe. It has none when it loses both.

Memory, vision, hearing, volition, all sensations disappear with the loss of the lobes. The cerebral lobes then are the one origin of sensations.

EXPERIMENTS ON THE DETERMINATION OF THE ROLE AND FUNCTIONS OF THE CEREBELLUM

I come now to the examination of the other parts of the cerebral mass.

1. A pigeon had the cerebellum removed by succeeding layers. During the extirpation of layers of the cerebellum, there appeared only a slight weakness and disharmony of movement.

In the middle layers, an almost universal agitation became manifest. The animal moved brusquely or irregularly. However, it retained both hearing and sight. At the removal of the last layers, the animal, whose ability to jump, fly, walk, and stand up was more and more altered by the preceding mutiliation, lost these faculties altogether. When the animal was placed on its back, it could not longer get up. Far from being calm as pigeons are, whose cerebral lobes have been removed, this animal became quite agitated, but never moved in a firm and determined manner. For instance, it saw the blow which threatened it, tried to avoid it, went through a thousand contortions to avoid it; yet it could not. When placed on its back, it tried to get up in vain, and finished by staying in the same position in spite of its efforts. Volition and sensations were retained: the possibility of executing gross movements existed also, but the coordination of these motions into regular and determined movements was no longer there.

2. The cerebellum was removed from another pigeon. Once arrived at the middle layers, I touched the medulla oblongata, resulting in a convulsive trembling. After this trembling had dissipated itself, I continued my operation. The incoordinated and impetuous movements reappeared in the same layers as in the preceding experiment. The animal lost the ability to balance itself, to walk, or fly; it was in an almost continuous agitation. It had volition and the ability to move, but could never move as it wished to.

3. I pricked with a needle the entire superior region of the cerebellum of a third pigeon. No indication of exaltation was present, but weakness, indetermination, and slight disharmony of movements was noticed I penetrated further in a forward direction, the weakness, indetermination, and disharmony of movement became more pronounced. I came to the last layers, the animal lost its balance almost entirely; its movements were undecided; and it was almost continually agitated.

4. The superior layers of the cerebellum from a fourth pigeon were removed. After this operation the animal saw and heard very well. It stood up, walked, flew, but in an undecided and unassured manner.

I continued my operation, the animal lost its balance almost completely. It had much trouble standing up and could only succeed in doing so by supporting itself with its wings and tail. When it walked, its tottering steps reminded one of a drunk animal. The pigeon was forced to use its wings in support of its legs and in spite of this help, it often appeared that it would fall and roll over. When the last layers were removed, all sense of balance, i.e. all the coordination between these efforts disappeared. The animal no longer walked, flew, or stood up, but I must again say that volition and attempts to execute these movements were still present.

5. I removed the cerebellum of a fifth pigeon by very thin slices, in order to follow in all details and to all degrees the way in which the animal changed from one perfectly balanced to one whose ability to fly, walk, stand up, was totally abolished. The animal gradually lost the ability to fly, then to walk, then to stand up, in the same ratio as parts of its cerebellum were removed. Particularly the ability to stand up changed by degrees before being completely lost. The animal, at first, was not able to stand up on its feet for a long time. It tottered almost all of the time. Then its legs were no longer sufficient to support it and it must bring in its wings and tail. Finally, all stability became impossible. The animal made incredible efforts to stay in one position but was unable to do so.

The ability to walk is also lost by degrees. At first, the animal walks in a somewhat unbalanced manner, almost comparable to that of a drunk. Soon it is forced to call the wings to the aid of its legs. Then it cannot walk any more at all. One can, at will, by careful extirpation suppress only the ability to fly or suppress the ability to fly and walk, or to remove with one stroke the ability to fly, walk, and stand. In removing the cerebellum, one abolishes all coordinated movements. The pigeon on which I made these experiments felt, after the removal of the first layers, only some weakness and experienced some hesitation in its movements. I wish to state here, concerning this weakness, that at the very moment of mutilation is the time when the weakness is most marked and that it then progressively disappears and does not return until or unless another mutilation takes place. After all layers had been removed as far as the center of the organ, the pigeon still saw and heard very well; seemed to be in good spirits and its head was alert. No one could have imagined that it lacked half the cerebellum. On the other hand, however, the animal walked in a tottering manner and in a rather agitated fashion. Soon it only walked with the help of its wings.

I continued the operation, the animal lost the ability to walk entirely. Its legs could no longer support it and the pigeon could only keep erect by leaning on its elbows, wings, and tail. Often it did try to walk or fly. However, these trials resembled more the attempts to fly and walk made by little birds when they leave the nest for the first time. If pushed forward, it rolled over its head. If pushed in a backward direction, over its tail.

I carried my operation even further. The animal lost in addition the ability to keep upright by help of elbows, wings, and tail. The pigeon rolled all over the table without being able to stay in one position. Finally the pigeon tired out and then kept for some minutes the last position it had been holding—either on its belly or its back. The pigeon was forced to stay on its back in spite of the pain this position caused it. The pigeon no longer knew how to change its position in spite of all the efforts he made. It saw and heard well. While in a resting position, the slightest menace or noise would start off a new series of contortions. But in spite of all these terrible contortions, the pigeon never showed any signs of convulsions.

* * * * *

1. The anterior part of the right cerebral lobe and the upper and central part of the left were removed from a pigeon. Sight weakened more and more as I advanced, but was totally lost when the layers around the central node of the lobes were removed. From the moment that sight was gone, hearing was lost, too; and with it went all intellectual and sensory faculties.

2. Another pigeon suffered removal of the exterior and posterior parts of the lobes extending almost to the central nerve. As this extirpation advanced, sight weakened gradually, then hearing, then all other faculties; and as soon as one was lost completely, all others were gone, too.

3. Operating on a third pigeon, I laid open the central node by gradually cutting away all posterior, anterior, and superior layers of the two lobes. The animal's ability to see weakened with the removal of each new layer and from the moment the animal no longer saw, it also lost its ability to hear; had no volition, no memory, no judgment and was for all purposes similar to an animal deprived of its lobes.

4. Thus—

(a) One can remove, from the front, or the back, or the top or the side, a certain portion of the cerebral lobes, without destroying their function. A small part of the lobe seems sufficient to exercise these functions.

(b) As the operation progresses, the exercise of these functions becomes weaker and is gradually lost. After certain limits have been surpassed, they are entirely extinguished. The cerebral lobes concur then in their entirety with all of their functions.

(c) Finally as one sensation is lost completely, all of them are. Consequently there is no different origin for any of the faculties nor for any of the sensations. The ability to feel, to judge, or want one thing resides then in the same place as the ability to feel, judge, or desire another. This faculty then is essentially one and resides in a single organ.

5. The different sense organs nevertheless have a distinct origin in the cerebral mass. We have already seen these actions of the retina and iris come from the corpora quadrigemina. Similarly, the sense of taste, smell, and hearing have, as does the sense of sight, their particular origin in the particular convolution giving rise to the respective nerves.

6. It is possible then by destroying separately each of these particular origins, to destroy separately each of the four senses arising from them. And one can, on the other hand, destroy at one time all of these senses by the destruction of the central organ which combines all of them.

* * * * *

1. We have just seen that it is possible to remove a certain portion of the cerebral lobes without destroying their functions completely. However, it is more than that. The lobe can recover these functions in their entirety after having lost them completely.

2. Operating on a pigeon, I laid open the central node by gradually cutting away successive layers. I stopped the operation as soon as the animal had lost completely the use of all senses and intellectual functions.

On the first day the two mutilated lobes swelled up enormously. This swelling started to go down on the second, and disappeared almost completely on the third day. The pigeon then began, bit by bit, to regain its sight, sense of hearing, judgment, volition, and other faculties. After six days, it had regained them completely, and it should certainly be mentioned that as soon as the pigeon had regained one of its faculties, it had regained them all.

3. Taking another pigeon, I carried the operation still further. The animal, as did the preceding one, lost all sensory and intellectual faculties but never recovered any of them completely.

4. Operating on a third pigeon, I pushed the operation further. All faculties were lost forever.

5. Thus, as long as not too much of the lobes is removed, they may regain in due time the exercise of their functions. Passing certain limits, however, the animal regains them only imperfectly and passing these new limits, it does not recover them at all. Finally, if one sensation comes back, all come back. If one faculty reappears, they all reappear.

* * * * *

1. Operating on a young rooster, I removed half of the cerebellum. The animal immediately lost all stability, all regularity of movement, and his bizarre and tottering walk reminded one of inebriation. Four days later the equilibrium was less disturbed and fifteen days later it was entirely regained.

2. I removed half of the cerebellum from a pigeon. The entire organ was removed from a chicken. After some time the pigeon recovered its balance; the chicken never regained it in spite of the fact that it survived the operation by four months.

3. I removed the upper part of the right corpora quadrigemina from one pigeon and the upper part of the left corpora quadrigemina from another. On the fourth day each pigeon saw a little through the affected eye. From that day on it saw better each day and regained sight after several days. The corpora quadrigemina and the cerebellum have the double privilege of regaining their functions after having lost them and to regain them in their entirety, although the organ itself is no longer complete.

* * * * *

1. Finally, if every part of the organ is removed, all of its functions are lost. If one part is left, all functions can be regained. This shows that each of these organs is only a single organ because the alteration of a single part changes everything and the conservation of one part permits all functions to be regained.

2. All of this substantiates my first experiments. Since each function is maintained, altered, or regained by a given organ, it belongs to that organ. Since each organ maintains, alters, or regains only one proper function, it is only this one function which is proper to it. The functions of these organs are then quite distinct. The organs themselves are quite distinct and each constitutes respectively a proper and specific organ or function.

* * * * *

1. While operating on a strong chicken, I laid open the the two cerebral lobes. Then I cut the right lobe along its width and the left one lengthwise—both along the center line and cutting as deep as I could go. The animal immediately exhibited the same phenomenon as if it had been totally deprived of both its lobes, that is to say, it had lost all sensory intellectual faculties. During the first six days, it did not hear, see, nor show volition—almost always in a trance, it only moved when disturbed. Both lobes were quite swollen. The seventh day the animal came and went by itself, heard somewhat, saw a little from his right eye (the one opposite the lobe cut lengthwise), but saw nothing through its left eye. The swelling went down. By the eighth day the animal made astonishing

progress–hearing very well and seeing through his right eye but not the left. It walked around and slept less and less often. Until now it had to be fed, but now it ate and drank by itself. The swelling disappeared. By the twelfth day the chicken had recovered all senses and faculties except sight through its left eye. By the fiftieth day, the chicken was no different from one which had not undergone the operation. One thing was still lacking–sight through the left eye; something which it never regained although I let it survive for six months after the operation.

2. We have seen earlier that when one sense is lost due to mutilation of the lobe, we can conclude that all others are lost. There was no doubt that the lobe opposite the eye through which the chicken no longer saw, had lost all of its other functions, too. In effect, after removing the lobe opposite the eye through which it did see, the animal was in all respects one which had lost both lobes.

3. Taking another chicken I made the inverse operation. I cut the right lobe lengthwise from end to end. The animal lost sight in its left eye, but on the seventh day it began to see a little through that eye and on the eighth recovered sight completely. I then removed the entire left lobe. In regaining sight in the left eye, the animal had at the same time regained all other sensory and intellectual faculties.

4. Operating on a young rooster, I cut both cerebral lobes lengthwise from end to end. Immediately both lobes swelled up and the animal lost all sensory and intellectual faculties. Then the swelling went down and the animal, bit by bit, regained all faculties previously lost. At the end of seven to eight days it had completely recovered.

5. On another young rooster, I cut the two lobes along the width, running the scalpel along the center line from side to side. The animal immediately lost all faculties and senses and never regained any of them. It survived, however, for several months.

6. Using two pigeons, I cut the cerebellum lengthwise on one; on the other, along the width. In each case the cerebellum swelled. The equilibrium was at first disturbed. After several days, however, the swelling went down, both regained balance, walked, flew, and stood upright as before.

7. I cut the cerebellum of a chicken along the width, it lost its balance but regained it twelve days later. On another chicken I cut it longitudinally–it lost its balance but regained it.

8. Thus, a longitudinal transsection of the cerebral lobes permits reunion of the two severed parts and reintegration of all its functions. While transverse section of the lobes does not permit such reunion and all functions are lost without recovery. In the cerebellum, however, both transverse and longitudinal sectioning is followed by perfect reintegration of the organ and its functions.

9. The reason for this is obvious. A complete tranverse sectioning of the cerebral lobes completely separates a part of the organ from its roots. And this part separated in such a way, dies. Such a transsection resembles a real loss of substance and as shown previously if such a loss surpasses certain limits, it leaves the organ forever without its functions.

10. In the cerebellum, on the other hand, no transsection separates the organ from its roots. The two severed parts are then able to reunite and this junction reintegrates the function of that organ.

GENERAL CONCLUSIONS

1. The cerebral lobes are the exclusive origin of the sensations, perceptions, and volition.

2. All sensations, all perceptions, and all volition occupy concurrently the same seat in these organs. The faculty of sensation, perception, and volition is then essentially one faculty.

3. The cerebral lobes, the cerebellum, and the corpora quadrigemina can lose part of the substance without losing their functions. They can regain them after having lost them completely.

4. The spinal cord and the medulla oblongata have a direct effect, the corpora quadrigemina, the cerebral lobes, and the cerebellum a crossed effect.

In the last analysis, the cerebral lobes, the cerebellum, the corpora quadrigemina, the medulla oblongata, the spinal cord, the nerves, all of the essential and various parts of the nervous system have specific properties, proper functions, distinct effects, and in spite of this marvelous diversity of properties, of functions and effects, they constitute nevertheless a unified system. When one point in the nervous system becomes excited, it excites all others; one point irritated, irritates all. There is community of reaction. Unity is the great reigning principle; it is everywhere; dominates everything. The nervous system is then only one single system.

James Mill: 1773-1836

ANALYSIS OF THE PHENOMENA OF THE HUMAN MIND *

1829

THOUGHT succeeds thought; idea follows idea, incessantly. If our senses are awake, we are continually receiving sensations, of the eye, the ear, the touch, and so forth; but not sensations alone. After sensations, ideas are perpetually excited of sensations formerly received; after those ideas, other ideas: and during the whole of our lives, a series of those two states of consciousness, called sensations, and ideas, is constantly going on. I see a horse: that is a sensation. Immediately I think of his master: that is an idea. The idea of his master makes me think of his office; he is a minister of state: that is another idea. The idea of a minister of state makes me think of public affairs; and I am led into a train of political ideas; when I am summoned to dinner. This is a new sensation, followed by the idea of dinner, and of the company with whom I am to partake it. The sight of the company and of the food are other sensations; these suggest ideas without end; other sensations perpetually intervene, suggesting other ideas: and so the process goes on.

In contemplating this train of feelings, of which our lives consist, it first of all strikes the contemplator, as of importance to ascertain, whether they occur casually and irregularly, or according to a certain order.

With respect to the *Sensations*, it is obvious enough that they occur, according to the order established among what we call the objects of nature, whatever those objects are; to ascertain more and more of which order is the business of physical philosophy in all its branches.

Of the order established among the objects of nature, by which we mean the objects of our senses, two remarkable cases are all which here we are called upon to notice; the *Synchronous Order* and the *Successive Order*. The synchronous order, or order of simultaneous existence, is the order in space; the successive order, or order of antecedent and consequent existence, is the order in time. Thus the various objects in my room, the chairs, the tables, the books, have the synchronous order, or

* James Mill's *Analysis* is usually said to represent the peak of associationism. The chapter reproduced here is that entitled "The Association of Ideas." It is taken from the 1869 edition, published by Longmans, Green, Reoder and Dyer, London, pp. 70-116.

order in space. The falling of the spark, and the explosion of the gunpowder, have the successive order, or order in time.

According to this order, in the objects of sense, there is a synchronous, and a successive, order of our sensations. I have *Synchronically*, or at the same instant, the sight of a great variety of objects; touch of all the objects with which my body is in contact; hearing of all the sounds which are reaching my ears; smelling of all the smells which are reaching my nostrils; taste of the apple which I am eating; the sensation of resistance both from the apple which is in my mouth, and the ground on which I stand; with the sensation of motion from the act of walking. I have *Successively* the sight of the flash from the mortar fired at a distance, the hearing of the report, the sight of the bomb, and of its motion in the air, the sight of its fall, the sight and hearing of its explosion, and lastly, the sight of all the effects of that explosion.

Among the objects which I have thus observed synchronically, or successively; that is, from which I have had synchronical or successive sensations; there are some which I have so observed frequently; others which I have so observed not frequently: in other words, of my sensations some have been frequently synchronical, others not frequently; some frequently successive, others not frequently. Thus, my sight of roast beef, and my taste of roast beef, have been frequently *Synchronical;* my smell of a rose, and my sight and touch of a rose, have been frequently synchronical; my sight of a stone, and my sensations of its hardness, and weight, have been frequently synchronical. Others of my sensations have not been frequently synchronical: my sight of a lion, and the hearing of his roar; my sight of a knife, and its stabbing a man. My sight of the flash of lightning, and my hearing of the thunder, have been often *Successive;* the pain of cold, and the pleasure of heat, have been often successive; the sight of a trumpet, and the sound of a trumpet, have been often successive. On the other hand, my sight of hemlock, and my taste of hemlock, have not been often successive: and so on.

It so happens, that of the objects from which we derive the greatest part of our sensations, most of those which are observed synchronically, are frequently observed synchronically; most of those which are observed successively, are frequently observed successively. In other words, most of our synchronical sensations, have been frequently synchronical; most of our successive sensations, have been frequently successive. Thus, most of our synchronical sensations are derived from the objects around us, the objects which we have the most frequent occasion to hear and see; the members of our family; the furniture of our houses; our food; the instruments of our occupations or amusements. In like manner, of those sensations which we have had in succession, we have had the greatest number repeatedly in succession; the sight of fire, and its warmth; the touch of snow, and its cold; the sight of food, and its taste.

Thus much with regard to the order of *Sensations;* next with regard to the order of *Ideas*.

As ideas are not derived from objects, we should not expect their orders to be derived from the order of objects; but as they are derived from sensations, we might by analogy expect, that they would derive their order from that of the sensations; and this to a great extent is the case.

Our ideas spring up, or exist, in the order in which the sensations existed, of which they are the copies.

This is the general law of the "Association of Ideas"; by which term, let it be remembered, nothing is here meant to be expressed, but the order of occurrence.

In this law, the following things are to be carefully observed:

1. Of those sensations which occurred synchronically, the ideas also spring up synchronically. I have seen a violin, and heard the tones of the violin, the visible appearance of the violin at the same time occurs to me. I have seen the sun, and the sky in which it is placed synchronically. If I think of the one, I think of the other at the same time.

One of the cases of synchronical sensations, which deserves the most particular attention, is, that of the several sensations derived from one and the same object; a stone, for example, a flower, a table, a chair, a horse, a man.

From a stone I have had, synchronically, the sensation of colour, the sensation of hardness, the sensations of shape, and the size, the sensation of weight. When the idea of one of these sensations occurs, the ideas of all of them occur. They exist in my mind synchronically; and their synchronical existence is called the idea of the stone; which, it is thus plain, is not a single idea, but a number of ideas in a particular state of combination.

Thus, again, I have smelt a rose, and looked at, and handled a rose, synchronically; accordingly the name rose suggests to me all those ideas synchronically; and this combination of those simple ideas is called my idea of the rose.

My idea of an animal is still more complex. The word thrush, for example, not only suggests an idea of a particular colour and shape, and size, but of song, and flight, and nestling, and eggs, and callow young, and others.

My idea of a man is the most complex of all; including not only colour, and shape, and voice, but the whole class of events in which I have observed him either the agent or the patient.

2. As the ideas of the sensations which occurred synchronically, rise

synchronically, so the ideas of the sensations which occurred successively, rise successively.

Of this important case of association, or of the successive order of our ideas, many remarkable instances might be adduced. Of these none seems better adapted to the learner than the repetition of any passage, or words; the Lord's Prayer, for example, committed to memory. In learning the passage, we repeat it; that is, we pronounce the words, in successive order, from the beginning to the end. The order of the sensations is successive. When we proceed to repeat the passage, the ideas of the words also rise in succession, the preceding always suggesting the succeeding, and no other. Our suggests Father, Father suggests which, which suggests art; and so on, to the end. How remarkably this is the case, any one may convince himself, by trying to repeat backwards, even a passage with which he is as familiar as the Lord's Prayer. The case is the same with numbers. A man can go on with the numbers in the progressive order, one, two, three, &c. scarcely thinking of his act; and though it is possible for him to repeat them backward, because he is accustomed to subtraction of numbers, he cannot do so without an effort.

Of witnesses in courts of justice it has been remarked, that eye-witnesses, and ear-witnesses, always tell their story in the chronological order; in other words, the ideas occur to them in the order in which the sensations occurred; on the other hand, that witnesses, who are inventing, rarely adhere to the chronological order.

3. A far greater number of our sensations are received in the successive, than in the synchronical order. Of our ideas, also, a number is infinitely greater that rise in the successive than the synchronical order.

4. In the successive order of ideas, that which precedes, is sometimes called the suggesting, that which succeeds, the suggested idea; not that any power is supposed to reside in the antecedent over the consequent; suggesting, and suggested, mean only antecedent and consequent, with the additional idea, that such order is not casual, but, to a certain degree, permanent.

5. Of the antecedent and consequent feelings, or the suggesting, and suggested; the antecedent may be either sensations or ideas; the consequent are always ideas. Any idea may be excited with either a sensation or an idea. The sight of the dog of my friend is a sensation, and it excites the idea of my friend. The idea of Professor Dugald Stewart delivering a lecture, recalls the idea of the delight with which I heard him; that, the idea of the studies in which it engaged me; that, the trains of thought which succeeded; and each epoch of my mental history, the succeeding one, till the present moment; in which I am endeavouring to present to others what appears to me valuable among the innumerable ideas of which this lengthened train has been composed.

6. As there are degrees in sensations, and degrees in ideas; for one sensation is more vivid than another sensation, one idea more vivid than another idea; so there are degrees in association. One association, we say, is stronger than another: First, when it is more permanent than another; Secondly, when it is performed with more certainty; Thirdly, when it is performed with more facility.

It is well known, that some associations are very transient, others very permanent. The case which we formerly mentioned, that of repeating words committed to memory, affords an apt illustration. In some cases, we can perform the repetition, when a few hours, or a few days have elapsed; but not after a longer period. In others, we can perform it after the lapse of many years. There are few children in whose minds some association has not been formed between darkness and ghosts. In some this association is soon dissolved; in some it continues for life.

In some cases the association takes place with less, in some with greater certainty. Thus, in repeating words, I am not sure that I shall commit mistakes, if they are imperfectly got; and I may at one trial repeat them right, at another wrong: I am sure of always repeating those correctly, which I have got perfectly. Thus, in my native language, the association between the name and the thing is certain; in a language with which I am imperfectly acquainted, not certain. In expressing myself in my own language, the idea of the thing suggests the idea of the name with certainty. In speaking a language with which I am imperfectly acquainted, the idea of the thing does not with certainty suggest the idea of the name; at one time it may, at another not.

That ideas are associated in some cases with more, in some with less facility, is strikingly illustrated by the same instance, of a language with which we are well, and a language with which we are imperfectly, acquainted. In speaking our own language, we are not conscious of any effort; the associations between the words and the ideas appear spontaneous. In endeavouring to speak a language with which are imperfectly acquainted, we are sensible of a painful effort: the associations between the words and ideas being not ready, or immediate.

7. The causes of strength in association seem all to be resolvable into two; the vividness of the associated feelings; and the frequency of the association.

In general, we convey not a very precise meaning, when we speak of the vividness of sensations and ideas. We may be understood when we say that, generally speaking, the sensation is more vivid than the idea; or the primary, than the secondary feeling; though in dreams, and in delirium, ideas are mistaken for sensations. But when we say that one sensation is more vivid than another, there is much more uncertainty. We can distinguish those sensations which are pleasurable, and those which are painful, from such as are not so; and when we call the pleasurable and painful more vivid, than those which are not so, we speak intelligibly. We can also distinguish degrees of pleasure, and of pain; and when we call the sensation of the higher degree more vivid than the sensation of the lower degree, we may again be considered as expressing a meaning tolerably precise.

In calling one *Idea* more vivid than another, if we confine the appellation to the ideas of such sensations as may with precision be called more or less vivid; the sensations of pleasure and pain, in their various degrees, compared with sensations which we do not call either pleasurable or painful; our language will still have a certain degree of precision. But what is the meaning which I annex to my words, when I say, that my idea of the taste of the pine-apple which I tasted yesterday is vivid; my idea of the taste of the foreign fruit which I never tasted but once in early life, is not vivid? If I mean that I can more certainly distinguish the more recent, than the more distant sensations, there is still some precision in my language; because it seems true of all my senses, that if I compare a distant sensation with the present, I am less sure of its being or not being a repetition of the same, than if I compare a recent sensation with a present one. Thus, if I yesterday had a smell of a very peculiar kind, and compare it with the present smell, I can judge more accurately of the agreement or disagreement of the two sensations, than if I compared the present with one much more remote. The same is the case with colours, with sounds, with feelings of touch, and of resistance. It is therefore sufficiently certain, that the idea of the more recent sensation affords the means of a more accurate comparison, generally, than the idea of the more remote sensation. And thus we have three cases of vividness, of which we can speak with some precision: the case of sensations, as compared with ideas; the case of pleasurable and painful sensations, and their ideas as compared with those which are not pleasurable or painful; and the case of the more recent, compared with the more remote.

That the association of two ideas, but for once, does in some cases, give them a very strong connection, is within the sphere of every man's experience. The most remarkable cases are probably those of pain and pleasure. Some persons who have experienced a very painful surgical operation, can never afterwards bear the sight of the operator, however strong the gratitude which they may actually feel towards him. The meaning is, that the sight of the operator, by a strong association, calls up so vividly the idea of the pain of the operation, that it is itself pain. The spot on which a tender maiden parted with her lover, when he embarked on the voyage from which he never returned, cannot afterwards be seen by her without an agony of grief.

These cases, also, furnish an apt illustration of the superiority which the sensation possesses over the idea, as an association cause. Though the sight of the surgeon, the sight of the place, would awaken the ideas which we have described, the mere thought of them might be attended with no peculiar effect. Those persons who have the association of frightful objects with darkness, and who are transported with terrors when placed in the dark, can still think of darkness without any emotion.

The same cases furnish an illustration of the effect of recency on the strength of association. The sight, of the affecting spot by the maiden, of the surgeon by the patient, would certainly produce a more intense emotion, after a short, than after a long interval. With most persons, time would weaken, and at last dissolve, the association.

So much with regard to vividness, as a cause of strong associations. Next, we have to consider frequency or repetition; which is the most remarkable and important cause of the strength of our associations.

Of any two sensations, frequently perceived together, the ideas are associated. Thus, at least, in the minds of Englishmen, the idea of a soldier, and the idea of a red coat are associated; the idea of a clergyman, and the idea of a black coat; the idea of a Quaker, and of a broad-brimmed hat; the idea of a woman and the idea of petticoats. A peculiar taste suggests the idea of an apple; a peculiar smell the idea of a rose. If I have heard a particular air frequently sung by a particular person, the hearing of the air suggests the idea of the person.

The most remarkable exemplification of the effect of degrees of frequency, in producing degrees of strength in the association, is to be found in the cases in which the association is purposely and studiously contracted; the cases in which we learn something; the use of words, for example.

Every child learns the language which is spoken by those around him. He also learns it by degrees. He learns first the names of the most familiar objects; and among familiar objects, the names of those which he most frequently has occasion to name; himself, his nurse, his food, his playthings.

A sound heard once in conjunction with another sensation; the word mamma, for example, with the sight of a woman, would produce no greater effect on the child, than the conjunction of any other sensation, which once exists and is gone forever. But if the word mamma is frequently pronounced, in conjunction with the sight of a particular woman, the sound will by degrees become associated with the sight; and as the pronouncing of the name will call up the idea of the woman, so the sight of the woman will call up the idea of the name.

The process becomes very perceptible to use, when, at years of reflection, we proceed to learn a dead or foreign language. At the first lesson, we are told, or we see in the dictionary, the meaning of perhaps twenty words. But it is not joining the word and its meaning once, that will make the word suggest its meaning to use another time. We repeat the two in conjunction, till we think the meaning so well associated with the word, that whenever the word occurs to use, the meaning will occur along with it. We are often deceived in this anticipation; and finding that the meaning is not suggested by the word, we have to renew the process of repetition, and this, perhaps, again, and again. By force of repetition the meaning is associated, at last, with every word of the language, and so perfectly, that the one never occurs to us without the other.

Learning to play on a musical instrument is another remarkable illustration of the effect of repetition in strengthening associations, in rendering those sequences, which, at first, are slow, and difficult, afterwards, rapid, and easy. At first, the learner, after thinking of each successive note, as it stands in his book, has each time to look out with care for the key or the string which he is to touch, and the finger he is to touch it with, and is every moment committing mistakes. Repetition is well known to be the only means of overcoming these difficulties. As the repetition goes on, the sight of the note, or even the idea of the note, becomes associated with the place of the key or the string; and that of the key or the string with the proper finger. The association for a time is imperfect, but at last becomes so strong, that it is performed with the greatest rapidity, without an effort, and almost without consciousness.

In few cases is the strength of association, derived from repetition, more worthy of attention, than in performing arithmetic. All men, whose practice is not great, find the addition of a long column of numbers, tedious, and the accuracy of the operation, by no means certain. Till a man has had considerable practice, there are few acts of the mind more toilsome. The reason is, that the names of the numbers, which correspond to the different steps, do not readily occur; that is, are not strongly associated with the names which precede them. Thus, 7 added to 5, make 12; but the antecedent, 7 added to 5, is not strongly associated with the consequent 12, in the mind of the learner, and he has to wait and search till the name occurs. Thus, again, 12 and 7 make 19; 19 and 8 make 27, and so on to any amount; but if the practice of the performer has been small, the association in each instance is imperfect, and the process irksome and slow. Practice, however, that is, frequency of repetition, makes the association between each of these antecedents and its proper consequent so perfect, that no sooner is the one conceived than the other is conceived, and an expert arithmetician can tell the amount of a long column of figures, with a rapidity, which seems almost miraculous to the man whose faculty of numeration is of the ordinary standard.

8. Where two or more ideas have been often repeated together, and the association has become very strong, they sometimes spring up in such close combinations as not to be distinguishable. Some cases of sensation are analogous. For example, when a wheel, on the seven parts of which the seven prismatic colours are respectively painted, is made to revolve rapidly, it appears not of seven colours, but of one uniform colour, white. By the rapidity of the succession, the several sensations cease to be distinguishable; they run, as it were, together, and a new sensation, compounded of all seven, but apparently a simple one, is the result. Ideas, also, which have been so often conjoined, that whenever one exists in the mind, the others immediately exist along with it, seem to run into one another, to coalesce, as it were, and out of many to form one idea; which idea, however in reality complex, appears to be no less simple, than any one of those of which it is compounded.

The word gold, for example, or the word iron, appears to express as simple an idea, as the word colour, or the word sound. Yet it is immediately seen, that the idea of each of those metals is made up of the separate ideas of several sensations; colour, hardness, extension, weight. Those ideas, however, present themselves in such intimate union, that they are constantly spoken of as one, not many. We say, our idea of iron, our idea of gold; and it is only with an effort that reflecting men perform the decomposition.

The idea expressed by the term weight, appears so perfectly simple, that he is a good metaphysician, who can trace its composition. Yet it involves, of course, the idea of resistance, which we have shewn above to compounded, and to involve the feeling attendant upon the contraction of muscles; and the feeling, or feelings, denominated Will; it involves the idea, not of resistance simply, but of resistance in a particular direction; the idea of direction, therefore, is included in it, and in that are involved the idea of extension, and of place and motion, some of the most complicated phenomena of the human mind.

The ideas of hardness and extension have been so uniformly regarded as simple, that the greatest metaphysicians have set them down as the copies of simple sensations of touch. Hartley and Darwin, were, I believe, the first who thought of assigning to them a different origin.

We call a thing hard, because it resists compression, or separation of parts; that is, because to compress it, or separate it into parts, what we call muscular force is required. The idea, then, of muscular action, and of all the feelings which go to it, are involved in the idea of hardness.

The idea of extension is derived from the muscular feelings in what we call the motion of parts of our own bodies; as for example, the hands. I move my hand along a line; I have certain sensations; on account of these sensations, I call the line long, or extended. The idea of lines in the direction of length, breadth, and thickness, constitutes the general idea of extension. In the idea of extension, there are included three of the most complex of our ideas; motion; time, which is included in motion; and space, which is included in direction. We are not yet prepared to explain the simple ideas which compose the very complex ideas, of motion, space, and time; it is enough at present to have shewn, that in the idea of extension, which appears so very simple, a great number of ideas are nevertheless included; and that this is a case of that combination of ideas in the higher degrees of association, in which the simple ideas are so intimately blended, as to have the appearance, not of a complex, but of a simple idea.

It is to this great law of association, that we trace the formation of our ideas of what we call external objects; that is, the ideas of a certain number of sensations, received together so frequently that they coalesce as it were, and are spoken of under the idea of unity. Hence, what we call the idea of a tree, the idea of a stone, the idea of a horse, the idea of a man.

In using the names, tree, horse, man, the names of what I call objects, I am referring, and can be referring, only to my own sensations; in fact, therefore, only naming a certain number of sensations, regarded as in a particular state of combination; that is, concomitance. Particular sensations of sight, of touch, of the muscles, are the sensations, to the ideas of which, colour, extension, roughness, hardness, smoothness, taste, smell, so coalescing as to appear one idea, I give the name, idea of a tree.

To this case of high association, this blending together of many ideas, in so close a combination that they appear not many ideas, but one idea, we owe, as I shall afterwards more fully explain, the power of classification, and all the advantages of language. It is obviously, therefore, of the greatest moment, that this important phenomenon should be well understood.

9. Some ideas are by frequency and strength of association so closely combined, that they cannot be separated. If one exists, the others exist along with it, in spite of whatever effort we make to disjoin them.

For example; it is not in our power to think of colour, without thinking of extension; or of solidity, with figure. We have seen colour constantly in combination with extension, spread as it were, upon a surface. We have never seen it except in this connection. Colour and extension have been invariably conjoined. The idea of colour, therefore, uniformly comes into the mind, bringing that of extension along with it; and so close is the association, that it is not in our power to dissolve it. We cannot, if we will, think of colour, but in combination with extension. The one idea calls up the other, and retains it, so long as the other is retained.

This great law of our nature is illustrated in a manner equally striking, by the connection between the ideas of solidity and figure. We never have the sensations from which the idea of solidity is derived, but in conjunction with the sensations whence the idea of figure is derived. If we handle anything solid, it is always either round, square, or of some other form. The ideas correspond with the sensations. If the idea of solidity rises, that of figure rises along with it. The idea of figure which rises, is, of course, more obscure than that of extension; because, figures being innumerable, the general idea is exceedingly complex, and hence, of necessity, obscure. But, such as it is, the idea of figure is always present when that of solidity is present; nor can we, by any effort, think of the one without thinking of the other at the same time.

Of all the cases of this important law of association, there is none more extraordinary that what some philosophers have called, the acquired perceptions of sight.

When I lift my eyes from the paper on which I am writing, I see the chairs, and tables, and walls of my room, each of its proper shape, and at its proper distance. I see, from my window, trees, and meadows, and horses, and oxen, and distant hills. I see each of its proper size, of its proper form, and at its proper distance; and these particulars appear as immediate informations of the eye, as the colours which I see by means of it.

Yet, philosophy has ascertained, that we derive nothing from the eye whatever, but sensations of colour; that the idea of extension, in which size, and form, and distance are included, is derived from sensations, not in the eye, but in the muscular part of our frame. How, then is it, that we receive accurate information, by the eye, of size, and shape, and distance? By association merely.

The colours upon a body are different, according to its figure, its distance, and its size. But the sensations of colour, and what we may here, for brevity, call the sensations of extension, of figure, of distance, have been so often united, felt in conjunction, that the sensation of the colour is never experienced without raising the ideas of the extension, the figure, the distance, in such intimate union with it, that they not only cannot be separated, but are actually supposed to be seen. The sight, as it is called, of figure, or distance, appearing, as it does, a simple sensation, is in reality a complex state of consciousness; a sequence, in which the antecedent, a sensation of colour, and the consequent, a number of ideas, are so closely combined by association, that they appear not one idea, but one sensation.

Some persons, by the folly of those about them, in early life, have formed associations between the sound of thunder, and danger to their lives. They are accordingly in a state of agitation during a thunder storm. The sound of the thunder calls up the idea of danger, and no effort they can make, no reasoning they can use with themselves, to show how small the chance that they will be harmed, empowers them to dissolve the spell, to break the association, and deliver themselves from the tormenting idea, while the sensation or the expectation of it remains.

Another very familiar illustration may be adduced. Some persons have what is called an antipathy to a spider, a toad, or a rat. These feelings generally originate in some early fright. The idea of danger has been on some occasion so intensely excited along with the touch or sight of the animal, and hence the association so strongly formed, that it cannot be dissolved. The sensation, in spite of them, excites the idea, and produces the uneasiness which the idea imports.

The following of one idea after another idea, or after a sensation, so certainly that we cannot prevent the combination, nor avoid having the consequent feeling as often as we have the antecedent, is a law of association, the operation of which we shall afterwards find to be extensive, and bearing a principal part in some of the most important phenomena of the human mind.

As there are some ideas so intimately blended by association, that it is not in our power to separate them; there seem to be others, which it is not in our power to combine. Dr. Brown, in exposing some errors of his predecessors, with respect to the acquired perceptions of sight, observes: "I cannot blend my notions of the two surfaces, a plane, and a convex, as one surface, both plane and convex, more than I can think of a whole which is less than a fraction of itself, or a square of which the sides are not equal." The case, here, appears to be, that a strong association excludes whatever is opposite to it. I cannot associate the two ideas of assafoetida, and the taste of sugar. Why? Because the idea of assafoetida is so strongly associated with the idea of another taste, that the idea of that other taste rises in combination with the idea of assafoetida, and of course the idea of sugar does not rise. I have one idea associated with the word pain. Why can I not associate pleasure with the word pain? Because another indissoluble association springs up, and excludes it. This is, therefore, only a case of indissoluble association; but one of much importance, as we shall find when we come to the exposition of some of the more complicated of our mental phenomena.

10. It not unfrequently happens in our associated feelings, that the antecedent is of no importance farther than it introduces the consequent. In these cases, the consequent absorbs all the attention, and the antecedent is instantly forgotten. Of this a very intelligible illustration is afforded by what happens in ordinary discourse. A friend arrives from a distant country, and brings me the first intelligence of the last illness, the last words, the last acts, and death of my son. The sound of the voice, the articulation of every word, makes its sensation in my ear; but

it is to the ideas that my attention flies. It is my son that is before me, suffering, acting, speaking, dying. The words which have introduced the ideas, and kindled the affections, have been as little heeded, as the respiration which has been accelerated, while the ideas were received.

It is important in respect to this case of association to remark, that there are large classes of our sensations, such as many of those in the alimentary duct, and many in the nervous and vascular systems, which serve, as antecedents, to introduce ideas, as consequents; but as the consequents are far more interesting than themselves, and immediately absorb the attention, the antecedents are habitually overlooked; and though they exercise, by the trains which they introduce, a great influence on our happiness or misery, they themselves are generally wholly unknown.

That there are connections between our ideas and certain states of the internal organs, is proved by many familiar instances. Thus, anxiety, in most people, disorders the digestion. It is no wonder, then, that the internal feelings which accompany indigestion, should excite the ideas which prevail in a state of anxiety. Fear, in most people, accelerates, in a remarkable manner, the vermicular motion of the intestines. There is an association, therefore, between certain states of the intestines, and terrible ideas; and this is sufficiently confirmed by the horrible dreams to which men are subject from indigestion; and the hypochondria, more or less afflicting, which almost always accompanies certain morbid states of the digestive organs. The grateful food which excites pleasurable sensations in the mouth, continues them in the stomach; and, as pleasures excite ideas of their causes, and these of similar causes, and causes excite ideas of their effects, and so on, trains of pleasurable ideas take their origin from pleasurable sensations in the stomach. Uneasy sensations in the stomach, produce analogous effects. Disagreeable sensations are associated with disagreeable circumstances; a train is introduced, in which, one painful idea following another, combinations, to the last degree afflictive, are sometimes introduced, and the sufferer is altogether overwhelmed by dismal associations.

In illustration of the fact, that sensations and ideas, which are essential to some of the most impotant operations of our minds, serve only as antecedents to more important consequents, and are themselves so habitually overlooked, that their existence is unknown, we may recur to the remarkable case which we have just explained, of the idea introduced by the sensations of sight. The minute gradations of colour, which accompany varieties of extension, figure, and distance, are insignificant. The figure, the size, the distance, themselves, on the other hand, are matters of the greatest importance. The first having introduced the last, their work is done. The consequents remain the sole objects of attention, the antecedents are forgotten; in the present instance, not completely; in other instances, so completely, that they cannot be recognized.

11. Mr. Hume, and after him other philosophers, have said that our ideas are associated according to three principles: Contiguity in time and place, Causation, and Resemblance. The Contiguity in time and place, must mean, that of the sensations; and so far it is affirmed, that the order of the ideas follows that of the sensations. Contiguity of two sensations in time, means the successive order. Contiguity of two sensations in place, means the synchronous order. We have explained the mode in which ideas are associated, in the synchronous, as well as, the successive order, and have traced the principle of contiguity to its proper source.

Causation, the second of Mr. Hume's principles, is the same with contiguity in time, or the order of succession. Causation is only a name for the order established between an antecedent and a consequent; that is, the established or constant antecedence of the one, and consequence of the other. Resemblance only remains, as an alleged principle of association, and it is necessary to inquire whether it is included in the laws which have been above expounded. I believe it will be found that we are accustomed to see like things together. When we see a tree, we generally see more trees than one; when we see an ox, we generally see more oxen than one; a sheep, more sheep than one; a man, more men than one. From this observation, I think, we may refer resemblance to the law of frequency, of which it seems to form only a particular case.

Mr. Hume makes contrast a principle of association, but not a separate one, as he thinks it is compounded of Resemblance and Causation. It is not necessary for us to show that this is an unsatisfactory account of contrast. It is only necessary to observe, that, as a case of association, it is not distinct from those which we have above explained.

A dwarf suggests the idea of a giant. How? We call a dwarf a dwarf, because he departs from a certain standard. We call a giant a giant, because he departs from the same standard. This is a case, therefore, of resemblance, that is, of frequency.

Pain is said to make us think of pleasure; and this is considered a case of association by contrast. There is no doubt that pain makes us think of relief from it; because they have been conjoined, and the great vividness of the sensations makes the association strong. Relief from pain is a species of pleasure; and one pleasure leads to think of another, from the resemblance. This is a compound case, therefore, of vividness and frequency. All other cases of contrast, I believe, may be expounded in a similar manner.

I have not thought it necessary to be tedious in expounding the observations which I have thus stated; for whether the reader supposes that resemblance is, or is not, an original principle of association, will not affect our future investigations.

12. Not only do simple ideas, by strong association, run together, and form complex ideas: but a complex idea, when the simple ideas which compose it have become so consolidated that it always appears as one, is capable of entering into combinations with other ideas, both simple and complex. Thus two complex ideas may be united together, by a strong association, and coalesce into one, in the same manner as two or more simple ideas coalesce into one. This union of two complex ideas into one, Dr. Hartley has called a duplex idea. Two also of these duplex, or doubly compounded ideas, may unite into one; and these again into other compounds, without end. It is hardly necessary to mention, that as two complex ideas unite to form a duplex one, not only two, but more than two may so unite; and what he calls a duplex idea may be compounded of two, three, four, or any number complex ideas.

Some of the most familiar objects with which we are acquainted furnish instances of these unions of complex and duplex ideas.

Brick is one complex idea, mortar is another complex idea; these ideas, with ideas of position and quantity, compose my idea of a wall. My idea of a plank is a complex idea, my idea of a rafter is a complex idea, my idea of a nail is a complex idea.

These, united with the same ideas of position and quantity, compose my duplex idea of a floor. In the same manner my complex idea of glass, and wood, and other, compose my duplex idea of a window; and these duplex ideas, united together, compose my idea of a house, which is made up of various duplex ideas. How many complex, or duplex ideas, are all united in the idea of furniture? How many more in the idea of merchandise? How many more in the idea called Every Thing?

Ernst Heinrich Weber: 1795-1878

CONCERNING TOUCH *

1834

In comparing objects and observing the distinction between them, we perceive not the difference between the objects, but the ratio of this difference to the magnitude of the objects compared. If we are comparing by touch two weights, the one of 30 and the other of 29 half-ounces, the difference is not more easily perceived than that between weights of 30 and 29 drachms. . . . Since the distinction is not perceived more easily in the former case than in the latter, it is clear that not the weights of the differences but their ratio are perceived. . . . Experience has taught us that apt and practised O's sense the difference between weights, if it is not less than the thirtieth part of the heavier weight, and that the same O's perceive the difference not less easily, if drachms are put in the place of half-cunces.

That which I have set forth with regard to weights compared by touch holds also of lines to be compared by sight. For, whether you compare longer or shorter lines, you will find that the difference is not sensed by most O's if the second line is less by a hundredth part. . . . The length in which the distinction resides, therefore, although (in the case of lines of 50 and 50.5 mm.) it is twice as small (as it is in the case of lines of 100 and 101 mm.), is nevertheless no less easily apprehended, for the reason that in both cases the difference of the compared lines is one hundredth of the longer line.

I have made no experiments upon comparison of tones by the ear. Delezenne, however, determined the j. n. d. of the b of 240 vs. As this author does not say that this difference is discriminated less easily in deeper, more easily in higher tones, and as I have never heard that a difference is more easily perceived in higher tones, . . . I imagine that in audition also not the absolute difference between the vibrations of two tones, but the relative compared with the number of vibrations of the tones is discriminated.

The observation, confirmed in several departments of sense, that in

* The paragraphs presented below constitute the first statement of Weber's Law. They form only a small part of the monograph whose title is cited. The translation is by E. B. Titchener. It is reprinted by the courtesy of the Houghton Mifflin Co., publishers of Rand's *The Classical Psychologists,* 1912.

observing the distinction between objects we perceive not the absolute but the relative differences, has again and again impelled me to investigate the cause of this phenomenon; and I hope that when this cause is sufficiently understood, we shall be able to judge more correctly regarding the nature of the senses.

Johannes Mueller: 1801-1858

THE SPECIFIC ENERGIES OF NERVES *
1838

THE senses, by virtue of the peculiar properties of their several nerves, make us acquainted with the states of our own body, and they also inform us of the qualities and changes of external nature, as far as these give rise to changes in the condition of the nerves. Sensation is a property common to all the senses; but the kind of sensation is different in each: thus we have the sensations of light, of sound, of taste, of smell, and of feeling, or touch. By feeling, or touch, we understand the peculiar kind of sensation of which the ordinary sensitive nerves generally—as, the nervus trigeminus, vagus, glossopharyngeal, and the spinal nerves,—are susceptible; the sensations of itching, of pleasure and pain, of heat and cold, and those excited by the act of touch in its more limited sense, are varieties of this mode of sensation. That which through the medium of our senses is actually perceived by the sensorium, is indeed merely a property or change of condition of our nerves; but the imagination and reason are ready to interpret the modifications in the state of the nerves produced by external influences as properties of the external bodies themselves. This mode of regarding sensations has become so habitual in the case of the senses which are more rarely affected by internal causes, that it is only on reflection that we perceive it to be erroneous. In the case of the sense of feeling or touch, on the contrary, where the peculiar sensations of the nerves perceived by the sensorium are excited as frequently by internal as by external causes, it is easily conceived that the feeling of pain or pleasure, for example, is a condition of the nerves, and not a property of the things which excite it. This leads us to the consideration of some general laws, a knowledge of which is necessary before entering on the physiology of the separate senses.

I. In the first place, it must be kept in mind that external agencies can give rise to no kind of sensation which cannot also be produced by internal causes, exciting changes in the condition of our nerves.

* Boring in his *History of Experimental Psychology*, page 78, has pointed out that whereas the doctrine of the specific energies of nerves had been implied or stated by many earlier writers, Müller deserves credit for its explicit and precise formulation. The material here presented is from a volume of his *Handbook of Physiology* which appeared in 1838. The translation is by William Braly. It is reprinted from *The Classical Psychologists* by permission of the Houghton Mifflin Co. Müller first advanced the theory in less detail in 1826.

In the case of the sense of touch, this is at once evident. The sensations of the nerves of touch (or common sensibility) are those of cold and heat, pain and pleasure, and innumerable modifications of these, which are neither painful nor pleasurable, but yet have the same kind of sensation as their element, though not in an extreme degree. All these sensations are constantly being produced by internal causes in all parts of our body endowed with sensitive nerves; they may also be excited by causes acting from without, but external agencies are not capable of adding any new element to their nature. The sensations of the nerves of touch are therefore states or qualities proper to themselves, and merely rendered manifest by exciting causes external or internal. The sensation of smell also may be perceived independently of the application of any odorous substance from without, the nerve of smell being thrown by an internal cause into the condition requisite for the production of the sensation. This perception of the sensation of odours without an external exciting cause, though not of frequent occurrence, has been many times observed in persons of an irritable nervous system; and the sense of taste is probably subject to the same affection, although it would be always difficult to determine whether the taste might not be owing to a change in the qualities of the saliva or mucus of the mouth; the sensation of nausea, however, which belongs to the sensations of taste, is certainly very often perceived as the result of a merely internal affection of the nerves. The sensations of the sense of vision, namely, color, light, and darkness, are also perceived independently of all external exciting cause. In the state of the most perfect freedom from excitement, the optic nerve has no other sensation than that of darkness. The excited condition of the nerve is manifested, even while the eyes are closed, by the appearance of light, or luminous flashes, which are merely sensations of the nerve, and not owing to the presence of any matter of light, and consequently are not capable of illuminating any surrounding objects. Every one is aware how common it is to see bright colours while the eyes are closed, particularly in the morning when the irritability of the nerves is still considerable. These phenomena are very frequent in children after waking from sleep. Through the sense of vision, therefore, we receive from external nature no impressions which we may not also experience from internal excitement of our nerves; and it is evident that a person blind from infancy in consequence of opacity of the transparent media of the eye, must have a perfect internal conception of light and colours, provided the retina and optic nerve be free from lesion. The prevalent notions with regard to the wonderful sensations supposed to be experienced by persons blind from birth when their sight is restored by operation, are exaggerated and incorrect. The elements of the sensation of vision, namely, the sensations of light, colour, and darkness, must have been previously as well known to such persons as to those of whom the sight has always been perfect.

If, moreover, we imagine a man to be from his birth surrounded merely by external objects destitute of all variety of colours, so that he could never receive the impressions of colours from without, it is evident that the sense of vision might nevertheless have been no less perfect in him than in other men; for light and colours are innate endowments of his nature, and require merely a stimulus to render them manifest.

The sensations of hearing also are excited as well by internal as by external causes; for, whenever the auditory nerve is in a state of excitement, the sensations peculiar to it, as the sounds of ringing, humming, &c. are perceived. It is by such sensations that the diseases of the auditory nerve manifest themselves; and, even in less grave, transient affections of the nervous system, the sensations of humming and ringing in the ears afford evidence that the sense of hearing participates in the disturbance.

No further proof is wanting to show that external influences give rise in our senses to no other sensations than those which may be excited in the corresponding nerves by internal causes.

II. The same internal cause excites in the different senses different sensations;—in each sense the sensations peculiar to it.

One uniform internal cause acting on all the nerves of the senses in the same manner, is the accumulation of blood in the capillary vessels of the nerve, as in congestion and inflammation. This uniform cause excites in the retina, while the eyes are closed, the sensation of light and luminous flashes; in the auditory nerve, humming and ringing sounds; and in the nerves of feeling, the sensation of pain. In the same way, also, a narcotic substance introduced into the blood excites in the nerves of each sense peculiar symptoms; in the optic nerves the appearance of luminous sparks before the eyes; in the auditory nerves tinnitus aurium; and in the common sensitive nerves the sensation of ants creeping over the surface.

III. The same external cause also gives rise to different sensations in each sense, according to the special endowments of its nerve.

The mechanical influence of a blow, concussion, or pressure excites, for example, in the eye the sensation of light and colours. It is well known that by exerting pressure upon the eye, when the eyelids are closed, we can give rise to the appearance of a luminous circle; by more gentle pressure the appearance of colours may be produced, and one color may be made to change to another. Children, waking from sleep before daylight, frequently amuse themselves with these phenomena. The light thus produced has no existence external to the optic nerve, it is merely a sensation excited in it. However strongly we press upon the eye in the dark, so as to give rise to the appearance of luminous flashes, these flashes, being merely sensations, are incapable of illuminating external objects. Of this any one may easily convince himself by experiment. I have in repeated trials never been able, by means of these luminous flashes in the eye, to recognise in the dark the nearest objects, or to see them better than before; nor could another person, while I produced by pressure on my eye the appearance of brilliant flashes, perceive in it the slightest trace of real light.

A mechanical influence excites also peculiar sensations of the auditory nerve; at all events, it has become a common saying, "to give a person what will make his ears ring," or "what will make his eyes flash fire," or "what will make him feel," so that the same cause, a blow, produces in the nerves of hearing, sight, and feeling, the different sensations proper to these senses. It has not become a part of common language that a blow shall be given which will excite the sense of smell, or or taste; nor would such sayings be correct; yet mechanical irritation of the soft palate, of the epiglottis and root of the tongue, excites the sensation of nauseau. The actions of sonorous bodies on the organ of hearing is entirely mechanical. A sudden mechanical impulse of the air upon the organ of hearing produces the sensation of a report of different degrees of intensity according to the violence of the impulse, just as an impulse upon the organ of vision gives rise to the sensation of light. If the action of the mechanical cause on the organ of hearing be of continued duration, the sound is also continued; and when caused by a rapid succession of uniform impulses, or vibrations, it has a musical character. If we admit that the matter of light acts on bodies by mechanical oscillation (the undulation theory), we shall have another example of a mechanical influence, producing different effects on different senses. These undulations, which produce in the eye the sensation of light, have no such effects on other senses; but in the nerves of feeling they produce the sensation of warmth.

The stimulus of electricity may serve as a second example of a uniform cause giving rise in different nerves of sense to different sensations. A single pair of plates of different metals applied so as to include the eye within the circle excites the sensation of a bright flash of light when the person experimented upon is in a dark room; and, even though the eye does not lie within the circle, if it be not distant from it,—as, for example, when one of the plates is applied to one of the eyelids, and the other to the interior of the mouth—the same effect will be produced, owing to a part of the current of electricity being diverted to the eye. A more intense electric stimulus gives rise to more intense sensations of light. In the organ of hearing, electricity excites the sensations of sound. Volta states that, while his ears were included between the poles of a battery of forty pairs of plates, he heard a hissing and pulsatory sound, which continued as long as the circle was closed. Ritter perceived a sound like that of the fiddle G at the moment of the closure of the galvanic circle.

The electricity of friction, developed by the electrical machine, excites in the olfactory nerves the odour of phosphorus. The application of plates of different metals to the tongue gives rise to an acid or a saline taste according to the length of the plates which are applied one above and the other beneath the tongue. The facts detailed with regard to the other senses are sufficient to show that these latter phenomena cannot be attributed to decomposition of the salts of the saliva.

The effects of the action of electricity on the nerves of common sensation or feeling, are neither the sensation of light, of sound, of smell, nor of taste, but those proper to the nerves of feeling, namely, the sensations of pricking, of a blow, &c.

Chemical influences also probably produce different effects on different nerves of sense. We have, of course, but few facts illustrating their action on these nerves; but we know that in the sensitive nerves of the skin they excite the different kinds of common sensation,—as the sensations of burning, pain, and heat; in the organ of taste, sensations of taste; and, when volatile, in the nerves of smell, the sensations of odors. Without the infliction of great injury on the textures, it is impossible to apply chemical agents to the nerves of the higher senses, sight and hearing, except through the medium of the blood. Chemical substances introduced into the blood act on every nerve of sense, and excite in such a manifestation of its properties. Hence the internal sensations of light and sound, which are well known to result from the action of narcotics.

IV. The peculiar sensations of each nerve of sense can be excited by several distinct causes internal and external.

The facts on which this statement is founded have been already mentioned; for we have seen that the sensation of light in the eye is excited:

1. By the undulations or emanations which from their action on the eye are called light, although they have many other actions than this; for instance, they effect chemical changes, and are the means of maintaining the organic processes in plants.

2. By mechanical influences; as concussion, or a blow.

3. By electricity.

4. By chemical agents, such as narcotics, digitalis, &c. which, being absorbed into the blood, give rise to the appearance of luminous sparks, &c. before the eyes independently of any external cause.

5. By the stimulus of the blood in the state of congestion.

The sensation of sound may be excited in the auditory nerve:

1. By mechanical influences, namely, by the vibrations of sonorous bodies imparted to the organ of hearing through the intervention of media capable of propagating them.

2. By electricity.

3. By chemical influences taken into the circulation; such as the narcotics, or alterantia nervina.

4. By the stimulus of the blood.

The sensation of odors may be excited in the olfactory nerves:

1. By chemical influences of a volatile nature,—odorous substances.

2. By electricity.

The sensation of taste may be produced:

1. By chemical influences acting on the gustatory nerves either from without or through the medium of the blood; for, according to Magendie, dogs taste milk injected into their blood-vessels, and begin to lap with their tongue.

2. By electricity.

3. By mechanical influences; for we must refer to taste the sensation of nausea produced by mechanically irritating the velum palati, epiglottis, and root of the tongue.

The sensations of the nerves of touch or feeling are excited:

1. By mechanical influences; as sonorous vibrations, and contact of any kind.

2. By chemical influences.

3. By heat.

4. By electricity.

5. By the stimulus of the blood.

V. Sensation consists in the sensorium receiving through the medium of the nerves, and as the result of the action of an external cause, a knowledge of certain qualities or conditions, not of external bodies, but of the nerves of sense themselves; and these qualities of the nerves of sense are in all different, the nerve of each sense having its own peculiar quality or energy.

The special susceptibility of the different nerves of sense for certain influences,—as of the optic nerve for light, of the auditory nerve for vibrations, and so on,—was formerly attributed to these nerves having each a specific irritability. But this hypothesis is evidently insufficient to explain all the facts. The nerves of the senses have assuredly a specific irritability for certain influences; for many stimuli, which exert a violent action upon one organ of sense, have little or no effect upon another: for example, light, or vibrations so infinitely rapid as those of light, act only on the nerves of vision and common sensation; slower vibrations, on the nerves of hearing and common sensation, but not upon those of vision; odorous substances only upon the olfactory nerves. The external stimuli must therefore be adapted to the organ of sense—must be "homogeneous": thus light is the stimulus adapted to the nerve of vision; while vibrations of less rapidity, which act upon the auditory nerve, are not adapted to the optic nerve, or are indifferent to it; for if the eye be touched with a tuning-fork while vibrating, a sensation of tremors is excited in the conjunctiva, but no sensation of light. We have seen, however, that one and the same stimulus, as electricity, will produce different sensations in the different nerves of the senses; all the nerves are susceptible of its action, but the sensations in all are different. The same is the case with other stimuli, as chemical and mechanical influences. The hypothesis of a specific irritability of the nerves of the senses for certain stimuli, is therefore insufficient; and we are compelled to ascribe, with Aristotle, peculiar energies to each nerve,—energies which are vital qualities of the nerve, just as contractility is the vital property of muscle. The truth of this has been rendered more and more evident in recent times by the investigation of the so-called "subjective" phenomena of the senses by Elliot, Darwin, Ritter, Goethe, Purkinje, and Tjort. Those phenomena of the senses, namely, are now styled "subjective," which are produced, not by the usual stimulus adapted to the particular nerve of sense, but by others which do not usually act upon it. These important phenomena were long spoken of as "illusions of the senses," and have been regarded in an erroneous point of view; while they are really true actions of the senses, and must be studied as fundamental phenomena in investigations into their nature.

The sensation of sound, therefore, is the peculiar "energy" or "quality" of the auditory nerve; the sensation of light and colours that of the optic nerve; and so of the other nerves of sense. An exact analysis of what takes place in the production of a sensation would of itself have led to this conclusion. The sensations of heat and cold, for example, make us acquainted with the existence of the imponderable matter of caloric, or of peculiar vibrations in the vicinity of our nerves of feeling. But the nature of this caloric cannot be elucidated by sensations, which is in reality merely a particular state of our nerves; it must be learnt by the study of the physical properties of this agent, namely, of the laws of its radiation, its development from the latent state, its property of combining with and producing expansion of other bodies, &c. All this again, however, does not explain the peculiarity of the sensation of warmth as a condition of the nerves. The simple fact devoid of all theory is this, that warmth, as a sensation, is produced whenever the matter of caloric acts upon the nerves of feeling; and that cold as a sensation, results from this matter of caloric being abstracted from a nerve of feeling.

So, also, the sensation of sound is produced when a certain number of impulses or vibrations are imparted, within a certain time, to the auditory nerve: but sound, as we perceive it, is a very different thing from a succession of vibrations. The vibrations of a tuning-fork, which to the ear give the impression of sound, produce in a nerve of feeling or touch the sensation of tickling; something besides the vibrations must consequently be necessary for the production of the sensation of sound, and that something is possessed by the auditory nerve alone. Vision is too be regarded in the same manner. A difference in the intensity of the action of the imponderable agent, light, causes an inequality of sensation at different parts of the retina: whether this action consists in impulses or undulations, (the undulation theory,) or in an infinitely rapid current of imponderable matter, (the emanation theory,) is a question here of no importance. The sensation of moderate light is produced where the action of the imponderable agent on the retina is not intense; of bright light where its action is stronger, and of darkness or shade where the imponderable agent does not fall; and thus results a luminous image of determinate form according to the distribution of the parts of the retina differently acted on. Color is also a property of the optic nerve; and when excited by external light, arises from the peculiarity of the so-called colored rays, or of the oscillations necessary for the production of the impression of color,—a peculiarity, the nature of which is not at present known. The nerves of taste and smell are capable of being excited to an infinite variety of sensations by external causes; but each taste is due to a determinate condition of the nerve excited by the external cause; and it is ridiculous to say that the property of acidity is communicated to the sensorium by the nerve of taste, while the acid acts equally upon the nerves of feeling, though it excites there no sensation of taste.

The essential nature of these conditions of the nerves, by virtue of which they see light and hear sound,—and the essential nature of sound as a property of the auditory nerve, and of light as a property of the optic nerve, of taste, of smell, and of feeling,—remains, like the ultimate causes of natural phenomena generally, a problem incapable of solution. Respecting the nature of the sensation of the color "blue," for example, we can reason no farther; it is one of the many facts which mark the limits of our powers of mind. It would not advance the question to suppose the peculiar sensations of the different senses excited by one and the same cause, to result from the propagations of vibrations of the nervous principle of different rapidity to the sensorium. Such an hypothesis, if at all tenable, would find its first application in accounting for the different sensations of which a single sense is susceptible; for example, in explaining how the sensorium received the different impressions of blue, red, and yellow, or of an acute and a grave tone, or of painful and pleasurable sensations, or of the sensations of heat and cold, or of the tastes of bitter, sweet, and acid. It is only with this application that the hypothesis is worthy of regard: tones of different degrees of acuteness are certainly produced by vibrations of sonorous bodies of different degrees of rapidity; and a slight contact of a solid body, which singly excites in a nerve of common sensation merely the simple sensation of touch, produces in the same nerve when repeated rapidly, as the vibrations of a sonorous body, the feeling of tickling; so that possibly a pleasurable sensation, even when it arises from internal causes independently of external influences, is due to the rapidity of the vibrations of the nervous principle in the nerves of feeling.

The accuracy of our discrimination by means of the senses depends on the different manner in which the conditions of our nerves are affected by different bodies; but the preceding considerations show us the impossibility that our senses can ever reveal to us the true nature and essence of the material world. In our intercourse with external nature it is always our own sensations that we become acquainted with, and from them we form conceptions of the properties of external objects, which may be relatively correct; but we can never submit the nature of the objects themselves to that immediate perception to which the state of the different parts of our own body are subjected in the sensorium.

VI. The nerve of each sense seems to be capable of one determinate kind of sensation only, and not of those proper to the other organs of sense; hence one nerve of sense cannot take the place and perform the function of the nerve of another sense.

The sensation of each organ of sense may be increased in intensity till it become pleasurable, or till it becomes disagreeable, without the specific nature of the sensation being altered, or converted into that of another organ of sense. The sensation of dazzling light is an unpleasant sensation of the organ of vision; harmony of colours, an agreeable one. Harmonious and discordant sounds are agreeable and disagreeable sensations of the organ of hearing. The organs of taste and smell have their pleasant and unpleasant tastes and odors; the organ of touch its pleasurable and painful feelings. It appears, therefore, that, even in the most excited condition of an organ of sense, the sensation preserves its specific character. It is an admitted fact that the sensations of light, sound, taste, and odors, can be experienced only in their respective nerves; but in the case of common sensation this is not so evidently the case, for it is a question whether the sensation of pain may not be felt in the nerves of the higher senses—whether, for example, violent irritation of the optic nerve may not give rise to the sensation of pain. This question is difficult of solution. There are filaments of the nerves of common sensation distributed in the nerves of the other organs of sense: the nostrils are supplied with nerves of common sensation from the second division of the nervus trigeminus in addition to the olfactory nerves; the tongue has common sensibility as well as taste, and may retain the one while it loses the other; the eye and organ of hearing likewise are similarly endowed.

To determine this question, it is necessary to institute experiments on the isolated nerves of special sense themselves. As far as such experiments have hitherto gone, they favor the view that the nerves of sense are susceptible of no other kind of sensation than that peculiar to each, and are not endowed with the faculty of common sensibility.

Among the well-attested facts of physiology, again, there is not one to support the belief that one nerve of sense can assume the functions of another. The exaggeration of the sense of touch in the blind will not in these days be called seeing with the fingers; the accounts of the power of vision by the fingers and epigastrium, said to be possessed in the so-called magnetic state, appear to be mere fables, and the instances in which it has been pretended to practise it, cases of deception. The nerves of touch are capable of no other sensation than that of touch or feeling. Hence, also, no sounds can be heard except by the auditory nerve; the vibrations of bodies are perceived by the nerves of touch as mere tremors wholly different in its nature from sound; though it is indeed even now not rare for the different modes of action of the vibrations of bodies upon the sense of hearing, and upon that of feeling, to be confounded. Without the organ of hearing with its vital endowments, there would be no such a thing as sound in the world, but merely vibrations; without the organ of sight, there would be no light, color, nor darkness, but merely a corresponding presence or absence of the oscillations of the imponderable matter of light.

VII. It is not known whether the essential causes of the peculiar "energy" of each nerve of sense is seated in the nerve itself, or in the parts of the brain and spinal cord with which it is connected; but it is certain that the central portions of the nerves included in the encephalon are susceptible of their peculiar sensations, independently of the more peripheral portion of the nervous cords which form the means of communication with the external organs of sense.

The specific sensibility of the individual senses to particular stimuli,—owing to which vibrations of such rapidity or length as to produce sound are perceived, only by the senses of hearing and touch, and mere mechanical influences, scarcely at all by the sense of taste,—must be a property of the nerves themselves; but the peculiar mode of reaction of each sense, after the excitement of its nerve, may be due to either of two conditions. Either the nerves themselves may communicate impressions different in quality to the sensorium, which in every instance remains the same; or the vibrations of the nervous principle may in every nerve be the same and yet give rise to the perception of different sensations in the sensorium, owing to the parts of the latter with which the nerves are connected having different properties.

The proof of either of these propositions I regard as at present impossible.

VIII. The immediate objects of the perception of our senses are merely particular states induced in the nerves, and felt as sensations either by the nerves themselves or by the sensorium; but inasmuch as the nerves of the senses are material bodies, and therefore participate in the properties of matter generally occupying space, being susceptible of vibratory motion, and capable of being changed chemically as well as by the action of heat and electricity, they make known to the sensorium, by virtue of the changes thus produced in them by external causes, not merely their own condition, but also properties and changes of condition of external bodies. The information thus obtained by the senses concerning external nature, varies in each sense, having a relation to the qualities or energies of the nerve.

Qualities which are to be regarded rather as sensations or modes of reaction of the nerves of sense, are light, color, the bitter and sweet tastes, pleasant and unpleasant odours, painful and pleasant impressions on the nerves of touch, cold and warmth: properties which may belong wholly to external nature are "extension," progressive and tremulous motion, and chemical change.

All the senses are not equally adapted to impart the idea of "extension" to the sensorium. The nerve of vision and the nerve of touch, being capable of an exact perception of this property in themselves, make us acquainted with it in external bodies. In the nerves of taste, the sensation of extension is less distinct, but is not altogether deficient; thus we are capable of distinguishing whether the seat of a bitter or sweet taste be the tongue, the palate, or the fauces. In the sense of touch and sight, however, the perception of space is most acute. The retina of the optic nerve has a structure especially adapted for this perception; for the ends of the nervous fibres in the retina are, as Treviramus discovered, so arranged as to be at last perpendicular to its inner surface, and by their papillar extremities form a pavement-like composite membrane. On the great number of these terminal fibrils depends the delicate power of discriminating the position of bodies in space possessed by the sense of vision; for each fibre represents a greater or less field of the visible world, and imparts the impression of it to the sensorium.

The sense of touch has a much more extended sphere of action for the perception of space than has the sense of vision; but its perception of this quality of external bodies is much less accurate; and considerable portions of the surface of the body or skin are in many instances represented in the sensorium by very few nervous fibres; hence, in many parts of the surface, impressions on two points considerably removed from each other are, as E. H. Weber has shown, felt as one impression. Although the senses of vision, touch, and taste are all capable of perceiving the property of extension in space, yet the quality of the sensations which give the conception of extension is different in each of these senses; the sensation in one is an image of which the essential quality is light; in another, a perception of extension with any of the modifications of the quality of touch, between pain, cold, heat, and pleasure; in the third, a perception of extension with the quality of taste.

John Stuart Mill: 1806-1873

PSYCHOLOGY AND ETHOLOGY *

1843

CHAPTER III

That There Is, or May Be, a Science of Human Nature

1. It is a common notion, or at least it is implied in many common modes of speech, that the thoughts, feelings, and actions of sentient beings are not a subject of science, in the same strict sense in which this is true of the objects of outward nature. This notion seems to involve some confusion of ideas, which it is necessary to begin by clearing up.

Any facts are fitted, in themselves, to be a subject of science, which follow one another according to constant laws; although those laws may not have been discovered, nor even be discoverable by our existing resources. Take, for instance, the most familiar class of meteorological phenomena, those of rain and sunshine. Scientific inquiry has not yet succeeded in ascertaining the order of antecedence and consequence among these phenomena, so as to be able, at least in our regions of the earth, to predict them with certainty or even with any high degree of probability. Yet no one doubts that the phenomena depend on laws, and that these must be derivative laws resulting from known ultimate laws, those of heat, electricity, vaporisation, and elastic fluids. Nor can it be doubted that if we were acquainted with all the antecedent circumstances, we could, even from those more general laws, predict (saving difficulties of calculation) the state of the weather at any future time.

A case may be conceived of an intermediate character between the perfection of science and this its extreme imperfection. It may happen that the greater causes, those on which the principal part of the phenomena depends, are within the reach of observation and measurement; so that if no other causes intervened, a complete explanation could be given not only of the phenomenon in general, but of all the variations and modifications which it admits of. But inasmuch as other, perhaps many other causes, separately insignificant in their effects, co-operate or conflict in many or in all cases with those greater causes, the effect, accordingly, presents more or less of aberration from what would be produced by the greater causes alone. Now if these minor causes are

* These chapters are from Mill's *A System of Logic*, 1843.

not so constantly accessible, or not accessible at all to accurate observation, the principal mass of the effect may still, as before, be accounted for, and even predicted; but there will be variations and modifications which we shall not be competent to explain thoroughly, and our predictions will not be fulfilled accurately, but only approximately.

It is thus, for example, with the theory of the tides. No one doubts that Tidology (as Dr. Whewell proposes to call it) is really a science. As much of the phenomena as depends on the attraction of the sun and moon is completely understood, and may in any, even unknown, part of the earth's surface be foretold with certainty; and the far greater part of the phenomena depends on those causes. But circumstances of a local or casual nature, such as the configuration of the bottom of the ocean, the degree of confinement from shores, the direction of the wind, &c., influence in many or in all places the height and time of the tide; and a portion of these circumstances being either not accurately knowable, not precisely measurable, or not capable of being certainly foreseen, the tide in known places commonly varies from the calculated result of general principles by some difference that we cannot explain, and in unknown ones may vary from it by a difference that we are not able to foresee or conjecture. Nevertheless, not only is it certain that these variations depend on causes, and follow their causes by laws of unerring uniformity; not only, therefore, is tidology a science, like meteorology, but it is what, hitherto at least, meteorology is not, a science largely available in practice. General laws may be laid down respecting the tides; predictions may be founded on those laws, and the result will in the main, though often not with complete accuracy, correspond to the predictions.

2. The science of human nature is of this description. It falls far short of the standard of exactness now realised in Astronomy; but there is no reason that it should not be as much a science as Tidology is, or as Astronomy was when its calculations had only mastered the main phenomena, but not the perturbations.

The phenomena with which this science is conversant being the thoughts, feelings, and actions of human beings, it would have attained the ideal perfection of a science if it enabled us to foretell how an individual would think, feel, or act throughout life, with the same certainty with which astronomy enables us to predict the places and the occultations of the heavenly bodies. It needs scarcely be stated that nothing approaching to this can be done. The actions of individuals could not be predicted with scientific accuracy, were it only because we cannot foresee the whole of the circumstances in which those individuals will be placed. But further, even in any given combination of (present) circumstances, no assertion, which is both precise and universally true, can be made respecting the manner in which human beings will think, feel, or act.

This is not, however, because every person's modes of thinking, feeling, and acting do not depend on causes; nor can we doubt that if, in the case of any individual, our data could be complete, we even now know enough of the ultimate laws by which mental phenomena are determined to enable us in many cases to predict, with tolerable certainty, what, in the greater number of supposable combinations of circumstances, his conduct or sentiments would be. But the impressions and actions of human beings are not solely the result of their present circumstances, but the joint result of those circumstances and of the characters of the individuals; and the agencies which determine human character are so numerous and diversified, (nothing which has happened to the person throughout life being without its portion of influence,) that in the aggregate they are never in any two cases exactly similar. Hence, even if our science of human nature were theoretically perfect, that is, if we could calculate any character as we can calculate the orbit of any planet, *from given data;* still, as the data are never all given, nor ever precisely alike in different cases, we could neither make positive predictions, nor lay down universal propositions.

Inasmuch, however, as many of those effects which it is of most importance to render amenable to human foresight and control are determined, like the tides, in an incomparably greater degree by general causes, than by all partial causes taken together; depending in the main on those circumstances and qualities which are common to all mankind, or at least to large bodies of them, and only on a small degree on the idiosyncrasies of organisation or the peculiar history of individuals; it is evidently possible, with regard to all such effects, to make predictions which will *almost* be verified, and general propositions which are almost always true. And whenever it is sufficient to know how the great majority of the human race, or of some nation or class of persons, will think, feel, and act, these propositions are equivalent to universal ones. For the purposes of political and social science this *is* sufficient. An approximate generalisation is, in social inquiries, for most practical purposes equivalent to an exact one; that which is only probable when asserted of individual human beings, indiscriminately selected, being certain when affirmed of the character and collective conduct of masses.

It is no disparagement, therefore, to the science of Human Nature that those of its general propositions which descend sufficiently into detail to serve as a foundation for predicting phenomena in the concrete are for the most part only approximately true. But in order to give a genuinely scientific character to the study, it is indispensable that these approximate generalisations, which in themselves would amount only to the lowest kind of empirical laws, should be connected deductively with the laws of nature from which they result—should be resolved into the properties of the causes on which the phenomena depend. In other words, the science of Human Nature may be said to exist in proportion as the approximate truths which compose a practical knowledge of mankind can be exhibited as corollaries from the universal laws of human nature on which they rest, whereby the proper limits of those approximate truths would be shown, and we should be enabled to deduce others for any new state of circumstances, in anticipation of specific experience.

CHAPTER IV

Of the Laws of Mind

3. The subject of Psychology is the uniformities of succession, the laws, whether ultimate or derivative, according to which one mental state succeeds another—is caused by, or at least is caused to follow, another. Of these laws, some are general, others more special. The following are examples of the most general laws.

First, Whenever any state of consciousness has once been excited in us, no matter by what cause, an inferior degree of the same state of consciousness, a state of consciousness resembling the former, but inferior in intensity, is capable of being reproduced in us, without the presence of any such cause as excited it at first. Thus, if we have once seen or touched an object, we can afterwards think of the object, though it be absent from our sight or from our touch. If we have been joyful or grieved at some event, we can think of or remember our past joy or grief, though no new event of a happy or painful nature has taken place. When a poet has put together a mental picture of an imaginary object, a Castle of Indolence, a Una, or a Hamlet, he can afterwards think of the ideal object he has created without any fresh act of intellectual combination. This law is expressed by saying, in the language of Hume, that every mental impression has its idea.

Secondly, These ideas, or secondary mental states, are excited by our impressions, or by other ideas, according to certain laws which are called Laws of Association. Of these laws the first is, that similar ideas tend to excite one another. The second is, that when two impressions have been frequently experienced (or even thought of), either simultaneously or in immediate succession, then whenever one of these impressions, or the idea of it, recurs, it tends to excite the idea of the other. The third law is, that greater intensity in either or both of the impressions is equivalent, in rendering them excitable by one another, to a greater frequency of conjunction. These are the laws of ideas, on which I shall not enlarge in this place, but refer the reader to works professedly psychological, in particular to Mr. James Mill's *Analysis of the Phenomena of the Human*

Mind, where the principal laws of association, along with many of their applications, are copiously exemplified, and with a masterly hand.

These simple or elementary Laws of Mind have been ascertained by the ordinary methods of experimental inquiry; nor could they have been ascertained in any other manner. But a certain number of elementary laws having thus been obtained, it is a fair subject of scientific inquiry how far those laws can be made to go in explaining the actual phenomena. It is obvious that complex laws of thought and feeling not only may, but must be generated from these simple laws. And it is to be remarked that the case is not always one of Composition of Causes: the effect of concurring causes is not always precisely the sum of the effects of those causes when separate, nor even always an effect of the same kind with them. Reverting to the distinction which occupies so prominent a place in the theory of induction, the laws of the phenomena of mind are sometimes analogous to mechanical, but sometimes also to chemical laws. When many impressions or ideas are operating in the mind together, there sometimes takes place a process of a similar kind to chemical combination. When impressions have been so often experienced in conjunction that each of them calls up readily and instantaneously the ideas of the whole group, those ideas sometimes melt and coalesce into one another, and appear not several ideas, but one, in the same manner, as when the seven prismatic colours are presented to the eye in rapid succession the sensation produced is that of white. But as in this last case it is correct to say that the seven colours when they rapidly follow one another *generate* white, but not that they actually *are* white; so it appears to me that the Complex Idea, formed by the blending together of several simpler ones, should, when it really appears simple, (that is, when the separate elements are not consciously distinguishable in it), be said to *result from*, or *be generated by*, the simple ideas, not to *consist* of them. Our idea of an orange really *consists* of the simple ideas of a certain colour, a certain form, a certain taste and smell, &c., because we can, by interrogating our consciousness, perceive all these elements in the idea. But we cannot perceive, in so apparently simple a feeling as our perception of the shape of an object by the eye, all that multitude of ideas derived from other senses, without which it is well ascertained that no such visual perception would ever have had existence; nor, in our idea of Extension, can we discover those elementary ideas of resistance derived from our muscular frame in which it has been conclusively shown that the idea originates. These, therefore, are cases of mental chemistry, in which it is proper to say that the simple ideas generate, rather than that they compose, the complex ones.

CHAPTER V

Of Ethology, or the Science of the Formation of Character

Although, however, there is scarcely any mode of feeling or conduct which is, in the absolute sense, common to all mankind; and though the generalisations which assert that any given variety of conduct or feeling will be found universally, (however nearly they may approximate to truth within given limits of observation,) will be considered as scientific propositions by no one who is at all familiar with scientific investigation; yet all modes of feeling and conduct met with among mankind have causes which produce them; and in the propositions which assign those causes will be found the explanation of the empirical laws, and the limiting principle of our reliance on them. Human beings do not all feel and act alike in the same circumstances; but it is possible to determine what makes one person, in a given position, feel or act in one way, another in another; how any given mode of feeling and conduct, compatible with the general laws (physical and mental) of human nature, has been, or may be, formed. In other words, mankind have not one universal character, but there exist universal laws of the Formation of Character. And since it is by these laws, combined with the facts of each particular case, that the whole of the phenomena of human action and feeling are produced, it is on these that every rational attempt to construct the science of human nature in the concrete and for practical purposes must proceed.

3. The laws, then, of the formation of character being the principal object of scientific inquiry into human nature, it remains to determine the method of investigation best fitted for ascertaining them. And the logical principles according to which this question is to be decided must be those which preside over every other attempt to investigate the laws of very complex phenomena. For it is evident that both the character of any human being, and the aggregate of the circumstances by which that character has been formed, are facts of a high order of complexity. Now to such cases we have seen that the Deductive Method, setting out from general laws, and verifying their consequences by specific experience, is alone applicable. The grounds of this great logical doctrine have formerly been stated, and its truth will derive additional support from a brief examination of the specialties of the present case.

There are only two modes in which laws of nature can be ascertained: deductively and experimentally, including under the denomination of experimental inquiry, observation as well as artificial experiment. Are the laws of the formation of character susceptible of a satisfactory investigation by the method of experimentation? Evidently not; because, even if we suppose unlimited power of varying the experiment, (which is abstractedly possible, though no one but an Oriental despot has that power, or, if he had, would probably be disposed to exercise it,) a still more essential condition is wanting—the power of performing any of the experiments with scientific accuracy.

The instances requisite for the prosecution of a directly experimental inquiry into the formation of character would be a number of human beings to bring up and educate from infancy to mature age; and to perform any one of these experiments with scientific propriety, it would be necessary to know and record every sensation or impression received by the young pupil from a period long before it could speak, including its own notions respecting the sources of all those sensations and impressions. It is not only impossible to do this completely, but even to do so much of it as should constitute a tolerable approximation. One apparently trivial circumstance which eluded our vigilance might let in a train of impressions and associations sufficient to vitiate the experiment as an authentic exhibition of the effects flowing from given causes. No one who has sufficiently reflected on education is ignorant of this truth: and whoever has not will find it most instructively illustrated in the writings of Rousseau and Helvetius on that great subject.

Under this impossibility of studying the laws of the formation of character by experiments purposely contrived to elucidate them there remains the resource of simple observation. But if it be impossible to ascertain the influencing circumstances with any approach to completeness even when we have the shaping of them ourselves, much more impossible is it when the cases are further removed from our observation, and altogether out of our control. Consider the difficulty of the very first step—of ascertaining what actually is the character of the individual in each particular case that we examine. There is hardly any person living, concerning some essential part of whose character there are not differences of opinion even among his intimate acquaintances; and a single action, or conduct continued only for a short time, goes a very little way towards ascertaining it. We can only make our observations in a rough way and *en masse*, not attempting to ascertain completely in any given instance what character has been formed, and still less by what causes; but only observing in what state of previous circumstances it is found that certain marked mental qualities or deficiencies *oftenest* exist. These conclusions, besides that they are mere approximate generalisations, deserve no reliance, even as such, unless the instances are sufficiently numerous to eliminate not only chance, but every assignable circumstance in which a number of the cases examined may happen to have resembled one another. So numerous and various, too, are the circumstances which form individual character, that the consequence of any particular combination is hardly ever some definite and strongly marked character, always found where that combination exists, and not otherwise. What is obtained, even after the most extensive and accurate observation, is merely a comparative result; as, for example, that in a given number of Frenchmen, taken indiscriminately, there will be found more persons of a particular mental tendency, and fewer of the contrary tendency, than among an equal number of Italians or English, similarly taken; or thus: of a hundred Frenchmen and an equal number of Englishmen, fairly selected, and arranged according to the degree in which they possess a particular mental characteristic, each number 1, 2, 3, &c., of the one series will be found to possess more of that characteristic than the corresponding number of the other. Since, therefore, the comparison is not one of kinds, but of ratios and degrees; and since in proportion as the differences are slight, it requires a greater number of instances to eliminate chance; it cannot often happen to any one to know a sufficient number of cases with the accuracy requisite for making the sort of comparison last mentioned; less than which, however, would not constitute a real induction. Accordingly there is hardly one current opinion respecting the characters of nations, classes, or descriptions of persons, which is universally acknowledged as indisputable.

4. Since, then, it is impossible to obtain really accurate propositions respecting the formation of character from observation and experiment alone, we are driven perforce to that which, even if it had not been the indispensable, would have been the most perfect mode of investigation, and which it is one of the principal aims of philosophy to extend; namely, that which tries its experiments not on the complex facts, but on the simple ones of which they are compounded, and after ascertaining the laws of the causes, the composition of which gives rise to the complex phenomena, then considers whether these will not explain and account for the approximate generalisations which have been framed empirically respecting the sequences of those complex phenomena. The laws of the formation of character are, in short, derivative laws, resulting from the general laws of mind, and are to be obtained by deducing them from those general laws by supposing any given set of circumstances, and then considering what, according to the laws of mind, will be the influence of those circumstances on the formation of character.

A science is thus formed, to which I would propose to give the name of Ethology, or the Science of Character, from ηθος a word more nearly corresponding to the term *character*, as I here use it, than any other word in the same language. The name is perhaps etymologically applicable to the entire science of our mental and moral nature; but if, as is usual and convenient, we employ the name Psychology for the science of the elementary laws of mind, Ethology will serve for the ulterior science which determines the kind of character produced in conformity to those general laws, by any set of circumstances, physical and moral. According to this definition, Ethology is the science which corresponds to the act of education, the widest sense of the term, including the formation of national or collective character, as well as individual. It would indeed be vain to expect (however completely the laws of the formation of character might be ascertained) that we could know so accurately the circumstances of any given case as to be able positively to predict the character that would be produced in that case. But we must remember that a degree of knowledge far short of the power of actual prediction is often of much practical value. There may be great power of influencing phenomena, with a very imperfect knowledge of the causes by which they are in any given instance determined. It is enough that we know that certain means have a *tendency* to produce a given effect, and that others have a tendency to frustrate it. When the circumstances of an individual or of a nation are in any considerable degree under our control, we may, by our knowledge of tendencies, be enabled to shape those circumstances in a manner much more favourable to the ends we desire than the shape which they would of themselves assume. This is the limit of our power, but within this limit the power is a most important one.

This science of Ethology may be called the Exact Science of Human Nature; for its truths are not, like the empirical laws which depend on them, approximate generalisations, but real laws. It is, however, (as in all cases of complex phenomena,) necessary to the exactness of the propositions that they should be hypothetical only, and affirm tendencies, not facts. They must not assert that something will always or certainly happen, but only that such and such will be the effect of a given cause, so far as it operates uncounteracted. It is a scientific proposition that bodily strength tends to make men courageous; not that it always makes them so; that an interest on one side of a question tends to bias the judgment; not that it invariably does so; that experience tends to give wisdom; not that such is always its effect. These propositions, being assertive only of tendencies, are not the less universally true because the tendencies may be frustrated.

James Braid: ca. 1795-1860

THE POWER OF THE MIND OVER THE BODY *

1846

Few publications have lately issued from the press so well calculated to excite general interest and inquiry, as Baron Von Reichenbach's *Researches on Magnetism.* The high reputation of the author, as well as that of his learned translator and annotator, Professor Gregory, who has furnished a condensed view of the subject in an English Dress, were all calculated to produce an effect—the greater, because the subject discussed was represented as bringing under our notice "a new imponderable," through which we should realize a clear and satisfactory solution of many problems in the mental and physical constitution of man, which had puzzled and perplexed alike the savage and the sage from the earliest ages.

The vast interest which the above-named brochure has created, is evinced by the extent to which it has been quoted, referred to, and reviewed in our numerous periodicals. Nor is it devoid of interest to observe the various awards of these different authorities. Thus, one quotes at great length, and not only with seriousness sets down the whole as fully established, but, moreover, with much self-complacency exults in the proof thereby adduced of the correctness of all the most extreme views he and other Mesmerists may have promulgated on certain points of this keenly debated science; whilst another writes a clever burlesque article holding up the whole speculation as worthy only of unsparing ridicule. Between these two extremes, again, we have every grade of approval or scepticism.

On the first announcement of Dr. Gregory's abstract of Baron Reichenbach's *Researches on Magnetism,* I lost no time in procuring a copy, which I perused with intense interest. I had not proceeded far, however, when my experience with hypnotic patients enabled me to perceive a source of fallacy, of which the Baron must either have been ignorant, or which he had entirely overlooked. From whatever cause this oversight

* The phenomena publicized by Mesmer and his followers were attributed to animal magnetism. Braid coined the modern term hypnotism, and attributed the phenomena entirely to the power of mind over body. He dealt with waking suggestion, as well as with hypnotism. While his best known publication was entitled *Neurypnology, or, the Rationale of Nervous Sleep; considered in Relation with Animal Magnetism* (1843), the pamphlet from which pages 3-19 and 31-36 are here reproduced seems to give more succinctly and concretely Braid's techniques and views. This pamphlet was published by John Churchill, London in 1846.

had arisen, I felt confident that, however carefully and perseveringly he had prosecuted his experiments, and however well-calculated they had been for determining mere physical facts, still no reliance could be placed upon the accuracy of conclusions drawn from premises assumed as true, where especial care had not been taken to guard against the source of fallacy to which I refer—viz., the important influence of the mental part of the process, which is in active operation with patients during such experiments. I therefore resolved to repeat his experiments, paying the strictest attention to this point; and, as I had anticipated, the results were quite opposed to the conclusions of Baron Reichenbach. It is with considerable diffidence that I venture to publish an opinion opposed to such high authority; but I shall briefly state the grounds of my own opinion, and leave it to others to repeat the experiments, and determine which opinion is nearer the truth. The observations which I have to submit may, moreover, prove suggestive to others, and enable them not only to avoid sources of fallacy with which I am familiar, but may also lead to the detection of many which may have escaped my own observation.

The great aim of Baron Reichenbach's researches in this department of science has been to establish the existence of a new imponderable, and to determine its qualities and powers in reference to matter and other forces, vital and inanimate. It unfortunately happens, however, that the only test of this alleged new force (with one solitary exception, and that as I thought by no means a satisfactory one) is the human nerve; and not only so, but it is further admitted that its existence can only be demonstrated by certain impressions imparted to, or experienced by, a comparatively small number of highly sensitive and nervous subjects. But it is an undoubted fact that with many individuals, and especially of the highly nervous, and imaginative, and abstractive classes, a strong direction of inward consciousness to any part of the body, especially if attended with the expectation or belief of something being about to happen, is quite sufficient to change the physical action of the part, and to produce such impressions from this cause alone, as Baron Reichenbach attributes to his new force. Thus every variety of feeling may be excited from an internal or mental cause—such as heat or cold, pricking, creeping, tingling, spasmodic twitching of muscles, catalepsy, a feeling of attraction or repulsion, sights of every form or hue, odours, tastes, and sounds, in endless variety, and so on, according as accident or intention may have suggested. Moreover, the oftener such impressions have been excited, the more readily may they be reproduced, under similar circumstances, through the laws of association and habit. Such being the fact, it must consequently be obvious to every intelligent and unprejudiced person, that no implicit reliance can be placed on the human nerve, as a test of this new power in producing effects from external impressions or influences, when precisely the same phenomena may arise from an internal or mental influence, when no external agency whatever is in operation.

In order to guard against this source of fallacy, therefore, I considered it would be the best mode to throw patients into the nervous sleep, and then operate on such of them as I knew had no use of their eyes during the sleep (for some patients have), and to take accurate notice of the results when a magnet capable of lifting fourteen pounds was drawn over the hand and other parts of the body without contact, after the manner described as performed by Baron Reichenbach in his experiments.

I experimented accordingly, and the results were, that in no instance was there the slightest effect manifested, unless when the magnet was brought so near as to enable the patient to feel the abstraction of heat, (producing a sensation of cold), when a feeling of discomfort was manifested, with a disposition to move the hand, or head, or face, as the case might be, from the offending cause. This indication was precisely the same when the armature was attached, as when the magnet was open; and in both cases, if I suffered the magnet to touch the patient, instantly the part was hurriedly withdrawn, as I have always seen manifested during the primary stage of hypnotism, when the patients were touched with any cold object. Now, inasmuch as patients in this condition, generally, if not always, manifest their perceptions of external impressions by the most natural movements, unless the natural law has been subverted by some preconceived notion or suggested idea to the contrary, and as I have operated with similar results upon a considerable number of patients, we have thus satisfactory proof that there was no real attractive power of a magnetic or other nature, tending to draw the patient, or any of his members, so as to cause an adhesion between his body and the magnet, as between the latter and iron, as Baron Reichenbach had alleged. I conclude, therefore, that the phenomena of apparent attraction manifested in his cases were due entirely to a mental influence; and I shall presently prove that this is quite adequate to the production of such effects.

But I must now give an extract, so as to state Baron Reichenbach's views, as expressed in Professor Gregory's abstract.

Magnets of 10 lbs. supporting power, when drawn along the body, without contact, produce certain sensations in a certain proportion of human beings. Occasionally, out of twenty, three, or four sensitive individuals are found; and in one case, out of twenty-two females examined by the author eighteen were found sensitive.

The sensation is rather unpleasant than agreeable, and is like an aura: in some cases warm, in other cool; or it may be a pricking, or the sensation of the creeping of insects on the skin; sometimes headache comes on rapidly. These effects occur when the patient does not see the magnet, nor know what is doing; they occur both in males and females, though more frequently in females; they are sometimes seen in strong, healthy people, but oftener in those whose health, though good, is not so vigorous, and in what are called nervous persons. Children are frequently found to be sensitive. Persons affected with spasmodic diseases, those who suffer from epilepsy, catalepsy, chorea, paralysis, and hysteria, are particularly sensitive. Lunatics and somnambulists are uniformly sensitive. The magnet is consequently an agent capable of affecting the living body. The object of the author is to solve some of the disputed questions, and to bring a number of phenomena under fixed physical laws.

Healthy sensitive subjects observe nothing farther than the sensations above noticed, and experience no inconvenience from the approach of magnets; but the diseased sensitive subjects experience different sensations, often disagreeable, and occasionally giving rise to fainting, to attacks of catalepsy, and to spasms so violent that they might possibly endanger life. In such cases, which generally include somnambulists, there occurs an extra-ordinary acuteness of the senses; smell and taste, for example, become astonishingly delicate and acute; many kinds of food become intolerable, and the perfumes most agreeable at other times become offensive. The patients hear and understand what is spoken three or four rooms off, and their vision is often so irritable, that, on the one hand, they cannot endure the sun's light, or that of a fire; while, on the other, they are able, in very dark rooms, to distinguish, not only the outlines, but also the colours of objects, where healthy people cannot distinguish anything at all. Up to this point, however strange the phenomena, there is nothing which may not be easily conceived, since animals and men differ very much in the acuteness of the senses, as is daily experienced.

Having met with a patient, Mlle. Nowotny, who was subject to catalepsy, who possessed such a high degree of acuteness of the senses, that "she could not endure the daylight, and in a dark night perceived her room as well lighted as it appeared to others in the twilight, so that she could quite well distinguish colours;" from a consideration of this circumstance, and remembering that the aurora borealis appears to be a phenomenon connected with terrestrial magnetism, or electro-magnetism, it occurred to the Baron "that possibly a patient of such acuteness of vision might see some luminous phenomenon about the magnet."

"The first experiment was performed by the patient's father;" no doubt by the suggestion of the Baron, and with the idea conveyed to him that some luminous appearance was likely to be discovered by the patient. It would be interesting to know whether the patient had not also been led, by some means, to understand the object of the inquiry, as such expectation, according to my own experience with such subjects, was quite adequate to the production of the expected phenomenon; and, moreover, once realized, it would be liable to recur ever after, under the same combination of circumstances.

In profound darkness, a horse-shoe magnet of nine elements, capable of carrying 80 lbs., was presented to the patient, the armature being removed; and she saw a distinct and continued luminous appearance, which uniformly disappeared, when the armature was applied.

The second experiment was made on her recovery from a cataleptic attack, when the excitability of her senses was greatest. She saw two luminous objects, one at each pole, (the magnet was open,) which disappeared on joining the poles, and reappeared on removing the armature. At the moment of breaking contact, the light was somewhat stronger. The appearance was the same at both poles, without any apparent tendency to unite. Next to the metal, she described a luminous vapour, surrounded by rays, which rays were in constant shooting motion, lengthening and shortening themselves incessantly, and presenting, as she said, a singularly beautiful appearance. There was no resemblance to an ordinary fire; the colour of the light was pure white, sometimes mixed with iridescent colours.

The next patient "was far more sensitive to the magnet than the former." She declared that, at the moment the armature was withdrawn, she had seen fire rise from the magnet, the height of a small hand, white, but mixed with red and blue.

Mlle. Maix.—As often as the armature was removed from a large magnet, in the dark, she instantly saw the luminous appearance above the poles, about a hand-breadth in height. But when affected with spasms, she was more sensitive, and the phenomenon increased in her eyes amazingly. She not only now saw the magnetic light at the poles much larger than before, but she also perceived currents of light proceeding from the whole external surface of the magnet, weaker than at the poles, but leaving in her eyes a dazzling impression, which did not for a long time disappear.

Mlle. Barbara Reichel saw the magnetic light not only in the dark, but also in such a twilight as permitted the author to distinguish objects, and to arrange and alter the experiments. The more intense the darkness, the brighter and larger she saw the emanations; the more sharp and defined their outline, and the more distinct the play of colours.

In the dark she saw the magnet giving out light, when shut, as well as when open, with this difference, that in the former case there were no points where the light appeared concentrated; but all the edges, joints, and corners of the magnet gave out short flame-like lights, uniform in size, and in a constant undulatory motion. From the large magnet these were about as long as the thickness of a little finger; when the armature was removed, however, the light was concentrated at the two poles, from which the flames arose to about the height of eight inches and a half, rather broader than the bar.

At each depression, where two plates of the magnet were laid together, there appeared smaller flames ending in point-like sparks on the edges and corner.

These small flames appeared blue, the chief light was white below, yellow higher up, then red and green at top. It was not motionless, but flickered and undulated, or contracted by starts continually, with an appearance as of rays shooting forth. There was no appearance of mutual attraction, or mutual tendency towards each other of the flames, or from one pole to the other; and as in the case of Mlle. Nowotny both poles presented the same appearance.

Mlle. Reichel was tested with a straight magnet. At the pole pointing to the north, or negative end of the magnet, the flame was larger than at the opposite end; it was sometimes undulating, sometimes starting, and shot out rays as in the horse-shoe magnet; it was red below, blue in the middle, green at top.

In order to enable the reader to form a correct estimate of what is represented in these several narratives, I have quoted the more important parts verbatim; and by comparing the results recorded by the different patients, no one can fail to be struck with the remarkable discrepancy in their description of what has been alleged as a physical fact. All expected, as I presume, to see light, and they saw light or flames accordingly; but let us remark another result: Mlle. Nowotny, in her most sensitive state, saw luminous vapour surrounded by rays which were in a constant shooting motion. "The colour of the light was nearly pure white, sometimes mixed with iridescent colours." The appearance was the same at both poles; the length of the flames, about one-half or three-fourths of an inch. Mlle. Maix, in her ordinary state, saw flames (from the same magnet I presume,) a hand breadth in height, and when in the more sensitive state they were much larger; and she now saw currents of flame proceeding from the whole external surface of the magnet, but weaker than at the poles.

Mlle. B. Reichel saw the magnet giving out light, not only when open, but also when closed. When open, the flames from the poles were about eight inches high, those at the joining of the plates of the magnet about a finger's breadth in length. "These small flames appeared blue, the chief light was white below, yellow higher up, then red, and green at top." As with the others, both poles seemed to have given out similar appearances of light and flame. This same patient being experimented on with the above straight bar magnet, about a foot and a half long, we are told that, "at the pole pointing to north, or negative end of the magnet, the flame was larger than at the opposite end;" and we are further told that, "it was red below, blue in the middle, and green at the top." When we advance to the flames seen to be given out by crystals, from the human hand, and other forms of matter, we have equally discordant descriptions as to colour and size of the flames as seen by different sensitive subjects. Now, to my mind, these discordant statements, as to the colour of the flames, are quite fatal to the notion of such representations proving a physical fact; and in an especial manner is that remark applicable to the statement of Mlle. Reichel, who not only saw the colour different which was emanating from a straight bar magnet from that of the horseshoe variety, but also described the size of the flame as larger from the north pole of the straight bar magnet than from the other end, whereas it was always seen by her, as well as by others, to be the same size at both poles of a horse-shoe magnet. If there be a physical reality in these alleged flames and colours, there ought to be no discrepancies of this sort; and the fact of such discordant statements having been made will tend to prepare the mind of the reader for the solution of the problem which I have now to submit.

In prosecuting the inquiry, Baron Reichenbach considered he had not only proved the existence of this new force, which produced all the physical effects enumerated, with streams of light from the poles, and the power of attracting the human body, and adhering to it, as steel to the magnet—I say he alleged that he had established such a force, not only as residing in the magnet, in addition to the ordinary magnetic force, but moreover, that it was found equally active in crystals, where it existed quite pure and distinct from ordinary magnetism. He also now ascertained that his subjects could discover "that from the finger points of healthy men, fiery bundles of light streamed forth, exactly as from the poles of magnets and of crystals visible to the sensitive." He alleges, moreover, that he had proved that where it was passive, it could be excited into activity by the sun's rays, by the moon's rays, by starlight, by heat, by chemical or mechanical action, and finally, that this luminous or phosphorescent appearance, and certain other peculiar properties, might be discovered by the highly sensitive in almost every place, and from nearly every object or form of matter, solid or fluid, animate or inanimate. Also, that it could be conducted through all other matter, and that all substances, not naturally actively charged with it, could be so temporarily, by proximity and contact of those which were actively charged.

I have already stated the wonderful power of the human mind, when inward consciousness is strongly directed to any part of a sensitive person, in changing physical action, and leading the subject to attribute to an external cause what may have arisen entirely from an internal or mental cause. It has also been stated that, when I resorted to a mode of operating which rendered the subjects more highly sensitive to external influences, and at the same time was calculated to obviate any source of fallacy, as to mental emotion or expectation being directed to the part from their seeing what was being done, the results were in direct opposition to what was represented as having been realized by the Baron. I have particularly adverted to this in respect to the alleged attraction of the magnet for the human frame; I have proved it to be equally so in respect to the human hand, and crystals, &c., where all sources of fallacy are guarded against. In my experience, moreover, with such cases, no light or flames have been perceived by patients either from the poles of a magnet, crystals, the points of the fingers, or other substance, unless the patients have been previously penetrated with some idea of the sort, or have been plied with such questions as were calculated to excite notions, when various answers were given accordingly, and when in the sleep, there appeared an equal aptitude to see something when neither magnet nor fingers were in the direction indicated, as when they were—a clear proof that the impressions were entirely imaginary, or mental in their origin.

I shall now proceed to detail the results of experiments with patients when wide awake, and when they had an opportunity of seeing what was being done, and expected something to happen; and also when the same patients saw nothing of what was doing, but supposed I was operating, and consequently expected something to occur.

With nearly all the patients I have tried, many of whom had never been hypnotised or mesmerised, when drawing the magnet or other object slowly from the wrist to the points of the fingers, various effects were realized, such as a change of temperature, tingling, creeping, pricking, spasmodic twitching, catalepsy of the fingers, or arm, or both; and reversing the motion was generally followed by a change of symptoms, from the altered current of ideas thereby suggested. Moreover; if any idea of what might be expected existed in the mind previously, or was suggested orally, during the process, it was generally very speedily realized. The above patients being now requested to look aside, or a screen having been interposed, so as to prevent their seeing what was being done, and they were requested to describe their sensations during the repetition of the processes, similar phenomena were stated to be realized, even when there was nothing whatever done, beyond watching them, and noting their responses. They believed the processes were being repeated, and had their minds directed to the part, and thus the physical action was excited, so as actually to lead them to believe and describe their feelings as arising from external impressions.

The above fact was most remarkably evinced in a young gentleman, twenty-one years of age. I first operated in this manner on his right hand, by drawing a powerful horse-shoe magnet over the hand, without contact, whilst the armature was attached. He immediately observed a sensation of cold follow the course of the magnet. I reversed the passes, and he felt it less cold, but he felt no attraction between his hand and the magnet. I then removed the cross-bar, and tried the effect with both poles alternatively, but still there was no change in the effect, and decidedly no proof of attraction between his hand and the magnet. In the afternoon of the same day I desired him to look aside and hold his hat between his eyes and his hand, and observe the effects when I operated on him, whilst he could not see my proceedings. He very soon described a recurrence of the same sort of sensations as those he felt in the morning, but they speedily became more intense and extended up the arm, producing rigidity of the member. In the course of two minutes this feeling attacked the other arm, and to some extent the whole body, and he was, moreover, seized with a fit of involuntary laughter, like that of hysteria, which continued for several minutes—in fact, until I put an end to the experiment. His first remark was, "Now this experiment clearly proves that there must be some intimate connection between mineral magnetism and Mesmerism, for I was most strangely affected, and could not possibly resist laughing during the extraordinary sensations with which my whole body was seized, as you drew the magnet over my hand and arm." I replied that I drew a very different conclusion from the experiments, as I had never used the magnet at all, nor held it, nor anything else, near to him; and that the whole proved the truth of my position as to the extraordinary power of mind over the body, and how mental impressions could change physical action.

I operated on two other gentlemen the same day, who were much older, and with decidedly marked effects in both, though less so than in the last case. The experiment being tried with a lady of fifty-six years of age, by drawing a gold pencil-case slowly from the wrist to the finger ends, a creeping, twitching, sensation was felt, which increased until it became very unpleasant, and excited a drawing, crampy feeling in the fingers of that hand. On causing her to look aside, watch, and describe her feelings during my subsequent operations, the results were similar, and that whilst I had done nothing; and the whole, therefore, was attributable to the power of the mind in changing the physical action.

Another interesting case of a married lady, I experimented with in presence of her husband, as follows. I requested her to place her hand on the table, with the palm upwards, so situated as to enable her to observe the process I was about to resort to. I had previously remarked, that by my drawing something slowly over the hand, without contact, whilst the patient concentrated her attention on the process, that she would experience some peculiar sensations in consequence. I took a pair of her scissors, and drew the bowl of the handle, slowly from the wrist downwards. I had only done so a few times, when she felt a creeping, chilly sensation, which was immediately followed by a spasmodic twitching of the muscles, so as to toss the hand from the table, as the members of a prepared frog are agitated when galvanised. I next desired her to place her other hand on the table, in like manner, but placed so, that by turning her head in the opposite direction, she might not see what was being done, and to watch her sensations in that hand, and tell us the result. In about the same length of time, similar phenomena were manifested, as with the other hand, although in this instance I had done nothing whatever, and was not near her hand. I now desired her to watch what happened to her hand, when I predicated that she would feel it become cold, and the result was as predicted, and vice versa, predicating that she would feel it become intensely hot, such was realized. When I desired her to think of the tip of her nose, the predicated result either of heat or cold, was speedily realized in that part.

Another lady, twenty-eight years of age, being operated on in the same manner, whilst looking at my proceedings, in the course of half-a-minute, described the sensation as that of the blood rushing into the fingers; and when the motion of my pencil-case was from below, upwards, the sensation was that of the current of blood being reversed, but less rapid in its motion. On resuming the downward direction, the original feeling recurred, still more powerfully that at first. This lady being requested now to look aside, whilst I operated, realized similar sensations, and that whilst I was doing nothing.

The husband of this lady, twenty-eight and a half years of age, came into the room, shortly after the above experiment was finished. She was very desirous of my trying the effect upon him, as he was in perfect health. I requested him to extend his right arm laterally, and let it rest on a chair with the palm upwards, to turn his head in the opposite direction, so that he might not see what I was doing, and to concentrate his attention on the feelings which might arise, during my process. In about half-a-minute he felt an aura like a breath of air passing along the hand; in a little after, a slight pricking, and presently a feeling passed along the arm, as far as the elbow, which he described as similar to that of being slightly electrified. All this, while I had been doing nothing, beyond watching what might be realized. I then desired him to tell me what he felt *Now*,–speaking in such a tone of voice, as was calculated to lead him to believe I was operating in some different manner. The result was that the former sensations ceased; but, when I requested him once more, to tell me what he felt now, the former sensations recurred. I then whispered to his wife, but in a tone sufficiently loud to be overheard by him, observe now, and you will find his fingers begin to draw, and hand will become clenched,–see how the little finger begins to move, and such was the case; see the next one also going in like manner, and such effects followed; and finally, the entire hand closed firmly, with a very unpleasant drawing motion of the whole flexor-muscles of the fore-arm. I did nothing whatever to this patient until the fingers were nearly closed, when I touched the palm of his hand with the point of my finger, which caused it to close more rapidly and firmly. After it had remained so for a short time, I blew upon the hand, which dissipated the previously existing mental impression, and instantly the hand became relaxed. The high respectability and intelligence of this gentleman rendered his testimony very valuable; and especially so, when he was not only wide awake, but had never been either mesmerised, hypnotised, or so tested before.

Another gentleman, twenty-one years of age, was tried by drawing a gold pencil-case along the palm of the hand, without contact. At the fourth traction, he looking at the part and my process, he described a cold aura following the course of the pencil, then a pricking, and after a few more courses, he described it as rather a warm pricking sensation; such as that experienced from the sun's rays concentrated on the skin by a lens. By reversing the passes, from the points of the fingers towards the wrist, the aura was changed, and he described the sensation as that of forcing back the blood in the veins, when they are much distended. I then proposed to experiment on his other hand, whilst his head was held aside, when similar sensations were realized, although on this occasion I had done nothing,—the whole results having arisen from his own concentration of inward consciousness, changing the physical action of the part, and recalling his former association of ideas in reference to the other hand. I thereupon explained to him the law, (for he was a very acute young gentleman,) which seemed to obtain in the production of such phenomena, and desired him to satisfy himself of the fact, by concentrating his attention on the upper part of his foot, and watching the result. Here, also, he experienced similar sensations to arise, even whilst he was aware that I was doing nothing; but the effects took place less rapidly than was the case in the former experiments with his hands. It is also worthy of remark, that this gentleman experienced very severe headache to result from these experiments, which, however, I was enabled very speedily to remove by another process.

A lady thirty years of age was requested to hold out her right hand over the arm of an easy chair, whilst she turned her head to the left, to prevent her from seeing what I was doing, and to watch and describe to me the feelings she experienced in the hand during my process, which was to be performed without contact. She very soon felt a pricking in the point of the third finger, which increased in intensity, and at length extended up the arm. I then asked her how her thumb felt, and presently the same feeling was transferred to it; and when asked to attend to the middle of the forearm, in like manner the feeling was presently perceived there. All the time I had been doing nothing; the whole was the result of her own mind acting on her hand and arm. I now took the large magnet, and allowed her to watch me drawing it slowly over the hand, when the feeling was much as before, only that she felt the cold from the steel when brought very near to the skin. It was precisely the same when closed as when opened, and the same sensations occurred when the north pole alone was approximated, or the south alone, or both together. She experienced no sense of attraction between her hand and the magnet from either pole, nor from both combined. I now requested this lady to keep a steady gaze upon the poles of the large horseshoe magnet, and tell me if she saw anything, (the rooms was not darkened nor was the light strong) but nothing was visible. I then told her to look steadily, and she would see flame or fire come out of the poles. In a little after this announcement she started, and said, "Now I see it, it is red; how strange my eyes feel," and instantly she passed into the hypnotic state. This lady had been repeatedly hypnotised. I now took the opportunity of testing her as to the alleged power of the magnet to attract her hand when asleep, but, as in the other cases, the results were quite the contrary—the cold of the magnet (and of either pole alike) caused her to withdraw her hand the moment it touched her. I now requested her to tell me what she saw (she being still in the sleep). She said she still saw the red light. I desired her to put her finger to the place where she saw it. This she declined to do, being afraid that it would burn her. I thereupon assured her that it would not burn her, upon which she pointed to the same place where the magnet was held before she went into the sleep, instead of to where it was now held, which was near to her face, but towards the opposite side of the chair. This lady does not see from under her closed eyelids when hypnotised, as some patients do; and the evidence her testimony affords in support of my opinion upon this subject is very conclusive, as she is a lady of very superior mental attainments, and one whose testimony merits unlimited confidence.

I beg to call particular attention to the fact, that in this latter case, as with the fifth of the vigilant cases narrated, the first experiments were tried without any magnet or other object being pointed at or drawn over them, and still the mental influence was quite sufficient to change the physical action, and produce decided and characteristic effects, where there could be no influence from without, of the nature alleged by Baron Reichenbach and the mesmerists.

I had long been familiar with the fact, that during a certain stage of hypnotism, patients may be made to give various manifestations, or declarations of their feelings and emotions, according to previously existing ideas, or suggestions imparted to them during the sleep; and, moreover, that such associations once formed, were liable to recur ever after, under a similar combination of circumstances. As occurs in ordinary dreaming, they seem generally at once to adopt the idea as a reality, without taking the trouble of reasoning on the subject as to the probability of such ideas being only imaginary; and their extreme mobility in the hypnotic state at a certain stage renders them prompt with their corresponding physical response. In proof of this, and how readily those inattentive to these facts may misapprehend what they see realized in such cases, I beg to submit the following interesting illustration. When in London lately, I had the pleasure of calling upon an eminent and excellent physician, who is in the habit of using mesmerism in his practice, in suitable cases, just as he uses any other remedy. He spoke of the extraordinary effects which he had experienced from the use of magnets applied during the mesmeric state, and kindly offered to illustrate the fact on a patient who had been asleep all the time I was in the room, and in that stage, during which I felt assured she could overhear every word of our conversation. He told me, that when he put the magnet into her hands, it would produce catalepsy of the hands and arms, and such was the result. He wafted the hands and the catalepsy ceased. He said that a mere touch of the magnet on a limb, would stiffen it, and such he proved to be the fact.

I now told him, that I had got a little instrument in my pocket, which although far less than his, I felt assured would prove quite as powerful, and I offered to prove this by operating on the same patient, whom I had never seen before, and who was in the mesmeric state when I entered the room. My instrument was about three inches long, the thickness of a quill, with a ring attached to the end of it. I told him that when put into her hands, he would find it catalepsize both hands and arms as his had done, and such was the result. Having reduced this by wafting, I took my instrument from her, and again returned it, in another position, and told him it would now have the very reverse effect—that she would not be able to hold it, and that although I closed her hands on it, they would open, and that it would drop out of them, and such was the case, —to the great surprise of my worthy friend, who now desired to be informed what I had done to the instrument to invest it with this new and apposite power. This I declined doing for the present; but I promised to do so, when he had seen some further proofs of its remarkable powers. I now told him that a touch with it, on either extremity would cause the extremity to rise and become cataleptic, and such was the result; that a second touch on the same point would reduce the rigidity, and cause it to fall, and such again was proved to be the fact. After a variety of other experiments, every one of which proved precisely as I had predicted, she was aroused. I now applied the ring of my instrument on the third finger of the right hand, from which it was suspended, and told the doctor, that when it was so suspended, it would send her to sleep. To this he replied, "it never will," but I again told him that I felt confident that it would send her to sleep. We then were silent, and very speedily she was once more asleep. Having aroused her, I put the instrument on the second finger of her left hand, and told the doctor that it would be found she could *Not* go to sleep, when it was placed there. He said he thought she would, and he sat steadily gazing at her, but I said firmly and confidently that she would not. After a considerable time the doctor asked her if she did not feel sleepy, to which she replied "not at all;" could you rise and walk? when she told him she could. I then requested her to look at the point of the fore-finger of her right hand, which I told the doctor would send her to sleep, and such was the result; and, after being aroused, I desired her to keep a steady gaze at the nail of the thumb of the left hand which could send her to sleep in like manner, and such proved to be the fact.

Having repaired to another room, I explained to the doctor the real nature and powers of my little and apparently magical instrument—that it was nothing more than my portmanteau-key and ring, and that what had imparted to it such apparently varied powers was merely the predictions which the patient had overheard me make to him, acting upon her in the peculiar state of the nervous sleep, as irresistible impulses to be affected, according to the results she had heard me predict. Had I predicted that she would see any flame, or colour, or form, or substance, animate or inanimate, I know from experience that such would have been realized, and responded to by her; and that, not from any desire on her part to impose upon others, but because she was self-deceived, the vividness of her imagination in that state, inducing her to believe as real, what were only the figments of fancy, suggested to her mind by the remarks of others. The power of suggestions of this sort also, in paralyzing or energising muscular power is truly astounding; and may all arise in perfect good faith with almost all patients who have passed into the second conscious state, and with some, during the first conscious stage; and with some weak-minded, or highly imaginative or credulous and concentrative people, even in the waking condition. The latter constitutes that class of subjects who manifest what are called the "vigilant phenomena." The true cause of these "vigilant phenomena" is not a physical influence from without, but a mental delusion from within, which paralyzes their reason, and independent volition, so that for the time being they are mere puppets in the hands of another person by whom they are irresistibly controlled, so that they can only see, or hear, or taste, or feel, or act, in accordance with his will and direction. They have their whole attention fixed on what may be said or signified by this alleged superior power, and consequently perceive impressions through the excited state of the organs of sense, called into operation which they could not perceive in their ordinary condition; and this sort of clairvoyance or thought-reading, the mesmerists attribute to some special influence, such as the new imponderable of Reichenbach. So soon as patients can be made to believe that in the waking state, the evidence of their senses is more trust-worthy than mere idea or suggested impressions; and that they can really exercise their own independent powers in opposition to the alleged power of the will of another, through his auricular suggestions or passes, and other manoeuvres, it will instantly be found that the spell is broken, and that rational beings can no longer be magnetically tied together, or to chairs, or tables, or the floor; or made to see an object of every colour and hue, or metamorphosed into every nature, form, or creature, the operator may incline and indite. It may have been interesting enough to have demonstrated that the human mind could be so subjugated and controlled; but, as I have formerly said, and now repeat, I do not consider the continual repetition of such experiments in the waking state, as at all proper, or free from the danger of throwing the faculties of the mind of such subjects into a permanently morbid condition.

It would be inconsistent with the scope of this paper to enter into an elaborate detail of my views as to the philosophical explanation of the modes of exciting and varying certain trains of ideas, and their consequent manifestations during the nervous sleep. The inquiry is not only curious, but also one of great interest, in respect to the power of the mind in controlling physical action, and of physical impressions in reacting on the mind. I have given a pretty ample discussion on these topics in a second edition of my little work on hypnotism, now preparing for the press, to which I beg leave to refer those who feel desirous of prosecuting the inquiry, and particularly those who desire to do so for curative purposes.

In conclusion, I beg particularly to remark, that, whilst my experiments and observations are opposed to the theoretical notions of Baron Reichenbach and the mesmerists, in all the more important points, they directly confirm the reality of the facts, as to the power which we possess of artifically producing certain phenomena by certain processes; as also of intensifying aspects which arise in a minor degree, spontaneously, or by the patient's own unaided efforts. They allege that the exciting cause is the impulsion into the body of the patient from without of a portion of this new force; whilst I attribute it to a subjective or personal influence, namely, that of the mind and body of the patient acting and re-acting on each other in a particular manner, from an intense concentration of inward consciousness of one idea, or train of ideas, which may, to a certain extent, be controlled and directed by others. The latter power, however, merely arises from the mental and physical impressions producing still greater concentration of the patient's attention in a particular direction; that is to say, by concentrating their attention to the point over which they see anything drawn, or upon which a mechanical, calorific, frigorific, or electric impression is made, whereby a greater supply of nervous influence, blood, and vital action, is drawn to the part from the physical and mental resources of the patient himself, and not from the person or substance exciting those physical impressions. They enable the patient more effectually to concentrate his own vital powers, and thus to energise function; on the same principle as a patient afflicted with anaesthesia, or loss of feeling, is able to hold an object in his hand whilst he looks at it, but will allow it to drop when his eyes are averted.

It is worthy of particular remark, that my researches prove the power of concentration of attention, as not only capable of changing physical action, so as to make some patients, in the wide-waking state, imagine that they see and feel from an external influence what is due entirely to an internal or mental cause; but I have extended the researches, so as to prove, that the same law obtains in respect to all the other organs of special sense, and different functions of the body. My theoretical views, therefore, instead of diminishing, rather enhance the value of this power as a means of cure. They strikingly prove how much may be achieved by proper attention to, and direction of, this power of the human mind over the physical frame, and vice versa, in ameliorating the ills which flesh is heir to. I beg further to remark, in support of my views, that in the experiments of Baron Reichenbach, and the mesmerists generally, all which I have endeavoured to prove as unnecessary for the production of the phenomena referred to their alleged mesmeric fluid, or new force; of the latter, there is under such circumstances, as yet no direct and satisfactory proof; and it is unphilosophical to attribute to a new and extraneous force what can be reasonably accounted for from the independent physical and psychiatric powers of the patient, which must necessarily be in active operation.

The results of my experiments satisfactorily prove the efficacy of the mind; and the remarkable power of the soul over the body.

Ernst Heinrich Weber: 1795-1878

THE SENSE OF TOUCH AND THE COMMON FEELING *

1846

THE smallest perceptible difference between two weights, which we can distinguish by the feeling of muscular exertion, appears according to my experiments to be that between weights which stand approximately in the relation of 39 to 40: that is to say, of which one is about 1/40 heavier than the other. By means of the feeling of pressure, which two weights make upon our skin, all we are able to distinguish is a difference of weight that amounts to only 1/30, so that the weights accordingly stand in the relation of 29 to 30.

If we look at one line after another, any one who possesses a very exceptional visual discrimination can according to my experiments discover a difference between two lines whose lengths are related as 50:51, or even as 100:101. Those who have a less delicate visual discrimination distinguish lines which are separated from one another by 1/25 of their length. The smallest perceptible difference of the pitch of two tones, (which are really in unison), that a musician perceives, if he hears two tones successively, is according to Delezenne 1/4 *Komma* (81/80) 1/4. A lover of music according to him distinguishes only about 1/2 *Komma* (81/80) 1/2. If the tones are heard simultaneously we cannot, according to Delezenne's experiments, perceive such small tonal differences. 1/4 *Komma* is nearly the relation of 160:161.

I have shown that the result in the determination of weight is the same, whether one takes ounces or half ounces; for it does not depend upon the number of grains that form the increment of weight, but depends on the fact that this increment makes up the thirtieth or fiftieth (should be fortieth) part of the weight which we are comparing with the second weight. This likewise holds true of the comparison of the length of two lines and of the pitch of two tones. It makes no difference whether we compare lines that are, say, two inches or one inch long, if we examine them successively, and can see them lying parallel to each other; and yet

* The part of this publication here reproduced is a restatement and amplification of the principle implied in Weber's paper of 1834, previously cited. The translation is by Benjamin Rand. Permission to reprint this translation has been granted by the Houghton Mifflin Co., publishers of *The Classical Psychologists*.

the extent by which the one line exceeds the other is in the former case twice as great as in the latter. To be sure, if both lines lie close together and parallel, we compare only the ends of the lines to discover how much the one line exceeds the other; and in this test the question is only how great that length of line which overlaps the other really is, and how near the two lines lie to one another.

So too in the comparison of the pitch of two tones, it does not matter whether the two tones are seven tonal stops (i.e. an octave) higher or lower, provided only they do not lie at the end of the tonal series, where the exact discrimination of small tonal differences becomes more difficult. Here again, therefore, it is not a question of the number of vibrations, by which the one tone exceeds the other, but of the relation of the numbers of the vibrations of the two tones. It would be conceivable, that we should pay attention only to the number of vibrations by which one tone exceeds the other. If we fix the eyes first upon one line and afterwards upon a second, and thus permit both to be pictured successively upon the most sensitive parts of the retina, and that we thereby perceived how much the second image exceeds the first, and conversely. For this is the way we compare two scale-units: we place one upon the other, so that they coincide, and thus perceive how much the one exceeds the other. From the fact, that we do not employ this method which is so very advantageous, it seems to follow, that we are unable to employ it, and that therefore the preceding impression left behind no such trace upon the retina, or in the brain, as would permit of comparison in the manner mentioned with succeeding impressions. That it is possible for us to proceed otherwise in the comparison of the length of two lines appears from the fact that we can compare two lines, which are longer than we can picture at once in their entirety on the most sensitive part of the retina. In this case we must move the eye and thereby cause the different parts of the same line to be pictured successively upon the same parts of the retina. Under these circumstances we must take account of the movement of the eye, and only thus do we form an idea of the length of the lines. Were the impressions of visible things, which we preserve in memory, traces, which the sensuous impressions left behind in the brain, and whose spatial relations correspond to the spatial relations of the sensuous impressions, and were thus so to speak photographs of the same, it would be difficult to remember a figure, which is larger than could be pictured at once wholly upon the sensitive part of the retina. It appears to me, indeed, as if a figure, which we can survey at a single glance, impressed itself better upon our memory and our imagination, than a figure, which we can survey only successively by moving the eyes; but we can nevertheless represent also the former by means of the imagination. But in this case the representation of the whole figure seems to be composed by us of the parts which we perceive all at once.

If we compare two lines, which are 20 and 21 *Linien* (i.e. 1/10 of an inch) long, the latter is 1/20 longer, but the absolute difference of length amounts to 1 *Linie*. If, on the other other hand, we compare two lines, which are 1 *Linie* and 1.05 *Linie* long, the difference amounts also to 1/20, but the line is only 1/20 *Linie* longer than the other. Consequently in the latter case the absolute difference is 20 times smaller. But 1/20 *Linie* is a size like a fine pinhole which lies at the very threshold of vision. The smallest possible point that we are able to see, is one whose diameter amounts to 1/20 *Linie*, and yet one who has a very good visual discrimination can distinguish in respect to their length two lines of which one is 1/20 *Linie* longer than the other. Two observers, before whom I placed such lines, both distinguished the longer from the shorter, and their visual discrimination extended even farther. I myself distinguished two lines, whose relative difference of length amounted to 1/20, and of which the one was between 1/17 and 1/18 *Linie* longer than the other. The apprehension of the relations of whole magnitudes, without our having measured the magnitudes by a smaller scale-unit, and without our having ascertained the absolute difference between them, is a most interesting psychological phenomenon. In music we apprehend the relations of tone, without knowing their rate of vibration (i.e., their absolute pitch); in architecture, the relation of spatial magnitudes, without having determined them by inches; and in the same way we apprehend the magnitudes of sensation or of force in the comparison of weights.

Herman von Helmholtz: 1821-1894

ON THE RATE OF TRANSMISSION OF THE NERVE IMPULSE *

1850

I HAVE found that there is a measurable period of time during which the effect of a stimulus consisting of a momentary electrical current applied to the iliac plexus of a frog is transmitted to the calf muscles at the entrance of the crural nerve. In the case of large frogs with nerves 50–60 mm. in length, which I preserved at a temperature of 2–6° C. while the temperature of the observation chamber was 11–15°, this period of time amounted to 0.0014 to 0.0020 of a second.

The stimulation of the nerve was given by means of an induction coil. By means of a special mechanical device, a second electrical current was transmitted to a galvanometer at the moment the original current was transmitted to the induction coil. I convinced myself that the error of measurement amounted to considerably less than 1/10 of the period of time with which we are here concerned. The current flowed through the induction coil until the stimulated gastrocnemius muscle had contracted sufficiently to lift a weight which was suspended by a platinum point on a gold-plated support. The lifting of the weight interrupted the current to the induction coil and to the galvanometer. The duration of the current, therefore, was exactly equal to the period elapsing from the application of the stimulation to the nerve to the commencement of the mechanical reaction of the muscle. The effect produced by the current on the galvanometer is proportional to the duration of the current. The time period may be calculated from the oscillation of the galvanometer when the oscillation which would result from known current is also known. I measured the deviation with mirror and telescope. In its essentials the procedure coincides with that of Pouillet for measurements of short periods of time.

The results are the following:

After a standard stimulus the time required for the muscle to lift the attached weight is longer the heavier the weight.

* This is Helmholtz's first brief report on the speed of the nerve impulse. It appeared in *Monatsberichten der Akademie der Wissenschaften zu Berlin*, January 21, 1850. Mrs. Alfred G. Dietze has made the translation.

Time is modified by varying the intensity of stimulation or sensitivity of the muscle, also the height to which the muscle lifts the weight.

Usually, but not always, the weight is lifted less high when the upper end of the sciatic nerve is stimulated than when the area adjacent to the muscle is stimulated. This fact coincides with the well-known findings of nerve degeneration, when the nerve is severed from the nerve center. In any case, an equal height of lifting may be brought about by reducing the force of the induction currents in the distal area. The galvanometer then indicates that, in stimulating the distal end of the nerve, the same mechanical effect regularly occurs earlier, than by stimulation of the proximal end. In the case of the same specimens, this difference is constant and is independent of the attached weights. In a series of observations with different specimens, the difference varied between 0.0014 and 0.0020 sec. The higher figures occurred on colder days. In experiments with smaller weights, the individual twitches are somewhat less regular, and the constant amount of difference must be calculated from the averages of the experimental series, while, in the case of 100 to 180 gr. weights, this amount may be found directly from a comparison of the individual recordings.

Hermann von Helmholtz: 1821-1894

THE YOUNG-HELMHOLTZ THEORY OF COLOR VISION *

1860

THEORY OF COLOR VISION

THE facts to be deduced from the laws of color-mixture, that three constituents of sensation which proceed independently of one another are produced by external stimulation, have received their more definite and more significant expression in the hypotheses, which assume, that these different constituents are excited and transmitted in different portions of the optic nerve; but that they simultaneously attain to consciousness, and thereby, so far as they have become excited from the same place of the retina, they are also localized in the same place of the field of vision.

Such a theory was first proposed by Thomas Young.[1] The more detailed development of it is essentially conditioned by the fact, that its author would ascribe to the sensitive nerves of the eye only the properties and capacities, which we positively know as belonging to the motor nerves of men and of animals. We have a much more favorable opportunity to discover these latter by experiments than is the case with the nerves of sensation, since we are able comparatively easily and definitely both to discern and to measure the finest changes of their excitation and

* Helmholtz rediscovered Young's brief statement of his tri-chromatic theory and referred to it in 1852, and included a fuller statement of it in his *Physiological Optics* in 1860. The present translation by Benjamin Rand, first published in *The Classical Psychologists* and reprinted by permission of the Houghton Mifflin Co., is from the second German edition, 1896.

[1] Thomas Young's theory of color vision is as follows: "From three simple sensations, with their combinations, we obtain seven primitive distinctions of colours; but the different proportions, in which they may be combined, afford a variety of traits beyond all calculation. The three simple sensations being red, green, and violet, the three binary combinations are yellow, consisting of red and green; crimson, of red and violet; and blue, of green and violet; and the seventh in order is white light, composed by all three united. But the blue thus produced by combining the whole of the green and violet rays, is not the blue of the spectrum, for four parts of green and one of violet make a blue differing very little from green; while the blue of the spectrum appears to contain as much violet as green: and it is for this reason that red and blue usually make a purple, deriving its hue from the predominance of the violet." Thomas Young's *A Course of Lectures on Natural Philosophy*. London, 1807, I, 440. [Editor's note: While Helmholtz refers to a 1807 publication by Young, Young's theory appeared as early as 1802 as shown by the selection reprinted on page 112 of these readings.]

excitability by means of the contractions occurring in the muscles, and their changes. What we furthermore have been able to ascertain concerning the structure, the chemical constitution, the excitability, the conductivity, and the electrical behavior of the sensitive nerves, harmonises so perfectly with the corresponding behavior of the motor nerves, that fundamental differences in the nature of their activity are extremely improbable, at least so far as these do not depend upon the other organic apparatus connected with them, upon which they exert their influence.

Now we know in regard to motor nerves only the contrast between the state of rest and of activity. In the former state the nerve can remain unaltered a long time without important chemical change or development of heat; and at the same time the muscle dependent upon the nerve remains lax. If we stimulate the nerve, heat develops in it material changes, electrical oscillations are shown, and the muscle is contracted. In a cut nerve-preparation the sensitiveness is quickly lost, probably on account of the expansion of the chemical constituents necessary for activity. Under the action of atmospheric oxygen, or better still of the arterial blood containing oxygen, the sensitiveness is wholly or partially slowly restored, save that these processes of restoration excite contractions of the muscle, or changes of electrical relation in nerve and muscle coincident with the activity. We are acquainted also with no external means which can produce this process of restoration so quickly and intensively, and which can permit it at the same time so suddenly to appear and again to cease, as would be necessary, if this process were to serve as the physiological basis of a powerful sensation occurring with precision.

If we confine our assumptions concerning the development of a theory of color vision to the properties belonging with certainty to the nerves, there is present in fairly secure outline the theory of Thomas Young.

The sensation of dark corresponds to the state of rest of the optic nerve, that of colored or white light to an excitement of it. The three simple sensations which correspond to the excitement only of a single one of the three nerve systems, and from which all the others can be composed, must correspond in the table of colors to the three angles of the color triangle.

In order to assume the finest possible color sensation not demonstrable by objective stimulus, it appears appropriate so to select the angles of the color triangle that its sides include in the closest possible way the curves of the colors of the spectrum.

Thomas Young has therefore assumed:

1. There are in the eye three kinds of nerve fibres. The excitation of the first produces the sensation of red; the excitation of the second, the sensation of green; the excitation of the third, the sensation of violet.

2. Objective homogeneous light excites these three kinds of fibres with an intensity which varies according to the length of the wave. The fibres sensitive to red are excited most strongly by light of the greatest

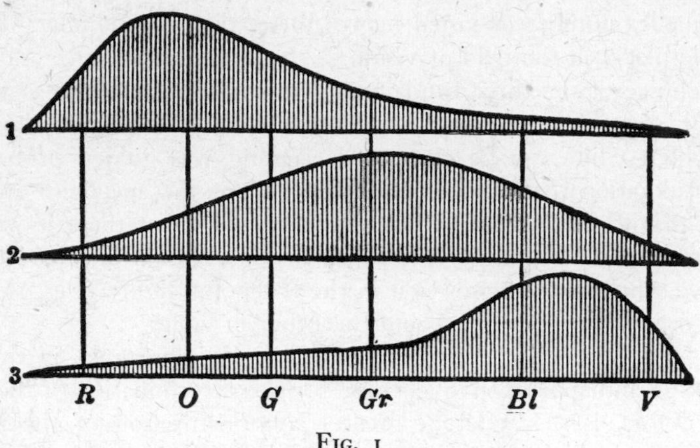

Fig. 1

wave-length; and those sensitive to violet by light of the smallest wave-length. Nevertheless, it is not precluded, but rather to be assumed, for the explanation of a series of phenomena, that each color of the spectrum excites all the kinds of fibres, but with different intensity. If we suppose in Fig. 1 the spectrum colors placed horizontally and in their natural order, beginning from red R up to violet V, the three curves may represent more or less exactly the strength of the excitation of the three kinds of fibres: no. 1 those sensitive to red; no. 2 those sensitive to green; and no. 3 those sensitive to violet.

The simple red excites strongly the fibres sensitive to red, and weakly the two other kinds of fibres; sensation: red.

The simple yellow excites moderately the fibres sensitive to red and green, weakly the violet; sensation: yellow.

The simple green excites strongly the fibres sensitive to green, much more weakly the two other kinds; sensation: green.

The simple blue excites moderately the fibres sensitive to green and violet, weakly the red; sensation: blue.

The simple violet excites strongly the fibres which belong to it, and weakly the others; sensation: violet.

The excitation of all the fibres of nearly equal strength gives the sensation of white, or of whitish colors.

Perhaps it may be objected at first view to this hypothesis, that three times the number of nerve fibres and nerve endings must be presumed than in the older assumption, according to which each separate nerve fibre was thought capable of transmitting all kinds of chromatic excitations. But I do not believe, that in this connection the supposition of Young is in contradiction with the anatomical facts. An hypothesis was previously discussed, which explains the accuracy of sight by the aid of much smaller number of visual nerve fibres, than the number of distinguishable places in the field of vision.

The choice of the three fundamental colors seems at first, as we have observed, somewhat arbitrary. Any other three colors might be chosen from which white can be composed. Young was guided probably by the consideration that the colors at the end of the spectrum appear to claim a privileged position. If we were not to select these it would be necessary to take for one of the fundamental colors a purple shade, and the curve which corresponds to it in the foregoing figure (Fig. 1), would have two maxima: one in red, and the other in violet.

The single circumstance, which is of direct importance in the mode of sensation and appears to give a clue for the determination of the fundamental colors, is the apparent greater color-saturation of the red and violet; a thing which also manifests itself, although indeed less markedly, for green. Since we style colors the more saturated the farther they are removed from white, we must expect that great saturation must belong particularly to those colors of the spectrum which produce most purely the simplest sensations of color. In fact, these colors, if they are very pure, have even with inferior brilliancy, something of an intensively glowing, almost dazzling quality. There are especially red, violet, or blue violet flowers, e.g. of the cameraria, whose colors display this characteristic blending of darkness and brilliancy. Young's hypothesis affords for this a simple explanation. A dark color can cause an intensive excitation of one of the three nerve systems, while the corresponding bright white causes a much weaker excitation of the same. The difference appears analogous to that between the sensation of very hot water upon a small portion of the skin and lukewarm water striking a greater surface.

In particular violet makes upon me this impression of a deeply saturated color. But inasmuch as the strictly violet rays, even when they occur in sunlight, are of slight intensity and are modified by fluorescence, ultramarine blue, which has far the advantage of greater intensity of light, produces an effect approximately equal to it. The strictly pure violet of the spectrum is very little known among the laity, since the violet pigments give nearly always the effect of a slight admixture of red, or appear very dark. For that very reason, the shades of the ultramarine blue coming near to the violet excite the general attention much more, are much better known, and are designated by a much older name,—that of blue,—than the violet strictly so called. In addition one has in the deep ultramarine blue of the cloudless sky a highly imposing, well-known, and constant example of this color.

In this fact I seek the reason why in former times blue has always been regarded as the one fundamental color. And the more recent observers, like Maxwell and A. Konig, who have sought to determine the composition of color, have also in part returned to it. For both of these had, to be sure, a more definite reason in the above mentioned elevation of the curve of the colors of the spectrum in violet.

It should still be mentioned that the Venetian school of painters, which creates effects chiefly by the intense richness of its color, is especially fond of putting in juxtaposition the three colors, red, green, and violet.

Furthermore, I decidedly question the opinion expressed by various investigators, that the need of designating primary sensations has manifested itself in the names of the colors, and that these might therefore give a clue for the determination of colors. Our forefathers had before them in colors a domain of vague distinctions. If they wanted to determine sharp degrees of difference they had first of all to look for good old examples of striking shade, which were everywhere known, and anywhere observable. The names for red led back to the Sanscrit rudhira-blood, and also "red." From this *refus*, *ruber*, *roth*, red, etc. For "blue" the Greeks have πορφύρεος and κυάνεος, which appear to refer to the sea; the Latins *coeruleus*, from *coelum*, the sky; the Germans *blau;* the English, blue; the Dutch, *blau;* the old German, *blaw;* which appear to lead to the English, "blow," that is, the color of the air. The names for green may be traced back to vegetation, πράσινος (leek-green), ποώδες (grass-green), *viridis* from *vis*, *virescere* (to grow strong); German: green, English: green, refer to "grow."

The oldest designations of color were very vague: ξανθός appears to have extended from golden yellow to blue green. It was clearly a difficult task to fix in sharp degrees of difference this vague domain. To-day even it is difficult for gifted children to learn the names of colors. One should not infer from these facts that the ancients were color blind.

That from the series of colors which may be stimulated by objective light, it is impossible to select three which can be regarded as fundamental sensations, has already been discussed. For this very reason A. Konig and C. Dieterici have distinguished a middle section of the spectrum, the colors of which we can no longer obtain by the mixture of the end-colors and one of the spectrum colors lying within it. The table of colors drawn according to the measurements of the same observers reveals the same fact in graphic representation. Just on this account the supposition is necessary for Thomas Young's theory, that every color of the spectrum excites simultaneously, even though in different intensity, not merely one, but two or all three, of the three nerve systems which are sensitive to color. At best the hypothesis of simplicity would be permissible for the end-colors of the spectrum, red and violet. But precisely in the case of violet we know, that the fluorescence of the retina produced by the violet rays must vitiate the sensation, and it appears to me not improbable, that the height of the curve between F and Y, found even by Maxwell, is conditioned by the fluorescence of the retina.

It further follows, that it must appear theoretically possible to produce sensations of more saturated colors through other conditions of excitation. That this is also practically possible, and that this demand can be actually fulfilled by Young's theory, I shall have to explain in the description of after-images.

The color theory of Thomas Young, above outlined, is, as compared with the general theory of nervous activity as it was worked out by Johannes Muller, a more special application of the law of specific sensations. Corresponding to its hypotheses the sensations of red, green, and violet would be regarded as determined by the specific energy of sensation of the corresponding three nerve systems. Any sort of excitation whatever, which can in any degree excite the nerve system aforesaid, would always be able to produce in it only its specific sensation. As for the cause of the particular quality of these sensations we hardly need look for it in the retina or the constitution of its fibres, but in the activity of the central parts of the brain associated with them.

I have up to the present kept the analysis of this theory relatively abstract in order to keep it as free as possible from farther hypothetical additions. Nevertheless, there are as great advantages for the certain understanding of such abstractions, if one tries to imagine for oneself pictures as concrete as possible, even though these occasion many a presupposition that is not directly necessary for the nature of the case. In this sense I permit myself to set forth Young's theory in the following somewhat more manifest form. That objections to these additions do not contradict the essence of Young's hypothesis, I have no need to explain.

1. Three kinds of photochemically decomposible substances are deposited in the end organs of the visual nerve fibres, which have different sensitiveness for the different parts of the spectrum. The three color values of the colors of the spectrum depend essentially upon the photochemical reaction of these three substances to the light. In the eyes of birds and reptiles besides colorless cones there occur in fact rods with red, and rods with yellow-green, drops of oil, which might produce a favoring of some simple light in their action upon the back element of these formations. In the case of human beings and other mammals nothing similar has up to the present time been found.

2. By the disintegration of all the substances sensitive to light, the nerve fibre laden therewith, is set into a state of excitation. There is only one

kind of activity capable of exciting sensation in every nerve fibre which accompanies the disintegration of the organic substance and the development of heat, as we know from our study of the nerves of muscles. These phenomena in the three systems of fibres are probably also thoroughly similar one to the other. They act differently in the brain only for the reason that they are united to different functioning parts of the brain. The nerve fibres need here as everywhere to play only the part of conducting wires, by which entirely similar electric currents which pass through them can precipitate or call forth the most various activities in the apparatus connected with the ends. These excitations of the three systems of fibre form the above separated three elementary excitations, provided always that the intensity of excitation, for which we still have no universally valid measure, is thereby made proportional to the strength of light. This does not present the intensity of the elementary excitation being any involved function whatever of the use of material or the negative variation of the current in the nerves, which latter phenomena might occasionally be employed as a measure of excitation.

3. In the brain the three systems of fibres stand in alliance with the three different functioning systems of ganglionic cells, which are perhaps spatially so close to one another, that those corresponding to the same parts of the retina lie close together. This appears to follow from recent investigations concerning the influence of lesions of the brain upon the field of vision.

Gustav Theodor Fechner: 1801-1887

ELEMENTS OF PSYCHOPHYSICS *

1860

WEBER'S law, that equal relative increments of stimuli are proportional to equal increments of sensation, is, in consideration of its generality and the wide limits within which it is absolutely or approximately valid, to be considered fundamental for psychic measurement. There are, however, limits to its validity as well as complications, which we shall have carefully to examine later. Yet even where this law ceases to be valid or absolute, the principle of psychic measurement continues to hold, inasmuch as any other relation between constant increments of sensation and variable increments of stimulus, even though it is arrived at empirically and expressed by an empirical formula, may serve equally well as the fundamental basis for psychic measurement, and indeed must serve as such in those parts of the stimulus scale where Weber's law loses its validity. In fact such a law, as well as Weber's law, will furnish a differential formula from which may be derived an integral formula containing an expression for the measurement of sensation.

This is a fundamental point of view, in which Weber's law, with its limitations, appears, not as limiting the application of psychic measurement, but as restricted in its own application toward that end and beyond which application the general principle of psychic measurement nevertheless continues to hold. It is not that the principle depends for its validity upon Weber's law, but merely that the application of the law is involved in the principle.

Accordingly investigation in the interest of the greatest possible generalization of psychic measurement has not essentially to commence with the greatest possible generalization of Weber's law, which might easily produce the questionable inclination to generalize the law beyond these limits solely in the interest of psychic measurement; but rather it may quite freely be asked how far Weber's law is applicable, and how far not; for the three methods which are used in psychic measurement are applicable even when Weber's law is not, and where these methods are applicable psychic measurement is possible.

* Fechner's modification of Weber's Law is the only part of Fechner's *Elements of Psychophysics* which has been published in English. It was translated by H. S. Langfeld, included in Rand's *The Classical Psychologists*, and is reprinted with the permission of the publishers and the translator.

In short, Weber's law forms merely the basis for the most numerous and important applications of psychic measurement, but not the universal and essential one. The most general and more fundamental basis for psychic measurement is rather those methods by which the relation between stimulus increments and sensation increment in general is determined, within, as well as without, the limits of Weber's law; and the development of these methods towards ever greater precision and perfection is the most important consideration in regard to psychic measurement.

And yet a great advantage would be lost, if so simple a law as Weber's law could not be used as an exact or at least sufficiently approximate basis for psychic measurement; just such an advantage as would be lost if we could not use the Kepler law in astronomy, or the laws of simple refraction in the theory of the dioptric instruments. Now there is just the same difficulty with these laws as with Weber's law. In the case of Kepler's law as with Weber's we abstract from deviations. In the case of simple lens refraction we abstract from optical aberration. In fact they may become invalid as soon as the simple hypotheses for which they are true no longer exist. Yet they will always remain decisive for the principal relations with which astronomy and dioptrics are concerned. Weber's law may in like manner, entirely lose its validity, as soon as the average or normal conditions under which the stimulus produces the sensation are unrealized. It will always, however, be decisive for these particular conditions.

Further, just as in physics and astronomy, so can we also in psychic measurement, neglect at first the irregularities and small departures from the law in order to discover and examine the principal relations with which science has to do. The existence of these exceptions must not, however, be forgotten, inasmuch as the finer development and further progress of the science depends upon the determination and calculation of them, as soon as the possibility of doing so is given.

The determination of psychic measurement is a matter for outer psychophysics and its first applications lie within its boundary; its further applications and consequences, however, extend necessarily into the domain of inner psychophysics and its deeper meaning lies there. It must be remembered that the stimulus does not cause sensation directly but rather through the assistance of bodily processes with which it stands in more direct connection. The dependence, quantitatively considered, of sensation on stimulus, must finally be translated into one of sensation on the bodily processes which directly underlie the sensation—in short the psycho-physical processes; and the sensation instead of being measured by the amount of the stimulus, will be measured by the intensity of these processes. In order to do this, the relation of the inner process to the stimulus must be known. Inasmuch as this is not a matter of direct experience it must be deduced by some exact method. Indeed it is possible for this entire investigation to proceed along exact lines, and it cannot fail at some time or other to obtain the success of a critical study, if one has not already reached that goal.

Although Weber's law, as applied to the relation of stimulus to sensation, shows only a limited validity in the domain of outer psychophysics, it has, as applied to the relation to kinetic energy, or as referred to some other function of the psycho-physical process, in all probability an unlimited validity in the domain of inner psychophysics, in that all exceptions to the law which we find in the arousal of sensation by external stimulus, are probably due to the fact that the stimulus only under normal or average conditions engenders a kinetic energy in those inner processes proportional to its own amount. From this it may be foreseen, that this law, after it has been restated as a relation between sensation and the psycho-physical processes, will be as important, general, and fundamental for the relations of mind to body, as is the law of gravity for the field of planetary motion. And it also has that simplicity which we are accustomed to find in fundamental laws of nature.

Although, then, psychic measurement depends upon Weber's law only within limits in the domain of outer psycho-physics, it may well get its unconditional support from this law in the field of inner psychophysics. These are nevertheless for the present merely opinions and expectations, the verification of which lies in the future.

THE FUNDAMENTAL FORMULA AND THE MEASUREMENT FORMULA

Although not as yet having a measurement for sensation, still one can combine in an exact formula the relation expressed in Weber's law,—that the sensation difference remains constant when the relative stimulus difference remains constant,—with the law, established by the mathematical auxiliary principle, that small sensation increments are proportional to stimulus increments. Let us suppose, as has generally been done in the attempts to preserve Weber's law, that the difference between two stimuli, or, what is the same, the increase in one stimulus, is very small in proportion to the stimulus itself. Let the stimulus which is increased be called β, the small increase $d\beta$, where the letter d is to be considered not as a special magnitude, but simply as a sign that $d\beta$ is the small increment of β. This already suggests the differential sign. The relative stimulus increase therefore is $\frac{d\beta}{\beta}$. On the other hand, let the sensation which is dependent upon the stimulus be called γ, and let the small increment of the sensation which results from the increase of the stimulus by $d\beta$ be called $d\gamma$, where d again simply expresses the small increment. The terms $d\beta$ and $d\gamma$ are each to be considered as referring to an arbitrary unit of their own nature.

According to the empirical Weber's law, $d\gamma$ remains constant when $\frac{d\beta}{\beta}$ remains constant, no matter what absolute values $d\beta$ and β take; and according to the *a priori* mathematical auxiliary principle the changes $d\gamma$ and $d\beta$ remain proportional to one another so long as they remain very small. The two relations may be expressed together in the following equation: $d\gamma = \frac{\kappa d\beta}{\beta}$ (1) where κ is a constant (dependent upon the units selected for γ and β). In fact, if one multiplies βd and β by any number, so long as it is the same number for both, the proportion remains constant, and with it also the sensation difference $d\gamma$. This is Weber's law. If one doubles or triples the value of the variation $d\beta$ without changing the initial value β, then the value of the change $d\gamma$ is also doubled or tripled. This is the mathematical principle. The equation $d\gamma = \frac{\kappa d\beta}{\beta}$ therefore entirely satisfies both Weber's law and this principle; and no other equation satisfies both together. This is to be called the *fundamental formula*, in that the deduction of all consequent formulas will be based upon it.

The fundamental formula does not presuppose the measurement of sensation, nor does it establish any; it simply expresses the relation holding between small relative stimulus increments and sensations increments. In short, it is nothing more than Weber's law and the mathematical auxiliary principle united and expressed in mathematical symbols.

There is, however, another formula connected with this formula by infinitesimal calculus, which expresses a general quantitative relation between the stimulus magnitude as a summation of stimulus increments, and the sensation magnitude as a summation of sensation increments, in such a way, that with the validity of the first formula, together with the assumption of the fact of limen, the validity of this latter formula is also given.

Reserving for the future a more exact deduction, I shall attempt first to make clear in a general way the connection of the two formulas.

One can readily see, that the relation between the increments $d\gamma$ and $d\beta$ in the fundamental formula corresponds to the relation between the increments of a logarithm and the increments of the corresponding number. For as one can easily convince oneself, either from theory or from the table, the logarithm does not increase by equal increments when the corresponding number increases by equal increments, but rather when the latter increases by equal amounts; in other words, the increases in the logarithms remain equal, when the relative increases of the numbers remain equal. Thus, for example, the following numbers and logarithms belong together:

Number.	Logarithm.
10	1.000000
11	1.0413927
100	2.000000
110	2.0413927
1000	3.000000
1100	3.0413927

where an increase of the number 10 by 1 brings with it just as great an increase in the corresponding logarithm, as the increase of the number 100 by 10 or 1000 by 100. In each instance the increases in the logarithm is 0.0413927. Further, as was already shown in explaining the mathematical auxiliary principle, the increases in the logarithms are proportional to the increases of the numbers, so long as they remain very small. Therefore one can say, that Weber's law and the mathematical auxiliary principle are just as valid for the increases of logarithms and numbers in their relation to one another, as they are for the increases of sensation and stimulus.

The fact of the threshold appears just as much in the relation of a logarithm to its number as in the relation of sensation to stimulus. The sensation begins with values above zero, not with zero, but with a finite value of the stimulus—the threshold; and so does the logarithm begin with values above zero, not with a zero value of the number, but with a finite value of the number, the value 1, inasmuch as the logarithm of 1 is equal to zero.

If now, as was shown above, the increase of sensation and stimulus stands in a relation similar to that of the increase of logarithm and number, and, the point at which the sensation begins to assume a noticeable value stands in a relation to the stimulus similar to that which the point at which the logarithm attains positive value stands to the number, then one may also expect that sensation and stimulus themselves stand in a relation to one another similar to that of logarithm to number, which, just as the former (sensation and stimulus) may be regarded as made up of a sum of successive increments.

Accordingly the simplest relation between the two that we can write is $\gamma = \log \beta$.

In fact it will soon be shown that, provided suitable units of sensation and stimulus are chosen, the functional relation between both reduces to this very simple formula. Meanwhile it is not the most general formula that can be derived, but one which is only valid under the supposition of particular units of sensation and stimulus, and we still need a direct and absolute deduction instead of the indirect and approximate one.

The specialist sees at once how this may be attained, namely, by treating the fundamental formula as a differential formula and integrating it. In the following chapter one will find this done. Here it must be supposed already carried out, and those who are not able to follow the simple infinitesimal deduction, must be asked to consider the result as a mathematical fact. This result is the following functional formula between stimulus and sensation, which goes by the name of the measurement formula and which will not be further discussed:

$$\gamma = \kappa (\log \beta - \log b) \quad (2)$$

In this formula κ again stands for a constant, dependent upon the unit selected and also the logarithmic system, and a second constant which stands for the threshold value of the stimulus, at which the sensation γ begins and disappears.

According to the rule, that the logarithm of a quotient of two numbers may be substituted for the difference of their logarithms, . . . one can substitute for the above form of the measurement formula the following, which is more convenient for making deductions. $\gamma = \kappa \log \frac{\beta}{b}$ (3) From this equation it follows that the sensation magnitude γ is not to be considered as a simple function of the stimulus value β, but of its relation to the threshold value b, where the sensation begins and disappears. The relative stimulus value, $\frac{\beta}{b}$ is for the future to be called the fundamental stimulus value, or the fundamental value of the stimulus.

Translated in words, the measurement formula reads:

The magnitude of the sensation (γ) is not proportional to the absolute value of the stimulus (β), but rather to the logarithm of the magnitude of the stimulus, when this last is expressed in terms of its threshold value (b), i. e. that magnitude considered as unit at which the sensation begins and disappears. In short, it is proportional to the logarithm of the fundamental stimulus value.

Before we proceed further, let us hasten to show that that relation between stimulus and sensation, from which the measurement formula is derived, may be correctly deduced in turn from it, and that this latter thus finds its verification in so far as these relations are found empirically. We have here at the same time the simplest examples of the application of the measurement formula.

The measurement formula is founded upon Weber's law and the fact of the stimulus threshold; and both must follow in turn from it.

Now as to Weber's law. In the form that equal increments of sensation are proportional to relative stimulus increments, it may be obtained by differentiating the measurement formula, inasmuch as in this way one returns to the fundamental formula, which contains the expression of the law in this form.

In the form, that equal sensation differences correspond to equal relations to stimulus, the law may be deduced in quite an elementary manner as follows.

Let two sensations whose difference is to be considered, be called γ and γ^1, and the corresponding stimuli β and β^1. Then according to the measurement formula $\frac{\gamma = \kappa (\log \beta - \log b)}{\gamma^1 = \kappa (\log \beta^1 - \log b)}$ and likewise for the sensation difference $\gamma - \gamma^1 = \kappa (\log \beta - \log \beta^1)$ or since $\log \beta - \log \beta^1 = \log \frac{\beta}{\beta^1}$ $\gamma - \gamma^1 = \kappa \log \frac{\beta}{\beta^1}$. From this formula it follows, that the sensation difference is a function of the stimulus relation $\frac{\beta}{\beta^1}$, and remains the same no matter what values β, β^1 may take, so long as the relation remains unchanged, which is the statement of Weber's law.

In a later chapter we shall return to the above formula under the name of the difference formula, as one of the simplest consequences of the measurement formula.

As for the fact of the threshold, which is caused by the sensation of having zero value not at zero but at a finite value of the stimulus, it is so far contained in the measurement formula as γ does not, according to this formula, have the value zero when $\beta = 0$, but when β is equal to a finite value b. This follows as well from equation (2) as (3) of the measurement formula, directly from (2), and from (3) with the additional consideration of the fact, that when β equals b, $\log \frac{\beta}{b}$ equals log 1, and $\log 1 = 0$.

Naturally all deduction from Weber's law and the fact of the threshold will also be deductions from our measurement formula.

It follows from the former law, that every given increment of stimulus causes an ever decreasing increment in sensation in proportion as the stimulus grows larger, and that at high values of the stimulus it is no longer sensed, while on the other hand, at low values it may appear exceptionally strong.

In fact the increase of a large number β by a given amount is accompanied by a considerably smaller increase in the corresponding logarithm γ, than the increase of a small number β by the same amount. When the number 10 is increased by 10, (that is, reaches 20), the logarithm corresponding to 10, which is 1, is increased to 1.3010. When, however, the number 1000 is increased by 10, the logarithm corresponding to 1000, namely 3, is increased only to 3.0043. In the first case the logarithm is increased by 1–3 of its amount, in the latter case by about 1–700.

In connection with the fact of the threshold belongs the deduction that a sensation is further from the perception threshold the more the stimulus sinks under its threshold value. This distance of a sensation from the threshold, is represented in the same manner by the negative values of γ, according to our measurement formula, as the increase above the threshold is represented by the positive values.

In fact one sees directly from equation (2), that when β is smaller than b and with it log β smaller than log b, the sensation takes on negative values, and the same deduction follows in equation (3), in that $\frac{\beta}{b^1}$ becomes a proper fraction when $\beta < b$, and the logarithm of a proper fraction is negative.

In so far as sensations which are caused by a stimulus which is not sufficient to raise them to consciousness, are called unconscious, and those which affect consciousness are called conscious, we may say that the unconscious sensations are represented in our formula by negative, the conscious by positive values. We will return to this statement in a special chapter since it is of great importance, and perhaps not directly evident to everyone. For the present I shall not let it detain me longer.

According to the foregoing our measurement formula corresponds to experience:

1. In the cases of equality, where a sensation difference remains the same when the absolute intensity of the stimulus is altered (Weber's law).

2. In the cases of the thresholds, where the sensation itself ceases, and where its change becomes either imperceptible or barely perceptible. In the former case, when the sensation reaches its lower threshold; in the latter case, when it becomes so great that a given stimulus increase is barely noticed.

3. In the contrasting cases, between sensations which rise above the threshold of consciousness and those that do not reach it,–in short, conscious and unconscious sensations. From the above the measurement formula may be considered well founded.

In the measurement formula one has a general dependent relation between the size of the fundamental stimulus and the size of the corresponding sensation and not one which is valid only for the cases of equal sensations. This permits the amount of sensation to be calculated from a relative amount of the fundamental stimulus and thus we have a measurement of sensation.

Hermann von Helmholtz: 1821-1894

CONCERNING THE PERCEPTIONS IN GENERAL *

1867

THE sensations aroused by light in the nervous mechanism of vision enable us to form conceptions as to the existence, form and position of external objects. These ideas are called visual perceptions. In this third subdivision of Physiological Optics we must try to analyze the scientific results which we have obtained concerning the conditions which give rise to visual perceptions.

Perceptions of external objects being therefore of the nature of ideas, and ideas themselves being invariably activities of our psychic energy, perceptions also can only be the result of psychic energy. Accordingly, strictly speaking, the theory of perceptions belongs properly in the domain of psychology. This is particularly true with respect to the mode of the mental activities in the case of the perceptions and with respect to the determination of their laws. Yet even here there is a wide field of investigation in both physics and physiology, inasmuch as we have to determine, scientifically as far as possible, what special properties of the physical stimulus and of the physiological situation are responsible for the formation of this or that particular idea as to the nature of the external objects perceived. In this part of the subject, therefore, we shall have to investigate the special properties of the retinal images, muscular sensations, etc., that are concerned in the perception of a definite position of the observed object, not only as to its direction but as to its distance; how the perception of the form of a body of three dimensions depends on certain peculiarities of the images; and under what circumstances it will appear single or double as seen by both eyes, etc. Thus, our main purpose will be simply to investigate the material of sensation whereby we are enabled to form ideas, in those relations that are important for the perceptions obtained from them. This problem can be solved entirely by scientific methods. At the same time, we cannot avoid referring to

* The title of this selection is the subtitle used by Helmholtz in his *Physiological Optics* in discussing his empirical approach to visual perception. The translation is from the third German edition. It is reprinted by the permission of the Optical Society of America from *Helmholtz's Treatise on Physiological Optics,* edited by James P. C. Southall, 1925, III, 1-18.

psychic activities and the laws that govern them, as far as they are concerned with the perception of the senses. But the discovery and description of these psychic activities will not be regarded as an essential part of our present task, because then we might run the risk of losing our hold of established facts and of not adhering steadily to a method founded on clear, well-recognized principles. Thus, for the present at least, I think the psychological domain of the physiology of the senses should be kept separate from pure psychology, whose province really is to establish as far as possible the laws and nature of the processes of the mind.

Still we cannot altogether avoid speaking of the mental processes that are active in the sense-perceptions, if we wish to see clearly the connection between the phenomena and to arrange the facts in their proper relation to one another. And hence, to prevent any misconception of the plan I have in mind, I intend to devote the latter part of this chapter to a discussion of the conclusions which I think can be inferred with respect to these mental processes. And yet we know by experience that people very seldom come to any agreement as to abstract questions of this nature. The keenest thinkers, philosophers like Kant for instance, have long ago analyzed these relations correctly and demonstrated them, and yet there is no permanent and general agreement about them among educated people. And, therefore, in the subsequent chapters devoted specially to the theory of the visual perceptions, I shall endeavour to avoid all references to opinions as to mental activity, as involving questions that always have been, and perhaps always will be, subjects of debate between the various metaphysical schools; so as not to distract the reader's attention from those facts about which an agreement may possibly be reached, by wrangling over abstract propositions that are not necessarily involved in the problem before us.

Here I shall merely indicate at the outset certain general characteristics of the mental processes that are active in the sense-perceptions, because they will be constantly encountered in connection with the various subjects to be considered. Without some previous explanation of their general significance and wide range of activity, the reader might be apt in some special case to regard them as paradoxical and incredible.

The general rule determining the ideas of vision that are formed whenever an impression is made on the eye, with or without the aid of optical instruments, is that such objects are always imagined as being present in the field of vision as would have to be there in order to produce the same impression on the nervous mechanism, the eyes being used under ordinary normal conditions. To employ an illustration which has been mentioned before, suppose that the eye ball is mechanically stimulated at the outer corner of the eye. Then we imagine that we see an appearance of light in front of us somewhere in the direction of the bridge of the nose. Under ordinary conditions of vision, when our eyes are stimulated by light coming from outside, if the region of the retina in the outer corner of the eye is to be stimulated, the light actually has to enter the eye from the direction of the bridge of the nose. Thus, in accordance with the above rule, in a case of this kind we substitute a luminous object at the place mentioned in the field of view, although as a matter of fact the mechanical stimulus does not act on the eye from in front of the field of view nor from the nasal side of the eye, but, on the contrary, is exerted on the outer surface of the eyeball and more from behind. The general validity of the above rule will be shown by many other instances that will appear in the following pages.

In the statement of this rule mention is made of the ordinary conditions of vision, when the visual organ is stimulated by light from outside; this outside light, coming from the opaque objects in its path that were the last to be encountered, and having reached the eye along rectilinear paths through an uninterrupted layer of air. This is what is meant here by the normal use of the organ of vision, and the justification for using this term is that this mode of stimulation occurs in such an enormous majority of cases that all other instances where the paths of the rays of light are altered by reflections or refractions, or in which the stimulations are not produced by external light, may be regarded as rare exceptions. This is because the retina in the fundus of the firm eyeball is almost completely protected from the actions of all other stimuli and is not easily accessible to anything but external light. When a person is in the habit of using an optical instrument and has become accustomed to it, for example, if he is used to wearing spectacles, to a certain extent he learns to interpret the visual images under these changed conditions.

Incidentally, the rule given above corresponds to a general characteristic of all sense-perceptions, and not simply to the sense of sight alone. For example, the stimulation of the tactile nerves in the enormous majority of cases is the result of influences that affect the terminal extensions of these nerves in the surface of the skin. It is only under exceptional circumstances that the nerve-stems can be stimulated by more powerful agencies. In accordance with the above rule, therefore, all stimulations of cutaneous nerves, even when they affect the stem or the nerve-centre itself, are perceived as occurring in the corresponding peripheral surface of the skin. The most remarkable and astonishing cases of illusions of this sort are those in which the peripheral area of this particular portion of the skin is actually no longer in existence, as, for example, in case of a person whose leg has been amputated. For a long time after the operation the patient frequently imagines he has vivid sensations in the foot that has been severed. He feels exactly the places that ache on one toe or the other. Of course, in a case of this sort the stimulation can affect only what is left of the stem of the nerve whose fibres formerly terminated in the amputated toes. Usually, it is the end of the nerve in the scar that is stimulated by external pressure or by contraction of the scar tissue. Sometimes at night the sensations in the missing extremity get to be so vivid that the patient has to feel the place to be sure that his limb is actually gone.

Thus it happens, that when the modes of stimulation of the organs of sense are unusual, incorrect ideas of objects are apt to be formed; which used to be described, therefore, as illusions of the senses. Obviously, in these cases there is nothing wrong with the activity of the organ of sense and its corresponding nervous mechanism which produces the illusion. Both of them have to act according to the laws that govern their activity once for all. It is rather simply an illusion in the judgment of the material presented to the senses, resulting in a false idea of it.

The psychic activities that lead us to infer that in front of us at a certain place there is a certain object of a certain character, are equivalent to a conclusion, to the extent that the observed action on our senses enables us to form an idea as to the possible cause of this action; although, as a matter of fact, it is invariably simply the nervous stimulations that are perceived directly, that is, the actions, but never the external objects themselves. But what seems to differentiate them from a conclusion, in the ordinary sense of that word, is that a conclusion is an act of conscious thought. An astronomer, for example, comes to real conscious conclusions of this sort, when he computes the positions of the stars in space, their distances, etc., from the perspective images he has had of them at various times and as they are seen from different parts of the orbit of the earth. His conclusions are based on a conscious knowledge of the laws of optics. In the ordinary acts of vision this knowledge of optics is lacking. Still it may be permissible to speak of the psychic acts of ordinary perception as unconscious conclusions, thereby making a distinction of some sort between them and the common so-called conscious conclusions. And while it is true that there has been, and probably always will be, a measure of doubt as to the similarity of the psychic activity in the two cases, there can be no doubt as to the similarity between the results of such unconscious conclusions and those of conscious conclusions.

The unconscious conclusions derived from sensation are equivalent in their consequences to the so-called conclusions from analogy. Inasmuch as in an overwhelming majority of cases, whenever the parts of the retina in the outer corner of the eye are simulated, it has been found to be due to external light coming into the eye from the direction of the bridge of the nose, the inference we make is that it is so in every new case whenever this part of the retina is stimulated; just as we assert that every single individual now living will die, because all previous experience has shown that all men who were formerly alive have died.

But, moreover, just because they are not free acts of conscious thought, these unconscious conclusions from analogy are irresistible, and the effect of them cannot be overcome by a better understanding of the real relations. It may be ever so clear how we get an idea of a luminous phenomenon in the field of vision when pressure is exerted on the eye; and yet we cannot get rid of the conviction that this appearance of light is actually there at the given place in the visual field; and we cannot seem to comprehend that there is a luminous phenomenon at the place where the retina is stimulated. It is the same way in case of all the images that we see in optical instruments.

On the other hand, there are numerous illustrations of fixed and inevitable associations of ideas due to frequent repetition, even when they have no natural connection, but are dependent merely on some conventional arrangement, as, for example, the connection between the written letters of a word and its sound and meaning. Still to many physiologists and psychologists the connection between the sensation and the conception of the object usually appears to be so rigid and obligatory that they are not much disposed to admit that, to a considerable extent at least, it depends on acquired experience, that is, on psychic activity. On the contrary, they have endeavoured to find some mechanical mode of origin for this connection through the agency of imaginary organic structures. With regard to this question, all those experiences are of much significance which show how the judgment of the senses may be modified by experience and by training derived under various circumstances, and may be adapted to the new conditions. Thus, persons may learn in some measure to utilize details of the sensation which otherwise would escape notice and not contribute to obtaining any idea of the object. On the other hand, too, this new habit may acquire such a hold that when the individual in question is back again in the old original normal state, he may be liable to illusions of the senses.

Facts like these show the widespread influence that experience, training and habit have on our perceptions. But how far their influence really does extend, it would perhaps be impossible to say precisely at present. Little enough is definitely known about infants and very young animals, and the interpretation of such observations as have been made on them is extremely doubtful. Besides, no one can say that infants are entirely without experience and practice in tactile sensations and bodily movements. Accordingly, the rule given above has been stated in a form which does not anticipate the decision of this question. It merely expresses what the result is. And so it can be accepted even by those who have entirely different opinions as to the way ideas originate concerning objects in the external world.

Another general characteristic property of our sense-perceptions is, that we are not in the habit of observing our sensations accurately, except as they are useful in enabling us to recognize external objects. On the contrary, we are wont to disregard all those parts of the sensations that are of no importance so far as external objects are concerned. Thus in most cases some special assistance and training are needed in order to observe these latter subjective sensations. It might seem that nothing could be easier than to be conscious of one's own sensations; and yet experience shows that for the discovery of subjective sensations some special talent is needed, such as Purkinje manifested in the highest degree; or else it is the result of accident or of theoretical speculation. For instance, the phenomena of the blind spot were discovered by Mariotte from theoretical considerations. Similarly, in the domain of hearing, I discovered the existence of those combination tones which I have called summation tones. In the great majority of cases, doubtless it was accident that revealed this or that subjective phenomenon to observers who happened to be particularly interested in such matters. It is only when subjective phenomena are so prominent as to interfere with the perception of things, that they attract everybody's attention. Once the phenomena have been discovered, it is generally easier for others to perceive them also, provided the proper precautions are taken for observing them, and the attention is concentrated on them. In many cases, however—for example, in the phenomena of the blind spot, or in the separation of the overtones and combination tones from the fundamental tones of musical sounds, etc.—such an intense concentration of attention is required that, even with the help of convenient external appliances, many persons are unable to perform the experiments. Even the after-images of bright objects are not perceived by most persons at first except under particularly favourable external conditions. It takes much more practice to see the fainter kinds of after-images. A common experience, illustrative of this sort of thing, is for a person who has some ocular trouble that impairs his vision to become suddenly aware of the so-called *mouches volantes* in his visual field, although the causes of this phenomenon have been there in the vitreous humor all his life. Yet now he will be firmly persuaded that these corpuscles have developed as the result of his ocular ailment, although the truth simply is that, owing to his ailment, the patient has been paying more attention to visual phenomena. No doubt, also, there are cases where one eye has gradually become blind, and yet the patient has continued to go about for an indefinite time without noticing it, until he happened one day to close the good eye without closing the other, and so noticed the blindness of that eye.

When a person's attention is directed for the first time to the double images in binocular vision, he is usually greatly astonished to think that he had never noticed them before, especially when he reflects that the only objects he has ever seen single were those few that happened at the moment to be about as far from his eyes as the point of fixation. The great majority of objects, comprising all those that were farther or nearer than this point, were all seen double.

Accordingly, the first thing we have to learn is to pay heed to our individual sensations. Ordinarily we do so merely in case of those sensations that enable us to find out about the world around us. In the ordinary affairs of life the sensations have no other importance for us. Subjective sensations are of interest chiefly for scientific investigations only. If they happen to be noticed in the ordinary activity of the senses, they merely distract the attention. Thus while we may attain an extraordinary degree of delicacy and precision in objective observation, we not only fail to do so in subjective observations, but indeed we acquire the faculty in large measure of overlooking them and of forming our opinions of objects independently of them, even when they are so pronounced that they might easily be noticed.

The most universal sign by which subjective vision phenomena can be identified appears to be by the way they accompany the movement of the eye over the field of view. Thus, the after-images, the *mouches volantes*, the blind spot, and the *luminous dust* of the dark field all participate in the motions of the eye, and coincide successively with the various stationary objects in the visual field. On the other hand if the same phenomena recur again invariably at the same places in the visual field, they may be regarded as being objective and as being connected with external bodies. This is the case with contrast phenomena produced by after-images.

The same difficulty that we have in observing subjective sensations, that is, sensations aroused by internal causes, occurs also in trying to analyze the compound sensations, invariably excited in the same connection by any simple object, and to resolve them into their separate components. In such cases experience shows us how to recognize a compound aggregate of sensations as being the sign of a simple object. Accustomed to consider the sensation-complex as a connected whole, generally we are not able to perceive the separate parts of it without external help and support. Many illustrations of this kind will be seen in the following pages. For instance the perception of the apparent direction of an object from the eye depends on the combination of those sensations by which we estimate the adjustment of the eye, and on being able to distinguish those parts of the retina where light falls from those parts where it does not fall. The perception of the solid form of an object of three dimensions is the result of the combination of two different perspective views in the two eyes. The gloss of a surface, which is apparently a simple effect, is due to differences of colouring or brightness in the images of it in the two eyes. These facts were ascertained by theory and may be verified by suitable experiments. But usually it is very difficult, if not impossible, to discover them by direct observation and analysis of the sensations alone. Even with sensations that are much more involved and always associated with frequently recurring complex objects, the oftener the same combination recurs, and the more used we have become to regarding the sensation as the normal sign of the real nature of the object, the more difficult it will be to analyze the sensation by observation alone. By way of illustration, it is a familiar experience that the colours of a landscape come out much more brilliantly and definitely by looking at them with the head on one side or upside down than they do when the head is in the ordinary upright position. In the usual mode of observation all we try to do is to judge correctly the objects as such. We know that at a certain distance green surfaces appear a little different in hue. We get in the habit of overlooking this difference, and learn to identify the altered green of distant meadows and trees with the corresponding colour of nearer objects. In the case of very distant objects like distant ranges of mountains, little of the colour of the body is left to be seen, because it is mainly shrouded in the colour of the illuminated air. This vague blue-grey colour, bordered above by the clear blue of the sky or the red-yellow of the sunset glow, and below by the vivid green of meadows and forests, is very subject to variations by contrast. To us it is the vague and variable colour of distance. The difference in it may, perhaps, be more noticeable sometimes and with some illuminations than at other times. But we do not determine its true nature, because it is not ascribed to any definite object. We are simply aware of its variable nature. But the instant we take an unusual position, and look at the landscape with the head under one arm, let us say, or between the legs, it all appears like a flat picture; partly on account of the strange position of the image in the eye, and partly because, as we shall see presently, the binocular judgment of distance becomes less accurate. It may even happen that with the head upside down the clouds have the correct perspective, whereas the objects on the earth appear like a painting on a vertical surface, as the clouds in the sky usually do. At the same time the colours lose their associations also with near or far objects, and confront us now purely in their own peculiar differences. Then we have no difficulty in recognizing that the vague blue-grey of the far distance may indeed be a fairly saturated violet, and that the green of the vegetation blends imperceptibly through blue-green and blue into this violet, etc. This whole difference seems to me to be due to the fact that the colours have ceased to be distinctive signs of objects for us, and are considered merely as being different sensations. Consequently, we take in better their peculiar distinctions without being distracted by other considerations.

The connection between the sensations and external objects may interfere very much with the perception of their simplest relations. A good illustration of this is the difficulty about perceiving the double images of binocular vision when they can be regarded as being images of one and the same external object.

In the same way we may have similar experiences with other kinds of sensations. The sensation of the timbre of a sound, as I have shown elsewhere, consists of a series of sensations of its partial tones (fundamental and harmonics); but it is exceedingly difficult to analyze the compound sensation of the sound into these elementary components. The tactile sensation of wetness is composed of that of coldness and that of smoothness of surface. Consequently, on inadvertently touching a cold piece of smooth metal, we often get the impression of having touched something wet. Many other illustrations of this sort might be adduced. They all indicate that we are exceedingly well trained in finding out by our sensations the objective nature of the objects around us, but that we are completely unskilled in observing the sensations per se; and that the practice of associating them with things outside of us actually prevents us from being distinctly conscious of the pure sensations.

This is true also not merely with respect to qualitative differences of sensation, but it is likewise true with respect to the perception of space-relations. For example, the spectacle of a person in the act of walking is a familiar sight. We think of this motion as a connected whole, possibly taking note of some of its most conspicuous singularities. But it requires minute attention and a special choice of the point of view to distinguish the upward and lateral movements of the body in a person's gait. We have to pick out points or lines of reference in the background with which we can compare the position of his head. But look through an astronomical telescope at a crowd of people in motion far away. Their images are upside down, but what a curious jerking and swaying of the body is produced by those who are walking about! Then there is no trouble whatever in noticing the peculiar motions of the body and many other singularities of gait; and especially differences between individuals and the reasons for them, simply because this is not the everyday sight to which we are accustomed. On the other hand, when the image is inverted in this way, it is not so easy to tell whether the gait is light or awkward, dignified or graceful, as it was when the image was erect.

Consequently, it may often be rather hard to say how much of our apperceptions (*Anschauungen*) are derived by the sense of sight, how much is due directly to sensation, and how much of them, on the other hand, is due to experience and training. The main point of controversy between various investigators in this territory is connected also with this difficulty. Some are disposed to concede to the influence of experience as much scope as possible, and to derive from it especially all notion of space. This view may be called the empirical theory (*empiristische Theorie*). Others, of course, are obliged to admit the influence of experience in the case of certain classes of perceptions; still with respect to certain elementary apperceptions that occur uniformly in the case of all observers, they believe it is necessary to assume a system of innate apperceptions that are not based on experience, especially with respect to space-relations. In contradistinction to the former view, this may perhaps be called the intuition theory (*nativistische Theorie*) of the sense-perceptions.

In my opinion the following fundamental principles should be kept in mind in this discussion.

Let us restrict the word idea (*Vorstellung*) to mean the image of visual objects as retained in the memory, without being accompanied by any present sense-impressions; and use the term apperception (*Anschauung*) to mean a perception (*Wahrnehmung*) when it is accompanied by the sense-impressions in question. The term immediate perception (*Perzeption*) may then be employed to denote an apperception of this nature in which there is no element whatever that is not the result of direct sensations, that is, an apperception such as might be derived without any recollection of previous experience. Obviously, therefore, one and the same apperception may be accompanied by the corresponding sensations in very different measure. Thus idea and immediate perception may be combined in the apperception in the most different proportions.

A person in a familiar room which is brightly lighted by the sun gets an apperception that is abundantly accompanied by very vivid sensations. In the same room in the evening twilight he will not be able to recognize any objects except the brighter ones, especially the windows. But whatever he does actually recognize will be so intermingled with his recollections of the furniture that he can still move about in the room with safety and locate articles he is trying to find, even when they are only dimly visible. These images would be utterly insufficient to enable him to recognize the objects without some previous acquaintance with them. Finally, he may be in the same room in complete darkness, and still be able to find his way about in it without making mistakes, by virtue of the visual impressions formerly obtained. Thus, by continually reducing the material that appeals to the senses, the perceptual-image (*Anschauungsbild*) can ultimately be traced back to the pure memory-image (*Vorstellungsbild*) and may gradually pass into it. In proportion as there is less and less material appeal to the senses, a person's movements will, of course, become more and more uncertain, and his apperception less and less accurate. Still there will be no peculiar abrupt transition, but sensation and memory will continually supplement each other, only in varying degrees.

But even when we look around a room of this sort flooded with sunshine, a little reflection shows us that under these conditions too a large part of our perceptual-image may be due to factors of memory and experience. The fact that we are accustomed to the perspective distortions of pictures of parallelopipeds and to the form of the shadows they cast has much to do with the estimation of the shape and dimensions of the room, as will be seen hereafter. Looking at the room with one eye shut, we think we see it just as distinctly and definitely as with both eyes. And yet we should get exactly the same view in case every point in the room were shifted arbitrarily to a different distance from the eye, provided they all remained on the same lines of sight.

Thus in a case like this we are really considering an extremely multiplex phenomenon of sense; but still we ascribe a perfectly definite explanation to it, and it is by no means easy to realize that the monocular image of such a familiar object necessarily means a much more meagre perception than would be obtained with both eyes. Thus too it is often hard to tell whether or not untrained observers inspecting stereoscopic views really notice the peculiar illusion produced by the instrument.

We see, therefore, how in a case of this kind reminiscences of previous experiences act in conjunction with present sensations to produce a perceptual image (*Anschauungsbild*) which imposes itself on our faculty of perception with overwhelming power, without our being conscious of how much of it is due to memory and how much to present conception.

Still more remarkable is the influence of the comprehension of the sensations in certain cases, especially with dim illumination, in which a visual impression may be misunderstood at first, by not knowing how to attribute the correct depth-dimensions; as when a distant light, for example, is taken for a near one, or vice versa. Suddenly it dawns on us what it is, and immediately, under the influence of the correct comprehension, the correct perceptual image also is developed in its full intensity. Then we are unable to revert to the previous imperfect apperception.

This is very common especially with complicated stereoscopic drawings of forms of crystals and other objects which come out in perfect clearness of perception the moment we once succeed in getting the correct impression.

Similar experiences have happened to everybody, proving that the elements in the sense-perceptions that are derived from experience are just as powerful as those that are derived from present sensations. All observers who have thoroughly investigated the theory of the sense-perceptions, even those who were disposed to allow experience as little scope as possible, have always admitted this.

Hence, at all events it must be conceded that, even in what appears to the adult as being direct apperception of the senses, possibly a number of single factors may be involved which are really the product of experience; although at the time it is difficult to draw the line between them.

Now in my opinion we are justified by our previous experiences in stating that no indubitable present sensation can be abolished and overcome by an act of the intellect; and no matter how clearly we recognize that it has been produced in some anomalous way, still the illusion does not disappear by comprehending the process. The attention may be diverted from sensations, particularly if they are feeble and habitual; but in noting those relations in the external world, that are associated with these sensations, we are obliged to observe the sensations themselves. Thus we may be unmindful of the temperature-sensation of our skin when it is not very keen, or of the contact-sensations produced by our clothing, as long as we are occupied with entirely different matters. But just as soon as we stop to think whether it is warm or cold, we are not in the position to convert the feeling of warmth into that of coldness; maybe because we know that it is due to strenuous exertion and not to the temperature of the surrounding air. In the same way the apparition of light when pressure is exerted on the eyeball cannot be made to vanish simply by comprehending better the nature of the process, supposing the attention is directed to the field of vision and not, say, to the ear or the skin.

On the other hand, it may also be that we are not in the position to isolate an impression of sensation, because it involves the composite sense-symbol of an external object. However, in this case the correct comprehension of the object shows that the sensation in question has been perceived and used by the consciousness.

My conclusion is, that nothing in our sense-perceptions can be recognized as sensation which can be overcome in the perceptual image and converted into its opposite by factors that are demonstrably due to experience.

Whatever, therefore, can be overcome by factors of experience, we must consider as being itself the product of experience and training. By observing this rule, we shall find that it is merely the qualities of the sensation that are to be considered as real, pure sensation; the great majority of space-apperceptions, however, being the product of experience and training.

Still it does not follow that apperceptions, which persist in spite of our better conscious insight and continue as illusions, might not be due to experience and training. Our knowledge of the changes of colour produced in distant objects by the haziness of the atmosphere, of perspective distortions, and of shadow is undoubtedly a matter of experience. And yet in a good landscape picture we shall get the perfect visual impression of the distance and the solid form of the buildings in it, in spite of knowing that it is all depicted on canvas.

Similarly, our knowledge of the composite sound of the vowels is certainly obtained from experience; and yet we get the auditory-impression of the vowel sound by combining the individual tones of tuning forks (as I have demonstrated) and grasp the sound in its entirety, although in this instance we know that it is really compound.

Here we still have to explain how experience counteracts experience, and how illusion can be produced by factors derived from experience, when it might seem as if experience could not teach anything except what was true. In this matter we must remember, as was intimated above, that the sensations are interpreted just as they arise when they are stimulated in the normal way, and when the organ of sense is used normally.

We are not simply passive to the impressions that are urged on us, but we observe, that is, we adjust our organs in those conditions that enable them to distinguish the impressions most accurately. Thus, in considering an involved object, we accommodate both eyes as well as we can, and turn them so as to focus steadily the precise point on which our attention is fixed, that is, so as to get an image of it in the fovea of each eye; and then we let our eyes traverse all the noteworthy points of the object one after another. If we are interested in the general shape of the object and are trying to get as good an idea as we can of its relative dimensions, we assume a position such that, without having to turn the head, we can survey the whole surface, enabling us at the same time to view as symmetrically as possible those dimensions we wish to compare. Thus, in looking at an object, as, for example, a building with prominent horizontal and vertical lines, we like to stand opposite to it with the centres of rotation of the two eyes in a horizontal line. This position of the eyes can be controlled at any moment by separating the double images; which in the case mentioned here are in the same horizontal plane.

Unquestionably, our reason for choosing this definite mode of seeing is because in this way we can observe and compare most accurately; and, consequently, in this so-called normal use of the eyes we learn best how to compare our sensations with the reality. And so we obtain also the most correct and most accurate perceptions by this method.

But if, from necessity or on purpose, we employ a different mode of looking at objects, that is, if we view them merely indirectly or without focusing both eyes on them, or without surveying them all over, or if we hold the head in some unusual position, then we shall not be able to have as accurate apperceptions as when the eyes are used in the normal fashion. Nor are we so well trained in interpreting what we see under such circumstances as in the other case. Hence there is more scope for interpretation, although, as a rule, we are not clearly aware of this uncertainty in the explanation of our sense-perceptions. When we see an object in front of us, we are obliged to assign it to some definite place in space. We cannot think of it as having some dubious intermediate position between two different places in space. Without any recollections coming to our aid, we are wont to interpret the phenomenon as it would have to be interpreted if we had received the same impression in the normal and most accurate mode of observation. Thus certain illusions enter into the perception, unless we concentrate our eyes on the objects under observation, or when the objects are in the peripheral part of the visual field, or if the head is held to one side, or if we do not focus the object with both eyes at once. Moreover, the agreement between the images on the two retinas is most constant and regular in looking at distant objects. The fact that the horizontal floor usually happens to be in the lower part of the visual field, apparently influences the comparison of the fields of the two eyes in a peculiar manner. Thus, our judgment as to the position of near objects is not entirely correct when we observe them with the look tilted decidedly up or down. The retinal images presented in this way are interpreted just as if they had been obtained by looking straight ahead. We run across many illustrations of this sort. Our training in interpreting immediate perceptions is not equally good in all directions of the eyes, but simply for those directions which enable us to have the most accurate and most consistent perceptions. We transfer the latter to all cases, as in the instances just cited.

Now it is quite possible that the similarity between a visual impression of this kind and one of the possible impressions obtained by normal observation may not be so overwhelming and striking as to preclude many other comparisons and corresponding interpretations of that impression. In such cases the explanation of the impression varies. Without any change of the retinal images, the same observer may see in front of him various perceptual images in succession, in which case the variation is easy to recognize. Or else one observer may incline more toward one comparison and interpretation, and another toward another. This has been a source of much controversy in physiological optics, because each observer has been disposed to consider the apperception which he obtained by the most careful observations he could make as being the only valid one. But supposing that we have such confidence in the observers as to assume that their observations were careful and unprejudiced, and that they knew how to make them, it would not be proper in such cases to adopt one of the conflicting interpretations of the visual phenomenon as being the only correct one. And yet that is what they are disposed to do who try to derive the origin of perceptual images mainly from innate factors. The truth rather is, that in a case of this sort various perceptual images may be developed; and we should seek rather to discover what circumstances are responsible for the decision one way or the other.

It is true we meet with a difficulty here that does not exist in the other parts of the natural sciences. In many instances we have simply the assertions of individual observers, without being in the position to verify them by our own observation. Many idiosyncrasies are manifested in this region, some of which are doubtless due to the structure of the eyes, other to the habitual way of using the eyes, and others still perhaps to previous impressions and apperceptions. Of course, nobody save the person who has peculiarities of this nature can observe their effects, and nobody else can give an opinion about them. On the other hand, observation in this region is by no means so easy as might be supposed at first. Steady fixation of a point for a long time while observations are being made in indirect vision; controlling the attention; taking the mind away from the ordinary objective interpretation of sense-impression; estimation of difference of colour and of difference of space in the visual field—all these things take much practice. And hence a number of facts in this region cannot be observed at all without having had previous long training in making observations in physiological optics. It cannot be done even by persons who are skilled in making other kinds of observations. Thus, with respect to many matters we have to depend on the observations of a very limited number of individuals, and hence when the results found by somebody else are different, it is much harder in this subject than anywhere else to judge rightly whether secondary influences have not contributed in an observation of this sort. Accordingly, I must apprise the reader in advance that much of the material that is perhaps new in the following chapters may possibly be due to individual peculiarities of my own eyes. Under such circumstances, there was no alternative to me except to observe as carefully as possible the facts as they appeared to my own eyes, and to try to ascertain their connection. Discrepancies that have been found by other observers have been noted. But how widespread this or the other mode of vision may be, is something that has to be left to the future to determine.

Incidentally, the more the visual impressions are unlike the normal ones, the greater will be the variety of interpretation as a rule. This is a natural consequence of the view which I hold, and is an essential characteristic of the activity of psychic influences.

Heretofore practically nothing has been ascertained as to the nature of psychic processes. We have simply an array of facts. Therefore, it is not strange that no real explanation can be given of the origin of sense-perceptions. The empirical theory attempts to prove that at least no other forces are necessary for their origin beyond the known faculties of the mind, although these forces themselves may remain entirely unexplained. Now generally it is a useful rule in scientific investigation not to make any new hypothesis so long as known facts seem adequate for the explanation, and the necessity of new assumptions has not been demonstrated. That is why I have thought it incumbent to prefer the empirical view essentially. Still less does the intuition theory attempt to give any explanation of the origin of our perceptual images; for it simply plunges right into the midst of the matter by assuming that certain perceptual images of space would be produced directly by an innate mechanism, provided certain nerve fibres were stimulated. The earlier forms of this theory implied some sort of self-observation of the retina; inasmuch as we were supposed to know by intuition about the form of this membrane and the positions of the separate nerve terminals in it. In its more recent development, especially as formulated by E. Hering, there is an hypothetical subjective visual space, wherein the sensations of the separate nerve fibres are supposed to be registered according to certain intuitive laws. Thus in this theory not only is Kant's assertion adopted, that the general apperception of space is an original form of our imagination, but certain special apperceptions of space are assumed to be intuitive.

The naturalistic view has been called also a special theory of identity, because in it the perfect fusion of the impressions on the corresponding places of the two retinas has to be postulated. On the other hand, the empirical theory is spoken of as a theory of projection, because according to it the perceptual images of objects are projected in space by means of psychic processes. I should like to avoid this term, because both supporters and opponents of this view have often attached undue importance to the idea that this projection must take place parallel to the lines of direction; which was certainly not the correct description of the psychic process. And, even if this construction were admitted as being valid simply with respect to the physiological description of the process, the idea would be incorrect in very many instances.

I am aware that in the present state of knowledge it is impossible to refute the intuition theory. The reasons why I prefer the opposite view are because in my opinion:

1. The intuition theory is an unnecessary hypothesis.

2. Its consequences thus far invariably apply to perceptual images of space which only in the fewest cases are in accordance with reality and

with the correct visual images that are undoubtely present; as will be shown in detail later. The adherents of this theory are, therefore, obliged to make the very questionable assumption, that the space sensations, which according to them are present originally, arc continually being improved and overruled by knowledge which we have accumulated by experience. By analogy with all other experiences, however, we should have to expect that the sensations which have been overruled continued to be present in the apperception as a conscious illusion, if nothing else. But this is not the case.

3. It is not clear how the assumption of these original "space sensations" can help the explanation of our visual perceptions, when the adherents of this theory ultimately have to assume in by far the great majority of cases that these sensations must be overruled by the better understanding which we get by experience. In that case it would seem to me much easier and simpler to grasp, that all apperceptions of space were obtained simply by experience, instead of supposing that the latter have to contend against intuitive perceptual images that are generally false.

This is by way of justifying my point of view. A choice had to be made simply for the sake of getting at least some sort of superficial order amid the chaos of phenomena; and so I believed I had to adopt the view I have chosen. However, I trust it has not affected the correct observation and description of the facts.

Francis Galton: 1822-1911

CLASSIFICATION OF MEN ACCORDING TO THEIR NATURAL GIFTS *

1869

I HAVE no patience with the hypothesis occasionally expressed, and often implied, especially in tales written to teach children to be good, that babies are born pretty much alike, and that the sole agencies in creating differences between boy and boy, and man and man, are steady application and moral effort. It is in the most unqualified manner that I object to pretensions of natural equality. The experiences of the nursery, the school, the University, and of professional careers, are a chain of proofs to the contrary. I acknowledge freely the great power of education and social influences in developing the active powers of the mind, just as I acknowledge the effect of use in developing the muscles of a blacksmith's arm, and no further. Let the blacksmith labour as he will, he will find there are certain feats beyond his power that are well within the strength of a man of herculean make, even although the latter may have led a sedentary life. Some years ago, the Highlanders held a grand gathering in Holland Park, where they challenged all England to compete with them in their games of strength. The challenge was accepted, and the well-trained men of the hills were beaten in the foot-race by a youth who was stated to be a pure Cockney, the clerk of a London banker.

Everybody who has trained himself to physical exercises discovers the extent of his muscular powers to a nicety. When he begins to walk, to row, to use the dumb bells, or to run, he finds to his great delight that his thews strengthen, and his endurance of fatigue increases day after day. So long as he is a novice, he perhaps flatters himself there is hardly an assignable limit to the education of his muscles; but the daily gain is soon discovered to diminish, and at last it vanishes altogether. His maximum performance becomes a rigidly determinate quantity. He learns to an inch, how high or how far he can jump, when he has attained the highest state of training. He learns to half a pound, the force he can exert on the dynamometer, by compressing it. He can strike a blow

* This is Chapter 3 of *Hereditary Genius: An Inquiry into its Laws and Consequences*, published in 1869. The text is taken from the American edition published by D. Appleton & Co. in 1870. Galton proposes that mental ability is distributed in the manner which is characteristic of physical traits.

against the machine used to measure impact, and drive its index to a certain graduation, but no further. So it is in running, in rowing, in walking, and in every other form of physical exertion. There is a definite limit to the muscular powers of every man, which he cannot by any education or exertion overpass.

This is precisely analogous to the experience that every student has had of the working of his mental powers. The eager boy, when he first goes to school and confronts intellectual difficulties, is astonished at his progress. He glories in his newly-developed mental grip and growing capacity for application, and, it may be, fondly believes it to be within his reach to become one of the heroes who have left their mark upon the history of the world. The years go by; he competes in the examinations of school and college, over and over again with his fellows, and soon finds his place among them. He knows he can beat such and such of his competitors; that there are some with whom he runs on equal terms, and others whose intellectual feats he cannot even approach. Probably his vanity still continues to tempt him, by whispering in a new strain. It tells him that classics, mathematics, and other subjects taught in universities, are mere scholastic specialties, and no test of the more valuable intellectual powers. It reminds him of numerous instances of persons who had been unsuccessful in the competitions of youth, but who had shown powers in after-life that made them the foremost men of their age. Accordingly, with newly furbished hopes, and with all the ambition of twenty-two years of age, he leaves his University and enters a larger field of competition. The same kind of experience awaits him here that he has already gone through. Opportunities occur—they occur to every man—and he finds himself incapable of grasping them. He tries, and is tried in many things. In a few years more, unless he is incurably blinded by self-conceit, he learns precisely of what performances he is capable, and what other enterprises lie beyond his compass. When he reaches mature life, he is confident only within certain limits, and knows, or ought to know, himself just as he is probably judged of by the world, with all his unmistakable weakness and all his undeniable strength. He is no longer tormented into hopeless efforts by the fallacious promptings of overweening vanity, but he limits his undertakings to matters below the level of his reach, and finds true moral repose in an honest conviction that he is engaged in as much good work as his nature has rendered him capable of performing.

There can hardly be a surer evidence of the enormous difference between the intellectual capacity of men, than the prodigious differences in the numbers of marks obtained by those who gain mathematical honours at Cambridge. I therefore crave permission to speak at some length upon this subject, although the details are dry and of little general interest.

There are between 400 and 450 students who take their degrees in each year, and of these, about 100 succeed in gaining honours in mathematics, and are ranged by the examiners in strict order of merit. About the first forty of those who take mathematical honours are distinguished by the title of wranglers, and it is a decidedly creditable thing to be even a low wrangler; it will secure a fellowship in a small college. It must be carefully borne in mind that the distinction of being the first in this list of honours, or what is called the senior wrangler of the year, means a vast deal more than being the foremost mathematician of 400 or 450 men taken at hap-hazard. No doubt the large bulk of Cambridge men are taken almost at hap-hazard. A boy is intended by his parents for some profession; if that profession be either the Church or the Bar, it used to be almost requisite, and it is still important, that he should be sent to Cambridge or Oxford. These youths may justly be considered as having been taken at hap-hazard. But there are many others who have fairly won their way to the Universities, and are therefore selected from an enormous area. Fully one-half of the wranglers have been boys of note at their respective schools, and, conversely, almost all boys of note at schools find their way to the Universities. Hence it is that among their comparatively small number of students, the Universities include the highest youthful scholastic ability of all England. The senior wrangler, in each successive year, is the chief of these as regards mathematics, and this, the highest distinction, is, or was, continually won by youths who had no mathematical training of importance before they went to Cambridge. All their instruction had been received during the three years of their residence at the University. Now, I do not say anything here about the merits or demerits of Cambridge mathematical studies having been directed along a too narrow groove, or about the presumed disadvantages of ranging candidates in strict order of merit, instead of grouping them, as at Oxford, in classes, where their names appear alphabetically arranged. All I am concerned with here are the results; and these are most appropriate to my argument. The youths start on their three years' race as fairly as possible. They are then stimulated to run by the most powerful inducements, namely, those of competition, of honour, and of future wealth (for a good fellowship is wealth); and at the end of the three years they are examined most rigorously according to a system that they all understand and are equally well prepared for. The examination lasts five and a half hours a day for eight days. All the answers are carefully marked by the examiners, who add up the marks at the end and range the candidates in strict order of merit. The fairness and thoroughness of Cambridge examinations have never had a breath of suspicion cast upon them.

Unfortunately for my purposes, the marks are not published. They are not even assigned on a uniform system, since each examiner is permitted to employ his own scale of marks; but whatever scale he uses, the results as to proportional merit are the same. I am indebted to a Cambridge examiner for a copy of his marks in respect to two examinations, in which the scales of marks were so alike as to make it easy, by a slight proportional adjustment, to compare the two together. This was, to a certain degree, a confidential communication, so that it would be improper for me to publish anything that would identify the years to which these marks refer. I simply give them as groups of figures, sufficient to show the enormous differences of merit. The lowest man in the list of honours gains less than 300 marks, the lowest wrangler gains about 1,500 marks; and the senior wrangler, in one of the lists now before me, gained more than 7,500 marks. Consequently, the lowest wrangler has more than five times the merit of the lowest junior optime, and less than one-fifth the merit of the senior wrangler.

Scale of Merit Among the Men who Obtain Mathematical Honours at Cambridge

The results of two years are thrown into a single table.
The total number of marks obtainable in each year was 17,000.

Number of marks obtained by candidates.	*Number of candidates in the two years, taken together, who obtained those marks.*
Under 500	24[1]
500 to 1,000	74
1,000 to 1,500	38
1,500 to 2,000	21
2,000 to 2,500	11
2,500 to 3,000	8
3,000 to 3,500	11
3,500 to 4,000	5
4,000 to 4,500	2
4,500 to 5,000	1
5,000 to 5,500	3
5,500 to 6,000	1
6,000 to 6,500	0
6,500 to 7,000	0
7,000 to 7,500	0
7,500 to 8,000	1
	200

[1] I have included in this table only the first 100 men in each year. The omitted residue is too small to be important. I have omitted it lest, if the precise numbers of honour men were stated, those numbers would have served to identify the years. For reasons already given, I desire to afford no data to serve that purpose.

The precise number of marks obtained by the senior wrangler in the more remarkable of these two years was 7,634; by the second wrangler in the same year, 4,123; and by the lowest man in the list of honours, only 237. Consequently, the senior wrangler obtained nearly twice as many marks as the second wrangler, and more than thirty-two times as many as the lowest man. I have received from another examiner the marks of a year in which the senior wrangler was conspicuously eminent. He obtained 9,422 marks, whilst the second in the same year—whose merits were by no means inferior to those of second wranglers in general—obtained only 5,642. The man at the bottom of the same honour list had only 309 marks, or one-thirtieth the number of the senior wrangler. I have some particulars of a fourth very remarkable year, in which the senior wrangler obtained no less than ten times as many marks as the second wrangler, in the "problem paper." Now, I have discussed with practised examiners the question of how far the numbers of marks may be considered as proportionate to the mathematical power of the candidate, and am assured they are strictly proportionate as regards the lower places, but do not afford full justice to the highest. In other words, the senior wranglers above mentioned had more than thirty, or thirty-two times the ability of the lowest men on the lists of honours. They would be able to grapple with problems more than thirty-two times as difficult; or when dealing with subjects of the same difficulty, but intelligible to all, would comprehend them more rapidly in perhaps the square root of that proportion. It is reasonable to expect that marks would do some injustice to the very best men, because a very large part of the time of the examination is taken up by the mechanical labour of writing. Whenever the thought of the candidate outruns his pen, he gains no advantage from his excess of promptitude in conception. I should, however, mention that some of the ablest men have shown their superiority by comparatively little writing. They find their way at once to the root of the difficulty in the problems that are set, and, with a few clean, apposite, powerful strokes, succeed in proving they can overthrow it, and then they go on to another question. Every word they write tells. Thus, the late Mr. H. Leslie Ellis, who was a brilliant senior wrangler in 1840, and whose name is familiar to many generations of Cambridge men as a prodigy of universal genius, did not even remain during the full period in the examination room: his health was weak, and he had to husband his strength.

The mathematical powers of the last man on the list of honours, which are so low when compared with those of a senior wrangler, are mediocre, or even above mediocrity, when compared with the gifts of Englishmen generally. Though the examination places 100 honour men above him, it puts no less than 300 "poll men" below him. Even if we go so far as to allow that 200 out of the 300 refuse to work hard enough to get honours, there will remain 100 who, even if they worked hard, could not get them. Every tutor knows how difficult it is to drive abstract conceptions, even of the simplest kind, into the brains of most people—how feeble and hesitating is their mental grasp—how easily their brains are mazed—how incapable they are of precision and soundness of knowledge. It often occurs to persons familiar with some scientific subject to hear men and women of mediocre gifts relate to one another what they have picked up about it from some lecture—say at the Royal Institution, where they have sat for an hour listening with delighted attention to an admirably lucid account, illustrated by experiments of the most perfect and beautiful character, in all of which they expressed themselves intensely gratified and highly instructed. It is positively painful to hear what they say. Their recollections seem to be a mere chaos of mist and misapprehension, to which some sort of shape and organization has been given by the action of their own pure fancy, altogether alien to what the lecturer intended to convey. The average mental grasp even of what is called a well-educated audience, will be found to be ludicrously small when rigorously tested.

In stating the differences between man and man, let it not be supposed for a moment that mathematicians are necessarily one-sided in their natural gifts. There are numerous instances of the reverse, of whom the following will be found, as instances of hereditary genius, in the appendix to my chapter on "Science." I would especially name Leibnitz, as being universally gifted; but Ampere, Arago, Condorcet, and D'Alembert, were all of them very far more than mere mathematicians. Nay, since the range of examination at Cambridge is so extended as to include other subjects besides mathematics, the differences of ability between the highest and lowest of the successful candidates, is yet more glaring than what I have already described. We still find, on the one hand, mediocre men, whose whole energies are absorbed in getting their 237 marks for mathematics; and, on the other hand, some few senior wranglers who are at the same time high classical scholars and much more besides. Cambridge has afforded such instances. Its lists of classical honours are comparatively of recent date, but other evidence is obtainable from earlier times of their occurrence. Thus, Dr. George Butler, the Head Master of Harrow for very many years, including the period when Byron was a schoolboy, (father of the present Head Master, and of other sons, two of whom are also head masters of great public schools,) must have obtained that classical office on account of his eminent classical ability; but Dr. Butler was also senior wrangler in 1794, the year when Lord Chancellor Lyndhurst was second. Both Dr. Kaye, the late Bishop of Lincoln, and Sir E. Alderson, the late judge, were the senior wranglers and the first classical prizemen of their respective years. Since 1824, when the classical tripos was first established, the late Mr. Goulburn (brother of Dr. Goulburn, Dean of Norwich, and son of the well-known Serjeant Goulburn) was second wrangler in 1835, and senior classic of the same year. But in more recent times, the necessary labour of preparation, in order to acquire the highest mathematical places, has become so enormous that there has been a wider differentiation of studies. There is no longer time for a man to acquire the necessary knowledge to succeed to the first place in more than one subject. There are, therefore, no instances of a man being absolutely first in both examinations, but a few can be found of high eminence in both classics and mathematics, as a reference to the lists published in the "Cambridge Calendar" will show. The best of these more recent degrees appears to be that of Dr. Barry, late Principal of Cheltenham, and now Principal of King's College, London (the son of the eminent architect, Sir Charles Barry, and brother of Mr. Edward Barry, who succeeded his father as architect). He was fourth wrangler and seventh classic of his year.

In whatever way we may test ability, we arrive at equally enormous intellectual differences. Lord Macaulay (see under "Literature" for his remarkable kinships) had one of the most tenacious of memories. He was able to recall many pages of hundreds of volumes by various authors, which he had acquired by simply reading them over. An average man could not certainly carry in his memory one thirty-second—ay, or one hundredth—part as much as Lord Macaulay. The father of Seneca had one of the greatest memories on record in ancient times (see under "Literature" for his kinships). Porson, the Greek scholar, was remarkable for this gift, and, I may add, the "Porson memory" was hereditary in that family. In statesmanship, generalship, literature, science, poetry, art, just the same enormous differences are found between man and man; and numerous instances recorded in this book, will show in how small degree, eminence, either in these or any other class of intellectual powers, can be considered as due to purely special powers. They are rather to be considered in those instances as the result of concentrated efforts, made by men who are widely gifted. People lay too much stress on apparent specialities, thinking overrashly that, because a man is devoted to some particular pursuit, he could not possibly have succeeded in anything else. They might just as well say that, because a youth had fallen desperately in love with a brunette, he could not possibly have fallen in love with a blonde. He may or may not have more natural liking for the former type of beauty than the latter, but it is as probable as not that the affair was mainly or wholly due to a general amorousness of disposition. It is just the same with special pursuits. A gifted man is often capricious and fickle before he selects his occupation, but when it has been chosen, he devotes himself to it with a truly passionate ardour. After a man of genius has selected his hobby, and so adapted himself to it as to seem unfitted for any other occupation in life, and to be possessed of but one special aptitude, I often notice, with admiration, how well he bears himself when circumstances suddenly thrust him into a strange position. He will display an insight into new conditions, and a power of dealing with them, with which even his most intimate friends were unprepared to accredit him. Many a presumptuous fool has mistaken indifference and neglect for incapacity; and in trying to throw a man of genius on ground where he was unprepared for attack, has himself received a most severe and unexpected fall. I am sure that no one who has had the privilege of mixing in the society of the abler men of any great capital, or who is acquainted with the biographies of the heroes of history, can doubt the existence of grand human animals, of natures pre-eminently noble, of individuals born to be kings of men. I have been conscious of no slight misgiving that I was committing a kind of sacrilege whenever, in the preparation of materials for this book, I had occasion to take the measurement of modern intellects vastly superior to my own, or to criticize the genius of the most magnificent historical specimens of our race. It was a process that constantly recalled to me a once familiar sentiment in bygone days of African travel, when I used to take altitudes of the huge cliffs that domineered above me as I travelled along their bases, or to map the mountainous landmarks of unvisited tribes, that loomed in faint grandeur beyond my actual horizon.

I have not cared to occupy myself much with people whose gifts are below the average, but they would be an interesting study. The number of idiots and imbeciles among the twenty million inhabitants of England and Wales is approximately estimated at 50,000, or as 1 in 400. Dr. Segiun, a great French authority on these matters, states that more than thirty per cent of idiots and imbeciles, put under suitable instruction, have been taught to conform to social and moral law, and rendered capable of order, of good feeling, and of working like the third of an average man. He says that more than forty per cent have become capable of the ordinary transactions of life, under friendly control; of understanding moral and social abstractions, and of working like two-thirds of a man. And, lastly, that from twenty-five to thirty per cent come nearer and nearer to the standard of manhood, till some of them will defy the scrutiny of good judges, when compared with ordinary young men and women. In the order next above idiots and imbeciles are a large number of milder cases scattered among private families and kept out of sight, the existence of whom is, however, well known to relatives and friends; they are too silly to take a part in general society, but are easily amused with some trivial, harmless occupation. Then comes a class of whom the Lord Dundreary of the famous play may be considered a representative; and so, proceeding through successive grades, we gradually ascend to mediocrity. I know two good instances of hereditary silliness short of imbecility, and have reason to believe I could easily obtain a large number of similar facts.

To conclude, the range of mental power between—I will not say the highest Caucasian and the lowest savage—but between the greatest and least of English intellects, is enormous. There is a continuity of natural ability reaching from one knows not what height, and descending to one can hardly say what depth. I propose in this chapter to range men according to their natural abilities, putting them into classes separated by equal degrees of merit, and to show the relative number of individuals included in the several classes. Perhaps some persons might be inclined to make an offhand guess that the number of men included in the several classes would be pretty equal. If he thinks so, I can assure him he is most egregiously mistaken.

The method I shall employ for discovering all this, is an application of the very curious theoretical law of "deviation from an average." First, I will explain the law, and then I will show that the production of natural intellectual gifts comes justly within its scope.

The law is an exceedingly general one. M. Quetelet, the Astronomer-Royal of Belgium, and the greatest authority on vital and social statistics, has largely used it in his inquiries. He has also constructed numerical tables, by which the necessary calculations can be easily made, whenever it is desired to have recourse to the law. Those who wish to learn more than I have space to relate, should consult his work, which is a very readable octavo volume, and deserves to be far better known to statisticians than it appears to be. Its title is *Letters on Probabilities*, translated by Downes. Layton and Co. London: 1849.

So much has been published in recent years about statistical deductions, that I am sure the reader will be prepared to assent freely to the following hypothetical case:—Suppose a large island inhabited by a single race, who intermarried freely, and who had lived for many generations under constant conditions; then the average height of the male adults of that population would undoubtedly be the same year after year. Also—still arguing from the experience of modern statistics, which are found to give constant results in far less carefully-guarded examples—we should undoubtedly find, year after year, the same proportion maintained between the number of men of different heights. I mean, if the average stature was found to be sixty-six inches, and if it was also found in any one year that 100 per million exceeded seventy-eight inches, the same proportion of 100 per million would be closely maintained in all other years. An equal constancy of proportion would be maintained between any other limits of height we pleased to specify, as between seventy-one and seventy-two inches; between seventy-two and seventy-three inches; and so on. Statistical experiences are so invariably confirmatory of what I have stated would probably be the case, as to make it unnecessary to describe analogous instances. Now, at this point, the law of deviation from an average steps in. It shows that the number per million whose heights range between seventy-one and seventy-two inches (or between any other limits we please to name) can be predicted from the previous datum of the average, and of any one other fact, such as that of 100 per million exceeding seventy-eight inches.

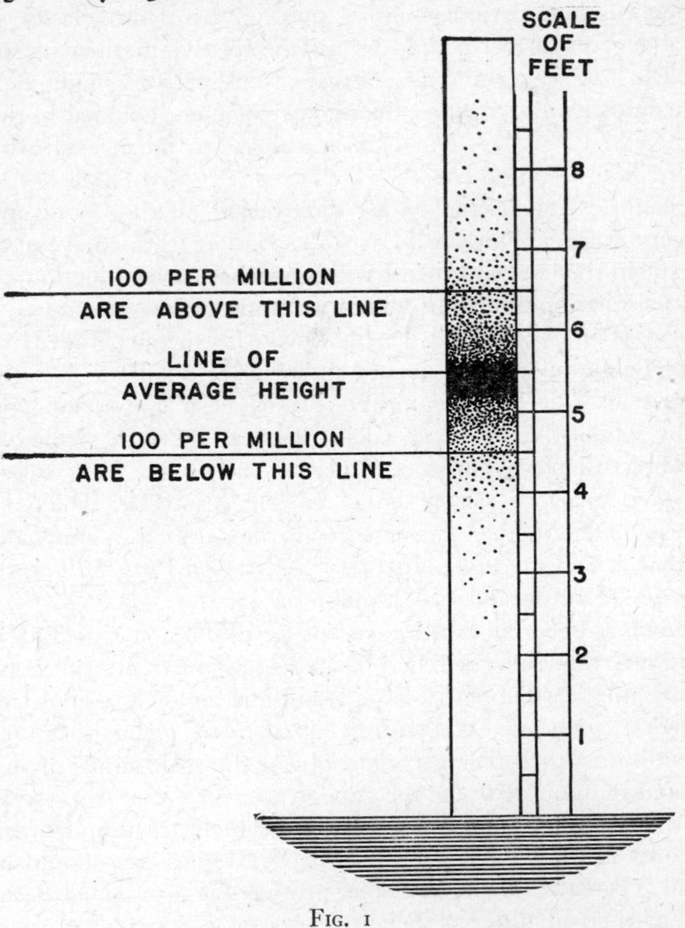

FIG. 1

The diagram on Figure 1 will make this more intelligible. Suppose a million of the men to stand in turns, with their backs against a vertical board of sufficient height, and their heights to be dotted off upon it. The board would then present the appearance shown in the diagram. The line of average height is that which divides the dots into two equal parts, and stands, in the case we have assumed, at the height of sixty-six inches. The dots will be found to be ranged so symmetrically on either side of the line of average, that the lower half of the diagram will be almost a precise reflection of the upper. Next, let a hundred dots be counted from above downwards, and let a line be drawn below them. According to the conditions, this line will stand at the height of seventy-eight inches. Using the data afforded by these two lines, it is possible, by the help of the law of deviation from an average, to reproduce, with extraordinary closeness, the entire system of dots on the board.

M. Quetelet gives tables in which the uppermost line, instead of cutting off 100 in a million, cuts off only one in a million. He divides the intervals between that line and the line of average, into eighty equal divisions, and gives the number of dots that fall within each of those divisions. It is easy, by the help of his tables, to calculate what would occur under any other system of classification we pleased to adopt.

This law of deviation from an average is perfectly general in its application. Thus, if the marks had been made by bullets fired at a horizontal line stretched in front of the target, they would have been distributed according to the same law. Wherever there is a large number of similar events, each due to the resultant influences of the same variable conditions, two effects will follow. First, the average value of those events will be constant; and, secondly, the deviations of the several events from the average, will be governed by this law (which is, in principle, the same as that which governs runs of luck at a gaming-table).

The nature of the conditions affecting the several events must, I say, be the same. It clearly would not be proper to combine the heights of men belonging to two dissimilar races, in the expectation that the compound results would be governed by the same constants. A union of two dissimilar systems of dots would produce the same kind of confusion as if half the bullets fired at a target had been directed to one mark, and the other half to another mark. Nay, an examination of the dots would show to a person, ignorant of what had occurred, that such had been the case, and it would be possible, by aid of the law, to disentangle two or any moderate number of superimposed series of marks. The law may, therefore, be used as a most trustworthy criterion, whether or no the events of which an average has been taken are due to the same or to dissimilar classes of conditions.

I selected the hypothetical case of a race of men living on an island and freely intermarrying, to ensure the conditions under which they were all supposed to live, being uniform in character. It will now be my aim to show there is sufficient uniformity in the inhabitants of the British Isles to bring them fairly within the grasp of this law.

For this purpose, I first call attention to an example given in Quetelet's book. It is of the measurements of the circumferences of the chests of a large number of Scotch soldiers. The Scotch are by no means a strictly uniform race, nor are they exposed to identical conditions. They are a mixture of Celts, Danes, Anglo-Saxons, and others, in various proportions, the Highlanders being almost purely Celts. On the other hand, these races, though diverse in origin, are not very dissimilar in character. Consequently, it will be found that their deviations from the average, follow theoretical computations with remarkable accuracy. The instance is as follows. M. Quetelet obtained his facts from the thirteenth volume of the *Edinburgh Medical Journal*, where the measurements are given in respect to 5,738 soldiers, the results being grouped in order of magnitude, proceeding by differences of one inch. Professor Quetelet compares these results with those that his tables give, and here is the result. The marvellous accordance between fact and theory must strike the most unpractised eye. I should say that, for the sake of convenience, both the measurements and calculations have been reduced to per thousandths:—

Measures of the chest in inches	*Number of men per 1,000, by experience*	*Number of men per 1,000, by calculation*	*Measures of the chest in inches*	*Number of men per 1,000, by experience*	*Number of men per 1,000, by calculation*
33	5	7	41	1,628	1,675
34	31	29	42	1,148	1,096
35	141	110	43	645	560
36	322	323	44	160	221
37	732	732	45	87	69
38	1,305	1,333	46	38	16
39	1,867	1,838	47	7	3
40	1,882	1,987	48	2	1

I will now take a case where there is a greater dissimilarity in the elements of which the average has been taken. It is the height of 100,000 French conscripts. There is fully as much variety in the French as in the English, for it is not very many generations since France was divided into completely independent kingdoms. Among its peculiar races are those of Normandy, Brittany, Alsatia, Provence, Bearne, Auvergne—each with their special characteristics; yet the following table shows a most striking agreement between the results of experience compared with those derived by calculation, from a purely theoretical hypothesis.

The greatest differences are in the lowest ranks. They include the men who were rejected from being too short for the army. M. Quetelet boldly ascribes these differences to the effect of fraudulent returns. It certainly seems that men have been improperly taken out of the second rank and

Height of Men	*Number of Men*	
	Measured	*Calculated*
Under 61.8	28,620	26,345
61.8 to 62.9	11,580	13,182
62.9 to 63.9	13,990	14,502
63.9 to 65.0	14,410	13,982
65.0 to 66.1	11,410	11,803
66.1 to 67.1	8,780	8,725
67.1 to 68.2	5,530	5,527
68.2 to 69.3	3,190	3,187
Above 69.3	2,490	2,645

put into the first, in order to exempt them from service. Be this as it may, the coincidence of fact with theory is, in this instance also, quite close enough to serve my purpose.

I argue from the results obtained from Frenchmen and from Scotchmen, that, if we had measurements of the adult males in the British Isles, we should find those measurements to range in close accordance with the law of deviation from an average, although our population is as much mingled as I described that of Scotland to have been, and although Ireland is mainly people with Celts. Now, if this be the case with stature, then it will be true as regards every other physical feature–as circumference of head, size of brain, weight of grey matter, number of brain fibres, &c; and thence, by a step on which no physiologist will hesitate, as regards mental capacity.

This is what I am driving at–that analogy clearly shows there must be a fairly constant average mental capacity in the inhabitants of the British Isles, and that the deviations from that average–upwards towards genius, and downwards towards stupidity–must follow the law that governs deviations from all true averages.

I have, however, done somewhat more than rely on analogy. I have tried the results of those examinations in which the candidates had been derived from the same classes. Most persons have noticed the lists of successful competitors for various public appointments that are published from time to time in the newspapers, with the marks gained by each candidate attached to his name. These lists contain far too few names to fall into such beautiful accordance with theory, as was the case with Scotch soldiers. There are rarely more than 100 names in any one of these examinations, while the chests of no less than 5,700 Scotchmen were measured. I cannot justly combine the marks of several independent examinations into one fagot, for I understand that different examiners are apt to have different figures of merit; so I have analysed each examination separately. I give a calculation I made on the examination last before me; it will do as well as any other. It was for admission into the Royal Military College at Sandhurst, December 1868. The marks obtained were clustered most thickly about 3,000, so I take that number as representing the average ability of the candidates. From this datum, and from the fact that no candidate obtained more than 6,500 marks, I computed the column B in the following table, by the help of Quetelet's numbers. It will be seen that Column B accords with column A quite as closely as the small number of persons examined could have led us to expect.

Number of Marks obtained by the Candidates	*Number of Candidates who obtained those marks*			
	A *According to fact*		*B* *According to theory*	
6,500 and above	0	73	0	72
5,800 to 6,500	1		1	
5,100 to 5,800	3		5	
4,400 to 5,100	6		8	
3,700 to 4,400	11		13	
3,000 to 3,700	22		16	
2,300 to 3,000	22		16	
1,600 to 2,300	8		13	
1,100 to 1,600	Either did not venture to complete, or were plucked.		8	
400 to 1,100			5	
below 400			1	

The symmetry of the descending branch has been rudely spoilt by the conditions stated at the foot of column A. There is, therefore, little room for doubt, if everybody in England had to work up some subject and then to pass before examiners who employed similar figures of merit, that their marks would be found to range, according to the law of deviation from an average, just as rigorously as the heights of French conscripts, or the circumferences of the chests of Scotch soldiers.

The number of grades into which we may divide ability is purely a matter of option. We may consult our convenience by sorting Englishmen into a few large classes, or into many small ones. I will select a system of classification that shall be easily comparable with the numbers of eminent men, as determined in the previous chapter. We have seen that 250 men per million become eminent; accordingly, I have so contrived the classes in the following table that the two highest, F and G, together with X (which includes all cases beyond G, and which are unclassed), shall amount to about that number—namely, to 248 per million:—

Classification of Men According to Their Natural Gifts

Grades of natural ability, separated by equal intervals		Numbers of men comprised in the several grades of natural ability, whether in respect to their general powers, or to special aptitudes							
		Proportionate, viz. one in	In each million of the same age	In total male population of the United Kingdom, viz. 15 millions, of the undermentioned ages:—					
Below average	Above average			20–30	30–40	40–50	50–60	60–70	70–80
a	A	4	256,791	651,000	495,000	391,000	268,000	171,000	77,000
b	B	6	162,279	409,000	312,000	246,000	168,000	107,000	48,000
c	C	16	63,563	161,000	123,000	97,000	66,000	42,000	19,000
d	D	64	15,696	39,800	30,300	23,900	16,400	10,400	4,700
e	E	413	2,423	6,100	4,700	3,700	2,520	1,600	729
f	F	4,300	233	590	450	355	243	155	70
g	G	79,000	14	35	27	21	15	9	4
x	X								
all grades below g	all grades above G	1,000,000	1	3	2	2	2	—	—
On either side of average			500,000	1,268,000	964,000	761,000	521,000	332,000	149,000
Total, both sides			1,000,000	2,536,000	1,928,000	1,522,000	1,042,000	664,000	298,000

The proportions of men living at different ages are calculated from the proportions that are true for England and Wales. (Census 1861, Appendix, p. 107.)

Example.—The class F contains 1 in every 4,300 men. In other words, there are 233 of that class in each million of men. The same is true of class f. In the whole United Kingdom there are 590 men of class F (and the same number of f) between the ages of 20 and 30; 450 between the ages of 30 and 40; and so on.

It will, I trust, be clearly understood that the numbers of men in the several classes in my table depend on no uncertain hypothesis. They are determined by the assured law of deviations from an average. It is an absolute fact that if we pick out of each million the one man who is naturally the ablest, and also the one man who is the most stupid, and divide the remaining 999,998 men into fourteen classes, the average ability in each being separated from that of its neighbours by equal grades, then the numbers in each of those classes will, on the average of many millions, be as is stated in the table. The table may be applied to special, just as truly as to general ability. It would be true for every examination that brought out natural gifts, whether held in painting, in music, or in statesmanship. The proportions between the different classes would be identical in all these cases, although the classes would be made up of different individuals, according as the examination differed in its purport.

It will be seen that more than half of each million is contained in the two mediocre classes a and A; the four mediocre classes a, b, A, B, contain more than four-fifths, and the six mediocre classes more than nineteen-twentieths of the entire population. Thus, the rarity of commanding ability, and the vast abundance of mediocrity, is no accident, but follows of necessity, from the very nature of these things.

The meaning of the word "mediocrity" admits of little doubt. It defines the standard of intellectual power found in most provincial gatherings, because the attractions of a more stirring life in the metropolis and elsewhere, are apt to draw away the abler classes of men, and the silly and the imbecile do not take a part in the gatherings. Hence, the residuum that forms the bulk of the general society of small provincial places, is commonly very pure in its mediocrity.

The class C possesses abilities a trifle higher than those commonly possessed by the foreman of an ordinary jury. D includes the mass of men who obtain the ordinary prizes of life. E is a stage higher. Then we reach F, the lowest of those yet superior classes of intellect, with which this volume is chiefly concerned.

On descending the scale, we find by the time we have reached f, that we are already among the idiots and imbeciles. We have seen that there are 400 idiots and imbeciles, to every million of persons living in this country; but that 30 per cent. of their number, appear to be light cases, to whom the name of idiot is inappropriate. There will remain 280 true idiots and imbeciles, to every million of our population. This ratio coincides very closely with the requirements of class f. No doubt a certain proportion of them are idiotic owing to some fortuitous cause, which may interfere with the working of a naturally good brain, much as a bit of dirt may cause a first-rate chronometer to keep worse time than an ordinary watch. But I presume, from the usual smallness of head and absence of disease among these persons, that the proportion of accidental idiots cannot be very large.

Hence we arrive at the undeniable, but unexpected conclusion, that eminently gifted men are raised as much above mediocrity as idiots are depressed below it; a fact that is calculated to considerably enlarge our ideas of the enormous differences of intellectual gifts between man and man.

I presume the class F of dogs, and others of the more intelligent sort of animals, is nearly commensurate with the f of the human race, in respect to memory and powers of reason. Certainly the class G of such animals is far superior to the g of humankind.

Wilhelm Wundt: 1832-1920

PRINCIPLES OF PHYSIOLOGICAL PSYCHOLOGY *

1873

AUTHOR'S PREFACE TO THE FIRST EDITION

THE work which I here present to the public is an attempt to mark out a new domain of science. I am well aware that the question may be raised, whether the time is yet ripe for such an undertaking. The new discipline rests upon anatomical and physiological foundations which, in certain respects, are themselves very far from solid; while the experimental treatment of psychological problems must be pronounced, from every point of view, to be still in its first beginnings. At the same time the best means of discovering the blanks that our ignorance has left in the subject matter of a developing science is, as we all know, to take a general survey of its present status. A first attempt, such as this book represents, must show many imperfections; but the more imperfect it is, the more effectively will it call for improvement. Moreover, it is especially true in this field of inquiry that the solution of many problems is intimately bound up with their relation to other groups of facts, facts that often appear remote and disconnected; so that the wider view is necessary, if we are to find the right path.

AUTHOR'S PREFACE TO THE FIFTH EDITION

When this book first came before the world, nearly eight and twenty years ago, the status of the science for which it hoped to prepare a place was very different from that of the physiological psychology of today. At that time only one successful attempt had been made—in Fechner's *Elemente der Psychophysik*—to throw the light of an exact procedure upon philosophical problems that might, in the last resort, be regarded as psychological. Fechner apart, the adventurer in "experimental psychology" was still reduced, in most instances, to borrow what he could from other disciplines, especially from the physiology of sense and nervous system. Today all this is changed; there is pouring in from all sides—

* The first edition of this work was published in 1873. It was frequently revised by Wundt. Part of the fifth German edition was translated by E. B. Titchener and published in 1910. Excerpts are here reprinted by permission of the Macmillan Co. and Allen & Unwin, Ltd.

from the psychological laboratories proper, from neighbouring disciplines, from every science that comes into contact with psychological problems—an amount of expository material that, even now, is hardly calculable. At that time the investigator who sought to employ accuracy of method in any question of psychology was challenged at every point, by philosophy as by natural science, to prove that his endeavours were legitimate. Today these doubts are hardly to be feared. But, to offset our advantage, there have appeared within psychology itself strongly divergent tendencies, some of which cover profound differences of principle regarding the problems and aims of the science, and the paths that it should pursue.

THE PROBLEM OF PHYSIOLOGICAL PSYCHOLOGY

As an experimental science, physiological psychology seeks to accomplish a reform in psychological investigation comparable with the revolution brought about in the natural sciences by the introduction of the experimental method. From one point of view, indeed, the change wrought is still more radical: for while in natural science it is possible, under favourable conditions, to make an accurate observation without recourse to experiment, there is no such possibility in psychology. It is only with grave reservations that what is called "pure self-observation" can properly be termed observation at all, and under no circumstances can it lay claim to accuracy. On the other hand, it is of the essence of experiment that we can vary the conditions of an occurrence at will and, if we are aiming at exact results, in a quantitatively determinable way. Hence even in the domain of natural science, the aid of the experimental method becomes indispensable whenever the problem set is the analysis of transient and impermanent phenomena, and not merely the observation of persistent and relatively constant objects. But conscious contents are at the opposite pole from permanent objects; they are processes, fleeting occurrences, in continual flux and change. In their case, therefore, the experimental method is of cardinal importance; it and it alone makes a scientific introspection possible. For all accurate observation implies that the object of observation (in this case the psychical process) can be held fast by the attention, and any changes that it undergoes attentively followed. And this fixation by the attention implies, in its turn, that the observed object is independent of the observer. Now it is obvious that the required independence does not obtain in any attempt at a direct self-observation, undertaken without the help of experiment. The endeavour to observe oneself must inevitably introduce changes into the course of mental events,—changes which could not have occurred without it, and whose usual consequence is that the very process which was to have been observed disappears from consciousness. The psychological experiment proceeds very differently. In the first place, it creates external conditions that look towards the production of a determinate mental process at a given moment. In the second place, it makes the observer so far master of the general situation, that the state of consciousness accompanying this process remains approximately unchanged. The great importance of the experimental method, therefore, lies not simply in the fact that, here as in the physical realm, it enables us arbitrarily to vary the conditions of our observations, but also and essentially in the further fact that it makes observation itself possible for us. The results of this observation may then be fruitfully employed in the examination of other mental phenomena, whose nature prevents their own direct experimental modification.

We may add that, fortunately for the science, there are other sources of objective psychological knowledge, which become accessible at the very point where the experimental method fails us. These are certain products of the common mental life, in which we may trace the operation of determinate psychical motives: chief among them are language, myth and custom. In part determined by historical conditions, they are also, in part, dependent upon universal psychological laws; and the phenomena that are referable to these laws form the subject-matter of a special psychological discipline, ethnic psychology. The results of ethnic psychology constitute, at the same time, our chief source of information regarding the general psychology of the complex mental processes. In this way, experimental psychology and ethnic psychology form the two principal departments of scientific psychology at large. They are supplemented by child and animal psychology, which in conjunction with ethnic psychology attempt to resolve the problems of psychogenesis. Workers in both these fields may, of course, avail themselves within certain limits of the advantages of the experimental method. But the results of experiment are here matters of objective observation only, and the experimental method accordingly loses the peculiar significance which it possesses as an instrument of introspection.

Wilhelm Preyer: 1842-1897

THE MIND OF THE CHILD *

1882

I PROPOSED to myself a number of years ago, the task of studying the child, both before birth and in the period immediately following, from the physiological point of view, with the object of arriving at an explanation of the origin of the separate vital processes. It was soon apparent to me that a division of the work would be advantageous to its prosecution. For life in the embryo is so essentially different a thing from life beyond it, that a separation must make it easier both for the investigator to do his work and for the reader to follow the exposition of its results. I have, therefore, discussed by itself, life before birth, the *Physiology of the Embryo*. The vital phenomena of the human being in the earliest period of his independent existence in the world are, again, so complicated and so various in kind, that here too a division soon appeared expedient. I separated the physical development of the newly-born and the very young child from his mental development, and have endeavored to describe the latter in the present book; at least, I hope that, by means of personal observations carried on for several years, I have furnished facts that may serve as material for a future description.

A forerunner of the work is a lecture, "Psychogenesis" (the Genesis of Mind), given before a scientific association at Berlin on the 3d of January, 1880, and soon after made public in my book. *Naturwissenschaftliche Thatsachen und Probleme (Facts and Problems of Natural Science)* Berlin, 1880.

This sketch has given manifold indictment to fresh observations. But great as is the number of occasional observations in regard to many children, I do not thus far know of diaries regularly kept concerning the mental development of individual children. Now precisely this chronological investigation of mental progress in the first and second years of life presents great difficulties, because it requires the daily registering of experiences than can be had only in the nursery. I have, notwithstanding, kept a complete diary from the birth of my son to the end of his third

* While several brief biographical accounts of child development appeared before 1882, Preyer's study was much more systematic and extensive than those of his predecessors. It contributed significantly toward the establishment of child psychology as a field of psychological science. The selection reproduced is Preyer's preface to the first edition, as presented in the English edition by D. Appleton and Co., 1888.

year. Occupying myself with the child at least three times a day—at morning, noon, and evening—and almost every day, with two trifling interruptions, and guarding him, as far as possible, against such training as children usually receive, I found nearly every day some fact of mental genesis to record. The substance of that diary has passed into this book.

No doubt the development of one child is rapid and that of another is slow; very great individual differences appear in children of the same parents even, but the differences are much more of time and degree than of the order in which the steps are taken, and these steps are the same in all individuals; that is the important matter. Desirable as it is to collect statistics concerning the mental development of many infants—the activity of their senses, their movements, especially their acquirement of speech—yet the accurate, daily repeated observation of one child—a child sound in health, having no brothers or sisters, and whose development was neither remarkably rapid nor remarkably slow—seemed at least quite as much to be desired. I have, however, taken notice, as far as possible, of the experiences of others in regard to other normal children in the first years of life, and have even compared many of these where opportunity offered.

But a description of the gradual appearance of brain-activity in the child, along with the most careful observation of his mental ripening, would be only a beginning. The development of mind, like the development of body, must be regarded as dating back far beyond the origin of the individual being.

If the infant brings into the world a set of organs which begin to be active only after a long time, and are absolutely useless up to that time—as, e.g., the lungs were before birth—then the question, To what causes do such organs and functions owe their existence? can have but one answer—heredity.

This, to be sure, explains nothing; but dim as the notion is, much is gained toward our understanding of the matter, in the fact that some functions are inherited while others are not.

What is acquired by experience is only a part. The question whether a function of the brain, on which everything depends in the development of the child's mind, is inherited or acquired, must be answered in each individual case, if we would not go astray in the labyrinth of appearances and hypotheses.

Above all, we must be clear on this point, that the fundamental activities of mind, which are manifested only after birth, do not originate after birth.

If they had previously no existence at all, we could not discover when they come or at what time. The substance of a hen's egg that has been fecundated, but is frozen as hard as a stone, certainly has no sensation;

but after thawing and three weeks' warming, that same substance, changed into a living chicken, has sensation.

The capacity of feeling, in case of the fulfillment of certain outward conditions, if it be not a property of the egg, must have originated during incubation from matter incapable of sentiency; that is, the material atoms must not only have arranged themselves in a different order, receiving through their union and separation different chemical properties, as actually happens; must not only have changed their physical properties—e.g., elasticity, solidity, etc., which are partly dependent on the chemical, partly independent of them—as likewise happens; but these atoms must have gained entirely new properties which were neither chemically nor physically indicated beforehand, were not to be assumed or predicated. For neither chemistry nor physics can attribute to the substances that constitute the egg other than chemical and physical properties. But if the warming, ventilation, evaporation, and liberation of carbonic acid have had their normal course during incubation, then these new mental properties present themselves, and that without the possibility of their being gained by imitation in the incubator. And these properties are similar to those of the beings that produced the egg. Hence, it must be admitted that these beings have imparted to the egg matter which contained, in addition to the known or physically and chemically discoverable properties, latent properties not chemically and physically discoverable—psychical, therefore, physiological—these being potential, so that warming, airing, etc., are necessary to their development. The same conditions are required for the development of the tissues and organs of the embryo, which likewise were not contained in the albumen, sugar, and fat, in the water and the salts of the egg; neither do their properties belong to those with which chemistry and physics are concerned, but they are like those of the generators of the egg.

Some parts of the contents of the egg, then, possess potentially properties unquestionably mental—the capacity of sensation, at least. And these parts must, at the same time, be those from which originate the cotyledons (of plants), the foundation of the embryo. As is well known, they are cellular forms with the power of independent movement, to which can not be denied, any more than to the lowest zoophytes, the capacity of discrimination. They grow and move by putting out and drawing in pseudopodia; they undoubtedly appropriate nourishment, require oxygen, multiply by division, conduct themselves in general like amoebae, or other simple living beings. The opinion that they possess a certain crude psychical endowment, sensation of an obscure sort, can not be refuted.

Everything goes to show a continuity in the capacity of sensation. This capacity does not spring afresh each time in the human being out of material incapable of sensation, but, as a hereditary property of the parts of the egg, is differentiated in these, and by stimulus from without is brought into action—the process being hardly discernible in the embryo protected from this stimulus, but plainly visible in the new-born child.

The mind of the new-born child, then, does not resemble a tabula rasa, upon which the senses first write their impressions, so that out of these the sum-total of our mental life arises through manifold reciprocal action, but the tablet is already written upon before birth, with many illegible, nay, unrecognizable and invisible, marks, the traces of the imprint of countless sensuous impressions of long-gone generations. So blurred and indistinct are these remains, that we might, indeed, suppose the tablet to be blank, so long as we did not examine the changes it undergoes in earliest youth. But the more attentively the child is observed, the more easily legible becomes the writing, not at first to be understood, that he brings with him into the world. Then we perceive what a capital each individual has inherited from his ancestors—how much there is that is not produced by sense-impressions, and how false is the supposition that man learns to feel, to will, and to think, only through his senses. Heredity is just as important as individual activity in the genesis of mind. No man is in this matter a mere upstart, who is to achieve the development of his mind (psyche) through his individual experience alone; rather must each one, by means of his experience, fill out and animate anew his inherited endowments, the remains of the experiences and activities of his ancestors.

It is hard to discern and to decipher the mysterious writing on the mind of the child. It is just that which constitutes a chief problem of this book.

Granville Stanley Hall: 1844-1922

THE CONTENTS OF CHILDREN'S MINDS *

1883

IN October, 1869, the Pedagogical Society of Berlin issued a circular requesting the masters of the eighty-four established schools of that city to ascertain how many of the children who entered the primary classes that fall had seen and could name certain common animals, insects, and plants, had taken certain walks, visited specified parks, museums, etc. It is more common in that country than in our own to connect songs, poems, reading exercises, and object lessons with the locality with which the child is most familiar, so that not only does the matter of elementary instruction vary considerably with the geographical, zoölogical, and botanical character of the different towns, and often even with the surroundings of different schools in the same city, but much importance is attached to stated holiday and half-holiday walks which teachers are expected to conduct with their pupils for educational purposes. To "determine the individuality of the children so far as conditioned by the concepts arising from their immediate environment," for statistical uses, was the express purpose of the questions proposed. It was expected that this "entrance examination" scheme, as it was humorously called, would show in a more definite form than ever before the psychic peculiarities of the different school districts of Berlin, upon which, from preliminary tests, locality seemed to exert a surprising influence. Besides a score or so of topographical questions, however—such as the public buildings, squares, chief streets, suburban pleasure resorts, etc.—others pertaining to the home, the farm, objects in natural history, and the aspects of the heavens were added, and finally the children were asked if they had any notion of God, Christ, could tell a Bible story, say a hymn or prayer, or had ever heard either of four of the best known of Grimm's tales. At first many of the children were questioned in classes, till, on account of intimidation in the presence of others, and other errors arising from a desire to appear wiser or not more ignorant than their mates, etc., it was found that more truthful results were obtained by questioning them in sections of eight or ten, altho this method nearly doubled the average ignorance displayed and quadrupled the work, which with one hundred

* Hall's paper is an important early contribution to both child psychology and educational psychology. The article first appeared in the *Princeton Review*, 1883, pp. 249-272. This article in its original form is reprinted in its entirety.

and thirty-eight questions was no small addition to that already required of the subordinate teachers to whom it was mainly entrusted. Of a little over two thousand children to whom these questions were put reliable results were thought to be obtained from about one half, while some teachers expressed the opinion that even they had no value owing to the haste and not unfrequently the unwillingness with which the work was undertaken.

It was with the advantages of many suggestions and not a few warnings from this attempt that the writer undertook, soon after the opening of the Boston schools in September last, to make out a list of questions suitable for obtaining an inventory of the contents of the mind of children of average intelligence on entering the primary schools of that city. All the local and many other of the German questions were for various reasons not suitable to children here, and the task of selecting those that should be so, tho perhaps not involving quite as many perplexing considerations as choosing an equally long list of normal words, was by no means easy. They must not be too familiar nor too hard and remote, but must give free and easy play to reason and memory. But especially, to yield most practical results, they must lie within the range of what children are commonly supposed or at least desired, by teachers and by those who write primary text-books and prescribe courses of instruction, to know. Many preliminary half-days of questioning small groups of children and receiving suggestions from many sources and the use of many primers, object-lesson courses, etc., now in use in this country were necessary before the first provisional list of one hundred and thirty-four questions was printed. The problem first in mind was strictly practical; viz., what may city children be assumed to know and have seen by their teachers when they enter school; altho other purposes more psychological shaped many other questions used later.

The difficulties and sources of possible error in the use of such questions are many. Not only are children prone to imitate others in their answers without stopping to think and give an independent answer of their own, but they often love to seem wise, and, to make themselves interesting, state what seems to interest us without reference to truth, divining the lines of our interest with a subtlety we do not suspect; if absurdities are doubted they are sometimes only the more protested, the faculties of some are benumbed and perhaps their tongues tied by bashfulness, while others are careless, listless, inattentive, and answer at random. Again, many questioners are brusque, lacking in sympathy or tact, or real interest or patience in the work, or perhaps regard it as trivial or fruitless. These and many other difficulties seemed best minimized by the following method which was finally settled upon and, with the cooperation of Mr. E. P. Seaver, superintendent of the Boston schools, put into operation. Four of the best trained and experienced kindergarten teachers were employed by the hour to question three children at a time in the dressing-room of the school by themselves alone, so as not to interrupt the school-work. No constraint was used, and, as several hours were necessary to finish each set, changes and rests were often needful, while by frequent correspondence and by meetings with the writer to discuss details and compare results uniformity of method was sought. The most honest and unembarrassed child's first answer to a direct question, e.g., whether it has seen a cow, sheep, etc., must rarely or never be taken without careful cross-questioning, a stated method of which was developed respecting many objects. If the child says it has seen a cow, but when asked its size points to its own finger-nail or hand and says, so big, as not unfrequently occurs, the inference is that it has at most only seen a picture of a cow, and thinks its size reproduced therein, and accordingly he is set down as deficient on that question. If, however, he is correct in size, but calls the color blue, does not know it as the source of milk, or that it has horns or hoofs,—several errors of the latter order have been generally allowed. A worm may be said to swim on the ground, butchers to kill only the bad animals, etc.; but when hams are said to grow on trees or in the ground, or a hill is described as a lump of dirt, or wool as growing on hens, as often occurs, deficiency is obvious. So many other visual and other notions that seem to adults so simple that they must be present to the mind with some completeness or not at all, are in the process of gradual acquisition element by element in the mind of a child, so that there must sometimes be confessedly a certain degree of arbitrariness in saying, as, except in cases of peculiar uncertainty, the questioners attempted to do, that the child has the concept or does not have it. Men's first names seem to have designated single striking qualities, but once applied they become general or specific names according to circumstances. Again, very few children knew that a tree had bark, leaves, trunk, and roots; but very few indeed had not noticed a tree enough for our "pass." Without specifying further details it may suffice here to say that the child was given the benefit of every doubt and credited with knowledge wherever its ignorance was not so radical as to make a chaos of what instruction and most primary text-books are wont to assume. It is important also to add that the questioners were requested to report manifest gaps in the child's knowledge in its own words, reproducing its syntax, pronunciation, etc.

About sixty teachers besides the above four have made returns from three or more children each. Many returns, however, are incomplete, careless, or show internal contradictions, and can be used only indirectly to control results from the other sources. From more than twice that number two hundred of the Boston children were selected as the basis of the following table. For certain questions and for many statistical purposes this number is much too small to yield very valuable results, but where, as in the majority of cases, the averages of these children taken by fiftics have varied less than ten per cent it is safe to infer that the figures have considerable representative worth and far more than they could have if the percentages were small. The precautions that were taken to avoid schools where the children come from homes representing extremes of either culture or ignorance, or to balance deviations from a conjectured average in one direction by like deviations in the other, and also to select from each school-room with the teacher's aid only children of average capacity and to dismiss each child found unresponsive or not acquainted with the English language, give to the percentages, it is believed, a worth which without these and other precautions to this end only far larger numbers could yield.

The following table shows the general results for a number of those questions which admit of categorical answers, only negative results being recorded; the italicized question in the "miscellaneous" class being based on only from forty to seventy-five children, the rest on two hundred, or in a few cases two hundred and fifty:

TABLE I

No.	*Name of the object or concept*	*Per cent of children ignorant of it*	*No.*	*Name of the object or concept*	*Per cent of children ignorant of it*
1	Beehive	80	1	Dew	78
2	Crow	77	2	What season it is	75.5
3	Bluebird	72.5	3	Seen hail	73
3	Ant	65.5	4	Seen rainbow	65
5	Squirrel	63	5	" sunrise	56.5
6	Snail	62	6	" sunset	53.5
7	Robin	60.5	7	" clouds	35
8	Sparrow	57.5	8	" stars	14
9	Sheep	54	9	" moon	7
10	Bee	52			
11	Frog	50	1	Concept of an island	87.5
12	Pig	47.5	2	" " a beach	55.5
13	Chicken	33.5	3	" " " woods	53.5
14	Worm	22	4	" " " river	48
15	Butterfly	20.5	5	" " " pond	40
16	Hen	19	6	" " " hill	28
17	Cow	18.5	7	" " " brook	15

TABLE I (continued)

No.	*Name of the object or concept*	*Per cent of children ignorant of it*
1	Growing wheat	92.5
2	Elm tree	91.5
3	Poplar tree	89
4	Willow	89
5	Growing oats	87.5
6	Oak tree	87
7	Pine	87
8	Maple	83
9	Growing moss	81.5
10	" strawberries	78.5
11	" clover	74
12	" beans	71.5
13	" blueberries	67.5
14	" blackberries	66
15	" corn	65.5
16	Chestnut tree	64
17	Planted a seed	63
18	Peaches on a tree	61
19	Growing potatoes	61
20	" buttercup	55.5
21	" rose	54
22	" grapes	53
23	" dandelion	52
24	" cherries	46
25	" pears	32
26	" apples	21
1	Where are the child's ribs	90.5
2	" " " " lungs	81
3	" " " " heart	80
4	" " " " wrists	70.5
5	Where are the ankles	65.5
6	" " " waist	52.5
7	" " " hips	45
8	" " " knuckles	36
9	" " " elbows	25
10	Know right and left hand	21.5
11	" cheek	18
12	" forehead	15
13	" throat	13.5
14	" knee	7
15	" stomach	6
1	Concept of a triangle	92
2	" " " square	56
3	" " " circle	35
4	The number five	28.5
5	" " four	17
6	" " three	8
1	Seen watchmaker at work	68
2	" file	65
3	" plough	64.5
4	" spade	62
5	" hoe	61
6	" bricklayer at work	44.5
7	" shoemaker at work	25
8	" axe	12
1	Know green by name	15
2	" blue by name	14
3	" yellow by name	13.5
4	" red by name	9
	Miscellaneous	
1	That leathern things come from animals	93.4
2	Maxim or proverb	91.5
3	Origin of cotton things	90
4	What flour is made of	89
5	Ability to knit	88
6	What bricks are made of	81.1
7	Shape of the world	70.3
8	Origin of woollen things	69

TABLE I (continued)

No.	*Name of the object or concept*	*Per cent of children ignorant of it*	*No.*	*Name of the object or concept*	*Per cent of children ignorant of it*
9	Never attended Kindergarten	67.5	15	Cannot sew	47.5
10	Never been in bathing	64.5	16	Cannot strike a given musical note	40
11	Can tell no rudiment of a story	58	17	Cannot beat time regularly	39
12	Not know wooden things are from trees	55	18	Have never saved cents at home	36
13	Origin of butter	50.5	19	Never been in the country	35.5
14	" meat from animals	48	20	Can repeat no verse	28
			21	Source of milk	20.5

The high rate of ignorance here indicated may surprise most who will be likely to read this report, because the childhood they know will be much above the average of intelligence here sought, as it may all, because the few memories of childhood which survive in adult life necessarily bear such slight traces of its imperfections and are from many causes so illusory. Skeins and spools of thread were said to grow on the sheep's back or on bushes, stockings on trees, butter to come from buttercups, flour to be made of beans, oats to grow on oaks, bread to be swelled yeast, trees to be stuck in the ground by God and rootless, meat to be dug from the ground, and potatoes to be picked from trees. Cheese is squeezed butter, the cow says "bow-wow," the pig purrs or burrows, worms are not distinguished from snakes, moss from the "toad's umbrella," bricks from stones, nor beans from trees. An oak may be known only as an acorn-tree or a button-tree, a pine only as a needle-tree, a bird's nest only as its bed, etc. So that while no one child has all these misconceptions none are free from them, and thus the liabilities are great that, in this chaos of half-assimilated impressions, half right, half wrong, some lost link may make utter nonsense or mere verbal cram of the most careful instruction, as in the cases of children referred to above who knew much by rote about a cow, its milk, horns, leather, meat, etc., but yet were sure from the picture-book that it was no bigger than a small mouse.

For 86 per cent of the above questions the average intelligence of thirty-six country children who were tested ranks higher than that of the city children of the table, and in many items very greatly. The subject-matter of primers for the latter is in great part still traditionally of country life; hence the danger of unwarranted presupposition is considerable. As our methods of teaching grow natural we realize that city life is unnatural, and that those who grow up without knowing the country are defrauded of that without which childhood can never be complete or normal. On the whole the material of the city is no doubt inferior in pedagogic value to country experience. A few days in the country at this age has raised

TABLE II

Name of the Object or Concept	*Per cent of Ignorance in 150 girls*	*Per cent of Ignorance in 150 boys*	*Per cent of Ignorance in 50 Irish Children*	*Per cent of Ignorance in 50 American Children*	*Per cent of Ignorance in 64 Kindergarten Children*
Beehive	81	75	86	70	61
Ant	59	60	74	38	26
Squirrel	69	50	66	42	43
Snail	69	73	92	72	62
Robin	69	44	64	36	29
Sheep	67	47	62	40	40
Bee	46	32	52	32	26
Frog	53	38	54	35	35
Pig	45	27	38	26	22
Chicken	35	21	32	16	22
Worm	21	17	26	16	9
Butterfly	14	16	26	8	9
Hen	15	14	18	2	14
Cow	18	12	20	6	10
Growing clover	59	68	84	42	29
" corn	58	50	60	68	32
" potatoes	55	54	62	44	34
" buttercup	50	51	66	40	31
" rose	48	48	60	42	33
" dandelion	44	42	62	34	31
" apples	16	16	18	12	5
Ribs	88	92	98	82	68
Ankles	58	52	62	40	38
Waist	53	52	64	32	36
Hips	50	47	72	31	24
Knuckles	27	27	34	12	23
Elbow	19	32	36	16	12

TABLE II (continued)

Name of the Object or Concept	*Per cent of Ignorance in 150 girls*	*Per cent of Ignorance in 150 boys*	*Per cent of Ignorance in 50 Irish Children*	*Per cent of Ignorance in 50 American Children*	*Per cent of Ignorance in 64 Kindergarten Children*
Right from left hand.	20	8	14	20	4
Wrist	21	34	44	9	19
Cheek	10	12	14	14	4
Forehead	10	11	12	10	7
Throat	10	18	14	16	14
Knee	4	5	2	10	2
Dew	64	63	92	52	57
What season it is	59	50	68	48	41
Hail	75	61	84	52	53
Rainbow	59	61	70	38	38
Sunrise	71	53	70	36	53
Sunset	47	49	52	32	29
Stars	15	10	12	4	7
Island	74	78	84	64	55
Beach	82	49	60	34	32
Woods	46	36	46	32	27
River	38	44	62	12	13
Pond	31	34	42	24	28
Hill	23	22	30	12	19
The number five	26	16	22	24	12
The number four ...	15	10	16	14	7
The number three ...	7	6	12	8	.0

the level of many a city child's intelligence more than a term or two of school training could do without it. It is there, too, that the foundations of a love of natural science are best laid. We cannot accept without many careful qualifications the evolutionary dictum that the child's mental development should repeat that of the race. Unlike primitive man the child's body is feeble and he is ever influenced by a higher culture about him. Yet from the primeval intimacy with the qualities and habits of plants, with the instincts of animals—so like those of children—with which hawking and trapping, the riding on instead of some distance behind horses, etc., made men familiar; from primitive industries and tools as first freshly suggested, if we believe Geiger, from the normal activities of the human organism, especially the tool of tools, the hand; from primitive shelter, cooking, and clothing, with which anthropological researches make us familiar, it is certain that not a few educational elements of great value can be selected and systematized for children, an increasing number of them in fact being already in use for juvenile games and recreations and for the vacation pastimes of adults. A country barn, a forest with its gloom and awe, its vague fears and indefinite sounds, is a great school at this age. The making of butter, which some teachers, after hearing so often that it grew inside eggs or on ice, or was made from buttermilk, think it worth while to make a thimbleful of it in a toy churn at school as an object-lesson; more acquaintance with birds, which, as having the most perfect senses, most constant motion in several elements, even Leopardi could panegyrize as the only real things of joy in the universe, and which the strange power of flight makes ideal beings with children, and whose nests were often said to grow on trees; more knowledge of kitchen-chemistry, of foods, their preparation and origin; wide prospects for the eyes—this is more pedagogic industrial training for young children, because more free and play-like, than sewing, or cooking, or whittling, or special trade-schools can be, as well as more hygienic. Many children locate all that is good and imperfectly known in the country, and nearly a dozen volunteered the statement that good people when they die go to the country—even here from Boston. It is things that live and, as it were, detach themselves from their background by moving that catch the eye and with it the attention, and the subjects which occupy and interest the city child are mainly in motion and therefore transient, while the country child has more solitude, and is likely to develop more independently and is less likely to be prematurely caught up into the absorbing activities and throbbing passions of manhood, and becomes more familiar with the experiences of primitive man. The city child knows a little of many more things and so is more liable to superficiality and has a wider field for error. At the same time it has two great advantages over the country child, in knowing more of human nature and in entering school with a much better developed sense of rhythm and all its important implications. On the whole, however, additional force seems thus given to the argument for excursions, by rail or otherwise, regularly provided for the poorer children who are causing the race to degenerate in the great centres of population, unfavourable enough for those with good homes or even for adults.

Words, in connection with rhyme, rhythm, alliteration, cadence, etc., or even without these simply as sound-pictures, often absorb the attention of children and yield them a really aesthetic pleasure either quite independently of their meaning or to the utter bewilderment of it. They hear fancied words in noises and sounds of nature and animals, and are persistent punners. As butterflies make butter to eat it or give it by squeezing, so grasshoppers give grass, bees give beads and beans, kittens grow on the pussy-willow, and all honey is from honeysuckles, and even a poplin dress is made of poplar-trees. When the cow lows it somehow blows its own horn; crows and scarecrows are confounded; and has some subtle relationship to aunt; angleworm suggests angle or triangle or ankle; Martie eats "tomarties;" a holiday is a day to "holler" on; Harry O'Neil is nicknamed Harry Oatmeal; isoceles is somehow related to sausages; October suggests knocked over: "I never saw a hawk, but I can hawk and spit too;" "I will not sing do re mi, but do re you;" "Miss Eaton will eat us"—these and many more from the questioners' notes, and the story of the child who, puzzled by the unfamiliar reflexive use of the verb, came to associate "now I lay me," etc., with a lama, or of another who was for years stultified as against a dead blank wall whenever the phrase "answer sought" occurred, suggest to us how, more or less consciously and more or less seriously, a child may be led, in the absence of corrective experience, to the most fantastic and otherwise unaccountable distortions of facts by shadowy word-spectres or husks. In many of the expressions quoted the child seems playing with relations once seriously held, and its "fun" to be joy over but lately broken mental fetters. Some at least of the not infrequently quite unintelligible statements or answers may perhaps be thus accounted for. Again, the child more than the adult thinks in pictures, gestures, and inarticulate sounds. The distinction between real and verbal knowledge has been carefully and constantly kept in mind by the questioners. Yet except a very few objects in the above table, as e.g. triangle and sparrow, a child may be said to know almost nothing of them, at least for school purposes, if he has no generally recognized name for them. The far greater danger is the converse, that only the name and not the thing itself will be known. To test for this was, with the exceptions presently to be noted, our constant aim, as it is that of true education to obviate it. The danger, however, is after all quite limited here, for the linguistic imperfections of children are far more often shown in combining words than in naming the concrete things they know or do not know. To name an object is a passion with them, for it is to put their own mark upon it, to appropriate it. From the talk which most children hear and use to book language is again an immense step. Words live only in the ear and mouth, and are pale and corpse-like when addressed to the eye. What we want, and indeed are likely soon to have, are carefully arranged child vocabularies and dictionaries of both verbal forms and meanings, to show teachers just the phonic elements and vocal combinations children have most trouble with, the words they most readily and surely acquire, their number and order in each thought-sphere—and the attributes and connotations most liable to confuse them. To that work it is believed the method here employed has already furnished valuable material in protocol soon to be augmented and digested.

To specify a few items more fully, the four color-questions were designed to test not color-blindness but the power to use color-names. The Holmgren worsteds were used, from which the child was asked to pick out, not colors like others to which its attention is directed without naming them, but the color named, to which he has no clue but the name. It did not seem safe to complicate the objects of the latter educational test with the former, so that some of those marked defective in the table may or may not have been color-blind. Excluding colored and Jewish children, both of whom seem to show exceptional percentages, and averaging the sexes, both Magnus and Jeffries found a little over two per cent of many thousand children color-blind. The children they tested, however, were much older than these, and two or three hundred is far too small a number to warrant us, were it otherwise allowable, in simply subtracting two per cent and inferring that the remainder were deficient only in knowledge of the color-word. Our figures, then, do not bear upon the question whether the color-sense itself is fully developed before the age of five or six or not. Again number cannot be developed to any practical extent without knowledge of the number-name. As Wundt's careful experiments show, the eye can apprehend but three of the smallest and simplest objects, unless they are arranged in some geometrical order, without taking considerable additional time to count. As the chromatic scale grades musical intervals or the names we count by graduate the vague sense of more or less, and later, as visible notes change all musical ideas and possibilities, so figures or number-signs almost create arithmetic. A child who seriously says a cat has three or five legs will pick out its own, e.g. fourth, seat in the fifth row in an empty school-room almost every time by happy guessing, and hold up "so many" fingers or blocks, when, if the number-name five or six were called for and nothing shown, it would be quite confused. In our tests the number-name was sought because it is that which is mainly serviceable for educational purposes. As to the physiological and geographical questions little need be said. Joint, flesh, and vein are often unknown terms, or joint is where the bone is broken, and there are stones in the knees. Within the skin is blood and something hard, perhaps wood. Physical self-consciousness, which is in little danger of becoming morbid at this age, begins with recognition of the hand, then of the foot, because these are the most mobile parts, but has not often reached the face at this age, and blushing is rare; while psychic self-consciousness is commonly only of pain, either internal, as of stomach-ache, or peripheral, of cuts, bruises, etc. The world is square, straight, or flat, and if the other side has been thought of it is all woods or water or ice, or where saved people or Protestants or anything much heard of but little seen are; if we go to the edge of the world we come to water or may fall off, or it may be like a house and we live on the top. The first notion of a hill may be of some particular pile of sand, perhaps on the moulding-board, three inches high, or a rubbish-heap in the back yard, or a slant where a sled will run along; but a comprehensive idea of hill with opposite sides, tho simpler and easier than most geographical categories, is by no means to be assumed.

If children are pressed to answer questions somewhat beyond their ken they often reply confusedly and at random, while if others beside them are questioned they can answer well; some are bolder and invent things on the spot if they seem to interest the questioner, while others catch quick and subtle suggestions from the form of the question, accent, gesture, feature, etc., so that what seems originality is really mind-reading, giving back our every thought and sometimes only a direct reproduction, with but little distortion because little apprehension, of what parents or teachers have lately told them. But there are certain elements which every tactful and experienced friend of children learns to distinguish from each of these with considerable accuracy—elements which, from whatever source, take or spring from deep roots in the childish heart, as distinct from all these as are Grimm's tales from those of some of our weakly juvenile weeklies. These are generally not easily accessible. I could not persuade an old nurse to repeat to me a nonsensical song I had half overheard that delighted a two-year-old child, and the brothers Grimm experienced a similar difficulty in making their collections. As many working men nail a horseshoe over their door for luck and many people really prefer to begin nothing important on Friday who will not confess to a trace of superstition in either case, so children cling to their "old credulities to nature dear," refusing every attempt to gain their full confidence or explore secret tracts in their minds, as a well-developed system of insane illusions may escape the scrutiny of the most skilful alienist. As a reasoning electric light might honestly doubt the existence of such things as shadows because, however near or numerous, they are always hidden from it, so the most intelligent adults quite commonly fail to recognize sides of their own children's souls which can be seen only by strategy. A boy and girl often play under my window as I write, and when either is quite alone unconscious words often reveal what is passing in their own minds, and it is often very absurd or else meaningless, but they run away with shame and even blushes if they chance to look up suddenly and catch me listening. Yet who of us has not secret regions of soul to which no friend is ever admitted, and which we ourselves shrink from full consciousness of? Many children half believe the doll feels cold or blows, that it pains flowers to tear or burn them, or that in summer when the tree is alive it makes it ache to pound or chop it. Of 48 children questioned 20 believed sun, moon, or stars to live, 15 thought a doll and

16 thought flowers would suffer pain if burned. Children who are accounted dull in school-work are more apt to be imaginative and animistic.

The chief field for such fond and often secret childish fancies is the sky. About three fourths of all questioned thought the world a plain, and many described it as round like a dollar, while the sky is like a flattened bowl turned over it. The sky is often thin, one might easily break through; half the moon may be seen through it, while the other half is this side; it may be made of snow, but is so large that there is much floor-sweeping to be done in heaven. Some thought the sun went down at night into the ground or just behind certain houses, and went across on or under the ground to go up out of or off the water in the morning, but 48 per cent of all thought that at night it goes or rolls or flies, is blown or walks, or God pulls it up higher out of sight. He takes it into heaven, and perhaps put it to bed, and even takes off its clothes and puts them on in the morning, or again it lies under the trees where the angels mind it, or goes through and shines on the upper side of the sky, or goes into or behind the moon, as the moon is behind it in the day. It may stay where it is, only we cannot see it, for it is dark, or the dark rains down so, and it comes out when it gets light so it can see. More than half the children questioned conceived the sun as never more than 40 degrees from the zenith, and, naturally enough, city children knew little of the horizon. So the moon comes around when it is a bright night and people want to walk, or forget to light some lamps; it follows us about and has nose and eyes, while it calls the stars into, under, or behind it at night, and they may be made of bits of it. Sometimes the moon is round a month or two, then it is a rim, or a piece is cut off, or it is half stuck or half buttoned into the sky. The stars may be sparks from fire-engines or houses, or, with higher intelligence, they are silver, or God lights them with matches and blows them out or opens the door and calls them in in the morning. Only in a single case were any of the heavenly bodies conceived as openings in the sky to let light or glory through, or as eyes of supernatural beings—a fancy so often ascribed to children and so often found in juvenile literature. Thunder, which anthropologists tell us, is or represents the highest God to most savage races, was apperceived as God groaning or kicking, or rolling barrels about, or turning a big handle, or grinding snow, walking loud, breaking something, throwing logs, having coal run in, pounding about with a big hammer, rattling houses, hitting the clouds, or clouds bumping or clapping together or bursting, or else it was merely ice sliding off lots of houses or cannon in the city or sky, hard rain down the chimney, or big rocks pounding, or piles of boards falling down, or very hard rain, hail, or wind. Lightning is God putting out his finger or opening a door, or turning on gas quick, or (very common) striking many matches at once, throwing stones and iron for sparks, setting paper afire, or it is light going outside and inside the sky, or stars falling. God keeps rain in heaven in a big sink, rows of buckets, a big tub or barrels, and they run over or he lets it down with a water hose through a sieve, a dipper with holes, or sprinkles or tips it down or turns a faucet. God makes it in heaven out of nothing or out of water, or it gets up by splashing up, or he dips it up off the roof, or it rains up off the ground when we don't see it. The clouds are close to the sky; they move because the earth moves and makes them. They are dirty, muddy things, or blankets, or doors of heaven, and are made of fog, of steam that makes the sun go, of smoke, of white wool or feathers and birds, or lace or cloth. In their changing forms very many children, whose very life is fancy, think they see veritable men, or more commonly, because they have so many more forms, animals, faces, and very often God, Santa Claus, angels, etc., are also seen. Closely connected with the above are the religious concepts so common with children. God is a big, perhaps blue, man, very often seen in the sky on or in clouds, in the church, or even street. He came in our gate, comes to see us sometimes. He lives in a big palace or a big brick or stone house on the sky. He makes lamps, babies, dogs, trees, money, etc., and the angels work for him. He looks like the priest, Frobel, papa, etc., and they like to look at him, and a few would like to be God. He lights the stars so he can see to go on the sidewalk or into the church. Birds, children, Santa Claus, live with him, and most but not all like him better than they do the latter. When people die they just go, or are put in a hole, or a box or a black wagon that goes to heaven, or they fly up or are drawn or slung up into the sky where God catches them. They never can get out of the hole, and yet all good people somehow get where God is. He lifts them up, they go up on a ladder or rope, or they carry them up, but keep their eyes shut so they do not know the way, or they are shoved up through a hole. When children get there they have candy, rocking-horses, guns, and everything in the toy-shop or picture-book, play marbles, top, ball, cards, hookey, hear brass bands, have nice clothes, gold watches, and pets, ice-cream and soda-water, and no school. There are men there who died in the war made into angels, and dolls with broken heads go there. Some think they must go through the church to get there, a few thought the horse-cars run there, and one said that the birds that grow on apple-trees are drawn up there by the moon. The bad place is like an oven or a police-station, where it burns, yet is all dark, and folks want to get back, and God kills people or beats them with a cane. God makes babies in heaven, tho the holy mother and even Santa Claus makes some. He lets them down or drops them, and the women or doctors catch them, or he leaves them on the sidewalk, or brings them down a wooden ladder backwards and pulls it up again, or mamma or the doctor or the nurse go up and fetch them sometimes in a balloon, or they fly down and lose off their wings in some place or other and forget it, or jump down to Jesus, who gives them around. They were also often said to be found in flour-barrels, and the flour sticks ever so long, you know, or they grow in cabbages, or God puts them in water, perhaps in the sewer, and the doctor gets them out and takes them to sick folks that want them, or the milkman brings them early in the morning, they are dug out of the ground, or bought at the baby-store. Sometimes God puts on a few things or else sends them along if he don't forget it; this shows that no one since Basedow believes in telling children the truth in all things.

Now a few children have or can be made to disclose no such ideas as the above, and indeed they seem to be generally already on the ebb at this age, and are sometimes timidly introduced by, as if, some say, it is like, or I used to think. Clear and confident notions on the above topics are the exception and not the rule, yet most have some of them, while some are common to many, indeed most, children. They represent a drift of consentient infantile philosophy about the universe not without systematic coherence, altho intimidated and broken through at every point by fragmentary truths, often only verbal indeed, without insight or realization of a higher order, so that the most diametrical contradictions often subsist peacefully side by side, and yet they are ever forming again at lower levels of age and intelligence. In all that is remote the real and ideal fade into each other like clouds and mountains in the horizon, or as poetry which keeps alive the standpoints of an earlier culture coexists with science. Children are often hardly conscious of them at all, and the very questions that bring them to mind and invite them to words at the same time often abash the child to the first disquieting self-consciousness of the absurdity of his fond fancies that have felt not only life but character into natural objects. Between the products of childish spontaneity, where the unmistakable child's mark is seen, and those of really happy suggestion by parents, etc., the distinction is as hard as anywhere along the line between heredity and tradition. It is enough that these fancies are like Galton's composite portraits, resultants in form and shading of the manifold deepest impression which what is within and what is without have together made upon the child's soul in these spheres of ideas. Those indicated above represent many strata of intelligence up through which the mind is passing very rapidly and with quite radical transformations. Each stratum was once with but a little elaboration, or is now somewhere, the highest culture, relegated to and arrested in an earlier and earlier stage as civilization and educational methods advance. Belief in the false is as necessary as it is inevitable, for the proper balance of head and heart, and happy the child who has believed or loved only healthy, unaffected, platonic lies like the above, which will be shed with its milk-teeth when more solid mental pabulum can be digested. It is possible that the present shall be so attractive and preoccupying that the child never once sends his thoughts to the remote in time and place, and that these baby-fancies—ever ready to form at a touch, and which made the impartation of truth, however carefully put, on these themes impossible before its time; which, when long forgotten, yet often reverberate, if their old chords be struck, in adults to the intensity of fanaticism or even delusion—shall be quite repressed. If so, one of the best elements of education which comes from long experience in laying aside a lower for a higher phase of culture of doubting opportunely, judiciously, and temperately, is lost.

De Quincey's pseudopia is thought by Dr. E. H. Clarks (*Visions*, p. 212) to be common with children; but altho about 40 were asked to describe what they saw with their eyes shut, it is impossible to judge whether they visualize in any such distinctive sense as Mr. Galton has described or only imagine and remember, often with Homeric circumstance, but with less than picturesque vividness. Childish thought is very largely in visual terms, hence the need of object (*anschauungs*) lessons, and hence, too, it comes that most of the above questions address the eye without any such intent. If phonic symbols could be made pictorial as they were originally, and as illustrated primers make them in a third and still remoter sense, the irrational elements in learning to read would be largely obviated. Again, out of 53 children 21 described the tones of certain instruments as colored. The colors, or *photisms*, thus suggested, tho so far as tested constant from week to week in the same child, had no agreement for different instruments, a drum, e.g., suggesting yellow (the favorite color of children) to one child and black or red to another, and the tone of a fife being described as pale or bright, light or dark colored, intensity and saturated varying greatly with different children. For this and other forms of association or analogies of sensation of a large and not yet explored class so common in children, many data for future study were gathered. This is also the case with their powers of time and tone reproduction, and their common errors in articulation, which have suggested other and more detailed researches, some of which are already in progress.

Each child was asked to name three things right and three things wrong to do, and nearly half could do so. In no case were the two confused, indicating not necessarily intuitive perception, but a general consensus in what is allowed and forbidden children at home, and how much better and more surely they learn to do than to know. Wrong things were specified much more readily and by more children than right things, and also in much greater variety. In about 450 answers 53 wrong acts are specified, while in over 350 answers only 34 different good acts are named. The more frequent answers are to mind and be good, or to disobey, be naughty, lie, and say bad words; but the answers of the girls differ from the boys in two marked ways, they more often name specific acts and nearly twice as often conventional ones, the former difference being most common in naming right, the latter in naming wrong things. Boys say it is wrong to steal, fight, kick, break windows, get drunk, stick pins into others, or to "sass," "cuss," shoot them, while girls are more apt to say it is wrong to not comb the hair, to get butter on the dress, climb trees, unfold the hands, cry, catch flies, etc. The right things seem, it must be confessed, comparatively very tame and unattractive, and while the genius of an Aristotle could hardly extract categories or infer intuitions by classification from either list, it is very manifest that the lower strata of conscience are dislike of dirt and fear. Pure intuitionalists may like to know that over a dozen children were found who convinced their questioners that they thought they ought not to say bad words if no one heard them, or lie if not found out, etc., or who felt sick at the stomach when they had been bad, but the soap and water or sand with which their mouths are sometimes washed after bad words in kindergartens, or the red pepper administered at home after lies, may possibly have something to do with the latter phenomenon.

For several hundred drawings, with the name given them by the child written by the teacher, the chief difference inferred is in concentration. Some make faint, hasty lines representing all the furniture of a room, or sky and stars, or all the objects they can think of, while others concentrate upon a single object. It is a girl with buttons, a house with a keyhole or steps, a man with a pipe or heels or ring grotesquely prominent. The development of observation and sense of form is best seen in the pictures of men. The earliest and simplest representation is a round head, two eyes and legs. Later comes mouth, then nose, then hair, then ears. Arms like legs at first grow directly from the head, rarely from the legs, and are seldom fingerless, tho sometimes it is doubtful whether several arms or fingers from head and legs without arms are meant. Of 44 human heads only 9 are in profile. This is one of the many analogies with the rock and cave drawings of primitive man, and suggests how Catlin came to nearly lose his life by "leaving out the other half" in drawing a profile portrait of an Indian chief. Last, as least mobile and thus attracting least attention, comes the body; first round like the head, then elongated, sometimes prodigiously, and sometimes articulated into several compartments, and in three cases divided, the upper part of the figure being in one place and the lower in another. The mind and not the eye alone is addressed, for the body is drawn and then the clothes are drawn on it (as the child dresses), diaphanous and only in outline.

Most draw living objects except the kindergarten children, who draw their patterns. More than two thirds of all objects are decidedly in action, and under 18 per cent word-pictures or scribbles called the name of the objects are made to imitate writing or letters, as sounds to imitate talking. The very earliest pencillings, commonly of three-year-old children, are mere marks to and fro, often nearly in the same line. Of 13 of these most were nearly in the angle described by Javal as corresponding to the earliest combination of finger and fore-arm movements and not far from the regulation slant of 52° taught in school penmanship.

Each child was asked to tell a verse or story to be recorded verbatim, and nearly half could do so. Children of this age are no longer interested in mere animal noises or rhymes or nonsense-words of the "Mother Goose" order, but everything to interest them deeply must have a cat, dog, bird, baby, another child, or possibly parent or teacher in it, must be dramatic and full of action, appeal to the eye as a "chalk-talk" or an object-lesson, and be copious of details, which need be varied but slightly to make the story as good as new for the twentieth time. A long gradation of abstractions culminates here. First, it is a great lesson for the child to eliminate touch and recognize objects by the eye alone. The first pictures are felt of, turned over with much confusion to find the surface smooth. To abstract from visual terms to words is still harder. Eyes and tongue must work together a long time before the former can be eliminated and stories told of objects first absent, then remote, then before unknown. Children must be far beyond this before they can be interested in e.g., fairy tales, and stories told interest them far more than if read to them no matter how apt the language. They are reproduced about as imperfectly as objects are drawn, only a few salient and disconnected points being seized at first, and sentence and sequence coming very slowly after many repetitions. Their own little faults may be woven in or ascribed to animals or even plants in a remote way which they themselves will feel at each stage, and the selfish birdie or the runaway squirrel or flowers as kind words may be referred to in case of need as a reserve moral capital. Why do we never teach maxims and proverbs which, when carefully selected, are found so effective at this age and teach the best morality embodied in the briefest and most impressive way?

Of the 36 per cent or 72 children of the table who never saved their pennies, 52 spend them for candy, which growing children need, but the adulterations of which are often noxious. Of toys, big things please them best. A recent writer in Austria fears that school savings-banks tend to call attention too early to money matters, and to cause its value to be dangerously overrated; but to pass the candy by and drop the cents where they are beyond their control for a year is much less pedagogic than to save them till a larger and more costly toy can be bought.

There are but 11 questions on which any comparison between the intelligence of the Boston and Berlin children can be made. On all of these except elementary number, where the average is nearly 20 per cent in favor of the Boston children, the figures vary surprisingly little despite local differences and another mode of questioning.

Table I. is based upon about equal number of boys and girls, and children of Irish and American parentage greatly predominate; there are 21 Germans, and 19 are divided between eight other nationalities. 14 per cent of all examined did not know their age; 6 per cent were four, 37 per cent were five, 25 per cent were six, 12 per cent were 7, and 2 per cent were eight years old. The returns were carefully tabulated to determine the influence of age, which seems surprisingly unpronounced, indicating, so far as the small numbers go, a slight value of age per se as an index of ripeness for school.

In Table II., columns 2 and 3 are based upon larger numbers and upon less carefully restricted selections from the aggregate returns. In 34 representative questions out of 49 the boys surpass the girls, as the German boys did in 75 per cent of the quite different Berlin questions. The girls excel in knowledge of the parts of the body, home and family life, thunder, rainbows, in knowledge of square, circle, and triangle, but not in that of cube, sphere, and pyramid, which is harder and later. Their stories are more imaginative, while their knowledge of things outward and remote, their power to sing and articulate correctly from dictation, their acquaintance with number and animals, is distinctly less than that of the boys. The Berlin report indicates that girls knew the four best of Grimm's tales nearly twice as frequently as the boys, but that in the concepts of God, Christ, and Bible stories the relation was exactly reversed, and proceeds to infer that the more common, near, or easy a notion is the more likely are the girls to excel the boys, and vice versa. Save possibly in the knowledge of the parts of the body, our returns do not particularly indicate this. Boys do seem, however, more likely than girls to be ignorant of common things right about them, where knowledge is wont to be assumed. Column 5 shows that the Irish children tested were behind others on nearly all topics. The Irish girls decidedly outrank the Irish boys, the advantage to the sex being outweighed by the wider knowledge of the boys of other nationalities. Whether, however, the five- and six-year-old Irish boys are not after all so constituted as to surpass their precocious American playmates later in school or adult life, as since Sigismund may think "slow" children generally do, is one of the most serious questions for the philosophical educator. Column 6 shows the advantage of the kindergarten children, without regard to nationality, over all others in a striking way. Most of the latter tested were from the charity kindergartens, so that superior intelligence of home surroundings can hardly be assumed. Many of them had attended kindergarten but a short time, and the questions were so ordered that the questioners who had a special interest in the kindergarten should not know till near the end of their tests whether or not they had ever attended it. On the other hand, a somewhat larger proportion of the children from the kindergarten had been in the country. Yet on the whole we seem to have here an illustration of the law that we really see not what is near or impresses the retina, but what the attention is called and held to, and what interests are awakened and words found for. Of nearly thirty primary teachers questioned as to the difference between children from kindergartens and others, four saw no difference, and all the rest thought them better fitted for school-work, instancing superior use of language, skill with the hand and slate, quickness, power of observation, singing, number, love of work, neatness, politeness, freedom from the benumbing school-bashfulness, or power to draw from dictation. Many thought them at first more restless and talkative generally—a trifling and transient fault.

There are many other details and more or less probable inferences, but the above are the chief. The work is laborious, involving about fifty thousand items in all; and as but few of the Berlin methods or results except statistical tables have been published, these results are it is believed to be in some degree the first opening of a new field, which should be specialized and single concept-groups subjected to more detailed study with larger numbers of children. It should also be applied to older children and youth, as the writer is already attempting to do. The difficulty is to get essential points to test for. If these are not characteristic and typical, all such work is worthless. We believe that not only practical educational conclusions of great scope and importance may be based on or illustrated by such results, but, who deeply sensible of many sources of inaccuracy which may limit their value, that they are of great importance for anthropology and psychology. It is characteristic of an educated man, says Aristotle in substance, not to require a degree of scientific exactness on any subject more than that which the subject admits. As scientific methods advance not only are increasingly complex matters subjected to them, but probabilities (which guide nearly all our acts) more and more remote from mathematical certainty are valued.

Steinthal tells an apposite story of six German gentlemen riding socially in a coupe all day, and as they approached the station where they were to separate one proposed to tell the vocation of each of the others, who were strangers to him, if they would write without hesitation an answer to the question "What destroys its own offspring?" One wrote, Vital force. "You," said the questioner, "are a biologist." Another wrote, War. "You," he said, "are a soldier." Another wrote,

Kronos, and was correctly pronounced a philologist; while the publicist revealed himself by writing Revolution, and the farmer by writing She-bear. This fable teaches the law of apperception. As Don Quixote saw an army in a flock of sheep and a giant in a windmill, as some see all things in the light of politics, others in that of religion, education, etc., so the Aryan races apperceived the clouds as cows and the rain as their milk, the sun as a horse, the lightning as an arrow, and so the children apperceive rain as God pouring down water; thunder as barrels, boards falling, or cannon; heaven as a well-appointed nursery, &c., &c. They bring more or less developed apperceiving organs with them into school, each older and more familiar concept gaining more apperceptive power over the newer concepts and percepts by use. The older impressions are on the lurch, as it were, for the new ones, and mental freedom and all-sidedness depends on the number and strength of these appropriating concepts. If there are very few, as with children, teaching is, as some one has well said, like pouring water from a big tub into a small narrow-necked bottle. A teacher who acts upon the now-everywhere-admitted fallacy that knowledge of the subject is all that is needed in teaching children pours at random on to more than into the children, talking to rather than with them, and gauging what he gives rather than what they receive. All now agree that the mind can learn only what is related to other things learned before, and that we must start from the knowledge that the children really have and develop this as germs, otherwise we are showing objects that require close scrutiny only to indirect vision, or talking to the blind of color. Alas for the teacher who does not learn more from his children than he can ever hope to teach them! Just in proportion as teachers do this do they cease to be merely mechanical and acquire interest, perhaps enthusiasm, and surely an all-compensating sense of growth in their work and life.

From the above tables it seems not too much also to infer:

1. That there is next to nothing of pedagogic value the knowledge of which it is safe to assume at the outset of school-life. Hence the need of objects and the danger of books and word-cram. Hence many of the best primary teachers in Germany spend from two to four or even six months talking of objects and drawing them before any beginning of what we till lately have regarded as primary-school work.

2. The best preparation parents can give their children for good school-training is to make them acquainted with natural objects, especially with the sights and sounds of the country and talk about them, and send them to good and hygienic as distinct from most fashionable kindergartens.

3. Every normal-school pupil should be required, as an essential part of his training, and every teacher on starting with a new class or in a new locality, to make sure that his efforts along some lines are not utterly

lost, should undertake to explore carefully section by section children's minds with all the tact and ingenuity he can command and acquire, to determine exactly what is already known.

4. The concepts which are most common in the children of a given locality are the earliest to be acquired, while the rarer ones are later. This order may generally be assumed in teaching as a natural one, e.g. apples first and wheat last (Cf. Table I.). This order, however, varies very greatly with every change of environment, so that the results of exploration of children's minds in one place cannot be assumed to be valid for those of another save within comparatively few concept-spheres.

Francis Galton: 1822-1911

INQUIRIES INTO HUMAN FACULTY AND ITS DEVELOPMENT *

1883

WHISTLES FOR AUDIBILITY OF SHRILL NOTES

I CONTRIVED a small whistle for conveniently ascertaining the upper limits of audible sound in different persons, which Dr. Wollaston had shown to vary considerably. He used small pipes, and found much difficulty in making them. I made a very small whistle from a brass tube whose internal diameter was less than one tenth of an inch in diameter. A plug was fitted into the lower end of the tube, which could be pulled out or pushed in as much as desired, thereby causing the length of the bore of the whistle to be varied at will. When the bore is long the note is low; when short, it is high. The plug was graduated, so that the precise note produced by the whistle could be determined by reading off the graduations and referring to a table.

On testing different persons I found there was a remarkable falling off in the power of hearing high notes as age advanced. The persons themselves were quite unconscious of their deficiency so long as their sense of hearing low notes remained unimpaired. It is an only too amusing experiment to test a party of persons of various ages, including some rather elderly and self-satisfied personages. They are indignant at being thought deficient in the power of hearing, yet the experiment quickly shows that they are absolutely deaf to shrill notes which the younger persons hear acutely, and they commonly betray much dislike to the discovery. Every one has his limit, and the limit at which sounds become too shrill to be audible to any particular person can be rapidly determined by this little instrument. Lord Raleigh and others have found that sensitive flames are powerfully affected by the vibrations of whistles that are too rapid to be audible to ordinary ears.

I have tried experiments with all kinds of animals on their powers of hearing shrill notes. I have gone through the whole of the Zoological

* This book is a collection of studies and essays, many of which had been published as journal articles during the decade preceding the appearance of the *Inquiries*. Nearly every item shows a striking originality. Included here are the invention of Galton's whistle, the first research on mental imagery, and the first investigation of the association of ideas.

Gardens, using an apparatus arranged for the purpose. It consists of one of my little whistles at the end of a walking stick—that is, in reality, a long tube; it has a bit of india-rubber pipe under the handle, a sudden squeeze upon which forces a little air into the whistle and causes it to sound. I hold it as near as is safe to the ears of the animals, and when they are quite accustomed to its presence and heedless of it, I make it sound; then if they prick their ears it shows that they hear the whistle; if they do not, it is probably inaudible to them. Still, it is very possible that in some cases they hear but do not heed the sound. Of all creatures, I have found none superior to cats in the power of hearing shrill sounds; it is perfectly remarkable what a faculty they have in this way. Cats, of course, have to deal with mice, and to find them out by their squealing. Many people cannot hear the shrill squeal of a mouse. Some time ago, singing mice were exhibited in London, and of the people who went to hear them, some could hear nothing, whilst others could hear a little, and others again could hear much. Cats are differentiated by natural selection until they have a power of hearing all the high notes made by mice and other little creatures that they have to catch. A cat that is at a very considerable distance, can be made to turn its ear round by sounding a note that is too shrill to be audible by almost any human ear. Small dogs also hear very shrill notes, but large ones do not. I have walked through the streets of a town with an instrument like that which I used in the Zoological Gardens, and made nearly all the little dogs turn round, but not the large ones. At Berne, where there appear to be more large dogs lying idly about the streets than in any other town in Europe, I have tried the whistle for hours together, on a great many large dogs, but could not find one that heard it. Ponies are sometimes able to hear very high notes. I once frightened a pony with one of these whistles in the middle of a large field. My attempts on insect hearing have been failures.

MENTAL IMAGERY

Anecdotes find their way into print, from time to time, of persons whose visual memory is so clear and sharp as to present mental pictures that may be scrutinised with nearly as much ease and prolonged attention as if they were real objects. I became interested in the subject and made a rather extensive inquiry into the mode of visual presentation in different persons, so far as could be gathered from their respective statements. It seemed to me that the results might illustrate the essential differences between the mental operations of different men, that they might give some clue to the origin of visions, and that the course of the inquiry might reveal some previously unnoticed facts. It has done all this more or less, and I will explain the results in the present and in the three following chapters.

It is not necessary to trouble the reader with my earlier tentative steps to find out what I desired to learn. After the inquiry had been fairly started it took the form of submitting a certain number of printed questions to a large number of persons. There is hardly any more difficult task than that of framing questions which are not likely to be misunderstood, which admit of easy reply, and which cover the ground of inquiry. I did my best in these respects, without forgetting the most important part of all—namely, to tempt my correspondents to write freely in fuller explanation of their replies, and on cognate topics as well. These separate letters have proved more instructive and interesting by far than the replies to the set questions.

The first group of the rather long series of queries related to the illumination, definition, and colouring of the mental image, and were framed thus:

Before addressing yourself to any of the Questions on the opposite page, think of some definite object—suppose it is your breakfast-table as you sat down to it this morning—and consider carefully the picture that rises before your mind's eye.

1. *Illumination*—Is the image dim or fairly clear? Is its brightness comparable to that of the actual scene?

2. *Definition*—Are all the objects pretty well defined at the same time, or is the place of sharpest definition at any one moment more contracted than it is in a real scene.

3. *Colouring*—Are the colours of the china, of the toast, bread-crust, mustard, meat, parsley, or whatever may have been on the table, quite distinct and natural?

The earliest results of my inquiry amazed me. I had begun by questioning friends in the scientific world, as they were the most likely class of men to give accurate answers concerning this faculty of visualising, to which novelists and poets continually allude, which has left an abiding mark on the vocabularies of every language, and which supplies the material out of which dreams and the well-known hallucinations of sick people are built.

To my astonishment, I found that the great majority of the men of science to whom I first applied protested that mental imagery was unknown to them, and they looked on me as fanciful and fantastic in supposing that the words "mental imagery" really expressed what I believed everybody supposed them to mean. They had no more notion of its true nature than a colour-blind man, who has not discerned his defect, has of the nature of colour. They had a mental deficiency of which they were unaware, and naturally enough supposed that those who affirmed they possessed it, were romancing. To illustrate their mental attitude it will be sufficient to quote a few lines from the letter of one of my correspondents, who writes:

> These questions presuppose assent to some sort of a proposition regarding the "mind's eye," and the "images" which it sees. . . . This points to some initial fallacy. . . . It is only by a figure of speech that I can describe my recollection of a scene as a "mental image" which I can "see" with my "mind's eye". . . . I do not see it . . . any more than a man sees the thousand lines of Sophocles which under due pressure he is ready to repeat. The memory possesses it, etc.

Much the same result followed inquiries made for me by a friend among members of the French institute.

On the other hand, when I spoke to persons whom I met in general society, I found an entirely different disposition to prevail. Many men and a yet larger number of women, and many boys and girls, declared that they habitually saw mental imagery, and that it was perfectly distinct to them and full of colour. The more I pressed and cross-questioned them, professing myself to be incredulous, the more obvious was the truth of their first assertions. They described their imagery in minute detail, and they spoke in a tone of surprise at my apparent hesitation in accepting what they said. I felt that I myself should have spoken exactly as they did if I had been describing a scene that lay before my eyes, in broad daylight, to a blind man who persisted in doubting the reality of vision. Reassured by this happier experience, I recommenced to inquire among scientific men, and soon found scattered instances of what I sought, though in by no means the same abundance as elsewhere. I then circulated my questions more generally among my friends and through their hands, and obtained the replies that are the main subject of this and of the three next chapters. They were from persons of both sexes, and of various ages, and in the end from occasional correspondents in nearly every civilised country.

I have also received batches of answers from various educational establishments both in England and in America, which were made after the masters had fully explained the meaning of the questions, and interested the boys in them. These have the merit of returns derived from a general census, which my other data lack, because I cannot for a moment suppose that the writers of the latter are a haphazard proportion of those to whom they were sent. Indeed I know of some who, disavowing all possession of the power, and of many others who, possessing it in too faint a degree to enable them to express what their experiences really were, in a manner satisfactory to themselves, sent no returns at all. Considerable statistical similarity was, however, observed between the sets of returns furnished by the schoolboys and those sent by my separate correspondents, and I may add that they accord in this respect with the oral information I have elsewhere obtained. The conformity of replies from so many different sources which was clear from the first, the fact of their apparent trustworthiness being on the whole much increased by cross-examination (though I could give one or two amusing instances of break-down), and the evident effort made to give accurate answers, have convinced me that it is a much easier matter than I had anticipated to obtain trustworthy replies to psychological questions. Many persons, especially women and intelligent children, take pleasure in introspection, and strive their very best to explain their mental processes. I think that a delight in self-dissection must be a strong ingredient in the pleasure that many are said to take in confessing themselves to priests.

Here, then, are two rather notable results: the one is the proved facility of obtaining statistical insight into the processes of other persons' minds, whatever *a priori* objection may have been made as to its possibility; and the other is that scientific men, as a class, have feeble powers of visual representation. There is no doubt whatever on the latter point, however it may be accounted for. My own conclusion is, that an over-ready perception of sharp mental pictures is antagonistic to the acquirement of habits of highly-generalized and abstract thought, especially when the steps of reasoning are carried on by words as symbols, and that if the faculty of seeing the pictures was ever possessed by men who think hard, it is very apt to be lost by disuse. The highest minds are probably those in which it is not lost, but subordinated, and is ready for use on suitable occasions. I am, however, bound to say, that the missing faculty seems to be replaced so serviceably by other modes of conception, chiefly, I believe, connected with the incipient motor sense, not of the eyeballs only but of the muscles generally, that men who declare themselves entirely deficient in the power of seeing mental pictures can nevertheless give life-like descriptions of what they have seen, and can otherwise express themselves as if they were gifted with a vivid visual imagination. They can also become painters of the Royal Academicians.

The facts I am now about to relate are obtained from the returns of 100 adult men, of whom 19 are Fellows of the Royal Society, mostly of very high repute, and at least twice, and I think I may say three times, as many more are persons of distinction in various kinds of intellectual work. As already remarked, these returns taken by themselves do not profess to be of service in a general statistical sense, but they are of much importance in showing how men of exceptional accuracy express themselves when they are speaking of mental imagery. They also testify to the variety of experiences to be met with in a moderately large circle. I will begin by giving a few cases of the highest, of the medium, and of the lowest order of the faculty of visualising. The hundred returns were first classified according to the order of the faculty, as judged to the best of my ability from the whole of what was said in them, and of what I knew from other sources of the writers; and the number prefixed to each quotation shows its place in the class-list.

VIVIDNESS OF MENTAL IMAGERY

(From returns, furnished by 100 men, at least half of whom are distinguished in science or in other fields of intellectual work)

Cases Where the Faculty is Very High

1. Brilliant, distinct, never blotchy.

2. Quite comparable to the real object. I feel as though I was dazzled, e.g. when recalling the sun to my mental vision.

3. In some instances quite as bright as an actual scene.

4. Brightness as in the actual scene.

5. Thinking of the breakfast-table this morning, all the objects in my mental picture are as bright as the actual scene.

6. The image once seen is perfectly clear and bright.

7. Brightness at first quite comparable to actual scene.

8. The mental image appears to correspond in all respects with reality. I think it is as clear as the actual scene.

9. The brightness is perfectly comparable to that of the real scene.

10. I think the illumination of the imaginary image is nearly equal to that of the real one.

11. All clear and bright; all the objects seem to me well defined at the same time.

12. I can see my breakfast-table or any equally familiar thing with my mind's eye, quite as well in all particulars as I can do if the reality is before me.

Cases Where the Faculty is Mediocre

46. Fairly clear and not incomparable in illumination with that of the real scene, especially when I first catch it. Apt to become fainter when more particularly attended to.

47. Fairly clear, not quite comparable to that of the actual scene. Some objects are more sharply defined than others, the more familiar objects coming more distinctly in my mind.

48. Fairly clear as a general image; details rather misty.

49. Fairly clear, but not equal to the scene. Defined, but not sharply; not all seen with equal clearness.

50. Fairly clear. Brightness probably at least one-half to two-thirds of original. (The writer is a physiologist.) Definition varies very much, one or two objects being much more distinct than the others, but the latter come out clearly if attention be paid to them.

51. Image of my breakfast-table fairly clear, but not quite so bright as the reality. Altogether it is pretty well defined; the part where I sit and its surroundings are pretty well so.

52. Fairly clear, but brightness not comparable to that of the actual scene. The objects are sharply defined; some of them are salient, and others insignificant and dim, but by separate efforts I can take a visualized inventory of the whole table.

53. Details of breakfast-table when the scene is reflected on are fairly defined and complete, but I have had a familiarity for many years with my own breakfast-table, and the above would not be the case with a table seen casually unless there were some striking peculiarity in it.

54. I can recall any single object or group of objects, but not the whole table at once. The things recalled are generally clearly defined. Our table is a long one; I can see in my mind pass my eyes all down the table and see the different things distinctly, but not the whole table at once.

Cases Where the Faculty is at the Lowest

89. Dim and indistinct, yet I can give an account of this morning's breakfast-table; split herrings, broiled chickens, bacon, rolls, rather light-coloured marmalade, faint green plates with stiff pink flowers, the girls' dresses, etc. etc. I can also tell where all the dishes were, and where the people sat (I was on a visit). But my imagination is seldom pictorial except between sleeping and waking, when I sometimes see rather vivid forms.

90. Dim and not comparable in brightness to the real scene. Badly defined with blotches of light; very incomplete.

91. Dim, poor definition; could not sketch from it. I have a difficulty in seeing two images together.

92. Usually very dim. I cannot speak of its brightness, but only of its faintness. Not well defined and very incomplete.

93. Dim, imperfect.

94. I am very rarely able to recall any object whatever with any sort of distinctness. Very occasionally an object or image will recall itself, but even then it is more like a generalized image than an individual image. I seem to be almost destitute of visualising power, as under control.

95. No power of visualising. Between sleeping and waking, in illness and in health, with eyes closed, some remarkable scenes have occasionally

presented themselves, but I cannot recall them when awake with eyes open, and by daylight, or under any circumstances whatever when a copy could be made of them on paper. I have drawn both men and places many days or weeks after seeing them, but it was by an effort of memory acting on study at the time, and assisted by trial and error on the paper or canvas, whether in black, yellow, or colour, afterwards.

96. It is only as a figure of speech that I can describe my recollection of a scene as a "mental image" which I can "see" with my "mind's eye." . . . The memory possesses it, and the mind can at will roam over the whole, or study minutely any part.

97. No individual objects, only a general idea of a very uncertain kind.

98. No. My memory is not of the nature of a spontaneous vision, though I remember well where a word occurs in a page, how furniture looks in a room, &c. The ideas not felt to be mental pictures, but rather the symbols of facts.

99. Extremely dim. The impressions are in all respects so dim, vague, and transient, that I doubt whether they can reasonably be called images. They are incomparably less than those of dreams.

100. My powers are zero. To my consciousness there is almost no association of memory with objective visual impressions. I recollect the breakfast-table, but do not see it.

These quotations clearly show the great variety of natural powers of visual representation, and though the returns from which they are taken have, as I said, no claim to be those of 100 Englishmen taken at haphazard, nevertheless, to the best of my judgment, they happen to differ among themselves in much the same way that such returns would have done. I cannot procure a strictly haphazard series for comparison, because in any group of persons whom I may question there are always many too indolent to reply, or incapable of expressing themselves, or who from some fancy of their own are unwilling to reply. Still, as already mentioned, I have got together several groups that approximate to what is wanted, usually from schools, and I have analysed them as well as I could, and the general result is that the above returns may be accepted as a fair representation of the visualising powers of Englishmen.

PSYCHOMETRIC EXPERIMENTS

When we attempt to trace the first steps in each operation of our minds, we are usually baulked by the difficulty of keeping watch, without embarrassing the freedom of its action. The difficulty is much more than the common and well-known one of attending to two things at once. It is especially due to the fact that the elementary operations of the mind are exceedingly faint and evanescent, and that it requires the utmost painstaking to watch them properly. It would seem impossible to give the required attention to the processes of thought, and yet to think as freely as if the mind had been in no way preoccupied. The peculiarity of the experiments I am about to describe is that I have succeeded in evading this difficulty. My method consists in allowing the mind to play freely for a very brief period, until a couple or so of ideas have passed through it, and then, while the traces or echoes of those ideas are still lingering in the brain, to turn the attention upon them with a sudden and complete awakening; to arrest, to scrutinise them, and to record their exact appearance. Afterwards I collate the records at leisure, and discuss them, and draw conclusions. It must be understood that the second of the two ideas was never derived from the first, but always directly from the original object. This was ensured by absolutely withstanding all temptation to reverie. I do not mean that the first idea was of necessity a simple elementary thought; sometimes it was a glance down a familiar line of associations, sometimes it was a well-remembered mental attitude or mode of feeling, but I mean that it was never so far indulged in as to displace the object that had suggested it from being the primary topic of attention.

I must add, that I found the experiments to be extremely trying and irksome, and that it required much resolution to go through with them, using the scrupulous care they demanded. Nevertheless the results well repaid the trouble. They gave me an interesting and unexpected view of the number of the operations of the mind, and of the obscure depths in which they took place, of which I had been little conscious before. The general impression they have left upon me is like that which many of us have experienced when the basement of our house happens to be under thorough sanitary repairs, and we realise for the first time the complex system of drains and gas and water pipes, flues, bell-wires, and so forth, upon which our comfort depends, but which are usually hidden out of sight, and with whose existence, so long as they acted well, we had never troubled ourselves.

The first experiments I made were imperfect, but sufficient to inspire me with keen interest in the matter, and suggested the form of procedure that I have already partly described. My first experiments were these. On several occasions, but notably on one when I felt myself unusually capable of the kind of effort required, I walked leisurely along Pall Mall, a distance of 450 yards, during which time I scrutinised with attention every successive object that caught my eyes, and I allowed my attention to rest on it until one or two thoughts had arisen through direct association with that object; then I took very brief mental note of them, and passed on to the next object. I never allowed my mind to ramble. The number of objects viewed was, I think, about 300, for I had subsequently repeated the same walk under similar conditions and endeavoured to estimate their number, with that result. It was impossible for me to recall, in other than the vaguest way, the numerous ideas that had passed through my mind; but of this, at least, I am sure, that samples of my whole life had passed before me, that many bygone incidents, which I never suspected to have formed part of my stock of thoughts, had been glanced at as objects too familiar to awaken the attention. I saw at once that the brain was vastly more active than I had previously believed it to be, and I was perfectly amazed at the unexpected width of the field of its everyday operations. After an interval of some days, during which I kept my mind from dwelling on my first experiences, in order that it might retain as much freshness as possible for a second experiment, I repeated the walk, and was struck just as much as before by the variety of ideas that presented themselves, and the number of events to which they referred, about which I had never consciously occupied myself of late years. But my admiration at the activity of the mind was seriously diminished by another observation which I then made, namely, that there had been a very great deal of repetition of thought. The actors in my mental stage were indeed very numerous, but by no means so numerous as I had imagined. They now seemed to be something like the actors in theatres where large processions are represented, who march off one side of the stage, and, going round by the back, come on again at the other. I accordingly cast about for means of laying hold of these fleeting thoughts, and, submitting them to statistical analysis, to find out more about their tendency to repetition and other matters, and the method I finally adopted was the one already mentioned. I selected a list of suitable words, and wrote them on different small sheets of paper. Taking care to dismiss them from my thoughts when not engaged upon them, and allowing some days to elapse before I began to use them, I laid one of these sheets with all due precautions under a book, but not wholly covered by it, so that when I leaned forward I could see one of the words, being previously quite ignorant of what the word would be. Also I held a small chronograph, which I started by pressing a spring the moment the word caught my eye, and which stopped of itself the instant I released the spring; and this I did so soon as about a couple of ideas in direct association with the word had arisen in my mind. I found that I could not manage to recollect more than two ideas with the needed precision, at least not in a general way; but sometimes several ideas occurred so nearly together that I was able to record three or even four of them, while sometimes I only managed one. The second ideas were, as I have already said, never derived from the first, but always direct from the word itself, for I kept my attention firmly fixed on the word, and the associated ideas were seen only by a half glance. When the two ideas had occurred, I stopped the chronograph and wrote them down, and the time they occupied. I soon got into the way of doing all this in a very methodical and automatic manner, keeping the mind perfectly calm and neutral, but intent and, as it were, at full cock and on hair trigger, before displaying the word. There was no disturbance occasioned by thinking of the forthcoming revulsion of the mind the moment before the chronograph was stopped. My feeling before stopping it was simply that I had delayed long enough, and this in no way interfered with the free action of the mind. I found no trouble in ensuring the complete fairness of the experiment, by using a number of little precautions, hardly necessary to describe, that practice quickly suggested, but it was a most repugnant and laborious work, and it was only by strong self-control that I went through my schedule according to programme. The list of words that I finally secured was 75 in number, though I began with more. I went through them on four separate occasions, under very different circumstances, in England and abroad, and at intervals of about a month. In no case were the associations governed to any degree worth recording, by remembering what had occurred to me on previous occasions, for I found that the process itself had great influence in discharging the memory of what had just been engaged in, and I, of course, took care between the experiments never to let my thoughts revert to the words. The results seem to me to be as trustworthy as any other statistical series that has been collected with equal care.

On throwing these results into a common statistical hotch-pot, I first examined into the rate at which these associated ideas were formed. It took a total time of 660 seconds to form the 505 ideas, that is, at about the rate of 50 in a minute, or 3000 in an hour. This would be miserably slow work in reverie, or wherever the thought follows the lead of each association that successively presents itself. In the present case, much time was lost in mentally taking the word in, owing to the quiet unobtrusive way in which I found it necessary to bring into view, so as not to distract the thoughts. Moreover, a substantive standing by itself is usually the equivalent of too abstract an idea for us to conceive properly without delay. Thus it is very difficult to get a quick conception of the word "carriage," because there are so many different kinds–two-wheeled, four-wheeled, open and closed, and all of them in so many different possible positions, that the mind possibly hesitates amidst an obscure sense of many alternatives that cannot blend together. But limit the idea to say a landau, and the mental association declares itself more quickly. Say a landau coming down the street to opposite the door, and an image of many blended landaus that have done so forms itself without the least hesitation.

Next, I found that my list of 75 words gone over 4 times, had given rise of 505 ideas and 13 cases of puzzle, in which nothing sufficiently definite to note occurred within the brief maximum period of about 4 seconds, that I allowed myself to any single trial. Of these 505 only 289 were different. The precise proportions in which the 505 were distributed in quadruplets, triplets, doublets, or singles, is shown in the uppermost lines of Table I. The same facts are given under another form in the lower lines of the Table, which show how the 289 different ideas were distributed in cases of fourfold, treble, double, or single occurrences.

TABLE I
RECURRENT ASSOCIATIONS

Total Number of Associations	*Occurring in*			
	Quadruplets	*Triplets*	*Doublets*	*Singles*
505	116	108	114	167
Per cent....100	23	21	23	33

Total Number of Different Associations	*Occurring*			
	Four Times	*Three Times*	*Twice*	*Once*
289	29	36	57	167
Per cent....100	10	12	20	58

I was fully prepared to find much iteration in my ideas, but had little expected that out of every hundred words twenty-three would give rise to exactly the same association in every one of the four trials; twenty-one to the same association in three out of the four, and so on, the experiments having been purposely conducted under very different conditions of time and local circumstances. This shows much less variety in the mental stock of ideas than I had expected, and makes us feel that the roadways of our minds are worn into very deep ruts. I conclude from the proved number of faint and barely conscious thoughts, and from the proved iteration of them, that the mind is perpetually travelling over familiar ways without our memory retaining any impression of its excursions. Its footsteps are so light and fleeting that it is only by such experiments as I have described that we can learn anything about them. It is apparently always engaged in mumbling over its old stores, and if any of these is wholly neglected for a while, it is apt to be forgotten, perhaps irrecoverably. It is by no means the keenness of interest and of the attention when first observing an object, that fixes it in the recollection.

We pore over the pages of a Bradshaw, and study the trains for some particular journey with the greatest interest; but the event passes by, and the hours and other facts which we once so eagerly considered become absolutely forgotten. So in games of whist, and in a large number of similar instances. As I understand it, the subject must have a continued living interest in order to retain an abiding place in the memory. The mind must refer to it frequently, but whether it does so consciously or unconsciously is not perhaps a matter of much importance. Otherwise, as a general rule, the recollection sinks, and appears to be utterly drowned in the waters of Lethe.

It would be very instructive to print the actual records at length, made by many experimenters, if the records could be clubbed together and thrown into a statistical form; but it would be too absurd to print one's own singly. They lay bare the foundations of a man's thoughts with curious distinctness, and exhibit his mental anatomy with more vividness and truth than he would probably care to publish to the world.

It remains to summarise what has been said in the foregoing memoir. I have desired to show how whole strata of mental operations that have lapsed out of ordinary consciousness, admit of being dragged into light, recorded and treated statistically, and how the obscurity that attends the initial steps of our thoughts can thus be pierced and dissipated. I then showed measurably the rate at which associations sprung up, their character, the date of their first formation, their tendency to recurrence, and their relative precedence. Also I gave an instance showing how the phenomenon of a long-forgotten scene, suddenly starting into consciousness, admitted in many cases of being explained. Perhaps the strongest of the impressions left by these experiments regards the multifariousness of the work done by the mind in a state of half-unconsciousness, and the valid reason they afford for believing in the existence of still deeper strata of mental operations, sunk wholly below the level of consciousness, which may account for such mental phenomena as cannot otherwise be explained. We gain an insight by these experiments into the marvellous number and nimbleness of our mental associations, and we also learn that they are very far indeed from being infinite in their variety. We find that our working stock of ideas is narrowly limited and that the mind continually recurs to the same instruments in conducting its operations, therefore its tracks necessarily become more defined and its flexibility diminished as age advances.

William James: 1842-1910

WHAT IS EMOTION? *

1884

THE physiologists who, during the past few years, have been so industriously exploring the functions of the brain, have limited their attempts at explanation to its cognitive and volitional performances. Dividing the brain into sensorial and motor centres, they have found their division to be exactly paralleled by the analysis made by empirical psychology, of the perceptive and volitional parts of the mind into their simplest elements. But the *aesthetic* sphere of the mind, its longings, its pleasures and pains, and its emotions, have been so ignored in all these researches that one is tempted to suppose that if either Dr. Ferrier or Dr. Munk were asked for a theory in brain-terms of the latter mental facts, they might both reply, either that they had as yet bestowed no thought upon the subject, or that they had found it so difficult to make distinct hypotheses, that the matter lay for them among the problems of the future, only to be taken up after the simpler ones of the present should have been definitively solved.

And yet it is even now certain that of two things concerning the emotions, one must be true. Either separate and special centres, affected to them alone, are their brain-seat, or else they correspond to processes occurring in the motor and sensory centres, already assigned, or in others like them, not yet mapped out. If the former be the case we must deny the current view, and hold the cortex to be something more than the surface of *projection* for every sensitive spot and every muscle in the body. If the latter be the case, we must ask whether the emotional *process* in the sensory or motor centre be an altogether peculiar one, or whether it resembles the ordinary perceptive processes of which those centres are already recognised to be the seat. The purpose of the following pages is to show that the last alternative comes nearest to the truth, and that the emotional brain-processes not only resemble the ordinary sensorial brain-processes, but in very truth, are nothing but such processes variously combined. The main result of this will be to simplify our notions of the possible complications of brain-physiology, and to make

* This essay, published in *Mind*, IX (1884), 188-204, constitutes James' first publication on the James-Lange theory of the emotions. Lange, a Dane, published quite independently the following year.

us see that we have already a brain-scheme in our hands whose applications are much wider than its authors dreamed. But although this seems to be the chief result of the arguments I am to urge, I should say that they were not originally framed for the sake of any such result. They grew out of fragmentary introspective observations, and it was only when these had already combined into a theory that the thought of the simplification the theory might bring to cerebral physiology occurred to me, and made it seem more important than before.

I should say first of all that the only emotions I propose expressly to consider here are those that have a distinct bodily expression. That there are feelings of pleasure and displeasure, of interest and excitement, bound up with mental operations, but having no obvious bodily expression for their consequence, would, I suppose, be held true by most readers. Certain arrangements of sounds, of lines, of colours, are agreeable, and others the reverse, without the degree of the feeling being sufficient to quicken the pulse or breathing, or to prompt to movements of either the body or the face. Certain sequences of ideas charm us as much as others tire us. It is a real intellectual delight to get a problem solved, and a real intellectual torment to have to leave it unfinished. The first set of examples, the sounds, lines, and colours, are either bodily sensations, or the images of such. The second set seem to depend on processes in the ideational centres exclusively. Taken together, they appear to prove that there are pleasures and pains inherent in certain forms of nerve-action as such, wherever that action occurs. The case of these feelings we will at present leave entirely aside, and confine our attention to the more complicated cases in which a wave of bodily disturbance of some kind accompanies the perception of the interesting sights or sounds, or the passage of the exciting train of ideas. Surprise, curiosity, rapture, fear, anger, lust, greed, and the like, become then the names of the mental states with which the person is possessed. The bodily disturbances are said to be the "manifestation" of these several emotions, their "expression" or "natural language;" and these emotions themselves, being so strongly characterized both from within and without, may be called the *standard* emotions.

Our natural way of thinking about these standard emotions is that the mental perception of some fact excites the mental affection called the emotion, and that this latter state of mind gives rise to the bodily expression. My thesis on the contrary is that *the bodily changes follow directly the* PERCEPTION *of the exciting fact, and that our feeling of same changes as they occur* IS *the emotion.* Common sense says, we lose our fortune, are sorry and weep; we meet a bear, are frightened and run; we are insulted by a rival, are angry and strike. The hypothesis here to be defended says that this order of sequence is incorrect, that the one mental state is not immediately induced by the other, that the bodily manifestations must first be interposed between, and that the more rational statement is that we feel sorry because we cry, angry because we strike, or tremble, because we are sorry, angry, or fearful as the case may be. Without the bodily states following on the perception, the latter would be purely cognitive in form, pale, colourless, destitute of emotional warmth. We might then see the bear, and judge it best to run, receive the insult and deem it right to strike, but we could not actually feel afraid or angry.

Stated in this crude way, the hypothesis is pretty sure to meet with immediate disbelief. And yet neither many nor far-fetched considerations are required to mitigate its paradoxical character, and possibly to produce conviction of its truth.

To begin with, readers of this Journal do not need to be reminded that the nervous system of every living thing is but a bundle of predispositions to react in particular ways upon the contact of particular features of the environment. As surely as the hermit-crab's abdomen presupposes the existence of empty whelk-shells somewhere to be found, so surely do the hound's olfactories imply the existence, on the one hand, of deer's or foxes' feet, and on the other, the tendency to follow up their tracks. The neural machinery is but a hyphen between determinate arrangements of matter outside the body and determinate impulses to inhibition or discharge within its organs. When the hen sees a white oval object on the ground, she cannot leave it; she must keep upon it and return to it, until at last its transformation into a little mass of moving chirping down elicits from her machinery an entirely new set of performances. The love of man for woman, or of the human mother for her babe, our wrath at snakes and our fear of precipices, may all be described similarly, as instances of the way in which peculiarly conformed pieces of the world's furniture will fatally call forth most particular mental and bodily reactions, in advance of, and often in direct opposition to, the verdict of our deliberate reason concerning them. The labours of Darwin and his successors are only just beginning to reveal the universal parasitism of each special creature upon other special relations stamped on its nervous system with it upon the scene.

Every living creature is in fact a sort of lock, whose wards and springs presuppose special forms of key—which keys however are not born attached to the locks, but are sure to be found in the world nearby as life goes on. And the locks are indifferent to any but their own keys. The egg fails to fascinate the hound, the bird does not fear the precipice, the snakes waxes not wroth at his kind, the deer cares nothing for the woman or the human babe. Those who wish for a full development of this point of view, should read Schneider's *Der thierische Wille*,—no other book shows how accurately anticipatory are the actions of animals, of the specific features of the environment in which they are to live.

Now among these nervous anticipations are of course to be reckoned the emotions, so far as these may be called forth directly by the perception of certain facts. In advance of all experience of elephants no child can but be frightened if he suddenly find one trumpeting and charging upon him. No woman can see a handsome little naked baby without delight, no man in the wilderness see a human form in the distance without excitement and curiosity. I said I should consider these emotions only so far as they have bodily movements of some sort for their accompaniments. But my first point is to show that their bodily accompaniments are much more far-reaching and complicated than we ordinarily suppose.

In the earlier books on Expression, written mostly from the artistic point of view, the signs of emotion visible from without were the only ones taken account of. Sir Charles Bell's celebrated *Anatomy of Expression* noticed the respiratory changes; and Bain's and Darwin's treatises went more thoroughly still into the study of the visceral factors involved, —changes in the functioning of glands and muscles, and in that of the circulatory apparatus. But not even a Darwin has exhaustively enumerated all the bodily affections characteristic of any one of the standard emotions. More and more, as physiology advances, we begin to discern how almost infinitely numerous and subtle they must be. The researches of Mosso with the plethysmograph have shown that not only the heart, but the entire circulatory system, forms a sort of sounding-board, which every change of our consciousness, however slight, may make reverberate. Hardly a sensation comes to us without sending waves of alternate constriction and dilatation down the arteries of our arms. The blood-vessels of the abdomen act reciprocally with those of the more outward parts. The bladder and bowels, the glands of the mouth, throat, and skin, and the liver, are known to be affected gravely in certain severe emotions, and are unquestionably affected transiently when the emotions are of a lighter sort. That the heart-beats and the rhythm of breathing play a leading part in all emotions whatsoever, is a matter too notorious for proof. And what is really equally prominent, but less likely to be admitted until special attention is drawn to the fact, is the continuous co-operation of the voluntary muscles in our emotional states. Even when no change of outward attitude is produced, their inward tension alters to suit each varying mood, and is felt as a difference of tone or of strain. In depression the flexors tend to prevail; in elation or belligerent excitement the extensors take the lead. And the various permutations and combinations of which these organic activities are susceptible, make it abstractly possible that no shade of emotion, however slight, should be without a bodily reverberation as unique, when taken in its totality, as is the mental mood itself.

The immense number of parts modified in each emotion is what makes it so difficult for us to reproduce in cold blood the total and integral expression of any one of them. We may catch the trick with the voluntary muscles, but fail with the skin, glands, heart, and other viscera. Just as an artificially imitated sneeze lacks something of the reality, so the attempt to imitate an emotion in the absence of its normal instigating cause is apt to be rather "hollow."

The next thing to be noticed is this, that every one of the bodily changes, whatsoever it be, is felt, acutely or obscurely, the moment it occurs. If the reader has never paid attention to this matter, he will be both interested and astonished to learn how many different local bodily feelings he can detect in himself as characteristic of his various emotional moods. It would be perhaps too much to expect him to arrest the tide of any strong gust of passion for the sake of any such curious analysis as this; but he can observe more tranquil states, and that may be assumed here to be true of the greater which is shown to be true of the less. Our whole cubic capacity is sensibly alive; and each morsel of it contributes its pulsations of feeling, dim or sharp, pleasant, painful, or dubious, to that sense of personality that every one of us unfailingly carries with him. It is surprising what little items give accent to these complexes of sensibility. When worried by any slight trouble, one may find that the focus of one's bodily consciousness is the contraction, often quite inconsiderable, of the eyes and brows. When momentarily embarrassed, it is something in the pharynx that compels either a swallow, a clearing of the throat, or a slight cough; and so on for as many more instances as might be named. Our concern here being with the general view rather than with the details, I will not linger to discuss these but, assuming the point admitted that every change that occurs must be felt, I will pass on.

I now proceed to urge the vital point of my whole theory, which is this. If we fancy some strong emotion, and they try to abstract from our consciousness of it all the feelings of its characteristic bodily symptoms, we find we have nothing left behind, no "mind-stuff" out of which the emotion can be constituted, and that a cold, a neutral state of intellectual perception is all that remains. It is true, that although most people, when asked, say that their introspection verifies this statement, some persist in saying theirs does not. Many cannot be made to understand the question. When you beg them to imagine away every feeling of laughter and of tendency to laugh from their consciousness of the ludicrousness of an object, and then to tell you what the feeling of its ludicrousness would be like, whether it be anything more than the perception that the object belongs to the class "funny," they persist in replying that the thing proposed is a physical impossibility, and that they always must laugh, if they see a funny object. Of course the task proposed is not the practical one of seeing a ludicrous object and annihilating one's tendency to laugh. It is the purely speculative one of subtracting certain elements of feeling from an emotional state supposed to exist in its fulness, and saying what the residual elements are. I cannot help thinking that all who rightly apprehend this problem will agree with the proposition above laid down. What kind of an emotion of fear would be left, if the feelings neither of quickened heart-beats nor of shallow breathing, neither of trembling lips nor of weakened limbs, neither of goose-flesh nor of visceral stirrings, were present, it is quite impossible to think. Can one fancy the state of rage and picture no ebullition of it in the chest, no flushing of the face, no dilatation of the nostrils, no clenching of the teeth, no impulse to vigorous action, but in their stead limp muscles, calm breathing, and a placid face? The present writer, for one, certainly cannot. The rage is as completely evaporated as the sensation of its so-called manifestations, and the only thing that can possibly be supposed to take its place is some cold-blooded and dispassionate judicial sentence, confined entirely to the intellectual realm, to the effect that a certain person or persons merit chastisement for their sins. In like manner of grief; what would it be without its tears, its sobs, its suffocation of the heart, its pang in the breast-bone? A feelingless cognition that certain circumstances are deplorable, and nothing more. Every passion in turn tells the same story. A purely disembodied human emotion is a nonentity. I do not say that it is a contradiction in the nature of things, or that pure spirits are necessarily condemned to cold intellectual lives; but I say that for us, emotion dissociated from all bodily feeling is inconceivable. The more closely I scrutinise my states, the more persuaded I become, that whatever moods, affections, and passions I have, are in very truth constituted by, and made up of, those bodily changes we ordinarily call their expression or consequence; and the more it seems to me that if I were to become corporeally anaesthetic, I should be excluded from the life of the affections, harsh and tender alike, and drag out an existence of merely cognitive or intellectual form. Such an existence, although it seems to have been the ideal of ancient sages, is too apathetic to be keenly sought after by those born after the revival of the worship of sensibility, a few generations ago.

But if the emotion is nothing but the feeling of the reflex bodily effects of what we call its "object," effects due to the connate adaptation of the nervous system to that object, we seem immediately faced by this objection: most of the objects of civilised men's emotions are things to which it would be preposterous to suppose their nervous systems connately adapted. Most occasions of shame and many insults are purely conventional, and vary with the social environment. The same is true of many matters of dread and of desire, and of many occasions of melancholy and regret. In these cases, at least, it would seem that the ideas of shame, desire, regret, &c., must first have been attached by education and association to these conventional objects before the bodily changes could possibly be awakened. And if in these cases the bodily changes follow the ideas, instead of giving rise to them, why not then in all cases?

To discuss thoroughly this objection would carry us deep into the study of purely intellectual Aesthetics. A few words must here suffice. We will say nothing of the argument's failure to distinguish between the idea of an emotion and the emotion itself. We will only recall the well-known evolutionary principle that when a certain power has once been fixed in an animal by virtue of its utility in presence of certain features of the environment, it may turn out to be useful in presence of other features of the environment that had originally nothing to do with either producing or preserving it. A nervous tendency to discharge being once there, all sorts of unforeseen things may pull the trigger and let loose the effects. That among these things should be conventionalities of man's contriving is a matter of no psychological consequence whatever. The most important part of my environment is my fellow-man. The consciousness of his attitude towards me is the perception that normally unlocks most of my shames and indignations and fears. The extraordinary sensitiveness of this consciousness is shown by the bodily modifications wrought in us by the awareness that our fellow-man is noticing us at all. No one can walk across the platform at a public meeting with just the same muscular innervation he uses to walk across his room at home. No one can give a message to such a meeting without organic excitement. "Stage-fright" is only the extreme degree of that wholly irrational personal self-consciousness which every one gets in some measure, as soon as he feels the eyes of a number of strangers fixed upon him, even though he be inwardly convinced that their feeling towards him is of no practical account. This being so, it is not surprising that the additional persuasion that my fellow-man's attitude means either well or ill for me, should awaken stronger emotions still. In primitive societies "Well" may mean handing me a piece of beef, and "Ill" may mean aiming a blow at my skull. In our "cultured age," "Ill" may mean cutting me in the street, and "Well," giving me an honorary degree. What the action itself may be is quite insignificant, so long as I can perceive in it intent or *animus*. That is the emotion-arousing perception; and may give rise to as strong bodily convulsions in me, a civilised man experiencing the treatment of an artificial society, as in any savage prisoner of war, learning whether his captors are about to eat him or to make him a member of their tribe.

But now, this objection disposed of, there arises a more general doubt.

Is there any evidence, it may be asked, for the assumption that particular perceptions do produce widespread bodily effects by a sort of immediate physical influence, antecedent to the arousal of an emotion or emotional idea? The only possible reply is, that there is most assuredly such evidence. In listening to poetry, drama, or heroic narrative, we are often surprised at the cutaneous shiver which like a sudden wave flows over us, and at the heart-swelling and the lachrymal effusion that unexpectedly catch us at intervals. In listening to music, the same is even more strikingly true. If we abruptly see a dark moving form in the woods, our heart stops beating, and we catch our breath instantly and before any articulate idea of danger can arise. If our friend goes near to the edge of a precipice, we get the well-known feeling of "all-overishness," and we shrink back, although we positively know him to be safe, and have no distinct imagination of his fall. The writer well remembers his astonishment, when a boy of seven or eight, at fainting when he saw a horse bled. The blood was in a bucket, with a stick in it, and, if memory does not deceive him, he stirred it round and saw it drip from the stick with no feeling save that of childish curiosity. Suddenly the world grew black before his eyes, his ears began to buzz, and he knew no more. He had never heard of the sight of blood producing faintness or sickness, and he had so little repugnance to it, and so little apprehension of any other sort of danger from it, that even at that tender age, as he well remembers, he could not help wondering how the mere physical presence of a pailful of crimson fluid could occasion in him such formidable bodily effects.

Imagine two steel knife-blades with their keen edges crossing each other at right angles, and moving too and fro. Our whole nervous organisation is "on-edge" at the thought; and yet what emotion can be there except the unpleasant nervous feeling itself, or the dread that more of it may come? The entire fund and capital of the emotion here is the senseless bodily effect the blades immediately arouse. This case is typical of a class: where an ideal emotion seems to precede the bodily symptoms, it is often nothing but a representation of the symptoms themselves. One who has already fainted at the sight of blood may witness the preparations for a surgical operation with uncontrollable heart-sinking and anxiety. He anticipates certain feelings, and the anticipation precipitates their arrival. I am told of a case of morbid terror, of which the subject confessed that what possessed her seemed, more than anything, to be the fear of fear itself. In the various forms of what Professor Bain calls "tender emotion," although the appropriate object must usually be directly contemplated before the emotion can be aroused, yet sometimes thinking of the symptoms of the emotion itself may have the same effect. In sentimental natures, the thought of "yearning" will produce real "yearning." And, not to speak of coarser examples, a mother's imagination of the caresses she bestows on her child may arouse a spasm of parental longing.

In such cases as these, we see plainly how the emotion both begins and ends with what we call its effects or manifestations. It has no mental status except as either the presented feelings, or the idea, of the manifestations; which latter thus constitute its entire material, its sum and substance, and its stock-in-trade. And these cases ought to make us see how in all cases the feeling of the manifestations may play a much deeper part in the constitution of the emotion than we are wont to suppose.

If our theory be true, a necessary corollary of it ought to be that any voluntary arousal of the so-called manifestations of a special emotion ought to give us the emotion itself. Of course in the majority of emotions, this test is inapplicable; for many of the manifestations are in organs over which we have no volitional control. Still, within the limits in which it can be verified, experience fully corroborates this test. Everyone knows how panic is increased by flight, and how the giving way to the symptoms of grief or anger increases those passions themselves. Each fit of sobbing makes the sorrow more acute, and calls forth another fit stronger still, until at last repose only ensues with lassitude and with the apparent exhaustion of the machinery. In rage, it is notorious how we "work ourselves up" to a climax by repeated outbreaks of expression. Refuse to express a passion, and it dies. Count ten before venting your anger, and its occasion seems ridiculous. Whistling to keep up courage is no mere figure of speech. On the other hand, sit all day in a moping posture, sigh, and reply to everything with a dismal voice, and your melancholy lingers. There is no more valuable precept in moral education than this, as all who have experience know; if we wish to conquer undesirable emotional tendencies in ourselves, we must assiduously, and in the first instance cold-bloodedly, go through the outward motions of those contrary dispositions we prefer to cultivate. The reward of persistency will infallibly come, in the fading out of the sullenness or depression, and the advent of real cheerfulness and kindliness in their stead. Smooth the brow, brighten the eye, contract the dorsal rather than the ventral aspect of the frame, and speak in a major key, pass the genial compliment, and your heart must be frigid indeed if it does not gradually thaw!

The only exceptions to this are apparent, not real. The great emotional expressiveness and mobility of certain persons often lead us to say "They would feel more if they talked less." And in another class of persons, the explosive energy with which passion manifests itself on critical occasions, seems correlated with the way in which they bottle it up during the intervals. But these are only eccentric types of character, and within each type the law of the last paragraph prevails. The sentimentalist is so constructed that "gushing" is his or her normal mode of expression. Putting a stopper on the "gush" will only to a limited extent cause more "real" activities to take its place; in the main it will simply produce listlessness. On the other hand the ponderous and bilious "slumbering volcano," let him repress the expression of his passions as he will, will find them expire if they get no vent at all; whilst if the rare occasions multiply which he deems worthy of their outbreak, he will find them grow in intensity as life proceeds.

I feel persuaded there is no real exception to the law. The formidable effects of suppressed tears might be mentioned, and the calming results of speaking out your mind when angry and having done with it. But these are also but specious wanderings from the rule. Every perception must lead to some nervous result. If this be the normal emotional expression, it soon expends itself, and in the natural course of things a calm succeeds. But if the normal issue be blocked from any cause, the currents may under certain circumstances invade other tracts, and there work different and worse effects. Thus vengeful brooding may replace a burst of indignation; a dry heat may consume the frame of one who fain would weep, or he may, as Dante says, turn to stone within; and then tears or a storming-fit may bring a grateful relief. When we teach children to repress their emotions, it is not that they may feel more, quite the reverse. It is that they may think more; for to a certain extent whatever nerve-currents are diverted from the regions below, must swell the activity of the thought-tracts of the brain.

The last great argument in favour of the priority of the bodily symptoms to the felt emotion, is the ease with which we formulate by its means pathological cases and normal cases under a common scheme. In every asylum we find examples of absolutely unmotivated fear, anger, melancholy, or conceit; and others of an equally unmotived apathy which persists in spite of the best of outward reasons why it should give way. In the former cases we must suppose the nervous machinery to be so "labile" in some one emotional direction, that almost every stimulus, however inappropriate, will cause it to upset in that way, and as a consequence to engender the particular complex of feelings of which the psychic body of the emotion consists. Thus, to take one special instance, if inability to draw deep breath, fluttering of the heart, and that peculiar epigastric change felt as "precordial anxiety," with an irresistible tendency to take a somewhat crouching attitude and to sit still, and with perhaps other visceral processes not now known, all spontaneously occur together in a certain person; his feeling of their combination is the emotion of dread, and he is the victim of what is known as morbid fear. A friend who has had occasional attacks of this most distressing of all maladies, tells me that in his case the whole drama seems to centre about the region of the heart and respiratory apparatus, that his main effort during the attacks is to get control of his inspirations and to slow his heart, and that the moment he attains to breathing deeply and to holding himself erect, the dread, *ipso facto*, seems to depart.

If our hypothesis be true, it makes us realise more deeply than ever how much our mental life is knit up with our corporeal frame, in the strictest sense of the term. Rapture, love, ambition, indignation, and pride, considered as feelings, are fruits of the same soil with the grossest bodily sensations of pleasure and of pain. But it was said at the outset that this would be affirmed only of what we then agreed to call the *standard* emotions; and that those inward sensibilities that appeared devoid at first sight of bodily results should be left out of our account. We had better, before closing, say a word or two about these latter feelings.

They are, the reader will remember, the moral, intellectual, and aesthetic feelings. Concords of sounds, of colours, of lines, logical consistencies, teleological fitnesses, affect us with a pleasure that seems ingrained in the very form of the representation itself, and to borrow nothing from any reverberation surging up from the parts below the brain. The Herbartian psychologists have tried to distinguish feelings due to the form in which ideas may be arranged. A geometrical demonstration may be as "pretty," and an act of justice as "neat" as a drawing or a tune, although the prettiness and neatness seem here to be a pure matter of sensation, and there to have nothing to do with sensation. We have then, or some of us seem to have, genuinely cerebral forms of pleasure and displeasure, apparently not agreeing in their mode of production with the so-called *standard* emotions we have been analysing. And it is certain that readers whom our reasons have hitherto failed to convince, will now start up at this admission, and consider that by it we give up our whole case. Since musical perceptions, since logical ideas, can immediately arouse a form of emotional feeling, they will say, is it not more natural to suppose that in the case of the so-called *standard* emotions, prompted by the presence of objects or the experience of events the emotional feeling is equally immediate, and the bodily expression something that comes later and is added on?

But a sober scrutiny of the cases of pure cerebral emotion gives little force to this assimilation. Unless in them there actually be coupled with the intellectual feeling a bodily reverberation of some kind, unless we actually laugh at the neatness of the mechanical device, thrill at the justice of the act, or tingle at the perfection of the musical form, our mental condition is more allied to a judgment of right than to anything else. And such a judgment is rather to be classed among awareness of truth: it is a cognitive act. But as a matter of fact the intellectual feeling hardly ever does exist thus unaccompanied. The bodily sounding-board is at work, as careful introspection will show, far more than we usually suppose. Still, where long familiarity with a certain class of effects has blunted emotional sensibility thereto as much as it has sharpened the taste and judgment, we do get the intellectual emotion, if such it can be called, pure and undefiled. And the dryness of it, the paleness, the absence of all glow, as it may exist in a thoroughly expert critic's mind, not only shows us what an altogether different thing it is from the *standard* emotions we considered first, but makes us suspect that almost the entire difference lies in the fact that the bodily sounding-board, vibrating in the one case as in the other mute. "Not so very bad" is, in a person of consummate taste, apt to be the highest limit of approving expression. *Rien ne me choque* is said to have been Chopin's superlative of praise of new music. A sentimental layman would feel, and ought to feel, horrified, on being admitted into such a critic's mind, to see how cold, how thin, how void of human significance, are the motives for favour or disfavour that there prevail. The capacity to make a nice spot on the wall will outweigh a picture's whole content; a foolish trick of words will preserve a poem; an utterly meaningless fitness of sequence in one musical composition set at naught any amount of "expressiveness" in another.

I remember seeing an English couple sit for more than an hour on a piercing February day in the Academy at Venice before the celebrated "Assumption" by Titian; and when I, after being chased from room to room by the cold, concluded to get into the sunshine as fast as possible and let the pictures go, but before leaving drew reverently near to them to learn with what superior forms of susceptibility they might be endowed, all I overheard was the woman's voice murmuring: "What a deprecatory expression her face wears! What self-abnegation! How unworthy she feels of the honour she is receiving!" Their honest hearts had been kept warm all the time by a glow of spurious sentiment that would have fairly made old Titian sick. Mr. Ruskin somewhere makes the (for him) terrible admission that religious people as a rule care little for pictures, and that when they do care for them they generally prefer the worst ones to the best. Yes! in every art, in every science, there is the keen perception of certain relations being right or not, and there is the emotional flush and thrill consequent there-upon. And these are two things, not one. In the former of them it is that experts and masters are at home. The latter accompaniments are bodily commotions that they may hardly feel, but that may be experienced in their fulness by Cretins and Philistines in whom the critical judgment is at its lowest ebb. The "marvels" of Science, about which so much edifying popular literature is written, are apt to be "caviare" to the men in the laboratories.

Cognition and emotion are parted even in this last retreat,—who shall say that their antagonism may not just be the one phase of the world-old struggle in which it seems pretty certain that neither party will definitively drive the other off the field.

To return now to our starting-point, the physiology of the brain. If we suppose its cortex to contain centres for the perception of changes in each special sense-organ, in each portion of the skin, in each muscle, each joint, and each viscus, and to contain absolutely nothing else, we still have a scheme perfectly capable of representing the process of the emotions. An object falls on a sense-organ and is apperceived by the appropriate cortical centre; or else the latter, excited in some other way, gives rise to an idea of the same object. Quick as a flash, the reflex currents pass down through their pre-ordained channels, alter the condition of muscle, skin and viscus; and these alterations, apperceived like the original object, in as many specific portions of the cortex, combine with it in consciousness and transform it from an object-simply-apprehended into an object-emotionally-felt. No new principles have to be invoked, nothing is postulated beyond the ordinary reflex circuit, and the topical centres admitted in one shape or another by all to exist.

It must be confessed that a crucial test of the truth of the hypothesis is quite as hard to obtain as its decisive refutation. A case of complete internal and external corporeal anesthesia, without motor alteration or alteration of intelligence except emotional apathy, would afford, if not a crucial test, at least a strong presumption, in favour of the truth of the view we have set forth; whilst the persistence of strong emotional feeling in such a case would completely overthrow our case. Hysterical anaesthesias seem never to be complete enough to cover the ground. Complete anesthesias from organic disease, on the other hand, are excessively rare. In the famous case of Remigius Leims, no mention is made by the reporters of his emotional condition, a circumstance which by itself affords no presumption that it was normal, since as a rule nothing ever is noticed without a pre-existing question in the mind. Dr. George Winter has recently described a case somewhat similar, and in reply to a question, kindly writes to me as follows:

> The case has been for a year and a half entirely removed from my observation. But so far as I am able to state, the man has characterised by a certain mental inertia and indolence. He was tranquil, and had on the whole the temperament of a phlegmatic. He was not irritable, not quarrelsome, went quietly about his farm-work, and left the care of his business and house-keeping to other people. In short, he gave one the impression of a placid countryman, who has no interests beyond his work.

Dr. Winter adds that in studying the case he paid no particular attention to the man's psychic condition, as this seemed *nebensachlich* to his main purpose. I should add that the form of my question to Dr. Winter could give him no clue as to the kind of answer I expected.

Of course, this case proves nothing, but it is to be hoped that asylum-physicians and nervous specialists may begin methodically to study the relation between anaesthesia and emotional apathy. If the hypothesis here suggested is ever to be definitively confirmed or disproved it seems as if it must be by them, for they alone have the data in their hands.

Hermann Ebbinghaus: 1850-1909

CONCERNING MEMORY *

1885

THE METHOD OF INVESTIGATION

In order to test practically, although only for a limited field, a way of penetrating more deeply into memory processes I have hit upon the following method.

Out of the simple consonants of the alphabet and our eleven vowels and diphthongs all possible syllables of a certain sort were constructed, a vowel sound being placed between two consonants.

These syllables, about 2300 in number, were mixed together and then drawn out by chance and used to construct series of different lengths, several of which each time formed the material for a test.

At the beginning a few rules were observed to prevent, in the construction of the syllables, too immediate repetition of similar sounds, but these were not strictly adhered to. Later they were abandoned and the matter left to chance. The syllables used each time were carefully laid aside till the whole number had been used, then they were mixed together and used again.

The aim of the tests carried on with these syllable series was, by means of repeated audible perusal of the separate series, to so impress them that immediately afterwards they could voluntarily just be reproduced. This aim was considered attained when, the initial syllable being given, a series could be recited at the first attempt, without hesitation, at a certain rate, and with the consciousness of being correct.

The following rules were made for the process of memorising:

1. The separate series were always read through completely from beginning to end; they were not learned in separate parts which were then joined together; neither were especially difficult parts detached and repeated more frequently. There was a perfectly free interchange between the reading and the occasionally necessary tests of the capacity to reproduce by heart. For the latter there was an important rule to the effect

* As is well known, this was the first experimental investigation of learning and retention. The entire monograph was translated by H. A. Ruger and Clara E. Bussenius and published by Teachers College, Columbia University, in 1913. Certain sections are reprinted by permission of the Bureau of Publications, Teachers College.

that upon hesitation the rest of the series was to be read through to the end before beginning it again.

2. The reading and the recitation of the series took place at a constant rate, that of 150 strokes per minute. A clockwork metronome placed at some distance was at first used to regulate the rate; but very soon the ticking of a watch was substituted, that being much simpler and less disturbing to the attention. The mechanism of escapement of most watches swings 300 times per minute.

3. Since it is practically impossible to speak continuously without variation of accent, the following method was adopted to avoid irregular variations: either three or four syllables were united into a measure and thus either the 1st, 4th, 7th, or the 1st, 5th, 9th . . . syllables were pronounced with a slight accent. Stressing of the voice was otherwise, as far as possible, avoided.

4. After the learning of each separate series a pause of 15 seconds was made, and used for the tabulation of results. Then the following series of the same test was immediately taken up.

5. During the process of learning the purpose of reaching the desired goal as soon as possible was kept in mind as much as was feasible. Thus, to the limited degree to which conscious resolve is of influence here, the attempt was made to keep the attention concentrated on the tiresome task and its purpose. It goes without saying that care was taken to keep away all outer disturbances in order to make possible the attainment of this aim. The smaller distractions caused by carrying on the test in various surroundings were also avoided as far as that could be done.

6. There was no attempt to connect the nonsense syllables by the invention of special associations of the mnemotechnik type; learning was carried on solely by the influence of the mere repetitions upon the natural memory. As I do not possess the least practical knowledge of the mnemotechnical devices, the fulfillment of this condition offered no difficulty to me.

7. Finally and chiefly, care was taken that the objective conditions of life during the period of the tests were so controlled as to eliminate too great changes or irregularities. Of course, since the tests extended over many months, this was possible only to a limited extent. But, even so, the attempt was made to conduct, under as similar conditions of life as possible, those tests the results of which were to be directly compared. In particular the activity immediately preceding the test was kept as constant in character as was possible. Since the mental as well as the physical condition of man is subject to an evident periodicity of 24 hours, it was taken for granted that like experimental conditions are obtainable only at like times of day. However, in order to carry out more than one test in a given day, different experiments were occasionally carried on to-

gether at different times of day. When too great changes in the outer and inner life occurred, the tests were discontinued for a length of time. Their resumption was preceded by some days of renewed training varying according to the length of the interruption.

The tests were made in two periods, in the years 1879–80 and 1883–84, and extended each over more than a year. During a long time preliminary experiments of a similar nature had preceded the definite tests of the first period, so that, for all results communicated, the time of increasing skill may be considered as past. At the beginning of the second period I was careful to give myself renewed training. This temporal distribution of the tests with a separating interval of more than three years gives the desired possibility of a certain mutual control of most of the results. Frankly, the tests of the two periods are not strictly comparable. In the case of the tests of the first period in order to limit the significance of the first fleeting grasp of the series in moments of special concentration, it was decided to study the series until two successive faultless reproductions were possible. Later I abandoned this method, which only incompletely accomplished its purpose, and kept to the first fluent reproduction. The earlier method evidently in many cases resulted in a somewhat longer period of learning. In addition there was a difference in the hours of the day appointed for the tests. Those of the later period all occurred in the afternoon hours between one and three o'clock; those of the earlier period were unequally divided between the hours of 10–11 A.M., 11–12 A.M., and 6–8 P.M., which for the sake of brevity I shall designate A, B, and C.

RETENTION AS A FUNCTION OF THE NUMBER OF REPETITIONS

The result of the fourth chapter was as follows: When in repeated cases I memorised series of syllables of a certain length to the point of their first possible reproduction, the times (or number of repetitions) necessary differed greatly from each other, but the mean values derived from them had the character of genuine constants of natural science. Ordinarily, therefore, I learned by heart homogeneous series under similar conditions with, on the average, a similar number of repetitions. The large deviations of the separate values from each other change the total result not at all; but it would require too much time to ascertain with exactness the number necessary for greater precision in detail.

What will happen, it may be asked, if the number of repetitions actually given to a certain series is less than is required for memorisation or if the number exceeds the necessary minimum?

The general nature of what happens has already been described.

Naturally the surplus repetitions of the latter alternative do not go to waste. Even though the immediate effect, the smooth and errorless reproduction, is not affected by them, yet they are not without significance in that they serve to make other such reproductions possible at a more or less distant time. The longer a person studies, the longer he retains. And, even in the first case, something evidently occurs even if the repetitions do not suffice for a free reproduction. By them a way is at least opened for the first errorless reproductions, and the disconnected, hesitating, and faulty reproductions keep approximating more and more to it.

These relations can be described figuratively by speaking of the series as being more or less deeply engraved in some mental substratum. To carry out this figure: as the number of repetitions increases, the series are engraved more and more deeply and indelibly; if the number of repetitions is small, the inscription is but surface deep and only fleeting glimpses of the tracery can be caught; with a somewhat greater number the inscription can, for a time at least, be read at will; as the number of repetitions is still further increased, the deeply cut picture of the series fades out only after ever longer intervals.

What is to be said in case a person is not satisfied with this general statement of a relation of dependence between the number of repetitions and the depth of the mental impression obtained, and if he demands that it be defined more clearly and in detail? The thermometer rises with increasing temperature, the magnetic needle is displaced to an increasing angle as the intensity of the electric current around it increases. But while the mercury always rises by equal spaces for each equal increase in temperature, the increase of the angle showing the displacement of the magnetic needle becomes less with a like increase in the electric current. Which analogy is it which holds for the effect of the number of repetitions of the series to be memorised upon the depth of the resulting impression? Without further discussion shall we make it proportional to the number of repetitions, and accordingly say that it is twice or three times as great when homogenous series are repeated with the same degree of attention twice or thrice as many times as are others? Or does it increase less and less with each and every constant increase in the number of repetitions? Or what does happen?

Evidently this question is a good one; its answer would be of theoretical as well as practical interest and importance. But with the resources hitherto at hand it could not be answered, nor even investigated. Even its meaning will not be quite clear so long as the words "inner stability" and "depth of impression" denote something indefinite and figurative rather than something clear and objectively defined.

Applying the principles developed in section 5, I define the inner stability of a series of ideas—the degree of its retainability—by the greater or less readiness with which it is reproduced at some definite time subsequent to its first memorisation. This readiness I measure by the amount of work saved in the relearning of any series as compared with the work necessary for memorising a similar but entirely new series.

The interval of time between the two processes of memorisation is of course a matter of choice. I choose 24 hours.

Since in the case of this definition we are not trying to settle a matter of general linguistic usage, it cannot be properly asked whether it is correct, but only whether it serves the purpose, or, at the most, whether it is applicable to the indefinite ideas connected with the notion of different depths of mental impression. The latter will probably be granted. But nothing can be said in advance as to how well it fulfills its purpose. That can be judged only after more extensive results have been obtained. And the character of the judgment will depend to a great extent on whether the results obtained with the help of this means of measurement fulfill the primary demand which we make with reference to any system of measurement. It consists in this,—that if any change whatever is made in the controllable conditions of that scale, the results obtained by the scale in its new form can be reduced to those of the old form by multiplication by some one constant. In our present case, for example, it would consequently be necessary to know whether the character of the results would remain the same if any other interval had been employed instead of that of 24 hours, arbitrarily chosen for measuring the after-effect of repetitions, or whether as a consequence the entire rationale of the results would be different, just as the absolute values are necessarily different. Naturally, this question cannot be decided *a priori.*

For ascertaining the relation of dependence between the increase in the number of repetitions of a series and the ever deeper impression of it which results, I have formulated the problem as follows: If homogeneous series are impressed to different extents as a result of different numbers of repetitions, and then 24 hours later are learned to the point of the first possible reproduction by heart, how are the resulting savings in work related to each other and to the corresponding number of former repetitions?

In order to answer the question just formulated, I have carried out 70 double tests, each of six series of 16 syllables each. Each double test consisted in this, that the separate series—each for itself—were first read attentively a given number of times (after frequently repeated readings they were recited by heart instead of read), and that 24 hours later I relearned up to the point of first possible reproduction the series thus impressed and then in part forgotten. The first reading was repeated 8, 16, 24, 32, 42, 53, or 64 times.

An increase of the readings used for the first learning beyond 64 repetitions proved impracticable, at least for six series of this length. For with this number each test requires about ¾ of an hour, and toward the end of this time exhaustion, headache, and other symptoms were often felt which would have complicated the conditions of the test if the number of repetitions had been increased.

If all the mean values are brought together in relation to this last value, the following table results:

I *After a preceding study of the series by X repetitions,*	*II* *They were just memorized 24 hours later in Y seconds*		*III* *The result therefore of the preceding study was a saving of T seconds,*		*IV* *Or for each of the repetitions, an average saving of D seconds*
X =	Y =	P.E.$_m$ =	T =	P.E.$_m$ =	D =
0	1270	7			
8	1167	14	103	16	12.9
16	1078	28	192	29	12.0
24	975	17	295	19	12.3
32	863	15	407	17	12.7
42	697	14	573	16	13.6
53	585	9	685	11	12.9
64	454	11	816	13	12.8
					m = 12.7

The simple relation approximately realised in these numbers is evident: the number of repetitions used to impress the series (Column I) and the saving in work in learning the series 24 hours later as a result of such impression (Co. III) increase in the same fashion. Division of the amount of work saved by the corresponding number of repetitions gives as a quotient a practically constant value (Co. IV).

RETENTION AND OBLIVISCENCE AS A FUNCTION OF THE TIME

All sorts of ideas, if left to themselves, are gradually forgotten. This fact is generally known. Groups or series of ideas which at first we could easily recollect or which recurred frequently of their own accord and in lively colors, gradually return more rarely and in paler colors, and can be reproduced by voluntary effort only with difficulty and in part. After a longer period even this fails, except, to be sure, in rare instances. Names, faces, bits of knowledge and experience that had seemed lost for years suddenly appear before the mind, especially in dreams, with every detail present and in great vividness; and it is hard to see whence they came and how they managed to keep hidden so well in the meantime. Psychologists–each in accordance with his general standpoint–interpret these facts from different points of view, which do not exclude each other entirely but still do not quite harmonise. One set, it seems, lays most importance on the remarkable recurrence of vivid images even after long periods. They suppose that of the perceptions caused by external impressions there remain pale images, "traces," which, although in every respect weaker and more flighty than the original perceptions, continue to exist unchanged in the intensity possessed at present. These mental images cannot compete with the much more intense and compact perceptions of real life; but where the latter are missing entirely or partly, the former domineer all the more unrestrainedly. It is also true that the earlier images are more and more overlaid, so to speak, and covered by the later ones. Therefore, in the case of the earlier images, the possibility of recurrence offers itself more rarely and with greater difficulty. But if, by an accidental and favorable grouping of circumstances, the accumulated layers are pushed to one side, then, of course, that which was hidden beneath must appear, after whatever lapse of time, in its original and still existent vividness.

For others the ideas, the persisting images, suffer changes which more and more affect their nature; the concept of obscuration comes in here. Older ideas are repressed and forced to sink down, so to speak, by the more recent ones. As time passes one of these general qualities, inner clearness and intensity of consciousness, suffers damage. Connections of ideas and series of ideas are subject to the same process of progressive weakening; it is furthered by a resolution of the ideas into their components, as a result of which the now but loosely connected members are eventually united in new combinations. The complete disappearance of the more and more repressed ideas occurs only after a long time. But one should not imagine the repressed ideas in their time of obscuration to be pale images, but rather to be tendencies, "dispositions," to recreate the image contents forced to sink down. If these dispositions are somehow supported and strengthened, it may happen at any one moment that the repressing and hindering ideas become depressed themselves, and that the apparently forgotten idea arises again in perfect clearness.

A third view holds that, at least in the case of complex ideas, oblivescence consists in the crumbling into parts and the loss of separate components instead of in general obscuration. The idea of resolution into component parts recently spoken of supplies here the only explanation:

The image of a complex object is dim in our memory not because as a whole with all its parts present and in order it is illuminated by a feebler light of consciousness, but it is because it has become incomplete. Some parts of it are entirely lacking. Above all the precise connection of those still extant is, in general, missing and is supplied only by the thought that some sort of union once existed between them; the largeness of the sphere in which, without being able to make a final decision, we think this or that connection equally probable, determines the degree of dimness which we are to ascribe to the idea in question.

Each of these opinions receives a certain, but not exclusive, support from the actual inner experiences, or experiences supposed to be actual, which we at times have. And what is the reason? It is that these fortuitous and easily obtained inner experiences are much too vague, superficial and capable of various interpretations to admit in their entirety of only a single interpretation, or even to let it appear as of preponderating probability. Who could, with even tolerable exactness, describe in its gradual course the supposed overlaying or sinking or crumbling of ideas? Who can say anything satisfactory about the inhibitions caused by series of ideas of different extent, or about the disintegration that a firm complex of any kind suffers by the use of its components in new connections? Everybody has his private "explanation" of these processes, but the actual conditions which are to be explained are, after all, equally unknown to all of us.

If one considers the limitation to direct, unaided observation and to the chance occurrence of useful experiences, there seems but little prospect of improvement in conditions. How will one for example determine the degree of obscuration reached at a certain point, or the number of fragments remaining? Or how can the probable course of inner processes be traced if the almost entirely forgotten ideas return no more to consciousness?

By the help of our method we have a possibility of indirectly approaching the problem just stated in a small and definitely limited sphere, and, by means of keeping aloof for a while from any theory, perhaps of constructing one.

After a definite time, the hidden but yet existent dispositions laid down by the learning of a syllable-series may be strengthened by a further memorisation of the series, and thereby the remaining fragments may be united again to a whole. The work necessary for this compared with that necessary when such dispositions and fragments are absent gives a measure for what has been lost as well as for what remains. The inhibition which idea-groups of different sorts or extents may occasion in relation to others must, as a result of the interposition of well defined complexes of ideas between learning and relearning, betray itself in the more or less increased work of relearning. The loosening of a bond of connection by some other use of its components can be investigated in a similar manner as follows: after a certain series has been studied, new combinations of the same series are memorised and the change in the amount of work necessary for relearning the original combination is then ascertained.

If syllable series of a definite kind are learned by heart and then left to themselves, how will the process of forgetting go on when left merely to the influence of time or the daily events of life which fill it? The determination of the losses suffered was made in the way described: after certain intervals of time, the series memorised were relearned, and the times necessary in both cases were compared.

The investigations in question fell in the year 1879–80 and comprised 163 double tests. Each double test consisted in learning eight series of 13 syllables each (with the exception of 38 double tests taken from 11–12 A.M. which contained only six series each) and then in relearning them after a definite time. The learning was continued until two errorless recitations of the series in question were possible. The relearning was carried to the same point; it occurred at one of the following seven times—namely, after about one third of an hour, after 1 hour, after 9 hours, one day, two days, six days, or 31 days.

No.	*I* *After X hours*	*II* *So much of the series learned was retained that in relearning a saving of Q% of the time of original learning was made*	*III* *P.E.m*	*IV* *The amount forgotten was thus equivalent to v% of the original in terms of time of learning*
	X =	Q =		v =
1	0.33	58.2	1	41.8
2	1.	44.2	1	55.8
3	8.8	35.8	1	64.2
4	24.	33.7	1.2	66.3
5	48.	27.8	1.4	72.2
6	6x24	25.4	1.3	74.6
7	31x24	21.1	0.8	78.9

It will probably be claimed that the fact that forgetting would be very rapid at the beginning of the process and very slow at the end should have been foreseen. However, it would be just as reasonable to be surprised at this initial rapidity and later slowness as they come to light here under the definite conditions of our experiment for a certain individual, and for a series of 13 syllables. One hour after the end of the learning, the forgetting had already progressed so far that one half the amount of the original work had to be expended before the series could be reproduced again; after 8 hours the work to be made up amounted to two thirds of the first effort. Gradually, however, the process became slower so that even for rather long periods the additional loss could be ascertained only with difficulty. After 24 hours about one third was always remembered; after 6 days about one fourth, and after a whole month fully one fifth of the first work persisted in effect. The decrease of this after-effect in the latter intervals of time is evidently so slow that it is easy to predict that a complete vanishing of the effects of the first memorisation of these series would, if they had been left to themselves, have occurred only after an indefinitely long period of time.

Henry Herbert Donaldson: 1857-1938

ON THE TEMPERATURE-SENSE *

1885

HISTORICAL

In the course of an investigation undertaken with Prof. G. Stanley Hall and under his direction, it was incidentally observed that the sensation of cold was felt only at definite spots on the skin.

The fact was noticed in this way: Then sensations of motion as derived from the skin were being studied by means of a metal point which was slowly drawn over the surface. When the motion of this point, which was controlled by a suitable apparatus, was very slow, it often happened that it seemed to stand still for a time or even be lost, when suddenly a sharp sensation of cold, distinctly localised, would recall its presence and position.

This occurred so often that I find in my protocol for April 18th, 1884, the note: "Point always felt as cold." This fact arrested my attention, and in connexion with the other work I made several maps of these cold-spots on different parts of the body. When the experiments had reached this point, an important paper by Magnus Blix came into my hands.

This investigator started from the law of the specific energies of nerves, and took up the study of the dermal sensations to determine, if possible, how well-founded was the contradiction which they apparently offered to this law. He employed unipolar elecrical stimulation, using a pin for his small electrode, and made use of an induction-current so weak that it did not generally cause pain. He thus produced at one spot on the skin a sensation of pain, at another pressure, at a third cold, and at a fourth heat. These spots were distinctly localised, and never superposed on one another. He gave special attention to the spots from which sensations of temperature were to be obtained. These he studied by means of a small metal tube drawn out to a conical point, and so arranged that a current of water could be kept flowing through it, thus enabling the observer to maintain the point at an approximately constant temperature.

* Blix in 1882 and Goldscheider in 1884 published independently on the discovery of the sensory spots of the skin. Donaldson's article, published in *Mind*, X (1885), 399-416, shows that his early findings, too, were arrived at independently. Donaldson's paper is presented because no English translations of Blix and Goldscheider's articles are available. Donaldson became acquainted with their work before publishing his own, and gives an adequate account of their methods and findings.

Using this instrument, he investigated various parts of the skin, and mapped out the heat-spots and cold-spots in several regions. Further, he applied the crucial test: a heat-spot and a cold-spot having been found, the warmed point was applied to both, then the cold. No sensation followed the application of the warmed point to the cold-spot, or the cold point to the heat-spot; thus showing the complete differentiation of these temperature-organs.

Where the epidermis is thicker, he found that the stimulus must be stronger to get the desired reaction. This suggests that the so-called spots may only be the more superficial portions of the nerve-bearing layer of the skin, which is in reality all sensitive. That this is not the case, is shown by the fact that the stimulus may be applied to a neutral spot for an unlimited time, without giving rise to a thermal sensation. The general bearing of these results on the current theories is kept in view throughout the paper. Blix, therefore, concluded that we have separate nerves for heat and cold, and that these have distinct terminations in the skin, which can be demonstrated.

Somewhat after the appearance of this paper by Blix, A. Goldscheider published the results of a very important series of experiments. He had been for some time studying the specific energies of nerves, and in this connexion was led to investigate the sensations of temperature. For detecting the cold-spots he used either fine brushes dipped in ether or capillary tubes filled with the same. For locating both the heat-spots and the cold-spots he used small brass tubes brought to a conical point at one end and closed by a rubber-stopper at the other; these could be heated or cooled as was desired. To exactly mark the spots when found, he used a thermaesthesiograph, by means of which a brush wet with Indian ink could be brought down quite exactly on the spot which had been previously stimulated. I regret, however, that he has given no account of precisely how he travelled over the skin with this apparatus, and thus developed his maps. Thus working, he found that temperature-sensations were roused only at definite spots. His maps show them as very much more abundant than either Blix or I found them.

As a rule the cold-spots are most abundant where the skin is most sensitive to cold, but what Goldscheider calls first-class spots, i.e., those which react strongly on moderate stimulation, may often be quite few in number, where the spots of all grades are numerous.

These spots are not alike on the symmetrical parts of the same individual, nor are they alike on the corresponding parts of different individuals. What has been said for the cold-spots holds true also for the heat-spots. These latter are on the whole less abundant than the former, and tend somewhat to occupy the spaces from which the former are absent. There are certain spots which are roused only by excessive temperatures. Goldscheider notes also that a spot often stimulated loses its sensibility, apparently becoming exhausted, for it does not react well until a more or less long period of rest has been allowed. When a heat-spot is over-heated, it sometimes happens that a hyperaesthesia is produced, so that even pressure from a perfectly neutral body gives rise to a sensation of heat. He calls attention to the often observed fact that the tactile and thermal sensibilities in different parts of the body do not vary uniformly, and he points out that the discriminative sensibility when measured on two thermal spots is, as a rule, much finer than when measured in the ordinary way, and that this discrimination is finer the more intense the stimulus. In certain parts, as, for instance, those in which it is finest, discrimination for tactile-sensations surpasses that for temperature-sensations.

These sensations of temperature can be roused by mechanical and electrical stimulation as well as thermal. In both cases the cold-spots are more easily discriminated than the heat-spots.

By sending a strong electrical current through the arm and parts of the hand and thus stimulating certain nerve-trunks, Goldscheider is able to get peripheral sensations of temperature; here, too, the sensations of cold tend to predominate. He finds these spots insensitive to pain or contact. A needle may be plunged into them, or excessive temperatures applied without causing any feelings of discomfort.

Goldscheider also mentions the commonly observed persistence of sensations after the removal of the stimulus.

In sketching a general theory of temperature-sensations, Goldscheider brings a certain amount of evidence against the views of Hering. This latter investigator, relying mainly on the fact that water of the same temperature may feel cold or warm according as the hand is brought into it from a warmer or a colder vessel, concluded that, when the susceptibility of the thermal apparatus is decreased from one kind of stimulus, e.g., heat, it is increased for the other, e.g., cold, and vice versa. The experiment which Goldscheider records is this: If one hand be put into a vessel of water at 40° C. and kept there for ten seconds, and if then both this hand and the one which during the meantime has been at the room-temperature be put into cold water, the warmed hand will feel the cold less distinctly than the one which has been kept in the air of the room. In going from a cold vessel to a hot one, heat is in the same way less distinctly felt by the hand which has been immersed. If, now, the view of Hering were correct, that the exhaustion for one stimulus was correlated with an increased sensitiveness to the other, we should expect the immersed hand to feel the change of temperature more acutely that the other; but this, we have seen, it does not do. Goldscheider therefore inclines to the older view of Weber.

Goldscheider's paper is further continued by an interesting discussion of the other sensations of the skin—pressure, pain and tickling; but with those we are not at present concerned.

In a communication to the Physiological Society at Berlin (Dec. 15th, 1884), Prof. Eulenberg states that he has been able, in the main, to corroborate the results of Blix and Goldscheider, but did not succeed in getting temperature-sensations by mechanical stimulation. In Eulenberg's paper, chemical stimulation is spoken of as having given positive results in Goldscheider's hands. As no mention is made of chemical stimulation in any of the published papers of Goldscheider which I have seen, I am inclined to think this statement erroneous.

The most recent paper is a note by Goldscheider in which he reaches the conclusion that the temperature-nerves often radiate from centres, and that these centres often coincide with the hair-follicles.

EXPERIMENTAL

In the statement of results it will be necessary to give them in chronological order to show how far they were independent. When first experimenting, a cold brass point, 1.5 mms. in diameter, was the only instrument used. With this I had found that cold was felt in spots, some spots giving an intense sensation, others a weak one; that the skin between these spots was not sensitive to cold; that the points were differently distributed in different parts of the same individual, and in similar parts of different individuals; that they were very small—as shown by the fact that unless a spot was carefully marked it could not be easily found again, for passing the point even very close to it did not rouse a sensation, as a rule; that they were permanent—once having been found they always could be found again; that they were easily exhausted—this being shown by the fact that, when the metal point was drawn down the arm and a certain number of points were observed, if it was again drawn down immediately, the number noticed on the second trip was almost always less than on the first, but if some minutes were allowed to elapse between the two trips, then the second result was, as a rule, like the first.

When I had gone thus far, Blix's paper was received. Blix, besides noting all the points above mentioned, found similar spots for heat, and found that what was true of the cold-spots was true of the heat-spots also, so far as their arrangement and distribution were concerned. He noticed also that the arrangement on symmetrical parts was not symmetrical; that the relative abundance of the two sorts of spots varied; that the heat-spots were rather less numerous; and that the two kinds were always distinct; further, he succeeded in getting them to react not only to thermal but also to electrical stimulation.

It was a simple matter to confirm Blix's observations on the heat-spots, and also his other observations on the temperature-sense. For this purpose the modification of the Kinesimeter already described was used. With regard to electrical stimulation there is something more to be said. Using unipolar stimulation, with a pin for the small electrode, the sensation of cold came out very plainly at certain spots, while the sensation of heat was by no means so clear, as it seemed to me, and tended strongly to go over into burning pain which was almost unbearable. There were also other spots at which the electrode caused a burning pain from the first. Wishing to try the effects of altering the temperature of the electrode, I fastened one wire of the secondary coil to my hollow tube, and, using that, was thus enabled to have my electrode at any desired temperature. The experiment was planned as follows. A heat-spot and a cold-spot were marked, then the electrode was cooled to 15° C., and by it a weak current was sent through the spots. The sensations of heat and cold followed, as was expected. The temperature was then raised to about 30° C., and again the current was applied. A sensation of heat was obtained at the proper point, but none of cold. So when the temperature was raised higher, the application of the current to the cold-spot gave no thermal sensation at all. Just what the meaning of this curious reaction is, I am not prepared to say, but my experiments on this subject are very concordant. These observations, taken in connexion with the fact that it is not very easy to get a good clear sensation of heat by electrical stimulation, indicate that further work is wanted here.

After the observations of Blix were thus corroborated, I continued the work in hopes of being able still to add something to the information already collected.

The investigation has proceeded on the assumption that these organs for heat and cold were in the skin. This idea is supported by the fact that a localised spot sensitive to temperature moves about as the skin is moved, and when the skin is raised, comes up with it. If then the organs are in the skin, it should be possible to cut them out and examine them histologically.

A cold-spot and heat-spot were localised on my own skin, and then cut out for me by Dr. Councilman. The bits of skin, about 3 mms. in diameter and the same in thickness, were treated by the gold chloride and formic acid method of Ranvier, hardened in alcohol, cut into serial sections perpendicular to the surface of the skin, and mounted in glycerine. For sectioning and mounting these specimens, I am indebted to Mr. H. F. Nachtrieb.

They had been marked with small dots of indelible ink, and the sections showed beneath the marking a slight inflammation. No difference could be made out between the spot at which cold had been felt and that at which heat was observed. There were numerous nerves beneath these spots, but they were almost as numerous in neighbouring parts. The result of the histological investigation then is so far completely negative. The cold-spot, it should be added, was taken from the middle of the lower leg on the anterior surface, while the heat-spot came from the middle of the volar surface of the forearm.

Thinking from this that the organs for the sensations of heat and cold might be quite independent of the papillary layer, I examined scars both on myself and others about the Laboratory. I also took the opportunity to examine some on patients at the Bay View Asylum. For this privilege I am indebted to Dr. Jones, the resident physician.

In the case of a woman with extensive burns (accident took place eighteen months ago), a large one on the arm, which had quite healed without much contraction, was very sensitive both to heat and cold. The point felt hotter on the scar than on the sound skin.

On the other arm the burn, in healing, had quite drawn together, and the bands of connective tissue beneath made the surface irregular. Here also both heat and cold were felt in spots, but were more intense on the superficial than on the deep parts of the scar.

In the case of a man who had two scars on his legs, consequent on deep incisions made some two years ago, the same sensitiveness was found, except for a line in the centre, about 3 mms. wide, where the scar was quite insensitive to contact, as well as to temperature. This line marked the place at which the incision had been made. For a little distance on either side of the line the point (either hot or cold) often gave rise to a pricking sensation. I later found the same pricking sensation from thermal stimulation of a large scar from a knife-wound on my own wrist made twenty years ago. Scars from boils are sensitive to temperature; and one case examined, in which the skin had been mechanically torn away for a space about 1 x 3 cms., and which was now healed, was exquisitely sensitive both to heat and cold.

It may further be added that the places on my own skin, from which the spots were removed, are now healed, 31 days having elapsed since excision, and are, so far as I can tell, as markedly sensitive to heat and cold respectively as they were before operation. I am aware that these observations do not accord with those of Weber. If I understand the statements of the facts as given by Weber, his experiments were made on wounds that had already healed, and therefore similar to those on which I have above reported. He found that a spatula at 8.7°–12.5° C. was not clearly distinguished from one at 45°–50° C., when applied to surfaces like burns on which the skin had been destroyed. The patients answered the question "hot" or "cold" as often wrongly as rightly, and occasionally, for three successive times, called the hot spatula cold, while on the uninjured part of the skin they could easily discriminate between them. The temperatures which I used were 12°–16° C. for cold, and 50°–55° C. for heat; but the application was made with a point only .9 mm. in diameter. The reason for the different results is, I think, this: When Weber rested his spatula on a thermally sensitive spot, the patient reacted correctly; but when it was between such spots, the patient had no thermal sensation and was forced to guess. That it is possible to find these thermally insensitive regions is pointed out by Blix and confirmed by my own experience. That they are sometimes quite large, even on sensitive parts, is plain, and furthermore I have noticed that on many scars the spots for the above temperatures were less abundant than on the sound skin. Finally I also found regions on the scars which were thermally insensitive, so that a spatula applied to them would have given the patient no idea of its temperature. This is to my mind the probable explanation of the contradiction here.

Later, Weber did make some observations on a fresh wound, from which the skin had been removed by a burn, and found it insensible to temperature-changes; but he did not study the regeneration of these nerves during the process of healing. Lussana has lately examined the scar of a burn in the case of a woman, the injury having occurred thirty-five years before the examination. Here the injury was very deep, and the extent some 10 x 12 cms. He states that in the region injured the temperature-sensibility is diminished, and concludes from this that this sensation is more delicate in the papillary layer than in the tissues beneath.

In this connexion it may be mentioned that, contrary to the explicit statement of Weber, I find the aesophagus, through its entire length, sensitive to temperature, both in myself and in a number of others. Some individuals do not distinguish clearly the temperature of a body in the aesophagus, but I have not found them as numerous as those that do. In one individual who was subject to certain dyspeptic attacks, accompanied by eructations, the temperature-sense in the aesophagus was apparently increased during the attacks. The tests were made with cold and hot water, at a temperature of 4° C. and about 50° C. The passage of the substance can, in my own case, be distinctly traced from one end of the aesophagus to the other, as a sensation of heat or cold. On entering the stomach, a slight sensation is felt, but this is by no means so clear as that from the aesophagus.

The usual statement of the parts endowed with temperature-sensations does not include the conjunctiva, but this is really quite sensitive.

From all this, it follows that the end-organs for the sensation of temperature will have to be found in the aesophagus and conjunctiva, as well as in the places usually named.

The observations can be summed up as follows:

The parts covered by skin have the temperature-organs in the skin. When the surfaces beneath the skin are tested, they are found insensitive to temperature.

The papillary layer is not necessary for temperature-sensations.

The nerves are generally regenerated in the healing of burns and other scars, except in certain places where the connective tissue is very dense.

Having done this much on the subject, I received Goldscheider's account of his own researches. The new points in his paper bearing on heat-sensation were—the number of spots found; their distribution; mechanical stimulation; their insensibility to pressure or pain; temperature-sensations from stimulation of nerve-trunks; and the increased discriminative sensibility on these spots.

In his maps the points are represented as much more numerous than they are in those presented by either Blix or myself. This is without doubt due to the fact that more intense stimuli, both for heat and cold, were used by Goldscheider than by either of us. His method was practically the same as that of Blix. Regarding the arrangement of these spots, both for temperature and pressure, his latest view is that they lie in lines radiating from centres, that these centres often coincide with the hairs in the hairy portions of the skin, and that in the hairless parts the arrangement of these spots is apparently the same. This statement I have not yet tested. He points out that these spots for both heat and cold can be roused by mechanical stimulation; a slight tapping over the surface where a temperature-spot is located giving rise to the sensations of heat or cold, the latter responding the more readily of the two. These experiments I have repeated, and the results are certainly very striking. Puncturing a temperature-spot also gives rise to temperature-sensations.

Moreover, he points out that these spots are insensible to pain or pressure. Repeating these experiments, I find complete analgesia in these spots, for a needle can be run into them without giving the slightest sensation of pain; but at the same time I have not been able to satisfy myself that I do not feel pressure.

In certain cases Goldscheider succeeded in getting sensation of temperature by electrical stimulation of the nerve-trunks in the arm, back of the hand, etc.

These observations I have also repeated, using very strong electrical currents which gave almost continuous pain, as recommended by Goldscheider. By stimulating nerves in the back of the hand, I have succeeded in getting peripheral sensations of both heat and cold, the latter sensation being the more frequent. The sensation was localized in small areas in all the cases which I observed.

I am able also to corroborate his statement that the discriminative sensibility is much finer for temperature than for tactile sensations.

Since the receipt of Goldscheider's paper, I have been able to make one independent contribution to this subject, which, so far as I am aware, is new.

Dr. M. Warfield called my attention, a short time since, to the fact that in a certain operation on the eye by Dr. Russell Murdoch, cocaine having been used, the patient recognised the presence of the knife on the eye by a sensation of cold. By the courtesy of Dr. Murdoch, I was enabled to examine the eyes of several patients at the Baltimore Eye and Ear Hospital. When the eye in these cases was completely insensible to pain, and felt no contact whatever, cold and warm bodies were readily distinguished. This observation I have been able to repeat on my own eye. By means of 5 per cent solution of muriate of cocaine the eye was rendered completely insensitive to pain on contact, but still readily felt heat and cold. Here we have the temperature-sensations completely isolated from the other dermal sensations in a way which is now capable of easy repetition, and important as furnishing another argument for the independence of the thermal apparatus.

This investigation has brought to light some new facts and results, which have, without doubt, their greatest importance in controlling other lines of work. Some of these results, as I have endeavoured to show, were independently worked out in this Laboratory: but, in presenting a claim for independence, I hope that I have still made it clear that to Blix belongs the priority; that Goldscheider's paper is very careful and complete; and that I am in a large measure indebted to both these observers

My thanks are due to Prof. G. Stanley Hall for his aid and advice during this work. I also gladly take this opportunity to thank all those who have kindly placed themselves and their time at my disposal for experiment, and otherwise assisted me in this research.

James McKeen Cattell: 1860-1944

THE INFLUENCE OF THE INTENSITY OF THE STIMULUS ON THE LENGTH OF THE REACTION TIME *

1885

DURING the past two years, Dr. G. O. Berger and I have been carrying on a series of experiments in the Psychological Laboratory of the University of Leipsig, looking to determine the relation between the intensity of the stimulus and the length of the reaction time. Wundt, Exner, and others had already made experiments on this subject, but it seemed to need a more thorough investigation. We undertook to determine the influence of various intensities of the electric shock, and of light on the length of the simple reaction time, and on the reaction time complicated by the addition of simple cerebral operations.

The term "reaction time" is now generally understood. If one lifts one's hand as soon as possible after the sudden appearance of a light, the interval between the application of the stimulus and the beginning of the muscular contraction is a reaction time. In order to investigate the influence of various intensities of light on the length of this time, we used a light produced in Geissler's tube by an induction current from six Daniell cells. This light we took as Normal, and kept constant. We then arranged five weaker intensites by putting smoked glass before the light. The amount of light transmitted through the smoked glass we determined photometrically. If we set the intensity of the normal light VI = 1000, then the intensities of the lights would be

I.	*II.*	*III.*	*IV.*	*V.*	*VI.*
1	7	23	123	315	1000

We further obtained two still brighter lights (VII and VIII) by means of lenses, but could not determine with our photometer the relation of these to the normal intensity. The observer sat in the dark, and looked through a telescopic tube at the point where the light was to appear. The following table gives the average of 150 reactions made by each of us

* As indicated in Cattell's report, this investigation was carried out in Wundt's laboratory, which had been established in 1879. Cattell's paper was published in *Brain*, VIII, (1885), 512-515.

with the several intensities. No reactions at all were omitted in taking the average. The second line, marked M, gives the average of the variation of each from the average of all the reactions; that is, if A is the average of n reactions a, b, c, d, then

$$M = \frac{(A-a)+(A-b)+(A-c)\ \ldots}{n}$$

all the differences being taken as positive. M shows us how much the reactions differ from one another, and when we know the number of reactions, we can find the probable error of the average. In the table .001 seconds is taken as the unit of time.

TABLE I

Intensity	*I*	*II*	*III*	*IV*	*V*	*VI*	*VII*	*VIII*	*Average*
					B				
Time	308	235	208	200	192	195	177	168	210
M.	26	18	16	15	15	17	18	16	18
					C				
Time	251	175	160	148	147	143	135	128	161
M.	30	17	16	14	15	13	16	19	18

It will be seen from the table that when the light is taken very weak, just strong enough to be seen, the times are the longest (with one accidental exception, B between V and VI) the greater the intensity of the light, the shorter the time of the reaction. I cannot, however, formulate a general law from the table.

In substantially the same manner the relation between the strength of an electric shock and the length of the reaction time was determined. The shock was received on the left forearm, and the reaction made with the right hand. We used four intensities; the strongest, IV, somewhat painful, the weakest, I, just enough to be felt. The two intermediate intensities made up, as far as we could judge, four equal steps. The averages of 150 reactions by each observer on each intensity are given in the table.

TABLE II

Intensity	*I*	*II*	*III*	*IV*	*Average*
			B		
Time	182	163	158	160	166
M.	17	14	12	11	18
			C		
Time	164	155	132	131	145
M.	19	18	14	14	16

It will be noticed that with the electric shock, as with light, the time of the reaction becomes shorter as the stimulus becomes stronger. The differences are not, however, so great, and for the intensities III and IV, the times are about the same; with IV the reaction was probably retarded, because the shock was painful.

In connection with the experiments on the intensity of the light, we made others to determine whether or not the quality of the stimulus, that is, the colour of the light, has any influence on the length of the reaction time. The averages of 180 reactions made by each of the observers on each of the six colours used are given in the table.

TABLE III

	White	*Red*	*Yellow*	*Green*	*Blue*	*Violet*	*Average*
B.	196	203	192	196	199	201	198
C.	155	162	160	156	161	153	158

The table does not show any decided difference in the times for the several colours. Violet and green, which I have found (see last number of *Brain*) must act longer on the retina than the other colours, in order that a sensation may be called forth, do not seem to cause a longer reaction time; this is because the reaction is made on the light, without waiting until the colour has been distinguished.

The time is longer when it is necessary to distinguish the colours before the reaction is made. We can determine this time, if instead of always reacting as quickly as possible, we react if it is red, but not at all if it is blue. We thus add to the simple reaction time. We can further let the subject lift his right hand if the light is red, his left hand if it is blue; we then have, besides the time necessary for the simple reaction and for distinguishing the colour, the time it takes to make a choice between two motions. The results of experiments made with three intensities of light (V, III, and I) are given in the table.

TABLE IV

		B			*C*	
	V	*III*	*I*	*V*	*III*	*I*
Reaction Time	189	218	273	189	209	303
Reaction with Perception Time	238	293	373	274	328	417
Reaction with Perception and Will Time	287	320	393	356	388	495
Perception Time	49	75	100	85	119	114
Will Time	49	27	20	82	60	78

It seems from the table that the time it takes to see or perceive a colour becomes shorter as the intensity of the light becomes stronger, but that the will time is not a function of the intensity of the stimulus.

James McKeen Cattell: 1860-1944

THE TIME IT TAKES TO SEE AND NAME OBJECTS *

1886

THE relation of the sensation to the stimulus and the time taken up by mental processes are the two subjects in which the best results have been reached by experimental psychology. These results are important enough to prove those to be wrong who with Kant hold that psychology can never become an exact science. It would perhaps be convenient to call the work done by Weber, Fechner and their followers in determining the relation of the sensation to the stimulus Psychophysics, and to confine the term Psychometry to the work done by Wundt and others in measuring the rapidity of mental processes. Psychometry seems to be of as great psychological interest as Psychophysics, but it has not been nearly so fully and carefully worked over. This is partly due to the difficulties which lie in the way of determining the time taken up by mental processes. Such a time cannot be directly measured; the experimenter can only determine the period passing between an external event exciting mental processes and a motion made after the mental processes have been completed. It is difficult or impossible to analyse this period, to give the time required for the purely physiological operations, and to decide what mental processes have taken place, and how much time is to be allotted to each. Experimenters have also met with two other difficulties. The physical apparatus used seldom produces the stimulus in a satisfactory manner or measures the times with entire accuracy, and must be so delicate and complicated that it requires the greatest care to operate with it and keep it in order. The other difficulty lies in the fact that the times measured are artificial, not corresponding to the times taken up by mental processes in our ordinary life. The conditions of the experiments place the subject in an abnormal condition, especially as to fatigue, attention and practice, and the method has often been such that the times given are too short, because the entire mental process has not been measured, or too long, because some other factor has been included in the time recorded. Considering therefore the difficulty of

* From *Mind*, XI, (1886), 63-65. Cattell's studies of word perception had considerable influence upon educational psychology as well as upon experimental psychology.

analysing the period measured, the inaccuracies of the recording apparatus, and the artificial and often incorrect methods of making the experiments, we have reason to fear that the results obtained by the psychologist in his laboratory do not always give the time it takes a man to perceive, to will and to think. Wundt has done much toward obviating these difficulties, carefully analysing the various operations, and improving the apparatus and methods. It has seemed to me, however, worth the while to make a series of experiments altogether doing away with involved methods and complicated apparatus, and looking to determine the time we usually require to see and name an object, such as a letter or a color.

1. I pasted letters on a revolving drum (a physiological kymograph) and determined at what rate they could be read aloud, as they passed by a slit in a screen. It was found that the time varied with the width of the slit. When the slit was 1 cm. wide (the letters being 1 cm. apart) one letter was always in view; as the first disappeared the second took its place, &c. In this case it took the nine persons experimented on (university teachers and students) from $\frac{1}{3}$ to $\frac{1}{5}$ sec. to read each letter. This does not however give the entire time needed to see and name a single letter, for the subject was finding the name of the letter just gone by at the same time that he was seeing the letter then in view. As the slit in the screen is made smaller the processes of perceiving and choosing cannot so well take place simultaneously, and the times become longer; when the slit is 1 mm. wide the time is $\frac{1}{2}$ sec., which other experiments I have made prove to be about the time it takes to see and name a single letter. When the slit on the contrary is taken wider than 1 cm., and two or more letters are always in view, not only do the processes of seeing and naming overlap but while the subject is seeing one letter, he begins to see the ones next following, and so can read them more quickly. Of the nine persons experimented on four could read the letters faster when five were in view at once, but were not helped by a sixth letter; three were not helped by a fifth and two not by a fourth letter. This shows that while one idea is in the centre, two, three or four additional ideas may be in the background of consciousness. The second letter in view shortens the time about $\frac{1}{40}$, the third $\frac{1}{60}$, the fourth $\frac{1}{100}$, the fifth $\frac{1}{200}$ sec.

2. I find it takes about twice as long to read (aloud, as fast as possible) words which have no connexion as words which make sentences, and letters which have no connexion as letters which make words. When the words make sentences and the letters words, not only do the processes of seeing and naming overlap, but by one mental effort the subject can recognize a whole group of words or letters, and by one will-act choose the motions to be made in naming them, so that the rate at which

the words and letters are read is really only limited by the maximum rapidity at which the speech-organs can be moved. As the result of a large number of experiments the writer found that he had read words not making sentences at the rate of ¼ sec. each, words making sentences (a passage from Swift) at the rate of ⅛ sec. per word. Letters not making words were read in $1/40$ sec. less time than words not making sentences; capital and small letters were read at the same rate, small German letters slightly and capital German letters considerably more slowly than the Latin letters. The experiments were repeated on eleven other subjects, confirming these results; the time required to read each word when the words did not make sentences varying between ¼ and ½ sec. When a passage is read aloud at a normal rate, about the same time is taken for each word as when words having no connexion are read as fast as possible. The rate at which a person reads a foreign language is proportional to his familiarity with the language. For example, when reading as fast as possible the writer's rate was, English 138, French 167, German 250, Italian 327, Latin 434 and Greek 484; the figures giving the thousandths of a second taken to read each word. Experiments made on others strikingly confirm these results. The subject does not know that he is reading the foreign language more slowly than his own; this explains why foreigners seem to talk so fast. This simple method of determining a person's familiarity with a language might be used in school-examinations.

3. The time required to see and name colours and pictures of objects was determined in the same way. The time was found to be about the same (over ½ sec.) for colours as for pictures, and about twice as long as for words and letters. Other experiments I have made show that we can recognise a single colour or picture in a slightly shorter time than a word or letter, but take longer to name it. This is because in the case of words and letters the association between the idea and name has taken place so often that the process has become automatic, whereas in the case of colours and pictures we must by a voluntary effort choose the name. Such experiments would be useful in investigating aphasia.

A more detailed account of these experiments, and of the methods used, will be found in Wundt's *Philosophische Studien*, ii. 4.

James McKeen Cattell: 1860-1944

EXPERIMENTS ON THE ASSOCIATION OF IDEAS *

1887

THE Association of Ideas has been a favourite subject with psychologists from Aristotle on, yet the results have not been very definite from the scientific point of view. An important paper by Mr. Galton first applied experimental methods to the subject, and put it in a way where scientific advance was possible. Professor Wundt at once saw the importance of this work, and took it up in his laboratory with improved apparatus and methods. Nothing further has, however, been published on the subject, which is a pity, as experimental psychology seems to have its most hopeful outlook in this direction.

Experiments I described in a paper contributed to *Mind*, Nos. 42–4, on "The Time taken up by Cerebral Operations," showed that about ⅖ sec. was needed to see and name a word. When the physiological factors and the time taken up in seeing the word were eliminated, it was found that about ⅒ sec. was spent in finding the name belonging to the printed symbol. The time was longer for letters, which we do not read as often as words, and still longer (about ¼ sec.) for colours and pictures. I called the time passing, while the motor expression was being found, a "Will-time." The process is, however, largely automatic, and consists in carrying out an association previously formed between the concept and the expression. There is no break between such a process and the other processes I am about to describe.

I

If an object is named in a foreign instead of in one's native language, the association between concept and expression is less intimate and takes up more time. It is an open question as to how far concepts are formed without the aid of words, and it is not evident what mental process takes place when an object is named in a foreign language, it depending, of

* Experimentation on the association of ideas, begun by Galton during his walks in London, was moved to the laboratory by Wundt. Cattell was one of Wundt's students who contributed most to this subject. The present article appeared in *Mind*, XII, (1887), 68-74.

course, on the familiarity of the language. It need scarcely be said that we know almost nothing as to the physical basis of memory and thought; we may hope that psychometric experiments, such as I am about to describe, will contribute something towards the study of this subject. In the paper above mentioned I showed how we can determine the time it takes to see and name the picture of an object; in like manner the time we need to name the picture in a foreign language can be measured. I must refer the reader to that paper for a detailed account of apparatus and methods. .001 sec. is taken as the unit of time, B (Dr. G. O. Berger) and C (the writer) are the two subjects; after these designations there is given the average time taken in all the experiments made, and the mean variation of these measurements from the average; after this is given a second average and mean variation, found by dropping the most irregular times in accordance with the method I have described. The number of experiments made on each subject is given in parenthesis. The experiments were made at Leipsig during the first half of the year 1885.

German-English: Long Words (78)

B	593	281	573	116	C	411	85	389	55

These numbers show that foreign languages take up much time even after they have been learned, and may lead us once more to weigh the gain and loss of a polyglot life.

II

A great part of our time is spent in calling to mind things we already know. Memory is no transcendental process outside of space and time; this paper shows just how much time it takes to remember, and we have every reason to believe that the time passes while certain changes in the brain call forth other changes. I give below the time it took B and C to remember certain facts, examples of the necessary associations with which the mind is continually busy. A well-known city was given, and the subject named the country in which it is situated; a month was given, and the season to which it belongs was named, and in like manner the preceding or following month; an eminent author was given, and the subject named the language in which he wrote; a distinguished man, and his calling was named. In the last two cases below, the subject respectively added and multiplied numbers of one place. At first sight this mental operation may seem to consist of a mathematical calculation, and to be altogether different from the others; it is however not unlike them, being essentially an act of memory.

	B				C			
City-Country (52)	348	53	333	35	462	120	413	65
Month-Season (26)	415	55	410	31	310	63	306	16
Month-Following Month (26)	345	45	327	25	389	172	384	61
Month-Preceding Month (26)	763	245	619	129	832	233	815	160
Author-Language (78)	417	80	402	53	350	57	337	32
Man-Calling (78)	465	89	440	62	368	95	326	53
Addition	221	46	223	23	336	77	299	36
Multiplication	389	71	369	38	544	225	507	158

The mental processes considered above are by no means invented for the sake of experiment, but are such as make up a considerable part of life. We see that it took the subjects $\frac{2}{5}$ to $\frac{4}{5}$ sec. to call to mind facts with which they were familiar. The times needed in the different cases are of interest. The time of addition was the shortest of all; B needed 168, C 208 longer to multiply than to add; it took twice as long to call to mind the foregoing as the following month. It will be noticed that the times of the two subjects correspond closely (the average time in the eight examples given is 420 for B, 436 for C); the differences of time in the several cases are explained by the character and pursuits of the subjects, and in turn throw light back upon these. For example, B is a teacher of mathematics, C has busied himself more with literature; C knows quite as well as B that $5 + 7 = 12$, yet he needs $\frac{1}{10}$ sec. longer to call it to mind; B knows quite well as C that Dante was a poet, but needs $\frac{1}{10}$ second longer to think of it. Such experiments lay bare the mental life in a way that is startling and not always gratifying.

The numbers given are the averages from many measurements; the mean variation shows how greatly the separate determinations vary from the average. This variation is partly owing to changing conditions of the brain, so that the same process never takes place exactly the same time; it is, however, largely due to the fact that the mental operations under the same class are not equally simple, and consequently require different times. Just as it takes less time to add 2 to 3 than to multiply 2 by 3, so it takes less time to add 2 to 3 than to add 6 to 7. Owing to the normal variation in the time of the same mental process, we should not place too much reliance on a small number of measurements; it will, however, be worth our while to notice a few examples. In giving the country in which the city is situated, as average of three trials, both B and C took the shortest time for Paris (212, 278), and the longest time for Geneva (403, 485). In giving the language in which an author wrote, as average of the three trials, B took the shortest for Luther (227) and Goethe (265), and the longest for Aristotle (591) and Bacon (565); C took the shortest time for Plato (224) and Shakespeare (258), the longest for Chaucer (503) and Plautus (478). In the case of Luther B took 244, in the case of Goethe 102 less time than C; in the case of Shakespeare C took 186 less time than B. It should be borne in mind that B is a German, C an American. In giving the calling of eminent men the order was as follows, the shortest times being placed first:—B—Poet (355), Warrior, Historian, Philosopher, Artist, Reformer, Man of Science (657); C—Poet (291), Artist, Historian, Warrior, Philosopher, Reformer, Man of Science (421). With both subjects Poets come first and Man of Science last. It is easier to think of Homer as a poet than of Darwin as a man of science.

III

In the experiments so far considered a question was asked which admitted but one answer; the association was necessary, and the interval passing while it was being formed might be called a "Recollection-time." A question can, however, be so arranged that beside the act of recollection a certain choice as to the answer must be made, and in this case a little more time is needed. Below is given the inverse of several of the cases we have considered; a country being given, some city situated in it had to be named, etc. The last line gives the time needed to think of a work by a given author.

				Country-City (26)					
B	400	72	357	45	C	346	75	340	48
				Season-Month (26)					
	561	92	548	36		435	99	399	54
				Language-Author (78)					
	663	200	702	110		519	137	523	83
				Author-Work (26)					
	1076	397	1095	287		763	308	596	127

It will be seen that it took no longer to name a city when the country was given than the reverse; in this case there was but little choice, as there is in each country one particular city which was named almost as a matter of course. It took, however, considerably longer to name a month when the season was given and an author when a language was given than the reverse. A choice had in the former case to be made, and further, as Steinthal has before remarked, the mind moves more readily from the part to the whole than from the whole to the part. It will be noticed that the naming a work by a given author is one of the most difficult associations considered in this paper. As to the time taken up by the separate associations, I must again call attention to the fact that it is largely determined by accidental variation. This variation could only be eliminated by making a large number of experiments, and in this case we should no longer have the time taken up by associations in our daily life, but the minimum recollection-time, which would tend to become the same for different classes of associations as they became equally familiar. In naming a city, C needed the longest time for Brussels (1042) and Pekin (1001); the shortest time for Athens (214) and Philadelphia (222), his home. In naming an author, less time was needed for English, German and Italian, where Shakespeare, Goethe and Dante at once occurred, than in the three other languages used, French, Latin and Greek. In naming a work by a given author C needed the longest time or Chaucer (*Canterbury Tales* 1898), Aristotle (*Logic* (sic) 1522), and Bacon (*Novum Organum* 1388); the shortest time for Milton (*Paradise Lost* 328), Dante (*Inferno* 373), and Goethe (*Faust* 393).

IV

We now come to consider certain classes of associations in which the mind is allowed a larger degree of liberty. The times required in eight such cases are given. A noun representing a class of objects was given and a particular example was named (river-Rhine); a picture of an object was shown, and instead of naming the entire picture the subject was required to select some part of the object and name it (picture of a ship-sail); a concrete noun was in the same way given and a part of the object was named; both the pictures and names of objects were shown, and the subject said what the thing is used for or what it does (horse-ride or trot); a substantive had to be found for an adjective (blue-sky), a subject for an intransitive (swim-fish) and an object for a transitive verb (write-letter).

	Thing-Example (52)							
B	727	216	663	102	C	537	179	457	95
	Picture-Part of Object (52)							
	399	96	368	40		447	162	415	69
	Substantive-Part of Object (26)							
	578	128	568	85		439	135	404	82

			Picture-Property (52)				
358	105	325	49	372	121	370	78
			Adjective-Substantive (26)				
879	278	823	186	351	86	307	41
			Verb-Subject (26)				
765	366	584	166	527	171	497	107
			Verb-Object (26)				
654	242	561	139	379	122	317	86

The times given need no long comment. The most difficult associations seem to be the finding of a special example when the class is given, and the subject for a verb; in both of these cases the times needed were irregular, as is shown by the large mean variation. B took 111, C 146 longer to find a subject than to find an object for a verb, the mind moving logically in the latter direction. In identifying a particular object the mind was inclined to choose either one immediately at hand or to go back to the home of childhood. Thus out of the 52 cases B thought of an object in the room, C 20 times; of objects identified with the early home B 22, C 19 times. In the other cases this was mostly impossible, but also here either a very recent or an early association was formed in all except 6 out of the 104 cases.

We have lastly to consider the time it takes to form a judgment or opinion. I choose three cases in which the results could conveniently be averaged. In the first case the subject estimated the length of a line drawn horizontally on a card 10 cm. long, 50 lines being used varying in length from 1 to 50 mm. In the second case the subject estimated the number of short perpendicular lines on a card, the number varying between 4 and 15. In the third case the names of two eminent men were shown, the subject decided which of them he thought to be the greater.

				Length of line (150)					
B	1124	242	1127	154	C	664	124	664	88
				Number of Lines (26)					
	183	57	180	35		319	74	313	45
				Eminent Men (26)					
	667	143	604	80		558	171	522	112

I made rather a large number of determinations with the lines, as I wished to find the ratio between the length of the line and the average error (psychophysical law,) and between the error and the time taken up in coming to a decision. I think it however desirable to still further increase the number of experiments before publishing the results. In judging as to the relative greatness of eminent men, as might be foreseen, the times were shortest when the judgment was easiest, more especially if the subject had already compared the men together (Homer, Virgil). The nature of the judgments is not without interest; but can better be considered when I come to print similar experiments which I have made on a larger number of subjects.

The associations we have been considering in this paper are in their nature fixed or limited, and we have concerned ourselves chiefly with the time taken up. The conditions of the experiment can however be so arranged that one idea is allowed to suggest another somewhat as in our ordinary thinking. I shall shortly have ready experiments in this direction in which both the time and the nature of the association will be considered.

Francis Galton: 1822-1911

CO-RELATIONS AND THEIR MEASUREMENT, CHIEFLY FROM ANTHROPOMETRIC DATA *

1888

"CO-RELATION or correlation of structure" is a phrase much used in biology, and not least in that branch of it which refers to heredity, and the idea is even more frequently present than the phrase; but I am not aware of any previous attempt to define it clearly, to trace its mode of action in detail, or to show how to measure its degree.

Two variable organs are said to be co-related when the variation of the one is accompanied on the average by more or less variation of the other, and in the same direction. Thus the length of the arm is said to be co-related with that of the leg, because a person with a long arm has usually a long leg, and conversely. If the co-relation be close, then a person with a very long arm would usually have a very long leg; if it be moderately close, then the length of his leg would usually be only long, not very long; and if there were no co-relation at all then the length of his leg would on the average be mediocre. It is easy to see that co-relation must be the consequence of the variations of the two organs being partly due to common causes. If they were wholly due to common causes, the co-relation would be perfect, as is approximately the case with the symmetrically disposed parts of the body. If they were in no respect due to common causes, the co-relation would be nil. Between these two extremes are an endless number of intermediate cases, and it will be shown how the closeness of co-relation in any particular case admits of being expressed by a simple number.

To avoid the possibility of misconception, it is well to point out that the subject in hand has nothing whatever to do with the average proportions between the various limbs, in different races, which have been often discussed from early times up to the present day, both by artists and by anthropologists. The fact that the average ratio between the stature and the cubit is as 100 to 37, or thereabouts, does not give the slightest information about the nearness with which they vary together.

* From the *Proceedings* of the Royal Society of London, XV, (1888), 135-145. The correlation method, an essential tool of psychology and of several other fields of science, was first suggested in this paper. It was later modified by Pearson to its present form (Pearson's r).

It would be an altogether erroneous inference to suppose their average proportion to be maintained so that when the cubit was, say, one-twentieth longer than the average cubit, the stature might be expected to be one-twentieth greater than the average stature, and conversely. Such a supposition is easily shown to be contradicted both by fact and theory.

The relation between the cubit and the stature will be shown to be such that for every inch, centimetre, or other unit of absolute length that the cubit deviates from the mean length of cubits, the stature will on the average deviate from the mean length of statures to the amount of 2.5 units, and in the same direction. Conversely, for each unit of deviation of stature, the average deviation of the cubit will be 0.26 unit. These relations are not numerically reciprocal, but the exactness of the co-relation becomes established when we have transmuted the inches or other measurement of the cubit and of the stature into units dependent on their respective scales of variability. We thus cause a long cubit and an equally long stature, as compared to the general run of cubits and statures, to be designated by an identical scale-value. The particular unit that I shall employ is the value of the probable error of any single measure in its own group. In that of the cubit, the probable error is 0.56 inch = 1.42 cm.; in the stature it is 1.75 inch = 4.44 cm. Therefore the measured lengths of the cubit in inches will be transmuted into terms of a new scale, in which each unit = 0.56 inch, and the measured lengths of the stature will be transmuted into terms of another new scale in which each unit is 1.75 inch. After this has been done, we shall find the deviation of the cubit as compared to the mean of the corresponding deviations of the stature, to be as 1 to 0.8. Conversely, the deviation of the stature as compared to the mean of the corresponding deviations of the cubit will also be as 1 to 0.8. Thus the existence of the co-relation is established, and its measure is found to be 0.8.

Now as to the evidence of all this. The data were obtained at my anthropometric laboratory at South Kensington. They are of 350 males of 21 years and upwards, but as a large proportion of them were students, and barely 21 years of age, they were not wholly fullgrown; but neither that fact nor the small number of observations is prejudicial to the conclusions that will be reached. They were measured in various ways, partly for the purpose of this inquiry. It will be sufficient to give some of them as examples. The exact number of 350 is not preserved throughout, as injury to some limb or other reduced the available number by 1, 2, or 3 in different cases. After marshalling the measures of each limb in the order of their magnitudes, I noted the measures in each series that occupied respectively the positions of the first, second, and third quarterly divisions. Calling these measures in any one series, Q_1, M, and Q_3, I take M, which is the median or middlemost value, as that whence the deviations are to be measured, and ½ $(Q_3 - Q_1) = Q$, as the probable error of any single measure in the series. This is practically the same as saying that one-half of the deviations fall within the distance to ± Q from the mean value, because the series run with fair symmetry. In this way I obtained the following value of M and Q, in which the second decimal must be taken as only roughly approximate. The M and Q of any particular series may be identified by a suffix, thus M_c, Q_c might stand for those of the cubit, and M_s, Q_s for those of the stature.

TABLE I

	M.		*Q.*	
	Inch	*Centim.*	*Inch*	*Centim.*
Head length	7.62	19.35	0.19	0.48
Head breadth	6.00	15.24	0.18	0.46
Stature	67.20	170.69	1.75	4.44
Left middle finger	4.54	11.53	0.15	0.38
Left cubit	18.05	45.70	0.56	1.42
Height of right knee	20.50	52.00	0.80	2.03

NOTE.—The head length is its maximum length measured from the notch between and just below the eyebrows. The cubit is measured with the hand prone and without taking off the coat; it is the distance between the elbow of the bent left arm and the tip of the middle finger. The height of the knee is taken sitting when the knee is bent at right angles, less the measured thickness of the heel of the boot.

Tables were then constructed, each referring to a different pair of the above elements, like Tables II and III, which will suffice as examples of the whole of them. It will be understood that the Q value is a universal unit applicable to the most varied measurements, such as breathing capacity, strength, memory, keenness of eyesight, and enables them to be compared together on equal terms notwithstanding their intrinsic diversity. It does not only refer to measures of length, though partly for the sake of compactness, it is only those of length that will be here given as examples. It is unnecessary to extend the limits of Table II, as it includes every line and column in my MS. table that contains not less than twenty entries. None of the entries lying within the flanking lines and columns of Table II were used.

The measures were made and recorded to the nearest tenth of an inch. The heading of 70 inches of stature includes all records between 69.5 and 70.4 inches; that of 69 includes all between 68.5 and 69.4, and so on.

The values derived from Table II, and from other similar tables, are entered in Table III, where they occupy all the columns up to the last three, the first of which is headed "smoothed." These smoothed values were obtained by plotting the observed values, after transmuting them as

TABLE II

Stature in inches.	*Length of left cubic in inches, 348 adult males.*								*Total cases*
	Under 16.5	*16.5 and under 17.0*	*17.0 and under 17.5*	*17.5 and under 18.0*	*18.0 and under 18.5*	*18.5 and under 19.0*	*19.0 and under 19.5*	*19.5 and above*	
71 and above	..	..	..	1	3	4	15	7	30
70	..	..	..	1	5	13	11	..	30
69	..	1	1	2	25	15	6	..	50
68	..	1	3	7	14	7	4	2	48
67	..	1	7	15	28	8	2	..	61
66	..	1	7	18	15	6	..	..	48
65	..	4	10	12	8	2	..	..	36
64	..	5	11	2	3	..	..	..	21
Below 64	9	12	10	3	1	..	..	..	34
	9	25	49	61	102	55	38	9	348

above described into their respective Q units, upon a diagram such as is shown in the figure. The deviations of the "subject" are measured parallel to the axis of y in the figure, and those of the mean of the corresponding values of the "relative" are measured parallel to the axis of x. When the stature is taken as the subject, the median positions of the corresponding cubits, which are given in the successive lines of Table III, are marked with small circles. When the cubit is the subject, the mean positions of the corresponding statures are marked with crosses. The firm line in the figure is drawn to represent the general run of the small circles and crosses. It is here seen to be a straight line, and it was similarly found to be straight in every other figure drawn from the different pairs of co-related variables that I have as yet tried. But the inclination of the line to the vertical differs considerably in different cases. In the present one the inclination is such that a deviation of 1 on the part of the subject, whether it be stature or cubit, is accompanied by a mean deviation on the part of the relative, whether it be cubit or stature, of 0.8. This decimal fraction is consequently transmuted into inches. If the stature be taken as the subject, then Q_s is associated with $Q_c \times 0.8$; that is, a deviation of 1.75 inches in the one with 0.56×0.8 of the other. This is the same as 1 inch of stature being associated with a mean length of cubit equal to 0.26 inch. Conversely, if the cubit be taken as the subject, then Q_c is associated with $Q_s \times 0.8$; that is, a deviation of 0.56 inch in the one with 1.75×0.8 of the other. This is the same as 1 inch of cubit being associated with a mean length of 2.5 inches of stature. If centimetre be read for inch the same holds true.

Six other tables are now given in a summary form, to show how well calculation on the above principles agrees with observation.

From Table IV the deductions given in Table V can be made; but they may be made directly from tables of the form of Table III, whence Table IV was itself derived.

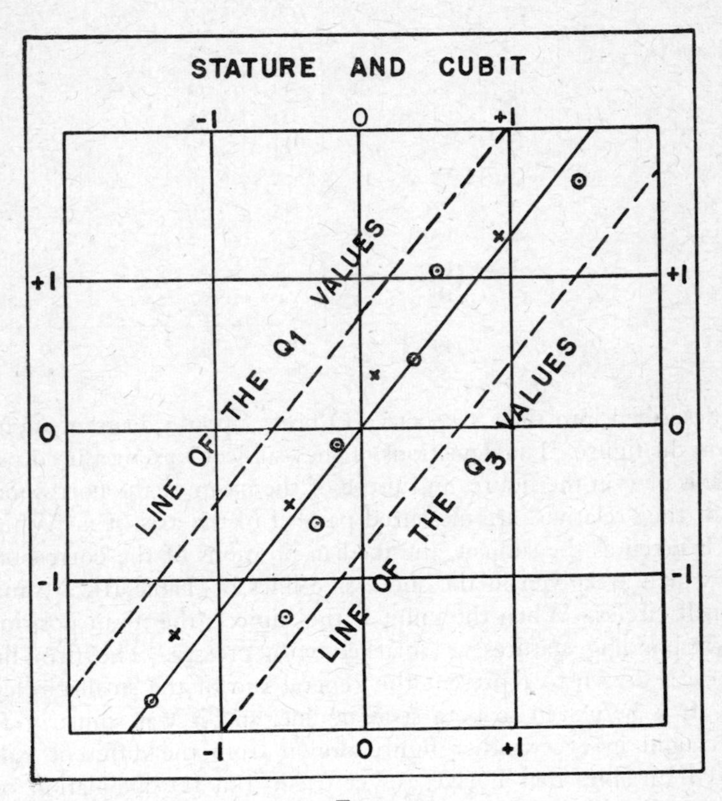

FIG. 1

When the deviations of the subject and those of the mean of the relatives are severally measured in units of their own Q, there is always a regression in the value of the latter. This is precisely analogous to what was observed in kinship, as I showed in my paper read before this Society on "Hereditary Stature" (*Roy. Soc. Proc.*, XL, (1886), 42). The statures of kinsmen are co-related variables; thus, the stature of the father is correlated to that of the adult son, and the stature of the adult son to that of the father; the stature of the uncle to that of the adult nephew, and the stature of the adult nephew to that of the uncle, and so on; but the index of co-relation, which is what I there called "regression," is different in the different cases. In dealing with kinships there is usually no need to reduce the measures to units of Q, because the Q values are alike in all the kinsmen, being of the same value as that of the population at large. It however happened that the very first case that I analysed was different in this respect. It was the reciprocal relation between the statures of what I called the "mid-parent" and the son. The mid-parent is an ideal progenitor, whose stature is the average of that of the father on the one hand and of that of the mother on the other, after her stature has been transmuted into its male equivalent by the multiplication of the factor of 1.08. The Q of the mid-parental statures was found to be 1.2, that of the population dealt with was 1.7. Again, the mean deviation measured in inches of the statures of the sons was found to be two-thirds of the deviation of the mid-parents, while the mean deviation in inches of the mid-parent was one-third of the deviation of the sons. Here the regression, when calculated in Q units, is in the first case from $\frac{1}{1.2}$ to $\frac{2}{3} \times 1.7 = 1$ to 0.47, and in the second case from $\frac{1}{1.7}$ to $\frac{1}{3} \times \frac{1}{1.2} = 1$ to 0.44, which is practically the same.

The rationale of all this will be found discussed in the paper on "Hereditary Stature," to which reference has already been made, and in the appendix to it by Mr. J. D. Hamilton Dickson. The entries in any table, such as Table II, may be looked upon as the values of the vertical ordinates to a surface of frequency, whose mathematical properties were discussed in the above-mentioned appendix, therefore I need not repeat them here. But there is always room for legitimate doubt whether conclusions based on the strict properties of the ideal law of error would be sufficiently correct to be serviceable in actual cases of co-relation between variables that conform only approximately to that law. It is therefore exceedingly desirable to put the theoretical conclusions to frequent test, as has been done with these anthropometric data. The result is that anthropologists may now have much less hesitation than before, in availing themselves of the properties of the law of frequency of error.

I have given in Table V a column headed $\sqrt{(1 - r^2)} = f$. The meaning of f is explained in the paper on "Hereditary Stature." It is the Q value of the distribution of any system of x values, as x_1, x_2, x_3, &c., round the mean of all of them, which we may call X. The knowledge of f enables dotted lines to be drawn, as in the figure above, parallel to the line of M values, between which one half of the x observations, for each value of y, will be included. This value of f has much anthropological interest of its own, especially in connexion with M. Bertillon's system of anthropometric identification, to which I will not call attention now.

TABLE III.—Stature $M_s = 67.2$ inches; $Q_s = 1.75$ inch. Left Cubit $M_c = 18.05$ inches; $Q_c = 0.56$ inch.

No. of cases.	Stature.	Deviation from M_s reckoned in		Mean of corresponding left cubits.	Deviation from M_c reckoned in			Smoothed values Multiplied by Q_c	Added to M_c
		Inches	Units of Q_s		Inches	Units of Q_c Observed	Smoothed		
	inches			inches					
30	70.0	+2.8	+1.60	18.8	+0.8	+1.42	+1.30	+0.73	18.8
50	69.0	+1.8	+1.03	18.3	+0.3	+0.53	+0.84	+0.47	18.5
38	68.0	+0.8	+0.46	18.2	+0.2	+0.36	+0.38	+0.21	18.3
61	67.0	−0.2	−0.11	18.1	+0.1	+0.18	−0.08	−0.04	18.0
48	66.0	−1.2	−0.69	17.8	−0.2	−0.36	−0.54	−0.30	17.8
36	65.0	−2.2	−1.25	17.7	−0.3	−0.53	−1.00	−0.56	17.5
21	64.0	−3.2	−1.83	17.2	−0.8	−1.46	−1.46	−0.80	17.2

No. of cases	Left Cubit	Deviation from M_c reckoned in		Mean of corresponding statures	Deviation from M_s reckoned in			Smoothed values multiplied by Q_s	Added to M_s
		Inches	Units of Q_c		Inches	Units of Q_s Observed	Smoothed		
	inches			inches					
38	19.25	+1.20	+2.14	70.3	+3.1	+1.8	+1.70	+3.0	70.2
55	18.75	+0.70	+1.25	68.7	+1.5	+0.9	+1.00	+1.8	69.0
102	18.25	+0.20	+0.36	67.4	+0.2	+0.1	+0.28	+0.5	67.7
61	17.75	−0.30	−0.53	66.3	−0.9	−0.5	−0.43	−0.8	66.4
49	17.25	−0.80	−1.42	65.0	−2.2	−1.3	−1.15	−2.0	65.2
25	16.75	−1.30	−2.31	63.7	−3.5	−2.0	−1.85	−3.2	64.0

It is not necessary to extend the list of examples to show how to measure the degree in which one variable may be co-related with the combined effect of n other variables, whether these be themselves co-related or not. To do so, we begin by reducing each measure into others, each having the Q of its own system for a unit. We thus obtain a set of values that can be treated exactly in the same way as the measures of a single variable were treated in Tables II and onwards. Neither is it necessary to give examples of a method by which the degree may be measured, in which the variables in a series each member of which is the summed effect of n variables, may be modified by their partial co-relation. After transmuting the separate measures as above, and then summing them, we should find the probable error of any one of them to be $\sqrt{n}$ if the variables were perfectly independent, and n if they were rigidly and perfectly co-related. The observed value would be always somewhere intermediate between these extremes, and would give the information that is wanted.

To conclude, the prominent characteristics of any two co-related variables, so far at least as I have as yet tested them, are four in number. It is supposed that their respective measures have been first transmuted into others of which the unit is in each case equal to the probable error of a single measure in its own series. Let $y =$ the deviation of the subject, which ever of the two variables may be taken in that capacity; and let x_1, x_2, x_3, &c., be the corresponding deviations of the relative, and let the mean of these be X. Then we find: (1) that $y = rX$ for all values of y; (2) that r is the same, whichever of the two variables is taken for the subject; (3) that r is always less than 1; (4) that r measures the closeness of co-relation.

TABLE IV

No. of cases	*Length of head*	*Mean of corresponding statures*		*No. of cases*	*Height*	*Mean of corresponding lengths of head*	
		Observed	*Calculated*			*Observed*	*Calculated*
32	7.90	68.5	68.1	26	70.5	7.72	7.75
41	7.80	67.2	67.8	30	69.5	7.70	7.72
46	7.70	67.6	67.5	50	68.5	7.65	7.68
52	7.60	66.7	67.2	49	67.5	7.65	7.64
58	7.50	66.8	66.8	56	66.5	7.57	7.60
34	7.40	66.0	66.5	43	65.5	7.57	7.69
26	7.30	66.7	66.2	31	64.5	7.54	7.65

TABLE IV (Continued)

No. of cases	Height	Mean of corresponding length of left middle finger		No. of cases	Length of left middle finger	Mean of corresponding statures	
		Observed	Calculated			Observed	Calculated
30	70.5	4.71	4.74	23	4.80	70.2	69.4
50	69.5	4.55	4.68	49	4.70	68.1	68.5
37	68.5	4.57	4.62	62	4.60	68.0	67.7
62	67.5	4.58	4.56	63	4.50	67.3	66.9
48	66.5	4.50	4.50	57	4.40	66.0	66.1
37	65.5	4.47	4.44	35	4.30	65.7	65.3
20	64.5	4.33	4.38				

No. of cases	Left middle finger	Mean of corresponding lengths of left cubit		No: of cases	Length of left cubit	Mean of corresponding length of left middle finger	
		Observed	Calculated			Observed	Calculated
23	4.80	18.97	18.80	29	19.00	4.76	4.75
50	4.70	18.55	18.49	32	18.70	4.64	4.69
62	4.60	18.24	18.18	48	18.40	4.60	4.62
62	4.50	18.00	17.87	70	18.10	4.56	4.55
57	4.40	17.72	17.55	37	17.80	4.49	4.48
34	4.30	17.27	17.24	31	17.50	4.40	4.41
				28	17.20	4.37	4.34
				24	16.90	4.32	4.28

No. of cases	Length of head	Mean of corresponding breadths of head		No. of cases	Breadth of head	Mean of corresponding lengths of head	
		Observed	Calculated			Observed	Calculated
32	7.90	6.14	6.12	27	6.30	7.72	7.84
41	7.80	6.05	6.08	36	6.20	7.72	7.75
46	7.70	6.14	6.04	53	6.10	7.65	7.65
52	7.60	5.98	6.00	58	6.00	7.68	7.60
58	7.50	5.98	5.96	56	5.90	7.50	7.55
34	7.40	5.96	5.91	37	5.80	7.55	7.50
26	7.30	5.85	5.87	30	5.70	7.45	7.46

TABLE IV (Continued)

No. of cases	*Stature*	*Mean of corresponding heights of knee*		*No. of cases*	*Height of knee*	*Mean of corresponding statures*	
		Observed	*Calculated*			*Observed*	*Calculated*
30	70.0	21.7	21.7	23	22.2	70.5	70.6
50	69.0	21.1	21.3	32	21.7	69.8	69.6
38	68.0	20.7	20.9	50	21.2	68.7	68.6
61	67.0	20.5	20.5	68	20.7	67.3	67.7
49	66.0	20.2	20.1	74	20.2	66.2	66.7
36	65.0	19.7	19.7	41	19.7	65.5	65.7
				26	19.2	64.3	64.7

No. of cases	*Left cubit*	*Mean of corresponding heights of knee*		*No. of cases*	*Height of knee*	*Mean of corresponding left cubit*	
		Observed	*Calculated*			*Observed*	*Calculated*
29	19.0	21.5	21.6	23	22.25	18.98	18.97
32	18.7	21.4	21.2	30	21.75	18.68	18.70
48	18.4	20.8	20.9	52	21.25	18.38	18.44
70	17.1	20.7	20.6	69	20.75	18.15	18.17
37	17.8	20.4	20.2	70	20.25	17.75	17.90
31	17.5	20.0	19.9	41	19.75	17.55	17.63
28	17.2	19.8	19.6	27	19.25	17.02	17.36
23	16.9	19.3	19.2				

Table V

Subject	*Relative*	*In units of Q* $r.$	$\sqrt{(1-r^2)} = f$	*In units of ordinary measure* *As 1 to*	f
Stature	Cubit	0.8	0.60	0.26	0.45
Cubit	Stature			2.5	1.4
Stature	Head length	0.35	0.93	0.38	1.63
Head length	Stature			3.2	0.17
Stature	Middle finger ...	0.7	0.72	0.06	0.10
Middle finger	Stature			8.2	1.26
Middle finger	Cubit	0.85	0.61	3.13	0.34
Cubit	Middle finger ...			0.21	0.09
Head length	Head breadth ...	0.45	0.89	0.43	0.16
Head breadth	Head length			0.48	0.17
Stature	Height of knee ..	0.9	0.44	0.41	0.35
Height of knee ...	Stature			1.20	0.77
Cubit	Height of knee ..	0.8	0.60	1.14	0.64
Height of knee ...	Cubit			0.56	0.45

James McKeen Cattell: 1860-1944

MENTAL TESTS AND MEASUREMENTS *

1890

PSYCHOLOGY cannot attain the certainty and exactness of the phsysical sciences, unless it rests on a foundation of experiment and measurement. A step in this direction could be made by applying a series of mental tests and measurements to a large number of individuals. The results would be of considerable scientific value in discovering the constancy of mental processes, their interdependence, and their variation under different circumstances. Individuals, besides, would find their tests interesting, and, perhaps, useful in regard to training, mode of life or indication of disease. The scientific and practical value of such tests would be much increased should a uniform system be adopted, so that determinations made at different times and places could be compared and combined. With a view to obtaining agreement among those interested, I venture to suggest the following series of tests and measurements, together with methods of making them.

The first series of ten tests is made in the Psychological Laboratory of the University of Pennsylvania on all who present themselves, and the complete series on students of Experimental Psychology. The results will be published when sufficient data have been collected. Meanwhile, I should be glad to have the tests, and the methods of making them, thoroughly discussed.

The following ten tests are proposed:

1. Dynamometer Pressure.
2. Rate of Movement.
3. Sensation-areas.
4. Pressure causing Pain.
5. Least noticeable difference in Weight.
6. Reaction-time for Sound.
7. Time for naming Colours.
8. Bi-section of a 50 cm. line.
9. Judgment of 10 seconds time.
10. Number of Letters remembered on once Hearing.

* From *Mind*, XV, (1890), 373-380. In this paper, Cattell introduced the term "mental tests," and proposed a standard series of tests. Galton was already applying a standard series of measurements, including some psychological measurements, in his Anthropometric Laboratory at the South Kensington Museum.

It will be noticed that the series begins with determinations rather bodily than mental, and proceeds through psychophysical to more purely mental measurements.

The tests may be readily made on inexperienced persons, the time required for the series being about an hour. The laboratory should be conveniently arranged and quiet, and no spectators should be present while the experiments are being made. The amount of instruction the experimentee should receive, and the number of trials he should be given, are matters which ought to be settled in order to secure uniformity of result. The amount of instruction depends on the experimenter and experimentee, and cannot, unfortunately, be exactly defined. It can only be said that the experimentee must understand clearly what he has to do. A large and uniform number of trials would, of course, be the most satisfactory, the average, average variation, maximum and minimum being recorded. Time is, however, a matter of great importance if many persons are to be tested. The arrangement most economical of time would be to test thoroughly a small number of persons, and a large number in a more rough-and-ready fashion. The number of trials I allow in each test is given below, as also whether I consider the average or "best" trial the most satisfactory for comparison.

Let us now consider the tests in order.

1. *Dynamometer pressure*—The greatest possible squeeze of the hand may be thought by many to be a purely physiological quantity. It is, however, impossible to separate bodily from mental energy. The "sense of effort" and the effects of volition on the body are among the questions most discussed in psychology and even in metaphysics. Interesting experiments may be made on the relation between volitional control or emotional excitement and dynamometer pressure. Other determinations of bodily power could be made (in the second series I have included the "archer's pull" and pressure of the thumb and forefinger), but the squeeze of the hand seems the most convenient. It may be readily made, cannot prove injurious, is dependent on mental conditions, and allows comparison of right- and left-handed power. The experimentee should be shown how to hold the dynamometer in order to obtain the maximum pressure. I allow two trials with each hand (the order being right, left, right, left), and record the maximum pressure of each hand.

2. *Rate of movement*—Such a determination seems to be of considerable interest, especially in connexion with the preceding. Indeed, its physiological importance is such as to make it surprising that careful measurements have not hitherto been made. The rate of movement has the same psychological bearings as the force of movement. Notice, in addition to the subjects already mentioned, the connexion between force and rate of movement on the one hand and the "four temperaments" on

the other. I am now making experiments to determine the rate of different movements. As a general test, I suggest the quickest possible movement of the right hand and arm from rest through 50 cm. A piece of apparatus for this purpose can be obtained from Clay & Torbensen, Philadelphia. An electric current is closed by the first movement of the hand, and broken when the movement through 50 cm. has been completed. I measure the time the current has been closed with the Hipp chronoscope, but it may be done by any chronographic method. The Hipp chronoscope is to be obtained from Peyer & Favarger, Neuchatel. It is a very convenient apparatus, but care must be taken in regulating and controlling it.

3. *Sensation-areas*—The distance on the skin by which two points must be separated in order that they may be felt as two is a constant, interesting both to the physiologist and psychologist. Its variation in different parts of the body (from 1 to 68 mm.) was a most important discovery. What the individual variation may be, and what inferences may be drawn from it, cannot be foreseen; but anything which may throw light on the development of the idea of space deserves careful study. Only one part of the body can be tested in a series such as the present. I suggest the back of the closed right hand, between the tendons of the first and second fingers, and in a longitudinal direction. Compasses with rounded wooden or rubber tips should be used, and I suggest that the curvature have a radius of 5 mm. This experiment requires some care and skill on the part of the experimenter. The points must be touched simultaneously, and not too hard. The experimentee must turn away his head. In order to obtain exact results, a large number of experiments would be necessary, and all the tact of the experimenter will be required to determine, without undue expenditure of time, the distance at which the touches may just be distinguished.

4. *Pressure causing pain*—This, like the rate of movement, is a determination not hitherto much considered, and if other more important tests can be devised they might be substituted for these. But the point at which pressure causes pain may be an important constant, and in any case it would be valuable in the diagnosis of nervous diseases and in studying abnormal states of consciousness. The determination of any fixed point or quantity in pleasure or pain is a matter of great interest in theoretical and practical ethics, and I should be glad to include some test in the present series. To determine the pressure causing pain, I use an instrument (to be obtained from Clay & Torbensen) which measures the pressure applied by a tip of hard rubber 5 mm. in radius. I am now determining the pressure causing pain in different parts of the body; for the present series I recommend the centre of the forehead. The pressure should be gradually increased, and the maximum read from the indicator

after the experiment is complete. As a rule, the point at which the experimentee says the pressure is painful should be recorded, but in some cases it may be necessary to record the point at which signs of pain are shown. I make two trials, and record both.

5. *Least noticeable difference in weight*—The just noticeable sensation and the least noticeable difference in sensation are psychological constants of great interest. Indeed, the measurement of mental intensity is probably the most important question with which experimental psychology has at present to deal. The just noticeable sensation can only be determined with great pains, if at all: the point usually found being in reality the least noticeable difference for faint stimuli. This latter point is itself so difficult to determine that I have postponed it to the second series. The least noticeable difference in sensation for stimuli of a given intensity can be more readily determined, but it requires some time, and consequently not more than one sense and intensity can be tested in a preliminary series. I follow Mr. Galton in selecting "sense of effort" or weight. I use small wooden boxes, the standard one weighing 100 gms. and the others 101, 102, up to 110 gms. The standard weight and another (beginning with 105 gms.) being given to the experimentee, he is asked which is the heavier. I allow him about 10 secs. for decision. I record the point at which he is usually right, being careful to note that he is always right with the next heavier weight.

6. *Reaction-time for sound*—The time elapsing before a stimulus calls forth a movement should certainly be included in a series of psychophysical tests: the question to be decided is what stimulus should be chosen. I prefer sound; on it the reaction-time seems to be the shortest and most regular, and the apparatus is most easily arranged. I measure the time with a Hipp chronoscope, but various chronographic methods have been used. There is need of a simpler, cheaper and more portable apparatus for measuring short times. Mr. Galton uses an ingenious instrument, in which the time is measured by the motion of a falling rod, and electricity is dispensed with, but this method will not measure times longer than about ⅓ sec. In measuring the reaction-time, I suggest that three valid reactions be taken, and the minimum recorded. Later, the average and mean variation may be calculated.

7. *Time for naming colours*—A reaction is essentially reflex, and, I think, in addition to it, the time of some process more purely mental should be measured. Several such processes are included in the second series; for the present series I suggest the time needed to see and name a colour. This time may be readily measured for a single colour by means of suitable apparatus but for general use sufficient accuracy may be attained by allowing the experimentee to name ten colours and taking the average. I paste coloured papers (red, yellow, green and blue) 2 cm.

square, 1 cm. apart, vertically on a strip of black pasteboard. This I suddenly uncover and start a chronoscope, which I stop when the ten colours have been named. I allow two trials (the order of colours being different in each) and record the average time per colour in the quickest trial.

8. *Bisection of a 50 cm. line*—The accuracy with which space and time are judged may be readily tested, and with interesting results. I follow Mr. Galton in letting the experimentee divide an ebony rule (3 cm. wide) into two equal parts by means of a movable line, but I recommend 50 cm. in place of 1 ft., as with the latter the error is so small that it is difficult to measure, and the metric system seems preferable. The amount of error in mm. (the distance from the true middle) should be recorded, and whether it is to the right or left. One trial would seem to be sufficient.

9. *Judgment of 10 sec. time*—This determination is easily made. I strike on the table with the end of a pencil, and again after 10 seconds, and let the experimentee in turn strike when he judges an equal interval to have elapsed. I allow only one trial and record the time, from which the amount and direction of error can be seen.

10. *Number of letters repeated on once hearing*—Memory and attention may be tested by determining how many letters can be repeated on hearing once. I name distinctly and at the rate of two per second six letters, and if the experimentee can repeat these after me I go on to seven, then eight, &c.; if the six are not correctly repeated after three trials (with different letters), I give five, four, &c. The maximum number of letters which can be grasped and remembered is thus determined. Consonants only should be used in order to avoid syllables.

Experimental psychology is likely to take a place in the educational plan of our schools and universities. It teaches accurate observation and correct reasoning in the same way as the other natural sciences, and offers a supply of knowledge interesting and useful to everyone. I am at present preparing a laboratory manual which will include tests of the senses and measurements of mental time, intensity and extensity, but it seems worth while to give here a list of the tests which I look on as the more important in order that attention may be drawn to them, and co-operation secured in choosing the best series of tests and the most accurate and convenient methods. In the following series, fifty tests are given, but some of them include more than one determination.

Sight

1. Accommodation (short sight, over-sight, and astigmatism).
2. Drawing Purkinje's figures and the blind-spot.
3. Acuteness of colour vision, including lowest red and highest violet visible.
4. Determination of the field of vision for form and colour.
5. Determination of what the experimentee considers a normal red, yellow, green and blue.
6. Least perceptible light, and least amount of colour distinguished grey.
7. Least noticeable difference in intensity, determined for stimuli of three degrees of brightness.
8. The time a colour must work on the retina in order to produce a sensation, the maximum sensation and a given degree of fatigue.
9. Nature and duration of after-images.
10. Measurement of amount of contrast.
11. Accuracy with which distance can be judged with one and with two eyes.
12. Test with stereoscope and for struggle of the two fields of vision.
13. Errors of perception, including bisection of line, drawing of square, &c.
14. Colour and arrangement of colours preferred. Shape of figure and of rectangle preferred.

Hearing

15. Least perceptible sound and least noticeable difference in intensity for sounds of three degrees of loudness.
16. Lowest and highest tone audible. Least perceptible difference in pitch for C, C′, C″, and point where intervals and chords (in melody and harmony) are just noticed to be out of tune.
17. Judgment of absolute pitch and of the nature of intervals, chords and dischords.
18. Number and nature of the overtones which can be heard with and without resonators.
19. Accuracy with which direction and distance of sounds can be judged.
20. Accuracy with which a rhythm can be followed and complexity of rhythm can be grasped.
21. Point at which loudness and shrillness of sound become painful. Point at which beats are the most disagreeable.
22. Sound of nature most agreeable. Musical tone, chord, instrument and composition preferred.

Taste and Smell

23. Least perceptible amount of cane-sugar, quinine, cooking salt and sulphuric acid, and determination of the parts of the mouth with which they are tasted.
24. Least perceptible amount of camphor and bromine.
25. Tastes and smells found to be peculiarly agreeable and disagreeable.

Touch and Temperature

26. Least noticeable pressure for different parts of the body.
27. Least noticeable difference in pressure, with weights of 10, 100 and 1000 gms.
28. Measurement of sensation-areas in different parts of the body.
29. Accuracy with which the amount and direction of the motion of a point over the skin can be judged.
30. Least noticeable difference in temperature.
31. Mapping out of heat, cold and pressure spots on the skin.
32. The point at which pressure and heat and cold cause pain.

Sense of Effort and Movement

33. Least noticeable difference in weight, in lifting weights of 10, 100 and 1000 gms.
34. Force of squeeze of hands, pressure with thumb and forefinger and pull as archer.
35. Maximum and normal rate of movement.
36. Accuracy with which the force, extent and rate of active and passive movements can be judged.

Mental Time

37. The time stimuli must work on the ear and eye in order to call forth sensations.
38. The reaction-time for sound, light, pressure and electrical stimulation.
39. The perception-time for colours, objects, letters and words.
40. The time of naming colours, objects, letters and words.
41. The time it takes to remember and to come to a decision.
42. The time of mental association.
43. The effects of attention, practice and fatigue on mental time.

Mental Intensity

44. Results of different methods used for determining the least noticeable difference in sensation.
45. Mental intensity as a function of mental time.

Mental Extensity

46. Number of impressions which can be simultaneously perceived.
47. Number of successive impressions which can be correctly repeated, and number of times a larger number of successive impressions must be heard or seen in order that they may be correctly repeated.
48. The rate at which a simple sensation fades from memory.
49. Accuracy with which intervals of time can be remembered.
50. The correlation of mental time, intensity and extensity.

John Dewey: 1859-

THE REFLEX ARC CONCEPT IN PSYCHOLOGY *

1896

THAT the greater demand for a unifying principle and controlling working hypothesis in psychology should come at just the time when all generalizations and classifications are most questioned and questionable is natural enough. It is the very cumulation of discrete facts creating the demand for unification that also breaks down previous lines of classification. The material is too great in mass and too varied in style to fit into existing pigeon-holes, and the cabinets of science break of their own dead weight. The idea of the reflex arc has upon the whole come nearer to meeting this demand for a general working hypothesis than any other single concept. It being admitted that the sensori-motor apparatus represents both the unit of nerve structure and the type of nerve function, the image of this relationship passed over psychology, and became an organizing principle to hold together the multiplicity of fact.

In criticising this conception it is not intended to make a plea for the principles of explanation and classification which the reflex arc idea has replaced; but, on the contrary, to urge that they are not sufficiently displaced, and that in the idea of the sensori-motor circuit, conceptions of the nature of sensation and of action derived from the nominally displaced psychology are still in control.

The older dualism between sensation and idea is repeated in the current dualism of peripheral and central structures and functions; the older dualism of body and soul finds a distinct echo in the current dualism of stimulus and response. Instead of interpreting the character of sensation, idea and action from their place and function in the sensori-motor circuit, we still incline to interpret the latter from our preconceived and preformulated ideas of rigid distinctions between sensations, thoughts and acts. The sensory stimulus is one thing, the central activity, standing for the idea, is another thing, and the motor discharge, standing for the

* From the *Psychological Review,* III, (1896), 357-370, reprinted by permission of the American Psychological Association and the author. While Dewey was not attempting to found a school of psychology, his general standpoint was that of functionalism. In addition, the present article may be considered a forerunner of Gestalt, and as a criticism, in advance, of behaviorism.

act proper, is a third. As a result, the reflex arc is not a comprehensive, or organic unity, but a patchwork of disjoined parts, a mechanical conjunction or unallied processes. What is needed is that the principle underlying the idea of the reflex arc as the fundamental psychical unity shall react into and determine the values of its constitutive factors. More specifically, what is wanted is that sensory stimulus, central connections and motor responses shall be viewed, not as separate and complete entities in themselves, but as divisions of labor, functioning factors, within the single concrete whole, now designated the reflex arc.

What is the reality so designated? What shall we term that which is not sensation-followed-by-idea-followed-by-movement, but which is primary; which is, as it were, the psychical organism of which sensation, idea and movement are the chief organs? Stated on the physiological side, this reality may most conveniently be termed coordination. This is the essence of the facts held together by and subsumed under the reflex arc concept. Let us take, for our example, the familiar child-candle instance. (James, *Psychology*, I,. 25.) The ordinary interpretation would say the sensation of light is a stimulus to the grasping as a response, the burn resulting is a stimulus to withdrawing the hand as response and so on. There is, of course, no doubt that is a rough practical way of representing the process. But when we ask for its psychological adequacy, the case is quite different. Upon analysis, we find that we begin not with a sensory stimulus, but with a sensori-motor coordination, the optical-ocular, and that in a certain sense it is the movement which is primary, and the sensation which is secondary, the movement of body, head and eye muscles determining the quality of what is experienced. In other words, the real beginning is with the act of seeing; it is looking, and not a sensation of light. The sensory quale gives the value of the act, just as the movement furnishes its mechanism and control, but both sensation and movement lie inside, not outside the act.

Now if this act, the seeing, stimulates another act, the reaching, it is because both of these acts fall within a larger coordination; because seeing and grasping have been so often bound together to reinforce each other, to help each other out, that each may be considered practically a subordinate member of a bigger coordination. More specifically, the ability of the hand to do its work will depend, either directly or indirectly, upon its control, as well as its stimulation, by the act of vision. If the sight did not inhibit as well as excite the reaching, the latter would be purely indeterminate, it would be for anything or nothing, not for the particular object seen. The reaching, in turn, must both stimulate and control the seeing. The eye must be kept upon the candle if the arm is to do its work; let it wander and the arm takes up another task. In other words, we now have an enlarged and transformed coordination;

the act is seeing no less than before, but it is now seeing-for-reaching purposes. There is still a sensori-motor circuit, one with more content or value, not a substitution of a motor response for a sensory stimulus.

Now take the affairs at its next stage, that in which the child gets burned. It is hardly necessary to point out again that this is also a sensori-motor coordination and not a mere sensation. It is worth while, however, to note especially the fact that it is simply the completion, or fulfillment, of the previous eye-arm-hand coordination and not an entirely new occurrence. Only because the heat-pain quale enters into the same circuit of experience with the optical-ocular and muscular quales, does the child learn from the experience and get the ability to avoid the experience in the future.

More technically stated, the so-called response is not merely *to* the stimulus; it is *into* it. The burn is the original seeing, the original optical-ocular experience enlarged and transformed in its value. It is no longer mere seeing; it is seeing-of-a-light-that-means-pain-when-contact-occurs. The ordinary reflex arc theory proceeds upon the more or less tacit assumption that the outcome of the response is a totally new experience; that it is, say, the substitution of a burn sensation for a light sensation through the intervention of motion. The fact is that the sole meaning of the intervening movement is to maintain, reinforce or transform (as the case may be) the original quale; that we do not have the replacing of one sort of experience by another, but the development (or as it seems convenient to term it) the mediation of an experience. The seeing, in a word, remains to control the reaching, and is, in turn, interpreted by the burning.

The discussion up to this point may be summarized by saying that the reflex arc idea, as commonly employed, is defective in that it assumes sensory stimulus and motor response as distinct psychical existences, while in reality they are always inside a coordination and have their significance purely from the part played in maintaining or reconstituting the coordination; and (secondly) in assuming that the quale of experience which precedes the "motor" phase and that which succeeds it are two different states, instead of the last being always the first reconstituted, the motor phase coming in only for the sake of such mediation. The result is that the reflex arc idea leaves us with a disjointed psychology, whether viewed from the standpoint of development in the individual or in the race, or from that of the analysis of the mature consciousness. As to the former, in its failure to see that the arc of which it talks is virtually a circuit, a continual reconstitution, it breaks continuity and leaves us nothing but a series of jerks, the origin of each jerk to be sought outside the process of experience itself, in either an external pressure of "environment," or else in an unaccountable spontaneous variation from within the "soul" or the "organism." As to the latter, failing to see the unity of activity, no matter how much it may prate of unity, it still leaves us with sensation or peripheral stimulus; idea, or central process (the equivalent of attention); and motor response, or act, as three disconnected existences, having to be somehow adjusted to each other, whether through the intervention of an extra-experimental soul, or by mechanical push and pull.

Before proceeding to a consideration of the general meaning for psychology of the summary, it may be well to give another descriptive analysis, as the value of the statement depends entirely upon the universality of its range of application. For such an instance we may conveniently take Baldwin's analysis of the reactive consciousness. In this there are, he says (*Feeling and Will*, p. 60), "three elements corresponding to the three elements of the nervous arc. First, the receiving consciousness, the stimulus–say a loud, unexpected sound; second, the attention involuntarily drawn, the registering element; and, third, the muscular reaction following upon the sound–say flight from fancied danger." Now, in the first place, such an analysis is incomplete; it ignores the status prior to hearing the sound. Of course, if this status is irrelevant to what happens afterwards, such ignoring is quite legitimate. But is it irrelevant either to the quantity or the quality of the stimulus?

If one is reading a book, if one is hunting, if one is watching in a dark place on a lonely night, if one is performing a chemical experiment, in each case, the noise has a very different psychical value; it is a different experience. In any case, what proceeds the "stimulus" is a whole act, a sensori-motor coordination. What is more to the point, the "stimulus" emerges out of this coordination; it is born from it as its matrix; it represents as it were an escape from it. I might here fall back upon authority, and refer to the widely accepted sensation continuum theory, according to which the sound cannot be absolutely *ex abrupto* from the outside, but is simply a shifting of focus of emphasis, a redistribution of tensions within the former act; and declare that unless the sound activity had been present to some extent in the prior coordination, it would be impossible for it now to come to prominence in consciousness. And such a reference would be only an amplification of what has already been said concerning the way in which the prior activity influences the value of the sound sensation. Or, we might point to cases of hypnotism, monoidealism and absent-mindedness, like that of Archimedes, as evidences that if the previous coordination is such as rigidly to lock the door, the auditory disturbance will knock in vain for admission to consciousness. Or, to speak more truly in the metaphor, the auditory activity must already have one foot over the threshold, if it is ever to gain admittance.

But it will be more satisfactory, probably, to refer to the biological side of the case, and point out that as the ear activity has been evolved on account of the advantage gained by the whole organism, it must stand in the strictest histological and physiological connection with the eye, or hand, or leg, or whatever other organ has been the overt center of action. It is absolutely impossible to think of the eye center as monopolizing consciousness and the ear apparatus as wholly quiescent. What happens is a certain relative prominence and subsidence as between the various organs which maintain the organic equilibrium.

Furthermore, the sound is not a mere stimulus, or mere sensation; it again is an act, that of hearing. The muscular response is involved in this as well as sensory stimulus; that is, there is a certain definite set of the motor apparatus involved in hearing just as much as there is in subsequent running away. The movement and posture of the ear, the tension of the ear muscles, are required for the "reception" of the sound. It is just as true to say that the sensation of sound arises from a motor response as that the running away is a response to the sound. This may be brought out by reference to the fact that Professor Baldwin, in the passage quoted, has inverted the real order as between his first and second elements. We do not have first a sound and then activity of attention, unless sound is taken as mere nervous shock or physical event, not as conscious value. The conscious sensation of sound depends upon the motor response having already taken place; or, in terms of the previous statement (if stimulus is used as a conscious fact, and not as a mere physical event) it is the motor response or attention which constitutes that, which finally becomes the stimulus to another act. Once more, the final "element," the running away, is not merely motor, but is sensori-motor, having its sensory value and its muscular mechanism. It is also a coordination. And, finally, this sensori-motor coordination is not a new act, supervening upon what preceded. Just as the "response" is necessary to constitute the stimulus, to determine it as sound and as this kind of sound, of wild beast or robber, so the sound experience must persist as a value in the running, to keep it up, to control it. The motor reaction involved in the running is, once more, into, not merely to, the sound. It occurs to change the sound, to get rid of it. The resulting quale, whatever it may be, has its meaning wholly determined by reference to the hearing of the sound. It is that experience mediated. What we have is a circuit, not an arc or broken segment of a circle. This circuit is more truly termed organic than reflex, because the motor response determines the stimulus, just as truly as sensory stimulus determines movement. Indeed, the movement is only for the sake of determining the stimulus, of fixing what kind of a stimulus it is, of interpreting it.

I hope it will not appear that I am introducing needless refinements and distinctions into what, it may be urged, is after all an undoubted fact, that movement as response follows sensation as stimulus. It is not a question of making the account of the process more complicated, though it is always wise to beware of that false simplicity which is reached by leaving out of account a large part of the problem. It is a question of finding out what stimulus or sensation, what movement and response mean; a question of seeing that they mean distinctions of flexible function only, not of fixed existence; that one and the same occurrence plays either or both parts, according to the shift of interest; and that because of this functional distinction and relationship, the supposed problem of the adjustment of one to the other, whether by superior force in the stimulus or an agency *ad hoc* in the center or the soul, is a purely self-created problem.

We may see the disjointed character of the present theory, by calling to mind that it is impossible to apply the phrase "sensori-motor" to the occurrence as a simple phrase of description; it has validity only as a term of interpretation, only, that is, as defining various functions exercised. In terms of description, the whole process may be sensory or it may be motor, but it cannot be sensori-motor. The "stimulus," the excitation of the nerve ending and of the sensory nerve, the central change, are just as much, or just as little, motion as the events taking place in the motor nerve and the muscles. It is one uninterrupted, continuous redistribution of mass in motion. And there is nothing in the process, from the standpoint of description, which entitles us to call this reflex. It is redistribution pure and simple; as much so as the burning of a log, or the falling of a house or the movement of the wind. In the physical process, as physical, there is nothing which can be set off as stimulus, nothing which reacts, nothing which is response. There is just a change in the system of tensions.

The same sort of thing is true when we describe the process purely from the psychical side. It is now all sensation, all sensory quale; the motion, as physically described, is just as much sensation as is sound or light or burn. Take the withdrawing of the hand from the candle flame as example. What we have is a certain visual-heat-pain-muscular-quale, transformed into another visual-touch-muscular-quale—the flame now being visible only at a distance, or not at all, the touch sensation being altered, etc. If we symbolize the original visual quale by v, the temperature by h, the accompanying muscular sensation by m, the whole experience may be stated as vhm-vh*m-vhm'*; *m* being the quale of withdrawing, *m'* the sense of the status after the withdrawal. The motion is not a certain kind of existence; it is a sort of sensory experience interpreted, just as is candle flame, or burn from candle flame. All are on a par.

But, in spite of all this, it will be urged, there is a distinction between stimulus and response, between sensation and motion. Precisely; but we ought now to be in a condition to ask of what nature is the distinction, instead of taking it for granted as a distinction somehow lying in the existence of the facts themselves. We ought to be able to see that the ordinary conception of the reflex arc theory, instead of being a case of plain science, is a survival of the metaphysical dualism, first formulated by Plato, according to which the sensation is an ambiguous dweller on the border land of soul and body, the idea (or central process) is purely psychical, and the act (or movement) purely physical. Thus the reflex arc formulation is neither physical (or physiological) nor psychological; it is a mixed materialistic-spiritualistic assumption.

If the previous descriptive analysis has made obvious the need of a reconsideration of the reflex arc idea, of the nest of difficulties and assumptions in the apparently simple statement, it is now time to undertake an explanatory analysis. The fact is that stimulus and response are not distinctions of existence, but teleological distinctions, that is, distinctions of function, or part played, with reference to reaching or maintaining an end. With respect to this teleological process, two stages should be discriminated, as their confusion is one cause of the confusion attending the whole matter. In one case, the relation represents an organization of means with reference to a comprehensive end. It represents an accomplished adaptation. Such is the case in all well developed instincts, as when we say that the contact of eggs is a stimulus to the hen to set; or the sight of corn a stimulus to peck; such also is the case with all thoroughly formed habits, as when the contact with the floor stimulates walking. In these instances there is no question of consciousness of stimulus *as* stimulus, of response *as* response. There is simply a continuously ordered sequence of acts, all adapted in themselves and in the order of their sequence, to reach a certain objective end, the reproduction of the species, the preservation of life, locomotion to a certain place. The end has got thoroughly organized into the means. In calling one stimulus, another response we mean nothing more than that such an orderly sequence of acts is taking place. The same sort of statement might be made equally well with reference to the succession of changes in a plant, so far as these are considered with reference to their adaptation to, say, producing seed. It is equally applicable to the series of events in the circulation of the blood, or the sequence of acts occurring in a self-binding reaper.

Regarding such cases of organization viewed as already attained, we may say, positively, that it is only the assumed common reference to an inclusive end which marks each member off as stimulus and response, that apart from such reference we have only antecedent and consequent; in other words, the distinction is one of interpretation. Negatively, it must be pointed out that it is not legitimate to carry over, without change, exactly the same order of considerations to cases where it is a question of *conscious* stimulation and response. We may, in the above case, regard, if we please, stimulus and response each as an entire act, having an individuality of its own, subject even here to the qualification that individuality means not an entirely independent whole, but a division of labor as regards maintaining or reaching an end. But in any case, it is an act, a sensori-motor coordination, which stimulates the response, itself in turn sensori-motor, not a sensation which stimulates a movement. Hence the illegitimacy of identifying, as is so often done, such cases of organized instincts or habits with the so-called reflex arc, or of transferring, without modification, considerations valid of this serial coordination of acts to the sensation-movement case.

The fallacy that arises when this is done is virtually the psychological or historical fallacy. A set of considerations which hold good only because of a completed process, is read into the content of the process which conditions this completed result. A state of things characterizing an outcome is regarded as a true description of the events which lead up to this outcome; when, as a matter of fact, if this outcome had already been in existence, there would have been no necessity for the process. Or, to make the application to the case in hand, considerations valid of an attained organization or coordination, the orderly sequence of minor acts in a comprehensive coordination, are used to describe a process, viz., the distinction of mere sensation as stimulus and of mere movement as response, which takes place only because such an attained organization is no longer at hand, but is in process of constitution. Neither mere sensation, nor mere movement, can ever be either stimulus or response; only an act can be that; the *sensation* as stimulus means the lack of and search for such an objective stimulus, or orderly placing of an act; just as mere movement as response means the lack of and search for the right act to complete a given coordination.

A recurrence to our example will make these formulae clearer. As long as the seeing is an unbroken act, which is as experienced no more mere sensation than it is mere motion (though the onlooker or psychological observer can interpret it into sensation and movement), it is in no sense the sensation which stimulates the reaching; we have, as already sufficiently indicated, only the serial steps in a coordination of *acts*. But now take a child who, upon reaching for bright light (that is, exercising the seeing-reaching coordination) has sometimes had a delightful exercise, sometimes found something good to eat and sometimes burned himself. *Now the response is not only uncertain, but the stimulus is equally uncertain; one is uncertain only in so far as the other is.* The real problem may be equally well stated as either to discover the right stimulus, to constitute the stimulus, or to discover, to constitute, the response. The question of whether to reach or to abstain from reaching is the question what sort of a bright light have we here? Is it the one which means playing with one's hands, eating milk, or burning one's fingers? The stimulus must be constituted for the response to occur. Now it is at precisely this juncture and because of it that the distinction of sensation as stimulus and motion as response arises.

The sensation or conscious stimulus is not a thing or existence by itself; it is that phase of a coordination requiring attention because, by reason of the conflict within the coordination, it is uncertain how to complete it. It is to doubt as to the next act, whether to reach or no, which gives the motive to examining the act. The end to follow is, in this sense, the stimulus. It furnishes the motivation to attend to what has just taken place; to define it more carefully. From this point of view the discovery of the stimulus is the "response" to possible movement as "stimulus." We must have an anticipatory sensation, an image, of the movements that may occur, together with their respective values, before attention will go to the seeing to break it up as a sensation of light, and of light of this particular kind. It is the initiated activities of reaching, which, inhibited by the conflict in the coordination, turn round, as it were, upon the seeing, and hold it from passing over into further act until its quality is determined. Just here the act as objective stimulus becomes transformed into sensation as possible, as conscious, stimulus. Just here also, motion as conscious response emerges.

In other words, sensation as stimulus does not mean any particular psychical *existence*. It means simply a function, and will have its value shift according to the special work requiring to be done. At one moment the various activities of reaching and withdrawing will be the sensation, because they are that phase of activity which sets the problem, or creates the demand for, the next act. At the next moment the previous act of seeing will furnish the sensation, being, in turn, that phase of activity which sets the pace upon which depends further action. Generalized, sensation as stimulus is always that phase of activity requiring to be defined in order that a coordination may be completed. What the sensation will be in particular at a given time, therefore, will depend entirely upon the way in which an activity is being used. It has no fixed quality of its own. The search for the stimulus is the search for exact conditions of action; that is, for the state of things which decides how a beginning coordination should be completed.

Similarly, motion, as response, has only a functional value. It is whatever will serve to complete the disintegrating coordination. Just as the discovery of the sensation marks the establishing of the problem, so the constitution of the response marks the solution of this problem. At one time, fixing attention, holding the eye fixed, upon the seeing and thus bringing out a certain quale of light is the response, because that is the particular act called for just then; at another time, the movement of the arm away from the light is the response. There is nothing in itself which may be labelled response. That one certain set of sensory quales should be marked off by themselves as "motion" and put in antithesis to such sensory quales as those of color, sound and contact, as legitimate claimants to the title of sensation, is wholly inexplicable unless we keep the difference of function in view. It is the eye and ear sensations which fix for us the problem; which report to us the conditions which have to be met if the coordination is to be successfully completed; and just the moment we need to know about our movements to get an adequate report, just that moment, motion miraculously (from the ordinary standpoint) ceases to be motion and becomes "muscular sensation." On the other hand, take the change in values of experience, the transformation of sensory quales. Whether this change will or will not be interpreted as movement, whether or not any consciousness of movement will arise, will depend upon whether this change is satisfactory, whether or not it is regarded as a harmonious development of a coordination, or whether the change is regarded as simply a means in solving a problem, an instrument in reaching a more satisfactory coordination. So long as our experience runs smoothly we are no more conscious of motion as motion than we are of this or that color or sound by itself.

To sum up: the distinction of sensation and movement as stimulus and response respectively is not a distinction which can be regarded as descriptive of anything which holds of psychical events or existences as such. The only events to which the terms stimulus and response can be descriptively applied are to minor acts serving by their respective positions to the maintenance of some organized coordination. The conscious stimulus or sensation, and the conscious response or motion, have a special genesis or motivation, and a special end or function. The reflex arc theory, by neglecting, by abstracting from, this genesis and this function gives us one disjointed part of a process as if it were the whole. It gives us literally an arc, instead of the circuit; and not giving us the circuit of which it is an arc, does not enable us to place, to center, the arc. This arc, again, falls apart into two separate existences having to be either mechanically or externally adjusted to each other.

The circle is a coordination, some of whose members have come into conflict with each other. It is the temporary disintegration and need of reconstitution which occasions, which affords the genesis of, the conscious distinction into sensory stimulus on one side and motor response on the other. The stimulus is that phase of the forming coordination which represents the conditions which have to be met in bringing it to a successful issue; the response is that phase of one and the same forming coordination which gives the key to meeting these conditions, which serves as instrument in effecting the successful coordination. They are therefore strictly correlative and contemporaneous. The stimulus is something to be discovered; and to be made out; if the activity affords its own adequate stimulation, there is no stimulus save in the objective sense already referred to. As soon as it is adequately determined, then and then only is the response also complete. To attain either, means that the coordination has completed itself. Moreover, it is the motor response which assists in discovering and constituting the stimulus. It is the holding of the movement at a certain stage which creates the sensation, which throws it into relief.

It is the coordination which unifies that which the reflex arc concept gives us only in disjointed fragments. It is the circuit within which fall distinctions of stimulus and response as functional phases of its own mediation or completion. The point of this story is in its application; but the application of it to the question of the nature of psychical evolution, to the distinction between sensational and rational consciousness, and the nature of judgment must be deferred to a more favorable opportunity.

THE POSTULATES OF A STRUCTURAL PSYCHOLOGY *

1898

BIOLOGY, defined in its widest sense as the science of life and of living things, falls into three parts, or may be approached from any one of three points of view. We may enquire into the structure of an organism, without regard to function,—by analysis determining its component parts, and by synthesis exhibiting the mode of its formation from the parts. Or we may enquire into the function of the various structures which our analysis has revealed, and into the manner of their interrelation as functional organs. Or, again, we may enquire into the changes of form and function that accompany the persistence of the organism in time, the phenomena of growth and of decay. Biology, the science of living things, comprises the three mutually interdependent sciences of morphology, physiology, and ontogeny.

This account is, however, incomplete. The life which forms the subject matter of science is not merely the life of an individual; it is species life, collective life, as well. Corresponding to morphology, we have taxonomy or systematic zoology, the science of classification. The whole world of living things is here the organism, and species and sub-species and races are its parts. Corresponding to physiology, we have that department of biology—it has been termed "oecology"—which deals with questions of geographical distribution, of the function of species in the general economy of nature. Corresponding to ontogeny we have the science of phylogeny (in Cope's sense): the biology of evolution, with its problems of descent and of transmission.

We may accept this scheme as a "working" classification of the biological sciences. It is indifferent, for my present purpose, whether or not the classification is exhaustive, as it is indifferent whether the reader regards psychology as a subdivision of biology or as a separate province of knowledge. The point which I wish now to make is this: that, employing the same principle of division, we can represent modern psychology as the exact counterpart of modern biology. There are three

* Reprinted from the *Philosophical Review,* VII, (1898), 449-465 by permission of Cornell University. Titchener's paper was the foundation stone of the American school of structural psychology.

ways of approaching the one, as there are the three ways of approaching the other; and the subject matter in every case may be individual or general. A little consideration will make this clear.

1. We find a parallel to morphology in a very large portion of "experimental" psychology. The primary aim of the experimental psychologist has been to analyze the structure of mind; to ravel out the elemental processes from the tangle of consciousness, or (if we may change the metaphor) to isolate the constituents in the given conscious formation. His task is a vivisection, but a vivisection which shall yield structural, not functional results. He tries to discover, first of all, what is there and in what quantity, not what it is there for. Indeed, this work of analysis bulks so largely in the literature of experimental psychology that a recent writer has questioned the right of the science to its adjective, declaring that an experiment is something more than a measurement made by the help of delicate instruments. And there can be no doubt that much of the criticism passed upon the new psychology depends on the critic's failure to recognize its morphological character. We are often told that our treatment of feeling and emotion, of reasoning, of the self is inadequate; that the experimental method is valuable for the investigation of sensation and idea, but can carry us no farther. The answer is that the results gained by dissection of the "higher" processes will always be disappointing to those who have not themselves adopted the dissector's standpoint. Protoplasm consists, we are told, of carbon, oxygen, nitrogen, and hydrogen; but this statement would prove exceedingly disappointing to one who had thought to be informed of the phenomena of contractility and metabolism, respiration and reproduction. Taken in its appropriate context, the jejuneness of certain chapters in mental anatomy, implying, as it does, the fewness of the mental elements, is a fact of extreme importance.

2. There is, however, a functional psychology, over and above this psychology of structure. We may regard mind, on the one hand, as a complex of processes, shaped and moulded under the conditions of the physical organism. We may regard it, on the other hand, as the collective name for a system of functions of the psychophysical organism. The two points of view are not seldom confused. The phrase "association of ideas," e.g., may denote either the structural complex, the associated sensation group, or the functional process of recognition and recall, the associating of formation to formation. In the former sense it is morphological material, in the latter it belongs to what I must name (the phrase will not be misunderstood) a physiological psychology.

Just as experimental psychology is to a large extent concerned with problems of structure, so is "descriptive" psychology, ancient and modern, chiefly occupied with problems of function. Memory, recognition, imagination, conception, judgment, attention, apperception, volition, and a host of verbal nouns, wider or narrower in denotation, connote, in the discussions of descriptive psychology, functions of the total organism. That their underlying processes are psychical in character is, so to speak, an accident; for all practical purposes they stand upon the same level as digestion and locomotion, secretion and excretion. The organism remembers, wills, judges, recognizes, etc., and is assisted in its life-struggle by remembering and willing. Such functions are, however, rightly included in mental science, inasmuch as they constitute, in sum, the actual, working mind of the individual man. They are not functions of the body, but functions of the organism, and they may—nay, they must—be examined by the methods and under the regulative principles of a mental "physiology." The adoption of these methods does not at all prejudice the ultimate and extra-psychological problem of the function of mentality at large in the universe of things. Whether consciousness really has a survival-value, as James supposes, or whether it is a mere epiphenomenon, as Ribot teaches, is here an entirely irrelevant question.

It cannot be said that this functional psychology, despite what we may call its greater obviousness to investigation, has been worked out either with as much patient enthusiasm or with as much scientific accuracy as has the psychology of mind structure. It is true, and it is a truth which the experimentalist should be quick to recognize and emphasize, that there is very much of value in "descriptive" psychology. But it is also true that the methods of descriptive psychology cannot, in the nature of the case, lead to results of scientific finality. The same criticism holds, as things stand, of individual psychology, which is doing excellent pioneer work in the sphere of function. Experimental psychology has added much to our knowledge, functional as well as structural, of memory, attention, imagination, etc., and will, in the future, absorb and quantify the results of these other, new coordinate branches. Still, I do not think that anyone who has followed the course of the experimental method, in its application to the higher processes and states of mind, can doubt that the main interest throughout has lain in morphological analysis, rather than in ascertainment of function. Nor are the reasons far to seek. We must remember that experimental psychology arose by way of reaction against the faculty psychology of the last century. This was a metaphysical, not a scientific, psychology. There is, in reality, a great difference between, say, memory regarded as a function of the psychophysical organism, and memory regarded as a faculty of the substantial mind. At the same time, these two memories are nearer together than are the faculty memory and the memories or memory complexes of psychological anatomy. There is, further, the danger that, if function is studied before structure has been fully elucidated, the student may fall into that acceptance of teleological explanation which is fatal to scientific advance; witness, if witness be necessary, the recrudescence of vitalism in physiology. Psychology might thus put herself for the second time, and no less surely though by different means, under the dominion of philosophy. In a word, the historical conditions of psychology rendered it inevitable that, when the time came for the transformation from philosophy to science, problems should be formulated, explicitly or implicitly, as static rather than dynamic, structural rather than functional. We may notice also the fact that elementary morphology is intrinsically an easier study than elementary physiology, and that scientific men are so far subject to the law of inertia, whose effects we see in the conservatism of mankind at large, that they prefer the continued application of a fruitful method to the adoption of a new standpoint for the standpoint's sake.

I may, perhaps, digress here for a moment, to raise and attempt to answer two questions which naturally suggest themselves: the questions whether this conservatism is wise, and whether it is likely to persist. I believe that both should be answered in the affirmative. As has been indicated above, the morphological study of mind serves, as no other method of study can, to enforce and sustain the thesis that psychology is a science, and not a province of metaphysics; and recent writing shows clearly enough that this truth has need of constant reiteration. Moreover, there is still so much to be done in the field of analysis (not simply analysis of the higher processes, though these will of course benefit in the long run, but also analysis of perception and feeling and idea) that a general swing of the laboratories towards functional work would be most regrettable. It seems probable, if one may presume to read the signs of the times, that experimental psychology has before it a long period of analytical research, whose results, direct and indirect, shall ultimately serve as basis for the psychology of function; unless, indeed, —and this is beyond predicting,—the demands laid upon psychology by the educationalist become so insistent as partially to divert the natural channels of investigation.

The remaining four psychologies may be dismissed with a briefer mention. 3. Ontogenetic psychology, the psychology of individual childhood and adolescence, is now a subject of wide interest, and has a large literature of its own. 4. Taxonomic psychology is not yet, and in all likelihood will not be, for some time to come, anything more than an ingredient in "descriptive," and a portion of individual, psychology. It deals with such topics as the classification of emotions, instincts and impulses, temperaments, etc., the hierarchy of psychological "selves," the typical mind of social classes (artists, soldiers, literary men), and so forth. 5. The functional psychology of the collective mind is, as might be expected, in a very rudimentary condition. We can delimit its sphere and indicate its problems; minor contributions to it may be found here and there in the pages of works upon psychology, logic, ethics, aesthetics, sociology, and anthropology; and a few salient points—the question, e.g., of the part played by the aesthetic sentiment in the make-up of a national mind—have been touched upon in essays. But we must have an experimental physiology of the individual mind, before there can be any great progress. 6. Lastly, the labors of the evolutionary school have set phylogenetic psychology upon a fairly secure foundation, and the number of workers is a guarantee of rapid advance in our understanding of mental development.

The object of the present paper is to set forth the state of current opinion upon the question of the structural elements of mind, their number and nature. It may be doubted, at first sight, whether anything like a consensus of opinion can be made out. "Every psychologist of standing," wrote Kulpe in 1893, "has his own laws of association." Every psychologist of standing in the year of grace 1898, so the reader may think, has his own favorite "unique" process. Does not Brentano advocate an ultimate "judgment," and James a "fiat of the will," and Stout an ultimate "thought"? Is there not the perennial controversy about the "third conscious element," the process of conation, the "activity experience"? Are not even the clear waters of the psychology of sensation troubled by the possibility of an "efferent" conscious process, a sensation of innervation? The questions are importunate, and cannot be lightly brushed aside. We will begin, therefore, by examining a test case: Brentano's irreducible "judgment." I select this, because Professor Ebbinghaus, in his recent Psychology, seems to put a structural interpretation upon it. He himself classifies the elements of mind (we shall return to this classification later) as sensations, ideas, and feelings; Brentano, he says, ranks alongside of ideas the element of judgment. If this account is correct, we must admit that the morphology of mind is still a battlefield for individual opinions; we shall hardly escape the difficulty by the mere statement that Ebbinghaus is an experimentalist, and Brentano not.

When, however, we turn to Brentano himself, the matter assumes a different complexion. Brentano's principal criterion of psychical, as contradistinguished from physical phenomena, is that of "intentional inexistence" or "immanent objectivity," which we may paraphrase as reference to contents, direction upon something as object. "Every psychical phenomenon contains in it something as object, though not every one in the same way. In ideation something is ideated, in judgment something admitted or rejected, in love and hate something loved and hated, in desire something desired, etc." This is evidently the language of function, not of structure. Indeed, Brentano uses the phrases *psychisches Phanomen* and *Seelenthatigkeit* interchangeably; his "fundamental" or "principal classes of psychical phenomena" are the "mental activities" of ideation (not "idea!"), judgment and interest (love and hate, the emotive processes). The spirit of his whole psychology is physiological; and when, on occasion, he discusses a point in anatomy, he leaves his reader in no doubt as to the shift of *venue*. Now the mental elements of the experimentalists, the bare sensation and the bare feeling, are abstractions, innocent of any sort of objective reference. We cannot fairly compare Brentano's "judgment" with them. Nay, more, we cannot fairly say that he would have posited an ultimate judgment process *if* he had adopted the anatomical point of view; since he has not adopted it, the speculation is absurd. The "psychology from the empirical standpoint" is a systematization of mental "activities," i.e., of the mental functions of the human organism.

This wave, then, has not overwhelmed us. Escaping it, we may turn now to the positive side of our enquiry. Our appeal will lie, in the first instance, to the experimentalists; but the omission of references to works on descriptive psychology is largely due to considerations of space, and does not by any means necessarily imply that the authors of these works differ from the writers quoted. Some of the "unique" processes still left outstanding will be taken up at the end of this discussion.

We set out from a point of universal agreement. Everyone admits that *sensations* are elementary mental processes. There is, it is true, diversity of opinion as to the range of contents that the term shall cover. Wundt identifies the peripherally excited and the centrally excited processes. "For the psychological attributes of a sensation the circumstance [of external or internal initiation] is entirely irrelevant. . . . It is only the central stimulus that always accompanies sensation." Kulpe retains the name "sensation" for both classes, but declares that they "must be treated separately, as they normally present characteristic differences." Ziehen and Ebbinghaus, on the other hand, draw a sharp line of distinction between the "sensation," which is externally aroused, and the "idea" (in Lotze's sense), which is its centrally aroused substitute, and so recognize two elements where Wundt and Kulpe see only one. The divergence, however, is not serious. It seems to depend, primarily, upon the admission or exclusion of genetic considerations. If we rule that these are foreign to a strictly morphological examination of mind, the question of one sense element or two becomes a problem set by analysis to analysis, capable of resolution by analytic methods; it is a subject for dispute "inside the ring," and is thus upon a quite different level from the question, e.g., of an elementary will process.—We may note, in passing, that the innervation sensation, while it remains as a theoretical possibility, has been generally given up by the experimental school.

Simple *affective* processes, again, are regarded by a large majority as elemental. Both Wundt and Kulpe are at some pains to make clear the essential difference between sensation and affection. Lehmann and Ebbinghaus are equally explicit. Ziehen does not give a place to feeling beside sensation and idea; his chapters are entitled "The Affective Tone of Sensation" and "The Affective Tone of Ideas," and his treatment makes affective tone an attribute coordinate with the intensity and quality of sensation and the clearness and contents (meaning) of idea. Nevertheless, he speaks in one passage of the cortical substrate of this tone as "an entirely new psychophysiological process." Munsterberg, on the other hand, denies the ultimateness of feeling altogether, and seeks to reduce it to the sensations accompanying movements of flexion and extension, reflexly released. There is, further, an "inside" controversy as to the number of affective qualities. But analysis will some day settle the question whether there are two of these (Kulpe), or two in the sphere of sensation and many more in that of idea (Ziehen), or an inexhaustible variety under the six heads of pleasantness and unpleasantness, tension and relaxation, excitement and tranquillization (Wundt).

It is natural, in view of the intrinsic difficulty of the subject, that the psychology of feeling should be in a less settled state than the psychology of sensation. All the more striking, when we consider the close relation that obtains between "feeling" and "will," is the unanimity with which experimentalists reject the doctrine of a specific will process. "There is no reason," writes Ebbinghaus, "for looking upon acts of will or appetitions as elementary forms of the mental life." And Wundt, Kulpe, Ziehen, and Munsterberg are of the same manner of thinking.

No fourth candidate for elemental rank has appeared. No trace has been found, in all the minute analysis of the last twenty years, of a mental krypton or argon. It seems safe, then, to conclude that the ultimate processes are two, and two only, sensations and affections, though we must not forget that the first class, that of sensations, includes the two well-defined sub-species, "sensation" and "idea."

How, now, are these different processes to be distinguished? What is our justification for looking upon them as last things of mind? Disregarding function, and trying to answer the question upon the anatomical plane, we can point at least to three valid criteria. We may refer to experience itself, and note that sensation and affection are irreducible for introspection. The one cannot be derived from, identified with, the other; they "look" different or "feel" different, however far analysis be pushed. Or we may have recourse to physiology. Since the structure of mind is conditioned upon the physical organization, we may differentiate sensation and affection by reference to their physical substrates. Or, again, we may seek a descriptive formula, which shall sum up the essential characteristics of the two processes. It is in this sense that Wundt is speaking, when he says that sensation qualities range between maxima of *difference*, and affective qualities between maxima of *opposition* or antithesis. Any one of these statements is adequate to the psychological requirements. The last of them, however, as Wundt's exposition shows, implies that we are already familiar with the *attributes* of which sensation and affection are constituted. We must devote a brief space to their consideration.

Once more, we set out from a point of universal agreement. "There are two indispensable determinants of every psychical element, quality and intensity." But discussion is now slow to begin. For these two attributes or determinants are, evidently, of different kinds. Quality is specific and individual; it is quality that makes the elemental process a blue or a sweet, a pleasant or a *c* of the third octave. Intensity, on the contrary, is a general attribute, common to all modalities of sensation and qualities of affection. Hence, while some psychologists rank the two determinations together, as coordinate, others set aside quality for itself, and count intensity along with extent and duration as equipollent characteristics, whether of all the mental elements or of certain great groups of qualities. There is also much difference of opinion as to the precise place to be ascribed to the attributes of extent and duration. For Wundt, who holds a genetic theory, psychological space is the resultant of a two-dimensional system of qualitative local signs multipled into, or fused with, a one-dimensional intensive system of sensations aroused by movement. It is, primarily, tactual or visual. Psychological time, in the same way, is the resultant of qualitatively varied feelings multiplied into, or fused with, the same intensive system of sensations. The affective processes, in abstraction, are timeless; the primary sources of temporal ideas are audition and "internal touch." It follows that space and time, extent and duration, can be predicated only of formations, not of elements. Spatial arrangement (Wundt makes no distinction between "spatial arrangement" and "space" as "absolute contents") cannot "be an original attribute of the elements, analogous to the intensity or quality of sensations;" it "results from the bringing together of these elements," which means the "arising of new psychical conditions;" and the same thing is true of time. Opposed to this genetic theory is the nativistic view, represented for space, e.g., by Stumpf, according to which every sensation has about it something of tridimensionality, a certain bigness or voluminousness, and every elemental process a certain duration.

It is, indeed, hardly possible to keep the psychological problem of space and time clear of epistemology, on the one hand, and of psychogenesis, on the other. It would, perhaps, be unwise to make any attempt to do so, in a work meant to serve the purpose of instruction; for the attempt would involve a total disregard of historical conditions. Nevertheless, there can be little doubt as to the anatomical facts. I am wholly unable to conceive of a sensation or affective process as timeless, as lacking duration; analysis of mind as it is leaves me, always, with a process-lasting-some-time. I am equally unable to conceive of a visual sensation or sensation of pressure as spaceless, punctual; analysis leaves me, always, with a process-spread-out. On the other hand, I feel no constraint to regard the spreading-out as tridimensional. Neither does the surface itself necessarily imply the depth perception, nor need the relation of the surface to the ideating subject be present in consciousness. And the other sensations, tones, tastes, etc., as well as the affections seem to be entirely devoid of space attributes. In mental morphology, the perfect element (say, a sensation of color) shows us quality, intensity, duration, and superficial extension.

A similar difficulty confronts us with regard to the attribute of clearness. Variation in degree of clearness of the constituent processes in ideas is the anatomical equivalent of what is functionally termed the "distribution of attention." Wundt places degree of clearness on the same level with spatial and temporal arrangement. "As these attributes [clearness and obscurity, distinctness and indistinctness] arise always and only from the interconnection of the various psychical formations, they cannot be considered as determinants of the psychical elements." Yet, on Wundt's own principle of relativity, the same thing would be true of sensation intensity; we cannot say anything of the intensity of a sensation unless a formation—at least two sensations, side by side—be there for "comparison." Moreover, we must exclude genetic arguments here as before. If we make analytic introspection the test, we cannot but admit that the ultimate sensation may be conceived of as clear or obscure.

I conclude, then, that the affective element is constituted of quality, intensity, and duration; the sense element (sensation or idea) of quality, intensity, duration, clearness, and (in some cases) extent. Quality is intrinsic and individual; intensity and clearness are "relative" characteristics; duration and extent are, very probably, extrinsic translations into structure of the lowest terms of a functional series. And the corollary is that the "elements" of the experimentalists, as they themselves have been the first to urge, are artifacts, abstractions, usefully isolated for scientific ends, but not found in experience save as connected with their like.

It is unnecessary to pursue further our examination of structural psychology. Just as morphology proper, passing beyond the cell, becomes a morphology of organs, so does structural psychology, passing beyond the elementary processes, become an anatomy of functional complexes. The experimental psychologies deal, as do the descriptive works, with the perceptions and emotions and actions handed down in popular and psychological tradition. Kulpe, working out a distinction which was quite clearly drawn in the physiological psychology of the younger Mill, has reduced all the "higher" processes to two structural patterns: mixtures of intensities and qualities (fusions), and connections of spatial and temporal attributes (colligations). This reduction marks a decided step in advance; but its chief value lies in the suggestion of a plan of arrangement for the results gained by analysis of the basal functions. A discussion of these results themselves would far transgress the limits of the present paper.

What remains, now, is to assure ourselves that the various "unique" processes of current psychology, not recognized in the preceding analysis, are conceived of in terms of function, and not in terms of structure. There is no room for doubt of this, in the case of Stout's *Analytic Psychology*. The author's use of the phrase "mental functions," his constant reference to Brentano, his insistence upon mental "activity," are indications enough. In view of the similarity of standpoint, it may be interesting to compare his final classification with that of Brentano. The latter, as we have seen, ranks ideation, judgment, and interest as the fundamental functions of mind. Stout distinguishes two primary attitudes of consciousness: the cognitive and the volitional. Cognition includes thought and sentience as "fundamentally distinct mental functions," and thought, again, subdivides into simple apprehension and judgment. Volition, in its turn, includes "two fundamentally distinct modes of reference to an object," feeling and conation. We have, then, five "fundamental modes of consciousness," grouped under the two primary conscious attitudes. The difference between Brentano and Stout is at least as apparent as their agreement.

James' "fiat of the will," or "express consent to the reality of what is attended to," is also a functional process:

> This consent . . . seems a subjective experience *sui generis*, which we can designate but not define. We stand here exactly where we did in the case of belief. When an idea *stings* us in a certain way, makes as it were a certain electric connection with our self, we believe that it *is* a reality. When it stings us in another way, makes another connection with our self, we say *let it be* a reality. To the words "is" and "let it be" correspond peculiar attitudes of consciousness which it is vain to seek to explain.

Lastly, I may refer in this connection to Dr. Irons' contention that emotion is an "irreducible" process, an "ultimate and primary aspect of mind." Dr. Irons has stated that the method of his enquiry is not genetic; and his definition of emotion as "feeling attitude" implies that it is not anatomical. But while his words are the words of function ("cognition," etc.), his criticism is very largely criticism of the morphologists. It would seem that he has not fully recognized the difference between the two standpoints. No one among the experimentalists has hitherto expressed a doubt—I venture to assert that no one ever will—as to the composite nature of the emotive process.

The burden of the argument has been that there is reasonable agreement, within the experimental camp, as to the postulates of a purely structural psychology, whereas there is pretty radical disagreement among the psychologists of function. Let it not be supposed, now, that this latter state of affairs is anything else than a disadvantage for psychology at large; above all, let it not be thought that the experimentalist rejoices at the lack of unanimity among his colleagues. It is a commonplace of the biological sciences that structure and function are correlative terms, and that advance in knowledge of the one conditions and is conditioned by advance in the understanding of the other. Only, in psychology, functional analysis—required by the living of our daily life—had been carried out to a degree sufficient for the successful prosecution of anatomical work, before the experimental method appeared. Structural psychology might proceed far on its way, even if the psychology of function had halted at Kant or, for that matter, at Aristotle. I believe that physiological psychology (in the sense of this paper) has a great future; and I subscribe fully to all that has been said of the critical subtlety of Brentano's discussions, of the delicacy of discrimination shown in Stout's recent book, of the genius of James' work. Nevertheless, I believe as firmly that the best hope for psychology lies today in a continuance of structural analysis, and that the study of function will not yield final fruit until it can be controlled by the genetic and, still more, by the experimental method—in the form both of laboratory experimenting and of interpretation of that natural experiment which meets us in certain pathological cases.

Edward Lee Thorndike: 1874-

ANIMAL INTELLIGENCE *

1898

THIS monograph is an attempt at an explanation of the nature of the process of association in the animal mind. Inasmuch as there have been no extended researches of a character similar to the present one either in subject-matter or experimental method, it is necessary to explain briefly its standpoint.

Our knowledge of the mental life of animals equals in the main our knowledge of their sense-powers, of their instincts or reactions performed without experience, and of their reactions which are built up by experience. Confining our attention to the latter, we find it the opinion of the better observers and analysts that these reactions can all be explained by the ordinary associative processes without aid from abstract, conceptual, inferential thinking. These associative processes then, as present in animals' minds and as displayed in their acts, are my subject-matter. Any one familiar in even a general way with the literature of comparative psychology will recall that this part of the field has received faulty and unsuccessful treatment. The careful, minute and solid knowledge of the sense-organs of animals finds no counterpart in the realm of associations and habits. We do not know how delicate or how complex or how permanent are the possible associations of any given group of animals. And although one would be rash who said that our present equipment of facts about instincts was sufficient or that our theories about it were surely sound, yet our notion of what occurs when a chick grabs a worm are luminous and infallible compared to our notion of what happens when a kitten runs into the house at the familiar call. The reason that they have satisfied us as well as they have is just that they are so vague. We say that the kitten associates the sound "kitty kitty" with the experience of nice milk to drink, which does very well for a commonsense answer. It also suffices as a rebuke to those who would have the kitten ratiocinate about the matter, but it fails to tell what real mental content is present. Does the kitten feel "sound of call, memory-image of milk

* From the *Psychological Review Monograph Supplements*, 1898, No. 8. Reprinted by permission of the American Psychological Association and the author. Thorndike's monograph, portions of which are reproduced here, was among the earliest laboratory researches on animal learning.

in a saucer in the kitchen, thought of running into the house, a feeling, finally, of 'I will run in' "? Does he perhaps feel only the sound of the bell and an impulse to run in, similar in quality to the impulses which make a tennis player run to and fro when playing? The word "association" may cover a multitude of essentially different processes, and when a writer attributes anything that an animal may do to association, his statement has only the negative value of eliminating reasoning on the one hand and instinct on the other. His position is like that of a zoologist who should to-day class an animal among the "worms." To give to the word a positive value and several definite possibilities of meaning is one aim of this investigation.

Although no work in this field is enough like the present investigation to require an account of its results, the method hitherto in use invites comparison by its contrast and as I believe, by its faults. In the first place, most of the books do not give us a psychology, but rather a eulogy, of animals. They have all been about animal intelligence, never about animal stupidity. Though a writer derides the notion that animals have reason, he hastens to add that they have marvelous capacity of forming associations, and is likely to refer to the fact that human beings only rarely reason anything out, that their trains of ideas are ruled mostly by association, as if, in this latter, animals were on a par with them. The history of books on animals' minds thus furnishes an illustration of the well-nigh universal tendency in human nature to find the marvelous wherever it can. We wonder that the stars are so big and so far apart, that the microbes are so small and so thick together, and for much the same reason wonder at the things animals do. They used to be wonderful because of the mysterious, God-given faculty of instinct, which could almost remove mountains. More lately they have been wondered at because of their marvelous mental powers in profiting by experience. Now imagine an astronomer tremendously eager to prove the stars as big as possible, or a bacteriologist whose great scientific desire is to demonstrate the microbes to be very, very little! Yet there has been a similar eagerness on the part of many recent writers on animal psychology to praise the abilities of animals. It cannot help leading to partiality in deductions from facts and more especially in the choice of facts for investigation. How can scientists who write like lawyers, defending animals against the charge of having no power of rationality, be at the same time impartial judges on the bench? Unfortunately the real work in this field has been done in this spirit. The levelheaded thinkers who might have won valuable results have contented themselves with arguing against the theories of the eulogists. They have not made investigations of their own.

In the second place, the facts have generally been derived from anecdotes. Now quite apart from such pedantry as insists that a man's word about a scientific fact is worthless unless he is a trained scientist, there are really in this field special objections to the acceptance of the testimony about animals' intelligent acts which one gets from anecdotes. Such testimony is by no means on a par with testimony about the size of a fish or the migration of birds, etc. For here one has to deal not merely with ignorant or inaccurate testimony, but also with prejudiced testimony. Human folk are as a matter of fact eager to find intelligence in animals. They like to. And when the animal observed is a pet belonging to them or their friends, or when the story is one that has been told as a story to entertain, further complications are introduced. Nor is this all. Besides commonly misstating what facts they report, they report only such facts as show the animal at his best. Dogs get lost hundreds of times and no one ever notices it or sends an account of it to a scientific magazine. But let one find his way from Brooklyn to Yonkers and the fact immediately becomes a circulating anecdote. Thousands of cats on thousands of occasions sit helplessly yowling, and no one takes thought of it or writes to his friend, the professor; but let one cat claw at the knob of a door supposedly as a signal to be let out, and straightway this cat becomes the representative of the cat-mind in all the books. The unconscious distortion of the facts is almost harmless compared to the unconscious neglect of an animal's mental life until it verges on the unusual and marvelous. It is as if some denizen of a planet where communication was by thought-transference, who was surveying humankind and reporting their psychology, should be oblivious to all our intercommunication save such as the psychical-research society has noted. If he should further misinterpret the cases of mere coincidence of thoughts as facts comparable to telepathic communication, he would not be more wrong than some of the animal psychologists. In short, the anecdotes give really the abnormal or supernormal psychology of animals.

Further, it must be confessed that these vices have been only ameliorated, not obliterated, when the observation is first-hand, is made by the psychologist himself. For as men of the utmost skill have failed to prove good observers in the field of spiritualistic phenomena, so biologists and psychologists before the pet terrier or hunted fox often become like Samson shorn. They, too, have looked for the intelligent and unusual and neglected the stupid and normal.

Finally, in all cases, whether of direct observation or report by good observers or bad, there have been three defects. Only a single case is studied, and so the results are not necessarily true of the type; the observation is not repeated, nor are the conditions perfectly regulated; the previous history of the animal in question is not known. Such observations may tell us, if the observer is perfectly reliable, that a certain thing takes place; but they cannot assure us that it will take place universally among the animals of that species, or universally with the same animal.

Nor can the influence of previous experience be estimated. All this refers to means of getting knowledge about what animals do. The next question is, "What do they feel?" Previous work has not furnished an answer or the material for an answer to this more important question. Nothing but carefully designed, crucial experiments can. In abandoning the old method one ought to seek above all to replace it by one which will not only tell more accurately what they do, and give much-needed information how they do it, but also inform us what they feel while they act.

To remedy these defects, experiment must be substituted for observation and the collection of anecdotes. Thus you immediately get rid of several of them. You can repeat the conditions at will, so as to see whether or not the animal's behavior is due to mere coincidence. A number of animals can be subjected to the same test, so as to attain typical results. The animal may be put in situations where its conduct is especially instructive. After considerable preliminary observation of animals' behavior under various conditions, I chose for my general method one which, simple as it is, possesses several other marked advantages besides those which accompany experiment of any sort. It was merely to put animals when hungry in inclosures from which they could escape by some simple act, such as pulling at a loop of cord, pressing a lever, or stepping on a platform. (A detailed description of these boxes and pens will be given later.) The animal was put in the inclosure, food was left outside in sight, and his actions observed. Besides recording his general behavior, special notice was taken of how he succeeded in doing the necessary act (in case he did succeed), and a record was kept of the time that he was in the box before performing the successful pull, or clawing, or bite. This was repeated until the animal had formed a perfect association between the sense-impression of the interior of that box and the impulse leading to the successful movement. When the association was thus perfect, the time taken to escape was, of course, practically constant and very short.

If, on the other hand, after a certain time the animal did not succeed, he was taken out, but not fed. If, after a sufficient number of trials, he failed to get out, the case was recorded as one of complete failure. Enough different sorts of methods of escape were tried to make it fairly sure that association in general, not association of a particular sort of impulse, was being studied. Enough animals were taken with each box or pen to make it sure that the results were not due to individual peculiarities. None of the animals used had any previous acquaintance with any of the mechanical contrivances by which the doors were opened. So far as possible the animals were kept in a uniform state of hunger, which was practically utter hunger. That is, no cat or dog was experimented on, when the experiment involved any important question of fact or theory, unless I was sure that his motive was of the standard strength. With chicks this is not practicable, on account of their delicacy. But with them dislike of loneliness acts as a uniform motive to get back to the other chicks. Cats (or rather kittens), dogs and chicks were the subjects of the experiments. All were apparently in excellent health, save an occasional chick.

DESCRIPTION OF APPARATUS

The shape and general apparatus of the boxes which were used for the cats is shown by the accompanying drawing of box K. Unless special

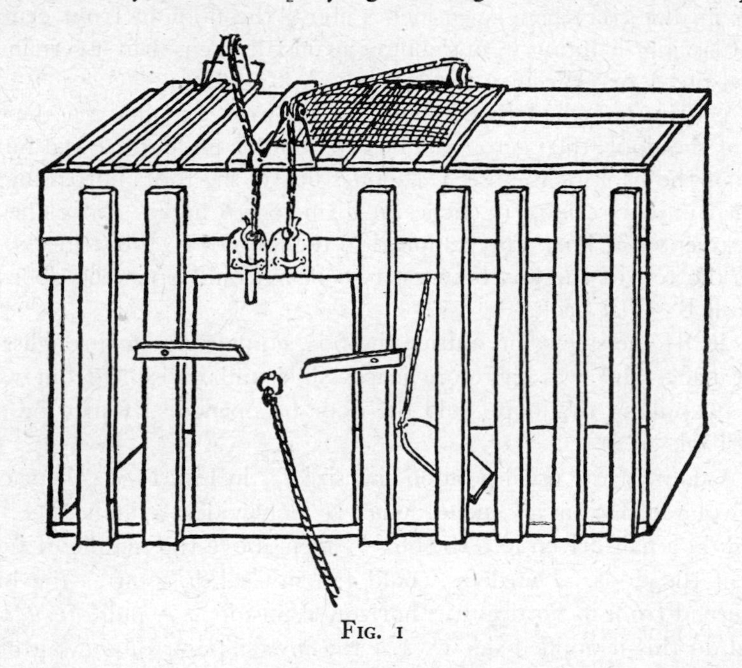

FIG. 1

figures are given, it should be understood that each box is approximately 20 inches long, by 15 broad, by 12 high. Except where mention is made to the contrary, the door was pulled open by a weight attached to a string which ran over a pulley and was fastened to the door, just as soon as the animal loosened the bolt or bar which held it. Especial care was taken not to have the widest openings between the bars at all near the lever, or wire loop, or what not, which governed the bolt on the door. For the animal instinctively attacks the large openings first, and if the mechanism which governs the opening of the door is situated near one of them, the animal's task is rendered easier. You do not then get the association-process so free from the helping hand of instinct as you do if you make the box without reference to the position of the mechanism to be set up within it. These various mechanisms are so simple that a verbal description will suffice in most cases. The facts which the reader should note are the nature of the movement which the cat had to make, the nature of the object at which the movement was directed, and the position of the object in the box. In some special cases attention will also be called to the force required. In general, however, that was very slight (20 to 100 grams if applied directly). The various boxes will be designated by capital letters.

A. A string attached to the bolt which held the door ran up over a pulley on the front edge of the box, and was tied to a wire loop (2½ inches in diameter) hanging 6 inches above the floor in front center of box. Clawing or biting it, or rubbing against it even, if in a certain way, opened the door. We may call this box A "O at front."

B. A string attached to the bolt ran up over a pulley on the front edge of the door, then across the box to another pulley screwed into the inside of the back of the box 1¼ inches below the top, and passing over it ended in a wire loop (3 inches in diameter) 6 inches above the floor in back center of box. Force applied to the loop or to the string as it ran across the top of the box between two bars would open the door. We may call B "O at back."

B1. In B1 the string ran outside the box, coming down through a hole at the back, and was therefore inaccessible and invisible from within. Only by pulling the loop could the door be opened. B1 may be called "O at back 2d."

C. A door of the usual position and size (as in Fig. 1) was kept closed by a wooden button 3½ inches long, ⅞ inch wide, ½ inch thick. This turned on a nail driven into the box ½ inch above the middle of the top edge of the door. The door would fall inward as soon as the button was turned from its vertical to a horizontal position. A pull of 125 grams would do this if applied sideways at the lowest point of the button 2¼ inches below its pivot. The cats usually clawed the button round by downward pressure on its top edge, which was 1¼ inches above the nail. Then, of course, more force was necessary. C may be called "Button."

D. The door was in the extreme right of the front. A string fastened to the bolt which held it ran up over a pulley on the top edge and back to the top edge of the back side of the box (3 inches in from the right side) and was there firmly fastened. The top of the box was of wire screening and arched over the string ¾ inch above it long its entire length. A slight pull on the string anywhere opened the door. This box was 20 × 16, but a space 7 × 16 was partitioned off at the left by a wire screen. D may be called "String."

D1 was the same box as B, but had the string fastened firmly at the back instead of running over a pulley and ending in a wire loop. We may call it "String 2d."

E. A string ran from the bolt holding the door up over a pulley and down to the floor outside the box, where it was fastened 2 inches in front of the box and 1½ inches to the left of the door (looking from the inside). By poking a paw out between the bars and pulling this string inward the door would be opened. We may call E "String outside."

EXPERIMENTS WITH CATS

In these various boxes were put cats from among the following. I give approximately their ages while under experiment.

No.		No.	
1.	*8–10 months*	7.	*3–5 months*
2.	*5–7 months*	8.	*6–6½ months*
3.	*5–11 months*	10.	*4–8 months*
4.	*5–8 months*	11.	*7–8 months*
5.	*3–5 months*	12.	*4–6 months*
6.	*3–5 months*	13.	*18–19 months*

The behavior of all but 11 and 13 was practically the same. When put into the box the cat would show evident signs of discomfort and of an impulse to escape from confinement. It tries to squeeze through any opening; it claws and bites at the bars or wire; it thrusts its paws out through any opening and claws at everything it reaches; it continues its efforts when it strikes anything loose and shaky; it may claw at things within the box. It does not pay very much attention to the food outside, but seems simply to strive instinctively to escape from confinement. The vigor with which it struggles is extraordinary. For eight or ten minutes it will claw and bite and squeeze incessantly. With 13, an old cat, and 11, an uncommonly sluggish cat, the behavior was different. They did not struggles vigorously or continually. On some occasions they did not even struggle at all. It was therefore necessary to let them out of some box a few times, feeding them each time. After they thus associate climbing out of the box with getting food, they will try to get out whenever put in. They do not, even then, struggle so vigorously or get so excited as the rest. In either case, whether the impulse to struggle be due to an instinctive reaction to confinement or to an association, it is likely to succeed in letting the cat out of the box. The cat that is clawing all over the box in her impulsive struggle will probably claw the string or loop or button so as to open the door. And gradually all the other nonsuccessful impulses will be stamped out and the particular impulse leading to the successful act will be stamped in by the resulting pleasure, until, after many trials, the cat will, when put in the box, immediately claw the button or loop in a definite way.

The starting point for the formation of any association in these cases, then, is the set of instinctive activities which are aroused when a cat feels discomfort in the box either because of confinement or a desire for food. This discomfort, plus the sense-impression of a surrounding, confining wall, expresses itself, prior to any experience, in squeezings, clawings, bitings, etc. From among these movements one is selected by success. But this is the starting point only in the case of the first box experienced. After that the cat has associated with the feeling of confinement certain impulses which have led to success more than others and are thereby strengthened. A cat that has learned to escape from A by clawing has, when put into C or G, a greater tendency to claw at things than it instinctively had at the start, and a less tendency to squeeze through holes. A very pleasant form of this decrease in instinctive impulses was noticed in the gradual cessation of howling and mewing. However, the useless instinctive impulses die out slowly, and often play an important part even after the cat has had experience with six or eight boxes. And what is important in our previous statement, namely, that the activity of an animal when first put into a new box is not directed by any appreciation of that box's character, but by certain general impulses to act, is not affected by this modification. Most of this activity is determined by heredity; some of it, by previous experience.

My use of the words instinctive and impulse may cause some misunderstanding unless explained here. Let us, throughout this book, understand by instinct any reaction which an animal makes to a situation without experience. It thus includes unconscious as well as conscious acts. Any reaction, then, to totally new phenomena, when first experienced, will be called instinctive. Any impulse then felt will be called an instinctive impulse. Instincts include whatever the nervous system of an animal, as far as inherited, is capable of. My use of the word will, I hope, everywhere make clear what fact I mean. If the reader gets the fact meant in mind it does not in the least matter whether he would himself call such a fact instinct or not. Any one who objects to the word may substitute "hocus-pocus" for it wherever it occurs. The definition here made will not be used to prove to disprove any theory, but simply as a signal for the reader to imagine a certain sort of fact.

The word impulse is used against the writer's will, but there is no better. Its meaning will probably become clear as the reader finds it in actual use, but to avoid misconception at any time I will state now that impulse means the consciousness accompanying a muscular innervation apart from that feeling of the act which comes from seeing oneself move, from feeling one's body in a different position, etc. It is the direct feeling of the doing as distinguished from the idea of the act done gained through eye, etc. For this reason I say "impulse and act" instead of simply "act." Above all, it must be borne in mind that by impulse I never mean the motive to the act. In popular speech you may say that hunger is the

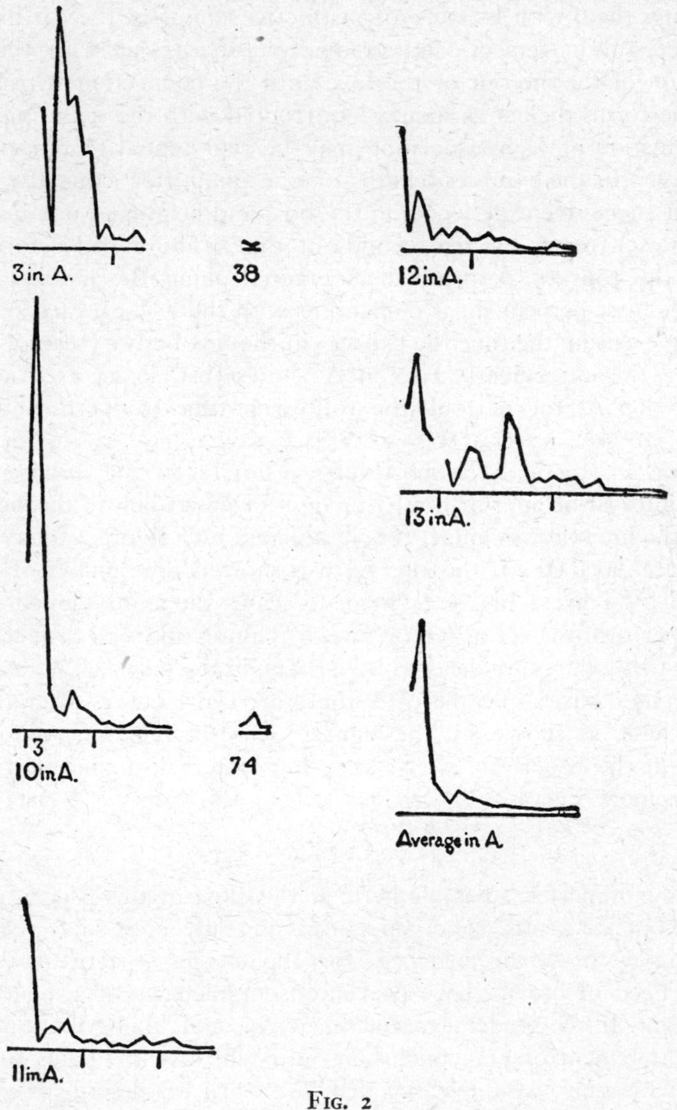

FIG. 2

impulse which makes the cat claw. That will never be the use here. The word motive will always denote that sort of consciousness. Any one who thinks that the act ought not to be thus subdivided into impulse and deed may feel free to use the word act for impulse or impulse and act throughout, if he will remember that the act in this aspect of being felt as to be done or as doing is in animals the important thing, is the thing which gets associated, while the act as done, as viewed from outside, is a secondary affair. I prefer to have a separate word, impulse, for the former, and keep the word act for the latter, which it commonly means.

Starting, then, with its store of instinctive impulses, the cat hits upon the successful movement, and gradually associates it with the sense-impression of the interior of the box until the connection is perfect, so that it performs the act as soon as confronted with the sense-impression. The formation of each association may be represented graphically by a time-curve. In these curves lengths of one millimeter along the abscissa represent successive experiences in the box, and heights of one millimeter above it each represents ten seconds of time. The curve is formed by joining the tops of perpendiculars erected along the abscissa 1 mm. apart (the first perpendicular coinciding with the y line), each perpendicular representing the time the cat was in the box before escaping. Thus, in Fig. 2 the curve marked 12 in A shows that, in 24 experiences or trials in box A, cat 12 took the following times to perform the act, 160 sec., 30 sec., 90 sec., 60, 15, 28, 20, 30, 22, 11, 15, 20, 12, 10, 14, 10, 8, 8, 5, 10, 8, 6, 6, 7. A short vertical line below the abscissa denotes that an interval of approximately 24 hours elapsed before the next trial. Where the interval was longer it is designated by a figure 2 for two days, 3 for three days, etc. If the interval was shorter, the number of hours is specified by 1 hr., 2 hrs., etc. In many cases the animal failed in some trial to perform the act in ten or fifteen minutes and was then taken out by me. Such failures are denoted by a break in the curve either at its start or along its course. In some cases there are short curves after the main ones. These, as shown by the figures beneath, represent the animal's mastery of the association after a very long interval of time, and may be called memory curves.

CONCLUSION

I do not think it is advisable here, at the close of this paper, to give a summary of its results. The paper itself is really only such a summary of the most important evidence, for the extent of territory covered and the need of brevity have prevented completeness in explanation or illustration. If the reader cares here, at the end, to have the broadest possible statement of our conclusions and will take the pains to supply the right meaning, we might say that our work has described a method, crude but promising, and has made the beginning of an exact estimate of just what associations, simple and compound, an animal can form, how quickly he forms them, and how long he retains them. It has described the method of formation, and, on the condition that our subjects were representative, has rejected reason, comparison or inference, perception of similarity, and imitation. It has denied the existence in animal consciousness of any important stock of free ideas or impulses, and so has denied that animal association is homologous with the association of human psychology. It has homologized it with a certain limited form of human association. It has proposed, as necessary steps in the evolution of human faculty, a vast increase in the number of associations, signs of which appear in the primates, and a freeing of the elements thereof into independent existence. It has given us an increased insight into various mental processes. It has convinced the writer, if not the reader, that the old speculations about what an animal could do, what it thought, and how what it thought grew into what human beings think, were a long way from the truth, and not on the road to it.

Finally, I wish to say that, although the changes proposed in the conception of mental development have been suggested somewhat fragmentarily and in various connections, that has not been done because I think them unimportant. On the contrary, I think them of the utmost importance. I believe that our best service has been to show that animal intellection is made up of a lot of specific connections, whose elements are restricted to them, and which subserve practical ends directly, and to homologize it with the intellection involved in such human associations as regulate the conduct of a man playing tennis. The fundamental phenomenon which I find presented in animal consciousness is one which can harden into inherited connections and reflexes, on the one hand, and thus connect naturally with a host of the phenomena of animal life; on the other hand, it emphasizes the fact that our mental life has grown up as a mediation between stimulus and reaction. The old view of human consciousness is that it is built up out of elementary sensations, that very minute bits of consciousness come first and gradually get built up into the complex web. It looks for the beginnings of consciousness to little feelings. This our view abolishes and declares that the progress is not from little and simple to big and complicated, but from direct connections to indirect connections in which a stock of isolated elements plays a part, is from "pure experience" or undifferentiated feelings, to discrimination, on the one hand, to generalizatons, abstractions, on the other. If, as seems probable, the primates display a vast increase of associations, and a stock of free-swimming ideas, our view gives to the line of descent a meaning which it never could have so long as the question was the vague one of more or less "intelligence." It will, I hope, when supported by an investigation of the mental life of the primates and of the period in child life when these directly practical associations become overgrown by a rapid luxuriance of free ideas, show us the real history of the origin of human faculty. It turns out apparently that a modest study of the facts of association in animals has given us a working hypothesis for a comparative psychology.

Edward Lee Thorndike: 1874-
Robert Sessions Woodworth: 1869-

THE INFLUENCE OF IMPROVEMENT IN ONE MENTAL FUNCTION UPON THE EFFICIENCY OF OTHER FUNCTIONS *

1901

GENERAL STATEMENT

THIS is the first of a number of articles reporting an inductive study of the facts suggested by the title. It will comprise a general statement of the results and of the methods of obtaining them, and a detailed account of one type of experiment.

The word "function" is used without any rigor to refer to the mental basis of such things as spelling, multiplication, delicacy in discrimination of size, force of movement, marking *a's* on a printed page, observing the word *boy* in a printed page, quickness, morality, verbal memory, chess playing, reasoning, and so forth. Function is used for all sorts of qualities in all sorts of performances from the narrowest to the widest, e.g., from attention to the word "fire" pronounced in a certain tone, to attention to all sorts of things. By the word "improvement" we shall mean those changes in the workings of functions which psychologists would commonly call by that name. Its use will be clear in each case and the psychological problem will never be different, even if the changes studied be not such as everyone would call improvements. For all purposes "change" may be used instead of "improvement" in the title. By "efficiency" we shall mean the status of a function which we use when comparing individuals or the same individual at different times, the status on which we would grade people in that function. By other function we mean any function differing in any respect whatever from the first. We shall at times use the word "function-group" to mean those cases where most psychologists would say that the same operation occurred with different data. The function attention, for instance, is really a vast group of functions.

* This publication was a pioneer contribution in the transfer of training. Portions of it are here reprinted from the *Psychological Review*, VIII (1901), 247-261 by permission of the American Psychological Association and of the authors.

Our chief method was to test the efficiency of some function or functions, then to give training in some other function or functions until a certain amount of improvement was reached, and then to test the first function or set of functions. Provided no other factors were allowed to affect the tests, the difference between the test before and the test after training measures the influence of the improvement in the trained functions on the functions tested.

It is possible to test the general question in a much neater and more convenient way by using, instead of measures of a function before and after training with another, measures of the correlation between the two functions. If improvement in one function increases the efficiency of another and there has been improvement in one, the other should be correlated with it; the individuals who have high rank in the one should have a higher rank in the other than the general average. Such a result might also be brought about by a correlation of the inborn capacities for those functions. Finding correlation between two functions thus need not mean that improvement in one has brought increased efficiency in the other. But the absence of correlation does mean the opposite. In an unpublished paper Mr. Clark Wissler, of Columbia University demonstrates the absence of any considerable correlation between the functions measured by the tests given to students there. Miss Naomi Norsworthy, of Teachers College, has shown (the data were presented in part at the Baltimore meeting; the research is not yet in print) that there is no correlation between accuracy and speed in marking on a printed page misspelled words, words containing *r* and *e*, the word *boy*, and in marking semicircles on a page of different geometrical figures.

Perhaps the most striking method of showing the influence or lack of influence of one function on another is that of testing the same function-group, using cases where there are very slightly different data. If, for instance, we test a person's ability to estimate a series of magnitudes differing each from the next very slightly, and find that he estimates one very much more accurately than its neighbors on either side, we can be sure that what he has acquired from his previous experience or from the experience of the test is not improvement in the function-group of estimating magnitudes but a lot of particular improvements in estimating particular magnitudes, improvements which may be to a large extent independent of one another.

The experiments, finally, were all on the influence of the training on efficiency, on ability as measured by a single test, not on the ability to improve. It might be that improvement in one function might fail to give in another improved ability, but succeed in giving ability to improve faster than would have occurred had the training been lacking.

The evidence given by our experiments makes the following conclusions seem probable:

It is misleading to speak of sense discrimination, attention, memory, observation, accuracy, quickness, and so forth, as multitudinous separate individual functions are referred to by any one of these words. These functions may have little in common. There is no reason to suppose that any general change occurs corresponding to the words "improvement of the attention," or "of the power of observation," or "of accuracy."

It is even misleading to speak of these functions as exercised within narrow fields as units. For example, "attention to words" or "accurate discrimination of lengths" or "observation of animals" or "quickness of visual perception" are mythological, not real entities. The words do not mean any existing fact with anything like the necessary precision for either theoretical or practical purposes, for, to take a sample case, attention to the meaning of words does not imply equal attention to their length, nor attention to certain letters in them equal attention to other letters.

The mind is, on the contrary, on its dynamic side a machine for making particular reactions to particular situations. It works in great detail, adapting itself to the special data of which he has had experience. The word *attention*, for example, can properly mean only the sum total of a lot of particular tendencies to attend to particular sorts of data, and ability to attend can properly mean only the sum total of all the particular abilities and inabilities, each of which may have an efficiency largely irrespective of the efficiencies of the rest.

Improvement in any single mental function need not improve the ability in functions commonly called by the same name. It may injure it.

Improvement in any single mental function rarely brings about equal improvement in any other function, no matter how similar, for the working of every mental function-group is conditioned by the nature of the data in each particular case.

The very slight amount of variation in the nature of the data necessary to affect the efficiency of a function-group makes it fair to infer that no change in the data, however slight, is without effect on the function. The loss in the efficiency of a function trained with certain data, as we pass to data more and more unlike the first, makes it fair to infer that there is always a point where the loss is complete, a point beyond which the influence of the training has not extended. The rapidity of this loss, that is, its amount in the case of data very similar to the data on which the function was trained, makes it fair to infer that this point is nearer than has been supposed.

The general consideration of the cases of retention or of loss of practice effect seems to make it likely that spread of practice occurs only where identical elements are concerned in the influencing and influenced function.

The particular samples of the influence of training in one function on the efficiency of other functions chosen for investigation were as follows:

1. The influence of certain special training in the estimation of magnitudes on the ability to estimate magnitudes of the same general sort, i.e., lengths or areas or weights, differing in amount, in accessory qualities (such as shape, color, form), or in both. The general method was here to test the subject's accuracy of estimating certain magnitudes, e.g., lengths of lines. He would, that is, guess the length of each. Then he would practice estimating lengths within certain limits until he attained a high degree of proficiency. Then he would once more estimate the lengths of the preliminary test series. Similarly with weights, areas, and so forth. This is apparently the sort of thing that happens in the case of a tea-taster, tobacco-buyer, wheat-taster, or carpenter, who attains high proficiency in judging magnitudes or, as we ambiguously say, in delicacy of discriminating certain sense data. It is thus like common cases of sense training in actual life.

2. The influence of training in observing words containing certain combinations of letters (e.g., s and e) or some other characteristic of the general ability to observe words. The general method here was to test the subject's speed and accuracy in picking out and marking certain letters, words containing certain letters, words of a certain length, geometric figures, misspelled words, and so forth. He then practiced picking out and marking words of some one special sort until he attained a high degree of proficiency. He was then re-tested. The training here corresponds to a fair degree with the training one has in learning to spell, to notice forms and endings in studying foreign languages, or in fact in learning to attend to any small details.

3. The influence of special training in memorizing on the general ability to memorize. Careful tests of one individual and a group test of students confirmed Professor James' result (see *Principles of Psychology*, I, 666-68). These tests will not be described in detail.

These samples were chosen because of their character as representative mental functions, because of their adaptability to quantitative interpretations, and partly because of their convenience. Such work can be done at odd times without any bulky or delicate apparatus. This rendered it possible to secure subjects. In all the experiments to be described we tested the influence of improvement in a function on other functions closely allied to it. We did not in sense-training measure the influence of training one sense on others, nor in the case of training of the attention the influence of training in noticing words on, say, the ability to do mental arithmetic or to listen to a metaphysical discourse. For common observation seemed to give a negative answer to this question, and some considerable preliminary experimentation by one of us supported such a negative. Mr. Wissler's and Miss Norsworthy's studies are apparently conclusive, and we therefore restricted ourselves to the more profitable inquiry.

A SAMPLE EXPERIMENT

There was a series of about 125 pieces of paper cut in various shapes (area test series). Of these 13 were rectangles of almost the same shape and of sizes from 20 to 90 sq. cm. (series 1), 27 others were triangles, circles, irregular figures, and so forth, within the same limits of size (series 2). A subject was given the whole series of areas and asked to write down the area in sq. cm. of each one. In front of him was a card on which three squares, 1, 25, and 100 sq. cm. in area respectively, were drawn. He was allowed to look at them as much as he pleased but not to superpose the pieces of paper on them. No other means of telling the areas were present. After being thus tested the subject was given a series of paper rectangles, from 10 to 100 sq. cm. in area and of the same shape as those of series 1. These were shuffled and the subject guessed the area of one, then looked to see what it really was and recorded his error. This was continued and the pieces of paper were kept shuffled so that he could judge their area only from their intrinsic qualities. After a certain amount of improvement had been made he was retested with the "area test series" in the same manner as before.

The function trained was that of estimating areas from 10 to 100 sq. cm. with the aid of the correction of wrong tendencies supplied by ascertaining the real area after each judgment. We will call this "function a." A certain improvement was noted. What changes in the efficiency of closely allied functions are brought about by this improvement? Does the improvement in this function cause equal improvement (1) in the function of estimating areas of similar size but different shape without the correction factor, or (2) in the function of estimating identical areas without the correction factor? (3) In any case, how much improvement was there? (4) Is there as much improvement in the function of estimating dissimilar shapes as similar? The last is the most important question.

We get the answer to (1) and part of (3) by comparing in various ways the average errors of the test areas of dissimilar shape in the before and after-tests. These are given in Table I. The average errors for the last trial of the areas in the training series similar in size to the test series are given in the same table.

The function of estimating series 2 (same sizes, different shapes) failed evidently to reach an efficiency equal to that of the function trained. Did it improve proportionately as much?

TABLE I

TEST SERIES 2

Subject	*Average error before training*	*Average error after training*	*Training series Average error at end of training*
T.	15.8	11.1	2.3
Be	28.0	5.2	3.1
Br.	22.5	18.7	3.3
J.W.	12.7	21.0	1.5 approx.
W(2)	17.0	20.0	4.0 approx.
E.B.	10.5	7.0	0.4

TABLE II

	Proportion of error after to error before training	
Subject	*Test Series 1*	*Series Training*
T	0.70	0.575
Be	0.19	0.56
Br.	0.83	0.53
J.W.	1.75	0.77 approx.
W(2)	1.18	0.83 approx.
E.B.	0.75	0.13

TABLE III

					Proportion of error after to error before training		
Subject	*Average error before training of series*	*Average error after training of series*	*Average error after training of same sizes in training series*	*Average error after training of series*	*Series 1*	*Series 2*	*Areas of training series identical with Series 1*
	1	*1*		*2*			
T	9.0	6.0	2.1	11.1	0.70	0.67	0.31
Be	21.9	6.4	1.8	5.2	0.19	0.29	0.45
Br	24.2	14.7	3.7	18.7	0.83	0.61	0.37
J.W.	7.7	8.6	1.5 app.	21.0	1.75	1.11	0.77 app.
W(2)	11.6	3.3 app.	4.0 app.	20.0	1.18	0.28 app.	0.83 app.
E.B.	9.8	4.1	0.4	7.9	0.75	0.42	0.08

This is a hard question to answer exactly, since the efficiency of function a increases with great rapidity during the first score or so of trials, so that the average error of even the first twenty estimates made is below that of the first ten, and that again is below that of the first five. Its efficiency at the start depends thus on what you take to be the start. The fact is that the first estimate of the training series is not an exercise of function a at all and that the correction influence increases up to a certain point which we cannot exactly locate. The fairest method would seem to be to measure the improvement in function a from this point and compare with that improvement the improvement in the other function or functions in question. This point is probably earlier in the series than would be supposed. If found, it would probably make the improvement in function a greater than that given in our percentages.

The proportion of average error in the after-test to that in the before-test is greater in the case of the test series than in the case of the first and last estimations of the areas of the same size in the training series, save in the case of Be. The proportions are given in Table II.

Question 2 is answered by a comparison of the average errors, before and after training, of Series 1, (identical areas) given without the correction factor. The efficiency reached in estimating without the correction factor (see column 2 of Table III) is evidently below that reached in "function a." The results there in the case of the same areas are given in column 3.

The function of estimating an area while in the frame of mind due to being engaged in estimating a limited series of areas and seeing the extent of one's error each time, is evidently independent to a large extent of the function of judging them after the fashion of the tests.

If we ask whether the function of judging without correction improved proportionately as much as function a, we have our previous difficulty about finding a starting point for a. Comparing as before the first 100 estimates with the last 100, we get the proportions in the case of the areas identical with those in the test. These are given in column 7. The proportions in the case of the test areas (series 1; same shape) are given in column 6. A comparison of columns 6 and 7 thus gives more or less of an answer to the question, and column 6 gives the answer to the further one: "How much improvement was there?"

We can answer question 4 definitely. Column 5 repeats the statement of the improvement in the case of the test areas of different shape, and by comparing column 6 with it we see that in every case save that of Be there was more improvement when the areas were similar in shape to those of the training series. This was, of course, the most important fact to be gotten at.

To sum up the results of this experiment, it has been shown that the improvement in the estimation of rectangles of a certain shape is not equaled in the case of similar estimations of areas of different shapes. The function of estimating areas is really a function-group, varying according to the data (shape, size, and so forth). It has also been shown that even after mental standards of certain limited areas have been acquired, the function of estimating with these standards constantly kept alive by noticing the real area after each judgment, is a function largely independent of the function of estimating them with the standards fully acquired by one to two thousand trials, but not constantly renewed by so noticing the real areas. Just what happened in the training was the partial formation of a number of associations. These associations were between sense impressions of particular mental attitude or frame of mind, and a number of ideas or impulses.

What was there in this to influence other functions, other processes than these particular ones? There was first of all the acquisition of certain improvements in mental standards of areas. These are of some influence in judgments of different shapes. We think, "This triangle or circle or trapezoid is about as big as such and such a rectangle, and such a rectangle would be 49 sq. cm." The influence is here by means of an idea that may form an identical element in both functions. Again, we may form a particular habit of making a discount for a tendency to a constant error discovered in training series. We may say, "I tend to judge with a minus error" and the habit of thinking of this may be beneficial in all cases. The habit of bearing this judgment in mind or of unconsciously making an addition to our first impulse is thus an identical element of both functions. This was the case with Be. That there was no influence due to a mysterious transfer of practice, to an unanalyzable property of mental functions, is evidenced by the total lack of improvement in the functions tested in the case of some individuals.

On pushing our conception of the separateness of different functions to its extreme, we were led to ask if the function of estimating one magnitude might not be independent even of the functions of estimating magnitudes differing only slightly from the first. It might be that even the judgment of areas of 40-50 sq. cm. was not a single function, but a group of similar functions, and that ability might be gained in estimating one of these areas without spreading to the others. The only limits that must necessarily be set to this subdivision would be those of the mere sensing of small differences.

If, on the contrary, judgments of nearly equal magnitudes are acts of a single function, ability gained in one should appear in the others also. The results of training should diffuse readily throughout the space covered by the function in question and the accuracy found in judgments of different magnitudes within this space should be nearly constant.

The differences found should simply be such as would be expected from chance.

The question can be put to test by comparing the actual difference between the average errors made, in judging each of neighboring magnitudes, with the probable difference as computed from the probability curve. If the actual difference greatly exceeds the probable difference, it is probably significant of some real difference in the subject's ability to judge the two magnitudes. He has somehow mastered one better than the other. No matter how this has come about, if it is a fact, then clearly ability in the one has not been transferred to the other.

Our experiments afford us a large mass of material for testing this question. In the "training series," we have a considerable number (10 to 40) of judgments of each of a lot of magnitudes differing from each other by slight amounts. We have computed the accuracy of the judgment of each magnitude (as measured by the error of mean square), and then compared the accuracy for each with that for the adjacent magnitudes. We find many instances in which the difference between the errors for adjacent magnitudes is largely in excess of the probable difference. And the number of such instances greatly exceeds what can be expected from chance.

These great differences between the errors of adjacent magnitudes are strikingly seen in the curves on Figure 3. The ordinates of these curves represent the mean square error of judgments of areas of 10 to 100 square centimeters, and for 3 individuals. The dots above and below each point of the curve give the limits of error of that value, as determined by the formula $\frac{u}{\sqrt{2n}}$ in which u is the error of mean square, and n the number of cases. These limits are such that the odds are about 2 to 1 more exactly 683 to 317, that the true value lies inside them. The dots thus furnish a measure of the reliability of the curve at every point. These curves are all irregular, with sudden risings and fallings that greatly obscure their general course. Psychologists are familiar of old with irregularities of this kind, and are wont to regard them as effects of chance, and so to smooth out the curve. But as we find more irregularity than can reasonably be attributed to chance, we conclude that our curves at least should not be smoothed out, and that the sudden jumps, or some of them, signify real differences in the person's ability.

If, for example, we examine Figure 1, we notice a number of sudden jumps, or points at which the errors in judging adjacent magnitudes differed considerably from each other. The most significant of these jumps are at 10-11, 36-37, 41-42, 65-66, 66-67, 83-84, and 98-99 sq. cm. The question is whether such a jump as that at 41-42 indicates greater ability to judge 42 sq cm., or whether the observed difference is simply due to chance and the relatively few cases (here 10 for each area). A vague appeal to chance should not be allowed, in view of the possibility of calculating the odds in favor of each side of the question. This can be done by a fairly simple method. We can consider two adjacent areas as practically equal, so far as concerns Weber's law or any similar law.

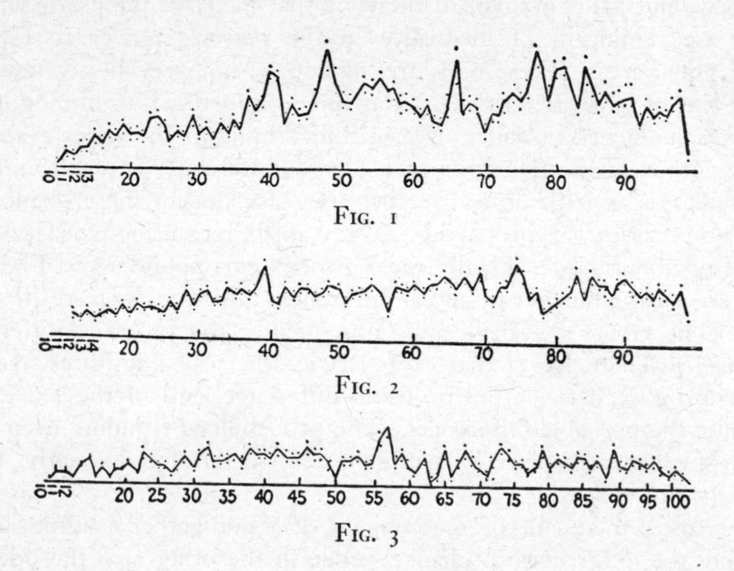

FIG. 1

FIG. 2

FIG. 3

The average errors found for the two would thus be practically two determinations of the same quantity, and should differ only as two determinations of the same quantity may probably differ.

We wish then, to compare the actual difference between the errors for 41 and 42 sq. cm. with the probable difference. The error—we use through the "error of mean square," and the measure of reliability based on it—this error is here 6.2 and 3.1 sq. cm. respectively. The actual difference is 3.1 sq. cm. To find the probable difference, we first find the limits of error or reliability of each determination, as described above, and then find the square root of the sums of the squares of these limits of error. The limits are here 1.0 and 0.7 and the probable difference 1.2 sq. cm. The actual difference is 2.6 times the probable. In this whole series we find 6 other instances in which the actual difference is over 2 times the probable. From the probability integral we find that, in the long run, 46 actual differences to the thousand would exceed twice the probable. The question is, therefore, what is the probability of finding as many as 7 such differences in a series of 90? This is a form of the familiar problem in probabilities; to find the chances that an event whose probability is p shall occur at least r times out of a possible n. The solution depends on an application of the binomial theorem, and may be evaluated by means of logarithms. In the present case, the value found is 0.1209 or about ⅛.

Instead of vaguely saying that the large jumps seen in the curves may be due to chance, we are now able to state that the odds are 7 to 1 against this view, and 7 to 1 in favor of the view that the large jumps, or some of them, are significant of inequality in the person's power to estimate nearly equal areas. These odds are, of course, not very heavy from the standpoint of scientific criticism. But they are fortified by finding, as we do, the same general balance of probability in all of the series examined. In one other series, the number of large differences is small, and the probability is as large as 0.2938 that they are due to mere chance. In three other series, this probability is very small, measuring 0.0025, 0.0025, 0.0028 or about 1-400. Finally, in the series corresponding to Figure 3, there are a large number of actual differences which far exceed the probable. (The errors are small, and consequently the probable differences are small.) There are 31 that exceed twice the probable difference, and of these 9 exceed twice the probable difference, and of these 9 exceed 3.5 times the probable differences. The probability of finding even these 9 is so small that six-place logarithms cannot determine it exactly, but it is less than 0.000001.

In 4 cases, then, out of 6 examined, it is altogether inadmissible to attribute the differences to chance, while in the other two the odds are against doing so. The probability that the differences in all the series are due to chance is, of course, many times smaller. The differences are therefore not chance, but significant; the ability to judge one magnitude is sometimes demonstrably better than the ability to judge the next magnitude; one function is better developed than its neighbor. The functions of judging nearly equal magnitudes are, sometimes at least, largely separate and independent. A high degree of ability in one sometimes coexists with a low degree of ability in the others.

Edward Lee Thorndike: 1874-

MEASUREMENT OF TWINS *

1905

THE following is a summary of the results of a study of the comparative importance of original nature and training in the case of fifty pairs of twins. A detailed account of the investigation will be published shortly.

THE RESEMBLANCES OF TWINS AND SIBLINGS

From the information at hand, which is not so satisfactory as information I hope to obtain during the next few years, the resemblance of twins in mental traits is roughly twice that of ordinary siblings; according to the actual figures of my measurements of siblings, more than twice. I have reason, however, to believe that the correlation coefficients obtained for siblings are affected by constant errors which make them too low; namely, the selection of mentally alike pairs by the conditions of the methods of obtaining siblings and the absence of suitable data to make sufficient correction for attenuation. Table I gives the facts.

I use the words "resemblance of" and "likeness of" as synonyms for "coefficients of correlation between." A resemblance of .50 means, a Pearson correlation coefficient of .50. I use the terms A test, word test, misspelled word test, opposites test, addition and multiplication to mean the tests, or at times the abilities measured by the tests, to describe which

TABLE I

THE RESEMBLANCES OF TWINS AND SIBLINGS COMPARED

Ability	*Coefficients of Correlation* *Twins*	*Siblings*
"A" test	.69	.32
Word test	.71	.29
Opposites test	.90	.30

* From the *Journal of Philosophy, Psychology and Scientific Method*, II (1905), 547-553. Reprinted by permission of the publishers and the author. This study represents the first joint application of two new techniques, correlation and mental tests, to the problem of twin resemblance.

would take too much space. I give for siblings the obtained results. Since the correction for attenuation had to be made in an imperfect form, the true resemblances are probably somewhat higher, but not over .40.

THE RESEMBLANCES OF YOUNG AND OF OLD TWINS

The older twins show no closer resemblance than the younger twins, and the chances are surely four to one that with an infinite number of twins tested the 12-14 year olds would not show a resemblance .15 greater than the 9-11 year olds. The facts are given in Table II.

TABLE II

THE RESEMBLANCES OF YOUNG AND OLD TWINS COMPARED

	In Corrected Coefficients		*In Raw Coefficients*	
	Twins 9-11	*Twins 12-14*	*Twins 9-11*	*Twins 12-14*
1) "A" test	.66	.73	.58	.67
2) Word test	.81	.62	.62	.49
3) Misspelled word test	.76	.74	.76	.74
4) Addition	.90	.54	.83	.46
5) Multiplication	.91	.69	.81	.53
6) Opposites	.96	.88	.79	.78
Marks in 1), 2) and 3) combined			.71	.69
Marks in 4), 5) and 6) combined			.90	.75
Averages	.83	.70	.75	.64

THE RESEMBLANCES IN TRAITS LITTLE AND IN TRAITS MUCH SUBJECT TO TRAINING

The variations in the closeness of resemblance of the twins in the different traits show little, and possibly no, direct correlation with the amount of opportunity for environmental influences. The traits most subject to training (addition and multiplication) do show closer resemblances than the traits moderately subject to training (the "A" test and word test); but on the other hand show less close resemblances than the traits moderately subject to training (the misspelled word test and opposites test). The hypothesis that the true resemblance varies in amount inversely with the amount of opportunity for environmental influence would not be irreconcilable with the facts, and the hypothesis that the differences between the different traits are due to chance (including in that term the variable errors of the measurements and the possibility of the unequal inheritance of different traits) is the most probable of all. The difference between the traits most subject and those least subject to training is no greater than the median difference between any one trait of the six and any other. Surely there is no evidence here of any large contribution from similarity of training to similarity of achievement. The facts are given in Table III.

THE RESEMBLANCES IN MENTAL TRAITS COMPARED WITH THE RESEMBLANCES IN PHYSICAL TRAITS

It is highly probable from the facts so far given that the similarity of twins in ancestry and conditions of conception and birth accounts for almost all of their similarity in mental achievement,—that only a small fraction of it can be attributed to similarity in training. On general principles it is also highly probable that similarity of ancestry and conditions of conception will produce equal similarity in original physical nature and in original mental nature. Certain resemblances in original physical nature are in all probability neither increased nor decreased by such similarities and differences of home training as act upon twins and non-related children, respectively, within a group such as ours; e.g., resemblances in cephalic index, ratio of height sitting to total height, eye color and hair color. Other resemblances in original physical nature are increased and decreased slightly and perhaps not at all; e.g., circumference of head, length of head, width of head, length of forearm and length of finger joints.

If then, the resemblances of twins were almost entirely due to original nature, we should expect them to be only slightly in excess of the resemblances in physical traits. The existence of the latter as a fact may properly be taken as a partial verification of the former as a general hypothesis. The evidence of its existence is given in Table IV.

TABLE III

THE RESEMBLANCES OF TWINS IN TRAITS LITTLE AND IN TRAITS MUCH SUBJECT TO TRAINING

	Coefficients of Correlation	*Averages*
1) "A" test	.69	.70
2) Word test	.71	
3) Misspelled word test	.80	.85
6) Opposites	.90	
4) Addition	.75	.795
5) Multiplication	.84	
Marks in 1), 2) and 3) combined	.70 (raw)	
Marks in 4), 5) and 6) combined	.82 (raw)	

SUMMARY AND CRITICISM

These facts prove that among one hundred twins living and attending school in New York City in 1903-4, the mental resemblances of a twin pair are about twice as great as those of a pair of siblings similarly chosen, are as great or nearly as great in the case of the younger as of the older half of the group, are as great or nearly as great in the case of the "A," word, misspelled word and opposites test as in the case of addition and multiplication, and are only slightly, if at all, greater than resemblances in physical traits which could have been caused, in some cases, only by original nature.

The facts are easily, simply and completely explained by one simple hypothesis: namely, that the natures of the germ-cells—the conditions of conception—cause whatever similarities and differences exist in the original natures of men, that these conditions influence body and mind equally, and that in life the differences in modification of body and mind produced by such differences as obtain between the environments of present-day New York City public school children are slight.

Certain other hypotheses seem possible at first sight, but become involved in great difficulties when one tries to explain all the facts by any of them. These difficulties I will point out briefly.

TABLE IV

THE RESEMBLANCES OF TWINS IN MENTAL AND IN PHYSICAL TRAITS

In Mental Traits		*In Physical Traits*	
1. "A" test	.69	11. Cephalic index	.76
2. Word test	.71	12. Ht. sitting/ht.	.76
3. Misspelled	.80	13. Height	.78
4. Addition	.75	14. Height sitting	.83
5. Multiplication	.84	15. Circ. of head	.75
6. Opposites	.90	16. Width of head	.86
7. Combined mark in 1-3	.70	17. Arm length	.72
8. Combined mark in 4-6	.82	18. Finger length	.71

7, 8 and 12-15 are raw correlations and the correction of attenuation might raise them by .01 or .02

Median of 1-6	.78	Average of	11-12	.76 (possibly .77)
		"	13-18	.77 (possibly .78 or .79)
Average of 1-6	.78	Median of	13-18	.77 (possibly .78 or .79)
		"	11-18	.76 (possibly .77)
Average of 7-8	.76 (Possibly .80)	Average of	11-18	.76 (possibly .77)

It may be said that all that has been proved of the twins is that they are alike in general mental maturity (o.e., in the points of development which they have reached).

Traits like those tested are of course influenced by maturity directly and indirectly through the relation between maturity and advance in school and the relation between the latter and certain of the traits tested. But maturity is by no means the total cause of efficiency in these traits. Nor is it a cause comparable in amount of influence with individual differences apart from maturity. Nor is there any evidence that there is any greater resemblance of twins in maturity than in other factors, such as eyesight. If maturity were the total cause of efficiency in the six traits measured, these traits should in the same individual show perfect correlation with each other. They do not, nor, indeed enough correlation to assign maturity a very important place as a contributory cause. If resemblance in maturity were the cause of the resemblances found, these should be largest in the traits most subject to maturity. The opposite is the case.

It may be said that all that has been proved of the twins is that the environmental conditions from 9 to 14 years count little; that the similarities in environment in utero and during childhood are left as possible causes of the resemblances found; and that these are the real causes. But that the conditions in utero are the cause of the resemblances of related individuals is disproved by the fact that paternal is as great as maternal resemblance in the case of those traits where parents and offspring have been compared; and that similarities in environment from 0 to 9 years should produce a far greater effect on the children's abilities to add, multiply, mark misspelled words and write opposites than do similarities in environment from 9 to 15 is a notion utterly devoid of probability.

It is equally difficult to accept original nature as a cause of a moderate amount of the resemblance found and to explain the rest as due to training. Suppose, for instance, that some one assumes that the force of the germ-natures,—of the conditions of conception, is sufficient to produce a resemblance of .20 in siblings and .40 in twins in mental traits. He must be then willing to believe that the likeness in training of a twin pair is enough greater than the likeness in training of a sibling pair, two or three years apart in age, to make the .40 rise to .80, whereas the .20 rises only to .40 or less. He must also be willing to believe either that inborn mental make-up is inherited by a totally different law from that regulating inborn physical make-up or else that the similarities in training of twins will raise .40 to .80 in physical traits such as cephalic index, and that the similarities in training of siblings will raise the .20 only to .40 or .50. He must also place the bulk of influence of this training previous to the tenth year and assume that it is of such a generalized sort as would raise the resemblances in marking A's or words containing r and e as much as that in multiplication.

Doubtless we all feel a repugnance to assigning so little efficacy to environmental forces as the facts of this study seem to demand; but common opinion also feels a repugnance to believing that the mental resemblances of twins, however caused, are as great as the physical resemblances. Yet they are. I can not here discuss the general facts and detailed studies which bear upon the question of the amount of influence of such likenesses and differences in environment as existed in the case of these twins.

I shall also spend but little time in comments upon the application of the facts so far presented to theories of education and human action and to the practical problems of social control. The inferences with respect to the enormous importance of original nature in determining the behavior and achievements of any man in comparison with his fellows of the same period of civilization and conditions of life are obvious. All theories of human life must accept as a first principle the fact that human beings at birth differ enormously in mental capacities and that these differences are largely due to similar differences in their ancestry. All attempts to change human nature must accept as their most important condition the limits set by original nature to each individual.

We must be careful, however, not to confuse two totally different things: (1) the power of the environment,—for instance, of schools, laws, books and social ideals,—to produce differences in the relative achievements of men, and (2) the power of the environment to produce differences in absolute achievement. It has been shown that the relative differences in certain mental traits which were found in these one hundred children are due almost entirely to differences in ancestry, not in training; but this does not in the least deny that better methods of training might improve all their achievements fifty per cent, or that the absence of training, say in spelling and arithmetic, might decrease the corresponding achievements to zero. Similarly, the fact that Mr. Rockefeller has amassed one of the great fortunes of the age is undoubtedly due almost exclusively to his original capacity, not to circumstances; but this does not deny that it is almost exclusively circumstances which make the average wealth of men to-day greater than it was a thousand years ago or that future changes in the environment might, without any change in capacity make nine men out of ten the owners of automobiles, racehorses, tall hats and the other blessings of wealth.

The argument has been limited entirely to the causes which make one person differ from another in mental achievements under the same general conditions of life at the beginning of the twentieth century in New York

City as pupils in its school system. If the resemblance of twins had been measured in the case of a group made up partly of New York City school children and partly of children of equal capacity brought up in the wilds of Africa, the variability of the group in addition and multiplication would have increased and the correlation coefficients would rise. They would then measure the influence of original nature plus the now much increased influence of the environment.

The relative impotence of such similarities of home training as existed in our fifty pairs of twins to create similarities of achievement does, however, make one suspect that the magnitude of the influence of the training given by schools, periods of civilization and the like has been exaggerated. For other reasons, also, I imagine this to be the case, but to prove or disprove it, one would need data quite different from the records of these hundred twins.

It is, then, folly to conclude that the inheritance of mental capacities from immediate ancestry implies the futility of education and social control in general—the wisdom of fatalism and laissez faire. Such studies as this merely prove the existence of and measure one determinant of human intellect and character and demonstrate that the influences of the environment are differential, the product varying not only in accord with the environmental force itself, but also in accord with the original nature upon which it operates. We may even expect that education will be doubly effective, once society recognizes the advantage from or need of wise investment. If it is true, for example, that the Negro is by nature unintellectual and joyous, this does not imply that he may not be made more intelligent by wiser training or misanthropic and ugly-tempered by the treatment he now receives. It does mean that we should be stupid to expect the same results from him that we should from an especially intellectual race like the Jews, and he will stand with equanimity a degree of disdain which a Celt would requite with dynamite and arson.

To the real work of man for man,—the increase of achievement through the improvement of the environment,—the influence of heredity offers no barrier. But to the popular demands from education and social reforms it does. For the common man does not much appreciate absolute happiness or absolute betterment. He does not rejoice that he and his children are healthier, happier and more supplied with noble pleasures than were his ancestors of a thousand years ago. His complaint is that he is not so well off as some of those about him; his pride is that he is above the common herd. The common man demands relative superiority,—to be above those of his own time and locality. If his son leads the community, he does not mind his real stupidity; to be the handsomest girl in the county is beauty enough. Social discontent comes from the knowledge or fancy that one is below others in welfare. The effort of children in school, of men in labor and of women in the home is, except as guided by the wise instincts of nature or more rarely by the wisdom of abstract thought, to rise above some one who seems higher. Thus the prizes which most men really seek are, after all, in large measure given or withheld by original nature. In the actual race of life, which is not to get ahead, but to get ahead of somebody, the chief determining factor is heredity.

Alfred Binet: 1857-1911
Theophile Simon: 1873-

UPON THE NECESSITY OF ESTABLISHING A SCIENTIFIC DIAGNOSIS OF INFERIOR STATES OF INTELLIGENCE *

1905

We here present the first rough sketch of a work which was directly inspired by the desire to serve the interesting cause of the education of subnormals.

In October, 1904, the Minister of Public Instruction named a commission which was charged with the study of measures to be taken for insuring the benefits of instruction to defective children. After a number of sittings, this commission regulated all that pertained to the type of establishment to be created, the conditions of admission into the school, the teaching force, and the pedagogical methods to be employed. They decided that no child suspected of retardation should be eliminated from the ordinary school and admitted into a special class, without first being subjected to a pedagogical and medical examination from which it could be certified that because of the state of his intelligence, he was unable to profit, in an average measure, from the instruction given in the ordinary schools.

But how the examination of each child should be made, what methods should be followed, what observations taken, what questions asked, what tests devised, how the child should be compared with normal children, the commission felt under no obligation to decide. It was formed to do a work of administration, not a work of science.

It has seemed to us extremely useful to furnish a guide for future Commissions' examination. Such Commissions should understand from the beginning how to get their bearings. It must be made impossible for those who belong to the Commission to fall into the habit of making haphazard decisions according to impressions which are subjective, and consequently uncontrolled. Such impressions are sometimes good, some-

* This article first appeared in *L'Année Psychologique*, XI (1905), 163-190. The present text is from a translation by Elizabeth S. Kite, published by Williams and Wilkins Co., Baltimore, 1916, under the title *The Development of Intelligence.* Reprinted by permission of Dr. Henry H. Goddard.

times bad, and have at all times too much the nature of the arbitrary, of caprice, of indifference. Such a condition is quite unfortunate because the interests of the child demand a more careful method. To be a member of a special class can never be a mark of distinction, and such as do not merit it, must be spared the record. Some errors are excusable in the beginning, but if they become too frequent, they may ruin the reputation of these new institutions. Furthermore, in principle, we are convinced, and we shall not cease to repeat, that the precision and exactness of science should be introduced into our practice whenever possible, and in the great majority of cases it is possible.

The problem which we have to solve presents many difficulties both theoretical and practical. It is a hackneyed remark that the definitions, thus far proposed, for the different states of subnormal intelligence, lack precision. These inferior states are indefinite in number, being composed of a series of degrees which mount from the lowest depths of idiocy, to a condition easily confounded with normal intelligence. Alienists have frequently come to an agreement concerning the terminology to be employed for designating the difference of these degrees; at least, in spite of certain individual divergence of ideas to be found in all questions, there has been an agreement to accept *idiot* as applied to the lowest state, *imbecile* to the intermediate, and *moron (débile)* to the state nearest normality. Still among the numerous alienists, under this common and apparently precise terminology, different ideas are concealed, variable and at the same time confused. The distinction between idiot, imbecile, and moron is not understood in the same way by all practitioners. We have abundant proof of this in the strikingly divergent medical diagnoses made only a few days apart by different alienists upon the same patient.

Dr. Blin, physician of the Vaucluse Asylum, recently drew the attention of his fellow physicians to these regrettable contradictions. He states that the children who are sent to the colony come provided with several dissimilar certificates. "One child, called imbecile in the first certificate, is marked idiot in the second, feeble-minded (débile) in the third, and degenerate in the fourth." M. Damaye, former house surgeon of Dr. Blin, adds this observation: "One would have only to look through several folders of records belonging to children of the colony, in order to collect almost the same number of different diagnoses." Perhaps this last affirmation is a little exaggerated, but a statistical study would show the exact truth on this point.

We cannot sufficiently deplore the consequence of this state of uncertainty recognized today by all alienists. The simple fact, that specialists do not agree in the use of the technical terms of their science, throws suspicion upon their diagnoses, and prevents all work of comparison. We ourselves have made similar observations. In synthesizing the diagnoses made by Mr. Bourneville upon patients leaving the Bicetre, we found that in the space of four years only two feeble-minded individuals have left his institution although during that time the Bureau of Admission has sent him more than thirty. Nothing could show more clearly than this change of label, the confusion of our nomenclature.

What importance can be attached to public statistics of different countries concerning the percentage of backward children if the definition for backward children is not the same in all countries? How will it be possible to keep a record of the intelligence of pupils who are treated and instructed in a school, if the terms applied to them, feeble-minded, retarded, imbecile, idiot, vary in meaning according to the doctor who examines them? The absence of a common measure prevents comparison of statistics, and makes one lose all interest in investigations which may have been very laborious. But a still more serious fact is that, because of lack of methods, it is impossible to solve those essential questions concerning the afflicted, whose solution presents the greatest interest; for example, the real results gained by the treatment of inferior states of intelligence by doctor and educator; the educative value of one pedagogical method compared with another; the degree of curability of incomplete idiocy, etc. It is not by means of *a priori* reasonings, of vague considerations, of oratorical displays, that these questions can be solved; but by minute investigation, entering into the details of fact, and considering the effects of the treatment for each particular child. There is but one means of knowing if a child, who has passed six years in a hospital or in a special class, has profited from that stay, and to what degree he has profited; and that is to compare his certificate of entrance with his certificate of dismissal, and by that means ascertain if he shows a special amelioration of his condition beyond that which might be credited simply to the considerations of growth. But experience has shown how imprudent it would be to place confidence in this comparison, when the two certificates come from different doctors, who do not judge in exactly the same way, or who use different words to characterize the mental status of patients.

It might happen that a child, who had really improved in school, had received in the beginning the diagnosis of moron (débile), and on leaving, the prejudicial diagnosis of imbecile, simply because the second doctor spoke a different language from the first. If one took these certificates literally, this case would be considered a failure. On the contrary, the appearance of amelioration would be produced if the physician who delivered the certificate of dismissal had the habit of using higher terms than the one who furnished the certificate of entrance. One can even go further. The errors which we note, do not necessarily emanate from the disagreement of different physicians. It would suffice for the same physician to deliver the two certificates, if he did not employ for each one the same criterion; and it would certainly be possible for him to vary unconsciously after an interval of several years if he had nothing to guide him but his own subjective impressions. Might not the same thing also happen if his good faith as a physician happened to be in conflict with the interests of the institution which he directed? Might he not unconsciously as it were, have a tendency to lower the mental status of patients on entering and to raise it on dismissal, in order to emphasize the advantages of the methods which he had applied? We are not incriminating anyone, but simply calling attention to methods actually in use which, by their lack of precision, favor the involuntary illusions of physicians and relatives, in a word, of all those who, having an interest in the amelioration of the condition of the defective child, would have a tendency to confound their desires with the reality.

Perhaps someone will raise an objection and say this uncertainty has no special application to diagnosis of the degrees of mental debility; it is also to be found in mental pathology and, in a general way, in the diagnosis of all maladies; it is the result of the empirical nature which is characteristic of clinical studies. It might be added, that, if anyone took the trouble to make a statistical study of the divergence in the diagnosis of different physicians upon the same patient, it would probably be found that the percentage of disagreement is very great in all branches of medicine.

We believe it worth while to examine their objection because it permits us to enter more deeply into the analysis of the question. The disagreements of practitioners might come from three very different classes of causes:

1. Ignorance, that is, the lack of aptitude of certain physicians. This is an individual failure, for which abstract science is not responsible. It is certain that, even when the symptoms of a disease are absolutely clear, such a physician might fail to recognize them through incapacity. There are many accountants who make mistakes in calculation, but these errors do not discredit mathematics. A physician might not be able to recognize a "p.g." if he is himself a "p.g."

2. The variable meaning of terms. Since the same expression has a different sense according to the person who uses it, it is possible that the disagreement of diagnosis may be simply a disagreement of words, due to the use of different nomenclature.

3. Lack of precision in the description of the symptoms which reveal or which constitute a certain particular malady; different physicians do not examine the same patient in the same manner and do not give the symptoms the same importance; or, it may be they make no effort to

find out the precise symptoms, and no effort to analyze carefully in order to distinguish and interpret them.

Of these three kinds of error, which is the one that actually appears in the diagnosis of inferior states of intelligence? Let us set aside the first. There remain the faults of nomenclature, and the insufficiency of methods of examination.

The general belief seems to be that the confusion arises wholly from an absence of a uniform nomenclature. There is some truth in this opinion. It can be proved by a comparison of terms used by authors belonging to the different countries. Even in France the terms differ somewhat according to the physician, the order of the admitted subdivisions not being rigorously followed. The classification of Magnan is not that of Voisin, and his, in turn, differs from that of Bourneville. Undoubtedly it would be a good work to bring about a unification of this nomenclature as has been done for the standard of measurements and for electric units. But this reform in itself is not sufficient and we are very sure that they deceive themselves who think that at bottom this is only a question of terminology. It is very much more serious. We find physicians who, though using the same terminology, constantly disagree in their diagnosis of the same child. The examples cited from M. Blin prove this. There the doctors had recourse to the terminology of Morel, who classifies those of inferior intelligence as idiots, imbeciles and *débiles*. Notwithstanding this use of the same terms, they do not agree in the manner of applying them. Each one according to his own fancy, fixes the boundary line separating these states. It is in regard to the facts that the doctors disagree.

In looking closely one can see that the confusion comes principally from a fault in the method of examination. When an alienist finds himself in the presence of a child of inferior intelligence, he does not examine him by bringing out each one of the symptoms which the child manifests and by interpreting all symptoms and classifying them; he contents himself with taking a subjective impression, an impression as a whole, of his subject, and of making his diagnosis by instinct. We do not think that we are going too far in saying that at the present time very few physicians would be able to cite with absolute precision the objective and invariable sign, or signs, by which they distinguish the degrees of inferior mentality.

Alfred Binet: 1857-1911
Theophile Simon: 1873-

THE DEVELOPMENT OF THE BINET-SIMON SCALE *

1905-1908

NEW METHODS FOR THE DIAGNOSIS OF THE INTELLECTUAL LEVEL OF SUBNORMALS [1]

Our purpose is to be able to measure the intellectual capacity of a child who is brought to us in order to know whether he is normal or retarded. We should therefore, study his condition at the time and that only. We have nothing to do either with his past history or with his future; consequently we shall neglect his etiology, and we shall make no attempt to distinguish between acquired and congenital idiocy; for a stronger reason we shall set aside all consideration of pathological anatomy which might explain his intellectual deficiency. So much for his past. As to that which concerns his future, we shall exercise the same abstinence; we do not attempt to establish or prepare a prognosis and we leave unanswered the question of whether this retardation is curable, or even improvable. We shall limit ourselves to ascertaining the truth in regard to his present mental state.

Furthermore, in the definition of this state, we should make some restrictions. Most subnormal children, especially those in the schools, are habitually grouped in two categories, those of backward intelligence, and those who are unstable. This latter class, which certain alienists call moral imbeciles, do not necessarily manifest inferiority of intelligence; they are turbulent, vicious, rebellious to all discipline; they lack sequence of ideas, and probably power of attention. It is a matter of great delicacy

* The material here reprinted is chosen from two of Binet and Simon's articles, one dated 1905, one 1908, which were translated by Elizabeth S. Fite and published in 1916 by the Training School at Vineland, N. J., under the title, *The Development of Intelligence in Children.* We are indebted to Dr. Henry H. Goddard for permission to republish sections of these translations. Successive sections are reprinted from pages 37-45, 182-183, 184, 237-239, 261-265, 272-273, of *The Development of Intelligence.* The title and dates of the article from which each section is chosen are given in a footnote to the section. Needless to say, these passages give only an abbreviated account of the development of the first test of intelligence.

[1] From *L'Année Psychologique,* XI (1905), 191-244.

to make the distinction between children who are unstable, and those who have rebellious dispositions. Elsewhere we have insisted upon the necessity of instructors not treating as unstable, that is as pathological cases, those children whose character is not sympathetic with their own. It would necessitate a long study, and probably a very difficult one, to establish the distinctive signs which separate the unstable from the undisciplined. For the present we shall not take up this study. We shall set the unstable aside, and shall consider only that which bears upon those who are backward in intelligence.

This is not, however, to be the only limitation of our subject because backward states of intelligence present several different types. There is the insane type—or the type of intellectual decay—which consists in a progressive loss of former acquired intelligence. Many epileptics, who suffer from frequent attacks, progress toward insanity. It would be possible and probably very important, to be able to make the distinction between those with decaying intelligence on the one hand, and those of inferior intelligence on the other. But as we have determined to limit on the side also, the domain of our study, we shall rigorously exclude all forms of insanity and decay. Moreover we believe that these are rarely present in the schools, and need not be taken into consideration in the operation of new classes for subnormals.

Another distinction is made between those of inferior intelligence and degenerates. The latter are subjects in whom occur clearly defined, episodical phenomena, such as impulsions, obsessions, deliriums. We shall eliminate the degenerates as well as the insane.

Lastly, we should say a word upon our manner of studying those whom alienists call idiots but whom we here call of inferior intelligence. The exact nature of this inferiority is not known; and today without other proof, one very prudently refuses to liken this state to that of an arrest of normal development. It certainly seems that the intelligence of these beings has undergone a certain arrest; but it does not follow that the disproportion between the degree of intelligence and the age is the only characteristic of their condition. There is also in many cases, most probably a deviation in the development, a perversion. The idiot of fifteen years, who, like a baby of three, is making his first verbal attempts, can not be completely likened to a three-year old child, because the latter is normal, but the idiot is not. There exists therefore between them, necessarily, differences either apparent or hidden. The careful study of idiots shows, among some of them at least, that whereas certain faculties are almost wanting, others are better developed. They have therefore certain aptitudes. Some have a good auditory or musical memory, and a whole repertoire of songs; others have mechanical ability. If all were carefully examined, many examples of these partial aptitudes would probably be found.

Our purpose is in no wise to study, analyze, or set forth the aptitudes of those of inferior intelligence. That will be the object of a later work. Here we shall limit ourselves to the measuring of their general intelligence. We shall determine their intellectual level, and, in order the better to appreciate this level, we shall compare it with that of normal children of the same age or of an analogous level. The reservations previously made as to the true conception of arrested development, will not prevent our finding great advantage in a methodical comparison between those of inferior and those of normal intelligence.

To what method should we have recourse in making our diagnosis of the intellectual level? No one method exists, but there are a number of different ones which should be used cumulatively, because the question is a very difficult one to solve, and demands rather a collaboration of methods. It is important that the practitioner be equipped in such a manner that he shall use, only as accessory, the information given by the parents of the child, so that he may always be able to verify this information, or, when necessary, dispense with it. In actual practice quite the opposite occurs. When the child is taken to the clinic the physician listens a great deal to the parents and questions the child very little, in fact scarcely looks at him, allowing himself to be influenced by a very strong presumption that the child is intellectually inferior. If, by a chance not likely to occur, but which would be most interesting some time to bring about, the physician were submitted to the test of selecting the subnormals from a mixed group of children, he would certainly find himself in the midst of grave difficulties, and would commit many errors especially in cases of slight defect.

The organization of methods is especially important because, as soon as the schools for subnormals are in operation, one must be on his guard against the attitude of the parents. Their sincerity will be worth very little when it is in conflict with their interests. If the parents wish the child to remain in the regular school, they will not be silent concerning his intelligence. "My child understands everything," they will say, and they will be very careful not to give any significant information in regard to him. If, on the contrary, they wish him to be admitted into an institution where gratuitous board and lodging are furnished, they will change completely. They will be capable even of teaching him how to simulate mental debility. One should, therefore, be on his guard against all possible frauds.

In order to recognize the inferior states of intelligence we believe that three different methods should be employed. We have arrived at this synthetic view only after many years of research, but we are now certain that each of these methods renders some service. These methods are:

1. *The medical method*, which aims to appreciate the anatomical, physiological, and pathological signs of inferior intelligence.

2. *The pedagogical method*, which aims to judge of the intelligence according to the sum of acquired knowledge.

3. *The psychological method*, which makes direct observations and measurements of the degree of intelligence.

From what has gone before it is easy to see the value of each of these methods. The medical method is indirect because it conjectures the mental from the physical. The pedagogical method is more direct; but the psychological is the most direct of all because it aims to measure the state of the intelligence as it is at the present moment. It does this by experiments which oblige the subject to make an effort which shows his capability in the way of comprehension, judgment, reasoning, and invention.

The Psychological Method

The fundamental idea of this method is the establishment of what we shall call a measuring scale of intelligence. This scale is composed of a series of tests of increasing difficulty, starting from the lowest intellectual level that can be observed, and ending with that of average normal intelligence. Each group in the series corresponds to a different mental level.

This scale properly speaking does not permit the measure of the intelligence, because intellectual qualities are not superposable, and therefore cannot be measured as linear surfaces are measured, but are on the contrary, a classification, a hierarchy among diverse intelligences; and for the necessities of practice this classification is equivalent to a measure. We shall therefore be able to know, after studying two individuals, if one rises above the other and to how many degrees, if one rises above the average level of other individuals considered as normal, or if he remains below. Understanding the normal progress of intellectual development among normals, we shall be able to determine how many years such an individual is advanced or retarded. In a word we shall be able to determine to what degrees of the scale idiocy, imbecility, and moronity correspond.

The scale that we shall describe is not a theoretical work; it is the result of long investigations, first at the Saltpetriere, and afterwards in the primary schools of Paris, with both normal and subnormal children. These short psychological questions have been given the name of tests. The use of tests is today very common, and there are even contemporary authors who have made a specialty of organizing new tests according to theoretical views, but who have made no effort to patiently try them out in the schools. Theirs is an amusing occupation, comparable to a person's making a colonizing expedition into Algeria, advancing always only upon the map, without taking off his dressing gown. We place but slight confidence in the tests invented by these authors and we have borrowed nothing from them. All the tests which we propose have been repeatedly tried, and have been retained from among many, which after trial have been discarded. We can certify that those which are here presented have proved themselves valuable.

We have aimed to make all our tests simple, rapid, convenient, precise, heterogeneous, holding the subject in continued contact with the experimenter, and bearing principally upon the faculty of judgment. Rapidity is necessary for this sort of examination. It is impossible to prolong it beyond twenty minutes without fatiguing the subject. During this maximum of twenty minutes, it must be turned and turned about in every sense, and at least ten tests must be executed, so that not more than about two minutes can be given to each. In spite of their interest, we were obliged to proscribe long exercises. For example, it would be very instructive to know how a subject learns by heart a series of sentences. We have often tested the advantage of leaving a person by himself with a lesson of prose or verse after having said to him, "Try to learn as much as you can of this in five minutes." Five minutes is too long for our test, because during that time the subject escapes us; it may be that he becomes distracted or thinks of other things; the test loses its clinical character and becomes too scholastic. We have therefore reluctantly been obliged to renounce testing the rapidity and extent of the memory by this method. Several other equivalent examples of elimination could be cited. In order to cover rapidly a wide field of observation, it goes without saying that the tests should be heterogeneous.

Another consideration. Our purpose is to evaluate a level of intelligence. It is understood that we here separate natural intelligence and instruction. It is the intelligence alone that we seek to measure, by disregarding in so far as possible, the degree of instruction which the subject possesses. He should, indeed, be considered by the examiner as a complete ignoramus knowing neither how to read nor write. This necessity forces us to forego a great many exercises having a verbal, literary or scholastic character. These belong to a pedagogical examination. We believe that we have succeeded in completely disregarding the acquired information of the subject. We give him nothing to read, nothing to write, and submit him to no test in which he might succeed by means of rote learning. In fact we do not even notice his inability to read if a case occurs. It is simply the level of his natural intelligence that is taken into account.

But here we must come to an understanding of what meaning to give to that word so vague and so comprehensive, "the intelligence." Nearly all the phenomena with which psychology concerns itself are phenomena of intelligence; sensation, perception, are intellectual manifestations as much as reasoning. Should we therefore bring into our examination the measure of sensation after the manner of the psycho-physicists? Should we put to the test all of his psychological processes? A slight reflection has shown us that this would indeed be wasted time.

It seems to us that in intelligence there is a fundamental faculty, the alteration or the lack of which, is of the utmost importance for practical life. This faculty is judgment, otherwise called good sense, practical sense, initiative, the faculty of adapting one's self to circumstances. To judge well, to comprehend well, to reason well, these are the essential activities of intelligence. A person may be a moron or an imbecile if he is lacking in judgment; but with good judgment he can never be either. Indeed the rest of the intellectual faculties seem of little importance in comparison with judgment. What does it matter, for example, whether the organs of sense function normally? Of what import that certain ones are hyperesthetic, or that others are anesthetic or are weakened? Laura Bridgman, Helen Keller and their fellow-unfortunates were blind as well as deaf, but this did not prevent them from being very intelligent. Certainly this is demonstrative proof that the total or even partial integrity of the senses does not form a mental factor equal to judgment. We may measure the acuteness of the sensibility of subjects; nothing could be easier. But we should do this, not so much to find out the state of their sensibility as to learn the exactitude of their judgment.

The same remark holds good for the study of the memory. At first glance, memory being a psychological phenomenon of capital importance, one would be tempted to give it a very conspicuous part in an examination of intelligence. But memory is distinct from and independent of judgment. One may have good sense and lack memory. The reverse is also common. Just at the present time we are observing a backward girl who is developing before our astonished eyes a memory very much greater than our own. We have measured that memory and we are not deceived regarding it. Neverthless that girl presents a most beautifully classic type of imbecility.

As a result of all this investigation, in the scale which we present we accord the first place to judgment; that which is of importance to us is not certain errors which the subject commits, but absurd errors, which prove that he lacks judgment. We have even made special provision to encourage people to make absurd replies. In spite of the accuracy of this directing idea, it will be easily understood that it has been impossible to permit of its regulating exclusively our examinations. For example, one can not make tests of judgment on children of less than two years when one begins to watch their first gleams of intelligence. Much is gained when one can discern in them traces of coordination, the first delineation of attention and memory. We shall therefore bring out in our lists some tests of memory; but so far as we are able, we shall give these tests such a turn as to invite the subject to make absurd replies, and thus under cover of a test of memory, we shall have an appreciation of their judgment.

Measuring Scale of Intelligence

General recommendations. The examination should take place in a quiet room, quite isolated, and the child should be called in alone without other children. It is important that when a child sees the experimenter for the first time, he should be reassured by the presence of someone he knows, a relative, an attendant, or a school superintendent. The witness should be instructed to remain passive and mute, and not to intervene in the examination either by word or gesture.

The experimenter should receive each child with a friendly familiarity to dispel the timidity of early years. Greet him the moment he enters, shake hands with him and seat him comfortably. If he is intelligent enough to understand certain words, awaken his curiosity, his pride. If he refuses to reply to a test, pass to the next one, or perhaps offer him a piece of candy; if his silence continues, send him away until another time. These are little incidents that frequently occur in an examination of the mental state, because in its last analysis, an examination of this kind is based upon the good will of the subject.

We here give the technique of each question. It will not suffice simply to read what we have written in order to be able to conduct examinations. A good experimenter can be produced only by example and imitation, and nothing equals the lesson gained from the thing itself. Every person who wishes to familiarize himself with our method of examination should come to our school. Theoretical instruction is valuable only when it merges into practical experience. Having made these reservations, let us point out the principal errors likely to be committed by inexperienced persons. There are two: the first consists in recording the gross results without making psychological observations, without noticing such little facts as permit one to give to the gross results their true value. The second error, equally frequent, is that of making suggestions. An inexperienced examiner has no idea of the influence of words; he talks too much, he aids his subject, he puts him on the track, unconscious of the help he is thus giving. He play the part of the pedagogue, when he should remain psychologist. Thus his examination is vitiated. It is a difficult art to be able to encourage a subject, to hold his attention, to make him do his best without giving aid in any form by an unskillful suggestion.

THE DEVELOPMENT OF INTELLIGENCE IN THE CHILD[1]

"The Measurement of Intelligence" is, perhaps, the most oft repeated expression in psychology during these last few years. Some psychologists affirm that intelligence can be measured; others declare that it is impossible to measure intelligence. But there are still others, better informed, who ignore these theoretical discussions and apply themselves to the actual solving of the problem. The readers of *L'Année* know that for some time we have been trying approximations, but they were not so well thought out as are those which we now present.

We have constantly kept in mind the point of view of pedagogy, normal as well as pathological. For several years we have tried to gather all the data and material capable of shedding light upon the intellectual and moral character of children. This is by no means the minor part of pedagogy, the least important, nor the least difficult. We set for ourselves the following program: first, to determine the law of the intellectual development of children and to devise a method of measuring their intelligence; and, second, to study the diversity of their intellectual aptitudes.

We hope that we shall be able to keep faithfully to this rather extensive program, and especially that we shall have the time and the strength to realize it, but already we see that the subject is far richer than we at first imagined. Our minds always tend to simplify nature. It had seemed to us sufficient to learn how to measure the child's intelligence. This measurement we now set forth, which if not complete is at least established upon correct lines, and already usable.

This measurement is taken by means of a series of tests, the gradation of which constitutes what we call a "Measuring Scale of Intelligence." It is important, above all, to set forth these tests with sufficient precision to enable any one to repeat them correctly who will take the trouble to assimilate them.

Classification of the tests according to age. We here give the series of tests ranged according to the ages at which the majority of children succeed in them. This constitutes our measuring scale of intelligence. (Descriptions of the tests, given in a later section of Binet and Simons' article, are not included in these readings.—Editor)

[1] From *L'Année Psychologique*, XIV (1908), 1-90.

Three years

Show eyes, nose, mouth
Name objects in a picture
Repeat 2 figures
Repeat a sentence of 6 syllables
Give last name

Four years

Give sex
Name key, knife, penny
Repeat 3 figures
Compare 2 lines

Five years

Compare 2 boxes of different weights
Copy a square
Repeat a sentence of 10 syllables
Count 4 sous
Put together two pieces in a game of "patience"

Six years

Repeat a sentence of 16 syllables
Compare two figures from an esthetic point of view
Define by use only, some simple objects
Execute 3 simultaneous commissions
Give one's age
Distinguish morning and evening

Seven years

Indicate omissions in drawings
Give the number of fingers
Copy a written sentence
Copy a triangle and a diamond
Repeat 5 figures
Describe a picture
Count 13 single sous
Name 4 pieces of money

Eight years

Read selection and retain two memories
Count 9 sous. (3 single and 3 double)
Name four colors
Count backward from 20–9
Compare 2 objects from memory
Write from dictation

Nine years

Give the date complete (day, month, day of the month, year)
Name the days of the week
Give definitions superior to use
Retain 6 memories after reading
Make change, 4 sous from 20 sous
Arrange 5 weights in order

Ten years

Name the months
Name 9 pieces of money
Place 3 words in 2 sentences
Answer 3 comprehensive questions
Answer 5 comprehensive questions

Eleven years

Criticize sentences containing absurdities
Place 3 words in 1 sentence
Find more than 60 words in 3 minutes
Give abstract definitions
Place disarranged words in order

Twelve years	*Thirteen years*
Repeat 7 figures	Paper cutting
Find 3 rhymes	Reversed triangle
Repeat a sentence of 26 syllables	Give differences of meaning
Interpret pictures	
Problem of facts	

The Use of the Measuring Scale of Intelligence

Our principal conclusion is that we actually possess an instrument which allows us to measure the intellectual development of young children whose age is included between three and twelve years. This method appears to us practical, convenient and rapid. If one wishes to know summarily whether a child has the intelligence of his age, or if he is advanced or retarded, it suffices to have him take the tests of his age; and the performance of these tests certainly does not require more than thirty minutes which should be interrupted by ten minutes rest if one thinks this necessary for the child.

Furthermore when one wishes to be more precise, or to make a closer approximation, one may make many more tests; if the child is seven years old, he may attempt the tests of eight, nine and ten years for example. One would also be able after an interval of several days to substitute analogous tests.

One question remains to be examined. To what purpose are these studies? In reading the reflections which we have interspersed in the course of our treatise, it will be seen that a profound knowledge of the normal intellectual development of the child would not only be of great interest but useful in formulating a course of instruction really adapted to their aptitudes. We fear that those who have drawn up the programs actually in force, are educated men who in their work have been led more by the fancies of their imaginations than by well-grounded principles. The pedagogical principle which ought to inspire the authors of programs seems to us to be the following: the instruction should always be according to the natural evolution of the child, and not precede it by a year or two. In other words the child should be taught only what he is sufficiently mature to understand; all precocious instruction is lost time, for it is not assimilated. We have cited an example of it in regard to the date, which is taught in the Maternal School, but which is not known and assimilated before the age of nine years. This is only one example, but it is eloquent; it shows the error of what has hitherto been done; it suggests a method which will enable us to improve upon the past,—a method less literary, less rapid, and even extremely laborious, for it demands that one establish by careful investigations the normal evolution of a child's intelligence, in order to make all our programs and methods of instruction conform to that evolution, when it is once known. If by this labor we have succeeded in showing the necessity for a thorough investigation conducted after this plan, our time has not been lost. But we are far from flattering ourselves that we have inaugurated a reform. Reforms in France do not succeed except through politics, and we cannot readily imagine a secretary of state busying himself with a question of this kind. What is taught to children at school! As though legislators could become interested in that!

It now remains to explain the use of our measuring scale which we consider a standard of the child's intelligence. Of what use is a measure of intelligence? Without doubt one could conceive many possible applications of the process, in dreaming of a future where the social sphere would be better organized than ours; where every one would work according to his known aptitudes in such a way that no particle of psychic force should be lost for society. That would be the ideal city. It is indeed far from us. But we have to remain among the sterner and the matter-of-fact realities of life, since we here deal with practical experiments which are the most commonplace realities.

We are of the opinion that the most valuable use of our scale will not be its application to the normal pupils, but rather to those of inferior grades of intelligence.

It is well known, as we have often affirmed, that the alienists are not agreed on the definitions of the words *idiot*, *imbecile* and *moron*. There are as many definitions as writers. Moreover the formulae employed and the processes of diagnosis in use, are so vague that the most conscientious author is not sure of remaining constantly consistent with himself. How, for instance, can one make use of formulae of diagnosis, founded on difference of degree, when these differences are not measured? Finally, the most serious criticisms that one can make of the actual medical practice is that if by chance, a child of normal intelligence were presented at a clinic, the alienist would not be able to know that he is dealing with a normal child. He will be unable for a very simple reason; he does not know what is necessary in order for a child to be normal; let us add that everyone is equally ignorant of how an individual intelligence can be studied and measured.

During the past year one of us examined 25 children who for various reasons had been admitted to Sainte-Anne and later confined at the Bicetre, at Salpetriere, or at other places. We applied the procedure of our measuring scale to all these children, and thus proved that *three of them were at age in intelligence, and two others were a year advanced beyond the average.*

On reflection, these cases should not surprise us; and it is not necessary to be in touch with questions of mental medicine to inveigh against arbitrary segregation. One ought to confine a child of normal intelligence, or even of super-normal, if he has epilepsy, or irresistible impulses which constitute a danger to his neighbors or to himself. But it is none the less true that the doctors who were obliged to diagnose these cases, have had to judge the degree of intelligence of these children; it is very interesting to show the errors of diagnosis which have been committed in this regard. To two of these children who showed normal intelligence we regret to say that the term *mental debility* had been applied without consideration. The third had received the term, truly extraordinary of its kind, of "*enfant idiot.*" The child was named T-----, aged seven years. A doctor had written concerning him, "Idiotic, with attacks of furious anger. Wishes to bite. Does not know how to read or write." This last is a little too naive. Since the normal child does not know how to read and write at seven years, to be astonished that T----- who is just seven is still illiterate, is like reproaching a three year old baby for not knowing how to play the piano. Finally, one of these children who was a year in advance, was classed as a moron; and as to the other nothing was said concerning his mentality. Nothing could show more clearly, that with the means which it has at its command, the mental clinic is not in a position to diagnose correctly a child's intelligence.

In terminating this account, it will suffice to make a very brief allusion to the appreciation of penal responsibility; there also our scale will render service. The problems of penal responsibility such as are actually placed before the tribunals, are most complex and recently have caused discussions that are highly curious on account of the attention which has been paid to words rather than to things. We have scarcely the space here to make the multiple distinctions which would be necessary in making clear the real situation. It will suffice to remark that in certain cases experts have to give their opinion on the degree of intelligence of an accused person; and that according to their customary point of view which consists in distinguishing health from illness they are preoccupied in learning if the accused should or should not enter the group of feebleminded. It is strange that so far, no other criterion than a subjective impression can guide them; they weigh each case with their good sense, which presupposes in the first place that everybody's good sense is equal to every other person's.

We suggest to them that they should use the six differentiating tests that we have described above. By the methodical employment of these tests, they will arrive at precise and controllable conclusions, which at the same time cannot help but enhance in the mind of the judges the value of the medico-legal appraisement of the alienists.

These examples to which we could add many others show that the methods of measuring the individual intelligence have not a speculative interest alone; by the direction, by the organization of all the investigations, psychology has furnished the proof (we do not say for the first time but in a more positive manner than ever before), that it is in a fair way to become a science of great social utility.

Ivan Petrovitch Pavlov: 1849-1936

SCIENTIFIC STUDY OF THE SO-CALLED PSYCHICAL PROCESSES IN THE HIGHER ANIMALS *

1906

THE subject of to-day's address, delivered in honour of Thomas Huxley, an eminent representative of natural science and a most energetic champion of that greatest biological principle (the doctrine of evolution), is the naturalistic investigation of the psychical processes in the higher animal.

I shall begin with an actual case which occurred in my laboratory a few years ago. Among my collaborators was a young doctor with an active mind capable of appreciating the joys and triumphs of investigation. Great was my astonishment when this loyal friend of science became profoundly disturbed on hearing of our plans to investigate the psychical activity of the dog in that same laboratory and by the same means which we had been using for the solution of physiological questions. All of our arguments were ineffective; he prophesied and hoped for only failure. The cause of this, as far as we could understand, was his idea that the psychical life of man and that of the higher animals was so individual and exalted that it not only did not lend itself to investigation, but would even be sullied by our rude physiological methods. Although this, gentlemen, may have been a somewhat exaggerated example, I believe it is characteristic and typical. In dealing with the highest vital phenomena, the fact must not be overlooked, that a systematic appreciation of natural science to the last limits of life will not be able to avoid misconception and opposition from those who are accustomed to regard these phenomena from another point of view and are convinced that this point of view is unassailable.

This is why I feel it obligatory first to explain exactly and clearly my

* This address, read in honor of Thomas Huxley, at the Charing Cross Medical School, London, on October 1, 1906, was one of Pavlov's earliest statements concerning the conditioned reflex. Abstracts of the address were published in 1906 by the *British Medical Journal, Lancet,* and *Science.* The present full text is reprinted from Chapter 4 of *Lectures on Conditioned Reflexes,* 1928, by permission of International Publishers.

point of view concerning the psychical activities of the higher animals, and secondly to pass from the preliminaries to the subject itself as soon as possible. I have referred intentionally to psychical activities as "so-called." If the naturalist hopes to make a complete analysis of the activity of the higher animals, he has not the right to speak of the psychical processes of these animals, and he can not so speak without deserting the principles of natural science. This is natural science—the work of the human mind applied to nature, and the investigation of nature without any kind of assumption or explanation from sources other than nature itself. Were the investigator to speak of the psychical faculties of the higher animals, he would be transferring ideas from his own inner world to nature, repeating the procedure of his predecessors who were accustomed, on observing nature, to apply to its inanimate phenomena their own thoughts, wishes and sensations. The naturalist must consider only one thing: what is the relation of this or that external reaction of the animal to the phenomena of the external world? This response may be extremely complicated in comparison with the reaction of any inanimate object, but the principle involved remains the same.

Strictly speaking, natural science is under obligation to determine only the precise connection which exists between a given natural phenomenon and the response of the living organism to that phenomenon, or, in other words, to ascertain completely how a living being maintains itself in constant equilibrium with its environment. This assertion can hardly be contested, and is further supported by the fact that it receives daily more and more general acceptance in the investigation of the lower and intermediate stages of the zoological scale. The question is simply whether this rule is already applicable to the examination of the higher functions of the higher vertebrates. A serious endeavour to institute enquiries in that direction is, as it appears to me, the only reasonable answer to the question. I and my many collaborators began this work some years ago and we have recently devoted ourselves to it almost exclusively. I would now ask your attention to an account, first, of the most important results of this enquiry, which seem to me to be very instructive; and secondly, to an account of the inferences which may be drawn from it.

Our experiments have been performed exclusively on the dog, in which the particular reaction used was an unimportant physiologic process—the secretion of saliva. The experimenter was always working with a perfectly normal animal, i.e., an animal which was not subjected to abnormal influences during the experiment. Exact observations on the work of the salivary glands could be made at any moment by means of a simple method. Saliva flows, as we all know, when something is given the dog to eat or is introduced forcibly into his mouth. Both the quality and the quantity of the saliva, under these conditions, is strictly dependent upon the quality and quantity of the substances brought into the dog's mouth. In this well-known physiological process we have before us a reflex. The idea of reflex action as a special elementary function of the nervous system is an old and established truism of physiology. It is the reaction of the organism to the external world, effected through the nervous system, by which an external stimulus is transformed into a nervous process and transmitted along a circuitous route (from the peripheral endings of the centripetal nerve, along its fibres to the apparatus of the central nervous system, and out along the centrifugal path until, reaching one or another organ, it excites its activity). This reaction is specific and permanent. Its specificity is a manifestation of a close and peculiar relation of the external phenomenon to the physiological action, and is founded on the specific sensibility of the peripheral nerve endings in the given nervous chain. These specific reflex actions in normal life, or to state it much more accurately, in the absence of abnormal vital conditions, are constant and unchanging.

The responses of the salivary glands to external influences are, however, not limited by the above-mentioned ordinary reflex actions. We all know that the salivary glands begin to secrete, not only when the stimulus of appropriate substances is impressed on the interior surface of the mouth, but that they also often begin to secrete when other receptive surfaces, including the eye and the ear, are stimulated. The actions last mentioned are, however, generally considered apart from physiology and receive the name of psychical stimuli.

We shall take another course, and shall endeavour to restore to physiology what properly belongs to it. These exceptional manifestations unquestionably have much in common with ordinary reflex action. Every time that such a flow of saliva begins it is attributable to the occurrence of some special stimulus among the external influences that may be recognised. On very careful exercise of his attention the observer perceives that the number of spontaneous flows of saliva forms a rapidly diminishing series, and it is in the highest degree probable that those extremely infrequent flows of saliva, for which no particular cause is at first sight apparent, are, in reality, the result of some stimulus invisible to the eye of the observer. From this it follows that the centripetal paths are always stimulated primarily, and the centrifugal paths secondarily, with the interposition, of course, of the central nervous system. Now these are actually all the elements of a reflex action, the only missing points being exact data as to the operation of the stimulus in the central nervous system. Are we familiar with this last mechanism in the ordinary reflexes? Speaking generally, then, our phenomena are reflexes, but the difference between these newly recognised reflexes and the long-known ones is certainly immense, for they have been assigned to quite different departments of science. Physiology has, therefore, before it the problem of evaluating this difference experimentally, and of establishing the essential properties of the reflexes which have been newly recognized.

In the first place they arise from all the body surfaces which are sensitive to stimulation, even from such regions as the eye and the ear, from which an ordinary reflex action affecting the salivary glands is never known to proceed. It must be mentioned that usual salivary reflexes may originate not only from the cavity of the mouth but also from the skin and nasal cavity; the skin, however, produces this effect only when it is subjected to some destructive process such as cutting or erosion by caustics, while the nasal cavity produces this effect only through the contact of vapours or gases, such as ammonia, which cause local irritation, but never through the agency of usual odours. In the second place, a conspicuous feature of these reflexes is that they are in the highest degree inconstant. All stimuli applied to the mouth of the dog unfailingly give a positive result with reference to the secretion of saliva, but the same objects when presented to the eye, the ear, etc., may sometimes be efficient and sometimes not. In consequence only of the last-mentioned fact have we provisionally called the new reflexes "conditioned reflexes," and for the sake of distinction we have called the old ones "unconditioned."

Every conditioned stimulus becomes totally ineffective on repetition. The shorter the interval between the separate repetitions of the conditioned reflex the more quickly is the reflex extinguished. The extinguishing of one conditioned reflex does not affect the operation of the others. Spontaneous restoration of extinguished conditioned reflexes does not occur until after the lapse of one, two, or more hours, but there is a way in which our reflex may be restored immediately. All that is necessary is to obtain a repetition of the *un*conditioned reflex, as, for instance, by pouring a weak solution of acid into the dog's mouth and then either showing it to him or letting him smell it. The action of the last-mentioned stimulus, which was previously quite obliterated, is now restored in its full extent. The following fact can be regularly observed: If for a long time, several days or weeks continuously, a certain kind of food is shown to the animal without it being given to him to eat, it loses its power of stimulating from a distance, that is, its power of acting from the eye, the nose, etc. These last-mentioned facts show plainly the close connection which exists between the stimulant effects of various properties of the substance—namely, the effects of the properties which excite secretion of saliva when the substance is in the mouth—and the effects of other properties of the same substance acting upon other receptive surfaces of the body. This material gives us the ground for assuming that the conditioned reflex in some way originates owing to the existence of the unconditioned reflex. And at the same time we may perceive the main features of the mechanism which gives rise to the conditioned reflex. When an object is placed in the mouth of the dog, some of its properties excite the simple reflex apparatus of the salivary glands; and for the production of our conditioned reflex that action must synchronise with the action of other properties of the same object influencing other receptive regions of the body whence the excitation is conveyed to other parts of the central nervous system. Just as the stimulant effects due to certain properties of an object placed in the mouth (unconditioned reflex) may coincide with a number of stimuli arising from other objects, so all these manifold stimuli may by frequent repetition be turned into conditioned stimuli for the salivary glands. Such stimuli may arise from the man who feeds the dog or who forcibly introduces certain articles into the dog's mouth, or they may owe their origin to the general environment in which this takes place. For this reason the above-mentioned experiments, by which the laws of the conditioned reflexes must be determined, require for their performance a well-trained experimenter who can really investigate only the action of the given conditioned stimulus or a definite number of such stimuli, without unconsciously introducing new stimuli with each successive repetition. If this last condition is not realised the laws in question will naturally be obscured. It must be remembered that in feeding a dog or forcing something into his mouth, each separate movement and each variation of a movement may by itself represent a conditioned stimulus. If that is the case, and if our hypothesis as to the origin of the conditioned reflex is correct, it follows that any natural phenomenon chosen at will may be converted into a conditioned stimulus. This has, in effect, been proved to be true. Any visual stimulus, any desired sound, any odour, and the stimulation of any part of the skin, either by mechanical means or by the application of heat or cold, have never failed in our hands to stimulate the salivary glands, although before they were all ineffective for that purpose. This was accomplished by applying the stimuli simultaneously with the action of the salivary glands, their action having been evoked by the giving of certain kinds of food, or by forcing certain substances into the dog's mouth. These artificial conditioned reflexes, the product of our training, showed exactly the same properties as the previously described natural conditioned reflexes. As regards their extinction and restoration they followed essentially the same laws as the natural conditioned reflexes. Thus we have the right to say, that our analysis of the origin of conditioned reflexes is proved by the facts.

Now that so much had been adduced on the subject we may advance further than was possible at the outset in the understanding of conditioned reflexes. In the manifestations of nervous energy which have up to the present time been submitted to careful scientific examination (our old specific reflex), the stimuli with which we had to do were comparatively few in number, but very constant in their action, and there was abundant evidence of a constant connection existing between the external influences and definite physiological effects. Now, however, in another more complicated part of the nervous system we encounter a new phenomenon, namely, the conditioned stimulus. On the one hand, this nervous apparatus becomes responsible in the highest degree, i.e., it is susceptible to the most varied external stimuli, but, on the other hand, these stimuli are not constant in their operation and are not definitely associated with certain physiological effects. At any given moment we find comparatively few circumstances favourable for these stimuli becoming active in the organism for a longer or shorter time and producing distinct physiological results.

The introduction of the idea of conditioned stimuli into physiology seems to me to be justified for many reasons. In the first place, it corresponds to the facts that have been adduced, since it represents a direct inference from them. In the second place, it is in agreement with the general mechanical hypotheses of natural science. In many kinds of apparatus and machinery, even of simple construction, certain forces can not develop their action unless at the proper time the necessary conditions are present. In the third place, it is completely covered by the ideas of facilitation (*Bahnung*) and inhibition, ideas which have been sufficiently elaborated in recent physiological literature. Finally, in these conditioned stimuli, looked at from the point of view of general biology, we have a most perfect mechanism of adaptation, or, what amounts to the same thing, a very delicate mechanism for maintaining an equilibrium with the surrounding medium. The body has the capacity to react in a sensitive way to the phenomena of the outer world, even the most insignificant, coinciding even temporarily with the essential become their indicators or, as they may be called, their signalling stimuli. The delicacy of the reaction shows itself both in the production of the conditioned stimulus and in its disappearance when it ceases to be a proper signal. There must be assumed to exist at this point one of the chief mechanisms for further discrimination in the nervous system. In view of all this, it is permissible, I think, to regard the idea of conditioned stimuli as the fruit of previous labours of biologists, and to consider my present report as illustrating the result of this work on a most complicated subject. It would be unreasonable to attempt to determine at present the limits of the immense field thus opened and to partition it. The following must be regarded as, and nothing more than, a provisional arrangement of material that has been collected, giving only the points indispensable for purposes of explanation.

There are reasons for considering the process of the conditioned reflex to be elementary, namely, a process which consists only in the coincidence of any one of the innumerable indifferent external stimuli with a state of excitation of a point in a definite part of the central nervous system. Now a path is established between the former indifferent stimulus and this given point. The first argument in favour of this hypothesis is the repeated occurrence of this phenomenon: the conditioned reflex may be obtained in all dogs, and it may be produced by all imaginable stimuli. In the second place, there is the certainty of its occurrence; under definite conditions it is reproduced inevitably. We see, therefore, that the process is not complicated by any other (and unknown) conditions. It may here be mentioned that various conditioned stimuli which had been rendered effective were applied at a distance, as from another room; the experimenter, who for the purpose of obtaining the conditioned reflex usually either gave the dog something to eat or put a substance of some kind into the dog's mouth, was not now in close proximity to the animal, but the result of the stimuli was, nevertheless, the same.

It has already been stated that every imaginable phenomenon of the outer world affecting a specific receptive surface of the body may be converted into a conditioned stimulus. After conditioned reflexes had been obtained from the eye, the ear, the nose, and the skin, it was a matter of interest to know what relation the cavity of the mouth had to the general question, and whether a conditioned reflex originated in the mouth. The answer to the inquiry could not be a simple one, because in this case not only the receptive surfaces for the stimuli of the conditioned and of the unconditioned reflex, but also the stimuli themselves were all brought together. Careful observations, however, have made it possible to separate the conditioned stimulus from the unconditioned stimulus even in this instance. When inedible, irritant substances were many times in succession forcibly introduced into the dog's mouth, we could observe the following facts:

If, for instance, a certain amount of acid was poured into the dog's mouth many times in succession, on each fresh repetition of this procedure, there was regularly a greater flow of saliva; the same thing was repeated on a series of successive days until a certain maximum was attained, whereupon for a considerable time the secretion remained constant. If the experiments were stopped for some days the quantity of saliva secreted became much less. This fact could be very simply explained as follows. On the first administration of the acid solution the secretion of saliva depended principally, or even exclusively, on the unconditioned reflex which the acid caused, while the subsequently occurring increase in secretion pointed to a conditioned reflex gradually formed under the influence of the same acid, and having as its receptor surface also the mouth cavity.

We will now consider the conditions which determine the formation of conditioned reflexes. This question taken comprehensively is naturally a vast one. The following account will serve to give you only a slight idea of the full compass of this vast subject.

Although there are great differences in the time required for the establishing of a conditioned reflex, some relations have been seen to exist. From our experiments it is evident that the intensity of the stimulus is of essential importance. We have some dogs in which the cooling or warming of a definite place on the skin acted as a conditioned stimulus for the salivary glands. A temperature of zero or 1 °C. in an experiment repeated 20 or 30 times caused saliva to flow, whilst a temperature of 4° or 5° C. in an experiment repeated 100 times gave no effect whatever. Exactly the same thing occurs with high temperatures. Heat of 45° C. applied as a conditioned stimulus showed similarly no action after even 100 applications; a temperature of 50°, on the other hand, caused a secretion of saliva after from 20 to 30 applications. In contradistinction to this we must state with regard to acoustic stimuli that very loud sounds such as the violent ringing of a bell did not, in comparison with weaker stimuli, quickly establish a conditioned reflex. It can be assumed that powerful acoustic stimuli call out some other important reaction in the body (e.g., motor), which hinders the development of the salivary response.

There is another group of related phenomena which deserves mention. When an odour not naturally exciting the salivary reflex—that of camphor, for instance—is by means of a special apparatus diffused, this diffusion of the odour must be made to coincide 10 or 20 times with the action of the unconditioned stimulus, such as acid poured into the dog's mouth. But if some of the odouriferous material is added to the acid, the new odour after one or two administrations acts as a conditioned stimulus. It should be asked whether the important circumstance in this experiment is the exact coincidence in time of the conditioned reflex or something else.

For the sake of brevity I will entirely omit the technical details, such as by what methods the conditioned reflexes are best obtained; whether with food or with non-food substances; how many times the various stimuli may be applied in a day; with what length of intermissions, and so on. Next in order comes the important question, What are the stimuli that the nervous system of the dog recognises as individual phenomena in the outer world? Or, in other words, What are the elements of a stimulus? With regard to this a good deal of evidence is in existence already. If the application of cold to a definite area of the skin (a circle having a diameter of from four to five centimetres) acts as a conditioned stimulus for the salivary glands, the application of cold to any other portion of the skin causes secretion of saliva on the very first occasion. This shows that the stimulation by cold is generalised over a considerable part of the skin, or perhaps even over the whole of it. But the application of cold to the skin is very clearly distinguished as such from the application of heat and from mechanical stimulation. Each of these stimuli must be elaborated separately in order to give a conditioned reflex. Just as in the case of cold, the application to the skin of heat as a conditioned stimulus, also generalises itself. This is equivalent to saying that if an application made to one place on the skin stimulates the salivary glands, an application made to another cutaneous area will also produce a secretion of saliva. Totally different results were yielded by mechanical stimulation of the skin, such as rubbing with a coarse brush (by means of a special apparatus). When this treatment applied to a certain area of the skin had become converted into a conditioned stimulus, the same treatment applied to another place on the skin remained completely ineffective. Other forms of mechanical stimulation, such as pressure with a sharp or blunt object, proved themselves less effective. Apparently the first mechanical stimulus formed only a small part of the latter.

Stimulation by musical sounds or by noises is remarkably convenient for determining the discriminating or analytical faculty of the nervous system of the dog. In this respect the precision of our reaction is very great. If a certain note of an instrument is employed as a conditioned stimulus, it often happens that not only all the notes adjoining it but even those differing from it by a quarter of a tone fail to produce any effect. Musical timbre (quality) is recognised with similar or even with much greater precision. An external agent acts as a conditioned stimulus not only when it comes on the scene but also when it disappears, so that either its beginning or its end may be made the stimulus. Of course, a separate analysis has to be undertaken in order to explain the nature of such stimuli.

We have hitherto spoken of the analytical ability of the nervous system as it presents itself to us in, so to say, a finished state. But we have now accumulated material which contains evidence of a continuous and great increase of this ability if the experimenter persists in subdividing and varying the conditioned stimuli. Here, again, is a new field of enormous extent.

In the material relating to the various conditioned stimuli, there are not a few cases in which can be seen an evident connection between the intensity of a stimulus and its effect. As soon as a temperature of 50°C. had begun to provoke a flow of saliva, it was found that even 30° C. had a similar but lesser effect. An analogous result may be observed in cases of mechanical stimulation. A diminished rate of rubbing with the brush (5 strokes instead of 25 to 30 strokes per minute) gives less saliva than the ordinary rate of rubbing, and accelerated rubbing (up to 60 strokes per minute) gives more saliva.

Furthermore, combinations consisting of stimuli of the same kind and also of stimuli of different kinds were tried. The simplest example is a combination of different musical tones, such as a chord consisting of three tones. When this is employed as a conditioned stimulus, the tones played in pairs and each separate tone of the chord produce an effect but the pairs produce less saliva than the three together, and the notes played separately less than those played in pairs. The case becomes more complicated when we employ as a conditioned stimulus a combination of stimuli of different kinds, that is, of stimuli acting upon different receptive surfaces. Only a few of such combinations have been provisionally experimented with. In these cases, one of the stimuli generally became a conditioned stimulus. In a combination in which rubbing and cold were employed the former was preponderant as a conditioned stimulus, while the application of cold taken by itself produced an effect hardly perceptible. But if an attempt is made to convert the weaker stimulus separately into a conditioned stimulus it soon acts energetically. If we now apply the two stimuli together, we have before us an increased effect resulting from the summation of stimuli.

The following problem had for its object the explanation of what happens to an active conditioned stimulus when a new stimulus is added to it. In the cases that we examined we saw that the action of the previously formed conditioned stimulus was disturbed when a new stimulus of like kind was added to it. A new similar odour inhibited the operation of another odour which was already a conditioned stimulus; a new musical note likewise impeded the action of a note employed as a conditioned stimulus, and just previously applied. It is not without interest, I think, to mention that we started with these experiments with another object in view. We were intending to form a new conditioned reflex with the aid of another conditioned reflex which had been previously formed. We accordingly experimented with combinations of dissimilar stimuli. Researches in this direction are well advanced. We have to discriminate between different cases. Some examples may be given. Scratching (or rubbing with a brush) may be a ready and effective conditioned stimulus. When we add to it the ticking of a metronome, applying both stimuli simultaneously, the scratching immediately loses its efficacy as a stimulant during the first applications (first phase); and this loss extends over some days but returns again, notwithstanding the addition of the metronome, and now our double stimulus has nearly the same effect as the scratching alone (second phase); later, scratching, when applied simultaneously with the metronome, ceases to act and the influence of this double stimulus now comes to an end altogether (third phase). When the glare of an ordinary electric lamp is added to scratching which is a conditioned stimulus, the scratching at first produces exactly the same effect as before when it was without the lamp, but afterwards the combination of scratching and the luminous stimulus ceases to act. Apparently a phenomenon of the same kind was observed when the action of other mechanical stimuli was experimented with instead of the scratching which had been made to play the part of a conditioned stimulus. In the first place, secretion of saliva was caused by pressure with a sharp as well as with a blunt object, but to a less degree than by scratching; on repetition, however, the effect of the pressure stimulus became progressively less, until finally, it altogether disappeared.

We may assume that a part of the stimulation by the sharp and blunt objects was identical with scratching, and that this component was responsible for the action of these objects during their first applications. But a part of the action was special; it led in the course of time to a destruction of the influence of the first. In these inhibitions we see the following phenomenon which in all experiments of this kind is regularly repeated. After a conditioned stimulus had been applied together with another one which inhibited its action, the effect of the first one tried alone was greatly weakened, and sometimes even arrested completely. This is either an after-effect of the inhibiting stimulus which was added, or it is the extinguishing of the conditioned reflex because in the experiment with the added stimulus the conditioned reflex had not been strengthened by the unconditioned reflex.

The inhibition of the conditioned reflex is observed also in the converse case. When you have a combination of agents acting as a conditioned stimulus, in which, as has been already stated, one of the agents by itself produces almost no effect, then frequent repetition of the powerfully acting stimulus alone, without the other one, leads to a marked inhibition of its action, almost to the point of its annihilation. The relative magnitudes of all these manifestations of stimulation and inhibition are closely dependent on the conditions under which they originate.

The following is an example. We assume that the stimulus of scratching is acting as a conditioned reflex in the following manner: In the first place nothing but scratching was employed for 15 seconds, then acid was poured into the dog's mouth, scratching being continued up to the end of one minute. If you now apply scratching for a full minute, you get a copious secretion of saliva. Try to keep up this reflex, that is, continue the scratching for a second minute, and only then pour acid into the dog's mouth. If you do this several times in succession, the effect of the scratching will quickly diminish during the first minute and will ultimately cease altogether. In order that the scratching may regain its efficiency during the first minute, it is only necessary to repeat the experiment several times; indeed, its effect will be even greater than it was in the previous experiments.

We have observed a similar course of events also in the exact measurement of the inhibitory effect.

Finally, it may be mentioned that the attempt was made to form conditioned reflexes from the traces of the latest remnants or after effects, both of a conditioned and of an unconditioned stimulus. This was accomplished by allowing a conditioned stimulus to act for one minute immediately before the unconditioned stimulus, or by even three minutes earlier. There was always an interval of a few seconds to several minutes between the stimuli. In all these cases the conditioned reflex developed. But in the cases in which the conditioned stimulus was applied three minutes before the unconditioned one, and was separated from the latter by an interval of two minutes, we obtained a result which, although quite unexpected and extremely peculiar, always occurred. When scratching, for example, was applied to a certain spot on the skin as a conditioned stimulus, after it became active we found that scratching of any other place also produced an effect; cold or heat applied to the skin, new musical sounds, optical stimuli, and odours—all these had the same effect as the conditioned stimulus. The unusually copious secretion of saliva and the extremely expressive movements of the animal attracted our attention. During the action of the conditioned stimulus the dog behaved exactly as if the acid which served as the unconditioned stimulus had been actually poured into its mouth.

It may appear that this phenomenon is of a different order from those with which we have hitherto been occupied. The fact is that in the earlier experiments at least one coincidence of the conditioned stimulus with the unconditioned one was necessary; but in these experiments, phenomena which had never occurred simultaneously with an unconditioned reflex were acting as conditioned stimuli. Here an unquestionable difference naturally comes to light, but at the same time there is seen an essential property of these phenomena which they have in common with the former ones; that is, the existence of an easily excitable point in the central nervous system, to which, as a result of its condition, are directed all the essential stimuli from the external world that affect the cells of the highest part of the brain.

I now bring to a close my cursory and very incomplete summary of the data which have been obtained in this new field of research. Three characteristic features of this subject deeply impress the investigator. In the first place, these phenomena are easily accessible for exact investigation, being in this respect scarcely inferior to the ordinary physiological phenomena. I refer to the ease with which they may be repeated—beyond all expectation—to their uniformity under similar conditions of experimentation, and to the fact that they are suitable for experimental analysis. In the second place, there is the possibility of considering this subject objectively. The introduction of a few subjective considerations which we admitted now and again for purposes of comparison seemed on further reflection to be an act of violence or an affront to a serious intellectual endeavour. In the third place, the subject involves an unusual number of stimulating questions for the investigator.

Under what heading is the subject to be classified? To what part of physiology does it correspond? The reply to this question presents no difficulities. It corresponds partly to what was, in former days, the physiology of the special sense organs, and partly to the physiology of the central nervous system.

Up to the present time the physiology of the eye, ear, and other receptor organs has been regarded almost exclusively in its subjective aspect; this presented some advantages, but at the same time, of course, limited the range of enquiry. Investigation by the method of conditioned stimuli in higher animals avoids this limitation, and a number of important questions in this field of research can be at once examined with the aid of all the immense resources which experiments on animals place in the hand of the physiologist. Owing to the shortness of the time that remains it is impossible to give illustrations of such questions. The investigation of conditioned reflexes is even of greater importance for the physiology of the highest parts of the central nervous system. Hitherto this department of physiology, throughout most of its extent, has been cluttered with foreign ideas, borrowed from psychology, but now there is a possibility of its being liberated from such harmful dependence. The conditioned reflexes disclose before us the vast field of the relations and reactions of animals to nature; this is a subject of immense extent and one that must be treated objectively. The physiologist can and must examine these reactions, using in connection with them progressive and systematic removal of parts of the central nervous system in order that he may ultimately arrive at an exact knowledge of the mechanism involved. And here arise at once some urgent and practical questions.

Still one point remains. What relation is there between psychological data and the facts just described? What points of mutual correspondence are there? Who will occupy himself with these relations? and when? This relationship may be interesting even now, but it must be confessed that physiology has at present no serious reason for discussing it. Its immediate problem is to collect and to analyse the endless amount of objective material which presents itself. But it is plain that the conquest which physiology has yet to make consists for the most part of the actual solution of those questions which hitherto have vexed and perplexed humanity. Mankind will possess incalculable advantages and extraordinary control over human behaviour when the scientific investigator will be able to subject his fellow men to the same external analysis as he would employ for any natural object, and when the human mind will contemplate itself not from within but from without.

Must I say something about the relationship which exists between medicine and the subject of my address? Physiology and medicine are fundamentally inseparable. If the physician is in his actual practice, and even more important, in his ideals, a mechanic of the human organism, then inevitably every fresh discovery in physiology will sooner or later increase his power over this extraordinary machine, his power to conserve and repair this mechanism. It is extremely gratifying to me that in honouring the memory of a great naturalist and man of science I am able to make use of ideas and facts which from this single successful point of view promises to throw light upon the highest and most complicated part of the animal mechanism. I am fully persuaded of, and boldly express my confidence in, the ultimate triumph of this new method of research and I avow it the more fearlessly because Thomas Huxley, who is an example to all of us, fought with rare courage for the freedom and the rights of the scientific point of view.

James Rowland Angell: 1869-

THE PROVINCE OF FUNCTIONAL PSYCHOLOGY *

1907

FUNCTIONAL psychology is at the present moment little more than a point of view, a program, an ambition. It gains its vitality primarily perhaps as a protest against the exclusive excellence of another starting point for the study of the mind, and it enjoys for the time being at least the peculiar vigor which commonly attaches to Protestantism of any sort in its early stages before it has become respectable and orthodox. The time seems ripe to attempt a somewhat more precise characterization of the field of functional psychology than has as yet been offered. What we seek is not the arid and merely verbal definition which to many of us is so justly anathema, but rather an informing appreciation of the motives and ideals which animate the psychologist who pursues this path. His status in the eye of the psychological public is unnecessarily precarious. The conceptions of his purposes prevalent in non-functional circles range from positive and dogmatic misapprehension, through frank mystification and suspicion up to moderate comprehension. Nor is this fact an expression of anything peculiarly abstruse and recondite in his intentions. It is due in part to his own ill-defined plans, in part to his failure to explain lucidly exactly what he is about. Moreover, he is fairly numerous and it is not certain that in all important particulars he and his confreres are at one in their beliefs. The considerations which are herewith offered suffer inevitably from this personal limitation. No psychological council of Trent has as yet pronounced upon the true faith. But in spite of probable failure it seems worth while to hazard an attempt at delineating the scope of functionalist principles. I formally renounce any intention to strike out new plans; I am engaged in what is meant as a dispassionate summary of actual conditions.

Whatever else it may be, functional psychology is nothing wholly new. In certain of its phases it is plainly discernible in the psychology of Aristotle and in its more modern garb it has been increasingly in evidence

* This paper, more than any other, outlines the platform of the functional school of psychology. It is reprinted by permission of the author and of the American Psychological Association, publisher of the *Psychological Review*, where the article appeared (1907), XIV, 61-91.

since Spencer wrote his *Psychology* and Darwin his *Origin of Species*. Indeed, as we shall soon see, its crucial problems are inevitably incidental to any serious attempt at understanding mental life. All that is peculiar to its present circumstances is a higher degree of self-consciousness than it possessed before, a more articulate and persistent purpose to organize its vague intentions into tangible methods and principles.

A survey of contemporary psychological writing indicates as was intimated in the preceding paragraph, that the task of functional psychology is interpreted in several different ways. Moreover, it seems to be possible to advocate one or more of these conceptions while cherishing abhorrence for the others. I distinguish three principal forms of the functional problem with sundry subordinate variants. It will contribute to the clarification of the general situation to dwell upon these for a moment, after which I propose to maintain that they are substantially but modifications of a single problem.

I

There is to be mentioned first the notion which derives most immediately from contrast with the ideals and purposes of structural psychology so-called. This involves the identification of functional psychology with the effort to discern and portray the typical operations of consciousness under actual life conditions, as over against the attempt to analyze and describe its elementary and complex contents. The structural psychology of sensation, e.g., undertakes to determine the number and character of the various unanalyzable sensory materials, such as the varieties of color, tone, taste, etc. The functional psychology of sensation would on the other hand find its appropriate sphere of interest in the determination of the character of the various sense activities as differing in their modus operandi from one another and from other mental processes such as judging, conceiving, willing and the like.

In this its older and more pervasive form functional psychology has until very recent times had no independent existence. No more has structural psychology for that matter. It is only lately that any motive for the differentiation of the two has existed and structural psychology—granting its claims and pretensions of which more anon—is the first, be it said, to isolate itself. But in so far as functional psychology is synonymous with descriptions and theories of mental action as distinct from the materials of mental constitution, so far it is everywhere conspicuous in psychological literature from the earliest times down.

Its fundamental intellectual prepossessions are often revealed by the classifications of mental process adopted from time to time. Witness the Aristotelian bipartite division of intellect and will and the modern tripartite division of mental activities. What are cognition, feeling and will but three basally distinct modes of mental action? To be sure this classification has often carried with it the assertion, or at least the implication, that these fundamental attributes of mental life were based upon the presence in the mind of corresponding and ultimately distinct mental elements. But so far as concerns our momentary interest this fact is irrelevant. The impressive consideration is that the notion of definite and distinct forms of mental action is clearly in evidence and even the much-abused faculty psychology is on this point perfectly sane and perfectly lucid. The mention of this classic target for psychological vituperation recalls the fact that when the critics of functionalism wish to be particularly unpleasant, they refer to it as a bastard offspring of the faculty psychology masquerading in biological plumage.

It must be obvious to any one familiar with psychological usage in the present year of grace that in the intent of the distinction herewith described certain of our familiar psychological categories are primarily structural—such for instance as affection and image—whereas others immediately suggest more explicit functional relationships—for example, attention and reasoning. As a matter of fact it seems clear that so long as we adhere to these meanings of the terms structural and functional every mental event can be treated from either point of view, from the standpoint of describing its detectable contents and from the standpoint of characteristic mental activity differentiable from other forms of mental process. In the practice of our familiar psychological writers both undertakings are somewhat indiscriminately combined.

The more extreme and ingenuous conceptions of structural psychology seem to have grown out of an unchastened indulgence in what we may call the "states of consciousness" doctrine. I take it that this is in reality the contemporary version of Locke's "idea." If you adopt as your material for psychological analysis the isolated "moment of consciousness," it is very easy to become so absorbed in determining its constitution as to be rendered somewhat oblivious to its artificial character. The most essential quarrel which the functionalist has with structuralism in its thoroughgoing and consistent form arises from this fact and touches the feasibility and worth of the effort to get at mental process as it is under the conditions of actual experience rather than as it appears to a merely postmortem analysis. It is of course true than for introspective purposes we must in a sense always work with vicarious representatives of the particular mental processes which we set out to observe. But it makes a great difference even on such terms whether one is engaged simply in teasing apart the fibers of its tissues. The latter occupation is useful and for certain purposes essential, but it often stops short of that which is as a life phenomenon the most essential, i.e., the modus operandi of the phenomenon.

As a matter of fact many modern investigations of an experimental kind largely dispense with the usual direct form of introspection and concern themselves in a distinctly functionalistic spirit with a determination of what work is accomplished and what the conditions are under which it is achieved. Many experiments in memory and association, for instance, are avowedly of this character.

The functionalist is committed *vom Grunde auf* to the avoidance of that special form of the psychologist's fallacy which consists in attributing to mental states without due warrant, as part of their overt constitution in the moment of experience, characteristics which subsequent reflective analysis leads us to suppose they must have possessed. When this precaution is not scrupulously observed we obtain a sort of *pate de foie gras* psychology in which the mental conditions portrayed contain more than they every naturally would or could hold.

It should be added that when the distinction is made between psychic structure and psychic function, the anomalous position of structure as a category of mind is often quite forgotten. In mental life the sole appropriateness of the term structure hinges on the fact that any amount of consciousness can be regarded as a complex capable of analysis, and the terms into which our analyses resolve such complexes are the analogues—and obviously very meager and defective ones at that—of the structures of anatomy and morphology.

The fact that mental contents are evanescent and fleeting marks them off in an important way from the relatively permanent elements of anatomy. No matter how much we may talk of the preservation of psychical dispositions, nor how many metaphors we may summon to characterize the storage of ideas in some hypothetical deposit chamber of memory, the obstinate fact remains that when we are not experiencing a sensation or an idea it is, strictly speaking, non-existent. Moreover, when we manage by one or another device to secure that which we designate the same sensation or the same idea, we not only have no guarantee that our second edition is really a replica of the first, we have a good bit of presumptive evidence that from the content point of view the original never is and never can be literally duplicated.

Functions, on the other hand, persist as well in mental as in physical life. We may never have twice exactly the same idea viewed from the side of sensuous structure and composition. But there seems nothing whatever to prevent our having as often as we will contents of consciousness which mean the same thing. They function in one and the same practical way, however discrepant their momentary texture. The situation is rudely analogous to the biological case where very different structures may under different conditions be called on to perform identical functions; and the matter naturally harks back for its earliest analogy to the instance of protoplasm where functions seem very tentatively and imperfectly differentiated. Not only then are general functions like memory persistent, but special functions such as the memory of particular events are persistent and largely independent of the specific conscious contents called upon from time to time to subserve the functions.

When the structural psychologists define their field as that of mental process, they really preempt under a fictitious name the field of function, so that I should be disposed to allege fearlessly and with a clear conscience that a large part of the doctrine of psychologists of nominally structural proclivities is in point of fact precisely what I mean by one essential part of functional psychology, i.e., an account of psychical operations. Certain of the official exponents of structuralism explicitly lay claim to this as their field and do so with a flourish of scientific rectitude. There is therefore after all a small but nutritious core of agreement in the structure-function apple of discord. For this reason, as well as because I consider extremely useful the analysis of mental life into its elementary forms, I regard much of the actual work of my structuralist friends with highest respect and confidence. I feel, however, that when they use the term structural as opposed to the term functional to designate their scientific creed they often come perilously near to using the enemy's colors.

Substantially identical with this first conception of functional psychology, but phrasing itself somewhat differently, is the view which regards the functional problem as concerned with discovering how and why conscious processes are what they are, instead of dwelling as the structuralist is supposed to do upon the problem of determining the irreducible elements of consciousness and their characteristic modes of combination. I have elsewhere defended the view that however it may be in other sciences dealing with life phenomena, in psychology at least the answer to the question "what" implicates the answer to the questions "how" and "why."

Stated briefly the ground on which this position rests is as follows: In so far as you attempt to analyze any particular state of consciousness you find that the mental elements presented to your notice are dependent upon the particular exigencies and conditions which call them forth. Not only does the affective coloring of such a psychical moment depend upon one's temporary condition, mood and aims, but the very sensations themselves are determined in their qualitative texture by the totality of circumstances subjective and objective within which they arise. You cannot get a fixed and definite color sensation, for example, without keeping perfectly constant the external and internal conditions in which it appears. The particular sense quality is in short functionally determined by the necessities of the existing situation which it emerges to meet. If you inquire then deeply enough what particular sensation you have in a given case, you always find it necessary to take account of the manner in which, and the reasons why, it was experienced at all. You may of course, if you will, abstract from these considerations, but in so far as you do so, your analysis and description is manifestly partial and incomplete. Moreover, even when you do so abstract and attempt to describe certain isolable sense qualities, your descriptions are of necessity couched in terms not of the experienced quality itself, but in terms of the conditions which produced it, in terms of some other quality with which it is compared, or in terms of some more overt act to which the sense stimulation led. That is to say, the very description itself is functionalistic and must be so. The truth of this assertion can be illustrated and tested by appeal to any situation in which one is trying to reduce sensory complexes, e.g., colors or sounds, to their rudimentary components.

II

A broader outlook and one more frequently characteristic of contemporary writers meets us in the next conception of the task of functional psychology. This conception is in part a reflex of the prevailing interest in the larger formulae of biology and particularly the evolutionary hypotheses within whose majestic sweep is nowadays included the history of the whole stellar universe; in part it echoes the same philosophical call to new life which has been heard as pragmatism, as humanism, even as functionalism itself. I should not wish to commit either party by asserting that functional psychology and pragmatism are ultimately one. Indeed, as a psychologist I should hesitate to bring down on myself the avalanche of metaphysical invective which has been loosened by pragmatic writers. To be sure pragmatism has slain its thousands, but I should cherish scepticism as to whether functional psychology would the more speedily slay its tens of thousands by announcing an offensive and defensive alliance with pragmatism. In any case I only hold that the two movements spring from similar logical motivation and rely for their vitality and propagation upon forces closely germane to one another.

The functional psychologist then in his modern attire is interested not alone in the operations of mental process considered merely of and by and for itself, but also and more vigorously in mental activity as part of a larger stream of biological forces which are daily and hourly at work before our eyes and which are constitutive of the most important and most absorbing part of our world. The psychologist of this stripe is wont to take his cue from the basal conception of the evolutionary movement, i.e., that for the most part organic structures and functions possess their present characteristics by virtue of the efficiency with which they fit into the extant conditions of life broadly designated the environment. With this conception in mind he proceeds to attempt some understanding of the manner in which the psychical contributes to the furtherance of the sum total of organic activities, not alone the psychical in its entirety, but especially the psychical in its particularities–mind as judging, mind as feeling, etc.

This is the point of view which instantly brings the psychologist cheek by jowl with the general biologist. It is the presupposition of every philosophy save that of outright ontological materialism that mind plays the stellar role in all the environmental adaptations of animals which possess it. But this persuasion has generally occupied the position of an innocuous truism or at best a jejune postulate, rather than that of a problem requiring, or permitting, serious scientific treatment. At all events, this was formerly true.

This older and more complacent attitude toward the matter is, however, being rapidly displaced by a conviction of the need for light on the exact character of the accommodatory service represented by the various great modes of conscious expression. Such an effort if successful would not only broaden the foundations for biological appreciation of the intimate nature of accommodatory process, it would also immensely enhance the psychologist's interest in the exact portrayal of conscious life. It is of course the latter consideration which lends importance to the matter from our point of view. Moreover, not a few practical consequences of value may be expected to flow from this attempt, if it achieves even a measurable degree of success. Pedagogy and mental hygiene both await the quickening and guiding counsel which can only come from a psychology of this stripe. For their purposes a strictly structural psychology is as sterile in theory as teachers and psychiatrists have found it in practice.

As a concrete example of the transfer of attention from the more general phases of consciousness as accommodatory activity to the particularistic features of the case may be mentioned the rejuvenation of interest in the quasi-biological field which we designate animal psychology. This movement is surely among the most pregnant with which we meet in our own generation. Its problems are in no sense of the merely theoretical and speculative kind, although, like all scientific endeavor, it poses an intellectual and methodological background on which such problems loom large. But the frontier upon which it is pushing forward its explorations is a region of definite, concrete fact, tangled and confused and often most difficult of access, but nevertheless a region of fact, accessible like all other facts to persistent and intelligent interrogation.

That many of the most fruitful researches in this field have been achievements of men nominally biologists rather than psychologists in no wise affects the merits of the case. A similar situation exists in the experimental psychology of sensation where not a little of the best work has been accomplished by scientists not primarily known as psychologists.

It seems hardly too much to say that the empirical conceptions of the consciousness of the lower animals have undergone a radical alteration in the past few years by virtue of the studies in comparative psychology. The splendid investigations of the mechanism of instinct, of the facts and methods of animal orientation, of the scope and character of the several sense processes, of the capabilities of education and the range of selective accommodatory capacities in the animal kingdom, these and dozens of other similar problems have received for the first time drastic scientific examination, experimental in character wherever possible, observational elsewhere, but observational in the spirit of conservative non-anthropomorphism as earlier observations almost never were. In most cases they have to be sure but shown the way to further and more precise knowledge, yet there can be but little question that the trail which they have blazed has success at its farther end.

One may speak almost as hopefully of human genetic psychology which has been carried on so profitably in our own country. As so often in psychology, the great desideratum here, is the completion of adequate methods which will insure really stable scientific results. But already our general psychological theory has been vitalized and broadened by the results of the genetic methods thus far elaborated. These studies constantly emphasize for us the necessity of getting the longitudinal rather than the transverse view of life phenomena and they keep immediately in our field of vision the basic significance of growth in mental process. Nowhere is the difference more flagrant between a functional psychology and the more literal-minded type of structural psychology. One has only to compare with the better contemporary studies some of the pioneer work in this field, conceived in the more static and structuralistic manner, as Preyer's for example was, to feel at once the difference and the imsensely greater significance both for theory and for practice which issues from the functional and longitudinal descriptions.

The assertions which we have permitted ourselves about genetic psychology are equally applicable to pathological psychology. The technique of scientific investigation is in the nature of the case often different in this field of work from that characteristic of the other ranges of psychological research. But the attitude of the investigator is distinctly functionalistic. His aim is one of a thoroughly vital and generally practical kind leading him to emphasize precisely those considerations which our analysis of the main aspects of functional psychology disclose as the goal of its peculiar ambitions.

It is no purpose of mine to submerge by sheer tour de force the individuality of these various scientific interests just mentioned in the regnant personality of a functional psychology. But I am firmly convinced that the spirit which gives them birth is the spirit which in the realms of general psychological theory bears the name functionalism. I believe, therefore, that their ultimate fate is certain, still I have no wish to accelerate their translation against their will, nor to inflict upon them a label which they may find odious.

It should be said, however, in passing, that even on the side of general theory and methodological conceptions, recent developments have been fruitful and significant. One at least of these deserves mention.

We find nowadays both psychologists and biologists who treat consciousness as substantially synonymous with adaptive reactions to novel situations. In the writings of earlier authorities it is often implied that accommodatory activities may be purely physiological and non-psychical in character. From this view-point the mental type of accommodatory act supervenes on certain occasions and at certain stages in organic development, but it is no indispensable feature of the accommodatory process.

It seems a trifle strange when one considers how long the fundamental conception involved in this theory has been familiar and accepted psychological doctrine that its full implication should have been so reluctantly recognized. If one takes the position now held by all psychologists of repute, so far as I am aware, that consciousness is constantly at work building up habits out of coordinations imperfectly under control; and that as speedily as control is gained the mental direction tends to automatism, it is only a step to carry the inference forward that consciousness immanently considered is *per se* accommodation to the novel. Whether conscious processes have been the precursors of our present instinctive equipment depends on facts of heredity upon which a layman may hardly speak. But many of our leaders answer strongly in the affirmative, and such an answer evidently harmonizes with the general view now under discussion.

To be sure the further assertion that no real organic accommodation to the novel ever occurs, save in the form that involves consciousness, requires for its foundation a wide range of observation and a penetrating analysis of the various criteria of mentality. But this is certainly a common belief among biologists today. Selective variation of response to stimulation is the ordinary external sign indicative of conscious action. Stated otherwise, consciousness discloses the form taken on by primary accommodatory process.

It is not unnatural perhaps that the frequent disposition of the functional psychologist to sigh after the flesh-pots of biology should kindle the fire of those consecrated to the cause of a pure psychology and philosophy freed from the contaminating influence of natural science. As a matter of fact, alarms have been repeatedly sounded and the faithful called to subdue mutiny. But the purpose of the functional psychologist has never been, so far as I am aware, to scuttle the psychological craft for the benefit of biology. Quite the contrary. Psychology is still for a time at least to steer her own untroubled course. She is at most borrowing a well-tested compass which biology is willing to lend and she hopes by its aid to make her ports more speedily and more surely. If in use it prove treacherous and unreliable, it will of course go overboard.

This broad biological ideal of functional psychology of which we have been speaking may be phrased with a slight shift of emphasis by connecting it with the problem of discovering the fundamental utilities of consciousness. If mental process is of real value to its possessor in the life and world which we know, it must perforce be by virtue of something which it does that otherwise is not accomplished. Now life and world are complex and it seems altogether improbable that consciousness should express its utility in one and only one way. As a matter of fact, every surface indication points in the other direction. It may be possible merely as a matter of expression to speak of mind as in general contributing to organic adjustment to environment. But the actual contributions will take place in many ways and by multitudinous varieties of conscious process. The functionalist's problem then is to determine if possible the great types of these processes in so far as the utilities which they present lend themselves to classification.

The search after the various utilitarian aspects of mental process is at once suggestive and disappointing. It is on the one hand illuminating by virtues of the strong relief into which it throws the fundamental resemblances of processes often unduly severed in psychological analysis. Memory and imagination, for example, are often treated in a way designed to emphasize their divergences almost to the exclusion of their functional similarities. They are of course functionally but variants on a single and basal type of control. An austere structuralism in particular is inevitably disposed to magnify differences and in consequence under its hands mental life tends to fall apart; and when put together again it generally seems to have lost something of its verve and vivacity. It appears stiff and rigid and corpse-like. It lacks the vital spark. Functionalism tends just as inevitably to bring mental phenomena together, to show them focalized in actual vital service. The professional psychologist, calloused by long apprenticeship, may not feel this distinction to be scientifically important. But to the young student the functionalistic stress upon community of service is of immense value in clarifying the intricacies of mental organization. On the other hand the search of which we were speaking is disappointing perhaps in the paucity of the basic modes in which these conscious utilities are realized.

Ultimately all the utilities are possibly reducible to selective accommodation. In the execution of the accommodatory activity the instincts represent the racially hereditary utilities, many of which are under the extant conditions of life extremely anomalous in their value. The sensory-algedonic-motor phenomena represent the immediate short circuit unreflective forms of selective response. Whereas the ideational-algedonic-motor series at its several levels represents the long circuit response under the influence of the mediating effects of previous experience. This experience serves either to inhibit the propulsive power intrinsic to the stimulus, or to reinforce this power by adding to it its own dynamic tendencies. This last variety of action is the peculiarly human form of mediated control. On its lowest stages, genetically speaking, it merges with the purely immediate algedonic type of response. All the other familiar psychological processes are subordinate to one or more of these groups. Conception, judgment, reasoning, emotion, desire, aversion, volition, etc., simply designate special varieties in which these generic forms appear.

III

The third conception which I distinguish is often in practice merged with the second, but it involves stress upon a problem logically prior perhaps to the problem raised there and so warrants separate mention. Functional psychology, it is often alleged, is in reality a form of psychophysics. To be sure, its aims and ideals are not explicitly quantitative in the manner characteristic of that science as commonly understood. But it finds its major interest in determining the relations to one another of the physical and mental portions of the organism.

It is undoubtedly true that many of those who write under functional prepossessions are wont to introduce frequent references to the physiological processes which accompany or condition mental life, Moreover, certain followers of this faith are prone to declare forthwith that psychology is simply a branch of biology and that we are in consequence entitled, if not indeed obliged, to make use where possible of biological materials. But without committing ourselves to so extreme a position as this, a mere glance at one familiar region of psychological procedure will disclose the leanings of psychology in this direction.

The psychology of volition affords an excellent illustration of the necessity with which descriptions of mental process eventuate in physiological or biological considerations. If one take the conventional analysis of a voluntary act drawn from some one or other of the experiences of adult life, the descriptions offered generally portray ideational activities of an anticipatory and deliberative character which serve to initiate immediately or remotely certain relevant expressive movements. Without the execution of the movements the ideational performances would be as futile as the tinkling cymbals of Scripture. To be sure, many of our psychologists protest themselves wholly unable to suggest why or how such muscular movements are brought to pass. But the fact of their occurrence or of their fundamental import for any theory of mental life in which consciousness is other than an epiphenomenon, is not questioned.

Moreover, if one considers the usual accounts of the ontogenesis of human volitional acts one is again confronted with intrinsically physiological data in which reflexes, automatic and instinctive acts are much in evidence. Whatever the possibilities, then, of an expurgated edition of the psychology of volition from which should be blotted out all reference to contaminating physiological factors, the actual practice of our representative psychologists is quite otherwise, and upon their showing volition cannot be understood either as regards its origin or its outcome without constant and overt reference to these factors. It would be a labor of supererrogation to go on and make clear the same doctrine as it applies to the psychology of the more recondite of the cognitive processes; so intimate is the relation between cognition and volition in modern psychological theory that we may well stand excused from carrying out in detail the obvious inferences from the situation we have just described.

Now if someone could but devise a method for handling the mind-body relationships which would not when published immediately create cyclonic disturbances in the philosophical atmosphere, it seems improbable that this disposition of the functional psychologists to inject physiology into his cosmos would cause comment and much less criticism. But even parallelism, that most insipid, pale and passionless of all the inventions begotten by the mind of man to accomplish this end, has largely failed of its pacific purpose. It is no wonder, therefore, that the more rugged creeds with positive programs to offer and a stock of red corpuscles to invest in their propagation should also have failed of universal favor.

This disposition to go over into the physiological for certain portions of psychological doctrine is represented in an interesting way by the frequent tendency of structural psychologists to find explanation in psychology substantially equivalent to physiological explanation. Professor Tichener's recent work on *Quantitative Psychology* represents this position very frankly. It is cited here with no intent to comment disparagingly upon the consistency of the structuralist position, but simply to indicate the wide-spread feeling of necessity at certain stages of psychological development for resort to physiological considerations.

Such a functional psychology as I have been presenting would be entirely reconciliable with Miss Calkins' "Psychology of selves" (so ably set forth by her in her presidential address last year) were it not for her extreme scientific conservatism in refusing to allow the self to have a body, save as a kind of conventional biological ornament. The real psychological self, as I understand her, is pure disembodied spirit—an admirable thing of good religious and philosophic ancestry, but surely not the thing with which we actually get through this vale of tears and not a thing before which psychology is under any obligation to kotow.

It is not clear that the functional psychologist because of his disposition to magnify the significance in practice of the mind-body relationships is thereby committed to any special theory of the character of these relationships, save as was said a moment since, that negatively he must seemingly of necessity set his face against any epiphenomenalist view. He might conceivably be an interactionist, or a parallelist or even an advocate of some wholly outworn creed. As a matter of fact certain of our most ardent functionalists not only cherish highly definite articles of faith as regards this issue, they would even go so far as to test functional orthodoxy by the acceptance of these tenets. This is to them the most momentous part of their functionalism, their holy of holies. It would display needless temerity to attempt within the limitations of this occasion a formulation of doctrine wholly acceptable to all concerned. But I shall venture a brief reference to such doctrine in the effort to bring out certain of its essentials.

The position to which I refer regards the mind-body relation as capable of treatment in psychology as a methodological distinction rather than a metaphysically existential one. Certain of its expounders arrive at their view by means of an analysis of the genetic conditions under which the mind-body differentiation first makes itself felt in the experience of the individual. This procedure clearly involves a direct frontal attack on the problem.

Others attain the position by flank movement, emphasizing to begin with the insoluble contradictions with which one is met when the distinction is treated as resting on existential differences in the primordial elements of the cosmos. Both methods of approach lead to the same goal, however, i.e., the conviction that the distinction has no existence on the genetically lower and more naif stages of experience. It only comes to light on a relatively reflective level and it must then be treated as instrumental if one would avoid paralogisms, antimonies and a host of other metaphysical nightmares. Moreover, in dealing with psychological problems this view entitles one to reject at least temporarily as irrelevant the question whether mind causes changes in neural action and conversely. The previous question is raised by defenders of this type of doctrine if one insists the lineage of your idea of causality, insisting that such a searching of one's intellectual reins will always disclose the inappropriateness of the inquiry as formulated above. They urge further that the profitable and significant thing is to seek for a more exact appreciation of the precise conditions under which consciousness is in evidence and the conditions under which it retires in favor of the more exclusively physiological. Such knowledge so far as it can be obtained is on a level with all scientific and practical information. It states the circumstances under which certain sorts of results will appear.

One's view of this functionalistic metaphysics is almost inevitably colored by current philosophical discussion as to the essential nature of consciousness. David Hume has been accused of destroying the reality of mind chiefly because he exorcised from it relationships of various kinds. If it be urged, as has so often been done, that Hume was guilty of pouring out the baby with the bath, the modern philosopher makes good the disaster not only by pouring in again both baby and bath, but by maintaining that baby and bath, mind and relations, are substantially one. Nor is this unity secured after the manner prescribed by the good Bishop Berkeley. At all events the metaphysicians to whom I refer are not fond of being called idealists. But the psychological functionalist who emphasizes the instrumental nature of the mind-body distinction and the metaphysician who regards mind as a relation are following roads which are at least parallel to one another if not actually convergent.

Whether or not one sympathizes with the views of that wing of the functionalist party to which our attention has just been directed it certainly seems a trifle unfair to cast up the mind-body difficulty in the teeth of the functionalist as such when on logical grounds he is no more guilty than any of his psychological neighbors. No courageous psychology of volition is possible which does not squarely face the mind-body problem, and in point of fact every important description of mental life contains doctrine of one kind or another upon this matter. A literally pure psychology of volition would be a sort of hanging-garden of Babylon, marvelous but inaccessible to psychologists of terrestrial habit. The functionalist is a greater sinner than others only in so far as he finds necessary and profitable a more constant insistence upon the translation of mental process into physiological process and conversely.

IV

If we now bring together the several conceptions of which mention has been made it will be easy to show them converging upon a common point. We have to consider (1) functionalism conceived as the psychology of mental operations in contrast to the psychology of mental elements; or, expressed otherwise, the psychology of the how and why of consciousness as distinguished from the psychology of the what of consciousness. We have (2) the functionalism which deals with the problem of mind conceived as primarily engaged in mediating between the environment and the needs of the organism. This is the psychology of the fundamental utilities of consciousness; (3) and lastly we have functionalism described as psychophysical psychology, that is the psychology which constantly recognizes and insists upon the essential significance of the mind-body relationship for any just and comprehensive appreciation of mental life itself.

The second and third delineations of functional psychology are rather obviously correlated with each other. No description of the actual circumstances attending the participation of mind in the accommodatory activities of the organism could be other than a mere empty schematism without making reference to the manner in which mental processes eventuate in motor phenomena of the physiological organism. The overt accommodatory act is, I take it, always sooner or later a muscular movement. But this fact being admitted, there is nothing for it, if one will describe accommodatory processes, but to recognize the mind-body relations and in some way give expression to their practical significance. It is only in this regard, as was indicated a few lines above, that the functionalist departs a trifle in his practice and a trifle more in his theory from the rank and file of his colleagues.

The effort to follow the lead of the natural sciences and delimit somewhat rigorously—albeit artificially—a field of inquiry, in this case consciousness conceived as an independent realm, has led in psychology to a deal of excellent work and to the uncovering of much hidden truth. So far as this procedure has resulted in a focusing of scientific attention and endeavor on a relatively narrow range of problems the result has more than justified the means. And the functionalist by no means holds that the limit of profitable research has been reached along these lines. But he is disposed to urge in season and out that we must not forget the arbitrary and self-imposed nature of the boundaries within which we toil when we try to eschew all explicit reference to the physical and physiological. To overlook this fact is to substitute a psychology under injunction for a psychology under free jurisdiction. He also urges with vigor and enthusiasm that a new illumination of this preempted field can be gained by envisaging it more broadly, looking at it as it appears when taken in perspective with its neighboring territory And if it be objected that such an inquiry however interesting and advantageous is at least not psychology, he can only reply: psychology is what we make it, and if the correct understanding of mental phenomena involves our delving in regions which are not at first glance properly mental, what recks it, provided only that we are nowhere guilty of untrustworthy and unverifiable procedure, and that we return loaded with the booty for which we set out, and by means of which we can the better solve our problem?

In its more basal philosophy this last conception is of course intimately allied to those appraisals of mind which emphasize its dominantly social characteristics, its rise out of social circumstances and the pervasively social nature of its constitutive principles. In our previous intimations of this standpoint we have not distinguished sharply between the physical and the social aspect of environment. The adaptive activities of mind are very largely of the distinctly social type. But this does not in any way jeopardize the genuineness of the connection upon which we have been insisting between the psychophysical aspects of a functional psychology and its environmental adaptive aspects.

It remains then to point out in what manner the conception of functionalism as concerned with the basal operations of mind is to be correlated with the other two conceptions just under discussion. The simplest view to take of the relations involved would apparently be such as would regard the first as an essential propaedeutic to the other two. Certainly if we are intent upon discerning the exact manner which mental process contributes to accommodatory efficiency, it is natural to begin our undertaking by determining what are the primordial forms of expression peculiar to mind. However plausible in theory this conception of the intrinsic logical relations of these several forms of functional psychology, in practice it is extremely difficult wholly to sever them from one another.

Again like the biological accommodatory view the psychophysical view of functional psychology involves as a rational presupposition some acquaintance with mental processes as these appear to reflective consciousness. The intelligent correlation in a practical way of physiological and mental operations evidently involves a preliminary knowledge of the conspicuous differentiations both on the side of conscious function and on the side of physiological function.

In view of the considerations of the last few paragraphs it does not seem fanciful nor forced to urged that these various theories of the problem of functional psychology really converge upon one another, however divergent may be the introductory investigations peculiar to each of the several ideals. Possibly the conception that the fundamental problem of the functionalist is one of determining just how mind participates in accommodatory reactions, is more nearly inclusive than either of the others, and so may be chosen to stand for the group. But if this vicarious duty is assigned to it, it must be on clear terms of remembrance that the other phases of the problem are equally real and equally necessary. Indeed the three things hang together as integral parts of a common program.

The functionalist's most intimate persuasion leads him to regard consciousness as primarily and intrinsically a control phenomenon. Just as behavior may be regarded as the most distinctly basic category of general biology in its functional phase so control would perhaps serve as the most fundamental category in functional psychology, the special forms and differentiations of consciousness simply constituting particular phases of the general process of control. At this point the omnipresent captious critic will perhaps arise to urge that the knowledge process is no more truly to be explained in terms of control than is control to be explained in terms of knowledge. Unquestionably there is from the point of view of the critic a measure of truth in this contention. The mechanism of control undoubtedly depends if one assumes the vitalistic point of view for one's more final interpretations, if one regards the furtherance of life in breadth and depth and permanence as an end in itself, and if one derives his scale of values from a contemplation of the several contributions toward this end represented by the great types of vital phenomena, with their apex in the moral, scientific and aesthetic realms, one must certainly find control a category more fundamental than the others offered by psychology. Moreover, it may be urged against the critic's attitude that even knowledge itself is built up under the control mechanism represented by selective attention and apperception. The basic character of control seems therefore hardly open to challenge.

One incidental merit of the functionalist program deserves a passing mention. This is the one method of approach to the problem with which I am acquainted that offers a reasonable and cogent account of the rise of reflective consciousness and its significance as manifested in the various philosophical disciplines. From the vantage point of the functionalist position logic and ethics, for instance, are no longer mere disconnected items in the world of mind. They take their place with all the inevitableness of organic organization in the general system of control, which requires for the expression of its immanent meaning *as psychic* a theoretical vindication of its own inner principles, its modes of procedure and their results. From any other point of view, so far as I am aware, the several divisions of philosophical inquiry sustain to one another relations which are almost purely external and accidental. To the functionalist on the other hand they are and must be in the nature of the case consanguineous and vitally connected. It is at the point, for example, where the good, the beautiful and the true have bearing on the efficacy of accommodatory activity that the issues of the normative philosophical sciences becomes relevant. If good action has no significance for the enriching and enlarging of life, the contention I urge is futile, and similarly as regards beauty and truth. But it is not at present usually maintained that such is the fact.

These and other similar tendencies of functionalism may serve to reassure those who fear that in lending itself to biological influences psychology may lose contact with philosophy and so sacrifice the poise and balance and sanity of outlook which philosophy undertakes to furnish. The particular brand of philosophy which is predestined to functionalist favor cannot of course be confidently predicted in advance. But anything approaching a complete and permanent divorce of psychology from philosophy is surely improbable so long as one cultivates the functionalist faith. Philosophy cannot dictate scientific method here any more than elsewhere, nor foreordain the special facts to be discovered. But as an interpreter of the psychologist's achievements she will always stand higher in the functionalist's favor than in that of his colleagues of other persuasions, for she is a more integral and significant part of his scheme of the cosmos. She may even outgrow under his tutelage that "valiant inconclusiveness" of which the last of her long line of lay critics has just accused her.

A sketch of the kind we have offered is unhappily likely to leave on the mind an impression of functional psychology as a name for a group of genial but vague ambitions and good intentions. This, however, is a fault which must be charged to the artist and to the limitations of time and space under which he is here working. There is nothing vaguer in the program of the functionalist when he goes to his work than there is in the purposes of the psychologist wearing any other livery. He goes to his laboratory, for example, with just the same resolute interest to discover new facts and new relationships, with just the same determination to verify and confirm his previous observations, as does his colleague who calls himself perhaps a structuralist. But he looks out upon the surroundings of his science with a possibly greater sensitiveness to its continuity with other ranges of human interest and with certainly a more articulate purpose to see the mind which he analyzes as it actually is when engaged in the discharge of its vital functions. If his method tempts him now and then to sacrifice something of petty exactitude, he is under no obligation to yield, and in any case he has for his compensation the power which comes from breadth and sweep of outlook.

So far as he may be expected to develop methods peculiar to himself—so far, indeed, as in genetic and comparative psychology, for example, he has already developed such—they will not necessarily be iconoclastic and revolutionary, nor such as flout the methods already devised and established on a slightly different foundation. They will be distinctly complementary to all that is solid in these. Nor is it in any way essential that the term functionalism should cling to this new-old movement. It seems at present a convenient term, but there is nothing sacrosanct about it, and the moment it takes unto itself the pretense of scientific finality its doom will be sealed. It means to-day a broad and flexible and organic point of view in psychology. The moment it becomes dogmatic and narrow its spirit will have passed and undoubtedly some worthier successor will fill its place.

John Broadus Watson: 1878-

PSYCHOLOGY AS THE BEHAVIORIST VIEWS IT *

1913

PSYCHOLOGY as the behaviorist views it is a purely objective experimental branch of natural science. Its theoretical goal is the prediction and control of behavior. Introspection forms no essential part of its methods, nor is the scientific value of its data dependent upon the readiness with which they lend themselves to interpretation in terms of consciousness. The behaviorist, in his efforts to get a unitary scheme of animal response, recognizes no dividing line between man and brute. The behavior of man, with all of its refinement and complexity, forms only a part of the behaviorist's total scheme of investigation.

It has been maintained by its followers generally that psychology is a study of the science of the phenomena of consciousness. It has taken as its problem, on the one hand, the analysis of complex mental states (or processes) into simple elementary constituents, and on the other the construction of complex states when the elementary constituents are given. The world of the physical objects (stimuli, including here anything which may excite activity in a receptor), which forms the total phenomena of the natural scientist, is looked upon merely as means to an end. That end is the production of mental states that may be "inspected" or "observed." The psychological object of observation in the case of an emotion, for example, is the mental state itself. The problem in emotion is the determination of the number and kind of elementary constituents present, their loci, intensity, order of appearance, etc. It is agreed that introspection is the method par excellence by means of which mental states may be manipulated for purposes of psychology. On this assumption, behavior data (including under this term everything which goes under the name of comparative psychology) have no value per se. They possess significance only in so far as they may throw light upon conscious states. Such data must have at least an analogical or indirect reference to belong to the realm of psychology.

Indeed, at times, one finds psychologists who are sceptical of even this

* From the *Psychological Review*, XX (1913), 158-177. Reprinted by permission of the author and of the American Psychological Association. This paper is Watson's earliest publication on behaviorism.

analogical reference. Such scepticism is often shown by the question which is put to the student of behavior, "What is the bearing of animal work upon human psychology?" I used to have to study over this question. Indeed it always embarrassed me somewhat. I was interested in my own work and felt that it was important, and yet I could not trace any close connection between it and psychology as my questioner understood psychology. I hope that such a confession will clear the atmosphere to such an extent that we will no longer have to work under false pretences. We must frankly admit that the facts so important to us which we have been able to glean from extended work upon the senses of animals by the behavior method have contributed only in a fragmentary way to the general theory of human sense organ processes, nor have they suggested new points of experimental attack. The enormous number of experiments which we have carried out upon learning have likewise contributed little to human psychology. It seems reasonably clear that some kind of compromise must be effected: either psychology must change its viewpoint so as to take in facts of behavior, whether or not they have bearings upon the problems of "consciousness"; or else behavior must stand alone as a wholly separate and independent science. Should human psychologists fail to look with favor upon our overtures and refuse to modify their position, the behaviorists will be driven to using human beings as subjects and to employ methods of investigation which are exactly comparable to those now employed in the animal work. Any other hypothesis than that which admits the independent value of behavior material, regardless of any bearing such material may have upon consciousness, will inevitably force us to the absurd position of attempting to construct the conscious content of the animal whose behavior we have been studying. On this view, after having determined our animal's ability to learn, the simplicity or complexity of its methods of learning, the effect of past habit upon present response, the range of stimuli to which it ordinarily responds, the widened range to which it can respond under experimental conditions,—in more general terms, its various problems and its various ways of solving them,—we should still feel that the task is unfinished and that the results are worthless, until we can interpret them by analogy in the light of consciousness. Although we have solved our problem we feel uneasy and unrestful because of our definition of psychology: we feel forced to say something about the possible mental processes of our animal. We say that, having no eyes, its stream of consciousness cannot contain brightness and color sensations as we know them,—having no taste buds this stream can contain no sensations of sweet, sour, salt and bitter. But on the other hand, since it does respond to thermal, tactual and organic stimuli, its conscious content must be made up largely of these sensations; and we usually add, to protect ourselves against the reproach of being anthropomorphic, "if it has any consciousness." Surely this doctrine which calls for an analogical interpretation of all behavior data may be shown to be false: the position that the standing of an observation upon behavior is determined by its fruitfulness in yielding results which are interpretable only in the narrow realm of (really human) consciousness.

This emphasis upon analogy in psychology has led the behaviorist somewhat afield. Not being willing to throw off the yoke of consciousness he feels impelled to make a place in the scheme of behavior where the rise of consciousness can be determined. This point has been a shifting one. A few years ago certain animals were supposed to possess "associative memory," while certain others were supposed to lack it. One meets this search for the origin of consciousness under a good many disguises. Some of our texts state that consciousness arises at the moment when reflex and instinctive activities fail properly to conserve the organism. A perfectly adjusted organism would be lacking in consciousness. On the other hand whenever we find the presence of diffuse activity which results in habit formation, we are justified in assuming consciousness. I must confess that these arguments had weight with me when I began the study of behavior. I fear that a good many of us are still viewing behavior problems with something like this in mind. More than one student in behavior has attempted to frame criteria of the psychic—to devise a set of objective, structural and functional criteria which, when applied in the particular instance, will enable us to decide whether such and such responses are positively conscious, merely indicative of consciousness, or whether they are purely "physiological." Such problems as these can no longer satisfy behavior men. It would be better to give up the province altogether and to admit frankly that the study of the behavior of animals has no justification, than to admit that our search is of such a "will o' the wisp" character. One can assume either the presence or the absence of consciousness anywhere in the phylogenetic scale without affecting the problems of behavior one jot or one tittle; and without influencing in any way the mode of experimental attack upon them. On the other hand, I cannot for one moment assume that the paramecium responds to light; that the rat learns a problem more quickly by working at the task five times a day than once a day, or that the human child exhibits plateaux in his learning curves. These are questions which vitally concern behavior and which must be decided by direct observation under experimental conditions.

This attempt to reason by analogy from human conscious processes to the conscious processes in animals, and vice versa: to make consciousness, as the human being knows it, the center of reference of all behavior, forces us into a situation similar to that which existed in biology in Darwin's time. The whole Darwinian movement was judged by the bearing it had upon the origin and development of the human race. Expeditions were undertaken to collect material which would establish the position that the rise of the human race was a perfectly natural phenomenon and not an act of special creation. Variations were carefully sought along with the evidence for the heaping up effect and the weeding out effect of selection; for in these and the other Darwinian mechanisms were to be found factors sufficiently complex to account for the origin and race differentiation of man. The wealth of material collected at this time was considered valuable largely in so far as it tended to develop the concept of evolution in man. It is strange that this situation should have remained the dominant one in biology for so many years. The moment zoology undertook the experimental study of evolution and descent, the situation immediately changed. Man ceased to be the center of reference. I doubt if any experimental biologist today, unless actually engaged in the problem of race differentiation in man, tries to interpret his findings in terms of human evolution, or ever refers to it in his thinking. He gathers his data from the study of many species of plants and animals and tries to work out the laws of inheritance in the particular type upon which he is conducting experiments. Naturally, he follows the progress of the work upon race differentiation in man and in the descent of man, but he looks upon these as special topics, equal in importance with his own yet ones in which his interests will never be vitally engaged. It is not fair to say that all of his work is directed toward human evolution or that it must be interpreted in terms of human evolution. He does not have to dismiss certain of his facts on the inheritance of coat color in mice because, forsooth, they have little bearing upon the differentiation of the genus homo into separate races, or upon the descent of the genus homo from some more primitive stock.

In psychology we are still in that stage of development where we feel that we must select our material. We have a general place of discard for processes, which we anathematize so far as their value for psychology is concerned by saying, "this is a reflex"; "that is a purely physiological fact which has nothing to do with psychology." We are not interested (as psychologists) in getting all of the processes of adjustment which the animal as a whole employs, and in finding how these various responses are associated, and how they fall apart, thus working out a systematic scheme for the prediction and control of response in general. Unless our observed facts are indicative of consciousness, we have no use for them, and unless our apparatus and method are designed to throw such facts into relief, they are thought of in just as disparaging a way. I shall always remember the remark one distinguished psychologist made as he looked over the color apparatus designed for testing the responses of animals to monochromatic light in the attic at Johns Hopkins. It was this: "And they call this psychology!"

I do not wish unduly to criticize psychology. It has failed signally, I believe, during the fifty-odd years of its existence as an experimental discipline to make its place in the world as an undisputed natural science. Psychology, as it is generally thought of, has something esoteric in its methods. If you fail to reproduce my findings, it is not due to some fault in your apparatus or in the control of your stimulus, but it is due to the fact that your introspection is untrained. The attack is made upon the observer and not upon the experimental setting. In physics and in chemistry the attack is made upon the experimental conditions. The apparatus was not sensitive enough, impure chemicals were used, etc. In these sciences a better technique will give reproducible results. Psychology is other wise. If you can't observe 3–9 states of clearness in attention, your introspection is poor. If, on the other hand, a feeling seems reasonably clear to you, your introspection is again faulty. You are seeing too much. Feelings are never clear.

The time seems to have come when psychology must discard all reference to consciousness; when it need no longer delude itself into thinking that it is making mental states the object of observation. We have become so enmeshed in speculative questions concerning the elements of mind, the nature of conscious content (for example, imageless thought, attitudes, and Bewusseinslage, etc.) that I, as an experimental student, feel that something is wrong with our premises and the types of problems which develop from them. There is no longer any guarantee that we all mean the same thing when we use the terms now current in psychology. Take the case of sensation. A sensation is defined in terms of its attributes. One psychologist will state with readiness that the attributes of a visual sensation are *quality*, *extension*, *duration*, and *intensity*. Another will add *clearness*. Still another that of *order*. I doubt if any one psychologist can draw up a set of statements describing what he means by sensation which will be agreed to by three other psychologists of different training. Turn for a moment to the question of the number of isolable sensations. Is there an extremely large number of color sensations—or only four, red, green, yellow and blue? Again, yellow, while psychologically simple, can be obtained by superimposing red and green spectral rays upon the same diffusing surface! If, on the other hand, we say that every just noticeable difference in the spectrum is a simple sensation, and that every just noticeable increase in the white value of a given color gives simple sensations, we are forced to admit that the number is so large and the conditions for obtaining them so complex that the concept of sensation is unusable, either for the purpose of analysis or that of synthesis. Titchener, who has fought the most valiant fight in this country for a psychology based upon introspection, feels that these differences of opinion as to the number of sensations and their attributes; as to whether there are relations (in the sense of elements) and on the many others which seem to be fundamental in every attempt at analysis, are perfectly natural in the present undeveloped state of psychology. While it is admitted that every growing science is full of unanswered questions, surely only those who are wedded to the system as we now have it, who have fought and suffered for it, can confidently believe that there will ever be any greater uniformity than there is now in the answers we have to such questions. I firmly believe that two hundred years from now, unless the introspective method is discarded, psychology will still be divided on the question as to whether auditory sensations have the quality of "extension," whether intensity is an attribute which can be applied to color, whether there is a difference in "texture" between image and sensation and upon many hundreds of others of like character.

The condition in regard to other mental processes is just as chaotic. Can image type be experimentally tested and verified? Are recondite thought processes dependent mechanically upon imagery at all? Are psychologists agreed upon what feeling is? One states that feelings are attitudes. Another finds them to be groups of organic sensations possessing a certain solidarity. Still another and larger group finds them to be new elements correlative with and ranking equally with sensations.

My psychological quarrel is not with the systematic and structural psychologist alone. The last fifteen years have seen the growth of what is called functional psychology. This type of psychology decries the use of elements in the static sense of the structuralists. It throws emphasis upon the biological significance of conscious processes instead of upon the analysis of conscious states into introspectively isolable elements. I have done my best to understand the difference between functional psychology and structural psychology. Instead of clarity, confusion grows upon me. The terms sensation, perception, affection, emotion, volition are used as much by the functionalist as by the structuralist. The addition of the word "process" ("mental act as a whole," and like terms are frequently met) after each serves in some way to remove the corpse of "content" and to leave "function" in its stead. Surely if these concepts are elusive when looked at from a content standpoint, they are still more deceptive when viewed from the angle of function, and especially so when function is obtained by the introspection method. It is rather interesting that no function psychologist has carefully distinguished between "perception" (and this is true of the other psychological terms as well) as employed by the systematist, and "perceptual process" as used in functional psychology. It seems illogical and hardly fair to criticize the psychology which the systematist gives us, and then to utilize his terms without carefully showing the changes in meaning which are to be attached to them. I was greatly surprised some time ago when I opened Pillsbury's book and saw psychology defined as the "science of behavior." A still more recent text states that psychology is the "science of mental behavior." When I saw these promising statements I thought, now surely we will have texts based upon different lines. After a few pages the science of behavior is dropped and one finds the conventional treatment of sensation, perception, imagery, etc., along with certain shifts in emphasis and additional facts which serve to give the author's personal imprint.

One of the difficulties in the way of a consistent functional psychology is the parallelistic hypothesis. If the functionalist attempts to express his formulations in terms which make mental states really appear to function, to play some active role in the world of adjustment, he almost inevitably lapses into terms which are connotative of interaction. When taxed with this he replies that it is more convenient to do so and that he does it to avoid the circumlocution and clumsiness which are inherent in any thoroughgoing parallelism. As a matter of fact I believe the functionalist actually thinks in terms of interaction and resorts to parallelism only when forced to give expression to his views. I feel that *behaviorism* is the only consistent and logical functionalism. In it one avoids both the Scylla of parallelism and the Charybdis of interaction. Those time-honored relics of philosophical speculation need trouble the student of behavior as little as they trouble the student of physics. The consideration of the mind-body problem affects neither the type of problem selected nor the formulation of the solution of that problem. I can state my position here no better than by saying that I should like to bring my students up in the same ignorance of such hypotheses as one finds among the students of other branches of science.

This leads me to the point where I should like to make the argument constructive. I believe we can write a psychology, define it as Pillsbury, and never go back upon our definition: never use the terms consciousness, mental states, mind, content, introspectively verifiable, imagery, and the like. I believe that we can do it in a few years without running into the absurd terminology of Beer, Bethe, Von Uexkull, Nuel, and that of the so-called objective schools generally. It can be done in terms of stimulus and response, in terms of habit formation, habit integrations and the like. Furthermore, I believe that it is really worth while to make this attempt now.

The psychology which I should attempt to build up would take as a starting point, first, the observable fact that organisms, man and animal alike, do adjust themselves to their environment by means of hereditary and habit equipments. These adjustments may be very adequate or they may be so inadequate that the organism barely maintains its existence; secondly, that certain stimuli lead the organisms to make the responses. In a system of psychology completely worked out, given the stimuli the response can be predicted. Such a set of statements is crass and raw in the extreme, as all such generalizations must be. Yet they are hardly more raw and less realizable than the ones which appear in the psychology texts of the day. I possibly might illustrate my point better by choosing an everyday problem which anyone is likely to meet in the course of his work. Some time ago I was called upon to make a study of certain species of birds. Until I went to Tortugas I had never seen these birds alive. When I reached there I found the animals doing certain things: some of the acts seemed to work peculiarly well in such an environment, while others seemed to be unsuited to their type of life. I first studied the responses of the group as a whole and later those of individuals. In order to understand more thoroughly the relation between what was habit and what was hereditary in these responses, I took the young birds and reared them. In this way I was able to study the order of appearance of hereditary adjustments and their complexity, and later the beginnings of habit formation. My efforts in determining the stimuli which called forth such adjustments were crude indeed. Consequently my attempts to control behavior and to produce responses at will did not meet with much success. Their food and water, sex and other social relations, light and temperature conditions were all beyond control in a field study. I did find it possible to control their reactions in a measure by using the nest and egg (or young) as stimuli. It is not necessary in this paper to develop further how such a study should be carried out and how work of this kind must be supplemented by carefully controlled laboratory experiments. Had I been called upon to examine the natives of some of the Australian tribes, I should have gone about my task in the same way. I should have found the problem more difficult: the types of responses called forth by physical stimuli would have been more varied, and the number of effective stimuli larger. I should have had to determine the social setting of their lives in a far more careful way. These savages would be more influenced by the responses of each other than was the case with the birds. Furthermore, habits would have been more complex and the influences of past habits upon the present responses would have appeared more clearly. Finally, if I had been called upon to work out the psychology of the educated European, my problem would have required several lifetimes. But in the one I have at my disposal I should have followed the same general line of attack. In the main, my desire in all such work is to gain an accurate knowledge of adjustments and the stimuli calling them forth.

My final reason for this is to learn general and particular methods by which I may control behavior. My goal is not "the description and explanation of states of consciousness as such," nor that of obtaining such proficiency in mental gymnastics that I can immediately lay hold of a state of consciousness and say, "this, as a whole, consists of gray sensation number 350, of such and such extent, occurring in conjunction with the sensation of cold of a certain intensity; one of pressure of a certain intensity and extent," and so on *ad infinitum.* If psychology would follow the plan I suggest, the educator, the physician, the jurist and the business man could utilize our data in a practical way, as soon as we are able, experimentally, to obtain them. Those who have occasion to apply psychological principles practically would find no need to complain as they do at the present time. Ask any physician or jurist today whether scientific psychology plays a practical part in his daily routine and you will hear him deny that the psychology of the laboratories finds a place in his scheme of work. I think the criticism is extremely just. One of the earliest conditions which made me dissatisfied with psychology was the feeling that there was no realm of application for the principles which were being worked out in content terms.

What gives me hope that the behaviorist's position is a defensible one is the fact that those branches of psychology which have already partially withdrawn from the parent, experimental psychology, and which are consequently less dependent upon introspection are today in a most flourishing condition. Experimental pedagogy, the psychology of drugs, the psychology of advertising, legal psychology, the psychology of tests, and psychopathology are all vigorous growths. These are sometimes wrongly called "practical" or "applied" psychology. Surely there was never a worse misnomer. In the future there may grow up vocational bureaus which really apply psychology. At present these fields are truly scientific and are in search of broad generalizations which will lead to the control of human behavior. For example, we find out by experimentation whether a series of stanzas may be acquired more readily if the whole is learned at once, or whether it is more advantageous to learn each stanza separately and then pass to the succeeding. We do not attempt to apply our findings. The application of this principle is purely voluntary on the part of the teacher. In the psychology of drugs we may show the effect upon behavior of certain doses of caffeine. We may reach the conclusion that caffeine has a good effect upon the speed and accuracy of work. But these are general principles. We leave it to the individual as to whether the results of our tests shall be applied or not. Again, in legal testimony, we test the effects of recency upon the reliability of a witness's report. We test the accuracy of the report with respect to moving objects, stationary objects, color, etc. It depends upon the judicial machinery of the country to decide whether these facts are ever to be applied. For a "pure" psychologist to say that he is not interested in the questions raised in these divisions of the science because they relate indirectly to the application of psychology shows, in the first place, that he fails to understand the scientific aim in such problems, and secondly, that he is not interested in a psychology which concerns itself with human life. The only fault I have to find with these disciplines is that much of their material is stated in terms of introspection, whereas a statement in terms of objective results would be far more valuable. There is no reason why appeal should ever be made to consciousness in any of them. Or why introspective data should ever be sought during the experimentation, or published in the results. In experimental pedagogy especially one can see the desirability of keeping all of the results on a purely objective plane. If this is done, work there on the human being will be comparable directly with the work upon animals. For example, at Hopkins, Mr. Ulrich has obtained certain results upon the distribution of effort in learning—using rats as subjects. He is prepared to give comparative results upon the effect of having an animal work at the problem once per day, three times per day, and five times per day. Whether it is advisable to have the animal learn only one problem at a time or to learn three abreast. We need to have similar experiments made upon man, but we care as little about his "conscious processes" during the conduct of the experiment as we care about such processes in the rats.

I am more interested at the present moment in trying to show the necessity for maintaining uniformity in experimental procedure and in the method of stating results in both human and animal work, than in developing any ideas I may have upon the changes which are certain to come in the scope of human psychology. Let us consider for a moment the subject of the range of stimuli to which animals respond. I shall speak first of the work upon vision in animals. We put our animal in a situation where he will respond (or learn to respond) to one of two monochromatic lights. We feed him at the one (positive) and punish him at the other (negative). In a short time the animal learns to go to the light at which he is fed. At this point questions arise which I may phrase in two ways: I may choose the psychological way and say "does the animal see these two lights as I do, i.e., as two distinct colors, or does he see them as two grays differing in brightness, as does the totally color blind?" Phrased by the behaviorist, it would read as follows: "Is my animal responding upon the basis of the difference in intensity between the two stimuli, or upon the difference in wavelengths?" He nowhere thinks of the animal's response in terms of his own experiences of colors and grays. He wishes to establish the fact whether wave-length is a factor in that animal's adjustment. If so, length must be maintained in the different regions to afford bases for differential responses? If wave-length is not a factor in adjustment he wishes to know what difference in intensity will serve as a basis for response, and whether that same difference will suffice throughout the spectrum. Furthermore, he wishes to test whether the animal can respond to wave-lengths which do not affect the human eye. He is as much interested in comparing the rat's spectrum with that of the chick as in comparing it with man's. The point of view when the various sets of comparisons are made does not change in the slightest.

However we phrase the question to ourselves, we take our animal after the association has been formed and then introduce certain control experiments which enable us to return answers to the questions just raised. But there is just as keen a desire on our part to test man under the same conditions, and to state the results in both cases in common terms.

The man and the animal should be placed as nearly as possible under the same experimental conditions. Instead of feeding or punishing the human subject, we should ask him to respond by setting a second apparatus until standard and control offered no basis for a differential response. Do I lay myself open to the charge here that I am using introspection? My reply is not at all; that while I might very well feed my human subject for a right choice and punish him for a wrong one and thus produce the response if the subject could give it, there is no need of going to extremes even on the platform I suggest. But be it understood that I am merely using this second method as an abridged behavior method. We can go just as far and reach just as dependable results by the longer method as by the abridged. In many cases the direct and typically human method cannot be safely used. Suppose, for example, that I doubt the accuracy of the setting of the control instrument, in the above experiment, as I am very likely to do if I suspect a defect in vision? It is hopeless for me to get his introspective report. He will say: "There is no difference in sensation, both are reds, identical in quality." But suppose I confront him with the standard and the control and so arrange conditions that he is punished if he responds to the "control" but not with the standard. I interchange the positions of the standard and the control at will and force him to attempt to differentiate the one from the other. If he can learn to make the adjustment even after a large number of trials it is evident that the two stimuli do afford the basis for a differential response. Such a method may sound nonsensical, but I firmly believe we will have to resort increasingly to just such a method where we have reason to distrust the language method.

There is hardly a problem in human vision which is not also a problem in animal vision: I mention the limits of the spectrum, threshold values, absolute and relative, flicker, Talbot's law, Weber's law, field of vision, the Purkinje phenomenon, etc. Every one is capable of being worked out by behavior methods. Many of them are being worked out at the present time.

I feel that all the work upon the senses can be consistently carried forward along the lines I have suggested here for vision. Our results will, in the end, give an excellent picture of what each organ stands for in the way of function. The anatomist and the physiologist may take our data and show, on the one hand, the structures which are responsible for these responses, and, on the other, the physico-chemical relations which are necessarily involved (physiological chemistry of nerve and muscle) in these and other reactions.

The situation in regard to the study of memory is hardly different. Nearly all of the memory methods in actual use in the laboratory today yield the type of results I am arguing for. A certain series of nonsense syllables or other material is presented to the human subject. What should receive the emphasis are the rapidity of the habit formation, the errors, peculiarities in the form of the curve, the persistence of the habit so formed, the relation of such habits to those formed when more complex material is used, etc. Now such results are taken down with the subject's introspection. The experiments are made for the purpose of discussing the mental machinery involved in learning, in recall, recollection and forgetting, and not for the purpose of seeking the human being's way of shaping his responses to meet the problems in the terribly complex environment into which he is thrown, nor for that of showing the similarities and differences between man's methods and those of other animals.

The situation is somewhat different when we come to a study of the more complex forms of behavior, such as imagination, judgment, reasoning, and conception. At present the only statements we have of them are in content terms. Our minds have been so warped by the fifty-odd years which have been devoted to the study of states of consciousness that we can envisage these problems only in one way. We should meet the situation squarely and say that we are not able to carry forward investigations along all of these lines by the behavior methods which are in use at the present time. In extenuation I should like to call attention to the paragraph above where I made the point that the introspective method itself has reached a *cul-de-sac* with respect to them. The topics have become so threadbare from much handling that they may well be put away for a time. As our methods become better developed it will be possible to undertake investigations of more and more complex forms of behavior. Problems which are now laid aside will again become imperative, but they can be viewed as they arise from a new angle and in more concrete settings.

The hypothesis that all of the so-called "higher thought" processes go on in terms of faint reinstatements of the original muscular act (including speech here) and that these are integrated into systems which respond in serial order (associative mechanisms) is, I believe, a tenable one. It makes reflective processes as mechanical as habit. The scheme of habit which James long ago described—where each return or afferent current releases the next appropriate motor discharge—is as true for "thought processes" as for overt muscular acts. Paucity of "imagery" would be the rule. In other words, wherever there are thought processes there are faint contractions of the systems of musculature involved in the overt exercise of the customary act, and especially in the still finer systems of musculature involved in speech. If this is true, and I do not see how it can be gainsaid, imagery becomes a mental luxury (even if it really exists) without any functional significance whatever. If experimental procedure justifies this hypothesis, we shall have at hand tangible phenomena which may be studied as behavior material. I should say that the day when we can study reflective processes by such methods is about as far off as the day when we can tell by physico-chemical methods the difference in the structure and arrangement of molecules between living protoplasm and inorganic substances. The solutions of both problems await the advent of methods and apparatus.

Will there be left over in psychology a world of pure psychics, to use Yerkes' term? I confess I do not know. The plans which I most favor for psychology lead practically to the ignoring of consciousness in the sense that that term is used by psychologists today. I have virtually denied that this realm of psychics is open to experimental investigation. I don't wish to go further into the problem at present because it leads inevitably over into metaphysics. If you will grant the behaviorist the right to use consciousness in the same way that other natural scientists employ it—that is, without making consciousness a special object of observation—you have granted all that my thesis requires.

In concluding, I suppose I must confess to a deep bias on these questions. I have devoted nearly twelve years to experimentation on animals. It is natural that such a one should drift into a theoretical position which is in harmony with his experimental work. Possibly I have put up a straw man and have been fighting that. There may be no absolute lack of harmony between the position outlined here and that of functional psychology. I am inclined to think, however, that the two positions cannot be easily harmonized. Certainly the position I advocate is weak enough at present and can be attacked from many standpoints. Yet when all this is admitted I still feel that the considerations which I have urged should have a wide influence upon the type of psychology which is to be developed in the future. What we need to do is to start work upon psychology, making *behavior*, not *consciousness*, the objective point of our attack. Certainly there are enough problems in the control of behavior to keep us all working many lifetimes without ever allowing us time to think of consciousness *an sich*. Once launched in the undertaking, we will find ourselves in a short time as far divorced from an introspective psychology as the psychology of the present time is divorced from faculty psychology.

SUMMARY

1. Human psychology has failed to make good its claim as a natural science. Due to a mistaken notion that its fields of fact are conscious phenomena and that introspection is the only direct method of ascertaining these facts, it has enmeshed itself in a series of speculative questions which, while fundamental to its present tenets, are not open to experimental treatment. In the pursuit of answers to these questions, it has become further and further divorced from contact with problems which vitally concern human interest.

2. Psychology, as the behaviorist views it, is a purely objective, experimental branch of natural science which needs introspection as little as do the sciences of chemistry and physics. It is granted that the behavior of animals can be investigated without appeal to consciousness. Heretofore the viewpoint has been that such data have value only in so far as they can be interpreted by analogy in terms of consciousness. The position is taken here that the behavior of man and the behavior of animals must be considered on the same plane; as being equally essential to a general understanding of behavior. It can dispense with consciousness in a psychological sense. The separate observation of "states of consciousness" is, on this assumption, no more a part of the task of the psychologist than of the physicist. We might call this the return to a non-reflective and naive use of consciousness. In this sense consciousness may be said to be the instrument or tool with which all scientists work. Whether or not the tool is properly used at present by scientists is a problem for philosophy and not for psychology.

3. From the viewpoint here suggested the facts on the behavior of amoebae have value in and for themselves without reference to the behavior of man. In biology studies on race differentiation and inheritance in amoebae form a separate division of study which must be evaluated in terms of the laws found there. The conclusions so reached may not hold in any other form. Regardless of the possible lack of generality, such studies must be made if evolution as a whole is ever to be regulated and controlled. Similarly the laws of behavior in amoebae, the range of responses, and the determination of effective stimuli, of habit formation,

persistency of habits, interference and reinforcement of habits, must be determined and evaluated in and for themselves, regardless of their generality, or of their bearing upon such laws in other forms, if the phenomena of behavior are ever to be brought within the sphere of scientific control.

4. This suggested elimination of states of consciousness as proper objects of investigation in themselves will remove the barrier from psychology which exists between it and the other sciences. The findings of psychology become the functional correlates of structure and lend themselves to explanation in physico-chemical terms.

5. Psychology as behavior will, after all, have to neglect but few of the really essential problems with which psychology as an introspective science now concerns itself. In all probability even this residue of problems may be phrased in such a way that refined methods in behavior (which certainly must come) will lead to their solution.

Walter Samuel Hunter: 1889-

THE DELAYED REACTION IN ANIMALS AND CHILDREN *

1914

INTRODUCTION

THE experiments in this monograph aim at an analysis of typical mammalian behavior under conditions where the determining stimulus is absent at the moment of response. Associations were first set up between movements that led to food and a light which might be in any one of three boxes. Controls were used to make sure that the position of the light alone determined the reactions of the subject. Tests were then instituted in which the light was turned off before the reaction was made. The subject thus had to respond in the absence of the stimulus that hitherto had guided his reactions.

The nature of the present experiment may be further set forth by contrasting it with the following type of adjustment: A cat watches for a mouse and sees it appear at an open hole. The mouse vanishes before the cat can react, yet the cat goes over to the hole. There can be no question here but that the determining stimulus is absent at the moment of response, provided possible olfactory stimuli be neglected. Our experiment differs from this in complexity. If there were three holes that differed only in their several directions from the cat, and if in the past the mouse had appeared an equal number of times in all three holes, the conditions would be the same as in our tests. A selection between the three holes would need to be made on the basis of the immediately previous presence of the rat, if a correct reaction were to occur. If an animal can manifest behavior that does not lend itself to a "stimulus and response" explanation, this is one type of situation in which that behavior should appear. That, in fact, it is the situation par excellence for the eliciting of this behavior will, I believe, appear as this monograph progresses.

* Hunter's monograph of this title was published by Williams and Wilkins. Portions of the monograph (pages 1-2, 21-29 and 79-81) are here reprinted by permission of the publisher and the author. Hunter's research represented, as he indicates, the first successful attempt to set up a problem which requires the subject to respond to a stimulus after the stimulus has been removed.

In the present experiments, two main factual questions arise: (1) How long after the determining stimulus has disappeared can an animal wait and still react correctly? (2) Does the animal give any behavior cues as to its method of solving the problem? If so, what are they? With these data given, there remains the task of interpretation. If a selective response has been initiated and controlled by a certain stimulus, and if the response can still be made successfully in the absence of that stimulus, then the subject must be using something that functions for the stimulus in initiating and guiding the correct response. Our investigation thus forces us to the consideration of the functional presence of a representative factor in the behavior of animals and children. Not only this, but the problem of the nature of this representative factor confronts us. Is it an overt motor attitude, or not? If not, is it sensory or imaginal, i.e., ideational?

In the interpretative study, I shall proceed on the assumption that animals are conscious. What the nature of this consciousness is, it will be the task of this paper to help determine. (If the reader does not choose to follow this line of interpretation, he may state everything in neurological terms without marring the significance of this discussion.) But a propos of the term "image" or "idea," let it be said once for all that wherever these terms are used by the present writer with reference to animal consciousness, they should be supplemented by the phrase "or functionally equivalent process." I use the structural term chiefly for the sake of its brevity.

NOTES ON THE ANIMALS AND CHILDREN TESTED

Four classes of re-agents were used in the experiments whose description is to follow: white rats, dogs, raccoons (Procyon lotor) and children. A few words descriptive of these subjects will not be amiss.

1. Rats

Twenty-two rats were used during the entire course of the experiments. Five of these were normal adults and were used only in preliminary tests in which the purpose was the perfection of a method. The remaining seventeen (normal) were all started in the experiments when approximately four weeks old. All were vigorous, healthy animals whose records may stand as typical.

2. Dogs

The two dogs tested were mongrels in whom the rat terrier strain was dominant. They were very bright and intelligent looking, very active, playful and affectionate,–indeed they seemed to possess all the qualities that are attributed to intelligent dogs in countless anecdotes. This was the unanimous testimony of many observers. The two dogs, Blackie and Brownie, both females of the same litter, were secured from an animal dealer when they were small puppies and were started on the preliminary tests at about the age of five months. They were usually kept in a kennel out of doors and remained in excellent condition during the experiments. Of the two, Brownie was the more aggressive and, to the ordinary observer, appeared possibly the more intelligent.

3. Raccoons

Four raccoons, two males–Bob and Jack–and two females–Betty and Jill, were tested. Bob and Betty had been pets and were secured from their owner when about five or six months old. Jack and Jill were caught in the woods when about two and a half months old. Preliminary experiments were started almost immediately with all four. The raccoons were and remained in perfect health throughout the experiments. The only physical defects possessed by any of them were the cataracts which developed in Bob's eyes about a month after his purchase. Although this interfered with his accurate vision of objects and resulted in his colliding frequently with them, he was able to distinguish such changes in brightness as were necessary in the experiments. This fact was demonstrated conclusively by many control tests which will be described later. Of the four, Betty was the quietest and most timid. She was the least promising subject among them.

4. Children

Five children were used in the course of the present tests: two boys, Hd and L, and three girls, F, M, and H. H, Hd and L were each approximately six years old. M was about eight years old; and F, about two and a half. Hd and L were in kindergarten work, and M and H were in the graded schools. The indications were that they were children both of normal ability and of normal intellectual advancement for their ages. F was a bright little girl and made an excellent subject. All of the children were more or less timid at first; but this was overcome, in all save possibly H's case, before tests were begun. Particular pains were taken with F. The experimenter was in her company a great deal, and by the beginning of the tests was a gladly accepted play-fellow.

APPARATUS AND GENERAL METHOD

The plan of box A is presented in Fig. 1. (This box was used for the raccoons.) The box is made of ¼″ boards and is 2½′ high with doors

7¼″ wide and 13″ high. The light stimulus came from 3 c.p. 8 volt miniature carbon lamps, so wired that they might be switched on one at a time. The current was obtained from a 220 volt lighting circuit and

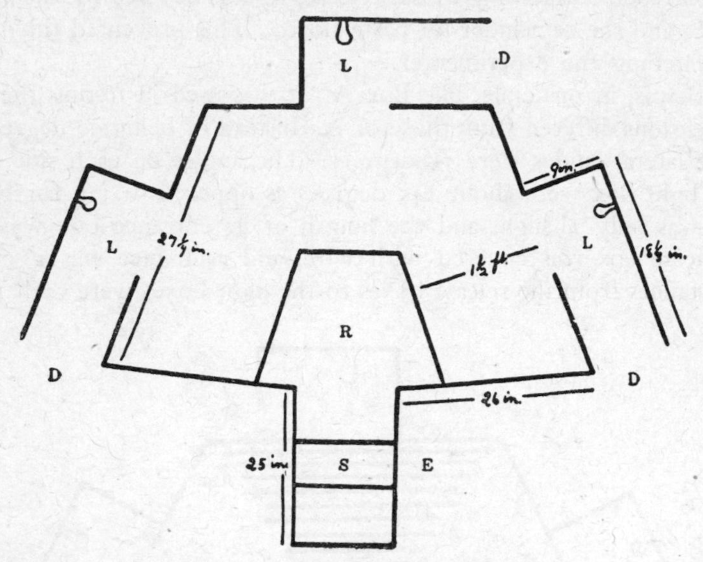

Fig. 1–Ground plan of Box A.

was passed through a lamp rheostat before reaching the discrimination box. The release box R was raised by means of a cord passed over a pulley in the ceiling and back to the experimenter at E. The first release box had glass over the top and sides. The right and left faces of the box were 12″ × 15½″. The front was 7½″ × 15½″. With this release box the distances to the entrances of the three light boxes (L) were unequal. Those at the sides were each 19¾″, while the distance straight in front was 20½″. These various inequalities were due to two causes: (1) The box had been planned originally for a different type of test and was only later arranged for the present experiment. (2) The release box, being covered with glass would have been too heavy to handle had it been made larger. During the course of the experiments, another release was made. This one was covered with wire of ½″ mesh. Its sides were 14½″ × 15½″; and its front was 9½″ × 15½″. The distances to the light boxes were now equal and of the dimensions indicated in Fig. 1.

Sliding doors were placed at the points marked D in the figure. They were controlled by strings which ran from them, through screw-eyes on the top of the box, to the experimenter at E.

A 16 c.p. light was suspended about four feet from the floor over the center of the apparatus. Its intensity was diminished approximately by two-thirds by wrapping the bulb in cloth. The three light boxes were covered in order to prevent light from entering them from above. Part of the entrance box leading to the release, R, was covered by the switchboard, S, and the remainder by paste board. This prevented the animals from watching the experimenter.

Box B was, in principle, like Box A. It was used in testing the dogs. Its dimensions differed from those of A. Instead of being 90 degrees, the extreme lateral angles were 75 degrees. The angles on each side of the middle light box were about 145 degrees as opposed to 127 for Box A. Box B was only 2′ high, and the length of its entrance box was 1′ 4″. The release box was covered with wire, and each face was 1′ × 10″. The distances from the release boxes to the light boxes were each 1½′.

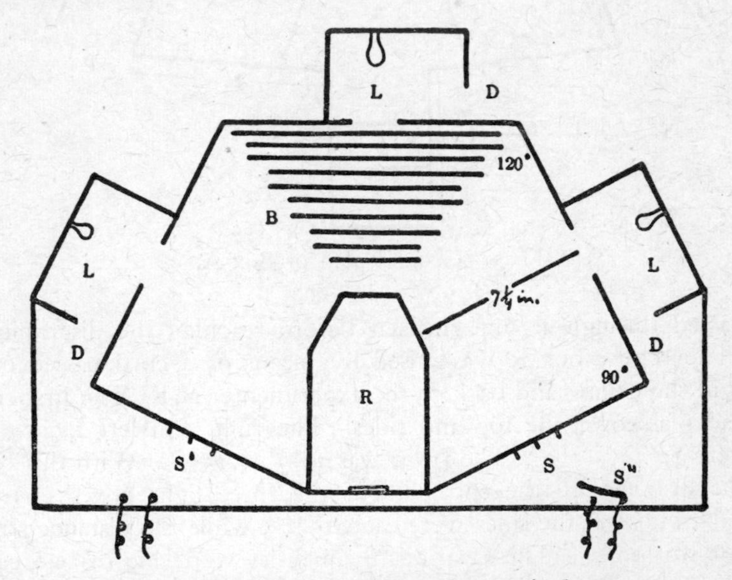

Fig. 2—Ground plan of Box C, D, exit door.

Fig. 2 is a ground plan of Box C. This box was used for rats. In addition to the data there given, the following points should be noted: The release box, R, was fastened by hinges so that when it was raised the three faces cleared the floor practically the same distance. The faces and the front half of the top of R are covered with glass; the rest is of wood. The doors leading into the light boxes are 4″ × 3″. Those leading out of the light boxes, called exit doors here, are 3″ × 2½″. The switches at S′ are for lights which are of the same intensity and wiring arrangements as those in the two preceding boxes. The switches at S turn the current into any or all of the paths from the release box to the light boxes. This current is obtained from a dry cell and is passed through the primary coil of a Porter inductorium. The strength of the current passing into the problem box was regulated so that the animals never became frightened by severe shocks. The current was never strong enough to cause the animals to squeak and only rarely did they attempt to jump over the strips. The brass strips from which the shocks were obtained (only one group, marked B, is shown in this figure), were very thin and lay flat on the floor of the box. Before being tacked down, they were given an acid bath which destroyed their lustre but left their conductivity practically unaffected for my purpose.

Box D, also used for rats, is similar to Box C in all save two respects: (1) It was not wired for punishment. (2) The doors leading from the light boxes could be closed with wooden slides. The use of these slides was discontinued shortly after the experiments began. Pieces of wire mesh were then used. These admitted the light and thus offered less opportunity for the animals to tell which box was open and which was closed.

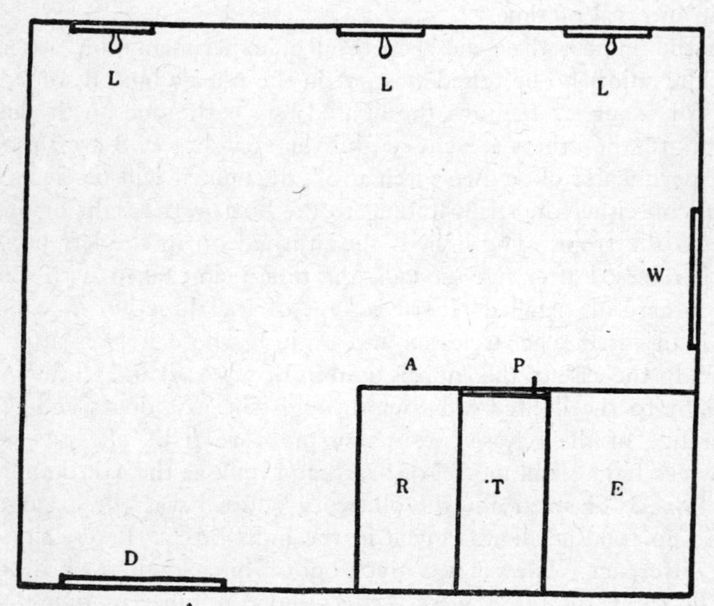

Fig. 3—Ground plan of apparatus used with children. D, door; W, window.

The apparatus (Fig. 3) which was used with children was constructed on the same principle as that described above for the other problem boxes. Three boards, each one foot square, were placed against the wall of a room 12′ × 14′. The middle square was seven feet distant from the release box, R. On each of these boards was mounted: (1) A 4 c.p. miniature electric light, L; and (2) just below the light, a push button. All three boards were painted black and were exact duplicates the one of the other. The front, A, of the release box was a lever which could be raised by a handle at P. The experimenter usually sat at E. T. is a table which held: (1) The candy used as a reward in the tests; (2) the switches regulating the lights and the buzzer; and (3) the buzzer. C is a curtain which hid the experimenter from the subject's view when the latter had left the release box. At first this curtain was also continued between R and T. Subsequently, this was found to be both inconvenient and unnecessary and its use was discontinued. The apparatus was wired so that any light could be turned on at will and so that any push button could be connected with the buzzer. Moving the switches was done without the subject's knowledge. The light was always turned on over the button that rang the buzzer. The child's problem was to find this button at the first trial when the light was on (in the learning series) and then (in the delayed reactions) after the light had been turned off for a certain interval of time.

With the animals the general method of experimentation was as follows: The animal to be tested was put in the release box, R, of problem Box C, for example. If, now, the lighted box is the one on the left, the exit doors of the others are closed and the switches at S are so set that if the experimenter close the switch at S″, the animal will receive a shock if it steps on either the strips leading to the box on the right or on those leading to the front. The light is then turned on in the left box. The animal is released after five seconds, the time being taken with a metronome. A careful, detailed record is kept of the direction in which the animal is oriented when released and of just where it goes after being released. In the case of the animals used in Boxes A, B and C, they should go straight to the lighted box, out through the exit doors and back to the entrance of the release box where they are fed. The rats used in Box D were fed a small morsel of bread and milk at the exit doors of the lighted boxes. Theoretically the olfactory control was not so good here as where no food at all was given in the light boxes. Practically, there was no difference. The rat was given only a bite, so almost no food fell on the floor; all the boxes were used an equal number of times; and all were frequently washed out. Whatever odor was present was so distributed as to afford no appreciable basis for discrimination. The results obtained with these rats, when compared with those where the olfactory control was better, support this statement. In any event, olfactory inequalities would persist after the light was turned out and would aid in delayed reactions only if associated with the light. More attention will be given to this possibility later in the discussion.

After the animal had been trained until it chose the lighted box almost perfectly, delays were begun. The light was turned off just as the animal reached the box. This was called the first stage of delay. At the second stage, the light was turned out when the animal was half way to the box. At the third stage, the light was turned out just as the experimenter started to raise the release box. Here there was a genuine delay, although a small one. The first two stages served primarily to adapt the animal emotionally to the sudden change from light to darkness. The rats and dogs usually ran so fast that their momentum was sufficient to carry them into the box when once they were started toward it. In any case they only needed to continue in the direction in which they were going. This, however, was not the case with the third stage. The light was put out before the animal started. Throughout these three stages, the animal was released promptly at the end of five seconds. From this stage on, where the animal was detained one or more seconds after the light was out before being released, it was obviously necessary to let the animal see the light before this was turned off. Occasionally, the interval thus required was more than five seconds. In these higher stages of delay, I always waited until I felt sure that the animal had seen the light, and then turned off the current while the animal was still oriented toward the source of light. Record was kept of any change in the orientation which an animal made after the light was turned off. How detailed these records were will be seen in the section on experimental results.

The delays were gradually increased in length until one was found at which the animal failed. They were then decreased until the animal was again making a high percentage of correct choices, when the intervals were again increased. An animal was thus tested twice for the limit of its ability to delay with the backgrounds surrounding the entrances to the light boxes all similar the one to the other. When this limit was found, the wall of the box about the entrance to c was covered with white cardboard; that about b, with a black; and that about a,[1] with a medium gray. If the animal's limit of delay was no better or was worse with this arrangement than before, the animal was dropped from the experiment. If the limit were better, the different backgrounds were removed and the similar ones used again. The limit of delay with these was then redetermined. If this third limit were greater than the second, the effect of training could be evoked as an explanation of the fact. But if it were markedly less than the second, the only cause could be an association between the backgrounds and the lights. The significance of this type of association will be dealt upon in detail later in this paper.

[1] a, b, and c will be used in this paper to designate the right, middle, and left light boxes respectively.

SUMMARY AND CONCLUSIONS

The following is a statement of the results and conclusions that have been reached as a result of the foregoing experiments and analyses:

1. The rats (one excepted), dogs, raccoons and children made successful reactions in situations where the customary determining stimulus was absent at the moment of response. The stimulus might appear in any one of three boxes. These boxes were qualitatively alike, but situated in different directions from the release box. At every trial, three possibilities of reaction confronted the subject. A selection had to be made and that box chosen in which the stimulus had appeared most recently.

2. The conditions under which the maximal delay was tested and the results obtained are indicated as follows:

(a) Different classes of subjects were used. Table I gives the maximum and minimum delays that were obtained from the different classes.

TABLE I

Subjects	*Min. delay*	*Max. delay*
Rats	either no learning or 3rd stage of delay	10 secs.
Dogs	2 secs.	5 mins.
Raccoons	3 secs.	25 secs.
Children	50 secs.	25 mins.

(b) Backgrounds of widely different grades of brightness did not affect the intervals of delay.

(c) The use of a large release which gave the animals the freedom of the interior of the box lengthened the intervals of delay in the case of some subjects.

(d) The use of two boxes as opposed to three lengthened the intervals of delay by increasing the accuracy of response.

(e) Neither punishment nor the particular number of trials per day appear to have affected the interval of delay.

3. An analysis of the possible cues that may have been used by the subjects in the solution of the present problem gave the following results: (a) Overt orienting attitudes were the probable cues for many reactions of the raccoons. These attitudes must be assumed as cues for the rats and dogs in order to explain their reactions. (b) Some intra-organic (non-orientation) factor not visible to the experimenter must be assumed in order to explain a significant number of the correct reactions of the raccoons and all of the successful reactions of the children. These cues fulfilled an ideational function. (c) All of the re-agents were influenced

by external stimuli that were constantly present from trial to trial, e.g., those given by the box itself. However, these could not be used as a basis for selective responses inasmuch as they were constant from trial to trial and hence could not furnish varying, or alternating, cues.

4. No animal that had used overt motor attitudes in solving the problem when the small release and similar backgrounds were used adopted another type of cue either when a large release or when backgrounds of different brightnesses were used.

5. The method used in the present tests for attacking the question of the functional presence of a representative factor in animal behavior is superior to that of imitation, use of tools and others that have been used in the past, because here it is possible to determine what stimulus controls the behavior. It is therefore possible to insure the absence of the stimulus at the moment of response.

6. The representative factor for which search has been instituted in this monograph stands primarily for "objects" and not movements. A technique that would make certain a control of the latter factor so as to insure its presence or absence at the will of the experimenter has not yet been perfected.

7. From a consideration of the theoretical advantages to be derived from interpreting this representative factor as sensory rather than as imaginal, a decision was reached in favor of the former alternative for all reagents save possibly the older children, H, Hd, M and L. Illustrations were given from human consciousness where a sensation performed a memory function or served as a link in a train of thought. Such cases have been termed "conscious attitudes" or "imageless thought." This function, as considered in this paper, was designated sensory thought.

8. The theory was advanced that such a function as sensory thought represents the highest grade of behavior in raccoons and probably also in children of some two and one-half years of age. This theory is supported by the hardly-to-be-doubted presence of sensations in animal consciousness and by the assumption that these sensations can function as the illustrations indicate that such processes do in human behavior. Such a theory seems more in accordance with the law of parsimony than would a theory which made images perform the representative function found in the raccoons and the child F.

9. From this theory, it follows that subjects may be put into at least four classes on the basis of the highest type of learning present in their behavior: (a) Absence of learning; (b) trial and error; (c) sensory thought, and (d) imaginal thought.

Walter Bradford Cannon: 1871-1945

RECENT STUDIES OF BODILY EFFECTS OF FEAR, RAGE, AND PAIN *

1914

DURING the past three years a series of investigations has been carried on in the Harvard Physiological Laboratory with the object of securing further insight into bodily changes accompanying pain and the major emotions. This work was the outgrowth of an interest in the inhibitory effect of pain and emotional excitement on digestive processes. The disturbances of digestion attending these affective states may considerably outlast the period of obvious excitement. What might be the occasion for the continuance of emotional disturbance in the body so long after the emotion-producing object has disappeared?

A suggestion that seemed reasonable was that the state of excitation was continued by secretion of the adrenal glands. These small bodies pour into the blood-stream a substance (adrenin, adrenalin, epinephrin) which exerts on structures innervated by the sympathetic nerves the same effects as are produced by impulses passing along those nerves. Thus the injection of adrenin will cause dilatation of the pupil, erection of hairs, inhibition of the movements of the alimentary canal, and other well-known consequences of sympathetic stimulation. But these glands are themselves stimulated by nerve impulses passing out by sympathetic pathways. It might be, therefore, that the bodily changes accompanying emotional excitement are produced initially by nerve impulses, that these impulses also rouse secretion of the adrenal glands, and that this secretion circulating in the blood continues by chemical influence changes nervously initiated.

By using as an indicator a strip of intestinal muscle, sensitive to adrenin in dilutions 1:20,000,000 parts, we were able to show that when a dog barks at a cat, and the cat reacts by signs of terror or by a raging counter attack, the cat's blood, taken near the opening of the adrenal veins, contains an increased adrenal secretion. Furthermore, stimulation in an anesthetized animal of afferent nerves which, if stimulated in the conscious animal would cause pain, likewise evoked an increased secretion from

* This is a summary of the results of some of Cannon's early studies of bodily changes in emotion. It is reprinted from the *Journal of Philosophy, Psychology and Scientific Methods*, XI (1914), 162-165, by permission of the Journal.

the adrenal glands. Pain, therefore, and such major emotions as fear and rage are accompanied by the discharge of a substance which can cause further excitation of organs innervated by the sympathetic system.

Certain remarkable effects of injecting adrenin have for many years been known. For example, it will cause liberation of sugar from the liver into the blood to such an extent that the sugar may appear in the urine (glycosuria). It will drive the blood from the abdominal viscera into the heart, lungs, central nervous system, and the limbs. It seems to act as an antidote to muscular fatigue. And it renders more rapid the coagulation of blood. The question at once arose after our first observations, does the adrenal secretion poured out in pain and emotional excitement likewise produce these effects? Our later researches have been concerned with answers to this question.

Emotional excitement and "painful" stimulation were proved to be accompanied by glycosuria. If a caged cat is frightened or made angry by a barking dog it is likely to be glycosuric. Students after a hard examination, and football players after a thrilling contest, also have, in many instances, glycosuria. The mere handling of a rabbit preparatory to an operation may nearly triple the sugar content of its blood.

If a muscle is fatigued, the threshold of irritability rises. It may rise as much as 600 per cent., but the average increase is approximately 200 per cent. If the fatigued muscle is allowed to rest, the former irritability is gradually regained, though two hours may pass before the recovery is complete. If a small dose of adrenalin is injected intravenously, or the adrenal glands are stimulated to secrete, we have found that the former irritability of the fatigued muscle may be recovered within three minutes. In this way adrenal secretion may largely restore efficiency after fatigue.

Fear and anger—as well as worry and distress—are attended, as already stated, by cessation of the contractions of the stomach and intestines. These mental states also reduce or temporarily abolish the secretion of gastric juice. Adrenin injected into the body has the same effect. Besides checking the functions of the alimentary canal, adrenin drives out the blood which, during digestive activity, floods the abdominal viscera. This blood flows all the more rapidly and abundantly through the heart, the lungs, the central nervous system, and the limbs.

If adrenin is injected in very minute amounts into the blood, the time which intervenes between removal of blood from the vessels and its clotting is greatly reduced. The same hastening of coagulation is observed if splanchnic impulses are excited, or an afferent nerve (e.g., the sciatic) is stimulated in a decerebrate animal, or if the animal is roused to fear or anger. The clotting time which, by the method used, was usually four or five minutes, was in some instances reduced to half a minute.

These profound effects of pain and fear and rage are not in the slightest degree directly subject to voluntary action. They are rather of the nature of reflexes, for they appear promptly, and result from impulses which traverse pathways already prepared in the nervous organization of the individual. Since the effects are reflex in character, and since reflexes are responses commonly useful to the body, it is pertinent to enquire regarding the utility of the changes above described.

The clue which gives these responses significance is found in considering the conditions which would accompany fear or great anger or pain. McDougall has pointed out the relation between these effective states and certain instincts. Thus fear is associated with the instinct to run, anger with the instinct to fight. The emotions in wild life would be roused in the presence of prey or the enemy—a situation that would not unnaturally involve both the pursuer and the pursued in a desperate run or a fight. In case of combat pain would add to the stimulus of the emotion, and thus there might ensue a supreme and prolonged struggle.

Under such circumstances the liberated sugar would be serviceable for the laboring muscles, for it is known to be the elective source of muscular energy. The adrenal secretion, by abolishing the effects of fatigue, would place the muscles unqualifiedly at the disposal of the nervous system. The shifting of the blood from the less insistent viscera of the abdomen to the organs of utmost value in critical physical struggle—the heart, lungs, limbs, and nervous system—would be of the greatest service in assuring efficient action of these organs. And if in the combat the vessels are injured, prompt clotting of the blood might help to prevent dangerous bleeding.

The emotional reactions above described may each be interpreted, therefore, as making the organism more efficient in the struggle which fear or rage or pain may involve. And that organism which, with the aid of adrenal secretions, best mobilizes its sugar, lessens its muscular fatigue, sends its blood to the vitally important organs, and provides against serious hemorrhage will stand the best chance of surviving in the struggle for existence.

Lewis Madison Terman: 1877-

THE MEASUREMENT OF INTELLIGENCE *

1916

NATURE OF THE STANFORD REVISION AND EXTENSION

ALTHOUGH the Binet scale quickly demonstrated its value as an instrument for the classification of mentally-retarded and otherwise exceptional children, it had, nevertheless, several imperfections which greatly limited its usefulness. There was a dearth of tests at the higher mental levels, the procedure was so inadequately defined that needless disagreement came about in the interpretation of data, and so many of the tests were misplaced as to make the results of an examination more or less misleading, particularly in the case of very young subjects and those near the adult level. It was for the purpose of correcting these and certain other faults that the Stanford investigation was planned.

Sources of Data

Our revision is the result of several years of work, and involved the examination of approximately 2300 subjects, including 1700 normal children, 200 defective and superior children, and more than 400 adults.

Tests of 400 of the 1700 normal children had been made by Childs and Terman in 1910–11, and of 300 children by Trost, Waddle, and Terman in 1911–12. For various reasons, however, the results of these tests did not furnish satisfactory data for a thoroughgoing revision of the scale. Accordingly a new investigation was undertaken, somewhat more extensive than the others, and more carefully planned. Its main features may be described as follows:

1. The first step was to assemble as nearly as possible all the results which had been secured for each test of the scale by all the workers of all countries. The result was a large sheet of tabulated data for each individual test, including percentages passing the test at various ages, conditions under which the results were secured, method of procedure, etc. After a comparative study of these data, and in the light of results

* From the book by this title published by the Houghton Mifflin Co. Pages 51-56 and 65-67 are reprinted with the permission of the publishers and the author. Terman's revision and extension of Binet and Simon's tests, known as the Stanford-Binet, was the first to have adequate standardization through the school years, and quickly became the most widely used individual intelligence test.

we had ourselves secured, a provisional arrangement of the tests was prepared for try-out.

2. In addition to the tests of the original Binet scale, 40 additional tests were included for try-out. This, it was expected, would make possible the elimination of some of the least satisfactory tests, and at the same time permit the addition of enough new ones to give at least six tests, instead of five, for each age group.

3. A plan was then devised for securing subjects who should be as nearly as possible representative of the several ages. The method was to select a school in a community of average social status, a school attended by all or practically all the children in the district where it was located. In order to get clear pictures of age differences the tests were confined to children who were within two months of a birthday. To avoid accidental selection, all the children within two months of a birthday were tested, in whatever grade enrolled. Tests of foreign-born children, however, were eliminated in the treatment of results. There remained tests of approximately 1000 children, of whom 905 were between 5 and 14 years of age.

4. The children's responses were, for the most part, recorded verbatim. This made it possible to re-score the records according to any desired standard, and thus to fit a test more perfectly to the age level assigned it.

5. Much attention was given to securing uniformity of procedure. A half-year was devoted to training the examiners, and another half-year to the supervision of the testing. In the further interests of uniformity all the records were scored by one person (the writer).

Method of Arriving at a Revision

The revision of the scale below the 14-year level was based almost entirely on the tests of the above-mentioned 1,000 unselected children. The guiding principle was to secure an arrangement of the tests and a standard of scoring which would cause the median mental age of the unselected children of each age group to coincide with the median chronological age. That is, a correct scale must cause the average child of 5 years to test exactly at 5, the average child at 6 to test exactly at 6, etc. Or, to express the same fact in terms of intelligence quotient, a correct scale must give a median intelligence quotient of unity, or 100 per cent, for unselected children of each age.

If the median mental age resulting at any point from the provisional arrangement of tests was too high or too low, it was only necessary to change the location of certain of the tests, or to change the standard of scoring, until an order of arrangement and a standard of passing were found which would throw the median mental age where it belongs.

We had already become convinced, for reasons too involved for presentation here, that no satisfactory revision of the Binet scale was possible on any theoretical considerations as to the percentage of passes which an individual test ought to show in a given year in order to be considered standard for that year.

As was to be expected, the first draft of the revision did not prove satisfactory. The scale was still too hard at some points, and too easy at others. In fact, three successive revisions were necessary, involving three separate scorings of the data and as many tabulations of the mental ages, before the desired degree of accuracy was secured. As finally revised, the scale gives a median intelligence quotient closely approximating 100 for the unselected children of each age from 4 to 14.

Since our school children who were above 14 years and still in the grades were retarded left-overs, it was necessary to base the revision above this level on the tests of adults. These included 30 business men and 150 "migrating" unemployed men tested by Mr. H. E. Knollin, 150 adolescent delinquents tested by Mr. J. Harold Williams, and 50 high-school students tested by the writer.

The extension of the scale in the upper range is such that ordinary intelligent adults, little educated, test up to what is called the "average adult" level. Adults whose intelligence is known from other sources to be superior are found to test well up toward the "superior adult" level, and this holds whether the subjects in question are well educated or practically unschooled. The almost entirely unschooled business men, in fact, tested fully as well as high-school juniors and seniors.

The following method was employed for determining the validity of a test. The children of each age level were divided into three groups according to intelligence quotient, those testing below 90, those between 90 and 109, and those with an intelligence quotient of 110 or above. The percentages of passes on each individual test at or near that age level were then ascertained separately for these three groups. If a test fails to show a decidedly higher proportion of passes in the superior IQ group than in the inferior IQ group, it cannot be regarded as a satisfactory test of intelligence. On the other hand, a test which satisfies this criterion must be accepted as valid or the entire scale must be rejected. Henceforth it stands or falls with the scale as a whole.

When tried out by this method, some of the tests which have been most criticized showed a high degree of reliability; certain others which have been considered excellent proved to be so little correlated with intelligence that they had to be discarded.

After making a few necessary eliminations, 90 tests remained, or 36 more than the number included in the Binet 1911 scale. There are 6 at each age level from 3 to 10, 8 at 12, 6 at 14, 6 at "average adult," 6 at "superior adult," and 16 alternative tests. The alternative tests, which are distributed among the different groups, are intended to be used only as substitutes when one or more of the regular tests have been rendered, by coaching or otherwise, undesirable.

Of the 36 new tests, 27 were added and standardized in the various Stanford investigations. Two tests were borrowed from the Healy-Fernald series, one from Kuhlmann, one was adapted from Bonser, and the remaining five were amplifications or adaptations of some of the earlier Binet tests.

ANALYSIS OF 1000 INTELLIGENCE QUOTIENTS

An extended account of the 1000 tests on which the Stanford revision is chiefly based has been presented in a separate monograph. This chapter will include only the briefest summary of some of those results of the investigation which contribute to the intelligent use of the revision.

The Distribution of Intelligence

The question as to the manner in which intelligence is distributed is one of great practical as well as theoretical importance. One of the most vital questions which can be asked by any nation of any age is the following: "How high is the average level of intelligence among our people, and how frequent are the various grades of ability above and below the average?" With the development of standardized tests we are approaching, for the first time in history, a possible answer to this question.

Most of the earlier Binet studies, however, have thrown little light on the distribution of intelligence because of their failure to avoid the influence of accidental selection in choosing subjects for testing. The method of securing subjects for the Stanford revision makes our results on this point especially interesting. It is believed that the subjects used for this investigation were as nearly representative of average American-born children as it is possible to secure.

The intelligence quotients for these 1000 unselected children were calculated, and their distribution was plotted for the ages separately. The distribution was found fairly symmetrical at each age from 5 to 14. At 15 the range is on either side of 90 as a median, and at 16 on either side of 80 as a median. That the 15- and 16-year-olds test low is due to the fact that these children are left-over retardates and are below average in intelligence.

The I Q's were then grouped in ranges of ten. In the middle group were thrown those from 96 to 105. The ascending groups including in order the I Q's from 106 to 115, 116 to 125, etc.; correspondingly with the descending groups. Figure 1 shows the distribution found by this grouping for the 905 children of ages 5 to 14 combined. The subjects above 14 are not included in this curve because they are left-overs and not representative of their ages.

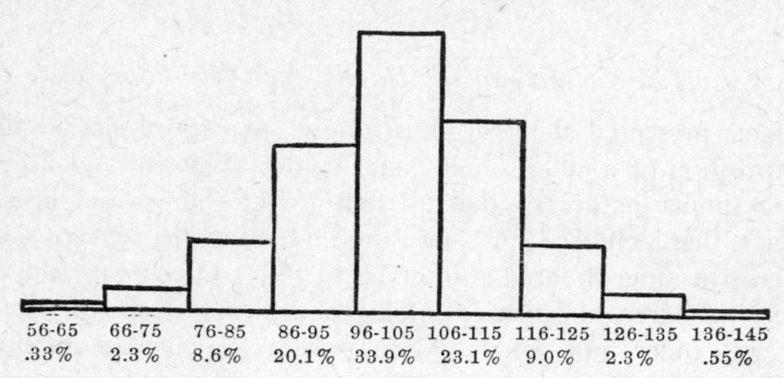

FIG. 1—Distribution of I Q's of 905 unselected children, 5-14 years of age.

The distribution for the ages combined is seen to be remarkably symmetrical. The symmetry for the separate ages was hardly less marked, considering that only 80 to 120 children were tested at each age. In fact, the range, including the middle 50 per cent of I Q's, was found practically constant from 5 to 14 years. The tendency is for the middle 50 per cent to fall (approximately) between 93 and 108.

Three important conclusions are justified by the above facts:

1. Since the frequency of the various grades of intelligence decreases gradually and at no point abruptly on each side of the median, it is evident that there is no definite dividing line between normality and feeble-mindedness, or between normality and genius. Psychologically, the mentally defective child does not belong to a distinct type, nor does the genius. There is no line of demarcation between either of these extremes and the so-called "normal" child. The number of mentally defective individuals in a population will depend upon the standard arbitrarily set up as to what constitutes mental deficiency. Similarly for genius. It is exactly as if we should undertake to classify all people into the three groups: abnormally tall, normally tall, and abnormally short.

2. The common opinion that extreme deviations below the median are more frequent than extreme deviations above the median seems to have no foundation in fact. Among unselected school children, at least, for every child of any given degree of deficiency there is another child as far above the average I Q as the former is below. We have shown elsewhere the serious consequences of neglect of this fact.

3. The traditional view that variability in mental traits becomes more marked during adolescence is here contradicted, as far as intelligence is concerned, for the distribution of I Q's is practically the same at each age from 5 to 14. For example, 6-year-olds differ from one another fully as much as do 14-year-olds.

The Validity of the Intelligence Quotient

The facts presented above argue strongly for the validity of the I Q as an expression of a child's intelligence status. This follows necessarily from the similar nature of the distributions at the various ages. The inference is that a child's I Q, as measured by this scale, remains constant. Re-tests of the same children at intervals of two to five years support the inference. Children of superior intelligence do not seem to deteriorate as they get older, nor dull children to develop average intelligence. Knowing a child's I Q, we can predict with a fair degree of accuracy the course of his later development.

The mental age of a subject is meaningless if considered apart from chronological age. It is only the ratio of retardation or acceleration to chronological age (that is, the I Q) which has significance.

It follows also that if the I Q is a valid expression of intelligence, as it seems to be, then the Binet-Simon "age-grade method" becomes transformed automatically into a "point-scale method," if one wants to use it that way. As such it is superior to any other point scale that has been proposed, because it includes a larger number of tests and its points have definite meaning.

Sex Differences

The question as to the relative intelligence of the sexes is one of perennial interest and great social importance. The ancient hypothesis, the one which dates from the time when only men concerned themselves with scientific hypotheses, took for granted the superiority of the male. With the development of individual phychology, however, it was soon found that as far as the evidence of mental tests can be trusted the average intelligence of women and girls is as high as that of men and boys.

If we accept this result we are then confronted with the difficult problem of finding an explanation for the fact that so few of those who have acquired eminence in the various intellectual fields have been women. Two explanations have been proposed: (1) That women become eminent less often than men simply for lack of opportunity and stimulus; and (2) that while the average intelligence of the sexes is the same, extreme variations may be more common in males. It is pointed out that not only are there more eminent men than eminent women, but that statistics also show a preponderance of males in institutions for the mentally defective. Accordingly it is often said that women are grouped closely about the average, while men show a wider range of distribution.

Many hundreds of articles and books of popular or quasi-scientific nature have been written on one aspect or another of this question of sex difference in intelligence; but all such theoretical discussions taken together are worth less than the results of one good experiment. Let us see what our 1000 I Q's have to offer toward a solution of the problem.

1. When the I Q's of the boys and girls were treated separately there was found a small but fairly constant superiority of the girls up to the age of 13 years. At 14, however, the curve for the girls dropped below that for boys.

The supplementary data, including the teachers' estimates of intelligence on a scale of five, the teachers' judgments in regard to the quality of the school work, and records showing the age-grade distribution of the sexes, were all sifted for evidence as to the genuineness of the apparent superiority of the girls age for age. The results of all these lines of inquiry support the tests in suggesting that the superiority of the girls is probably real even up to and including age 14, the apparent superiority of the boys of this age being fully accounted for by the more frequent elimination of 14-year-old girls from the grades by promotion to the high school.

2. However, the superiority of girls over boys is so slight (amounting at most ages to only 2 to 3 points in terms of I Q) that for practical purposes it would seem negligible. This offers no support to the opinion expressed by Yerkes and Bridges that "at certain ages serious injustice will be done individuals by evaluating their scores in the light of norms which do not take account of sex differences."

3. Apart from the small superiority of girls, the distribution of intelligence in the two sexes is not different. The supposed wider variation of boys is not found. Girls do not group themselves about the median more closely than do boys. The range of I Q including the middle fifty per cent is approximately the same for the two sexes.

4. When the results for the individual tests were examined, it was found that not many showed very extreme differences as to the per cent of boys and girls passing. In a few cases, however, the difference was rather marked.

The boys were decidedly better in arithmetical reasoning, giving differences between a president and a king, solving the form board, making change, reversing hands of clock, finding similarities, and solving the "induction test." The girls were superior in drawing designs from memory, aesthetic comparison, comparing objects from memory, answering the "comprehension questions," repeating digits and sentences, tying a bow-knot, and finding rhymes.

Accordingly, our data, which for the most part agree with the results of others, justify the conclusion that the intelligence of girls, at least up to 14 years, does not differ materially from that of boys either as regards the average level or the range of distribution. It may still be argued that the mental development of boys beyond the age of 14 years lasts longer and extends farther than in the case of girls, but as a matter of fact this opinion received little support from such tests as have been made on men and women college students.

The fact that so few women have attained eminence may be due to wholly extraneous factors, the most important of which are the following: (1) The occupations in which it is possible to achieve eminence are for the most part only now beginning to open their doors to women. Women's career has been largely that of home-making, an occupation in which eminence, in the strict sense of the word, is impossible. (2) Even of the small number of women who embark upon a professional career, a majority marry and thereafter devote a fairly large proportion of their energy to bearing and rearing children. (3) Both the training given to girls and the general atmosphere in which they grow up are unfavorable to the inculcation of the professional point of view, and as a result women are not spurred on by deep-seated motives to constant and strenuous intellectual endeavor as men are. (4) It is also possible that the emotional traits of women are such as to favor the development of the sentiments at the expense of innate intellectual endowment.

Intelligence of the Different Social Classes

Of the 1000 children, 492 were classified by their teachers according to social class into the following five groups: very inferior, inferior, average, superior, and very superior. A comparative study was then made of the distribution of I Q's for these different groups.

The data may be summarized as follows:—

1. The median I Q for children of the superior social class is about 7 points above, and that of the inferior social class about 7 points below, the median I Q of the average social group. This means that by the age of 14 inferior class children are about one year below, and superior class children one year above, the median mental age for all classes taken together.

2. That the children of the superior social classes make a better showing in the tests is probably due, for the most part, to a superiority in original endowment. This conclusion is supported by five supplementary lines of evidence: (a) the teachers' rankings of the children according

to intelligence; (b) the age-grade progress of the children; (c) the quality of the school work; (d) the comparison of older and younger children as regards the influence of social environment; and (e) the study of individual cases of bright and dull children in the same family.

3. In order to facilitate comparison, it is advisable to express the intelligence of children of all social classes in terms of the same objective scale of intelligence. This scale should be based on the median for all classes taken together.

As regards their responses to individual tests, our children of a given social class were not distinguishable from children of the same intelligence in any other social class.

The Relation of the I Q to the Quality of the Child's School Work

The school work of 504 children was graded by the teachers on a scale of five grades: very inferior, inferior, average, superior, and very superior. When this grouping was compared with that made on the basis of I Q, fairly close agreement was found. However, in about one case out of ten there was rather serious disagreement; a child, for example, would be rated as doing average school work when his I Q would place him in the very inferior intelligence group.

When the data were searched for explanations of such disagreements it was found that most of them were plainly due to the failure of teachers to take into account the age of the child when grading the quality of his school work. When allowance was made for this tendency there were no disagreements which justified any serious suspicion as to the accuracy of the intelligence scale. Minor disagreements may, of course, be disregarded, since the quality of school work depends in part on other factors than intelligence, such as industry, health, regularity of attendance, quality of instruction, etc.

The Relation Between I Q and Grade Progress

This comparison, which was made for the entire 1000 children, showed a fairly high correlation, but also some astonishing disagreements. Nine-year intelligence was found all the way from grade 1 to 7, inclusive; 10-year intelligence all the way from grade 2 to 7; and 12-year intelligence all the way from grade 3 to grade 8. Plainly the school's efforts at grading fail to give homogeneous groups of children as regards mental ability. On the whole, the grade location of the children did not fit their mental ages much better than it did their chronological ages.

When the data were examined, it was found that practically every child whose grade failed to correspond fairly closely with his mental age was either exceptionally bright or exceptionally dull. Those who tested between 96 and 105 I Q were never seriously misplaced in school. The very dull children, however, were usually located from one to three grades above where they belonged by mental age, and the duller the child the more serious, as a rule, was the misplacement. On the other hand, the very bright children were nearly always located from one to three grades below where they belonged by mental age, and the brighter the child the more serious the school's mistake. The child of 10-year mental age in the second grade, for example, is almost certain to be about 7 or 8 years old; the child of 10-year intelligence in the sixth grade is almost certain to be 13 to 15 years of age.

All this is due to one fact, and one alone: the school tends to promote children by age rather than ability. The bright children are held back, while the dull children are promoted beyond their mental ability. The retardation problem is exactly the reverse of what we have thought it to be. It is the bright children who are retarded, and the dull children who are accelerated.

The remedy is to be sought in differentiated courses (special classes) for both kinds of mentally exceptional children. Just as many special classes are needed for superior children as for the inferior. The social consequences of suitable educational advantages for children of superior ability would no doubt greatly exceed anything that could possibly result from the special instruction of dullards and border-line cases.

Special study of the I Q's between 70 and 79 revealed the fact that a child of this grade of intelligence never does satisfactory work in the grade where he belongs by chronological age. By the time he has attended school four or five years, such a child is usually found doing "very inferior" to "average" work in a grade from two to four years below his age.

On the other hand, the child with an I Q of 120 or above is almost never found below the grade for his chronological age, and occasionally he is one or two grades above. Wherever located, his work is always "superior" or "very superior," and the evidence suggests strongly that it would probably remain so even if extra promotions were granted.

Correlation Between I Q and the Teachers' Estimates of the Children's Intelligence

By the Pearson formula the correlation found between the I Q's and the teachers' rankings on a scale of five was .48. This is about what others have found, and is both high enough and low enough to be significant. That it is moderately high in so far corroborates the tests.

That it is not higher means that either the teachers or the tests have made a good many mistakes.

When the data were searched for evidence on this point, it was found, that the fault was plainly on the part of the teachers. The serious mistakes were nearly all made with children who were either over age or under age for their grade, mostly the former. In estimating children's intelligence, just as in grading their school success, the teachers often failed to take account of the age factor. For example, the child whose mental age was, say, two years below normal, and who was enrolled in a class with children about two years younger than himself, is often graded "average" in intelligence.

The tendency of teachers is to estimate a child's intelligence according to the quality of his school work in the grade where he happens to be located. This results in over-estimating the intelligence of older, retarded children, and underestimating the intelligence of the younger, advanced children. The disagreements between the tests and the teachers' estimates are thus found, when analyzed, to confirm the validity of the test method rather than to bring it under suspicion.

The Validity of the Individual Tests

The validity of each test was checked up by measuring it against the scale as a whole. For example, if 10-year-old children having 11-year intelligence succeed with a given test decidedly better than 10-year-old children who have 9-year intelligence, then either this test must be accepted as valid or the scale as a whole must be rejected. Since we know, however, that the scale as a whole has at least a reasonably high degree of reliability, this method becomes a sure and ready means of judging the worth of a test.

When the tests were tried out in this way it was found that some of those which have been most criticized have in reality a high correlation with intelligence. Among these are naming the days of the week, giving the value of stamps, counting thirteen pennies, giving differences between president and king, finding rhymes, giving age, distinguishing right and left, and interpretation of pictures. Others having a high reliability are the vocabulary tests, arithmetical reasoning, giving differences, copying a diamond, giving date, repeating digits in reverse order, interpretation of fables, the dissected sentence test, naming sixty words, finding omissions in pictures, and recognizing absurdities.

Among the somewhat less satisfactory tests are the following: repeating digits (direct order), naming coins, distinguishing forenoon and afternoon, defining in terms of use, drawing designs from memory, and aesthetic comparison. Binet's "line suggestion" test correlated so little with intelligence that it had to be thrown out. The same was also true of two of the new tests which we had added to the series for try-out.

Tests showing a medium correlation with the scale as a whole include arranging weights, executing three commissions, naming colors, giving number of fingers, describing pictures, naming the months, making change, giving superior definitions, finding similarities, reading for memories, reversing hands of clock, defining abstract words, problems of fact, bow-knot, induction test, and comprehension questions.

A test which makes a good showing on this criterion of agreement with the scale as a whole becomes immune to theoretical criticisms. Whatever it appears to be from mere inspection, it is a real measure of intelligence. Henceforth it stands or falls with the scale as a whole.

The reader will understand, of course, that no single test used alone will determine accurately the general level of intelligence. A great many tests are required; and for two reasons: (1) because intelligence has many aspects; and (2) in order to overcome the accidental influences of training or environment. If many tests are used no one of them need show more than a moderately high correlation with the scale as a whole. As stated by Binet, "Let the tests be rough, if there are only enough of them."

Wolfgang Köhler: 1887-

THE MENTALITY OF APES *

1917

Two sets of interests lead us to test the intelligence of the higher apes. We are aware that it is a question of beings which in many ways are nearer to man than to the other ape species; in particular it has been shown that the chemistry of their bodies, in so far as it may be perceived in the quality of the blood, and the structure of their most highly-developed organ, the brain, are more closely related to the chemistry of the human body and human brain-structure than to the chemical nature of the lower apes and *their* brain development. These beings show so many human traits in their "everyday" behaviour that the question naturally arises whether they do not behave with intelligence and insight under conditions which require such behaviour. This question expresses the first, one may say, naïve, interest in the intellectual capacity of animals. We wished to ascertain the degree of relationship between anthropoid apes and man in a field which seems to us particularly important, but on which we have as yet little information.

The second aim is theoretical. Even assuming that the anthropoid ape behaves intelligently in the sense in which the word is applied to man, there is yet from the very start no doubt that he remains in this respect far behind man, becoming perplexed and making mistakes in relatively simple situations; but it is precisely for this reason that we may, under the simplest conditions, gain knowledge of the nature of intelligent acts. The human adult seldom performs for the *first* time in his life tasks involving intelligence of so simple a nature that they can be easily investigated; and when in more complicated tasks adult men really find a solution, they can only with difficulty observe their own procedure. So one may be allowed the expectation that in the intelligent performances of anthropoid apes we may see once more in their plastic state processes with which we have become so familiar that we can no longer immediately recognize their original form: but which, because of their very simplicity, we should treat as the logical starting-point of theoretical speculation.

* Kohler's work first appeared in 1917, under the title *Intelligenzprufen an Anthropoiden.* The English translation of the second revised edition, under the title given above, was first published in 1924. Pages 1-9 and 265-269 are reprinted by permission of the author and of the publishers, Kegan Paul, Trench, Trubner & Co., London.

As all the emphasis in the following investigations is laid on the first question, the doubt may be expressed whether it does not take for granted a particular solution of the problems treated under the second. One might say that the question whether intelligent behaviour exists among anthropoid apes can be discussed only after recognizing the theoretical necessity of distinguishing between intelligent behaviour and behaviour of any other kind; and that, since association psychology, in particular, claims to derive from one single principle all behaviour which would come under consideration here, up to the highest level, even that attained by human beings, a theoretical point of view is already assumed by the formulation of problem I; and one which is antagonistic to association psychology.

This is a misconception. There is probably no association psychologist who does not, in his own unprejudiced observations, distinguish, and, to a certain extent, contrast, unintelligent and intelligent behaviour. For what is association psychology but the theory that one can trace back to the phenomena of a generally-known simple association type even those occurrences which, to unbiassed observation, do not at first seem corresponding to that type, most of all the so-called intelligent performances? In short, it is just these differences which are the starting-point of a strict association psychology; it is they which need to be theoretically accounted for; they are well known to the association psychologist. Thus, for instance, we find a radical representative of this school (Thorndike) stating the conclusion, drawn from experiments on dogs and cats: "I failed to find any act that even *seemed* due to reasoning." To anyone who can formulate his results thus, other behaviour must have seemed to be intelligent; he is already acquainted with the contrast in his observations, say of human beings, even if he discards it afterwards in theory.

Accordingly, if we are to inquire whether the anthropoid ape behaves intelligently, this problem can for the present be treated quite independently of theoretical assumptions, particularly those for or against the association theory. It is true that it then becomes somewhat indefinite; we are not to inquire whether anthropoid apes show something well defined, but whether their behaviour approximates to a type rather superficially known by experience, and which we call "intelligent" in contrast to other behaviour—especially in animals. But in proceeding thus, we are only dealing according to the nature of the subject; for clear definitions have no place at the beginning of sciences founded on experience; it is only as we advance towards results that we can mark our progress by the formulation of definitions.

Moreover, the type of human and, perhaps, animal behaviour to which the first question animadverts is not quite indefinite, even without a theory. As experience shows, we do not speak of behaviour as being intelligent, when human beings or animals attain their objective by a direct unquestionable route which clearly arises naturally out of their organization. But we tend to speak of "intelligence" when, circumstances having blocked the obvious course, the human being or animal takes a roundabout path, so meeting the situation. In unexpressed agreement with this, nearly all these observers who heretofore have sought to solve the problem of animal intelligence, have done so by watching animals in just such predicaments. Since animals below the stage of development of anthropoid apes give, in general, negative results, there has arisen out of these experiments the view widely held at present, i.e., that there is very little intelligent behaviour in animals. Only a small number of such experiments have been carried out on anthropoid apes, and they have not yet produced any very definite results. All the experiments described in the following pages are of one and the same kind: the experimenter sets up a situation in which the direct path to the objective is blocked, but a roundabout way left open. The animal is introduced into this situation, which can, potentially, be wholly surveyed. So we can see of what levels of behaviour it is capable, and, particularly, whether it can solve the problem in the possible "roundabout" way.

The experiments were at first applied to chimpanzees only, with the exception of a few cases taken for comparison, in which human beings, a dog, and hens were observed.

Seven of the animals belonged to the old branch of the anthropoid station which the Prussian Academy of Science maintained in Tenerife from 1912 to 1920. Of these seven the oldest, an adult female, was named Tschego, because of several characteristics which made us, perhaps wrongly, consider her a member of the Tschego species. (We are yet far from possessing a clear and systematized classification of the varieties of the chimpanzee.) The oldest of the smaller animals, called Grande, differed considerably in several respects from its comrades. But as the differences concern its general character rather than the behaviour investigated in the intelligence tests, a detailed description of them would be out of place here. The other five, two males (Sultan and Konsul), and three females (Tercera, Rana, and Chica), were of the usual chimpanzee type.

To the seven animals mentioned, two others were added later, both of which led to valuable observations, but both of which, to our regret, soon died. I shall briefly describe them in order to give an impression of the completely different "personalities" which exist among chimpanzees.

Nueva, a female ape, about the same age as the other little animals (four to seven years at the time of the majority of our experiments), differed from them bodily in her extraordinarily broad ugly face and an obviously pathological sparsity of hair on her unhealthy skin. But her ugliness was completely offset by a nature so mild and friendly, of such naïve confidence and quiet clarity as never fell to our lot to meet with in a chimpanzee before or after. Her childlike attachment we found to some extent in other animals when they were ill, and perhaps many of Nueva's good qualities can be explained by the fact that, from the beginning, she was the prey of a slowly-advancing disease; chimpanzee, on the whole, can do with a little suppression. We were particularly impressed by the way she would play for hours, quite contentedly with the simplest toys. Unfortunately the others tended to become lazy if they were not given any particular employment, or if they were not quarrelling, or inspecting each other's bodies. If a number of healthy children are left together all the time, without any particular occupation, the effect will not be in the line of a discreet, though playful activity. Nueva had been kept alone for many months. One must, however, not assume that the pleasant qualities of this animal were due to earlier educational influences. Unfortunately, education does not seem able to transform a naturally mischievous and wanton chimpanzee into an amiable being; moreover, Nueva was not "brought up" in the nursery sense; on the contrary, she showed that she was not used to being corrected at all. She regularly ate her excretions, and was first astonished and then extremely indignant when we took measures against this habit. On the second day of her stay at the station, the keeper threatened her, during this proceeding with a little stick, but she did not understand the meaning of the stick, and wanted to play with it. If food which she had, with complete naïveté, appropriated somewhere, was taken away from her she would bite, in her sudden rage, immediately; she was as yet without any inhibitions toward man; in fact, she showed herself completely naïve, and was, without doubt, less "cultured" than the station animals.

The male, Koko, judged to be about three years of age, was a type of chimpanzee not uncommonly met with: above his drum-taut stomach a pretty face with neatly parted hair, a pointed chin, and prominent eyes which seemed always discontentedly asking for something, giving the little fellow a native expression of sauciness. A large part of his existence was, in fact, spent in a kind of chronic indignation, either because there was not enough to eat, or because the children came too near him, or because someone who had just been with him left him again, or finally, because he could not remember to-day how he had solved a similar test yesterday. He would not complain; he would merely be indignant. Usually this mood was manifested by loud pommelling on the floor with both fists, and an agitated hopping up and down in one spot; in cases of great rage by glottal cramp-attacks which passed over quickly. (These we noticed also in other chimpanzees when they had attacks of rage, and very rarely in manifestations of joy.) Before such attacks, and in cases of minor excitement, he would utter a continual staccato o in that irregular characteristic rhythm which one hears from a slow-firing line of soldiers. In his angrily-uttered demands, and his wild indignation if they were not immediately satisfied, Koko resembled another egoist *par excellence*, Sultan. Luckily—and perhaps that is no accident—Koko was, at the same time, just as gifted as Sultan.

These are only two chimpanzees. For one who has seen Koko and Nueva alive, there is no doubt that in their own way they were as much unlike as two human children with fundamentally different characters, and one can set up as a general maxim that observations of one chimpanzee should never be considered typical for all of this species of animal. The experiments we describe in the following show that there are just as great individual differences in the intellectual field.

Practically all the observations were made in the first six months of 1914. They were frequently repeated later, but only a few additional experiments and repetitions (dating from the spring of 1916) are incorporated in this report, as, in general, the behaviour observed the first time was repeated; in any case, no important corrections had to be made in the earlier results.

Experiments of the kind described above may make very different calls upon the animlas to be tested, according to the situation in which they are put. In order to discover, even roughly, the zone of difficulty within which the testing of chimpanzees will be of any use, Mr. E. Teuber and I gave them a problem which seemed to us difficult, but not impossible, of solution for a chimpanzee. How Sultan behaved in this test should be sketched here as a preliminary example.

A long thin string is tied to the handle of a little open basket containing fruit; an iron ring is hung in the wire-roof on the animals' playground through which the string is pulled till the basket hangs about two metres above the ground; the free end of the string, tied into a wide open loop, is laid over the stump of a tree-branch about three metres away from the basket, and about the same height from the ground; the string forms an acute angle—the end being at the iron ring. Sultan, who has not seen the preparations, but who knows the basket well from his feeding-times, is let into the playground while the observer takes his place outside the bars. The animal looks at the hanging basket, and soon shows signs of lively agitation (on account of his unwonted isolation), thunders, in true chimpanzee style, with his feet against a wooden wall, and tries to get into touch with the other animals at the windows of the ape-house and wherever there is an outlook, at the bars; but the animals are out of sight, and the observer remains indifferent. After a time, Sultan suddenly makes for the tree, climbs quickly up to the loop, stops a moment, then, watching the basket, pulls the string till the basket bumps against the ring (at the roof), lets it go again, pulls a second time more vigorously so that the basket turns over, and a banana falls out. He comes down, takes the fruit, gets up again, and now pulls so violently that the string breaks, and the whole basket falls. He clambers down, takes the basket, and goes off to eat the fruit.

Three days later, the same experiment is repeated, except that the loop is replaced by an iron ring at the end of the rope, and the ring, instead of being put over the branch, is hung on a nail driven into a scaffolding (used for the animals' gymnastics). Sultan now shows himself free from all doubt, looks up at the basket an instant, goes straight up to the scaffolding, climbs it, pulls once at the cord, and lets it slip back, pulls again with all his might so that the cord breaks then he clambers down, and fetches his fruit.

The best solution of the problem which could be expected would be that the animal should take the loop or iron ring off the branch or nail and simply let the basket drop, etc. The actual behavior of the animal shows plainly that the hub of the situation, i.e., the rope connexion, is grasped as a matter of course, but the further course of action for the experiment is not very clear. The best solution is not even indicated. One cannot tell just why. Did Sultan perhaps not see the loose fixing of the loop to the branch or ring to the nail? If he had noticed it, would he have been able to solve it? Would he in any case expect the basket to fall to the ground if this fastening were loosened? Or does the difficulty lie in the fact that the basket would fall to the ground, and not straight into Sultan's hands? For we cannot even know whether Sultan really pulled at the cord to break it, and thus bring the basket to earth. So we have performed one experiment which, for a beginning, contains conditions too complicated to teach us much, and, therefore, we see the necessity of beginning the next examinations with elementary problems in which, if possible, the animal's conduct can have one meaning only.

The chimpanzee manifest intelligent behaviour of the general kind familiar in human beings. Not all their intelligent acts are externally similar to human acts, but under well-chosen experimental conditions, the type of intelligent conduct can always be traced. This applies, in spite of very important differences between one animal and another, even to the least gifted specimens of the species that have been observed here, and, therefore, must hold good for every member of the species, as long as it is not mentally deficient, in the pathological sense of the word. With this exception, which is presumably rare, the success of the intelligence tests in general will be more likely endangered by the person making the experiment than by the animal. One must learn and, if necessary, establish by preliminary observation, within what limits of difficulty and in what functions the chimpanzee *can possibly* show insight; negative or confused results from complicated and accidentally-chosen test-material, have obviously no bearing upon the fundamental question, and, in general, the experimenter should recognize that every intelligence test is a test, not only of the creature examined, but also of the experimenter himself. I have said that to myself quite often, and yet I have remained uncertain whether the experiments I performed may be considered "satisfactory" in this respect; without theoretical foundations, and in unknown territory, methodological mistakes may quite well have occurred; anyone who continues this work will be able to prevent them more easily.

At any rate, this remains true: Chimpanzees not only stand out against the rest of the animal world by severe morphological and, in the narrower sense, physiological, characteristics, but they also show a type of behaviour which counts as specifically human. As yet we know little of their neighbours on the other side, but according to the little we do know, with the results of this report, it is not impossible that, in this region of experimental tasks, the anthropoid is nearer to man *in intelligence too,* than to many of the lower monkey-species. So far, observations agree well with the theories of evolution; in particular, the correlation between intelligence, and the development of the brain, is confirmed.

The positive result of the investigation needs a limiting determination. It is, indeed, confirmed by experiments of a somewhat different nature, which will be recounted later; but a more complete picture will be formed when they are added, and in so far, our judgment of the intelligence of apes is left some scope. Of much greater importance is the fact that the experiments in which we tested these animals brought them into situations in which all essential conditions were actually visible, and the solution could be achieved immediately. This method of experimentation is as well adapted to the chief problem of insight as are any which can bring about the decision "yes" or "no"; in fact, it may be the very best method possible at present, as it yields very many, and very clear, results. But we must not forget that it is just in these experimental circumstances that certain factors hardly appear, or appear not at all, which are rightly considered to be of the greatest importance for *human* intelligence. We do not test at all, or rather only once in passing how far the chimpanzee is influenced by factors not present, whether things "merely thought about" occupy him noticeably at all. And most closely connected with this, is the following problem. In the method adopted so far we have not been able to tell how far back and forward stretches the time "in which the chimpanzee lives"; for we know that, though one can prove some effects of recognition and reproduction after considerable lapses of time —as is actually the case in anthropoids—this is not the same as "life for a longer space of time." A great many years spent with chimpanzees lead me to venture the opinion that, besides in the lack of speech, it is in the extremely narrow limits in *this* direction that the chief difference is to be found between anthropoids and even the most primitive human beings. The lack of an invaluable technical aid (speech) and a great limitation of those very important components of thought, so-called "images," would thus constitute the causes that prevent the chimpanzee from attaining even the smallest beginnings of cultural development. With special reference to the second fact, the chimpanzee, who is easily puzzled by the simplest optical complications, will indeed fare badly in "image-life," where even man has continually to be fighting against the running into one another, and melting together, of certain processes.

In the field of the experiments carried out here the insight of the chimpanzee shows itself to be principally determined by his optical apprehension of the situation; at times he even starts solving problems from a too visual point of view, and in many cases in which the chimpanzee *stops* acting with insight, it may have been simply that the structure of the situation was too much for his visual grasp (relative "weakness of form perception"). It is therefore difficult to give a satisfactory explanation of all his performances, so long as no detailed theory of form (Gestalt) has been laid as a foundation. The need for such a theory will be felt the more, when one remembers that, in this field of intelligence, *solutions* showing insight necessarily are of the same nature as the structure of the situations, in so far as they arise in dynamic processes *co-ordinated with* the situation.

One would like to have a standard for the achievements of intelligence described here by comparing with our experiments the performances of human beings (sick and well) and, above all, human children of different ages. As the results in this book have special reference to a particular method of testing and the special test-material of optically-given situations, the psychological facts established in human beings (especially children), under the same conditions, would have to be used. But such comparisons cannot be instituted, as, very much to the disadvantage of psychology, not even the most necessary facts of this sort have been ascertained. Preliminary experiments—some have been mentioned—have given me the impression that we are inclined to over-estimate the capabilities of children of all ages up to maturity, and even adults, who have had no special technical training in this type of performance. We are in a region of *terra incognita.* Educational psychology, engaged on the well-known quantitative tests for some time, has not yet been able to test how far normal, and how far mentally-deficient, children can go in certain situations. As experiments of this kind can be performed at the very tenderest age, and are certainly as scientifically valuable as the intelligence tests usually employed, it does not matter so much if they do not become immediately practicable for school and other uses. M. Wertheimer has been expressing this view for some years in his lectures; in this place, where the lack of human standards makes itself so much felt, I should like to emphasize particularly the importance and—if the anthropoids do not deceive us—the fruitfulness of further work in this direction.

Postscript.—When I finished this book, I received from Mr. R. M. Yerkes (of Harvard University) his work entitled *The Mental Life of Monkeys and Apes: a Study in Ideational Behaviour (Behaviour Monographs,* III, i, 1916). In this book some experiments of the type I have described are recorded. The anthropoid tested is an orang-utan, not a chimpanzee, but, as far as one can judge from the material given, the results agree with mine. Mr. Yerkes himself also thinks that insight must be attributed to the animal he tested.

Shepard Ivory Franz: 1874-1933
Karl Spencer Lashley: 1890-

THE RETENTION OF HABITS BY THE RAT AFTER DESTRUCTION OF THE FRONTAL PORTION OF THE CEREBRUM *

1917

Much has been written regarding the neurology of learning and especial attention has been directed to the cerebrum. Comparatively little evidence has been adduced to show what cerebral elements are used in the formation of habits, although recent experimental investigations show that the frontal positions of the cerebrum are utilized by monkeys, dogs, and cats. In only those animals with a highly developed brain is there a distinct differentiation of the frontal (as an association area) from the central (so-called motor and sensory-kinesthetic) area, and in fact the possibility of the histological differentiation of numerous areas of the brains of many of the lower animals is slight. The relatively simple and homogeneous character of the cerebral cortex in the rodents makes their cerebral physiology worthy of study, and there is the added advantage that the animals acquire habits rapidly and much information is at hand regarding their normal reactions.

At the same time, on account of their low cost and ease of housing, many different experiments on the brain may be made which are not possible with animals having larger and more highly developed brains. Such experiments on rats may be expected to give results of at least suggestive value respecting the functions of corresponding parts of more highly evolved brains. Thus, if it is found that these animals can acquire habits after the removal of certain small or large parts of the cerebrum, but not after the removal of other parts, or if they can retain but can not acquire habits after certain cerebral destructions, there will exist a basis for further extensive and intensive work on the so-called higher animals. The present work was undertaken with these objects in view.

* From *Psychobiology*, I, (1917-18), 3-7, 19-18. Reprinted by permission of the Williams and Wilkins Co. and of Dr. Lashley. This investigation, done jointly with Franz, was the beginning of a long series of researches which Lashley subsequently conducted. See "Brain Mechanisms and Intelligence" (1929) in this volume for a later significant publication by Lashley.

Several questions were posed, although the facts to answer only a few parts of these questions are now available. Some of the questions are: Do rats retain habits of recent formation after the destruction of certain cerebral regions? Do they retain habits of long standing, or those in which there has been an overtraining or over-learning? Can rats learn after the removal of the whole cortex? If learning and retention are possible after destruction of parts of the cortex, how much and what parts of the brain are necessary for, and what parts are normally used in the formation and the retention of habits? At the present time there are available results of experiments in which the frontal portions of the brain have been destroyed, and in which there have been destructions of two-thirds or more of the whole cortex (that of the cerebral convexity), but only those experiments dealing with the effects of frontal destructions will be reported here.

When the experiments were undertaken there was available a large number of rats which has been trained in a simple maze for other purposes and it was decided to use them in preliminary tests. The maze was built after the pattern of the Yerkes discrimination box (Fig. 1). It consists of a starting compartment (a) leading by a sliding door to a central alley (b), which at its outer end offers the alternatives of the cul de sac (c) and the alley (d) leading directly to the food (e). A maze of this character had decided advantages for the training of large numbers of animals but it is not altogether suitable for tests on retention on account of the speed with which it is learned and the degree of probability that any given correct trial is the result of chance. Incidental observations on the behavior of the animals in the maze are therefore of great importance for the determination of the retention of the habit.

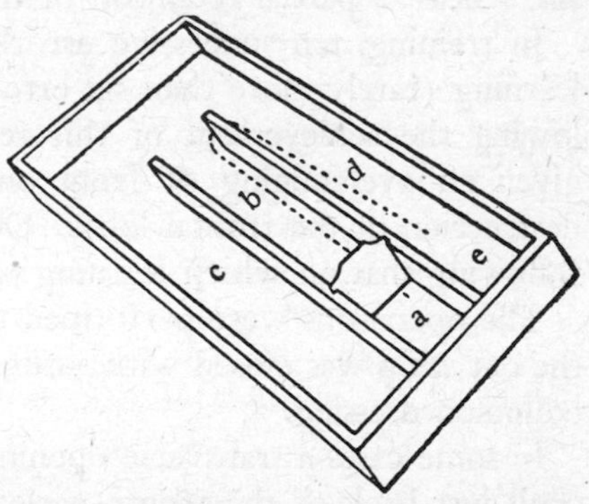

FIG. 1—Simple Maze. A, starting compartment; e, food. Dotted line shows the path taken by well-trained animals.

Two activities of the animals in the maze are to be especially noted, as their characteristics are evidences of learning or lack of learning, and of retention of the maze habits. These activities relate to the reactions at the door of the starting box and to the shortening of the path to the food. When first introduced into the starting compartment of the maze the rat sniffs at the wire cover, sides, and corners of the compartment and pays no particular attention to the door. When the door is first raised he almost always stands erect and sniffs at its lower edge before venturing into the first alley. With practice his reactions become centered on the door; he tries to push it up or sniffs at the crack under it. The moment that the experimenter touches the door to open it the rat turns with his head in the right front corner of the starting compartment and as soon as the door is raised high enough to admit his body craws out into the alley. This behavior is noted in the records of the different animals as "normal orientation to opening door."

In his first trials in the maze the rat spends much time in sniffing at the wire cover, the walls, and particularly the corners of the maze. The trained rat can go from the starting compartment to the food in 1.2 seconds. The minimum time on the first trial for any of the sixty rats that have been trained has been eight seconds and the modal time is about thirty seconds, most of which is spent in exploratory sniffing. With practice these exploratory movements disappear and the animal runs to the food without a pause. Many animals come to follow the path marked by the dotted line in Figure I. That is, they keep close to the right-hand wall of the middle alley and keep close to the end of the partition in rounding the turn. This cutting down of excess distance and absence of exploratory sniffing are characteristic of the later stages of learning and when they appear in retention tests are therefore conclusive evidence for at least a partial retention of the motor habits of the maze.

In training, ten successive errorless trials were taken as evidence for learning (rarely more than six errors are made in the hundred trials following the achievement of this record). Some of the rats were then given an overtraining of from one to two hundred trials before the destruction of the frontal lobes. Others were operated upon on the day following that on which learning was completed.

The operations were performed under ether anesthesia, and at the end the cut scalp was closed with sutures and was covered with a cotton and collodion dressing.

In some cases a transverse opening about 4 by 8 mm. was made in the skull just back of the fronto-parietal suture and the frontal area of the brain was destroyed by passing a narrow scalpel diagonally forward to the region of the olfactory bulbs and thence cutting out to the sides of the cranial cavity. In other cases two small trephine holes were made in the region of the suture and a spear-pointed needle was inserted through these, pushed through the frontal area and drawn to the sides to cut away the frontal regions. Owing to the small operation field it is not possible to determine the exact extent of the lesion at the time of operation but the possibility of using a large number of animals and of later determination of the extent of the destruction of tissue makes it possible to obtain records of some animals in which the exact lesion desired has been produced.

Most of the animals have been kept for two weeks or more after the operation and in many cases the absorption of the clot has progressed to such an extent that it seems advisable to wait until histological examinations of the brains can be made before describing the lesions in detail. Fourteen animals have been operated upon for destruction of the frontal lobes and of these eight have been autopsied. In these the gross lesion has been in every case as extensive as that indicated in Figure 2, and in three of the animals has extended back so as to involve the anterior two-thirds of the cortex.

Brief records of the animals studied are given below. Whenever possible, fifteen trials in the maze were obtained from each animal on the day following the operation. The time consumed in each of these trials in going from the starting compartment to the food dish and the number of errors, either of entering the cul de sac or of turning back upon the true pathway, was recorded. In the following records the total time consumed in these fifteen trials and the total number of errors are compared with the total time and errors of the first fifteen trials made by the same rat in its first training in the maze. The time and number of errors of the rat's first trial in the maze at the beginning of training are also compared with those of the first trial of the retention tests. In addition to this observations are reported on the general behavior of the animals in the maze.

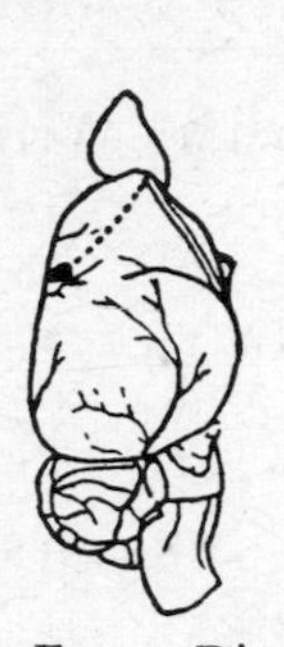
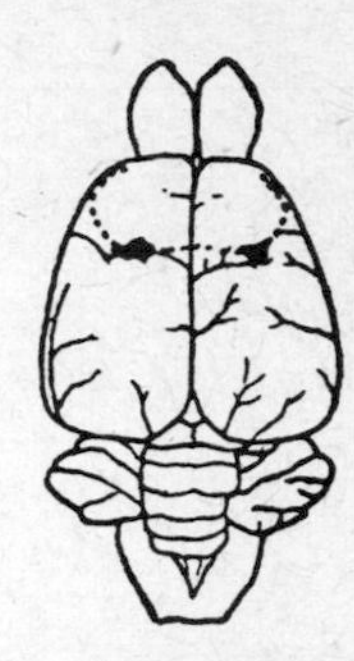

FIG. 2—Diagram of the extent of the lesion in Rat H1♀, as determined by gross dissection.

SUMMARY OF RESULTS OF EXPERIMENTS

The records of time and errors have been summarized in Table I. From the averages it appears that the rats which were not overtrained required 29 per cent less time for the first 15 trials after the destruction of the frontal lobes and made 53 per cent fewer errors than they did in learning the maze. This in itself is evidence for a partial retention of the habit. When considered in connection with the data on their behavior in the maze it shows that there was little if any loss that can not be accounted for by the distracting effects of the head bandages and the general shock effects of the operation. None of the animals showed the exploratory sniffing at cracks and corners which is so characteristic of the untrained rat in the maze. All were tested immediately after the retention tests by being placed in a strange cage with food and all spent at least thirty

TABLE I

THE TIME REQUIRED FOR REACHING THE FOOD AND THE NUMBER OF ERRORS MADE BY RATS IN LEARNING THE MAZE AND IN THE RETENTION TESTS AFTER THE DESTRUCTION OF THE FRONTAL LOBES

Number	*Training* First 15 trials Time	*Training* First 15 trials Errors	*Training* First trial	*Retention* First 15 trials Time	*Retention* First 15 trials Errors	*Retention* First trial
ANIMALS WITHOUT OVERTRAINING						
G2	188	5	15	54	1(?)	2.6
G1	117	8	10	159	2	45
H1	85	2	10	64	4	8
Totals	390	15	35	277	7	55.6
ANIMALS OVERTRAINED						
G1♂	1018	21	34	92	2	12
F1♀	640	19	15	44	2	4
F2♂	93	7	13	68	0	6
G3♂	359	11	11	55	1	8
F2♀	203	7	60	115	3	18
D1♀	566	23	18	57	2	1.8
B1♂	1797	33	32	137	2	12
F3♂	428	11	175	50	1	11
G4♂	135	2	20	51	0	2
G2♂	134	3	31	123	0	8
Totals	5408	137	399	791	13–	82.8

seconds in exploring the cage before pausing at the food, so that the lack of exploratory activities in the maze must be looked upon as due to retention of the habit and not to a general sluggishness resulting from the operations. The three rats which were not overtrained oriented in the starting compartment and two regularly followed the path marked in Figure 1. The abnormality of behavior of the third (G1 ♀) was probably due to loss of sensitivity of the vibrissae.

The animals which were overtrained required 87 per cent less time for the first fifteen trials after operation and made 90 per cent fewer errors than in their initial learning. This, in addition to the data on individual behavior in the maze shows that there was practically no loss of the habit resulting from the destruction of the frontal lobes.

There is an apparent difference in the amount of retention between animals which were over-trained and those which were trained only until they had learned the problem. This difference is probably not so great as is indicated by the averages because the long time spent by the non-overtrained group is the result of the inclusion of the rat G1 which spent a great deal of time in trying to remove the dressing from its head.

Only one animal did not show evidence of the maze habit after removal of the frontal portions of the brain. This animal showed such an amount of muscular weakness, or apathy, that the running of the maze was not attempted by it even after the fashion of an untrained animal. With this exception the tests gave indisputable evidence of the retention of the habit after the frontal portions of both hemispheres had been excised. Moreover, the evidence is more compelling because of some obvious behavior disturbances in a number of the animals. Thus, it has been reported of the second animal, G1 ♀ that, although the time for running the maze after the operation was greater than in the training series its other behavior relating directly to the maze was retained. The time variation (lengthening) was due entirely to changes in its physical condition other than those necessarily related to its maze activities. That this is so will be realized when it is remembered that the delays were made up of periods of scratching its head-dressing and of long stuporous or apathetic pauses. In the fourth animal the sensibility of the vibrissae was decreased, perhaps they were anesthetic, and the short times for running the maze after the operation are especially noteworthy. The twelfth and thirteenth animals were weak and spastic, and exhibited abnormal reactions in connection with the food dish, but both managed to find the correct path quite promptly. The time for the first fifteen trials of the thirteenth animal, G2 ♂, after operation was only slightly less than that of the corresponding period of training, but the long stuporous pauses account for much of the time that was taken.

As a whole, therefore, the experiments show that in the white rat the removal of large parts of the frontal portions of the brain does not greatly interfere with a learned reaction. This is the more remarkable since it seems probable that the so-called motor area is in that region and that in most, if not all, of the cases there was a destruction or abolition of the motor connections. While it can not be concluded with certainty, it seems likely that the motor derangements which were exhibited by many of the rats were due to the interference with the normal efferent impulses and not to the general anemia (from the hemorrhage of the operation). Some of the animals also showed obvious disturbances of sensibility, the observations indicating that in some the stimuli to the vibrissae and olfactory stimuli did not give normal effects. In view of the importance of these two forms of sensibility in the rat's reactions, we are led to wonder whether these retain their predominance in the animal's learned activities, or are replaced by other forms of sensibility, such as the general kinesthetic. Although the results give plain evidence of non-interference (relative, to be sure) with learned reactions when the frontal portions of the brain have been destroyed they also suggest that the habit reaction is not necessarily cortical in these animals. Other experiments which have been performed bear out this conclusion, but it seems best to reserve the account of these other tests until careful cerebral examinations have been completed.

Wolfgang Köhler: 1887-

PHYSICAL GESTALTEN *

1920

INTRODUCTION FOR PHILOSOPHERS AND BIOLOGISTS

When spatial, visual, auditory and intellectual processes are such as to display properties other than could be derived from the parts in summation, they may be regarded as unities illustrating what we mean by the word "*Gestalten.*"

In order to orient itself in the company of natural sciences, psychology must discover connections wherever it can between its own phenomena and those of the older disciplines. If this search fails, then psychology must recognize that its categories and those of natural science are incommensurable. And indeed a first glance does not give one much encouragement, for the *exactitude* of science does at first seem incompatible with inquiry in a field devoted to the study of compounds possessing their own "specific unity." When, further, it is said that these whole-phenomena disclose properties and influences that are "more than the sum of their parts," the suspicion becomes even greater that a search for them elsewhere than in psychology would somehow violate the fundamentals of exact science.

Let us nevertheless see whether physics discloses whole-phenomena of this type. At first we may despair of success, for without some guiding hints the immense domain of physics seems to reveal but little of the sort of thing we are seeking. However, we must not expect a ready-made answer to our problem right at the start. The thought and language of physics were established in accordance with other points of view than those with which our search is concerned; hence if these alone were consulted, they would hinder more than they might help—despite their admirable fitness for the purposes of the research physicist.

It seems wiser, therefore, to abandon the idea of reaching our goal immediately—i.e. by a systematic survey of the whole body of physics as ordinarily presented. Probably, if our search is to succeed at all, a

* From *Die Physichen Gestalten in Ruhe und in stationaren Zustand, Eine naturphilosophische Untersuchung*, Erlangen, 1920, as translated and abridged in *A Source Book of Gestalt Psychology* by Willis D. Ellis, Harcourt, Brace Co., N. Y., in 1938. Reprinted by permission of Kegan Paul, Trench, Trubner & Co. and the author.

more special point of departure and a less ambitious method will prove advantageous.

In biology the controversy has centered around the problem whether life processes can be explained physio-chemically or whether "vital" forces must be postulated. Indeed, the properties of life processes with which biology is concerned are not unlike the psychical phenomena responsible for the Gestalt problem in psychology. This does not mean, however, that the vitalists' doctrine in biology recommends itself as particularly fruitful, for *their* answer precludes the possibility of success in a search for physical Gestalten. The biologists have of course made some attempts at discovering analogies in physics, but thus far little more than vague comparisons with crystal formations have been achieved. The problem was formulated much too generally.

The closest approach between general biology and psychology occurs in the theory of nervous functions, particularly in the doctrine of the physical basis of consciousness. Here we have an immediate correspondence between mental and physical processes and the demand seems inescapable that at this point organic functions be thought of as participating in and exhibiting essentially Gestalt characteristics. The import and extraordinary significance of this was first recognized by Wertheimer who thereby attached to Gestalten a degree of reality far beyond any they had previously possessed. This implies, as Koffka emphasized, that central physiological processes cannot be regarded as sums of individual excitations, but as configured whole-processes.

Now we find ourselves in a very different position regarding physics, for the brief reference to biology has suggested the thing we lacked, viz. a special but far more concrete problem—and surely nothing is lost if one begins by attacking this problem alone. A successful solution here would supply not only the beginnings of a physiological Gestalt theory but also definite instances of physical (in this case neurological) Gestalten. If we were successful in a discovery of such Gestalten in physics we should be able to derive the principles necessary for a generally satisfactory outcome of our original search. If there are *some* cases of Gestalten in physics, even these few will suffice to guide subsequent inquiry. It follows that this special path—i.e. from individual instances of Gestalt processes in the nervous system to physics—may carry us into yet wider avenues eventually leading them back into biology and thus permit a much more comprehensive physical treatment not only of nervous but of all organic Gestalt processes.

INTRODUCTION FOR PHYSICISTS

Let us consider under what conditions a physical system attains a state which is independent of time (i.e. a state of equilibrium or a so-called stationary state). In general we can say that such a state is reached when a certain condition is satisfied for the system *as a whole*. The potential energy must have reached a minimum, the entropy a maximum, or the like. The solution of the problem demands not that forces or potentials assume particular values in individual regions, but that their total arrangement relative to one another in the whole system must be of a certain definite type. The state or process at any place therefore depends in principle on the conditions obtaining in all other parts of the system. If the laws of equilibrium or stationary state for the individual parts can be formulated separately, then these parts do not together constitute a *single* physical system, but each part is a system in itself.

Thus an electric circuit is a physical system precisely because the conditions prevailing at any given point are determined by those obtaining in all the other parts. Contrariwise, a group of electrical circuits completely insulated from each other constitutes a complex of independent, single systems. This complex is a "whole" *only* in the mind of one who chances to think of it as such; from the physical standpoint it is a summation of independent entities.

Now, although these facts are obviously familiar to physicists, they are often neglected in the theoretical treatment of biological problems. An example from the psychophysiology of space perception will illustrate this: when a number of stimuli act on different points of the sense organ at the same time, it has been the custom to interpret the action of each stimulus separately, and the total process has been considered a summation of the elementary processes which each stimulus would have aroused. A visual perception was thus physiologically ascribed to a mosaic of local nervous excitations in the visual cortex, each excitation corresponding to a single stimulus point on the retina and a single point of the object in space. Even Helmholtz proceeded in sense physiology upon this presupposition, although it is clear that the nervous system would have to satisfy very special conditions to make such a view tenable—namely, the nervous system could not be a *single physical system.*

For a time this method of treatment seemed adequate but, with the progress of psychology, difficulties began to appear which could not be covered up by the introduction of "psychological" hypotheses. And it was essentially this which led v. Ehrenfels to raise the "*Gestalt*" problem.

If, in the case of vision, we assume that each physically isolable stimulus produces an independent optical excitation, the problem, then, is to explain the unity of visual experience. As so-called optical illusions show, we do not see individual fractions of a thing; instead, the mode of appearance of each part depends not only upon the stimulation arising at *that* point but upon the conditions prevailing at other points as well. Since this fact does not bear out the assumption of isolated excitations, its explanation has been sought in terms of "higher mental processes." And yet, had it not been for this assumption probably no one would have thought to maintain that visual "Gestalten" occur only as products of mental activity. The *real* assumption, of course, was that to be scientific one had to treat wholes as bare aggregates.

The work of Wertheimer and Koffka has proceeded not on the basis just suggested but rather in conformity with our earlier remarks about physical systems. The facts of vision require that we treat them as properties of a *single* physical system in which the totality of stimulus conditions both individually and collectively is determined by the whole which they comprise. This mode of attack denies that the validity of the assumption was really scientific. It is the aim of this essay to support the Wertheimer hypothesis on physical grounds.

THE DERIVATION OF A FIRST PHYSICAL GESTALT FACTOR

The Characteristic Qualities of Stationary Somatic Fields

We feel and see Gestalten in the ordinary sense of the word when the spatial field of perception is *not* homogeneous. A tactual Gestalt is experienced only when a limited area of the skin is touched; colour differentiation is essential for the visual perception of Gestalten, etc. This leads us to inquire whether any significant changes occur in the nervous system when we turn from a homogeneous to an inhomogeneous field? If such changes *do* occur, does the nervous system itself possess Gestalt properties?

Let us assume that adjacent elements of a sensory surface correspond to adjacent elements in the neuro-somatic field and brain. And that every difference in position upon that sensory surface involves a corresponding change of place among the elements of the somatic field. This schematic view of nerve cell relations is to serve us merely as a preliminary sketch and lays claim to no more than that. Returning now to the question of homogeneity we find that if all points of a sensory surface are identically stimulated, the corresponding brain excitation will be likewise undifferentiated. With this in mind let us now consider certain types of excitation.

G. E. Muller has proposed a chemical theory of visual excitation according to which the processes of the retina and optic nerves involve reversible chemical reactions. This means that complementary colours are believed to initiate mutually opposite chemical processes in the optic system. We propose to generalize upon this view by assuming that all excitations in the somatic field are potentially reversible chemical reactions in a broad sense of the term.

In attacking the problem of variations of nervous activity let us consider once more the concept of stationary processes mentioned above, and notice, first, the several types of process of which this is one. These include (a) perfect equilibrium or rest, (b) stationary processes, (c) quasi-stationary processes, (d) periodic stationary processes, and (e) dynamic processes. A state of *equilibrium* is most simply illustrated by any physical body such as a book resting upon the table—let the book fall, however, and a *dynamic* process will arise. *Periodic stationary processes* are illustrated by membranes resonating with a constant and continuous vibration. A system is said to be in the stationary (or steady) state when the *same process* is going on in it continually, without changing any of its systemic properties. A steady stream of water in a pipe is an example. Change the conditions of a stationary process, however, and you have a dynamic process with accompanying changes of system-characteristics. A system is said to be in a quasi-stationary state when the process taking place in it changes very gradually with time—so gradually that the specifically *dynamic* factors are negligible. Gradual depletion in the electric current of a galvanic battery is an example.

In the nervous system the excitation produced by a continued stimulus does not, in general, remain constant with time; but the excitation of the sensory surface and the corresponding somatic field will, with sufficiently protracted stimulation, reach a stationary, or at least quasi-stationary, state.

There is to-day a general tendency to treat nerve activity as a case of reactions in dilute solutions, and this point of view is adopted here also. The most important solvent in nervous tissue is water, and since water enhances the ionization of molecules, it is likely that nervous substance (like all living matter) contains dissolved material that is to a large extent electrolytically dissociated. This would seem to justify the assumption that ionization of this type plays an essential part in the chemical reactions of the somatic field. Thus with constant external conditions, excitations in the somatic field may be considered quasi-stationary chemical reactions in dilute solutions in which ions participate. Hence the state prevailing at any given moment during the excitation is completely determined by the concentrations of reacting molecules and ions obtaining at that moment.

The Electric Behaviour of Inhomogeneously Stimulated Fields

It was proposed above that each adjacent element of a sensory surface be thought of as represented by similarly adjacent elements of the central nervous field. Let us now supplement this by the addition of certain physical principles; viz. the nature of field-excitation as illustrated by chemical reactions in dilute solutions. The manner in which neighbouring solutions affect one another is through diffusion or (what amounts to the same thing) equalization of osmotic pressures. This interrelationship of parts constitutes a physical system. We assume nervous elements to be so connected that diffusion can take place.

When the sensory surface is *in*homogeneously stimulated, reactions of the corresponding (stationary) nerve processes are *dis*similar. If two sensory areas are thus dissimilarly stimulated, then two different stationary processes of different concentration occur in the corresponding nerve areas. Hence all along the boundary between these there is a difference of osmotic pressure (with ensuing diffusion and migration of ions) and, owing to the difference in the velocity of the positive and negative ions, a consequent difference of electrostatic potential—and it follows that this potential difference is a function of the excitation-conditions of both somatic fields together. The principle of diffusion and consequent difference of electrical potential is applicable also to the case in which one area is stimulated while the other is devoid of stimulation. Indeed our theoretical considerations are verified by the fact that electromotive forces are operative between excited and unexcited regions not only in the nervous system but almost everywhere in living substance. Yet although electromotive forces in physiological processes have been widely studied (e.g. muscles, retina, etc.) the changes occurring in the somatic field in cases of spatially inhomogeneous excitations have not been investigated. If there is really a quantitative or qualitative difference in the excitations of adjacent fields under these conditions, then the following conclusions may be drawn:

1. Nervous fields excited by pressure, pain, or temperature stimuli display electromotive forces when circumscribed parts of the sensory surface are stimulated or when the type of stimulation is different at different places on this surface.

2. If the nerve regions corresponding to the two ear labyrinths are unequally stimulated, an osmotic communication of this dissimilarity will result, and a difference of electrical potential will arise between the two.

3. Most important of all is the nervous field corresponding to the retinas, for these are not peripheral sense organs like the cochlea, but parts of the brain itself. Two colours simultaneously seen have each a particular excitation-equivalent in the nervous system, and the contour

between them is the equivalent of an electromotive force in the nervous system between the two areas. The amount and direction of the potential difference are thus determined by the nature of the stimulating colours. If the two colours are gradually made to resemble one another, both the electromotive force and the contour diminish and disappear also. So long, however, as there is differentiation in the visual field—e.g. that of figure and ground—there will be a corresponding electromotive force in the nervous field. Figure perception is represented in the optic field by differences of potential along the entire outline or border of the figure. Similarly, movements of the eyes are governed almost completely by the contours of the things seen, and every executed eye-movement is accompanied by a change in the locus of electromotive force. Likewise a visual object is a total form bounded by definite contours enclosing a surface and this whole is experienced as set off against the surroundings in which it occurs. The less this condition of "being set off against" becomes, the less we are likely to consider the object a "thing." Along the boundaries of every perceived thing there arise electromotive forces in the optic sector of the nervous system.

According to these considerations one cannot treat the complex of physical processes which correspond to a given visual field as a mosaic of individual excitations in purely *geometrical* (as opposed to dynamic) interrelation. The process in the somatic field includes something *more* than this.

The First Physical Gestalt Factor

The foregoing has brought to light a factor which marks the distinction between homogeneously and inhomogeneously stimulated fields. The importance for our inquiry of the physical nature of this factor is that in apprehending it we are apprehending a simple *Gestalt* property of the systems we have studied. To elucidate this we now raise the question whether the characteristic properties of such physical systems are derivable from similar characteristics possessed by their *parts?* In answering this question let us suppose first that the "similar characteristic" of the parts is, say, the *weight* of each. In this case it is true that the characteristic quality of the whole *is* a sum of those of the parts and no more. But this does not resemble the cases of potential difference discussed above. In those cases the "difference" arose only when the two fields were in *physical communication*—it was not a mere difference between two previously existing potentials, but something that only came into being with the interplay of the two. The potential difference, then, is a primary characteristic of the *two* fields and impossible without *both* of them. The absolute potentials of the solutions taken alone would be another thing altogether, and it is in no sense true that the potential difference of the pair is derived additively from previously existing potentials. Indeed, the *reverse* is the case, for the electrical properties of the two parts are determined by those of the system as a whole. In instances of the kind we have discussed (osmotic communications of two solutions) the material nature (ionization, concentration) of the pair determines a new systemic property for the whole system, with simultaneous changes in the properties of the parts. In other words, when brought together the solutions communicate in a way such that a system of typical Gestalt attributes appears. A system of this kind is an internal unity precisely because its *parts* are determined by the material nature of the whole. From all of which it is self-evident that physics does not arbitrarily consider one group of parts a "whole" and another not, for the question is decided by very real and actual properties of the phenomena themselves.

Two characteristics of mental phenomena were considered by von Ehrenfels as criteria of Gestalten. First, when the separate stimuli (tones) of a melody are presented, one each to a number of persons, the totality of experiences is poorer than the total experience of *one* person to whom all the tones are presented. This criterion seems rather definitely to take for granted that both the stimuli and their specific "sensations" are all the while identical in themselves whether they are presented together or separately—and that the distinguishing feature of the richer experience rests upon a "*Gestaltqualitat*" added to the other elements. This, however, does not cover the facts. Actually von Ehrenfels's first criterion, though necessary, demands too little, for not only must the stimulations occur in a single phenomenal (or physiological) system, but they must also be able to influence each other reciprocally in the sense already suggested.

Von Ehrenfels's second criterion of phenomenal Gestalten is based on transposition, i.e. it is characteristic of phenomenal Gestalten that they may retain their specific properties even when the absolute constituents upon which they rest are varied in certain ways. While transposibility is undoubtedly a characteristic of many, it does not apply to all cases of Gestalten; thus this is a sufficient but not a necessary criterion and therefore it must be said that whereas the former criterion demanded too little, this one requires too much. The criterion is correct in this, however, that transposition demonstrates the independence of Gestalten of the specific parts contained in them.

ELECTROSTATIC STRUCTURES

"And-Summations" and "Physical Systems"

If the electromotive force in heterogeneous systems has not been recognized as a Gestalt property of such systems, perhaps these properties have also been overlooked in still *other* physical phenomena. To repeat our former question: Are there physical whole-states or whole structures in which the parts are not mere and-summations (Wertheimer, Koffka) of elementary individual states and individual structures? The first step is to determine an accurate and precise definition of the word "summation." An aggregate of "parts" or "pieces" is a genuine "sum" only when its constituents may be added together one after another without thereby causing any alteration in any of them; and conversely, a summation is that kind of togetherness from which any one or more units may be removed without any effect either on the ones remaining or on the ones removed. This preliminary characterization is, however, not sufficient for the purposes of the following inquiry. The grouping may under certain circumstances be quite unimportant, or it may be the essential feature of a "togetherness." The latter is a case of "summative grouping" when, although each piece occupies a definitely prescribed place, no change in property of the parts themselves is thereby involved. And again conversely: from a summative grouping, parts or pieces may be removed without any change occurring either in the distribution of the remaining ones or in those removed. If there are six coins on the table it will not alter them to be laid out as points of a six-sided figure, nor does any change of arrangement occur in the remaining ones when three are removed.

This specification of what summations are in physics is necessary in order that there be no misunderstanding when we come to speak of super-summative physical structures. Physical quantities are usually divided into scalar and vector quantities, both of which a first survey reveals to be summative. As regards the former: the *mass* of a system may be increased or decreased by specific amounts; the electrical *charge* of a system may be increased by partial charges until a desired sum of such charges is reached, and vice versa, the *energy* of a system may be removed in small quantities. Physics accordingly speaks of conservation of mass, electricity, and energy. With vectors the situation, while somewhat more complicated, is similar in that the addition of two or more vectors (e.g. velocities, forces) gives a vector that is the (vectorial) sum of those vectors.

We now turn to groupings and distributions. Three stones, one in Australia, another in Africa, and a third in the United States, might formally be said to constitute a group, but displacement of one has no effect on the others, nor upon their mutual relation. And this may be said also in general even when the stones are but 1 metre apart. Since such examples abound in our everyday experience, we are apt to acquire a deeply rooted prejudice about the nature of *all* groupings.

In physics it is not customary to investigate purely additive distributions because the investigation of a distribution consisting of *n* independent objects divides itself into *n* separate and distinct investigations. Contrariwise, when the independent displacement of particles in a distribution brings about reciprocal influences, the relations within such a distribution are no longer summative. In this case one displacement can and will determine other displacements—and we now have a "physical system." With increasing mutual dependence among the parts we reach systems where no displacement or change of state is without its influence throughout the entire system. An example of this can be seen in an electric charge, for changes in charge at one point of an insulated conductor involve immediate corresponding changes in the whole system. Physical systems and their distributions behave throughout differently from summative groupings of "objects"; the groupings of physical systems are of a non-additive nature and the distinctions between *distributions of physical objects*—where summation is possible—and distributions in *physical systems* must never be lost sight of.

The second law of thermodynamics deals specifically with physical systems and designates the *direction* taken by their processes. Consider an isolated system of constant mass, volume, and energy. What is meant when we say that each later state possesses a greater entropy or is "a more probable state" than the preceding one? Since the system at last reaches a maximum entropy, the "state of equilibrium" thus attained shows us, by comparison with earlier stages, in what manner the increase of entropy has occurred: according to the particular kind of system we find that temperature and pressure have become the same throughout and that there is now also a definite distribution of velocities in the entire system. Thus the second law, in referring to distribution, refers to the system as a *whole*, and any attempt to apply it to *parts* of a system would lead to extremely bad errors. This is because satisfaction of the second law by the *entire* system requires that one or more parts (considered alone) shall proceed in the *opposite* direction from that of the larger system. Consequently an attempt to derive the validity of this law additively from parts of a system would necessarily fail. The law of the system prescribes what must take place in the parts, not the reverse.

Electric Charge Structures

We have already mentioned the case of electrostatic distributions and our first example was also of electric phenomena. Taking up this matter again now we observe that, as a result of the conditions of equilibrium and the law of force between electric charges, the charge upon an insulated conductor is confined to its outer surface, and further that this surface is one of constant potential. The charge distributes itself in such a way that these two conditions are fulfilled. Since this distribution is, as we shall see, not a summative one, we shall, to avoid ambiguity, call it a *structure.*

Considering somewhat more closely the behaviour of a charge upon a conductor we find: (a) If the conductor is supplied at a given instant with an electric charge of any arbitrary distribution and thereafter left alone, there results a spontaneous arrangement of equilibrium distribution so rapid as practically to preclude an investigation of its course. If now the conductor remains undisturbed and ideally insulated, no change of this state takes place. Upon a conductor of definitely determined properties to which a certain charge is conveyed and whose state of charge is dependent only upon itself, one encounters either a definite, unchanging distribution of charge or an extremely brief dynamic displacement-process leading to a static distribution peculiar to this conductor. It is therefore correct to designate this distribution the "natural structure" of the charge upon the given conductor. (The mathematical expression of a natural structure would thus be called its "natural function.")

(b) It is impossible to decrease, increase, or displace any part of this charge alone; for with any such change there occurs a reaction throughout the entire natural structure. This does not refer, of course, to *amount* of charge which can be summatively increased or decreased without reference to structure. In a word *the structures of static charges upon conductors of given shape are physical Gestalten.*

Field Structures

We turn now to a consideration of the *fields* surrounding these electric structures. Whatever the medium between bodies may be in itself, we find in practice that the vicinity of a charged surface is a static field whose properties may be expressed in terms of the natural structure of the charge, hence also in terms of the conductor's shape. Just as equilibrium of an electric structure on a surface involves a constant potential throughout this surface, so also is the field in equilibrium characterized by its potential which satisfies the Laplace equation. Thus a field in equilibrium is itself a "structure," as follows from the fact that any effective change in the electric structure causes changes both in the structure of the charge and in the surrounding field. For simplicity's sake we spoke above of charge-structures alone, but this is really inadmissible, for a state of equilibrium in a charge is possible only when the structure is completed in its surrounding field. Finally also there is the question of electric (potential) energy which a charge possesses even when in a static state. Amount of energy depends not only upon the amount of charge but also upon the shape of conductor and hence upon the natural structure assumed by the charge. This dependence is due to the fact that when the structure is formed, as much energy will be transformed into heat as corresponds to the difference between the original energy and the remaining electrostatic energy. Hence we see that electrostatic energy is determined by the *entire* natural structure including, that is to say, the field also. Therefore the *complete* electric structure consists of charge and field and electrostatic energy together.

The following is an example of a weak Gestalt: a number of conductors, so isolated that there is but a negligible reciprocal influence between them, are connected by fine wires. When a charge is introduced into this system an electric current passes along the wires until there is a uniform potential throughout and hence a static state is reached. Nevertheless the structures assumed by the charge upon each conductor are (almost wholly) the *natural* structures of each. In other words, the structural moments of each conductor are in *principle* dependent upon the conditions of the whole system but in extreme cases their *specific* articulation is not noticeably influenced by *specific* events in remote parts of this system; the articulation of such limited regions depends instead upon the systemic conditions within each region itself.—Furthermore we may expect the mathematical treatment of weak Gestalten to be somewhat simpler than that of strong Gestalten. (This follows from the general principle that the method of attacking a problem is more or less determined by the object of study itself.) This simplification is due to the fact that the determining parts of a weak Gestalt (e.g. the several strong Gestalten) are finite in number. A *weak* Gestalt is nevertheless a *Gestalt* as may be determined by reference to the v. Ehrenfels criteria: the *structure* is unchanged even when the capacities of the conductors are increased or decreased proportionally (i.e. the structure is transposible: second criterion). It is shown that *steady electric currents* have Gestalt properties the same as those of static states, i.e. that there are also physical *processes* of a Gestalt character. This is also confirmed by reference to the v. Ehrenfels criteria.

SUMMARY

One point of view would be that nature is composed of independent elements whose purely additive total constitutes reality. Another that there are no such elements in nature, that all states and processes are real in a vast universal whole, and hence that all "parts" are but products of abstraction. The first proposition is completely wrong; the second hinders comprehension of the Gestalt principle more than it helps. Take for example the case of radioactive substances whose disintegrations occur according to their own laws and regardless of their surroundings. An outstanding exception such as this justifies us in rejecting the second hypothesis; this does not mean, however, that all states and processes are indifferent to other events around them. The *size* of an area beyond which interaction between a process and its surroundings may be ignored is a matter for specific determination; and the first step in all physical experimentation consists in making just this determination. The hypothesis of universal interaction, however, far from helping us in this, gives instead a picture of nature that is completely misleading.

If natural science has never been greatly concerned with the doctrine of universal interactionism, philosophy, unhampered by concrete examples of physical phenomena, has suffered all the more. The doctrine appears to be a complete acceptance of the Gestalt principle; in point of fact it only corrupts that principle. The trouble is, no one can take so general and indefinite an hypothesis seriously. "The whole world," which would really be involved in each investigation, cannot be manipulated in this way. The outcome, therefore, is either a romantic scepticism or a position such as this: to obtain a picture of nature we must, for better or worse, overlook universal interaction and deal only with the abstracted parts or pieces of nature. Hence we return in practice to the assumption of independent elements and their and-summations.

In psychology the situation is closely analogous. The worst enemy of a fruitful Gestalt theory—fruitful, i.e. because it is pledged to accept the concrete implications of its position—is the doctrine that only the total consciousness as such is directly given. But since nothing can be *done* with a reality of this sort, there remains on the one side a purely platonic agreement with the modern thesis, and on the other, a feeling that all abstractions are equally founded (better: equally unfounded) anyhow; and consciousness is thereupon treated as piecemeal as it was, say, by Hume. The outcome is a confused misdirection of emphasis leading eventually to a position diametrically opposite to Gestalt principles. The *important* point is missed: viz. the existence of self-enclosed, finitely extended Gestalten with their scientifically determinable, natural laws *(Eigengesetze)*. *In the physical world,* as has been shown in the foregoing pages, *it is precisely segregated physical systems to which the laws of nature apply.*

Whereas the doctrine of universal interactionism results in no responsible scientific inquiry, but leads in practice to a purely additive point of view, consideration of finite structures deals instead with definite, non-additive properties. The Gestalt principle, in harmony with its own empirical objects, involves a *finite* application and leads therefore to direct results. It would be indeed surprising if these results were not apparent in the treatment of biological and psychological problems.

The concepts of parts, of summations, etc., do not lose their important significance when we deal with Gestalt phenomena. One must be clear, however, about *what* it is to which the concepts are applied. (A distinction implicit in our previous treatment may make this clear.) In none of the Gestalt phenomena treated above have the physical components (electricity, electric current, migrating substance, etc.) been unconstrained (free) in their own structures; instead in each case there was a complex of *unchangeable conditions* spatially delimiting the structural material and at the same time specifically determining its *mode of extension.* The shape of a conductor was frequently mentioned in discussing strong Gestalten, but this form as well as other physical topography was not included in the Gestalten themselves, since *it* may exist whether the Gestalt phenomenon is present or not. The electric conductor was for our purposes the same whether charged or not. It follows that supra-summative Gestalt properties in no way imply supra-summative characteristics in their determining topography. It is for a Gestalt in such cases immaterial whether its topography be additively constituted or not. Hence we may readily assume that such topographies are physically composite. Therefore the term "part" may be used here in its ordinary meaning: we saw, for example, how two dissociated solutions of unequal ionic concentration could be brought together or separated. Only the stationary process occurring when they are together has any bearing on the Gestalt question, not the conditions obtaining in the two solutions separately. In this respect the physical conditions for the occurrence (and the properties) of a potential difference are not essentially different from the properties of the topography in which a stationary electric current develops. The entire system or any of its parts may exist, and the question whether or not an additive complex be involved has nothing to do with the question of the current-Gestalt. In general, distinguishing between Gestalten and their topographies at once frees one from conceptual difficulties, and apparent contradictions disappear. This clarification is especially helpful in the field of nerve physiology.

As against summations we have, in the case of Gestalten, finitely composed unities dependent upon a finite topography—and hence there are physical grounds why we are compelled to treat such organized wholes *as* unities. There is here nothing of a choice whereby, for example, we might at will think of one arrangement of parts rather than another. Instead the Gestalt laws observed by such phenomena and the specific structure spontaneously and objectively assumed *prescribe for us* what we are to recognize "as one thing." From which it follows that the moments of a structure, unlike the items of a geometrical grouping, are *not logically prior* to the total structure itself. To treat the moments of a Gestalt as if they *were* independent elements would be intrinsically and objectively fallacious. It would be intrinsically and objectively self-contradictory to treat a *structure* as one would a *geometric grouping* in which every element and its locus may be considered as independently variable factors. *A physical structure upon a given topography is not logically secondary relative to its moments.*

In physics the mode of thinking suitable for Gestalt problems is induced by *experience* itself. It is different in sciences that keep themselves remote from experience (e.g. modern philosophy) or are able only with great difficulty to make decisive observations (e.g. psychology and biology). Here the pressure of undeniable facts and hence restrictions upon purely additive thinking is lacking. Until recently it has been impossible to give conclusive answers to the speculations of additive thinking; *now*, however, from physics comes evidence to *demonstrate* the errors of such thinking.

Robert Mearns Yerkes: 1876-

PSYCHOLOGICAL EXAMINING IN THE UNITED STATES ARMY *

1921

On April 6, 1917, in connection with a meeting of a group of experimental psychologists which was at that time being held in Emerson Hall, Cambridge, Mass., a session was arranged by Messrs. Langfeld and Yerkes, with the approval of the chairman of the meeting, Mr. Titchener, for discussion of the relations of psychology to national defense. Capt. W. S. Bowen, instructor in military science and tactics, Harvard University, attended this meeting and made valuable suggestions concerning the possible role of psychology. At the conclusion of the discussion it was moved by Mr. Warren that a committee, consisting of Messrs. Yerkes, Bingham, and Dodge, be appointed to gather information concerning the possible relations of psychology to military affairs and to further the application of psychological methods to military problems.

On the evening of the same day at an informal conference of the members of this committee (Mr. Bingham's place was taken by Mr. Ogden) it was decided that the matter should be placed before the council of the American Psychological Association, so that the national organization rather than any restricted or local group might take action.

At the special meeting of the council of the American Psychological Association, which was held on the evening of April 21 and the morning of April 22 in Philadelphia, the president of the association reported the action taken in Cambridge and the results of his observations in Canada. After thorough discussion of the relations of psychology to the military situation it was voted by the council that the president be instructed to appoint committees from the membership of the American Psychological Association to render to the Government of the United States all possible assistance in connection with psychological problems arising in the military emergency.

* This report edited by Dr. Robert M. Yerkes, gives a picture of the first large-scale application of psychology to military problems. Excerpts are reprinted by permission of Dr. Yerkes. Selections are from pages 7, 8, 9-10, 99-100, 103-104, 114-119 of the *Memoirs of the National Academy of Sciences*, XV, 1921.

During the last week in April, in pursuance of the suggestions of the council of the American Psychological Association, the president, acting as chairman of the committee on methods for the psychological examining of recruits, prepared for transmission to the proper military authorities a plan for the examining of recruits, in which the function of the psychologist in dealing with intellectual deficiency and psychopathic tendencies, and his limitation, as an assistant of the military medical examiner, to the purely psychological aspects of the work was emphasized.

The evident necessity for developing methods of psychological examining especially adapted to military needs stimulated the chairman of the committee on methods of examining recruits to seek such financial aid as should render possible the organizing of an active committee for this special task. About the middle of May this need and opportunity were brought to the attention of the committee on provision for the feeble-minded (Philadelphia), whose secretary, Mr. Joseph P. Byers, immediately presented the matter to his board. It was promptly voted by this organization to offer the committee on methods facilities for work at The Training School, Vineland, N.J., and to meet the expenses of the work to an amount not to exceed $500. This sum was later increased to $700. On the basis of this offer of assistance, a committee, consisting of Messrs. Bingham, Goddard, Haines, Terman, Wells, Whipple, and Yerkes, was assembled at The Training School, Vineland, N.J., on May 28. It remained in session until June 9 when it adjourned for two weeks to make trial of methods which had been devised.

During the first two weeks it was decided to arrange a method of examining recruits in groups of 25 to 50, as an initial psychological survey. The group method, as finally agreed upon and printed for preliminary trial, consists of 10 different measurements.

From June 10 to 23 the various members of the committee conducted examinations by the above method in several parts of the country. In all, about 400 examinations were made, chiefly upon United States marines and candidates in officers' training camps. These measurements were analyzed by the committee and used as a basis for revision and the devising of methods of scoring.

On June 25 the committee resumed its sessions at Vineland and continued its work until Saturday, July 7, when it adjourned, on the completion of tentative methods of group and individual examining. At this time, the committee had in press five forms of group examination record blanks; an individual examination record blank, which provides special forms of measurement for illiterates, those who have difficulty with the English language, those who exhibit irregularities suggestive of psychopathic condition, those who are intellectually subnormal or inferior, and, finally, those who are distinctly supernormal; an examiners' guide, which contains directions for the conduct of examinations; and various types of special record sheet.

Before its adjournment the committee, through a joint committee of psychiatrists and psychologists, consisting of Drs. Copp, Meyer, Williams, Terman, Haines, (Bingham, alternate), and Yerkes, received assurance from the National Committee for Mental Hygiene that this committee would finance to the extent of $2,500 the trial of the above methods of psychological examining in various army and navy organizations—the work to be so planned as to test thoroughly the reliability and serviceableness of the methods, and to supply materials for their improvement, and for the development of satisfactory methods of scoring and reporting data of examinations.

This offer of assistance resulted in the prompt formulation of the following plan, which was successfully carried out:

Five groups of three men each are to be organized for immediate work in four different military establishments, each group to consist of a chief examiner and two assistants. The fifth group to be organized for statistical work.

The four examining groups are to work for one month in naval stations, army reorganization camps, or officers' training camps. It is proposed that approximately 1,000 men be examined at each place by the group method and approximately 200 by the individual method; further, that, so far as possible, the results of these examinations be correlated with industrial and military records or histories.

This work is to begin as soon after July 15 as possible. Records for examinations are to be shipped to the statistical unit in New York City as rapidly as possible, so that they may be scored and the results evaluated and correlated with a view to determining the best methods of scoring and desirable changes in methods of examining.

The examining of approximately 4,000 soldiers in accordance with the plan described above and the comparison of the results with officers' ratings of the men revealed a correlation of about 0.5, and in general justified the belief that the new methods would prove serviceable to the Army.

The achievements of the psychological service between September, 1917, and January, 1919, may at this point be summarized very briefly, since this memoir presents a detailed account of the work with reference especially to organization, methods and practical results.

After preliminary trial in four cantonments psychological examining was extended by the War Department to the entire Army, excepting only field and general officers. To supply the requisite personnel, a school for training in military psychology was established in the Medical

Officers' Training Camp, Fort Oglethorpe, Ga. Approximately 100 officers and more than 300 enlisted men received training at this school.

The work of mental examining was organized finally in 35 army training camps. A grand total of 1,726,966 men had been given psychological examination prior to January 31, 1919. Of this number about 42,000 were commissioned officers. More than 83,500 of the enlisted men included in the total had been given individual examination in addition to the group examination for literates, for illiterates, or both.

Between April 28, 1918, and January 31, 1919, 7,800 men (0.5 per cent) were reported with recommendations for discharge by psychological examiners because of mental inferiority. The recommendations for assignment to labor battalions because of low grade intelligence number 10,014 (0.6 per cent). For assignment to development battalions, in order that they might be more carefully observed and given preliminary training to discover, if possible, ways of using them in the Army, 9,487 men (0.6 per cent) were recommended.

During this same interval there were reported 4,780 men with mental age below 7 years; 7,875, between 7 and 8 years; 14,814, between 8 and 9 years; 18,878, between 9 and 10 years. This gives a total of 46,347 men under 10 years' mental age. It is extremely improbable that many of these individuals were worth what it cost the Government to maintain, equip, and train them for military service.

As originally conceived, psychological service within the medical department was to assist medical officers, and especially neuro-psychiatric officers, in discovering and eliminating men who were mentally unfit for military duty. It appeared, prior to actual trial, that reasonably well-planned methods of mental measurement should enable psychological examiners to discover mentally inferior recruits as soon as they arrived in camp and to make suitable recommendation concerning them to the medical officer. It was also believed that psychologists could assist neuropsychiatrists in the examination of psychotic individuals. The proposed role of the psychologist then was that of assistant to the army surgeon; the actual role, as a result of demonstration of values, was that of expert in scientific personnel work.

In interesting contrast with the original purpose of mental examining, as stated above, stands the following account of the purposes actually achieved by this service: (1) The assignment of an intelligence rating to every soldier on the basis of systematic examination; (2) the designation and selection of men whose superior intelligence indicates the desirability of advancement or special assignment; (3) the prompt selection and recommendation for development battalions of men who are so inferior mentally as to be unsuitable for regular military training; (4)

the provision of measurements of mental ability which shall enable assigning officers to build organizations of uniform mental strength or in accordance with definite specifications concerning intelligence requirements; (5) the selection of men for various types of military duty or for special assignments, as, for example, to military training schools, colleges or technical schools; (6) the provision of data for the formation of special training groups within the regiment or battery in order that each man may receive instruction suited to his ability to learn; (7) the early discovery and recommendation for elimination of men whose intelligence is so inferior that they can not be used to advantage in any line of military service.

Although it originally seemed that psychological examining naturally belonged to the Medical Department of the Army, and would there prove most useful, it subsequently became evident that this is not true, because the service rendered by psychological examiners is only in part medical in its relations and values. In the main its significance relates to placement, and its natural affiliation is with military personnel. For practical as well as logical reasons it would doubtless have been wiser had the service of the Division of Psychology been associated from the first with that of the Committee on Classification of Personnel in the Army, so that the psychological as well as occupational, educational and other important data might have been assembled by a single military agency and promptly rendered available for use in connection with the assignment of recruits. Thus also the organization of a special branch of the General Staff or of a personnel section of the Adjutant General's Office to deal with varied problems of military personnel might have been hastened and otherwise facilitated and the utilization of brain power as contrasted with man power in the ordinary sense rendered more satisfactory early in the emergency.

The services which are listed and briefly described below were rendered by psychologists under the direction of the Division of Psychology of the Surgeon General's Office. The problem of the division, as originally conceived, was to provide for the examination of recruits at the larger camps in this country and to report the results of examination to organization commanders, medical officers, and personnel adjutants for their use and information. Soon, however, other originally incidental services were introduced. The preceding sections have outlined the principal service and touched upon some auxiliary services. It is now the intention more systematically to outline the auxiliary services which ultimately came to be rendered to a variety of authorities and for a variety of purposes.

SERVICES TO ORGANIZATION COMMANDERS

After psychological examination an alphabetical list of the men in an organization with their corresponding grades was made on special report blanks. When possible, in divisional training camps, this report was delivered in person and discussed with the company commander by psychological officers. In some camps arrangements were made at an early date whereby psychological grades thus reported should be entered upon service records under "Remarks." At other camps this practice was forbidden until a final ruling from The Adjutant General of the Army was obtained which definitely permitted such entry. A mimeographed explanation of grades and scores was attached to all reports. When the reports were not delivered personally conferences of all officers of the regiment were sometimes held. Explanatory talks were usually made when officers or officers' training camp students were themselves being examined.

Commanding officers in divisional and replacement units found the ratings of considerable service in making transfers and assignments of men within their units. Questionnaires and other means of securing information showed that the following were the chief uses made of the ratings by company commanders:

(a) Assistance in the organization of the company in cases where many new recruits arrived at one time.

(b) Assistance in the selection within the company of men for special duties; for example, company clerk, orderly, post exchange detail, etc.

(c) As a check upon the officers' personal estimate of men and to direct particular attention to men whose ability had previously been either overlooked or overestimated. Such systematic use of the ratings as the calling in of all A and B men for personal interview by the captain or the inspection of men grouped by platoons of A, B, C, D, and E ratings are sometimes reported.

(d) Assistance in the selection of noncommissioned officers, acting noncommissioned officers, and candidates for noncommissioned officers' schools. In many camps, this use either as a sole or partial basis for such selection, was made obligatory by camp order; in others, such an order was not found necessary; but in no camp, so far as is known, were psychological grades entirely disregarded in making such selection.

(e) Assistance in the selection of men for officers' training school. Until forbidden to do so by General Orders, No. 74, the commanding officers in certain camps issued orders that such candidates must have A or B or, in some cases, C rating. In general, however, the psychological grade was considered simply as one of the chief factors to be taken into consideration.

(f) In several camps special training groups, based upon psychological ratings, were formed; the group with the higher rating was given more intensive and rapid special training. A major who assigned new recruits in his battalion into four groups, the A's, the B's, the C's, and the D's, thus describes the result of his experiment:

I went out to watch the platoons that were classified on the basis of your intelligence ratings. I was interested in seeing whether I could pick out the different platoons and classify them as to rank on the basis of their showing on the drill field. I had no difficulty in picking out the best, the medium and the lowest platoons. However, I could not distinguish between the A and B group, both of them seeming to execute the drill equally well. This may have been due to the fact that the B group was small in comparison to the other three, and consequently, had received more individual and therefore, better training. It was very evident that there was an apparent difference between the other three groups. If I should have graded them, I would have given the D and D-group 50 per cent; the C C and C-group, 75 per cent, and the A and B group 100 per cent. The A and B group would easily learn in one week what it would take the D and D-group two weeks to learn with the same amount of drilling each day. My plan was to rearrange the groups at the end of the first week, but I found no rearrangement necessary as the classification already made seemed to be correct. I watched the platoons in order to pick out any men who were not up to the standard of the group, but could not detect a single case that needed reclassifying.

This experiment was much more commonly tried in development battalions. At Camp Gordon, the chief psychological examiner spent the greater portion of his time for several months advising and lecturing to officers on methods of training.

(g) Many company commanders reported that psychological rating was consulted by them and found of assistance in deciding what should be done in disciplinary cases. Thus a man with a low psychological rating might be presumed not to have understood the full meaning of the offense which he had committed, and might be given another company punishment merely instead of being brought before a summary court martial. Numerous examinations were made at the request of company commanders in cases of men who were giving trouble through apparent inability to learn, through misconduct and the like, and special recommendations for treatment were made by the psychologist.

(h) The uses made of the psychological examination of officers are mentioned elsewhere. It needs only to be indicated here that psychological grades were commonly considered by superior officers in making assignments of their subordinates to special duty, in recommending promotions, in courts-martial and in examining for discharge for inefficiency.

SERVICES IN DEVELOPMENT BATTALIONS

Development battalions were first authorized in May, 1918. Their functions were "to relieve other organizations of all unfit men; to conduct intensive training with a view to developing such men; promptly to rid the service of all men who, after thorough trial and examination, are found physically, mentally, or morally incapable of performing the duties of a soldier." Psychological examinations in all camps resulted in the recommendation of a large number of men to such organizations on account of mental unfitness. In some camps orders were issued that no man should be so transferred without consideration of his psychological record. Later examinations inside the battalions themselves assisted the commanding officer and the medical officer in charge in the classification of men for training and other purposes. In at least eight camps special training companies in the battalion were formed primarily on the basis of psychological grades.

A War Department circular on "the instruction in English of soldiers who have not sufficient knowledge of the language," July, 1918, directed that

> From time to time the Psychological Division, Sanitary Corps, will be called upon to assist to the best interests of the service in determining the rate of progress of slow learning men and the reasons for their backwardness, to the end that all practical and scientific means may be used to determine the best training that should be given those undeveloped mentally as well as educationally.

Accordingly in many development battalions psychological officers became to all intents and purposes educational directors. Numerous requests that special psychological officers be assigned for full duty in development battalions had to be refused on account of the insufficient personnel of the Division of Psychology. At the request of Col. Lentz of the General Staff, Capt. Paterson was assigned to the development battalion at Camp Meade to make a special study of the methods whereby psychologists could be of special service in development battalions. Capt. Basset and Lt. Houser were sent by their commanding officers to the school for officers of development battalions held at Camp Meade. Afterwards Capt. Basset was transferred to the infantry and placed in command of the development battalion at Camp Logan.

In the elimination of totally unfit men, after trial in the development battalion, psychological recommendations were considered even more carefully and given greater weight than they had been in the original examination of recruits. Thus two camps reported that some 200 men previously recommended for rejection by psychologists and nevertheless accepted for service, ultimately reached the development battalions and were quickly discharged for mental deficiency.

SERVICES TO PSYCHIATRIC EXAMINERS

Theoretically the mode of cooperation between psychologist and psychiatrist was laid down in a joint memorandum signed by the chiefs of the two divisions involved. In practice, however, a great variety of methods for securing this cooperation was developed in the camps to meet the special local requirements of temporal order of examination, spatial location of examining stations, rush requirements and the like. The details of such methods are further described in the section on camp organizations. Typically different methods, for example, were in operation at Camps Lee, Dix, and Pike. Psychologists served with recruit examining boards in nearly all camps, and with disability boards, and in the neuropsychiatric wards of base hospitals. The fact that over 8,000 men, as the result of individual psychological examination, were discharged indicates the magnitude of this coordinated service.

SERVICES TO PERSONNEL OFFICERS

From the beginning of psychological examining, grades (or grades and scores) were reported to personnel officers for entry upon qualification cards. Personnel officers used these ratings for a variety of purposes, some of which are described below:

Before the trade tests were established psychological grades were used to a greater or less extent as a partial basis for occupational ratings; thus, for example, some personnel officers made a practice of giving no rating of "expert" in the skilled trades except in connection with a psychological grade of C or better. Sometimes in filling a special requisition calling for high-grade men of a given trade, they selected only the men of that trade having the highest psychological ratings. At a later date more definite information as to the probable intelligence of various occupational groups was furnished to the Committee on Classification of Personnel by the psychologists. One psychologist from the division, Maj. Hayes, was assigned to the trade tests laboratory at Newark to assist in the development and standardization of trade tests.

In numerous cases, where requisitions called for the transfer to another camp of Negro recruits capable of becoming noncommissioned officers or of filling other positions of special resonsibility, personnel officers made their selection solely on the basis of psychological rating. Occupational qualifications were often of no significance in these cases since so large a percentage of the men were farmers. Dependence was frequently placed upon the ratings in the assignments to stevedore regiments, pioneer infantry, labor battalions and the like. Psychological ratings were commonly used by personnel adjutants and commanding officers as a check upon the appropriateness of assignments of men to development battalions. Not only were psychologists' recommendations for special assignment closely followed in most camps, but the ratings were sometimes also used to prevent too numerous assignments; thus, in several camps where organization commanders were considered overzealous in raising the standard of their organization by such transfer, orders were issued from headquarters that no man should be transferred as inept without consideration of his psychological rating or in some cases without joint recommendation of transfer by psychologist and summary court officer.

Use of psychological grades in the balancing of mental strength of organizations has been mentioned in the account of the examining at Camp Lee in the fall of 1917. More intensive and systematic application of this principle was made later in several camps. The similar practice of assigning remainders from the depot brigade to special organizations such as antiaircraft and other machine gun battalions, artillery parks, and the like, after occupational needs of these organizations had been satisfied, was even more common. In several camps psychological examinations were made a final part of the special examination to determine fitness for overseas duty.

SERVICES TO JUDGE ADVOCATES

As mentioned above, psychological ratings were sometimes consulted by company commanders in considering cases of misconduct before court-martial charges should be made. Either independently or in connection with psychiatrists many offenders were given a special psychological examination to furnish courts-martial with evidence as to the responsibility of an accused. In several camps all stockade prisoners were examined as a matter of routine. Capt. Norton and Lieuts. Folsom and Lincoln were detailed for some months to assist in a complete mental and social survey of the entire prisoner population at Fort Leavenworth Disciplinary Barracks. By order of the Secretary of War all conscientious objectors were given special psychological examination.

SERVICES TO THE MORALE BRANCH OF THE GENERAL STAFF

Activities of the Division of Psychology played an important part in bringing about the organization of morale work. The chief of the division used every opportunity to promote interest in recommendations submitted by Col. E. L. Munson to the Surgeon General relative to "the need for a systematic plan for the psychological stimulation of troops in promoting fighting efficiency." To this end he organized two conferences for the discussion of the problem of controlling morale, and in addition provided members of the General Staff with pertinent information.

As commanding officer of the medical officers' training camp at Fort Oglethorpe, Ga., Col. Munson later had opportunity to put his ideas into effect. Under his instructions Maj. Foster, Capt. Frost, and Lieut. Anderson prepared plans for systematic morale work in the detention camp at Camp Greenleaf, and, with the assistance of enlisted men of the psychological service, School of Military Psychology, organized practical service for the camp. Subsequently this work was extended throughout Camp Greenleaf.

SERVICES TO THE COMMITTEE ON EDUCATION AND SPECIAL TRAINING

Majs. Terman and Yoakum were in succession employed as psychologists by the Committee on Education and Special Training of the War Department. In October, 1918, this committee requested the cooperation of the Division of Psychology in securing mental ratings of members of the Student Army Training Corps, to serve as partial basis for their admission, educational guidance, and assignment. Permission was given for the use of the alpha examination, and arrangements were made for administering the tests under direction of faculty members and with supervision of psychological officers who should be temporarily assigned for the work until others could be commissioned. The armistice prevented the extension of testing to the 209 schools which stated their desire to use the tests. Only 11 Student Army Training Corps units have reported results fully. In 104 others, reports are either incomplete or indicate that the tests will be used later. The total number of students in the colleges who were given the test is 11,500 and includes the Students' Army Training Corps, Reserve Officers' Training Corps, and men and women in the colleges and normal schools.

SERVICE THROUGH SPECIAL EXAMINATION

In addition to examination of the groups mentioned in the previous paragraphs, numerous special examinations have been made, usually by special request to the division. Candidates of the third officers' training camp, some 14,000 in number, were given the examination in February, 1919, by examiners detailed for the purpose from the four original camps. Examination *a* was used. Examinations of candidates at later officers' training camps were conducted by the chief psychological examiners at the camps involved. In the fourth and later series examination alpha was used. At later periods the tests served as "assisting guides" in making final selections for commissions.

Other special examinations were made as follows: Candidates for commissions in the personnel schools at Camp Meigs and elsewhere; civilian applicants for commission in the Quartermaster Corps at Camps Bowie and Sherman and in the Intensive Service Course at Camp Meigs; officers and civilian staff of the office of the Quartermaster General at Washington; aviation candidates at Camp Jackson; the chaplains' school at Camp Taylor; the Army Nurse Corps at Camps Kearny, Lee, Logan, and Sherman; the civilian personnel of the Civil Service Commission in Washington; soldier hospital attendants at St. Elizabeth's Hospital for the Insane, Washington; mental cases at the port of debarkation at Newport News; personnel of the Field Signal Service at Camp Alfred Vail, N.J.; secretaries of the Young Men's Christian Association and of the Knights of Columbus at Camps Sherman, Taylor, Travis, and elsewhere; 191 German war prisoners at Camp Sherman, and the war prison barracks guard at Fort Oglethorpe; prostitutes in cities near Camps Dix, Greenleaf, Hancock, Newport News, Sherman, and Travis.

SERVICES THROUGH DEVELOPMENT OF SPECIAL METHODS

At Camp Lewis practical methods were devised by psychologists to demonstrate the part played by trigger squeeze and breathing in determining accuracy and improvement in rifle practice. Complete account of the method is impossible in this place, but the following statement from the colonel of an infantry regiment who used the devices will make clear the chief points:

These devices accomplish the following:

(a) They demonstrate ocularly the manner in which a man aiming a rifle breathes, whether he is taking a full breath, or breathes irregularly.

(b) They demonstrate ocularly the manner in which a man pulls the trigger, whether by a squeeze or jerk; i. e., the manner of pulling the trigger at all stages of the aiming and releasing of the firing pin.

This possesses the following value in the instruction of the rifleman:

(a) It enables the instructor to see the errors in breathing and aiming at once.

(b) It enables the rifleman to see his own errors.

(c) It enables both instructor and rifleman to see when those errors have been corrected.

(d) From the foregoing it enables the instructor to decide when the recruit is proficient in aiming, breathing, and trigger squeezing, and prepared to pass on to instruction in firing the rifle.

(e) A practical test in breathing and trigger pull may be prescribed and determined by means of this device.

At Camp Upton formal tests of ability to understand and speak the English language were developed for the purpose of determining what men could not grasp (without special training in language) instruction in military drill. The tests gave measures of ability in five grades on a scale from 0 to 45 in the individual test and from 0 to 30 in the group test. The individual examination involved verbal answers to a set of questions graded in difficulty, and upon performance of directions similarly graded. In the group examinations the score depended upon the following of graded directions in connection with a series of pictures. The individual examination required on the average about 5 minutes, and the group test about 10 minutes.

At Camp Sherman certain tests to assist in selection were suggested by the chief psychological examiner and made part of the qualifications of enlisted men considered for intelligence work. Beside the psychological test those adopted were suited to measure discrimination of minute movements, localization of light, and deductive reasoning.

At Camp Jackson the chief psychological examiner assisted in the standardization of educational tests used to measure progress and ability in the Field Artillery Replacement Depot. When the armistice came he was engaged, by request of the commanding general, in developing further tests for the special selection and measurement of artillerists.

MISCELLANEOUS SERVICES

Minor services too numerous to mention were rendered by the Division to governmental and civilian agencies concerned either directly or indirectly with the war, and to industrial and educational institutions, in order that the practical values of methods of mental measurement might be widely demonstrated and the methods rapidly perfected. In return for these services the Division of Psychology received valuable assistance from many sources in accumulating data for the revision of methods and the evaluation of results.

Leonard Carmichael: 1898-

THE DEVELOPMENT OF BEHAVIOR IN VERTEBRATES EXPERIMENTALLY REMOVED FROM THE INFLUENCE OF EXTERNAL STIMULATION *

1926

THE behavior of an adult vertebrate differs radically from the behavior of a young individual of the same species. What are the factors which bring about this differential transformation? Is this modification of activity the result of environmentally conditioned learning or of the maturing of certain innate behavior patterns or "instincts"? The experiments recorded in this paper were undertaken in an effort to throw some additional empirical light upon certain phases of this question.

PART I. EXPERIMENTAL

The specific problem of the present investigation was the determination of the nature and the speed of the process by which developing vertebrates first acquire the ability to carry out muscular movements. The work was done upon the embryos of the frog (*Rana Sylvatica*) and the salamander (*Amblystoma Punctatum*). A relatively short time is required for the development of these embryos from fertilized eggs into larvae with well-coordinated swimming movements. The fundamental procedure of the investigation consisted in the comparison of the movements of larvae which were allowed to develop "normally" with the movements of larvae which were reared under such experimental conditions that they showed no gross bodily movements until released by the experimenter.

The embryos used in these experiments developed from eggs found in masses in small pools in the neighborhood of Princeton, New Jersey. In all cases the eggs were in very early stages of cell division when they when brought into the laboratory. The technique of the experiments,

* This investigation has provided the classical instance of the maturation of behavior. Reprinted from the *Psychological Review*, XXXIII, (1926), 51-58 by permission of the author and of the American Psychological Association.

save where noted to the contrary, was the same for both the *Rana* and *Amblystoma* embryos.

In the laboratory the protecting jelly was removed from the individual eggs. This somewhat tedious process was accomplished by holding a few of the jelly-surrounded eggs upon a piece of very damp paper toweling by means of a wide-mouthed pipette. Then, by the use of needles, the individual eggs were teased out the jelly. The bare eggs were kept at all times in covered glass dishes filled with tap water. The embryos were allowed to grow in these dishes until the head and tail "buds" could be observed. Body movements do not appear in these organisms until a stage much later than this early head and tail bud period; indeed at this stage the peripheral nervous system has not developed.

The embryos in this early head and tail bud stage were, in all of the experiments, divided into two similar groups. One of these sets, the *Control Group,* was placed in a development dish filled with tap water. The other set, the *Experimental Group,* was placed in a development dish filled with a solution of chloretone *(chlorbutanol).* Previous work had shown that living organisms placed in a solution containing certain concentrations of this drug continue to grow, but they never exhibit any body movements in response to external stimulation while they are under the influence of the anaesthetic. The present experiments confirmed this observation. Some little difficulty was experienced in determining the optimal concentration of the drug in which to raise the experimental groups. If the solution was too weak the embryos would show some slight movement in response to strong stimulation while still supposedly under the influence of the anaesthetic. When movement of this sort occurred the entire experimental group had to be discarded. On the other hand, if the solution was too strong the embryos developed morphological abnormalities. Typical of such defects was a great bloating of the body which either resulted in death or seriously interfered with the later observations on movement. The best concentrations of chloretone for the proper development of the *Rana* and *Amblystoma* embryos were found to be somewhat different. Good results were obtained with the frog embryos raised in a solution containing by weight, 3 parts of chloretone in 10,000 parts of water. Acceptable results however were secured in solutions differing slightly from those noted above.

In all cases the experimental and control groups were kept in covered glass dishes on the same table. No especial effort was made to regulate the temperature or the light of the room in which the investigation was carried on. Both the experimental and control groups were thus at all times subject to the same conditions. Morphologically the development of the control and the experimental embryos was, in the best examples, quite similar. In all cases the larvae in the tap water grew more rapidly in size than did those in the chloretone solution.

At a certain point, as previously noted by Drs. Herrick and Coghill, the developing embryos of the control group began to respond to the stimulation of slight touches of a slender rod. Very soon after such responses had been first elicited, both in the frog and salamander embryos, a coordination of responses was effected which culminated in rapid swimming movements. Similar stimulation elicited no movement in the experimental embryos at this stage or at any other period, so long as the animals lived and were kept in an anaesthetic solution of proper concentration. From day to day these drugged larvae showed a gradual morphological development; otherwise they were absolutely "inert."

In the organisms raised under these experimental conditions, therefore, bodily movement in response to external stimulation was absent during growth. Long before muscular response commenced in the normal embryo these experimental larvae were placed in the chloretone solution, and until released by the investigator they gave no evidence whatsoever of behavior.

The method of liberating each embryo from the influence of the drug consisted in lifting it with a pipette from the chloretone solution and placing it in a large dish of tap water. The time after the organism was placed in the unmedicated water until it elicited the first movement in response to the stimulation of a slender rod was taken by the use of a stop watch. The tables given below indicate this time to the nearest minute for the frog and salamander embryos.

Tables Showing the Time After Removing Embryo From Anaesthetic Before First Response to Stimulation was Observed

Table I

Amblystoma

Embryo number	1	2	3	4	5	6	7	8	9	10
Time in minutes	14	25	9	7	6	8	8	7	24	13
Embryo number	11	12	13	14	15	16	17	18		
Time in minutes	9	9	12	11	5	5	28	8		

Table II

Rana

Embryo number	1	2	3	4	5	6	7
Time in minutes	10	14	11	7	9	15	15

The conclusion of the present preliminary experiments is, therefore, that in a period of time which averages less than twelve minutes, embryos raised under conditions of absolute artificial inactivity are able to respond to external stimulation. In varying lengths of time after this first movement, but in all cases in less than thirty minutes, the previously drugged embryos showed coordinated swimming movements. In fact a number of the eighteen *Amblystoma* embryos swam so well in less than one half hour after they had shown the first sign of movement, that they could with difficulty, if at all, be distinguished from the members of the control group who had been free swimmers for five days.

PART II. THEORETICAL

May the results of this experiment be interpreted as giving additional support to the theory that the maturing of innate factors alone accounts for the development of the neuro-muscular mechanism upon which behavior depends? Certainly the results of the experiments recorded above seem to show that the reflex system of these organisms is able to function in a manner which is biologically useful to the animal in a very short time after the first signs of behavior are noted. But is this rapidity of development a sign that these swimming movements were already determined in the fertilized egg? May we class this behavior with those functions of which Professor Woodworth has written, "... the only question, regarding such traits, is whether the environment is going to be such as to enable this young individual to live and mature and unfold what is latent within it"? It does not seem to the present writer that this "maturation hypothesis" is necessarily substantiated by the fact discovered in the experiments reported above. Much recent work upon the development of the neuromuscular system, as I have shown elsewhere, points to the fact that the growth of this system can only be understood in terms of continuous living function. The intricate development of such interrelated structures as receptors, nerve trunks, central apparatus and motor end-organs appears to be determined by functional stimulation within the organism itself. The excitation and response of the elements of the neuromuscular system is itself a part of the growth process. It may thus be said that during growth these systems are continuously functioning, and yet before a certain stage has been reached they are not able to serve their typical *purpose* in the organism. This of course does not mean that development is non-functional and a mysteriously teleological event determined alone by certain elements of the original germ. Indeed, as Dr. Child has well said:

The older conception of ontogeny as a process of construction of a machine which, after construction is completed, begins to function seems less and less satisfactory as our knowledge advances. Living protoplasm is functioning at all times and development is a process of functional construction, that is, beginning with a given structure and function, the continuance of function modifies the structural substratum, and this in turn modifies further function and so on.

It should be remembered, too, that in the experiments recorded above, the swimming reaction was not perfect at the first trial. From the initial twitch to the fully coordinated swimming movements, a continuum of increasingly complex responses could be noted in each organism as it developed through the short period indicated above. It is at present impossible to state to what extent this apparent gradual perfection of behavior was due to a process analogous to very rapid learning, and how much of it was due to the gradual removal of the "masking" influence of the drug. The observations, however, show no sudden arrival of fitness.

For the reasons given above there is no obligation on the part of the student to assume that behavior in the experimental cases was the result *merely* of the maturation of certain innate factors.

Is it possible, on the other hand, to account for the result of these experiments without any reference to heredity? Dr. Kuo, for example, would dismiss the entire concept of heredity from a behavioristic psychology. May this program be applied to the experimental findings recorded above? It seems to the writer that the facts observed cannot be explained without any reference to heredity. The rapidity and uniformity of the development of the swimming reaction in the experimental larvae and the unmistakable differences in behavior between the frog and the salamander embryos, even when raised under apparently identical conditions, seems to suggest the basic importance of certain non-environmental influences in the development of responses.

Indeed, it is difficult to see how the facts recorded here, as well as the results of many similar experiments, can be explained save on the assumption that heredity and environment are *interdependently* involved in the perfection of behavior. Is development anything other than a process by which, what is in the last analysis, an hereditary "given" is transformed by an environmental "present"?

If this view be true it will appear that any attempted separation of the parts played by heredity and environment in the drama of development can be in logical terms only. Moreover, the sterile products of such verbal analysis are of more than dubious value to science; they may even do much positive harm in education or industry if applications are based upon them.

In summary, it may be said that the preliminary experiments recorded here successfully demonstrate that in a typical vertebrate form the development of the structures upon which behavior depends may apparently occur during a period when there is no observable response to environmental stimulation. The structures so developed however are not able at their initial appearance to serve the purpose which they ultimately perform in the adult organism. Theoretically, it is held that these facts do not demonstrate that behavior is alone dependent upon the maturation of certain hypothetical innate factors. Likewise the results do not show that all behavior may be explained alone in terms of environmental conditioning. It seems probable indeed that the development of behavior in this typical case, if not in all cases, can only be conceived as resulting from the *interdependent* action of both heredity and environment in determining the functional development of the individual.

Barbara Stoddard Burks: 1902-1943

THE RELATIVE INFLUENCE OF NATURE AND NURTURE UPON MENTAL DEVELOPMENT *

1928

INTRODUCTORY

To what extent are ordinary differences in mental level due to nature and to what extent they are due to nurture?

Few scientific problems have been the subject of so much speculation and controversy as the specific one with which this study deals. This is probably attributable to two facts: the practical and theoretical significance of the problem itself, and the extreme difficulty of gathering evidence which cannot be applied with more or less plausibility to support of either the nature or the nurture hypothesis.

The result has been that, since the appearance in 1869 of Galton's Hereditary Genius, nearly every study published in the field has been seized upon by both the hereditarians and the environmentalists and interpreted as favorable to the point of view of their own school. The high incidence of genius in certain strains and of feeble-mindedness in others; the consistent decrease in familial correlation coefficients for psychical traits as more and more remote degrees of relationship are considered; the stronger resemblance found between twins than that between ordinary siblings; the approximate constancy of intelligence level when measured in the same individuals over intervals of time; the marked differences in average intelligence which have never failed to appear in studies of groups who were dissimilar in racial, occupational, educational, or social status—all these phenomena might conceivably be due either to hereditary or to environmental forces or to both at once. Hence, none of them offers evidence which can be regarded as crucial.

However, the fact that no experiment has yet served to uncover in unambiguous terms the relative contributions of ordinary nature and

* This study is the first attempt to determine quantitatively the relative role played by heredity and by environment in causing variability in intelligence. It is reprinted from the Twenty-seventh Yearbook of the National Society for the Study of Education by permission of the Society. The sections reproduced are from Part 1, pp. 219-224 and 302-309.

nurture differences to differences in mental level does not invalidate the experimental data which have been accumulating for nearly sixty years. In revealing tendencies, suggesting profitable avenues of approach, and in actually indicating the existence of the problem itself, their contribution has been very great. Furthermore, they provide a substantial structure of fact which requires merely the impact of one additional experimental step to become invested with definite meaning. This additional step, by some means not yet employed, must isolate the effects of heredity and environment; then, in the light of our new knowledge, the wide factual background of previous data will assume its proper scientific perspective.

This step might be accomplished in one of two ways. The first would require the experimental control of either nature or nurture so that the effects of one or the other could be singly observed. The second would require the application of mathematical techniques to data collected in the ordinary way.

The second method offers us more than the first, ultimately, for in addition to isolating nature-nurture effects, it promises to yield an explanation of the actual mechanics underlying mental heredity. A start has been made towards developing such a scheme of mathematical analysis in the work of R. A. Fisher, who has already applied his techniques to the study of inherited physical traits with extremely interesting results. However, the method he employed will probably be inapplicable to the study of mental traits without important modifications, and is consequently at present out of question for students of mental heredity. This leaves the first, or empirical, method as the only possible attack at present.

The investigation in hand approaches the aspect of the problem which concerns heredity and home environment through a comparison of mental test resemblances obtaining between parents and their children on the one hand, with those obtaining between foster parents and their foster children on the other. Thus, it seeks to evaluate the effects of nature and of home nurture through a study of two kinds of familial resemblance, one of which is dependent upon nurture influence alone, and the other upon a combination of both nature and nurture influences. Through its use of foster parents and their foster children as subjects, it applies to its purpose the end results of the social experimentation which is going on in many homes all about us.

It should be emphasized at this point that whatever tendencies and conclusions can be found in this study are valid only for populations as homogeneous in racial extraction, social standards, and educational opportunities as that from which our subjects are drawn. The distribution of homes of the children studies in this investigation was probably nearly as variable in essential features as homes of the general American white population (though somewhat skewed toward a superior level). It was not as variable, however, as if the homes of southern Negroes, poor mountain whites, or Philippine Negritoes had been included; and consequently, home environment cannot be expected to have as large a proportional effect upon the mental differences of the children we studied as though they were being reared in families unselected as to race or geographical location throughout the world.

Reference should also be made to the educational opportunities of the children examined, which were good. (All children were living in California communities.) If the children had varied considerably in educational opportunity, so that a number of them had as limited amount of schooling as that, for example, of Gordon's English canal-boat children, and if, in addition, home environment and educational opportunity had been correlated, it would have been quite difficult to separate the effects of the two upon the mental variability of our children. In this study, not only is the possible complication of differences in educational opportunity averted, but the confusing issue of possible cumulative effects of schooling is averted as well, since the measuring instrument used—the Stanford-Binet test of intelligence—was standardized upon California school children covering the same age range as our children, who themselves had undergone a cumulative educational process.

Other factors causing real or apparent impairment in mental ability, such as language handicap, deafness, pathological trauma (as from spastic birth paralysis, lethargic encephalitis or other diseases leaving permanent mental deficiency) were also ruled out.

Thus, the study is based upon children homogeneous as to race and educational opportunity; sufficiently homogeneous in health and physique to avoid confusion; and about as variable in hereditary endowment and in home environment (including kindred social mores) as white children of ordinary communities.

The study does not purport to demonstrate what proportions of the total mental development of an individual are due to heredity and to environment. Biologists have frequently pointed out the futility of attempting such a demonstration, since any development whatever would be impossible without the contributions of both nature and nurture. But if we direct our attention to the contributions of ordinary differences in heredity and ordinary differences in environment to mental differences (i.e., I. Q. variance), it is possible to draw some significant conclusions. The causes which affect human differences, rather than the causes which condition the absolute developmental level of the human species have, after all, the more vital bearing upon social and educational problems.

Given a group of school children such as our subjects (which surely are representative of the largest single element in the American juvenile population), it will later be seen that the data fathered in this investigation lead to the conclusion that about 17 per cent of the variability of intelligence is due to differences in home environment. It will further appear that the best estimate the data afford of the extreme degree to which the most favorable home environment may enhance the I. Q., or the least favorable environment depress it, is about 20 I. Q. points. This amount is larger, no doubt, than some of the firmest believers in heredity would have anticipated, but smaller than the effects often attributed to nurture by holders of an extreme environmentalist's view. To the writer, these results constitute an important vindication of the potency of home environment. But even more significant appear to be the implications of these basic results, e.g., that not far from 70 per cent of ordinary white school children have intelligence that deviates less than 6 I. Q. points up or down from what they would have if all children were raised in a standard (average) home environment; that, while home environment in rare, extreme cases may account for as much as 20 points of increment above the expected, or congenital, level, heredity (in conjunction with environment) may account in some instances for increments above the level of the generality which are five times as large (100 points).

ESTIMATE OF TOTAL CONTRIBUTION OF HEREDITY

As has been noted above, a^2, or 33 percent, represents the proportion of I.Q. variance that is attributable to parental intelligence alone. Now, 37 per cent is the proportion of I.Q. variance that we have already found attributable to parental intelligence and environment, alone and in combination. It follows that, if we could, without at the same time narrowing the range of parental intelligence, level all other aspects of home environment to a standard or average, the variance of children's intelligence would be reduced by 37 minus 33, or 4 percent. The contribution of parental intelligence to variance would then be equal to .33/.96, or 34 percent.

Such a contribution corresponds to a multiple correlation of .34, or .58,—the multiple correlation (corrected for attenuation) which would be found between child's I.Q. and parental intelligence if the home environment of all families were made constant, but parental intelligence continued to vary as much as before. In this latter respect the coefficient differs radically in theory from the partial correlation coefficient, which in comparable situations has sometimes been interpreted erroneously. The partial correlation of I.Q. and parental intelligence with environment constant is here only .42, as contrasted with .58.

The value .58 probably represents fairly closely the actual degree of resemblance between children and their two parents based upon heredity alone. The undoubted fact that a small amount of parent-child resemblance due to environment, but not measured by the Whittier Scale, is still concealed in the coefficient probably enhances its value slightly. But the fact that parents were themselves molded in part by environment, and in consequence vary somewhat from their congenital mental level, and the further likelihood of slight random environmental effects (such as those from pre- and post-natal nutrition), suggest that the intrinsic genetic resemblance between parents and offspring is somewhat depressed thereby. The elevating and depressing effects undoubtedly cancel one another to some extent. The coefficient .58 can consequently be taken as a tentative approximation to the true genetic relation. Its probable error could in this case be computed similarly to the probable error of a regression coefficient if the coefficient .58 were not based upon correlations corrected for attenuation. It can only be observed that its probable error must be somewhat greater than the probable error (.06) of an ordinary regression coefficient based upon raw intercorrelations equivalent to the corrected ones used here.

We have now seen that the total contribution of systematic (or measurable) home environment is close to 17 percent, and that the contribution of home environment and parental intelligence together is represented by a multiple correlation coefficient (corrected) of .61, or by a percentage of .37. If not more than 35 or 40 percent of the variance of children's I.Q.'s is accounted for by reference to these factors, what contributes the other 60 or 65 percent.

Possibly a portion of this residual variance is due to the "random somatic effects of environment," to quote Fisher. But it seems reasonable to suppose that not a great deal is due to this effect, since numerous studies have shown a marked tendency for the I.Q. to remain constant over a period of years, while other studies have shown that identical twins correlate in intelligence about as closely as the reliability of the tests employed will permit. Probably the major share of the residual variance is due to congenital endowment, since in known modes of hereditary transmission the influence of heredity is always far stronger than parental correlations alone would indicate. This is necessarily the case because only half the chromosomes of each parent are passed on to the offspring. Hence, the parental deviation for any trait in question is determined by a number of factors other than the ones transmitted to the child. In hereditary traits such as stature, which are known to be influenced relatively little by ordinary differences in environment, the multiple correlation of child with parents is .64, but the contributions of heredity to variance approaches 100 percent. The closeness of our estimated value of the "genetic" multiple correlation for intelligence to this value of the multiple correlation for stature is striking. Probably, then, close to 75 or 80 percent of I.Q. variance is due to innate and heritable causes.

This estimate makes allowance for the 17 percent which the data of this study show is due to measurable home environment, plus an additional 5 or 10 percent due to the possible "random somatic effects of environment." In the opinion of the writer, the estimate is the most reasonable one that can be made from available data with available methods. But a determination of the total contribution of heredity can probably never be made beyond cavil until the genetic mechanics of mental heredity are first established by methods analogous to those used by Fisher in the study of physical traits.

A NUMERICAL ESTIMATE OF THE POTENCY OF HOME ENVIRONMENT TO RAISE OR DEPRESS THE I.Q.

One further angle of interpretation will be especially pertinent to the general problem of the possibilities and limitations of training. From a practical outlook the point to be raised is undoubtedly of even greater significance than the more general problem of the proportional contributions of nature and nurture to mental variability. It is concerned with the question: "How far, in terms of measurable I.Q., is environment potent to increase or inhibit the development of innate intelligence?"

It has been seen that empirical considerations, based upon facts given, strongly suggested that the "congenital mental level" of the foster children was not more than two or three points above 100 I.Q. But the average I.Q. level actually found in this group was 107. Can this discrepancy be accounted for through superior environmental advantages?

Probably it can be. The average mental age level of the foster fathers is 16 years, 11 months, and of the foster mothers is 16 years, 3 months. The average mid-parent level, 16–7, is about one standard deviation above that of parents in general.

The army intelligence data strongly imply that the average adult mental level of Americans is closer to 14 years than to the 16-year level which had been tentatively established previously. But the Army Alpha group test was different in many respects from individual tests, and psychologists have hesitated to assume without further evidence that the same outcome would necessarily hold for tests of the Binet type. However, our control data rather bear out the army conclusions when treated in the following manner: Summary cards for the cases were arranged from lowest to highest in order of father's mental age. Starting with the first case, the children's I.Q.'s were added and averaged as each additional case was inserted. When a point was reached at which the children's I.Q.'s averaged as close to 100 as our limited number of cases permitted (within three points of 100), the fathers' and mothers' mental ages for those cases were averaged separately and together with the following result:

		N
Fathers' mental age	12.9	21
Mothers' mental age	14.5	21
Average	13.7	

The same procedure was repeated with cases in which mothers' mental age was arranged from lowest to highest, with the result:

		N
Fathers's mental age	14.6	20
Mothers' mental age	12.4	20
Average	13.5	

Finally, first with the fathers and then with the mothers, and starting with 13.5 as a median, paired cases in which parent scores showed equal positive and negative deviations from 13.5 were selected until all possible pairs had been used. The average of fathers and mothers was 13.8 in the first instance and 14.1 in the second instance. The corresponding average I.Q.'s of children were 105 and 104, respectively, suggesting that 14 years may be a little high to represent the average adult level. But it seems justifiable on the basis of the foregoing to use 14 for an approximation to the truth. As the standard deviation of our mid-parent mental age is close to two years, the average level of the control parents (similarly of the foster parents) is about one standard deviation superior.

It is difficult to say just how high above the mean of the generality are the other environmental measures (culture index, Whittier index, income, etc.) because no satisfactory norms for unselected populations are available upon them. Since most of the correlations between the measures of environment and the measures of parental intelligence are quite high, a safe estimate would be that the total complex of environment (including parental intelligence) is between one half and one standard deviation above average.

The multiple correlation (corrected for attenuation), .42, can now be used as a regression coefficient for predicting the average standard score of the Foster Group. A positive increment of .42 times one standard deviation (or 15 I.Q. points) would equal 6 I.Q. points; or times one half a standard deviation would equal 3 I.Q. points. An increment of 3 to 6 I.Q. points would bring the I.Q. level of our foster children very close to that actually found (107), provided my judgment is correct that their average innate intelligence is about 102 or 103.

We may now go through some of the variables which were correlated with the I.Q.'s of the foster children and ascertain, when various factors of environment are, say, one standard unit above or below the mean of American communities, how much the I.Q.'s of the children have been shifted from their "congenital" value in consequence. The column in the following table headed "measured" is based upon raw correlations, and the column headed "actual" is based upon correlations corrected for attenuation. The values of Table I are found merely by multiplying the correlations of foster children's I.Q.'s with the factors in question by the S.D., 15, of the children's I.Q.'s.

TABLE I.—AVERAGE SHIFT, DUE TO ENVIRONMENT, IN POINTS OF I.Q., OF FOSTER CHILDREN, WHEN VARIOUS FACTORS ARE ONE S. D. ABOVE OR BELOW THE POPULATION MEAN

Factor	*Measured*	*Actual*
Foster father's mental age	1.0	1.4
Foster mother's mental age	2.9	3.5
Foster mid-parent mental age	3.0	..
Whittier rating of foster home	3.1	3.6
Culture rating of foster home	3.7	4.4
Total environment	5.3	6.3

The implications of this table seem to the writer of more profound significance than those of any other part of the study. While the intercorrelations between these environmental factors are so complex that the relative influences of the separate factors are probably not represented linearly by the differences in the corresponding I.Q. "shifts," the order of their influence is probably so indicated. From this argument two outstanding conclusions emerge:

1. The total effect of environmental factors one standard deviation up or down the scale is only about 6 points, or, allowing for a maximal oscillation in the corrected multiple correlation (.42) of as much as .20, the maximal effect almost certainly lies between 3 and 9 points.

2. Assuming the best possible environment to be three standard deviations above the mean of the population (which, if "environments" are distributed approximately according to the normal law, would only occur about once in a thousand cases,) the excess in such a situation of a child's I.Q. over his inherited level would lie between 9 and 27 points—or less if the relation of culture to I.Q. is curvilinear on the upper levels, as it well may be.

An influence of this magnitude, although significant, is emphatically not sufficient to account for genius upon a theory of environment.

Francis Galton, whose I.Q. in childhood Professor Terman has estimated to have been close to 200, was reared in a home of exceptional cultural advantages. Yet even without the possible 9 to 27 points contributed by his environment, he would still have ranked as a genius such as occurs in unselected populations only once in many thousands of individuals. Whether or not he would have succeeded in using his gifts with such telling effect if he had not had the training, education, and inspiring associates that were his, is of course another question. While many men and women have surmounted unbelievable obstacles to achieve eminence, there is no telling how many others, of weaker stamina, have crumpled by the way.

It is of further interest to note that, while the environmental conditions of gifted men, women, and children indisputably show a somewhat superior tendency, they are not, as a rule, so exceptional as those to which the fortunate young Galton was born. The average Barr rating of fathers of the California gifted children studied by Professor Terman is 12.77—a value close to that of the foster fathers and of the control fathers. Thus, the superiority of the gifted group must be due preponderantly to endowment and, on an average, less than 10 points of I.Q. must be due to environment. Home environment in the most favorable circumstances may suffice to bring a child just under the borderline of dullness up over the threshold of normality, and to make a slightly superior child out of a normal one; but it cannot account for the enormous mental differences to be found among human beings.

If environment cannot account for men, like Galton, who far and away outstrip the majority of their fellows coming even from such a favorable environment as theirs, still less can it account for an impressive number of eminent men whose early conditions of life have been of the kind that depress rather than enhance the I.Q.: men like Lincoln of the backwoods; Carlyle, whose simple peasant mother learned writing while he was at college so that she might correspond with him; Dickens, whose nursery was a London slum; or Canning, a neglected little boy who "longed for bread and butter" as he followed the ragged fortunes of a band of strolling players in eighteenth century England.

SUMMARY OF CONCLUSIONS

By methods which have permitted the effects of environment to be studied separately from those of heredity in conjunction with environment, this study has sought to evaluate the factors conditioning the intelligence of a group of white American school children living in ordinarily variable circumstances. The main conclusions thereby reached are as follows:

1. Home environment contributes about 17 percent of the variance in I.Q.: parental intelligence alone accounts for about 33 percent.

2. The total contribution of heredity (i.e., of innate and heritable factors) is probably not far from 75 or 80 percent.

3. Measurable environment one standard deviation above or below the mean of the population does not shift the I.Q. by more than 6 to 9 points above or below the value it would have had under normal environmental conditions. In other words, nearly 70 percent of school children have an actual I.Q. within 6 to 9 points of that represented by their innate intelligence.

4. The maximal contribution of the best home environment to intelligence is apparently about 20 I.Q. points, or less, and almost surely lies between 10 and 30 points. Conversely, the least cultured, least stimulating kind of American home environment may depress the I.Q. as much as 20 I.Q. points. But situations as extreme as either of these probably occur only once or twice in a thousand times in American communities.

5. With regard to character and personality traits, upon which the data presented are less reliable and less objective than those upon intelligence, the indications are that environment is at least as potent as in the case of intellectual traits—possibly much more potent.

A more comprehensive study of such traits, however, must await the future. Whatever clear contribution is made to the general nature-nurture problem by this investigation must rest only upon the data which deal with intelligence. On this point, it is believed that the study finds support for the conclusion reached by the first pioneer to study mental heredity by statistical methods—that heredity is a force in the determination of mental ability by the side of which all other forces are "dwarfed in comparison."

Karl Spencer Lashley: 1890-

BRAIN MECHANISMS AND INTELLIGENCE *

1929

OBJECT OF THE PRESENT EXPERIMENTS

THE experiments to be reported are an attempt to sample the activities of the rat, to determine the correlations among them, and to test the influence of certain neurological variables upon them. The limited number of tests and of subjects tested is an unavoidable defect of the study. The selection of tests may be more justly criticized. They all deal with some aspect of the learning process, and its relation to the problem of intelligence is not yet clearly established.

The great majority of recent discussions of learning in animals have developed under the influence of the doctrine of random activities and the elimination of useless movements. Habits are conceived as successions of movements, isolated save for simple associations with the preceding and subsequent links of the chain, as simple concatenations of conditioned reflexes. Such a view precludes any attempt to relate the findings from studies of animal learning with human insight or reactions to relations. Capacity to memorize has shown but low correlations with intelligence, measured by other criteria; and, to the extent that our studies of learning in animals are what they have purported to be, measures of mnemonic capacity, they are irrelevant to the problem of intelligence.

I began the study of cerebral function with a definite bias toward such an interpretation of the learning problem. The original program of research looked toward the tracing of conditioned-reflex arcs through the cortex, as the spinal paths of simple reflexes seemed to have been traced through the cord. The experimental findings have never fitted into such a scheme. Rather, they have emphasized the unitary character of every habit, the impossibility of stating any learning as a concatenation of reflexes, and the participation of large masses of nervous tissue in the functions rather than the development of restricted conduction-paths.

Likewise, attempts to analyze the maze and problem-box habits in terms of adequate stimulus and conditioned-reflex response have indicated

* Lashley's studies of brain localization have revolutionized concepts in this field. *Brain Mechanisms and Intelligence* offers the best single presentation of his methods and views. Pages 14-15, 28-35, and 120-131 of this work are reproduced by permission of the author and the University of Chicago Press.

that the problem is far from solved by the simple mechanical theories of learning. Random activity, association, and retention constitute only a small part of the totality of processes underlying the formation of such habits, and even with the rat in the maze there is more than a little indication that direct adaptive reactions and some process of generalization are of fundamental importance for the learning process. Evidence in support of this statement will be presented later. For the present I wish merely to emphasize that the interpretation of learning in animals as a simple conditioning is by no means established.

The primary requirements for the tests were that they be capable of giving fairly accurate quantitative results and that some objective estimate of their difficulty or complexity be possible. Of the available techniques, the learning tests alone could qualify. The results obtained seem to have justified their selection.

PROBLEMS AND SPECIAL METHODS

In planning the experiments the following questions seemed most pressing:

1. Are there situations for the rat in which a deterioration of learning ability after brain injury can be demonstrated, as well as those, like the double-platform box, in which no defect appears? If so, what determines the involvement or non-involvement of the capacity to acquire each particular activity? To test this, it was desirable to sample as many different activities as possible; and in preliminary experiments the multiple choice method of Yerkes (1916), the perseverance reaction of Hamilton (1916), the alternation problem of Carr (1917), a variety of latch boxes, pattern vision, and several tests of direct adaptation to changes in the maze were tried out, in addition to the problems finally selected.

2. Is the deterioration following cerebral lesion temporary or permanent? To test this it was necessary, when reduced learning ability had been demonstrated for one type of problem, to train upon another similar problem at a later date, allowing at least a sufficient interval for complete recovery from any shock or diaschisis effect.

3. What is the influence of the locus of injury upon the capacity to learn different types of problems? This necessitates testing the effects of lesions in all possible parts of the cortex upon the learning of a variety of problems.

4. What is the effect of the magnitude of the lesion upon various types of learning? This requires lesions of different magnitude in each of the areas studied.

5. What is the relation between the sensory components of the problem, the locus of injury, and the degree of deterioration? To test this

it was desirable to present problems offering different and controllable sensory cues.

6. What is the relation between the complexity of the habit and the degree of retardation after brain injury? To test this it was desirable to include several problems having the same sensorimotor basis and differing in the number of identical components included in each. Mazes most nearly meet this requirement but present the difficulty that one must either vary the pattern considerably, and so introduce other factors than the reduplication of parts, or risk obscuring results by permitting a large amount of transfer from one to another.

7. Is the capacity to remember affected in the same way as the capacity to learn? This calls for retention tests for the different types of situations studied.

8. When deterioration exists, is it due to sensory defect, to reduced motor control, to lowered efficiency of the mechanism of fixation, to a general functioning at a lower level of complexity, or what not? These questions demand a variety of tests and controls beyond immediate experimental possibility. They determined the inclusion of two problems, reversal of Maze I and the incline box, as tests of plasticity and of kinaesthesis.

It was desirable to observe the behavior of the same animals in a variety of situations, since only so could the effects of the same lesions in different situations be tested. This limited the number of problems which could be used to the capacity of the most retarded cases and made it necessary to discard the majority of the problem situations which were included in the preliminary tests. Most of these either required too great time for learning or failed to provide a clear-cut objective criterion of learning.

Ten problems were finally selected for study. To test the influence of complexity of problem on degree of deterioration three mazes were used; and for the permanence of defect, a fourth. For diversity of sensory components the brightness habit and the incline box were included. Retention tests for two mazes and the brightness habit, and a test for the ease of substituting one habit for another, completed the series. A detailed description of the problems follows.

1. *Maze III.*—This is a maze with eight culs-de-sac requiring alternate right and left turns in the true path (Fig. 1). It is arranged for automatic recording of errors. The animals were given 5 trials per day until 10 consecutive errorless trials were obtained. Time consumed and errors per trial were recorded. In case learning was much retarded, training was discontinued after 150 trials, which is more than seven times the average requirement of normal animals, and almost twice the upper range of normal cases.

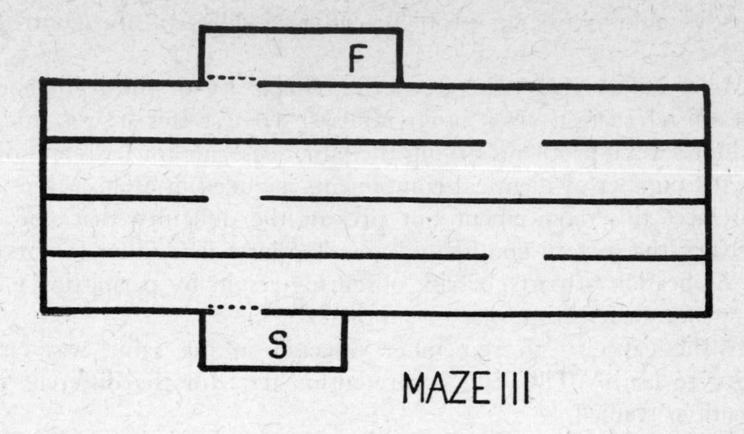

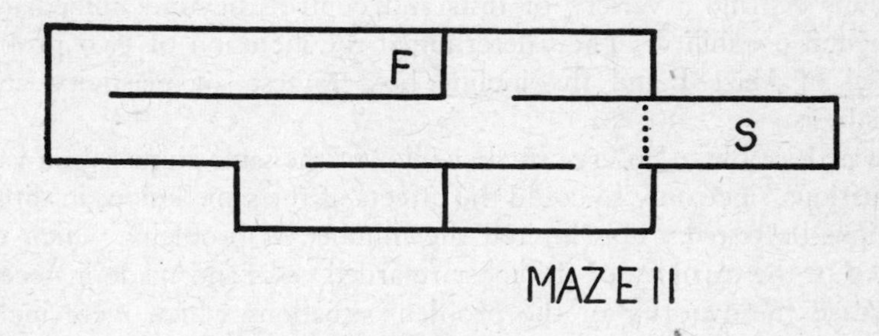

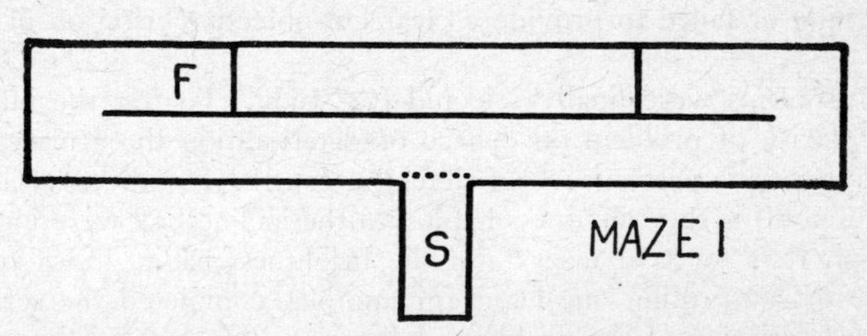

FIG. 1—Ground plans of the inclosed mazes used in the present study. S, starting compartments; F, food compartments. The broken lines represent trap doors which prevent return to the starting-box. Scale: 1 inch equals one foot.

2. *Maze II.*—This is a relatively simple maze having a straight path, with three culs-de-sac and the food compartment opening at the sides (Fig. 1). Training was continued at 5 trials per day until 10 consecutive errorless trials were obtained, or until 100 trials had been given. The latter is six times the average requirement for normal and three times the upper range of normal cases.

3. *Maze I.*—This is a simple T maze with one cul-de-sac to the right and food to the left (Fig. 1). With it, training was continued at 5 trials per day until 10 consecutive errorless trials were obtained, or until 60 trials had been given. The latter is four times the average requirement of normal animals and twice the upper limit of the range.

4. *Brightness discrimination.*—Animals were trained in a standard Yerkes box to choose the illuminated and avoid the darkened compartment. Training was continued at 10 trials per day until 30 consecutive errorless trials were obtained. No animal failed to reach this requirement.

5. *Retention of Maze III.*—Forty days after the completion of training on Maze III the animals were returned to it for tests of retention. These were given as were the original training tests and were continued to 10 consecutive errorless trials, or until 35 trials had been given. This is eighteen times the average requirement for relearning by normal animals and seven times the upper limit of their range.

6. *Retention of Maze I.*—On completion of retention tests for Maze III, a similar series was given for Maze I, with 5 trials per day to 10 consecutive errorless trials, or until 35 trials had been given. The latter is seven times the average requirements of normal animals and three times the upper limit of the normal range.

7. *Reversal of Maze I.*—After completion of the retention tests for Maze I the food was transferred to the cul-de-sac on the right and the animals trained to turn to the right and avoid the former correct path. Training was continued at 5 trials per day to 10 consecutive errorless trials, or until 50 trials had been given. The latter is four times the average requirement of normal animals and nearly three times the upper limit of their range.

8. *Retention of brightness discrimination.*—Retraining tests were given in the discrimination box until 30 consecutive errorless trials were obtained.

9. *Maze IV.*—This maze has the general plan of Maze III, but requires the animal to run along the edges of vertically placed boards, 3/16 inch in width, after the method devised by Miles (1927). Animals were given 5 trials per day to 10 consecutive errorless trials, or until 60 trials had been given. The latter is nine times the average requirement of normal animals and three times the upper limit of their range.

10. *Incline box.*—As a test of the possible loss of somesthetic sensitivity

some of the more deteriorated of the operated cases were trained in a problem box which required discrimination of the direction of slope of an inclined surface. The problem box is of essentially the same form as Maze I, arranged so that it may be tilted laterally at an angle of 12½° with either end elevated above the other. The box is inclosed, light-tight, and the alleys wired with punishment grills and with signal contacts which record the animal's position. The animals were trained to turn up the incline on leaving the starting-compartment. Ten trials per day were given until 30 consecutive errorless trials were obtained.

The animals were trained successively in these problems in the order in which they are listed above. In the majority of cases training in each problem was begun immediately upon the completion of the tests with the preceding problem, but with some of the cases having more extensive lesions, which lose weight under the conditions of training, it was necessary to introduce a rest period of a week or more between problems.

Hunger was used as the incentive in all the mazes; a combination of hunger and electric shock in the discrimination habits.

Fifty animals were subjected to cerebral lesion and started on the series of problems at an interval of from 10 to 30 days after operation, depending upon the rate of recovery from operation. Thirteen were discarded because of illness in the early stages of training or because of evidence of infection of the brain tissue at necropsy. Others died during the course of the experiment so that only 21 completed the series of problems. In addition 22 normal animals were started in the series of problems under similar training conditions. Six of these died during an epidemic of dysentery before completion of the series.

When symptoms of illness developed in any animal, training was discontinued immediately, and his record for the problem last completed was discarded, as a control of the effect of earlier undetected illness.

DISCUSSION OF EXPERIMENTAL RESULTS

At various points in the presentation of the data it has been necessary to postpone a final discussion and interpretation until all of the lines of evidence were at hand. The report of experiments on sensory functions completes the available material and opens the way for an attempt to analyze the nature of the defects consequent on brain injuries. The data are rather intricate and are closely related to results reported in earlier papers, so that a general statement of the findings, even at the expense of some repetition, will not be out of place as an introduction to a final discussion of the problems. The results for the various separate experiments will first be summarized, then taken up in their more general relations.

SUMMARY OF DATA

Maze I (one cul-de-sac).—Data for a similar maze are available from papers by Franz and Lashley (1917) and by Lashley and Franz (1917) and from some later unpublished experiments. Results with this and Maze I are sufficiently similar to justify treating the two as a single problem. The formation of the habit is slightly retarded by extensive lesions in any part of the cortex and to some degree in proportion to the magnitude of the lesions (average correlation for time, errors, and trials is 0.20). The habit is not abolished by any cerebral injury up to one-third of the entire cortex. I suspect that there is some interference when the lesions are more extensive, but have not conclusive evidence. Retention of the habit formed after operation is somewhat reduced.

Maze II (three culs-de-sac).—The initial formation of the habit is somewhat more retarded by cerebral lesion than is that of Maze I. The degree of retardation is proportional to the magnitude of lesion (average correlation is 0.58), and retardation occurs after lesions in various loci. Data on localization and retention are not available.

Maze III (eight culs-de-sac).—After cerebral lesions the rate of formation of this habit is much retarded, is independent of the locus of injury, and is closely proportional to the magnitude (average correlation is 0.75). Retention of the habit formed under these conditions is much inferior to normal. The habit is usually abolished by any lesion involving more than 15 per cent of the neopallium irrespective of its position. The degree of loss is proportional to the magnitude of the injury (average correlation is 0.69) and probably independent of locus.

Maze IV (open maze with eight culs-de-sac).—The formation of the habit is retarded by any cerebral lesion, in proportion to its extent (average correlation is 0.55). Data on retention are not available.

Brightness discrimination.—Studies of this habit are included in several earlier papers (Lashley, 1920, 1921a, 1922, 1926). The formation of the habit is not retarded by any cortical lesion up to 60 per cent of the entire neopallium. In three separate experiments operated animals have been slightly superior to the normal controls. There is no significant relation between the extent of cortical injury and the amount of practice required for learning. The retention of the habit formed after cerebral injury is not significantly inferior to that of normal animals. When the habit has been formed by a normal animal, it is abolished by destruction of the occipital portion of the cortex (area striata), and the degree of loss is proportional to the extent of injury (average correlation is 0.72). The habit is not abolished by extensive injuries to any other part of the cortex or to the corpus striatum even when it has been formed in the absence of the visual cortex. The formation of the habit is probably retarded by lesions within the visual nuclei of the thalamus.

Double-platform box.—Data on this, or on a somewhat similar problem box, have been reported by Lashley and Franz (1917), Lashley (1920), and Hunter (1926). The rate of formation of the habit is not influenced by any cortical injury up to 50 per cent and is independent of the magnitude and locus of the lesion. The habit is abolished by lesions within the frontal third of the cortex and by injuries in no other region. Not enough cases are available for a study of the influence of extent of injury upon postoperative retention.

Tests for the reversal of the habit of Maze I and learning of the incline box have not given useful data.

Sensory factors.—The tests upon the sensory and motor components of the habit of Maze III seem to establish the fact that the retardation in learning and the loss of the habit from brain lesion are not the result of any simple sensory or motor defect but can be explained only in terms of some higher-level organization. The results with the brightness habit likewise show that loss of this habit after destruction of the area striata is not accompanied by any indication of blindness to differences of luminosity, and seems referable to the associational rather than to purely sensory mechanisms.

The data raise more questions than they answer, but among their inconsistencies certain facts stand out as rather well established. In one phase or another the results with every habit indicate the importance of the total mass of tissue, and a certain lack of specificity in cerebral function.

NON-SPECIFICITY OF CEREBRAL STRUCTURES FOR LEARNING

The most surprising outcome of the work has been the number of lines of evidence pointing to the equivalence of function of all parts of the cerebral cortex for learning. When the first study of mass relations was undertaken I fully expected to obtain varied results from lesions in different areas, exhibited both through unlike effects upon the rate of learning and through qualitative differences in the solutions adopted by different animals. No indication of this has been obtained in any of the experiments. Selective effects upon habits already formed appear after diverse cerebral injuries, but in all tests upon learning subsequent to brain operations the effects of injuries to different areas seem to be qualitatively identical. There is no indication of a slower acquisition, which can be related to the locus of injury, of one rather than of another element of the problem. Even where specific functions are restricted to definite areas, as in the case of the double-platform and brightness habits, the separate parts of the functional areas do not seem to have diverse subordinate functions. The reduction in efficiency pervades every part of the performance equally after lesions to any part of the functional areas. It is the same, qualitatively and quantitatively, after equal lesions to diverse areas.

These facts seem to mean that the increase in efficiency of learning with increasing amounts of cortical material is not due to the aggregation of more and more diverse functions (visual, auditory, and kinaesthetic imagery or what not) contributed severally by different areas, as is implied in Munk's and Thorndike's theories of intelligence, but results from an increase in the amount or intensity of some qualitatively unitary thing which contributes to the efficiency of a variety of functions.

In a previous study I found that the function of the occipital cortex in brightness discrimination was unaffected by linear lesions which cut the transcortical fibers within the visual area, provided these lesions did not involve the destruction of a large area of the cortex. We know little of the paths of association or projection fibers in the rat's cortex. Marchi preparations after lesions to the occipital pole indicate that the majority of the occipito-thalamic fibers pass cephalad and laterad to enter the thalamus at about level 16 of our diagram. This means that many of the linear lesions described in the earlier study destroyed the majority of the occipito-thalamic fibers without disturbing the habit, although the habit is abolished by destruction of the cortical area which they supply.

The present study provides some additional evidence upon this point. In No. 1 the lesion divided the subcortical fibers throughout the length of both hemispheres; yet this animal made a better record than any normal one which I have trained on Maze III, and was superior to the average of normals in practically all tests. In No. 2 the lesion certainly involved a majority of the occipito-thalamic fibers without producing a significant retardation in learning.

Figure 30 shows the long axes of lesions which produced no serious retardation in animals tested for postoperative retention of Maze III. They clearly involve the long association tracts in every part of the cortex and indicate that, for the efficient performance of the maze habit, it is not necessary that any two cortical fields shall be in direct connection with one another.

I do not regard these observations upon the effects of linear lesions as conclusive against the specificity of function of association tracts, but certainly all of the positive evidence thus far obtained gives no indication of functionally restricted conduction within the cerebral cortex. It is perhaps what we should expect to find where the functions of different areas are not specific, and in this respect the experiments on cortex and association fibers seem in harmony.

This lack of specificity does not mean, however, that the functions of the cortex are not integrative, are not highly differentiated for each specific activity, but does imply that the functional differentiation must be largely independent of both the macroscopic and microscopic structural differentiation. How functional specificity can exist without structural is not clear from our present theories of nervous function, but in a later section I shall try to harmonize these apparently contradictory conceptions in discussing the assumptions concerning cerebral function which the facts of intelligent behavior seem to necessitate.

THE SYNAPSE IN RETENTION

We have today an almost universal acceptance of the theory that learning consists of modification of the resistance of specific synapses within definite conduction units of the nervous system. Sherrington's theory of relative synaptic resistance (1906), Kappers' theory of axone growth (1917), or Thorndike's theory of the formation of bonds (1913) may be taken as typical. In the theories nothing is implied as to the locus of these changes; for a given habit they may be restricted to a definite cerebral area or may be scattered uniformly throughout a cortex or may exist in any intermediate condition. In conformity with the doctrine of localization it is usually suggested that the region of alteration in conductivity is fairly restricted; but this is not an essential part of the theory, which, in fact, is too vaguely formulated to be capable of experimental test. Retention is thought to arise from the fact that the altered resistances, once established, are relatively permanent.

From such assumptions it must follow that, once a habit is formed, its retention depends upon the stability of the individual synapses and that this stability varies either with the nature of the intercellular connections themselves, as anatomical or chemical structures, or with the action of some disruptive processes of whose nature we have still no conception.

In the experiments upon the retention of habits formed after brain injury the accuracy of performance after initial learning was for many of the operated animals as great as that of the normal controls. Their time for traversing the maze was slightly greater, but this was obviously a function of the general rate of running and not of time consumed by integration at the critical points in the maze. The peculiarities of behavior observable during learning almost entirely disappeared with the perfecting of the habit, and in final performance there were no significant differences between the operated and control animals. For the learning of the maze we have no evidence that one part of the cortex rather than another is primarily concerned, and hence cannot conclude, as we do for the habit of brightness discrimination, that after the destruction of one part another learns vicariously. Thus there are no reasons for believing that the fundamental mechanism of the habit, once formed, differs in the normal and operated cases. The lowering of synaptic resistances to produce equal efficiencies should be equal, and equal changes should be equally stable.

But the habit of Maze III was lost more rapidly by animals with brain lesions than by normals, and to an extent somewhat proportional to the amount of cerebral destruction. This can only mean that the retention of the habit is conditioned by the total amount of functional tissue in the cortex and not, primarily, by the inherent properties of the synapses themselves. We seem confronted with the alternatives of devising some new hypothesis concerning the nature of the synaptic mechanism which will admit that its stability depends upon extrinsic factors or of facing the improbability of our whole theory of the mechanism of learning. The former can doubtless be done by making enough gratuitous assumptions concerning elementary neurophysiology. We might cite the facts of retroactive inhibition as evidence for extrinsic disruptive forces acting on the synapse, and posit inhibitors and inhibitors of inhibitors, as Pavlov (1927) has done; but the truth is that our hypotheses have so far exceeded our facts as to be beyond any experimental test, and the piling on of a few more speculations is likely to make the whole structure collapse of its own weight.

The synapse is, physiologically, a convention to describe the polarity of conduction in the nervous system of higher animals, together with some similarities of function in the central nervous system and in the neuromuscular junction. That these functions are due to the action of the intercellular membranes has not been directly demonstrated. Learning or processes so closely allied to learning that we cannot characterize their differences (adaptation, change in the sense of reaction, modifiability of behavior), have been found in organisms with a syncytial type of nervous system, so that it is not clear that the synapse is either essential or important for learning. The convention has been useful for dealing with some of the simpler physiological reactions but is not on that account the sine qua non of neurological theory.

THE MASS FACTOR IN CEREBRAL FUNCTION

Three types of experiments have now given significant correlations between the extent of cerebral lesion and the efficiency of performance of a habit mechanism. The types seem sufficiently diverse to avoid common sources of error. The rate of learning of the four mazes reported in this study is clearly a function of the total mass of tissue, and the evidence presented indicates that retentiveness as such for these habits is conditioned in the same way. Postoperative tests with Maze III show a similar relationship to the mass of the cortex as a whole. The correspondence is less close than for initial learning but is nevertheless significant. In the habit of brightness discrimination the mass effect is restricted to the performance of the habit after it has been acquired and to the occipital third of the cortex instead of to the entire cerebrum, as in the maze habits.

The only possible source of spurious correlation for the brightness habit seemed to be the production of scotoma. The controls of sensory function in the maze seem to rule out any similar possibility and leave the correlation as representative of some actual interference with the associative mechanisms of the cortex. The relationship is not an artifact arising from some peculiarity of the methods of training, from the shock of operation, from sense privation, or from the production of different amounts of paralysis. It can be interpreted only as a real relationship between the amount of cerebral tissue and the efficiency of its action.

In previous discussions of this factor of mass (1926) I pointed out that it might be either a result of the participation of a large number of equivalent conditioned reflex arcs passing through different parts of the cortex or an indication of some less specific dynamic function. If we assume that with improvement in a habit more and more similar bonds are formed among its elements, which in turn are responsible for increased efficiency in its performance, then partial destruction of these bonds might produce a loss proportional to the number rendered non-functional.

Evidence was adduced from the lack of effects of linear lesions that the reduplicated bonds could not be transcortical, and arguments against the existence of equivalent conduction systems in different parts of the cortex were suggested from the complexity of the habit and the failure of lesions ever to separate it into component parts; but the problem could not then be conclusively settled on the existing evidence.

The present experiments contribute three sets of data which further oppose the reduplication hypothesis:

1. They make it possible to extend the test of section of association fibers to those connecting the cortex with lower centers and give additional data on the effects of the interruption of large numbers of transcortical fibers. The thalamico-occipital fibers probably pass cephalad from the thalamus in the posterior part of the internal capsule, turn upward and outward at about level 15 of our diagrams, and, after passing around the anterior margin of the hippocampal lobes, turn caudad, in the thin sheet of white matter underlying the cortex, to reach the area striata. Thus any lesion which penetrates the fiber layer (as do all in

the present studies) at level 17 or farther back, must interrupt the projection tracts of the areas directly behind the lesion.

In the postoperative retention tests were 8 cases with rather narrow transverse lesions within this general area. These were Nos. 65, 67, 69, 70, 73, 74, 78, and 82. The average extent of lesions in these cases was 10.1 per cent. Their average errors in retraining were 14.0. The majority of the lesions must have severed at least half of the projection fibers of the occipital cortex, yet the average loss of the habit which they produced is not greater than expected from the actual magnitude of the lesion to the cortex alone. Numbers 101, 105, 107, 110, 113, and 116 had destruction of the areas caudad to the regions involved in the foregoing cases. Their average destruction was 27.3 per cent, and the average of their errors in postoperative retention tests was 456. Thus the destruction of the areas supplied by the projection fibers produces much more serious disturbance than an extensive injury to the fibers.

In training after operation there were three cases with linear injuries interrupting thalamico-occipital bundles. These were Nos. 2, 7, and 9. Their average destruction was 8.1 per cent; and average errors in learning, 87.3. This is considerably under the expectation from the regression coefficient for the whole group and indicates that the partial interruption of the projection tracts to the occipital areas did not produce a retardation.

The evidence upon this point is not yet complete, for every cortical lesion interrupts some association tracts as well as destroys a definite amount of cortex, so that our standard of comparison for lesions of any size may be partly determined by the interruption of fibers; but if this is accepted as a rejoinder to the preceding argument, it leads to the further conclusion that for learning or retention of the maze habit all projection and association paths are equipotential.

2. Contribution to the efficiency of performance of a habit by the summated action of equivalent bonds is understandable for habits which have already been formed. It is less obvious how their formation could be retarded by a reduction in the number of possible bonds before the bonds have been formed. For this to occur would require that only a limited number of bonds for any given performance can be formed readily in any part of the cortex—an assumption which is contradicted by the results with the visual discrimination habit which normally involves only the occipital cortex, yet is formed with equal facility in the absence of this area.

3. Even granting that such a limitation exists, it is still more difficult to understand, in terms of reduplication of bonds, how a habit which has been learned to equal efficiency of performance (i.e., to the establishment of equal numbers of bonds) by two animals with unequal amounts

of cortex should be more effectively retained by one than by the other, in accord with the amount of functional tissue.

The evidence thus seems opposed to the hypothesis that the correlations found are due to the reduplication of equivalent arcs, and we are forced to postulate some mechanism distributed throughout the cerebral cortex and capable of facilitating a variety of activities by its total mass rather than by specific integrations.

The results are in accord with a view which Bianchi (1922) has formulated clearly for the purpose of refutation:

Suppose for a moment that intelligence emanates from the cortical fields (arcs) (sic) like electricity from electric batteries; it becomes more intense and reaches a higher potential as the number of areas increases, just as the intensity of the electric current, ceteris paribus, increases with an increased number of batteries.

Far from accepting Bianchi's criticisms of such a theory, I find it the only expression which will adequately cover the facts reported.

Clark Leonard Hull: 1884-

SIMPLE TRIAL-AND-ERROR LEARNING: A STUDY IN PSYCHOLOGICAL THEORY *

1930

I

SCIENCE proceeds by a double movement. For the most part, scientific discoveries are accomplished by means of observation and experiment. Occasionally, however, it happens that a discovery is made by means of a more or less complex logical process or "gedanken experiment." Einstein's mathematical deduction and prediction of what may be observed in the behavior of light when it passes near the sun is perhaps as good an example of this as any.

Frequently, after the existence and characteristics of natural phenomena have been discovered empirically, it is seen that these things might very well have been deduced from facts and principles already known. When the deduction is thus performed, as a kind of afterthought, the process is more properly termed explanation. Actual prediction is more dramatic than explanation, but the two processes are logically very similar. A true deductive explanation possesses a quality of logical necessity closely akin to prediction regardless of when the empirical observation takes place. It is of the mass of such interlocking deductive explanations that scientific systems are made. In general, that science is most perfectly systematized which can show the greatest proportion of its phenomena as logically deducible from recognized principles and other known phenomena. Morever it seems reasonable that rival systems within a science may also be evaluated on the basis of this same criterion.

It is evident that much of what passes for explanation fails of this true deductive quality. It avails little merely to subsume a known phenomenon under some more or less general principle. It is true enough to say of any actual event that it is a case of conservation of energy, or of cause and effect. But such bare general principles of themselves alone can hardly enable one to deduce the existence and characteristics of

* This article presented Hull's first attempt to introduce a deductive-theoretical method into psychology, a method since carried much further by Hull and his co-workers. Reproduced from the *Psychological Review*, XXXVII, (1930), 241-256, by permission of the author and of the America Psychological Association.

natural phenomena. In a similar manner, the typical undergraduate behaviorist's glib explanation of the more complex forms of habit phenomena by saying of each that it is a case of stimulus and response, utterly fails of the true deductive quality. The same may be said of the fairly common, but equally futile, invocation of complexes, equilibrium, Gestalten, closures, Einsicht and the like for a similar purpose.

For an explanation to form the substance of a true system, the deduction must eventuate in some kind of genuine novelty as compared with what is contained in the original premises. This element of novelty is what was referred to above as a predictive quality in real explanation. The deductive process is a true generative activity. The known principles give rise to new knowledge as the result of a causal sequence in a high-class redintegrative organism. According to one plausible hypothesis, principles are symbolic habits which, as a result of their functional interaction within the organism possessing them, give rise to new and distinct habits. These latter constitute the new knowledge. Thus the new knowledge, while derived from the original principles, is not the principles, but something newly come into existence. By the accumulation of these bits of deductive explanation, scientific systems become enlarged very much as have systems of mathematics.

Perhaps no theorists have been more naive in their attempts at system construction than those who seek in the principles of stimulus-response the main explanation of those forms of behavior usually called mental. It may even be that, thus far, none have failed much worse in evolving the solid substance of genuine explanation. Even so, the author has considerable confidence in the possibilities of this point of view. As a concrete example in miniature of what is believed to be a desirable direction for this movement toward systematization to take, there is given the following account of a simple type of trial-and-error learning. This may be taken as a relatively uninvolved example of what has been spoken of above as a deductive explanation.

II

There appear to be a number of fairly distinct types of trial-and-error learning. The particular principles necessary to employ in their explanation, as well as the mode of combining the principles, differ somewhat according to the type of learning to be explained. Of the true trial-and-error learning, we have the relatively complex type exemplified by maze learning, where the obvious reinforcement of the conditioning process (or the lack of reinforcement) for the most part comes only at the end of a series or particular combination of trial acts. A strict deductive explanation of this type of learning presents special difficulties and very probably will turn out to involve some principles not needed for the explanation of the less complex types. A second and relatively simple type of trial-and-error learning is seen where each act or trial is definitely and immediately reinforced positively, if successful, or is followed by punishment (negative reinforcement) if unsuccessful. A still different, and perhaps simpler, type is where each trial act is reinforced, if successful, but is followed by no special stimulus (is merely unreinforced) if unsuccessful. It is this last type of learning only which we shall consider in the following paragraphs.

Numerous phenomena characteristic of this third type of learning call for explanation. These problems can perhaps best be formulated as a series of questions:

1. Why does the organism persist in its trials or attempts even after repeated failure?

2. Why, in case success does not result from its first attempts, does the organism vary its reactions, often over a very wide range?

3. What principle or mechanism limits the range of the variation of the reactions which an organism will make to any problem situation?

4. Why do organisms of the same general type sometimes differ so widely from each other in their reactions to the same (external) problem situation?

5. What principle determines the order of appearance of the several trial acts of a trial-and-error sequence?

6. Why, in the series of trial acts preceding the first success, does the organism often stupidly commit the same erroneous reaction repeatedly?

7. What constitutes success itself?

8. Why should the trial sequence come to an end as soon as success has been attained? Why should it not continue exactly as before?

9. Why, even after the successful reaction cycle has been performed one or more times, do reactions, repeatedly found to be unsuccessful, quite illogically continue sometimes to be made?

10. Why, in general, do these erroneous reactions become less and less frequent with each successful solution, and why do they at length cease altogether?

11. Why, for a particular organism, are certain trial-and-error problems so much more readily solved than are other? Why for certain organisms, is the same problem so much more difficult of solution than for other organisms, persumably of equally good natural endowment?

12. Why, on the whole, are the trial reactions in "blind" trial-and-error learning so much more likely to prove successful than would be a mere random sampling from the entire repertory of the organism's possible movements? Why is the organism so much more likely to try a success-

ful act early in the trial-and-error sequence than pure random sampling might be expected to bring about?

III

Let it be assumed, at the outset, that there exist a number of unconditioned stimuli, S_x, S_y, and S_z; and that these stimuli evoke in a certain organism the responses R_x, R_y, and R_z, respectively. It is assumed, further, that these responses involve the same "final common path" so that no two of them can take place simultaneously. Let S_1 represent a very mild neutral stimulus evoking at the outset no observable response whatever.

Now if S_1 should accompany S_x in the same stimulus complex a number of times there will be set up the conditioned reaction tendency

$$S_1 \longrightarrow R_x.$$

In a similar manner, if S_1 accompanies S_y in another stimulus complex a number of times there well be set up the conditioned reaction tendency

$$S_1 \longrightarrow R_y.$$

Similarly, there may also be set up the conditioned reaction tendency

$$S_1 \longrightarrow R_z.$$

Thus S_1 may come to possess a number of distinct and mutually incompatible excitatory tendencies or "bonds." Presumably each of these tendencies to action will have a strength or potency different from that of the others. For the sake of definiteness and simplicity of the logical consequences, we may let the strength of these excitatory tendencies stand, at this stage, in the ratio respectively of 3, 2, and 1. Lastly let it be assumed that reaction R_z is the one and only response which is biologically successful, i.e., the one which is followed by reinforcement and which terminates the stimulus S_1.

Under the conditions as assumed, what might logically be expected to result in case the organism should be stimulated by S_1, either alone or in conjunction with certain other approximately neutral stimuli? It is obvious at once that there will arise a kind of competition or rivalry among the three mutually incompatible excitatory tendencies. This competition may conveniently be represented thus:

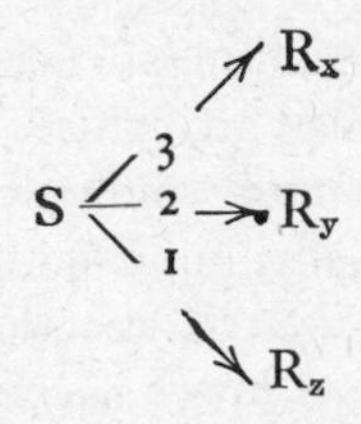

Since the excitatory tendency flowing from S_1 to R_x is strongest, this reaction will be the first trial act. By hypothesis this reaction will not be reinforced. According to the principle of experimental extinction this failure of reinforcement will weaken the tendency of S_1 to evoke R_x, leaving it, let us say, with a value of 2.1. But since this excitatory tendency, even after its weakening, is stronger than either of the other two, it will still be dominant. By hypothesis, S_1 continues without interruption. Accordingly, after the brief refractory phase following the R_x response, this same reaction will be repeated as the second trial act. A second experimental extinction at once reduces the tendency to R_x to a strength of 1.2. This leaves the tendency to R_y dominant to the beginning of the third trial. S_1 continues to act. Accordingly R_y is evoked as the third trial. Here, for the first time, we note the phenomenon of variability in the trial acts.

But since R_y will not be reinforced, this excitatory tendency also will suffer extinction, reducing it to 1.1. Meanwhile, R_x has spontaneously recovered to a strength of 1.5. By hypothesis, S_1 still persists. As a result, R_x is evoked as the fourth trial of the series. Failure of reinforcement at once reduces it to the value of .6. During this time R_y has recovered to 1.4, which gives it a position of dominance. S_1 accordingly evokes this reaction for a second time, as the fifth trial act of the trial-and-error series. Failure of reinforcement reduces its excitatory potentiality to .5. Meanwhile, R_x has recovered to a strength of .9, but this is not enough to equal that of R_z, which now for the first time becomes dominant. S_1 accordingly evokes R_z as the sixth trial of the series. By hypothesis this reaction is a success and is followed by reinforcement. Since this act also terminates S_1, R_z is the last trial of the first trial-and-error sequence or behavior cycle.

The second time the organism encounters the stimulus S_1 (the beginning of the second behavior cycle) the values of all the excitatory tendencies have increased over those existent at the conclusion of the previous behavior cycle. The tendency to R_x is dominant, and this reaction follows at once. The trial is unsuccessful, extinction follows, and stimulus S_1 persists. Thereupon R_y becomes dominant, and therefore becomes the second trial act. This also is an error. Meanwhile, R_x once more has recovered to a state of dominance, and it accordingly becomes the third trial. R_x is weakened again by failure of reinforcement, which leaves dominant the correct reaction R_z. This reaction brings the second problem cycle to a successful conclusion and R_z is reinforced a second time.

The third time the stimulus S_1 is encountered it finds the three excitatory tendencies is still a different combination of strengths. R_x is dominant and becomes the first trial, an error. Its consequent weakening leaves R_z dominant. S_1 accordingly evokes R_z as the second trial. This success, as before, is followed by reinforcement.

On the fourth occasion that the organism encounters the stimulus S_1, for the first time it finds R_z dominant at the outset. Accordingly the first trial act is a success. At this point the process of trial-and-error learning may be considered as functionally complete.

IV

We may now summarize the results of our deduction by answering the questions formulated above.

1. The organism persists in its attempts because the stimulus which evokes the attempts itself persists.

2. The organism varies its reaction, when one reaction fails, because the consequent weakening of the primarily dominant excitatory tendency leaves dominant a second and distinct excitatory tendency conditioned to the same stimulus situation.

3. The range or variety of reactions which may be evoked by a given problem situation is limited to the reactions which have become conditioned during the life of the organism to one or another stimulus component of that situation.

4. Organisms superficially quite similar in general constitution may differ very widely in the nature of their trial attempts at problem solution, because their previous life history has resulted in both qualitative and quantitative differences in their stock of excitatory tendencies evocable by the several stimulus components of the problem situation.

5. The principle which determines which of the possible trial acts shall be evoked first, second, third, etc., in the trial-and-error series is: That trial act is evoked at any given stage of the trial-and-error process which at that time is dominant, i.e., strongest.

6. The reason that the organism frequently, and apparently quite stupidly, tries an unsuccessful act over and over during the first problem cycle, despite failure of reinforcement, is quite simply that the several processes which are continually varying the strengths of the different excitatory tendencies may on more than one occasion leave any particular excitatory tendencies dominant. This may even result in the same erroneous act taking place two or more times in immediate succession, as in trials 1 and 2 of Behavior cycle I. (See Table I.)

7. Not enough is yet known concerning the psychology of learning to give a completely general definition of success in objective biological terms. In the case of hunger, success consists in the eating of food. Ordinarily the successful act results in the cessation of the persisting stimulus S_1. In the case of hunger, S_1 is generally considered to be the cramping of the walls of the upper digestive tract.

Table I

Table showing the progressive changes that would take place in a simple case of trial-and-error learning if the influence of experimental extinction each time should be to diminish an unreinforced excitatory tendency .9 points, the influence of spontaneous recovery should be to restore the loss from experimental extinction .3 points for each interval between successive trials (say one hour) and for the interval between problem cycles (say 24 hours) to restore two-thirds of the maximum diminution resulting from the experimental extinction of the preceding cycle. Each successful reaction reinforces its excitatory tendency by .3 points, this reinforcement being assumed to take place immediately.

	Behavior Cycle I.		*Behavior Cycle II.*		*Behavior Cycle III.*		*Behavior Cycle IV.*	
Trial No.	*Status of Excitatory Tendencies Preceding Reaction*		*Status of Excitatory Tendencies Preceding Reaction*		*Status of Excitatory Tendencies Preceding Reaction*		*Status of Excitatory Tendencies Preceding Reaction*	
1	x = 3.0 y = 2.0 z = 1.0	R_x	x = 2.2 y = 1.5 z = 1.3	R_x	x = 1.7 y = 1.2 z = 1.6	R_x	x = 1.4 y = 1.2 z = 1.9	R_z
2	x = 2.1 y = 2.0 z = 1.0	R_x	x = 1.3 y = 1.5 z = 1.3	R_y	x = .8 y = 1.2 z = 1.6	R_x		
3	x = 1.2 y = 2.0 z = 1.0	R_y	x = 1.6 y = .6 z = 1.3	R_x				
4	x = 1.5 y = 1.1 z = 1.0	R_x	x = .7 y = .9 z = 1.3	R_z				
5	x = .6 y = 1.4 z = 1.1	R_y						
6	x = .9 y = .5 z = 1.0	R_z						

8. The trials cease after success has been attained simply because success terminates the stimulus (S_1) which evokes the trials.

9. Erroneous acts continue to be made even after the correct solution has been "discovered" one or more times by successful trials because the

reinforcement, by success, of a weak excitatory tendency is not always great enough to make it equal in strength to excitatory tendencies which were originally more potent and which have had time to recover greatly from the effects of experimental extinction suffered just previous to the successful reaction.

10. The erroneous reactions become less and less frequent as the trial-and-error process continues, because the basic superiority in the strength of the excitatory tendencies leading to erroneous responses become less and less dominant. This in turn is owing (a) to the action of experimental extinction which continually weakens such erroneous reactions as chance to become functionally dominant, and (b) to the action of reinforcement which strengthens the excitatory tendency which, when dominant, evokes successful responses. Ultimately this process must lead to a state in which the successful excitatory tendency will be dominant at the very outset of a behavior cycle.

In this first case if success on the initial trial of a behavior cycle should chance to take place under circumstances such that the spontaneous recovery from extinction by the unsuccessful tendencies had not had time to take place (as might have happened if Cycle II. had begun very soon after the conclusion of Cycle I.), then we should expect to find errors made repeatedly after one or several perfect initial performances had occurred.

11. One problem is more readily solved than another for a given organism because in its particular stock of reaction tendencies the one tending to the successful reaction chances to be relatively stronger than in the other problem situation. In case the excitatory tendency evoking the successful reaction chances to be dominant at the outset, the correct reaction will be made at the first trial and no errors whatever will occur. On the other hand, the same problem may be more difficult for one organism than another, both of which can ultimately master it, because the previous history of the two organisms has so conditioned them that the successful tendency is relatively more dominant in one than in the other. Such relative similarity in the difficulty of problems for different specimens of a given type of organism as actually exists presumably depends upon the relative similarity in the stimulating situations encountered in their lives. This is usually considerable.

12. From the foregoing, it is obvious that trial-and-error learning, while "blind" in the sense that it is not assumed that there is available for its guidance and control any disembodied soul or spirit, is not blind in the sense that it does not operate according to recognized principles. In the first place, the trials are not made from the total repertory of the organism, but from only those movements which have by previous stimulation become conditioned to one or another stimulus component

of the problem situation. This fact at once automatically limits enormously the number of trial reactions from which selection must be made, and thus largely accounts for such efficiency as it displays. In the second place, of those acts which may be evoked by the stimulus situation, it seems reasonable to expect that in the long run the stronger excitatory tendencies will be more likely to evoke successful reactions than the weaker, and the weaker ones than those reactions within the repertoire of the organism, which have not become conditioned at all to any component of the problem stimulus complex. Since the trial acts are evoked in the order of their strength, this factor will also greatly favor an early success over a mere random sampling from the possible reactions of the organism. It is true that such a system would not always succeed early, and might fail completely of the solution of a problem. Unfortunately this also agrees with the facts of life. Problems are often solved only after much delay, and not infrequently they are not solved at all.

V

From the point of view of the longevity of hypotheses, it is extremely dangerous for them to become thoroughly definite and specific. The very definiteness of an hypothesis makes it possible to determine with relative ease whether its implications agree with the known phenomena which it proposes to explain. In case of failure to conform, the unambiguous nature of the comparison is peculiarly fatal. Worse yet, an unambiguous hypothesis is likely to permit the deductive forecast of what should be observed under various experimental conditions which may as yet be untried. A single well-planned experiment may at any moment yield results quite different from the deductive forecast, and thus topple the entire hypothetical structure. This, of course, is all quite as it should be. The healthy development of a science demands that the implications of its hypotheses be deduced as promptly and unambiguously as possible. This will make it possible for them, if verified by experiment, to be incorporated into the structure or system of the science; or, if found to disagree with experimental findings, the hypotheses may be recast or simply discarded as errors in the long trial-and-error process of system construction. At the least, such hypotheses may be credited with the virtue of having stimulated experimental research. But if an hypothesis be so vague and indefinite, or so lacking in relevancy to the phenomena which it seeks to explain that the results neither of previous experiments nor those of experiments subsequently to be performed may be deduced from it, it will be difficult indeed to prove it false. And if, in addition, the hypothesis should appear in some subtle fashion to the predilections of a culture in which it gains currency, it should enjoy a long and honored existence. Unfortunately, because of its very sterility and barrenness in the above deductive sense, such an hypothesis should have no status whatever in science. It savors more of metaphysics, religion, or theology.

Substantially the only significant criticism of the stimulus-response, or mechanistic movement in psychology, has been made by members of the Wertheimer branch of the Gestalt school, notably by W. Kohler and K. Koffka, particularly the latter. This painstaking criticism of theoretical stimulus-response constructs has been a distinct service to science. Better still, they have put forward a quite different set of principles to explain the same phenomena, which are proposed as alternative, because assumed to be superior, concepts. The issue has thus been joined in a manner quite frank and deliberate. Best of all the contest, instead of taking place in a field of pure speculation where a decision can rarely be reached, is to be conducted in the laboratory where the decision must ultimately be submitted to the impartial arbitration of the facts. That hypothesis, or set of hypotheses, which can show the highest achievement in the things which are recognized by scientists as the functions or virtues of hypotheses must in the end be judged the superior.

As a beginning in this direction there may be considered the above theoretical construct concerning one extremely limited type of trial-and-error learning. Here the question at once arises: are the concepts or principles, by which the Gestalt psychologists would explain the kind of behavior under consideration, of such a nature that answers to the above questions can also be deduced from them? The present writer is frank to confess that such concepts as closure, Pragnanz, Einsicht and the like appear to him either too vague or too general to permit any significant deductions whatever to be drawn. He is quite free to admit, however, that this may be due merely to his failure to grasp the true significance and virtue of these concepts. The real test is whether the Gestalt psychologists themselves can do so. It is entirely possible, of course, that they may repudiate in whole or in part the very existence of conditions implied in the questions propounded. In that event it would seem fair to expect an exhibition of the deductive explanation of parallel phenomena as they conceive them to exist.

VI

It is admitted on all hands that one of the very best tests of an hypothesis or explanatory system is to deduce correctly the result of experimental observations not yet made, particularly when the latter are made by observers disinterested in the outcome. This is a severe test, but it is a fair one, and no system should shrink from it. A number of such possibilities lie sufficiently near to the range of the very simple conditions assumed above for first-approximation forecasts of the outcome of certain experimental procedures to be ventures. Space is lacking for the presentation of but one of these. We shall make our own deduction from the same set of principles already employed. A friendly invitation is extended to the Gestalt psychologists, and to such other schools as put forward distinctive theories of learning, to exhibit in similar detail a similar deduction from their own principles. If no such deductive forecast can be derived, there will be an indication of immaturity, possibly of inadequacy. If a deduction is evolved in which recognized stimulus-response principles are employed, the indication will be that the psychology in question is not so distinct as might otherwise have been supposed. If a rigorous deduction from genuinely distinct principles should appear, but one in which the same outcome is arrived at as by the stimulus-response principles here employed, an extremely interesting situation of parallelism would be presented, which might very well be mutually illuminating to all parties to the discussion. Finally, if any two deductions should arrive at quite distinct forecasts as to the outcome of the experimental procedures, the laboratory may be evoked as the final court of appeal. Indeed, the laboratory must pass the final verdict even if there were no difference of opinion whatever.

Forecast: In cases of relatively simple trial-and-error learning by mammalian organisms below the anthropoids where, as above, but a single act is required for success; where the several trial acts are relatively distinct and uniform; and where the first one-fourth of the behavior cycles required for complete learning have been both fairly protracted and in fairly close succession: it is predicted that there will be a tendency for the proportion of erroneous acts (R_x and R_y) to successful acts (R_z) to be greater at the first trial act of new cycles when the new cycle begins a relatively long time after the conclusion of the preceding one than when it begins relatively soon after.

Deduction: From Table I it is quite obvious that if Behavior Cycle II. should begin at once after the conclusion of Cycle I., R_z will be dominant since the status of the excitatory tendencies will be:

$$x = .9$$
$$y = .5$$
$$z = 1.3$$

But if, instead, an hour intervenes, the relative strength of the tendencies will be:

$$x = 1.2$$
$$y = .8$$
$$z = 1.3$$

At this point R_z and R_x are about equally likely to take place. Or if, as a third alternative, still more time elapses between the close of Cycle I. and the beginning of the next cycle, R_x and R_y will both become progressively more dominant over R_z until at length we shall have the condition obtaining at the first trial act of Cycle II. as shown in Table I.

It must be especially emphasized that the type of learning here considered is not only very simple, but very special in its simplicity. Its nature is perhaps best indicated in the early parts of sections II. and III. It naturally will require some ingenuity fully to satisfy these conditions in an experiment. In particular it may be difficult to set up an experimental situation where all the components of the stimulus complex, except a single dynamic core (S_1), will remain practically neutral throughout the reaction sequence. However, ingenious experimentalists will be able to approach those conditions closely enough to make possible significant comparisons of results.

VII

In conclusion it may be observed that the behavior deduced above, particularly the persistence of effort at solution by means of varied response, is one of the most commonly remarked differences between behavior, usually called psychic or mental, and that of ordinary automatic machines. Indeed it is common, by way of contrast, to call such behavior "intelligent" and "purposive." It is the belief of the present author that these latter terms represent extremely important aspects of mammalian behavior, but that instead of being ultimate entities, all may be derived from certain combinations of more basic principles. It is believed, for example, that the account sketched above in section III. deduces a type of behavior which, if observed in an animal, would be called purposive by most psychologists though it does not show the type of purpose involving plan.

Moreover, if the type of explanation put forward above be really a sound deduction, it should be a matter of no great difficulty to construct parallel inanimate mechanisms, even from inorganic materials, which will genuinely manifest the qualities of intelligence, insight, and purpose, and which, in so far, will be truly psychic. Such a mechanism would represent a radically new order of automaticity, one not yet dreamed of by the ordinary designer of automatic machinery. That such mechanisms have not been constructed before is doubtless due to the paralyzing influence of metaphysical idealism. The appearance of such "psychic" mechanisms in the not very remote future may be anticipated with considerable confidence. Dr. H. D. Baernstein, in collaboration with the present author, has already succeeded in constructing an electro-chemical mechanism which shows the more important of the phenomena of the simple conditioned reflex. There has also been constructed a model which manifests the phenomenon of simple rote learning. It is not inconceivable that "psychic" machines may ultimately play an appreciable role in the life of industrialized communities. On the side of psychology it is possible that these mechanisms may dissolve the age-old problem of the opposition of mind to matter by practically demonstrating the characteristic mechanisms by means of which matter manifests the forms of behavior called psychic.

INDEX OF NAMES

(2)